GLOBAL ISSUES

SAGE was founded in 1965 by Sara Miller McCune to support the dissemination of usable knowledge by publishing innovative and high-quality research and teaching content. Today, we publish more than 750 journals, including those of more than 300 learned societies, more than 800 new books per year, and a growing range of library products including archives, data, case studies, reports, conference highlights, and video. SAGE remains majority-owned by our founder, and after Sara's lifetime will become owned by a charitable trust that secures our continued independence.

Los Angeles | London | Washington DC | New Delhi | Singapore | Boston

GLOBAL ISSUES

SELECTIONS FROM CQ RESEARCHER

2015 EDITION

$SAGE | CQ PRESS

Los Angeles | London | New Delhi
Singapore | Washington DC | Boston

Los Angeles | London | New Delhi
Singapore | Washington DC | Boston

FOR INFORMATION:

CQ Press
An Imprint of SAGE Publications, Inc.
2455 Teller Road
Thousand Oaks, California 91320
E-mail: order@sagepub.com

SAGE Publications Ltd.
1 Oliver's Yard
55 City Road
London EC1Y 1SP
United Kingdom

SAGE Publications India Pvt. Ltd.
B 1/I 1 Mohan Cooperative Industrial Area
Mathura Road, New Delhi 110 044
India

SAGE Publications Asia-Pacific Pte. Ltd.
3 Church Street
#10-04 Samsung Hub
Singapore 049483

Acquisitions Editor: Sarah Calabi
Senior Development Editor: Nancy Matuszak
Editorial Assistant: Katie Lowry
Production Editor: Kelly DeRosa
Typesetter: C&M Digitals (P) Ltd.
Cover Designer: Candice Harman
Marketing Manager: Amy Whitaker

Printed in the United States of America

ISBN 978-1-5063-0835-7

Library of Congress Control Number: 2015937070

This book is printed on acid-free paper.

SFI Certified Sourcing
www.sfiprogram.org
SFI-00453

15 16 17 18 19 10 9 8 7 6 5 4 3 2 1

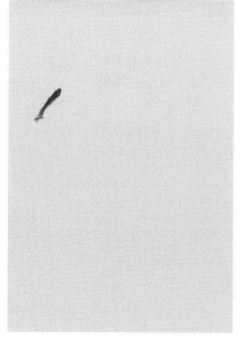

Contents

Annotated Contents

CONFLICT, SECURITY AND TERRORISM
Chemical and Biological Weapons

The Syrian government's use of nerve gas on rebel-controlled Damascus neighborhoods this summer focused renewed attention on the threat posed by chemical and biological weapons. The attacks, which killed up to about 1,400, led President Obama to threaten military retaliation. Syrian President Bashar al-Assad responded by agreeing to destroy his chemical arsenal. Chemical weapons have been outlawed since 1928, after the world saw the horrors of their effect in World War I. After Iraq used chemical weapons to kill tens of thousands of Iranians and Iraqi Kurds in the 1980s, a 1993 international accord strengthened enforcement of the ban. The Syrian gas attacks have spurred debate over whether chemical weapons are worse than conventional arms. Meanwhile, biological weapons also are outlawed, but some experts fear they could be used by terrorists.

Israeli-Palestinian Conflict

The decades-old conflict between Israelis and Palestinians might seem to have a simple solution: Create a Palestinian state next door to Israel in territory that the Jewish state seized from invading countries in 1967. But a "two-state solution" has eluded decades of attempts to reach agreement—most of them shepherded by American presidents and diplomats. Israeli and Palestinian leaders each charge the other with responsibility for the latest deadlock. Now, the Obama administration is warning that time is running out on the possibility of an accord. Indeed, hopes are dimming among both Israelis and Palestinians. However, a sense of urgency is building among neighboring Arab countries, which are being rocked by war and political turmoil. They have joined with Secretary of State John Kerry in trying to push both sides to the negotiating table over a new peace plan.

Iraq War: 10 Years Later

As the world marks the 12th anniversary of the U.S.-led invasion of Iraq, the war is fast fading from the memories of many Americans. After more than eight years of combat, the U.S. and Iraqi governments couldn't come to terms on keeping U.S. combat troops in the country. They were withdrawn at the end of 2011 except for a small contingent involved in training Iraqi forces. But Iraq remains mired in sectarian and religious conflict. In the United States, debates about the justification for the invasion have given way to arguments about whether Iraq is a budding democracy—an objective of the George W. Bush administration—or a new dictatorship. That dispute intersects with the question of whether U.S. withdrawal from Iraq will spur the country to solve its own problems or push it into friendlier relations with its anti-American neighbor, Iran.

Improving Cybersecurity

The Internet has brought profound changes across the globe, but its rapidly expanding criminal side threatens to undermine both its achievements and its promise. Today, thieves using computers can rob banks and steal corporate trade secrets from the other side of the world. Hackers opposed to U.S. policies can sabotage government websites, and some experts warn that a hostile country could bring the United States to a virtual standstill without firing a shot, such as by hacking into the power grid or disrupting transportation. New cybersecurity legislation has not been passed since 2002, and with new laws stalled in Congress, President Obama announced on Feb. 12, 2013, he had signed an executive order aimed at protecting government and businesses from "the rapidly growing threat from cyber-attacks." Meanwhile, some countries are moving to control Internet content, often in the name of cybersecurity.

Assessing the Threat from al Queda

Since carrying out the Sept. 11, 2001, attacks on the United States, al Qaeda has become more decentralized,

and some say stronger, with affiliates launching sectarian attacks in the Middle East, Somalia, Algeria and beyond. The ruthless Islamic State of Iraq and Greater Syria (ISIS) currently sweeping through Iraq, was a part of al Qaeda until February 2014, when it was expelled for excessive brutality. In Yemen, President Obama has launched more than 90 drone strikes against an al Qaeda affiliate there, known as Al Qaeda in the Arabian Peninsula, considered the most serious direct threat to the United States. Meanwhile, al Qaeda's traditional leadership in Pakistan is weaker as a result of U.S. drone strikes that peaked there in 2010 and the killing of Osama bin Laden by Navy SEALS in 2011. Counterterrorism experts are divided over how to define the al Qaeda of today, whether it continues to pose a danger to the West and how the United States should respond.

Unrest in the Arab World

The wave of popular uprisings that toppled dictators in Tunisia, Egypt, and Libya now appears to be stalling five years later. Egypt's democratically elected Islamist president has been ousted in a military coup, and other governments have held on by cracking down on protests or instituting modest reforms. Meanwhile, Syria is engulfed in a bloody civil war that now appears less and less likely to force President Bashar Assad from office. Some experts say the events have transformed political attitudes in Arab nations. Others stress that a majority of those countries still have authoritarian regimes. The political dramas are playing out against the backdrop of pressing economic problems, including high unemployment among Arab youths. In addition, the growing power of Islamist parties and groups is raising concerns among advocates of secular government and creating risks of sectarian disputes among different Muslim sects.

Transnational Crime

Instant global communications and open trade routes have been a boon to businesspeople and consumers—as well as to international criminals. "Transnational organized crime"—in U.N. and U.S government parlance—has been expanding over the past two decades, some officials say, threatening to overwhelm the legitimate world economy. Criminals have raced ahead of law enforcement in adapting to globalization and modern technology, experts argue, citing booming ivory and drug smuggling, human trafficking, piracy, cyber-theft and counterfeiting of luxury goods. Others counter that transnational crime is not new but simply a modern form of an old crime—smuggling—and that new technology also enables law enforcement to better track down criminals, even across borders. Both sides agree, however, that modern technology enables hackers, pirates, smugglers and others to inflict widespread damage more quickly than in the past. The intersection between internationally minded criminals and terrorism is another worry, with terrorists turning to crime to finance their operations.

Resurgent Russia

Russia is growing more assertive on the global stage, having regained its economic strength following the 1991 breakup of the Soviet Union. It has been most active in its own region, where a tug-of-war has broken out between Russia and the European Union (EU) as each tries to draw the nations of Eastern Europe and the Caucasus into its orbit. Ukrainian President Viktor Yanukovych recently reneged on an EU trade deal, reportedly after pressure from Moscow, touching off violent pro–EU protests throughout Ukraine. Russia's efforts to maintain influence over the former Soviet republics have fed speculation that President Vladimir Putin wants to reconstitute the Soviet bloc, which Russian officials deny. Meanwhile, Russia's relations with the United States have deteriorated, although the two countries are cooperating on hot-button issues such as Iran's nuclear program and Syria's civil war. Russia's relations with China are relatively good, however, even though the Chinese have eclipsed Russia economically in recent years.

INTERNATIONAL POLITICAL ECONOMY
U.S. Trade Policy

In 2013, after more than four years without pushing for new free-trade agreements, President Obama decided the time was ripe for America to again push for a more liberalized international trading system. The United States negotiated two massive regional free-trade pacts—one with 11 Asian and Pacific Rim countries and the other with the 28-member European Union. Together, the 40

countries comprise the lion's share of the world economy. Meanwhile, the World Trade Organization languished on the sidelines as negotiations over a slew of new regional agreements overshadowed the WTO's decade-long effort to broker a single global trade agreement. Hopes for the regional pacts reignited debates on whether free trade creates or costs U.S. jobs and helps or hurts human rights. Looming over the debates was booming China, whose conglomerates—most owned and subsidized by the state—conquered markets in both developing and developed nations.

Millennium Development Goals

World leaders from 189 countries gathered at the United Nations in 2000 to approve an ambitious plan to change the world. By 2015, they vowed, countries would meet broad, measurable objectives—which would become the eight Millennium Development Goals (MDGs)—designed to, among other things, eliminate extreme poverty and hunger, promote gender equality, achieve universal primary education, and fight HIV-AIDS, malaria, and other diseases. With the 2015 deadline approaching, some MDG targets appear out of reach. Others—such as halving the percentage of people living in extreme poverty and lacking access to safe drinking water—were met in 2010. But some critics say the MDGs have been inherently unfair because regions such as sub-Saharan Africa were far behind other regions at the outset, so they had much farther to go to meet the targets. As the international community prepares to draft new goals, it seeks lessons from the first round of MDGs on what works and what doesn't and whether goal setting is the best way to solve global problems.

Booming Africa

Once considered hopeless, much of sub-Saharan Africa is booming. Six of the world's ten fastest-growing economies currently are in Africa. High prices for the continent's oil and mineral exports have brought a surge of government revenue and investment, but the growth is occurring in commodity-poor countries as well. Better governance, less war, and the rapid spread of cell phones and other communication technologies are fostering growth even in nations with few natural resources. Debt forgiveness and the rise of China, India, and other emerging markets as trading partners and sources of investment also have spurred economies forward. Demographers say that with the continent's working-age population projected to expand by a third by 2020, Africa could benefit from a "demographic dividend" that would fuel sustained economic growth, even as populations in developed countries and Asia are growing older. Yet the population boom also poses challenges: Africa's economies must provide enough jobs for the growing number of workers with expectations of a better life.

U.S. Global Engagement

As concern grows about Russia's intentions in Ukraine and the civil war in Syria continues unabated, the United States faces increasing pressure from hawks to intervene militarily—though not with boots on the ground. But in the wake of the long wars in Iraq and Afghanistan, most Americans oppose involving U.S. troops in military actions abroad. Mindful of the potential for escalation and intent on shifting resources to domestic needs, the Obama administration has been using diplomacy and economic sanctions rather than bullets to assert American power. It has refused military aid to Ukraine but imposed economic sanctions in an attempt to stem what many view as an effort by Russian President Vladimir Putin to bring Ukraine under Moscow's control. In 2013, President Obama stopped short of bombing Syria after it used chemical weapons, instead sending aid for refugees of the war. Some U.S. allies applaud the administration's restraint, but others want to see more American muscle.

RELIGIOUS AND HUMAN RIGHTS
Free Speech at Risk

Governments around the globe have been weakening free-speech protections because of concerns about security or offending religious believers. After a phone-hacking scandal erupted in the British press and Muslims worldwide violently protested images in the Western media of the Prophet Muhammad, European nations enacted new restrictions on hate speech, and Britain is considering limiting press freedom. Autocratic regimes increasingly are jailing journalists and political dissidents or simply buying media companies to use them for propaganda and to negate criticism. Muslim countries are adopting and rigidly enforcing blasphemy laws, some of which carry the death penalty. Meanwhile, some governments are blocking or monitoring social media and cybertraffic, increasing the risk of arrest for those who freely express their thoughts online and dashing hopes that new technologies would allow unlimited distribution of information and opinion.

Islamic Sectarianism

Sectarian rifts are almost as old as Islam itself. They surfaced in 632, shortly after the death of the Prophet Muhammad, when Muslims disagreed over who should succeed him. Although the original sectarian split was violent, Islam's two major branches—Shiism and Sunnism—have co-existed peacefully more often than not over the centuries. But recently, sectarian tensions once again have erupted into full-scale violence in the wake of the U.S. invasion of Iraq and 2011's Arab Spring democracy movement. The volatile situation is not just about theology. Competition for power and privilege intensifies the hostility and distrust. In postwar Iraq, sectarian attacks killed 325 people in July 2011, the highest monthly toll since August 2010. Currently, the epicenter of the sectarian crisis is Syria, where the Sunni opposition is battling the Shiite Alawite regime of Bashar Assad. Experts fear the violence could engulf significant parts of the Middle East. Meanwhile, other countries have lined up on either side of the fight, with Iran, Russia and China supporting the Syrian regime and Saudi Arabia, Turkey, the Gulf States and the West supporting the rebels.

ENVIRONMENTAL ISSUES
Climate Change

The effects of climate change are steadily becoming more evident across the globe. Atmospheric concentrations of carbon dioxide—the main heat-trapping greenhouse gas produced by human activities—are the highest in 3 million years, and climbing. Scientists say climate change is increasing the frequency and severity of extreme weather events such as hurricanes, heat waves and droughts. Americans increasingly agree that climate change is real and human actions are contributing to it, but many nations around the world oppose measures designed to address the problem. Some experts want to start researching large-scale geoengineering technologies for cooling

Earth's climate, but many observers fear that these strategies could do more harm than good.

Global Hunger

New agricultural technology has enabled global food supplies to outstrip population growth, driving down the number of hungry people around the world from just over 1 billion in 1992 to 842 million in 2014—a 17 percent drop. But food shortages and undernourishment remain huge problems in developing countries. Hunger stems from weather-related disasters such as droughts and floods, as well as from war, poverty, overpopulation, poor farming practices, government corruption, difficulties transporting food to markets, climate change and waste. Hunger is severest in sub- Saharan Africa, where 25 percent of the population is undernourished. Developed countries and humanitarian organizations have become proficient at providing emergency relief and promoting higher-yield, environmentally friendly agricultural practices, but the outlook on global hunger remains murky. Experts expect an expanding global population and growing economic affluence in developing countries to increase the demand for food, even as climate change hampers the planet's ability to feed itself.

Preface

In this pivotal era of international policymaking, scholars, students, practitioners and journalists seek answers to such critical questions as: Is Moscow trying to recreate the Soviet bloc? Will new regional trade agreements create American jobs? Can Sunni-Shiite hostilities be resolved? Students must first understand the facts and contexts of these and other global issues if they are to analyze and articulate well-reasoned positions.

The 2015 edition of *Global Issues* provides comprehensive and unbiased coverage of today's most pressing global problems. This edition is a compilation of 16 recent reports from *CQ Researcher*, a weekly policy brief that unpacks difficult concepts and provides balanced coverage of competing perspectives. Each article analyzes past, present and possible political maneuvering, is designed to promote in-depth discussion and further research and helps readers formulate their own positions on crucial international issues.

This collection is organized into four subject areas that span a range of important international policy concerns: conflict, security, and terrorism; international political economy; religious and human rights; and environmental issues. Six of these reports are new to this edition.

Global Issues is a valuable supplement for courses on world affairs in political science, geography, economics and sociology. Citizens, journalists and business and government leaders also turn to it to become better informed on key issues, actors and policy positions.

CQ RESEARCHER

CQ Researcher was founded in 1923 as *Editorial Research Reports* and was sold primarily to newspapers as a research tool. The magazine was renamed and redesigned in 1991 as *CQ Researcher*. Today, students are its primary audience. While still used by hundreds of journalists and newspapers, many of which reprint portions of the reports, *Researcher's* main subscribers are now high school, college and public libraries. In 2002, *Researcher* won the American Bar Association's coveted Silver Gavel Award for magazine excellence for a series of nine reports on civil liberties and other legal issues.

Researcher staff writers—all highly experienced journalists—sometimes compare the experience of writing a *Researcher* report to drafting a college term paper. Indeed, there are many similarities. Each report is as long as many term papers—about 11,000 words—and is written by one person without any significant outside help. One of the key differences is that the writers interview leading experts, scholars and government officials for each issue.

Like students, staff writers begin the creative process by choosing a topic. Working with *Researcher's* editors, the writer identifies a controversial subject that has important public policy implications. After a topic is selected, the writer embarks on one to two weeks of intense research. Newspaper and magazine articles are clipped or downloaded, books are ordered and information is gathered from a wide variety of sources, including interest groups, universities and the government. Once the writers are well informed, they develop a detailed outline and begin the interview process. Each report requires a minimum of ten to fifteen interviews with academics, officials, lobbyists and people working in the field. Only after all interviews are completed does the writing begin.

CHAPTER FORMAT

Each issue of *CQ Researcher*, and therefore each selection in this book, is structured in the same way. A selection begins with an introductory overview, which is briefly explored in greater detail in the rest of the report.

The second section chronicles the most important and current debates in the field. It is structured around a number of key issues questions, such as "Has technology made speech freer?" and "Will expanding free trade create jobs for Americans?" This section is the core of each selection. The questions raised are often highly controversial and usually the object of much argument among scholars and practitioners. Hence, the answers provided are never conclusive, but rather detail the range of opinion within the field.

Following those issue questions is the "Background" section, which provides a history of the issue being examined. This retrospective includes important legislative and executive actions and court decisions to inform readers on how current policy evolved.

Next, the "Current Situation" section examines important contemporary policy issues, legislation under consideration and action being taken. Each selection ends with an "Outlook" section that gives a sense of what new regulations, court rulings and possible policy initiatives might be put into place in the next five to ten years.

Each report contains features that augment the main text: sidebars that examine issues related to the topic, a pro/con debate by two outside experts, a chronology of key dates and events and an annotated bibliography that details the major sources used by the writer.

CUSTOM OPTIONS

Interested in building your ideal CQ Press Issues book, customized to your personal teaching needs and interests? Browse by course or date, or search for specific topics or issues from our online catalog of *CQ Researcher* issues at http://custom.cqpress.com.

ACKNOWLEDGMENTS

We wish to thank many people for helping to make this collection a reality. Thomas J. Billitteri, managing editor of *CQ Researcher*, gave us his enthusiastic support and cooperation as we developed this edition. He and his talented staff of editors and writers have amassed a first-class collection of *Researcher* articles, and we are fortunate to have access to this rich cache. We also thankfully acknowledge the advice and feedback from current readers and are gratified by their satisfaction with the book.

Some readers may be learning about *CQ Researcher* for the first time. We expect that many readers will want regular access to this excellent weekly research tool. For subscription information or a no-obligation free trial of *Researcher*, please contact CQ Press at www.cqpress.com or toll-free at 1-866-4CQ-PRESS (1-866-427-7737).

We hope that you will be pleased by the 2015 edition of *Global Issues*. We welcome your feedback and suggestions for future editions. Please direct comments to Sarah Calabi, Acquisitions Editor for Political Science, CQ Press, an imprint of SAGE, 2600 Virginia Avenue, NW, Suite 600, Washington, DC 20037; or send e-mail to *Sarah.Calabi@sagepub.com*.

—The Editors of CQ Press

Contributors

Brian Beary, a freelance Irish journalist based in Washington, specializes in European Union (EU) affairs and is the U.S. correspondent for the daily newspaper, *Europolitics*. Originally from Dublin, he worked in the European Parliament for Irish MEP Pat "The Cope" Gallagher in 2000 and at the EU Commission's Eurobarometer unit on public opinion analysis. Beary also writes for the Brussels-based *Parliament Magazine* and *The Globalist*. His most recent report for *CQ Global Researcher* was "Emerging Central Asia." He also authored the recent CQ Press book, *Separatist Movements, A Global Reference.*

Roland Flamini is a Washington-based correspondent who specializes in foreign affairs. Fluent in six languages, he was *Time* bureau chief in Rome, Bonn, Beirut, Jerusalem and the European Common Market and later served as international editor at United Press International. While covering the 1979 Iranian Revolution for *Time*, Flamini wrote the magazine's cover story — in which Ayatollah Ruhollah Khomeini was named Man of the Year — and was promptly expelled because authorities didn't like what they read. His books include a study of Vatican politics in the 1960s, *Pope, Premier, President*. His most recent report for *CQ Global Researcher* was "Rising Tension Over Iran."

Alan Greenblatt covers foreign affairs for National Public Radio. He was previously a staff writer at *Governing* magazine and *CQ Weekly*, where he won the National Press Club's Sandy Hume Award for political journalism. He graduated from San Francisco State University in 1986 and received a master's degree in English literature from the University of Virginia in 1988. For the *CQ Researcher*, he wrote "Confronting Warming," "Future of the GOP" and "Immigration Debate." His most recent *CQ Global Researcher* reports were "Rewriting History" and "International Adoption."

Leda Hartman is a nationally award-winning print and public radio journalist who specializes in global affairs. Her articles have appeared in *The New York Times* and *The Christian Science Monitor*, and her radio stories have aired on programs such as "Morning Edition," "All Things Considered," "Marketplace" and "The World." She also was an editor for two public radio global affairs programs, "Latitudes" and the "World Vision Report."

Kenneth Jost has written more than 160 reports for *CQ Researcher* since 1991 on topics ranging from legal affairs and social policy to national security and international relations. He is the author of *The Supreme Court Yearbook* and *Supreme Court From A to Z* (both CQ Press). He is an honors graduate of Harvard College and Georgetown Law School, where he teaches media law as an adjunct professor. He also writes the blog Jost on Justice (http://jostonjustice.blogspot.com). His previous reports include "Police Misconduct" (2012) and "Policing the Police" (2000).

Reed Karaim, a freelance writer in Tucson, Ariz., has written for *The Washington Post, U.S. News & World Report, Smithsonian, American Scholar, USA Weekend* and other publications. He is the author of the novel, *If Men Were Angels*, which was selected for the Barnes & Noble Discover Great New Writers series. He is also the winner of the Robin Goldstein Award for Outstanding Regional Reporting and other journalism honors. Karaim is a graduate of North Dakota State University in Fargo.

Peter Katel is a *CQ Researcher* contributing writer who previously reported on Haiti and Latin America for *Time* and *Newsweek* and covered the Southwest for newspapers in New Mexico. He has received several journalism awards, including the Bartolomé Mitre Award for coverage of drug trafficking, from the Inter-American Press

Association. He holds an A.B. in university studies from the University of New Mexico. His recent reports include "Mexico's Future" and "3D Printing."

Danielle Kurtzleben reports on business and economics for *U.S. News & World Report* and previously worked at the Pew Research Center's Project for Excellence in Journalism. Originally from rural northern Iowa, Danielle holds a B.A. in English from Carleton College (Northfield, Minn.) and an M.A. in Global Communication from George Washington University's Elliott School for International Affairs. She has appeared on C-SPAN and the Washington, D.C., public radio affiliate, WAMU, and she is also a regular contributor to the career website Brazen Life.

Barbara Mantel is a freelance writer in New York City. She is a 2012 Kiplinger Fellow and has won several journalism awards, including the National Press Club's Best Consumer Journalism Award and the Front Page Award from the Newswomen's Club of New York for her Nov. 1, 2009, CQ Global Researcher report "Terrorism and the Internet." She holds a B.A. in history and economics from the University of Virginia and an M.A. in economics from Northwestern University.

Jason McLure is a New Hampshire-based freelance writer. Previously he was a campaign correspondent for Reuters and an Africa correspondent for Bloomberg News and *Newsweek* and worked for *Legal Times* in Washington, D.C. His writing has appeared in publications such as *The Economist, The New York Times* and *BusinessWeek*. His last *CQ Global Researcher* was "Booming Africa." His work has been honored by the Washington, D.C., chapter of the Society for Professional Journalists, the Maryland-Delaware-District of Columbia Press Association and the Overseas Press Club of America Foundation. He is also coordinator of the Committee to Free Eskinder Nega, a jailed Ethiopian journalist.

Tom Price is a Washington-based freelance journalist and a contributing writer for *CQ Researcher*. Previously, he was a correspondent in the Cox Newspapers Washington Bureau and chief politics writer for the *Dayton Daily News* and *The* (Dayton) *Journal Herald*. He is author or coauthor of five books including, with former U.S. Rep.

Tony Hall (D-Ohio), *Changing The Face of Hunger: One Man's Story of How Liberals, Conservatives, Democrats, Republicans and People of Faith Are Joining Forces to Help the Hungry, the Poor and the Oppressed.*

Jennifer Weeks is a Massachusetts freelance writer who specializes in energy, the environment and science. She has written for *The Washington Post, Audubon, Popular Mechanics* and other magazines and previously was a policy analyst, congressional staffer and lobbyist. She has an A.B. degree from Williams College and master's degrees from the University of North Carolina and Harvard. Her recent *CQ Researcher* reports include "Coastal Development" and "Managing Wildfires."

Global Issues,
2015 Edition

1

Chemical and Biological Weapons

Reed Karaim

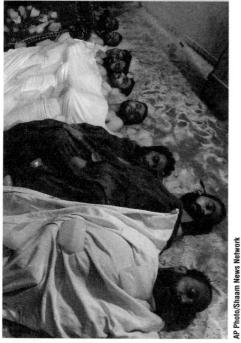

Civilians lie in a makeshift mortuary after being killed in a sarin gas attack on Damascus, Syria, on Aug. 21, 2013. Syrian forces under President Bashar al-Assad launched the attack against rebel forces in the city, according to Human Rights Watch and the U.S. and French governments. More than 1,400 people were killed, including hundreds of women and children, according to the U.S. government.

From *CQ Researcher*,
December 13, 2013.

AP Photo/Shaam News Network

As soon as the first rockets exploded around 2:45 a.m. on Aug. 21 in the Damascus suburb of Ghouta, in Syria, residents began experiencing horrific suffering: frothing at the mouth, fluid coming out of the eyes, convulsions and suffocation.[1]

Two hours later another round of rockets landed in the nearby neighborhood of Moadamiya. "We were praying in the mosque near the Turbi area, 400 meters away," an eyewitness later told the international advocacy group Human Rights Watch. "We heard the strike and went to the site to help the wounded . . . when we got there someone was screaming, 'Chemical! Chemical!' People covered their faces with shirts dunked in water. We didn't smell anything, but . . . if anyone entered the building where the rocket fell, they would faint."[2]

Human Rights Watch and United Nations inspectors later said the rockets carried sarin nerve gas. One drop of sarin fluid can make a person ill.[3] Estimates of the number of Syrians who died in the attacks range from the U.S. government's figure of more than 1,400 — including 426 children and other civilians — to 355, reported by Médicins Sans Frontières (Doctors Without Borders), the international humanitarian organization.[4]

Global outrage over the attacks sparked a renewed debate about how the world community should respond to chemical and biological weapons, and whether they are really any worse — morally or in their lethal effect — than conventional wartime arms. Both types of weapons kill people, some observers say, so making a distinction is meaningless. But others say chemical weapons are unique, in that they target defenseless civilians.

Most Chemical Weapons Have Been Destroyed

Nearly 82 percent of the world's declared chemical weapons have been destroyed since the Chemical Weapons Convention went into effect in 1997. Russia has the world's largest remaining stockpile of chemical weapons, about three times more than the United States. At least six countries are thought to have had or to still have undeclared chemical weapons.

Amount of Chemical Weapons Declared, Destroyed and Remaining, by Country (as of October, 2013)

Country	Metric Tons** Declared	Percent Destroyed (as of)	Metric Tons** Remaining
Albania	16	100% (2007)	0
South Korea	undisclosed	100% (2008)	0
India	1,000+	100% (2009)	0
United States	31,500	90% (intends by 2023)	3,150
Russia	40,000	76% (pledged by 2015-20)	9,600
Libya	26.3	85% (planning by end of 2016)	3.95
Iraq	unknown*	0%	NA
Syria	1,300	In process (first half of 2014)	NA

Note: Japan left 350,000 chemical munitions on Chinese soil during World War II. It is working with China to dispose of those weapons.

* When Iraq joined the Chemical Weapons Convention in 2009, it said an unknown quantity of chemical agents remained in bunkers that were bombed in 2003.

** A metric ton is 2,204.6 pounds.

Sources: Organisation for the Prohibition of Chemical Weapons; "Chemical and Biological Weapons Status at a Glance," Arms Control Association, October 2013, www.armscontrol.org/factsheets/cbwprolif, and telephone conversations with Arms Control Association personnel

The rockets fired on Damascus had almost certainly been fired by the government of President Bashar al-Assad against rebel forces in Syria's ongoing civil war, according to Human Rights Watch and the U.S. and French governments. Although chemical weapons such as sarin long have been prohibited by international treaty, at the time of the attacks Syria was one of five nations that hadn't signed the 1993 Convention on the Prohibition of Chemical Weapons, known simply as the Chemical Weapons Convention (CWC), which went into effect in 1997.

Although some evidence indicated that Syria had used chemicals weapons on a smaller scale earlier in the war, the Ghouta attack represented the first time a nation had launched a significant chemical weapons attack since Iraqi leader Saddam Hussein used them against Iran and Iraqi Kurds in the 1980s.

The United States and much of the global community quickly condemned Syria's action. "This attack is an assault on human dignity," said President Obama, adding that he would ask Congress to support a limited military strike against Syrian forces in response. "Here's my question for every member of Congress and every member of the global community: What message will we send if a dictator can gas hundreds of children to death in plain sight and pay no price?"[5]

Obama's comments were intended to reinforce a "red line" he had drawn earlier insisting that chemical weapons were outside of the acceptable international norms of behavior, even in war. But some critics of Obama's comment questioned the wisdom of taking a position that could require a military response.

"The lesson learned is: Never anchor yourself by drawing red lines because then you take away other options," says Gary Guertner, a professor at the University of Arizona in Tucson and former chairman of the Policy and Strategy Department at the U.S. Army War College.

Others observers, however, suggested Obama should have acted even more forcefully. "When it comes to saying this is horrible, we need to contain it. We need to draw the line," says Michael Rubin, a resident scholar at the conservative American Enterprise Institute and a former Pentagon official. "The president could have acted symbolically by immediately targeting the units that used the weapons."

Obama asked Congress to approve limited strikes on Syria in retaliation, but lawmakers from both parties indicated that Congress might not approve more military action in the Middle East. Nevertheless, facing even the possibility of a U.S. military strike, Syria agreed to sign the 1993 convention and open its chemical weapons arsenal for immediate inspection and dismantling.

Although the deal, largely brokered by Syria's key ally, Russia, meant the U.S. Congress never had to vote on whether to authorize the use of force, the debate over the threat represented by chemical and biological weapons — and how the world should respond to their use — has continued.

Chemical weapons have been considered unacceptable by the global community since the widespread use of poison gases in World War I killed or wounded thousands of soldiers. The Geneva Protocol banned them in 1928, and although scattered exceptions have occurred, the convention and the even stronger 1993 accord have largely kept chemical weapons off the world's battlefields.

"It's a real robust taboo that has developed over time," says Richard Price, a professor of political science at the University of British Columbia in Vancouver and the author of *The Chemical Weapons Taboo*. "What you saw in Syria, it's the first time they've been used in 25 years. That's a remarkable record for a weapon of warfare."

Biological weapons, which use disease microbes or toxins to attack their victims, have received less attention but also are outlawed by an international treaty, the 1972 Biological Weapons Convention, which went into force in 1975. Although biological agents rarely

North Korea Said to Have Large Stockpile

At least six countries are thought to have had or to still have undeclared chemical weapons, including North Korea, which is believed to have a large stockpile developed during a long-standing program.

Countries Suspected of Having Chemical Weapons

China — The United States alleged in 2003 that China had an "advanced chemical weapons research and development program," but a 2010 State Department report said there was insufficient evidence to confirm China's previous or current activities.

Egypt — Allegedly stockpiled chemical weapons and used them against Yemen in 1963-67; has never signed the Chemical Weapons Convention (CWC).

Iran — Denounces possession of chemical weapons; recent State Department assessments said Iran is "capable of weaponizing" chemical agents in a variety of delivery systems.

Israel — Believed to have had an offensive chemical weapons program in the past, but there is no conclusive evidence of an ongoing program; has not ratified the CWC.

North Korea — Has a "long-standing CW program" and a large stockpile of weapons, according to a 2012 U.S. intelligence assessment.

Sudan — Unconfirmed reports say that Sudan developed and used chemical weapons in the past; United States bombed what was alleged to be a chemical weapons factory in 1998. A 2005 State Department report questions whether Sudan was ever involved in chemical weapons manufacture.

Sources: Organisation for the Prohibition of Chemical Weapons; "Chemical and Biological Weapons Status at a Glance," Arms Control Association, October 2013, www.armscontrol.org/factsheets/cbwprolif, and telephone conversations with Arms Control Association personnel

have been used in warfare, some analysts consider them a greater potential threat, especially as a terrorist weapon.

Chemical and biological weapons often are discussed together, but weapons experts point out they require different resources to build and pose different challenges to find and neutralize. Building a chemical weapons arsenal requires a significant industrial capacity, the ability not only to manufacture large amounts of the chemical agents but also to load them in rockets or shells that can be fired at the enemy. The large-scale industrial plants, resources and personnel required mean chemical weapons are harder to hide than biological weapons.

The 1993 Chemical Weapons Convention established an inspection procedure for chemical weapons sites and timetables for destruction of chemical arsenals. Nearly all nations with significant stockpiles of such weapons, including the United States and Russia, have been proceeding with their destruction. The Organisation for the Prohibition of Chemical Weapons, a Hague-based agency that oversees implementation of the convention, says 81.7 percent of the world's declared chemical weapons have been destroyed.[6]

Biological weapons, such as anthrax or smallpox, can be grown in a lab, so they have a smaller "footprint" than chemical weapons, making them easier to hide. But many of the deadliest pathogens exist only in a limited number of research laboratories around the world. Thus, they are less available than the basic materials of chemical weapons.

The United States and other nations have boosted efforts to secure supplies of dangerous pathogens in recent years. The 1972 Biological Weapons Convention, however, does not have the same strong inspection mechanisms as the Chemical Weapons Convention, leading to greater concerns that these deadly agents could be secretly grown and weaponized.

As the world weighs options for dealing with chemical and biological weapons, here are some of the questions under discussion:

Are chemical weapons worse than other weapons of war?

Chemical weapons are one of the few categories of weapons specifically banned through international treaty.[7] But even during World War I, when they were used widely by both sides, they accounted for a relatively small percentage of overall casualties.

Up to 100,000 soldiers were killed by gas attacks in World War I — less than 1 percent of the war's fatalities, and more than 1 million were wounded by gas, or about 2 percent of the total; many were blinded.[8] In the Syrian conflict, 70 to 100 times as many people have died from conventional weapons — 105,000 to 150,000 deaths — as died in the gas attacks.[9]

Such disparities lead some analysts to question whether chemical weapons should be considered worse

than other weapons. "There's a sense people have that somehow chemical weapons are worse — more horrifying. But if you look at it coolly and rationally, it's not obvious that they are worse than shelling or guns, which have killed many more people," says Dominic Tierney, a political science professor at Swarthmore College in Pennsylvania.

Regardless of the casualty count, other analysts believe chemical weapons have characteristics that make them especially brutal.

"There is something unique about chemical weapons" because of "who they most effectively destroy: babies sleeping in their cribs and innocent civilians," says Greg Thielmann, a senior fellow at the Washington-based Arms Control Association, which supports effective arm control policies. "And the people they're least likely to destroy are prepared soldiers because soldiers can protect themselves against chemical weapons much more easily than they can against high explosives."

Rubin, the American Enterprise Institute scholar, notes that chemical weapons are less accurate than conventional weapons. "Conventional munitions have become more precise over time — more lethal while also more precise," he says. "The problem with chemical weapons is that they're notoriously imprecise — they're at the mercy of the wind, for example." That means they can only be counted on to sow terror or kill indiscriminately, he adds.

But other analysts say the relative military ineffectiveness of chemical weapons argues against the idea they are worse than other weapons. "Because they are hard to use in most battlefield situations, chemical weapons are usually less lethal than non-taboo weapons like high explosives," wrote Stephen M. Walt, a professor of international affairs at Harvard University in Cambridge, Mass.[10]

And in a civil war such as the Syrian conflict, where President Assad has regularly targeted civilian neighborhoods held by the opposition, Walt asked, "Does it really matter whether Assad is killing his opponents using 500-pound bombs, mortar shells, cluster munitions, machine guns, icepicks or sarin gas? Dead is dead, no matter how it is done."[11]

Rubin counters that chemical weapons can cause particularly brutal injuries, and that victims can suffer permanently scarred lungs, nerve damage and other lingering disabilities. "The more relevant issue is not how

From Anthrax to Mustard Gas

Chemical and biological weapons have a variety of characteristics.

A wide range of chemical and biological weapons have been developed in the past century, although only a limited number have been used on the battlefield. The earliest poison gases deployed in World War I were easily countered by simple gas masks, but before the war's end scientists had developed mustard gas, a blistering agent effective enough that it remained in chemical arsenals into the 21st century.

Chemical and biological weapons are outlawed today under international treaties. Much of the world's chemical arsenal has already been destroyed, and biological weapons are considered unlikely to be used by nations because of their unpredictable nature. Still, some countries, including the United States and Russia, are still in the process of destroying their chemical arsenals, and it is possible other hidden stockpiles exist. Both chemical and biological weapons are also considered attractive to terrorist groups because of the weapons' ability to cause widespread destruction and panic.

Here are some of the main chemical and biological agents that have been or could be used in weapons:[1]

• **Mustard gas** — Nearly odorless and hard to detect, sulfur mustard gas damages the skin and mucous membranes on contact. It is an organic chemical compound that derives its name from a faint smell of the mustard plant that sometimes accompanies it. Exposure can come through the skin, eyes, lungs or by drinking contaminated water. Death often occurs when the lungs fill up with fluid after their linings are destroyed. No antidote exists for mustard gas.

• **Sarin** — One of the first "nerve agent" chemical weapons, sarin is an oily liquid that evaporates quickly into a vaporous gas. It can cause convulsions, constriction of the chest and suffocation. It interrupts the operation of an enzyme that works as an "off switch" for muscles and glands, which then become constantly stimulated. Exposure by inhalation or touch can be deadly. Even a drop of sarin on the skin can cause serious injury. Antidotes exist, but must be administered quickly.

• **VX** —The most potent of all nerve agents, VX acts upon the body much like sarin does but more quickly. A miniscule drop can be fatal. An oily liquid that evaporates slowly, it lingers on surfaces for days and can kill within minutes. Early symptoms include blurred vision, chest tightness, drooling and excessive sweating, nausea and small, pinpoint pupils.

• **Anthrax** — An infectious disease caused by a bacteria found in soil, anthrax infects both domestic and wild animals around the world, often fatally, but rarely humans naturally. Anthrax is not contagious, but exposure to the miniscule spores, less than a thousandth of an inch in size, can lead to serious sickness or death. A person can become exposed by breathing in anthrax, ingesting contaminated food or liquids or through an open wound. Anthrax can be treated with antibiotics, if diagnosed quickly enough.

• **Smallpox** — A contagious and sometimes fatal disease that has killed tens of millions of civilians throughout history. Some historians believe the British used smallpox-contaminated blankets as a weapon against Native Americans in colonial America. Smallpox was eradicated in the 20th century through a worldwide vaccination program. But the smallpox virus still exists in laboratory samples and is considered a potential bioterrorism weapon today. Infection can come through face-to-face contact or by handling contaminated objects such as clothing, or breathing contaminated air in closed spaces. The United States maintains a large supply of smallpox vaccine in the event of an outbreak.

• **Pneumonic Plague** — A relative of the bubonic plague ("Black Death") that wiped out a third to a half of Europe's population in the Middle Ages, the pneumonic plague can be transmitted from person to person. Symptoms of the potentially fatal disease usually include fever, weakness and rapidly developing pneumonia. The United States has antibiotics that could be used to treat pneumonic plague. Like smallpox and other disease agents, it is considered most likely to be used as a weapon by terrorists or individuals rather than by a military force.

— *Reed Karaim*

---

[1]Most of the information in this sidebar on chemical and biological agents comes from the Centers for Disease Control and Prevention website. For more complete lists and further details, see "Chemical Weapons Information," www.cdc.gov/nceh/demil/chemical_agent .htm, and "General Fact Sheets on Specific Bioterrorism Agents," http://emergency.cdc.gov/bioterrorism/factsheets.asp.

AFP/Getty Images/Ali Al-Saadi

Photographs of Iraqi Kurds gassed by Iraqi President Saddam Hussein are displayed at a memorial in the Kurdish town of Halabja, in northern Iraq. By some estimates 50,000-60,000 Iranians and Kurds were killed or wounded in Iraqi gas attacks during the Iran-Iraq War in the 1980s, which led in part to the 1993 Chemical Weapons Convention.

painful the death is, but what happens to the walking wounded. You have a much greater chance of recovering from a bullet or shrapnel wound than you do recovering from mustard gas or sarin," Rubin says. "Once the hostilities end, you can really suffer the effects of this much more acutely than the effects of a bullet wound, often for the rest of your life."

But Tierney believes drawing a line around chemical weapons can have an unintended negative consequence. "If you say chemical weapons are unacceptable in Syria, you're implicitly saying that conventional weapons are acceptable," he says. "You have to be careful about drawing these lines because there's a way in which you legitimize war on the other side of the line."

Making the kind of weapon used the determining factor in one's response to a conflict, he says, misses a larger point. "What I'd like to see is less focus on the means by which leaders kill and more on the ends: How many people killed? Focus more on the amount of human suffering and the overall situation and less on the specific means."

The University of British Columbia's Price, however, says ruling chemical weapons out of bounds has limited the potential for mass destruction in war. When chemical weapons first came on the scene, they were seen as potential weapons of mass destruction, he says. "People thought, 'Oh my God, you're going to wipe out whole

cities.' And that's why there were efforts to curtail them. Chemical weapons have never lived up to that, . . . in part because of the restraints we've imposed."

Anything that gets the world to say someone has gone too far when it comes to making war should be considered a positive, he adds. "We ought to be grateful that we have some of these thresholds, at least, that galvanize humanitarian attention and response around the world," he says.

But for others, lumping chemical and biological weapons together with nuclear arms as "weapons of mass destruction," as some U.S. policymakers have done, overstates their capacity for destruction. "I've always had trouble with that trilogy," says the University of Arizona's Guertner. "Nuclear weapons are in a category all by themselves. Neither chemical nor biological weapons are going to cause mass casualties in the sense that nuclear weapons are."

Although chemical weapons are not as destructive as nuclear weapons, Rubin says that doesn't mean they're not unusually cruel weapons.

"The real question is, do we say chemical weapons should become normal in war? Ultimately, I would say no. You risk opening a Pandora's box if you do," he says. "You're erasing a line that was drawn almost 100 years ago, and then you have to debate about where you draw the new line."

Are biological weapons a serious threat to the United States?

A week after the Sept. 11, 2001, terrorist attacks on the United States, letters containing anthrax spores were mailed to offices of two U.S. senators and several news media outlets.[12] The Centers for Disease Control and Prevention (CDC) considers anthrax, an infectious disease that can cause sickness or death, "one of the most likely agents to be used in a biological attack."[13]

Five people died and 17 became seriously ill from the anthrax-contaminated letters. The FBI eventually concluded they were the work of one man, Bruce Ivins, an army scientist with access to anthrax in a government lab. Ivins, who committed suicide before he could be charged, had a history of psychological problems, and his alleged motives remain obscure.[14]

Still, coming on the heels of the 9/11 attacks, the letters raised fears the nation was vulnerable to a major biological attack by terrorists.[15] Since 2001, the government has spent more than $71 billion to beef up its defenses against biological weapons by creating better detection systems and increasing stockpiles of vaccines and other treatments.[16] But there has not been a significant biological attack in the United States in the 12 years since 9/11, leading to a debate over the likelihood of such an event.

A 2012 study by the Aspen Institute, a Washington think tank, concluded that "the threat of bioterrorism remains undiminished," in part because the bacteria and viruses that could be used in a bioweapon are found around the world. "Any nation with a developed pharmaceutical industry has the capability to produce potent 'military-grade' bioweapons," the study said.[17]

While terrorists probably cannot build a weapon as sophisticated as a weapon of mass destruction, the report said, there is "considerable evidence" they could produce bioweapons approaching the standard of such a weapon. The study noted that al Qaeda is now headed by Ayman al Zawahiri, a former Egyptian surgeon who earlier led the terrorist group's efforts to develop a biological weapon, and al Qaeda still appears intent on developing such a weapon.[18]

A bioweapon attack is "a serious potential threat," says Leonard Cole, an editor of the study and director of the University of New Jersey's Program on Terror Medicine and Security. Noting that smallpox killed an estimated 300 million people in the 20th century before it was eradicated, he says, "Anybody who fails to understand or acknowledge the potential for catastrophic consequences of a biological release is not facing reality."

But while they agree the consequences of an attack would be severe, other experts doubt the capability of terrorist groups to build a bioweapon capable of mass death. For example, they point to the failure of the Japanese cult Aum Shinrikyo, which managed to obtain a nonlethal version of anthrax and another disease agent, but was unable to create biological weapons from them despite having a member who had done Ph.D. work in virology. The group later released sarin gas in the Tokyo metro.[19]

"Biological weapons are extremely hard to develop. Even though lots of ingredients are available, it still takes

World War I Saw Deadliest Chemical Attacks

Toxic gas dispersed first by Germany and then by both sides killed 100,000 people. It is unknown how many Chinese were killed by Japan's 2,000 chemical weapons attacks in 1937-42 because Japan was dropping non-chemical bombs at the same time. In the 1980s, Iraq's use of chemical weapons during the Iran-Iraq War killed or wounded up to 60,000 people, prompting a worldwide ban on the use of such weapons in 1993.

Casualties from Chemical Weapons Attacks

Year	Event	What Happened	Estimated Deaths/ Casualties
1915-18	WWI	Poison gas used, first by Germany against the Allies and then by both sides.	100,000 deaths
1935-36	Second Italo-Ethiopian War	Italy used mustard gas against the Ethiopians.	15,000 casualties
1937-42	Japanese Invasion of China	Japan used variety of chemical agents in 2,000 attacks against the Chinese.	unknown
1962-67	Vietnam War	U.S. used herbicides against the North Vietnamese.	unknown
1980-88	Iran-Iraq War	Iraq used various gases against Iran and the Kurds.	Up to 60,000 casualties
1995	Terrorist Attack	Aum Shinrikyo cult releases sarin gas in Tokyo metro.	13 deaths
2013	Syrian Civil War	Government uses sarin gas against rebel forces.	Up to around 1,400 deaths

Sources: Javed Ali, "Chemical Weapons and the Iran-Iraq War: A Case Study in Noncompliance," *The Nonproliferation Review*, Spring 2001, pp. 43-58; Lina Grip and John Hart, "The use of chemical weapons in the 1935-36 Italo-Ethiopian War, SIPRI Arms Control and Non-proliferation Programme, October 2009; "Chemical Weapons: Frequently Asked Questions," Arms Control Association, October 2013; "The Shadow of Ypres: The history of chemical weapons," *The Economist*, Aug. 31, 2013

a lot of skill and knowledge to convert a sample of anthrax into a bomb capable of causing widespread casualties," says Gregory Koblentz, deputy director of the biodefense graduate program at George Mason University in Fairfax, Va. "So far, we've not seen a terrorist group capable of doing that."

However, a bipartisan congressional commission looking at terrorist threats in 2008 concluded there was a high likelihood terrorists would use a weapon of mass destruction in the next five years, and "terrorists are more likely to be able to obtain and use a biological weapon than a nuclear weapon."[20] The commission painted a nightmare scenario: "A recent study from the intelligence community projected that a one- to two-kilogram [2.2- to 4.4-pound] release of anthrax spores from a crop duster plane could kill more Americans than died in World War II (over 400,000)."[21]

But two experts who examined the commission's scenario found several holes in their example. Lynn Klotz, a senior fellow at the Center for Arms Control and Non-Proliferation in Washington, and science journalist and Arizona State University journalism professor Edward J. Sylvester concluded it would take much more than four pounds to cause mass casualties, and there were significant challenges in getting the anthrax safely loaded into a spray plane and dispersed into the air.

"We decided this was very improbable," says Klotz. "These are sort of scare tactics. The way I look at these things is, you have a big bio-defense effort underway and the more you scare Congress, the more likely you are to get funding."

Given the technical hurdles, Klotz says, "Any serious biological attack would have to be launched by a state program." But, any country doing so would likely face massive retaliation if discovered, he adds. "It would have to be a state willing to take a big risk. That's not to say that I don't think there is a risk [that bioweapons could be used], I just don't think it's as big as people think there is."

However, because biological programs are relatively easy to conceal, nations, including those with ties to international terrorism, could maintain them secretly, says Raymond Zilinskas, director of the Chemical & Biological Weapons Nonproliferation Program at the Monterey Institute of International Studies at Middlebury College in Vermont. "Does North Korea

have a biological weapons program? Does Iran have a biological weapons program? Does Syria have a biological weapons program? All these are black boxes," he says. "We don't know what's going on inside them."

He adds that Russia has three military microbiological institutes "still active and closed to all foreigners. You have to assume they have weaponized agents waiting to go, if the decision was made."

But Klotz says the indiscriminate nature of biological weapons — they present a danger to anyone using them and can't be controlled once released — makes them unattractive as weapons of war. He notes the U.S. government discontinued its biological weapons program in 1969, when President Richard M. Nixon became convinced "the United States would be safer without biological weapons."

Can the world rid itself of chemical and biological weapons?

The Convention on the Prohibition of Chemical Weapons is widely considered an example of a successful disarmament treaty. Now that Syria signed the convention in September, only four nations — Angola, Egypt, North Korea and South Sudan — have not signed it, and two others, Israel and Myanmar, have signed but not ratified it.[22]

The world's other 190 nations have ratified the convention, which stipulates they will never use, develop, produce, acquire, transfer or stockpile chemical weapons. Under the accord, nations that have chemical weapons also agree to destroy them and submit to international inspection and verification of their efforts.[23]

The Organisation for the Prohibition of Chemical Weapons says more than 80 percent of all existing weapons have been destroyed, including the bulk of the sizable U.S. and Soviet arsenals, where destruction is ongoing. Several analysts are optimistic the global community will eventually rid itself of these weapons.

"It's very realistic to believe it can be done. It is being done," says the University of Arizona's Guertner. Worldwide revulsion, combined with the fact "the military doesn't like them" because they are imprecise and ineffective against prepared soldiers provides momentum to continue disarmament, he says.

But Swarthmore's Tierney doubts the world will ever be free of the threat. "You're always going to find regimes that are going to try to use chemical weapons," he says. "They're not that difficult to produce, and they do have shock value. In fact, an unfortunate side effect of putting them in a special category is that it might make them more attractive to groups looking to have that shock effect."

Thielmann, the Arms Control Association fellow, says the world's reaction to Syria's chemical attacks increases the chances the holdouts to the convention could reconsider. "I don't think anyone could watch what is happening in Syria and say it would be safe to use chemical weapons," he says. "It creates a real threat that the international community will come down on them like a ton of bricks."

While some analysts can envision a world without chemical weapons, the situation surrounding biological weapons is more complex. Thielmann notes that the 1972 Biological Weapons Convention does not have the inspection and verification provisions found in the Chemical Weapons Convention, making it impossible to be sure what nations are doing.

Still, he says, "Diseases and plagues are very hard to control. It's just not the kind of weapon that military forces like to have. I think there is a possibility, even in our lifetimes, of seeing a time when both biological and chemical weapons won't be part of the arsenals of any nation."

Thielmann adds, however, that individuals or terrorist organizations are another matter. "There's a much longer time that we will worry about a small group of individuals using them as a terror weapon," he says.

The Aspen Institute's Cole believes the world will never be rid of the threat of biological weapons. "How can you? That would be the same as getting rid of all biological agents, all pathogens," he says. "It's like saying get rid of every micro-organism and you'll be rid of all biological weapons."

The University of British Columbia's Price worries more about the prospect of a terrorist group or other "non-state actor" acquiring a biological weapon than about the possibility of such a group building chemical weapons, because a biological weapon has a greater capacity to do widespread harm. But, he concedes, that very capability limits the attractiveness of such weapons.

"There's a much greater risk of falling prey to it yourself," he says. "If some group unleashed a deadly plague,

it could just as well kill them. The extra bit of restraint that provides has always proven very powerful in the case of biological weapons."

However, the Monterey Institute's Zilinskas believes it is becoming increasingly likely that someone will use a biological weapon, as more people get their hands on deadly pathogens.

"The whole biological, technical workforce is growing all the time," he says. "Someone is going to get greedy. Without any doubt, that's going to happen."

BACKGROUND

Primitive Attempts

Chemical and biological weapons may seem like modern inventions, but primitive forms of both were used in some of the earliest recorded instances of warfare.

The ancient Scythians, fierce horsemen who came from an area around the Black Sea, were known for their use of poison arrows, according to the Greek historian Herodotus, which may have helped them defeat Darius, the king of Persia, in 513 B.C.[24]

About 750 years later, in 256 A.D., a Persian army attacking the Roman-controlled city of Dara-Europos apparently used a chemical gas attack. According to University of Leicester archaeologist Simon James, evidence from the site indicates the Persians added bitumen and sulfur to fires to create a toxic cloud in tunnels into the city that killed at least 20 Roman soldiers.[25]

An example of a primitive early attempt to use a biological weapon occurred in 1346, when Tartars besieging the city of Kaffa, in what is now Ukraine, catapulted plague-contaminated corpses into the city.[26]

Evidence also suggests that British forces in the French-Indian Wars in 1763 may have given blankets used by smallpox victims to hostile Native American tribes with the hope of infecting them. Smallpox did ravage Native Americans around the time.[27] There is also circumstantial evidence indicating the British may have used the same strategy during the Revolutionary War.[28]

By 1899, the potential of chemical weapons was well enough understood in Europe that most major world powers agreed, in the Hague Convention, not to use "poison or poisoned arms" in warfare.[29] The treaty was the first significant attempt to control chemical weapons, but less than two decades later it would be ignored in the first great war of the 20th century.

World War I

On April 22, 1915, French and French-Algerian soldiers in the allied trenches near Ypres, Belgium, saw a greenish-yellow cloud billow from the enemy lines and roll toward them. The first significant chemical attack of World War I had begun.[30]

German soldiers had opened the valves on 6,000 cylinders of liquid chlorine, which formed a poisonous gas when it hit the air. Chlorine gas strips the lining from the lungs and bronchial tubes, leading to a buildup of fluid in the lungs that causes the victim to drown in his own fluids.[31]

"The effect of the gas was devastating," wrote historian Martin Gilbert.[32] The French and Algerian troops had no gas masks, and as the gas reached them thousands fell dead in the trenches. Others fled. A four-mile gap was blown in the allied lines, but the Germans, advancing carefully through the cloud in crude masks of moistened cotton, were unable to exploit the advantage. They had launched the gas attack as an experiment but didn't have sufficient reserves in place to press on.[33]

The attack and others that followed, directed at British-held parts of the line, caused widespread outrage in England and other nations sympathetic to the allied cause. British military officers quickly asked for authority to respond in kind.[34] On Sept. 25, in the battle of Loos, France, the British unleashed their own chlorine gas attack on German lines. It ended up illustrating the dangerously unpredictable nature of chemical weapons.

As the gas was about to be released, the wind shifted along parts of the British lines. At least one officer in charge of a gas canister decided not to release his load of chlorine, but he was overridden by orders from headquarters far behind the lines. When the gas was released, some of it simply hung in no man's land between the trenches and some drifted back into British-held territory, gassing hundreds of British soldiers; confusion reigned on the battlefield.[35]

Gas would continue to cause similar problems for the rest of the war. As gas masks and other defensive measures improved, soldiers would become more used to dealing with it and holding their positions. In a deadly chemical

weapons race, both sides tried to develop ever more deadly weapons to gain an advantage. In 1917, the Germans introduced mustard gas, a blistering agent that could disable a soldier simply by getting on his skin or into his eyes, where it could cause blindness.[36] It also lingered in the environment, presenting a danger long after an attack.

The effectiveness of chemical weapons in World War I is debated by historians and chemical weapons experts. Considering they caused only a small percentage of casualties and never led to a major shift in fortunes, some analysts have discounted their significance.

But Edward Spiers, a British historian and the author of *A History of Chemical and Biological Weapons*, says, "Contemporaries did not regard them as 'relatively ineffective.' In fact, their proportion of usage grew with each year of the war."

For the soldiers in the trenches, however, despite their having equipment and gaining experience that enabled them to survive chemical attacks, the psychological impact of the chemical weapons did not dissipate.

"In the ordinary soldier there was born a hatred of gas that steadily deepened as the war progressed," wrote Robert Harris and Jeremy Paxman in *A Higher Form of Killing*, a history of chemical and biological warfare.[37]

That revulsion only grew after the war, as the public learned more about conditions on the battlefield and the lingering health problems faced by gassing victims, according to Spiers. "The psychological fears of gas . . . magnified in some of the postwar imagery of temporarily blinded victims of mustard gas, coupled with fears of its future development — and especially aerial delivery over cities — all stoked the postwar reaction," he says.

In 1925 in Geneva, at a disarmament conference held under the auspices of the League of Nations, the leading military powers agreed to "the Prohibition of the Use in War of Asphyxiating, Poisonous or Other Gases, and of Bacteriological Methods of Warfare."[38]

Eventually, some 130 nations signed onto the so-called Geneva Protocol. But the strength of the prohibition soon was severely tested.

World War II

The prohibition against chemical weapons largely held on the battlefields during World War II, the largest and deadliest conflict in history. Before the war, Italy used

C H R O N O L O G Y

1915-1925 *Widespread use of poison gas during World War I leads to growing revulsion toward chemical weapons.*

1915 Germans use chlorine gas against the French at Ypres, Belgium, in first major chemical weapons attack of World War I (April 22). . . . British use chlorine gas in battle of Loos, France (Sept. 25).

1918 Germans lob more than half a million gas shells at allied troops in final attempt to break through allied lines in France in the Second Battle of the Marne.

1925 Geneva Protocol outlawing chemical and biological warfare is signed by most nations, U.S. signs but doesn't ratify the treaty. Japan does not sign.

1940-1945 *Major powers build up their chemical arsenals, but the prohibition against chemical weapons largely holds on World War II battlefields.*

1940 Japanese drop rice and wheat mixed with plague-carrying fleas over China and Manchuria, a primitive use of biological weapons against the civilian population.

1940-1945 Germany, the United States, Britain and Japan accumulate stockpiles of deadly chemical agents but never use them against each other during the war, partly in fear of retaliation.

1947-1972 *As the Cold War heats up, the United States and the Soviet Union build chemical and biological arsenals.*

1947 Soviet Union begins building secret factory in Zagorsk to produce smallpox for biological weapons.

1950 United States begins building secret biological weapons facility in Pine Bluff, Ark.

1969 President Richard M. Nixon orders the unilateral end of the U.S. biological weapons program.

1972 Biological Weapons Convention, which prohibits the research, use or stockpiling of biological agents, is negotiated. U.S. is early signatory.

1983-1993 *Iraq defies prohibition on chemical weapons without consequences. New international treaty seeks to eliminate chemical weapons.*

1983-1988 Iraq uses lethal mustard, phosgene and hydrogen-cyanide gases in Iran-Iraq War. Some 50,000 Iranians die from the attacks. World community does not interfere.

1988 Iraq uses hydrogen-cyanide and mustard gases against Kurds.

1993 Chemical Weapons Convention, calling for the elimination of chemical weapons, is negotiated.

2001-Present *Concerns raised by 9/11 terrorist attacks on United States give new urgency to efforts to control and defend against chemical and biological weapons.*

2001 Shortly after 9/11, letters containing anthrax are sent to news media offices and two U.S. senators, killing five people and infecting 17 others. FBI identifies Bruce Ivins, a government scientist, as the culprit, though some doubt his guilt; he commits suicide before being charged.

2003 Claiming Iraq still has chemical and biological weapons, President George W. Bush pushes the United States and its allies to invade. It is later determined Iraq had no such working weapons.

2012 President Obama warns Syria that use of chemical weapons in the country's civil war would cross an unacceptable "red line."

2013 Chemical weapons attacks in Damascus by Syrian military kill more than 1,400 people (Aug. 21). . . . President Obama says he will seek authorization from Congress for a limited military response to the Syrian chemical attacks (Aug. 31). . . . As part of a deal negotiated by Russia and the United States, Syria announces it will join the Chemical Weapons Convention and allow inspectors to enter the country to identify and dismantle its chemical weapons (September). . . . Organisation for the Prohibition of Chemical Weapons announces that Syria's most critical chemical weapons will be removed from the country by year's end (November).

Biological Weapons vs. Natural Occurrences

Sometimes it's difficult to tell the difference.

The use of biological weapons, which rely on disease agents, is not always easy to separate from natural occurrences. A sudden outbreak of plague, for example, could be caused by a weapon or a new, mutated version of the bacteria that causes the disease.

One of the strangest cases of confusion about a biological weapon and a natural occurrence may have occurred during the Cold War, when Secretary of State Alexander Haig publicly charged Soviet-backed forces in Laos and Cambodia with waging biological warfare.

In a 1981 speech in Berlin followed by a detailed report to Congress, Haig said Hmong fighters and others resisting the Soviet-backed forces in the two Southeast Asian countries told officials they had been sprayed from the air with a yellow substance, and that hundreds of casualties had resulted.[1]

U.S. investigators interviewed Hmong refugees and obtained small samples of the "yellow rain" to test. They concluded the samples included potentially deadly mycotoxins derived from fungi. If the samples were from a biological weapon released in the air, it would have violated the 1925 Geneva Protocol outlawing the use of chemical or biological weapons. It also would have been the first significant use of such a weapon during the Cold War.[2]

But Matthew S. Meselson and Julian Perry Robinson, scientific researchers from Harvard and the University of Sussex in England, respectively, wrote in 2008 that a scientist at the Chemical Defence Establishment at Porton Down had determined in 1982 that the principal component of the yellow rain was pollen.[3]

Repeated tests later confirmed that finding, and subsequent research indicated that bees in the region sometimes engaged in mass "cleansing flights" in which they released large amounts of yellow bee feces in the air. That was almost certainly what the Americans had publicly charged was a dangerous biological weapon.

Although the U.S. government never formally renounced the charges, the scientific evidence indicates the refugees either exaggerated their claims or confused the physical injuries caused by the effects of conventional arms — including from smoke inhalation and physical

Demonstrators at the Albanian Embassy in Skopje, Macedonia, hold a sign reading "Stop chemical weapons" on Nov. 14, 2013. They oppose possible plans to destroy Syrian chemical weapons in nearby Albania.

shock — with those caused by chemical weapons. The initial results indicating mycotoxins were also found to be suspect by later researchers, although it is possible that the bee droppings could have contained miniscule amounts of fungal material.[4]

"The lesson is, if you're going to investigate these type of allegations you need to lean on scientists, not political types. The other lesson is you need to be skeptical of refugee accounts until you get first-hand information," says Gary Guertner, a professor at the University of Arizona in Tucson who previously served as chairman of the Policy and Strategy Department at the U.S. Army War College.

— *Reed Karaim*

[1] Jonathan B. Tucker, "The "Yellow Rain Controversy: Lessons for Arms Control Compliance," *The NonProliferation Review*, Spring 2001, http://cns.miis.edu/npr/pdfs/81tucker.pdf.

[2] *Ibid.*

[3] Matthew S. Meselson and Julian Perry Robinson, "The Yellow Rain Affair: Lessons from a Discredited Allegation," in *Terrorism, War or Disease?* (2008), p. 76, http://belfercenter.ksg.harvard.edu/publication/18277/yellow_rain_affair.html.

[4] Tucker, *op. cit.*

chemical weapons, primarily mustard gas, in a campaign against the Ethiopian army in 1935-36, a precursor to the larger war.[39] Japan also used various forms of gas and other chemical and biological weapons during its invasion of China, but the actual death toll attributable to such weapons is undetermined because the Japanese were using conventional bombs simultaneously.[40] But the countries fighting in Europe, including Nazi Germany, refrained from battlefield gas attacks, and Japan and the United States never used chemical weapons against each other in the Pacific.

The major powers had built up significant chemical weapons arsenals between the world wars, but historians say the Geneva Protocol largely held, for several reasons. Revulsion stemming from the World War I experience partly explained the restraint. In addition, "President Roosevelt was staunchly against the use of gas," says the University of British Columbia's Price. "He personally found it abhorrent and said we will not be the first to use these weapons."

In England, Prime Minister Winston Churchill pressed his military commanders to consider using gas if the Germans invaded. But the commanders, many of whom had first-hand experience with gas in World War I, rejected the idea. "Clearly, I cannot make head against the parsons and the warriors at the same time," a frustrated Churchill wrote.[41]

Nazi leader Adolf Hitler had been gased and temporarily blinded during the end of his World War I military service. Historians have speculated the experience may have contributed to his reluctance to use chemical weapons on the battlefield — although it did nothing to stop him from gassing to death millions in his concentration camps.

Experts suggest that fear of retaliation may explain why the most powerful combatants in the war never engaged in chemical warfare. "Neither side felt like they were ready to prevail if the conflict took that turn," says Price. Despite stockpiles of chemical weapons, he adds, "both sides felt they were under-prepared."

China, the only theater of war where chemical weapons were used during the Second World War, also suffered the only significant deployment of biological weapons in modern warfare. Jeanne Guillemin, a senior adviser at the Massachusetts Institute of Technology Security Studies

A chemical company technician in Münster, Germany, demonstrates how to dispose of rocket-borne chemical warfare agents on Oct. 30, 2013. More than three-quarters of the world's declared chemical weapons have been destroyed since the 1993 Chemical Weapons Convention went into effect in 1997. At least six countries are thought to have had, or still have, undeclared chemical weapons.

Program, says the Japanese dropped disease agents from the air, contaminated water supplies and even introduced plague-infected fleas. They also conducted experiments on civilians and prisoners to measure the effectiveness of biological weapons.[42]

"The use of biological weapons in 1942 as the Japanese were retreating east from central China was likely quite extensive, although sorting out biological weapons casualties from victims of conventional weapons is difficult," Guillemin says. "Some have estimated the victims at 200,000 or so. Anthrax, glanders [an infectious disease], cholera, and typhoid were certainly used."

Japan's biological warfare and human experimentation have gotten little notice, Guillemin says, because after the war American officials suppressed information about the program in order to shield Japanese scientists and officials from prosecution in order to take advantage of Japan's germ warfare experiences for the U.S. bioweapons program. If the program and its consequences had come fully to light, Guillemin believes the future might have taken a different turn. "There was a critical juncture in late 1945 [and] early 1946 at which biological programs could have been legally eliminated," she says, "but that moment passed."

Instead, the United States and other nations continued to develop both biological and chemical agents. "Unfortunately, a real arms race developed between the Soviets and the U.S. over who could develop the most deadly chemical weapons. Further laboratory development went on for more than 25 years after World War II," says Paul Walker, a longtime arms control expert who runs the Washington office of Green Cross International, a global environmental organization headquartered in Geneva.

Despite the development and stockpiling of deadly chemical and biological agents, only a few cases of relatively small-scale use were reported in the next few decades. Egyptian forces involved in a civil war in Yemen used chemical weapons in the 1960s, and the Soviet Union may have supplied chemical weapons to fighters in Southeast Asia and Afghanistan in the 1970s.[43]

However, in the 1980s, during the eight-year Iraq-Iran War, Iraqi leader Saddam Hussein shattered the international prohibition against the use of chemical weapons when he made widespread use of them on the battlefield against the Iranians and against Kurdish communities inside Iraq, which were in a loose alliance with Iran. An estimated 50,000-60,000 Iranians were killed by a variety of chemical weapons, and up to 100,000 continue to suffer today from lingering health effects.[44]

Unlike the Obama administration's outrage at the gassing deaths of up to 1,400 Syrians earlier this year, the Ronald Reagan administration was mostly silent about the deaths of tens of thousands of Iranians and Kurds due to Saddam's chemical attacks. In fact, *The Washington Post* later found that the Reagan administration knew it was supplying materials to Iraq that were being used to make chemical weapons, but the administration considered stopping Iran's forces a priority.[45]

The initial response among other Western nations also was muted, although Iran protested to the United Nations and sent victims of the attacks to Europe in an effort to build international support for its cause.[46] "The world basically ignored the Iraqi use of chemical weapons against Iran," says Thielmann, the Arms Control Association fellow. "And the U.S., the most powerful nation in the world, decided to assist Saddam Hussein, the perpetrator of these attacks. . . . That was a terrible example of the world failing to enforce the [1925 Geneva] ban on chemical weapons."

However, the attacks against Kurdish civilians and growing concern about Iraq's behavior finally led the United States, the U.N. and other nations to speak out.[47] Iraq's chemical weapons use is thought to have spurred the global community to adopt the Convention on the Prohibition of Chemical Weapons in 1993, which contained stronger provisions than the Geneva Protocol had, allowing inspections and requiring the destruction of weapons stockpiles.[48]

Until the Syrian civil war, the only other use of chemical weapons since the convention was enacted occurred in 1994-1995, when Aum Shinrikyo, a Japanese cult that believed it was destined to rule the world, launched two sarin gas attacks in Tokyo. In the largest attack, Aum followers released sarin gas in three different trains in the Tokyo subway system. About 5,000 people were injured and a dozen died.[49]

The attacks raised concerns that similar groups could get access to chemical weapons — fears that only grew after the 9/11 attacks. Worried that terrorists or other rogue groups could get their hands on chemical weapons, governments around the world have been dismantling their chemical arsenals ever since.

CURRENT SITUATION

Syria Disarms

Change in Syria's chemical weapons status is occurring rapidly. In September the Assad regime announced it would submit to the Chemical Weapons Convention.

In mid-November, the Organisation for the Prohibition of Chemical Weapons (OPCW) announced that the most critical chemical weapons in Syria's arsenal will be removed from the country by the end of the year, while the rest will be removed by early February.[50] Once outside Syria, the country's declared arsenal of nearly 1,300 tons of chemical weapons will be destroyed in the "safest and soonest manner," no later than the end of June 2014, according to the OPCW Executive Council.[51]

Earlier in November, OPCW inspectors announced they had only one site left to check and had verified that Syria had destroyed 22 of the 23 sites the Syrian government said had been used to produce chemical weapons.[52] A week earlier, the OPCW announced that

And the Nobel Peace Prize Goes to. . . .

The Organisation for the Prohibition of Chemical Weapons won the 2013 award.

On Oct. 11, Thorbjorn Jagland, chairman of the Nobel Prize Committee, stepped to the podium in Oslo, Norway, to announce that, to the surprise of many, the Organisation for the Prohibition of Chemical Weapons (OPCW) had been awarded the 2013 Nobel Peace Prize.

The OPCW had not been considered a favorite to win the world's most prestigious humanitarian award, but Jagland noted that the organization has helped to define "the use of chemical weapons as a taboo under international law."[1]

Combined with the OPCW's recent investigation of Syria's chemical arsenal, the award brought international recognition to an agency that has largely worked behind the scenes during most of its existence. Secretary of State John Kerry joined those praising the organization, saying the OPCW "has taken extraordinary steps and worked with unprecedented speed" to respond to Syria's use of chemical weapons last summer. Kerry praised the "bravery and resolve" of OPCW inspectors who had traveled through the country during wartime to verify that Syria had used — and was shutting down — its chemical weapons operations.[2]

The OPCW was created in 1997 to serve as the watchdog for the Convention on the Prohibition of Chemical Weapons, an international accord outlawing the use, manufacture or possession of chemical weapons. Since then, the agency's 125 inspectors have conducted more than 5,000 inspections in 86 countries, often under difficult or dangerous circumstances.

Based in The Hague, Netherlands, the OPCW is a relatively small international agency, with an annual budget of about $100 million and a staff of 500. But it oversees one of the largest disarmament efforts in history. Only six nations — Angola, Egypt, North Korea, South Sudan, Israel and Myanmar — have either refused to sign or have not ratified the convention; 190 nations have joined.

To date, 64,124 tons of chemical agents — nearly 82 percent of the global declared stockpile of chemical weapons — have been destroyed in compliance with the convention, according to the OPCW. Individual nations are generally responsible for destroying their arsenals,

Turkish diplomat Ahmet Uzumcu, director-general of the Organisation for the Prohibition of Chemical Weapons, received the Nobel Peace Prize in Oslo, Norway, on Dec. 10, 2013.

Getty Images/Anadolu Agency/Irfan Cemiloglu

although they sometimes receive outside assistance. OPCW inspectors monitor the progress to make sure nations are complying with the treaty.[3] Most of the remaining global arsenal is in the United States and Russia, which are behind schedule in destroying their large chemical weapons stockpiles.

The delays have been attributed to the unexpected complexity of destroying the dangerous chemical agents in the weapons, according to James Lewis, a spokesman for the Center for Arms Control and Non-Proliferation, a Washington-based research organization. But both countries hope to done within the next 10 years.

— Reed Karaim

---

[1]"The Nobel Peace Prize for 2013," The Nobel Prize, Oct. 11, 2013, www.nobelprize.org/nobel_prizes/peace/laureates/2013/press.html.

[2]John Kerry, "Statement on Awarding of the Nobel Peace Prize to the Organisation for the Prohibition of Chemical Weapons," U.S. Department of State, Oct. 11, 2013, www.state.gov/secretary/remarks/2013/10/215318.htm.

[3]"Demilitarisation: Latest facts and figures," Organisation for the Prohibition of Chemical Weapons, Oct. 30, 2013, www.opcw.org/our-work/demilitarisation/.

Syria said the equipment at all the sites had been rendered inoperable.[53]

"This is much quicker than any other state," says Green Cross's Walker. "Everything I've heard from negotiators and inspectors has been very positive. They've said the Syrian government and military seem very committed to following through on their obligations under the Chemical Weapons Convention."

James Lewis, a spokesman for the Center for Arms Control and Non-Proliferation, says the Syrians could be hiding some facilities or weapons, but OPCW has 27 people in the country, and the Syrian government has made no effort to impede their investigation. He adds, "Syria runs a major risk of getting caught if it tries to cheat."

Rubin, the American Enterprise Institute scholar, doubts the sincerity of the Syrian effort. But, he says, "What I find most troubling is that if you have chemical weapons, use them once to the greatest effect and then cry uncle, you can escape [serious sanctions]." Syria is facing no significant retribution, he says, even though "here you have a thousand people killed."

Other Efforts

Although the OPCW's efforts in Syria have captured the world's attention, chemical weapons also have been dismantled and destroyed recently in several other countries.

The Chemical Weapons Convention calls for nations to declare their arsenals within 30 days of joining the accord and have destruction facilities — usually special incinerators — ready for testing by the second year; destruction of the most dangerous chemical weapons should commence in the third year and be complete within 10 years after signing.[54]

Many nations that joined the accord never developed chemical weapons, while others certified they had previously disposed of their arsenals. Albania, India and South Korea have destroyed their chemical weapons stockpiles and facilities under the accord. Libya is very close to finishing its chemical disarmament effort.[55]

Russia and the United States have the world's two largest chemical arsenals and are significantly behind schedule in destroying their chemical weapons. But Lewis, of the Center for Arms Control and Non-Proliferation, says the delays are due to the difficulty of destroying such large amounts of chemical weapons.

The United States, which originally listed 30,000 tons of nerve gases and other chemical agents in its arsenal, has destroyed 90 percent of that stockpile at an estimated cost of $28 billion, according to the center. The United States still has two facilities with chemical weapons — in Pueblo, Colo., and Blue Grass, Ky. It plans to complete destruction of its remaining arsenal by 2023 — 13 years past its original deadline.[56]

Russia has destroyed about 75 percent of its declared stockpile of 44,100 tons of chemical agents, according to the center. It hopes to complete its work between 2015 and 2020.[57]

"The sheer volume of these materials has been a problem, and [in the U.S.] there was a lot of backlash from the environmental community about how are you destroying this stuff," Lewis says. "We had a limited number of locations where we were burning it, and then the decision was made that we wouldn't do that anymore. We're using low-temperature destruction, which takes a long time."

The United States originally hoped to incinerate its stockpile at three sites, but concerns about moving the material safely across the country eventually led to creating nine disposal sites, according to Green Cross's Walker, who was involved in the early establishment of the program.

The process proved more time consuming and complicated than the Pentagon anticipated, he notes. As an alternative to high-temperature incineration, the United States turned to using chemical agents to neutralize the chemicals in the weapons and then incinerating the final product.

"Both countries are behind," Walker says. "But I must say that both countries have been fully committed."

Bioweapons Threats

America's effort to protect itself from a biological attack is proceeding along several fronts. Two key programs initiated after the 9/11 terror attacks are expanding the health care system's ability to respond to an attack and developing an early warning system to detect dangerous airborne biological elements.

The Biowatch detection system, established by President George W. Bush in 2003, now has sensors that analyze the air for dangerous microorganisms in 30 U.S. cities and is used during large spectator events. Plans also are

Does use of chemical weapons warrant military intervention?

YES
Patrick Christy
*Senior Policy Analyst,
Foreign Policy Initiative*

NO
John Mueller
*Political Scientist, Ohio State University; Senior
Fellow, Cato Institute; Author,* Atomic Obsession:
Nuclear Alarmism from Hiroshima to Al-Qaeda

Written for *CQ Researcher,* December 2013

Written for *CQ Researcher,* December 2013

When the use of chemical weapons by foreign entities threatens America's national security interests, military intervention is warranted. President Obama said as much in August 2012, when he drew a "red line" against Syrian dictator Bashar al-Assad's use or transfer of chemical weapons in Syria. However, Obama's failure to respond to Assad's subsequent use of chemical weapons was a mistake that has undermined our values and harmed U.S. interests in the Middle East and beyond.

Assad's repeated use of chemical weapons in 2013 was an open challenge to America's moral values and national security interests. The regime has slaughtered more than 1,500 people using chemical weapons in a conflict that has claimed more than 115,000 lives. He has employed death squads, missile strikes and chemical weapon attacks in his effort to terrorize the Syrian people into submission. These barbaric acts have helped facilitate the emergence of Islamist extremists in opposition-held territory, while Assad relies on Hezbollah and Iranian Revolutionary Guard Quds Force fighters to transform an uprising into a regional conflict. This cauldron of terror, regional instability and weapons of mass destruction directly threatens such U.S. allies as Jordan, Turkey and Israel.

Obama's failure to adequately enforce his own "red line" on Assad's use of chemical weapons undermines U.S. credibility and has created a crisis of confidence in Washington's ability to deter aggression. Secretary of State John Kerry was right when he warned, "we will have lost credibility in the world . . . if we turn our backs today."

Assad has gone unpunished for his crimes. The U.S.-Russian agreement on Assad's chemical weapons has not removed him from power and does not guarantee that he will surrender his chemical weapons. If anything, it gave him a green light to continue his indiscriminate violence against Syrian rebels and non-combatants, so long as he does not again use chemical weapons.

A U.S.-led military intervention in Syria would not have created Iraq 2.0. At a minimum, limited airstrikes to disable the Assad regime's chemical weapons delivery systems could have weakened its position. Indeed, since September 2007 Israel has launched various airborne campaigns against the regime's activities related to weapons of mass destruction or attempts to transfer advanced conventional weapons to Hezbollah. Without U.S. intervention, the killing continues, Assad remains in power and the growth of Islamist extremists is on the rise.

Those who began the movement to ban chemical weapons a century ago probably hoped it would eventually lead to elimination of all weapons and therefore the extinguishment of war.

But that hasn't happened, and the chemical weapon ban has been widely accepted, primarily because militaries generally have found them to be inferior weapons. After World War I, the largest armed conflict in which chemical weapons were used extensively, a British military history concluded that such weapons "made war uncomfortable . . . to no purpose."

A nuclear weapon certainly is a "weapon of mass destruction," because a single one can kill tens of thousands. But that does not hold for chemical weapons: Overall, chemical weapons were responsible for less than seven-tenths of 1 percent of World War I battle deaths and, on average, it took a ton of gas to register a single fatality. Moreover, soldiers incapacitated by gas usually returned to battle within a few days, while those wounded by bullets were frequently removed for much longer periods and were far more likely to die.

Those who insist it is morally reprehensible to kill people with gas in wars should be asked, "How would you prefer they be killed?"

Deaths inflicted by bullets generally appear quick and painless on television or in the movies because most viewers have an aversion to seeing blood spilled. Indeed, films that show lots of blood are officially categorized as "horror" movies and carry specific warnings for the viewer.

Admittedly, death by some gases can be painful. But it is difficult to see why dying from chemicals is worse than bleeding slowly to death after being punctured by a bullet, having an arm torn off by shrapnel or being repeatedly hacked by a machete — the weapon that has killed more people than any other in recent decades due to its extensive use in the 1994 Rwandan genocide.

Rather than leading to the end of war, the aversion to chemical weapons has helped trigger conflicts. Hostility to former Iraqi President Saddam Hussein — because he had used, and was presumed to possess, chemical weapons — was a key justification for the U.S. invasion of Iraq in 2003. The result was the violent deaths of well over 100,000 people. None of them by gas.

AFP/Getty Images/Jim Lopez

Mohammad Zayed, a student at Syria's Aleppo University, teaches local citizens to use gas masks on Sept. 15, 2013. An estimated 1,400 Syrians were killed last summer when the forces of Syrian President Bashar al-Assad gassed rebel-controlled areas near Damascus. After President Obama threatened military retaliation, Assad agreed to destroy his chemical arsenal.

underway to expand Biowatch and install new equipment, Biowatch Gen-3, but the program has been plagued by controversy, and some members of Congress have questioned the wisdom of continuing the effort.[58]

According to a *Los Angeles Times* investigation, Biowatch has signaled false attacks more than 100 times in various cities. At the same time, experts familiar with test results say the system isn't sensitive enough to reliably detect low, yet dangerous amounts of pathogens such as anthrax, smallpox or plague, according to *The Times*.[59]

In a 2012 statement, "The Truth about Biowatch," Department of Homeland Security Chief Medical Officer Alexander Garza wrote that the program had never reported a false positive.[60] But testifying before a congressional committee in the summer of 2013, Biowatch Program Manager Michael V. Walter acknowledged there have been false reports but said efforts to improve the program are underway.[61]

The United States also now has the personnel and supplies to deal with a biological attack. "We have huge national stockpiles of antibiotics against bacterial diseases, huge stockpiles of vaccines against smallpox and such diseases. These things are pretty up to date," says the Monterey Institute's Zilinskas.

While biodefense efforts under Bush were "tailored only to address the threat from biological terrorism and

biological weapons," says George Mason's Koblentz, the Obama administration has broadened the effort to include threats to public health "ranging from manmade outbreaks caused by terrorists to naturally occurring, emerging infectious diseases and pandemics."

The broader effort includes a focus on developing multi-use antibiotics and vaccines, says the Center for Arms Control and Non-Proliferation's Klotz. "That, I think, is the way to go. Anything you develop for natural disease would most naturally have an application for biological weapons as well."

Zilinskas believes the focus on versatile antibiotics reflects that the greatest public health threat still comes from a natural outbreak of a new, deadly disease strain. "What you've got to keep in the back of your mind all the time is that the biggest enemy we face in the biological area is nature," he says.

But experts point out that biological defense presents another challenge: The samples of pathogens needed to study dangerous diseases and prepare successful treatments and vaccines are the basic materials of the weapons. "Essentially, every country has culture collections that contain the pathogens that could be weaponized," says Zilinskas. "They're all dual use."

U.S. labs bolstered their security efforts after the 2001 anthrax letters. But Klotz says the expansion of biodefense research still has had a paradoxical effect. "Most of the knee-jerk response to the anthrax letters in 2001 was wrong," he says. "We started this huge biodefense program, most of it in secret. Before the anthrax attacks, there might have been a few hundred people working on anthrax. After 9/11, the biodefense sector blossomed to maybe up to 400 labs, with thousands of people working in them. If a terrorist wants to get into a lab, it's a lot easier. . . . We've increased the risk of theft, and the likelihood something will escape the lab by accident."

OUTLOOK
Complacency?

Looking 10 or 15 years down the road, many analysts profess optimism that the world's nations are largely ready to abandon chemical and biological weapons. They are less positive about the ability of the global community to keep such weapons out of the hands of smaller groups of people determined to do harm.

The University of British Columbia's Price says the idea that chemical weapons are "beyond the pale" has developed deep roots over the last century. "We're unmistakably at the point where we have what scholars would call a quite robust international norm. It's a combination of the legal restraints, the moral prohibition and just the sheer tradition of non-use," he says. "Do people want to go where even Hitler didn't go in World War II?"

Thielmann, at the Arms Control Association, believes Syria's agreement to sign the Chemical Weapons Convention could spur further movement among the remaining holdouts, particularly Egypt and Israel. "If we can pull this off with Syria, that's going to put a lot of pressure on other countries in the Middle East not to retain the option," he says. North Korea is likely to remain unyielding, he believes, "but if you can get to the point where the only country in the world that retains the option for chemical weapons is North Korea, you'll really have accomplished something."

Green Cross's Walker shares his optimism. However, he adds, even after the stockpiles have been destroyed, a significant number of chemical weapons sites contaminated by leaking weapons will remain, and cleaning those up could take many more years. The United States alone has more than 200 sites, he says.

"They were also dumped in every ocean," Walker says. "There is a long-time legacy issue about cleaning up old and abandoned chemical weapons."

Biological weapons are more troublesome, he says, "because of the potential for non-state actors to [use them to] gain a significant capability for destruction." Price also worries about "the pushing of genetic research, in particular. That's one area on the cutting edge of science [that] could produce different things with enormous capacity to do harm to humans."

The Aspen Institute's Cole worries someone will develop a hybrid pathogen, "an organism that is highly contagious, highly virulent or lethal and also highly durable. That would be a nightmare."

However, George Mason's Koblentz says, "There has been this shrinking list of countries that appear to be interested in biological weapons. I'm optimistic that we can eliminate these weapons and focus everyone's attention on how to use these technologies for beneficial purposes."

But, warns the American Enterprise Institute's Rubin, it's important to remember the damage caused by chemical weapons in World War I and other conflicts, and the lethal effects of diseases such as smallpox and anthrax.

"The danger is historical amnesia," Rubin says. The prohibitions have been successful "because of the memory of how horrific these weapons can be. However, the success of these organizations has meant that memory has faded with time. What the international community is facing is complacency."

NOTES

1. "Syria Chemical Attack: What we know," BBC News, Sept. 24, 2013, www.bbc.co.uk/news/world-middle-east-23927399. Also see "Attacks on Ghouta: Analysis of Alleged Use of Chemical Weapons in Syria," Human Rights Watch, September 2013, p. 4, www.hrw.org/reports/2013/09/10/attacks-ghouta-0.

2. *Ibid* (Human Rights Watch).

3. "Report on the Alleged Use of Chemical Weapons in the Ghouta Area of Damascus on 21 August 2013," United Nations Mission to Investigate Allegations of the Use of Chemical Weapons in the Syrian Arab Republic, www.un.org/disarmament/content/slideshow/Secretary_General_Report_of_CW_Investigation.pdf. Also see "Facts About Sarin," Centers for Disease Control and Prevention, May 20, 2013, www.bt.cdc.gov/agent/sarin/basics/facts.asp.

4. "Government Assessment of the Syrian Government's Use of Chemical Weapons on August 21, 2013," The White House, Aug. 30, 2013, www.whitehouse.gov/the-press-office/2013/08/30/government-assessment-syrian-government-s-use-chemical-weapons-august-21. See also "Syria: Thousands suffering neurotoxic symptoms treated in hospitals supported by MSF," Medicine Sans Frontiers, Aug. 24, 2013, www.msf.org/article/syria-thousands-suffering-neurotoxic-symptoms-treated-hospitals-supported-msf.

5. Aamer Madhani and Susan Davis, "Obama asks Congress to OK strike on Syria," *USA Today*, Aug. 31, 2013, www.usatoday.com/story/news/politics/2013/08/31/obama-makes-statement-on-syria/2751085/.

6. "Demilitarisation, Latest facts and figures," Organisation for the Prohibition of Chemical Weapons, Sept. 30, 3013, www.opcw.org/our-work/demilitarisation/.

7. An international treaty that would ban anti-personnel landmines has been signed by 150 nations, although not the United States. See: "Disarmament: Anti-Personnel Landmines Convention," United Nations Office at Geneva, www.unog.ch/80256EE600585943/(httpPages)/CA826818C8330D2BC1257180004B1B2E?OpenDocument.

8. "Brief History of Chemical Weapons Use," Organisation for the Prohibition of Chemical Weapons, www.opcw.org/about-chemical-weapons/history-of-cw-use/; also see Steven Erlanger, "A Weapon Seen as Too Horrible, Even in War," *The New York Times*, Sept. 6, 2013, www.nytimes.com/2013/09/07/world/middleeast/a-weapon-seen-as-too-horrible-even-in-war.html.

9. *Ibid.*

10. Stephen M. Walt, "Weapons Assad Uses Shouldn't Affect U.S. Policy," *The New York Times*, Aug. 26, 2013, www.nytimes.com/roomfordebate/2013/08/26/is-an-attack-on-syria-justified/type-of-weapons-assad-uses-shouldnt-affect-us-policy.

11. *Ibid.*

12. "Amerithrax or Anthrax Investigation," Famous Cases & Criminals, Federal Bureau of Investigation, www.fbi.gov/about-us/history/famous-cases/anthrax-amerithrax.

13. "Anthrax: Bioterrorism," Centers for Disease Control and Prevention, Aug. 29, 2013, www.cdc.gov/anthrax/bioterrorism/index.html.

14. Scott Shane, "Panel on Anthrax Inquiry Finds Case Against Ivins Persuasive," *The New York Times*, March 23, 2011, www.nytimes.com/2011/03/24/us/24anthrax.html?_r=0.

15. Joby Warrick, "FBI investigation of 2001 anthrax attacks concluded; U.S. releases details," *The Washington Post*, Feb. 20, 2010, www.washingtonpost.com/wp-dyn/content/article/2010/02/19/AR2010021902369.html.

16. Wil S. Hylton, "How Ready Are We for Bioterrorism," *The New York Times Magazine*, Oct. 26, 2011, www.nytimes.com/2011/10/30/magazine/how-ready-are-we-for-bioterrorism.html?pagewanted=all&_r=0.

17. "WMD Terrorism: An Update on the Recommendations of the Commission on the Prevention of Weapons of Mass Destruction Proliferation and Terrorism," The Aspen Institute Homeland Security Group, Nov. 15, 2012, www.aspeninstitute.org/sites/default/files/content/docs/hsi/AHSG%20WMD%20Paper%2011.15.12.pdf.

18. *Ibid.*

19. Philip C. Bleek, "Revisiting Aum Shinrikyo: New Insights into the Most Extensive Non-State Biological Weapons to Date," The Nuclear Threat Initiative, Dec. 11, 2011, www.nti.org/analysis/articles/revisiting-aum-shinrikyo-new-insights-most-extensive-non-state-biological-weapons-program-date-1/.

20. "World at Risk: Report of the Commission on the Prevention of WMD Proliferation and Terrorism," The Council on Foreign Relations, Dec. 3, 2008, www.cfr.org/terrorism/world-risk-report-commission-prevention-wmd-proliferation-terrorism/p17910.

21. Douglas Mackinnon, "Top Threat, Ignored," *The Baltimore Sun*, Dec. 4, 2009, http://articles.baltimoresun.com/2009-12-04/news/0912030063_1_biological-weapons-crop-duster-bioterrorism. For full report, see www.pharmathene.com/CPWMD_Interim_Report.pdf.

22. "Member States and States not Party," Organisation for the Prohibition of Chemical Weapons, www.opcw.org/news-room/member-states-and-states-not-party/.

23. "Overview of the Chemical Weapons Convention," Organisation for the Prohibition of Chemical Weapons, www.opcw.org/chemical-weapons-convention/about-the-convention/.

24. "Chronology of Major Events in the History of Biological and Chemical Weapons," James Martin Center for Nonproliferation Studies, August 2008, http://cns.miis.edu/cbw/pastuse.htm.

25. Sharon Jacobs, "Chemical Warfare, from Rome to Syria. A Timeline," *National Geographic News*, Aug. 22, 2013, http://news.nationalgeographic.com/news/2013/08/130822-syria-chemical-biological-weapons-sarin-war-history-science/.

26. "Chronology of Major Events in the History of Biological and Chemical Weapons," *op. cit.*

27. Jacobs, *op. cit.*

28. Colette Flight, "Silent Weapon: Smallpox and Biological Warfare," BBC History, Feb. 17, 2011, www.bbc.co.uk/history/worldwars/coldwar/pox_weapon_01.shtml.

29. "Chronology of Major Events in the History of Biological and Chemical Weapons," *op. cit.*

30. Robert Harris and Jeremy Paxman, *A Higher Form of Killing*, Random House Trade Paperback Edition (2002), p. 3.

31. *Ibid.*, pp. 3-4.

32. Martin Gilbert, *The First World War: A Complete History* (1994), p. 144.

33. Harris and Paxman, *op. cit.*, p. 4.

34. Gilbert, *op. cit.*, p. 145.

35. Robert Graves, *Good-bye to All That* (1958), pp. 151-159.

36. "Facts about Sulfur Mustard," Centers for Disease Control and Prevention, May 2, 2013, www.bt.cdc.gov/agent/sulfurmustard/basics/facts.asp.

37. Harris and Paxman, *op. cit.*, p. 17.

38. "1925 Geneva Protocol," United Nations Office for Disarmament Affairs, www.un.org/disarmament/WMD/Bio/1925GenevaProtocol.shtml.

39. Lina Grip and John Hart, "The use of chemical weapons in the Italo-Ethiopian War of 1935-36," SIPRI Arms Control and Non-proliferation Programme, October 2009, www.sipri.org/research/disarmament/chemical/publications/ethiopiapaper/.

40. Erlanger, *op. cit.*

41. "The history of chemical weapons: The Shadow of Ypres," *The Economist*, Aug. 31, 2013, www.economist.com/news/briefing/21584397-how-whole-class-weaponry-came-be-seen-indecent-shadow-ypres.

42. For more detail on Japanese biological experiments see: Jeanne Guillemin, *Biological Weapons: From the Invention of State-sponsored Programs to Contemporary Bioterrorism* (2005).

43. Glenn Kessler, "Kerry's claim that only three tyrants have used chemical weapons," *The Washington Post*, Sept. 5, 2013, www.washingtonpost.com/blogs/fact-checker/wp/2013/09/05/kerrys-claim-that-only-three-tyrants-have-used-chemical-weapons/.

44. "The history of chemical weapons: The Shadow of Ypres," *op. cit.* Also see Javed Ali, "Chemical Weapons and the Iran-Iraq War: A Case Study in Noncompliance," *The Nonproliferation Review*, Spring 2001, http://cns.miis.edu/npr/pdfs/81ali.pdf.

45. Michael Dobbs, "U.S. had Key Role in Iraq Buildup," *The Washington Post*, Dec. 30, 2002, www.commondreams.org/headlines02/1230-04.htm.

46. Ali, *op. cit.*

47. *Ibid.*

48. "The history of chemical weapons: The Shadow of Ypres," *op. cit.*

49. Yasuo Seto, "The Sarin Gas Attack in Japan and the Related Forensic Investigation," Organisation for the Prohibition of Chemical Weapons, June 1, 2001, www.opcw.org/news/article/the-sarin-gas-attack-in-japan-and-the-related-forensic-investigation/.

50. "OPCW Executive Council adopts plan for the destruction of Syria's chemical weapons programme in the first half of 2014," Organisation for the Prohibition of Chemical Weapons, Nov. 15, 2013, www.opcw.org/news/article/opcw-adopts-plan-for-destruction-of-syrias-chemical-weapons-programme-in-the-first-half-of-2014. Also see Alan Cowell, "Syria is said to Destroy all Chemical Weapons Production Sites," *The New York Times*, Oct. 31, 2013, file:///Users/rkaraim/Dropbox/Chemical%20weapons%202013/clips/Syria/Syria%20Is%20Said%20to%20Destroy%20All%20Chemical%20Arms%20Production%20Sites%20-%20NYTimes.com.webarchive.

51. "OPCW Executive Council adopts plan for the destruction of Syria's chemical weapons programme in the first half of 2014," *op. cit.*

52. Alan Cowell and Rick Gladstone, "Inspectors in Syria Have Only One Site Left to Check," *The New York Times*, Nov. 7, 2013, www.nytimes.com/2013/11/08/world/middleeast/syria.html.

53. Anne Barnard, "Syria Destroys Chemical Sites, Inspectors Say," *The New York Times*, Oct. 31, 2013, www.nytimes.com/2013/11/01/world/middleeast/syria.html.

54. James Lewis, "Fact Sheet: Chemical Weapons and their Destruction," The Center for Arms Control and Non-Proliferation, http://armscontrolcenter.org/issues/biochem/fact_sheet_cw/.

55. "Chemical and Biological Weapons Status at a Glance," Arms Control Association, October 2013, www.armscontrol.org/factsheets/cbwprolif.

56. Lewis, *op. cit.*

57. Diane Barnes, "U.N. Chief Urges Full Chemical Disarmament by 2018," Global Security Newswire, April 9, 2013, www.nti.org/gsn/article/un-chief-demands-chemical-disarmament-years-ahead-us-schedule/.

58. David Willman, "Biowatch's chief aim is off target, U.S. security officials say," *Los Angeles Times*, June 18, 2013, http://articles.latimes.com/2013/jun/18/nation/la-na-biowatch-20130619.

59. David Willman, "Biowatch Stands at a Crossroads," *Los Angeles Times*, Dec. 22, 2012, www.latimes.com/news/nationworld/nation/la-biowatch-dec-22-2012-m,0,7371184.story#axzz2kvkqwKdK.

60. Alexander Garza, "The Truth about Biowatch: The importance of Early Detection of a Biological Attack," U.S. Department of Homeland Security, July 12, 2012, https://www.dhs.gov/blog/2012/07/12/truth-about-biowatch.

61. Willman, "Biowatch's chief aim is off target, U.S. security officials say," *op. cit.*

BIBLIOGRAPHY

Selected Sources

Books

Gilbert, Martin, *The First World War: A Complete History*, Henry Holt and Co., 1994.

British historian Gilbert's comprehensive history of World War I includes the impact major gas attacks had, both on soldiers and strategy.

Guillemin, Jeanne, *American Anthrax: Fear, Crime, and the Investigation of the Nation's Deadliest Bioterror Attack*, Times Books, 2011.

A senior fellow in the Security Studies Program at the Massachusetts Institute of Technology examines America's most famous biological terror attack and the investigation that followed.

Harris, Robert, and Jeremy Paxman, *A Higher Form of Killing: The Secret History of Chemical and Biological Warfare*, Random House Trade Paperbacks, 2002.

A best-selling author (Harris) and a journalist look at the development of chemical and biological weapons through the 20th century.

Spiers, Edward M., *A History of Chemical and Biological Weapons*, Reaktion Books, 2010.

A professor of strategic studies at Leeds University in England examines the development of chemical and biological weapons over time and how the international response to these weapons also evolved.

Articles

"The history of chemical weapons: The Shadow of Ypres," *The Economist*, Aug. 31, 2013, www.economist.com/news/briefing/21584397-how-whole-class-weaponry-came-be-seen-indecent-shadow-ypres.

This short history of chemical weapons use from World War I on includes estimated fatalities from different conflicts.

Erlanger, Steven, "A Weapon Seen as Too Horrible, Even in War," *The New York Times*, Sept. 6, 2013, www.nytimes.com/2013/09/07/world/middleeast/a-weapon-seen-as-too-horrible-even-in-war.html.

The revulsion toward chemical weapons that followed World War I and their sporadic use since is reviewed, along with the debate about whether they are really worse than other weapons.

Plumer, Brad, "Everything you need to know about Syria's chemical weapons," *The Washington Post*, Sept. 5, 2013, www.washingtonpost.com/blogs/wonkblog/

wp/2013/09/05/everything-you-need-to-know-about-syrias-chemical-weapons.

A wealth of background information on chemical weapons is included in this summary, including what they do and how the world has decided to deal with them.

Strunsky, Steve, "Bioterrorism remains real threat a decade after Anthrax attack, expert says," (New Jersey) *Star-Ledger*, Nov. 15, 2012, www.nj.com/news/index.ssf/2012/11/bioterrorism_threat_remains_re.html.

The head of the Terror Medicine and Security Program at the University of Medicine and Dentistry of New Jersey believes the threat of a biological terrorist attack remains real but that the nation has lowered its guard.

Willman, David, "BioWatch's chief aim is off-target, U.S. security officials say," *Los Angeles Times*, June 18, 2013, http://articles.latimes.com/2013/jun/18/nation/la-na-biowatch-20130619.

America has invested more than $1 billion in a program to detect large biological attacks, but some officials say the program is misguided, according to this report, part of an investigative series on the Biowatch program.

Reports and Studies

"Attacks on Ghouta, Analysis of Alleged Use of Chemical Weapons in Syria," Human Rights Watch, 2013, www.hrw.org/reports/2013/09/10/attacks-ghouta-0.

The international human rights group says evidence strongly suggests the Syrian government was behind the horrific chemical weapons attacks there, backing U.S. and French assertions.

"National Biosurveillance Science and Technology Roadmap," National Science and Technology Council, Executive Office of the President, June 2013, www.whitehouse.gov/sites/default/files/microsites/ostp/biosurveillance_roadmap_2013.pdf.

This report updates the Obama administration's effort to coordinate efforts by federal, state and local governments, along with the private sector and international partners, to enhance the early detection of biological threats.

"Report of the OPCW on the Implementation of the Convention on the Prohibition of the Development, Production, Stockpiling and Use of Chemical Weapons and on their Destruction in 2011," Organization for the Prohibition of Chemical Weapons, Nov. 27, 2012, www.opcw.org/index.php?eID=dam_frontend_push&docID=16013.

The latest official report documents the progress that signatories to the international treaty banning chemical weapons have made in destroying their chemical arsenals.

Documentaries

"The Anthrax Files," Frontline, Oct. 10, 2011, www.pbs.org/wgbh/pages/frontline/anthrax-files/.

"Frontline," McClatchy Newspapers and ProPublica look back at the 2001 anthrax attacks in the United States and the FBI's conclusion that government scientist Bruce Ivins was responsible.

For More Information

Arms Control Association, 1313 L St., N.W., Suite 130, Washington, DC 20005; 202-463-8270; www.armscontrol.org. Founded in 1971, the association promotes public understanding of and support for effective arms control policies.

The Center for Arms Control and Non-Proliferation, 322 4th St., N.E., Washington, DC 20002; 202-546-0795; www.armscontrolcenter.org. Seeks to enhance international peace and security in the 21st century.

Foreign Policy Initiative, 11 Dupont Circle, N.W., Suite 325, Washington, DC 20036; 202-296-3322; www.foreignpolicyi.org. Promotes an active U.S. foreign policy committed to robust support for democratic allies, human rights and a strong American military.

Office of Health Affairs, Department of Homeland Security, Washington, DC 20528; 202-254-6479; www.dhs.gov/office-health-affairs. Leads and coordinates the government's biological and chemical defense activities and provides medical and scientific expertise to support the department's preparedness and response efforts.

Organisation for the Prohibition of Chemical Weapons, Johan de Wittlaan 32, 2517 JR, The Hague, Netherlands; +31 70 416 3300; www.opcw.org. Implements the 1993 Chemical Weapons Convention, through which 190 nations have agreed to rid themselves of chemical weapons.

U.S. Army Chemical Materials Activity, CMA Headquarters (Public Affairs Office), AMSCM-PA, E4585 Hoadley Rd., Aberdeen Proving Ground, MD 21010, 800-488-0648; www.cma.army.mil/home.aspx. Responsible for safely storing and destroying the nation's chemical weapons in compliance with the Chemical Weapons Convention.

2

Israeli-Palestinian Conflict

Peter Katel

A Jewish settler confronts an Israeli soldier who stopped him from interfering with Palestinian farmers trying to plant trees on their land near Susia, an Israeli settlement in the West Bank, on Feb. 11, 2012. President Obama, in a visit to the West Bank last March, urged the Israelis and Palestinians to return to the negotiating table to resolve their decades-long conflict.

AFP/Getty Images/Hazem Bader

From *CQ Researcher*,
June 21, 2013.

It's been 20 years since President Bill Clinton and the leaders of Israel and the Palestinian people dramatically joined hands on a deal that was supposed to lead to a permanent solution of their bitter, decades-long conflict.

The agreement, signed on the White House lawn, might have ended in creation of a Palestinian state existing peacefully next to Israel. That outcome remains in reach if both sides compromise, President Barack Obama said during a March visit to Israel and the West Bank.[1] His speech launched what American officials called the last, best chance for a peaceful resolution.

"We're running out of time," Secretary of State John Kerry told a major pro-Israel advocacy group, the American Jewish Committee, in early June. "And let's be clear: If we do not succeed now — and I know I'm raising those stakes — but if we do not succeed now, we may not get another chance."[2]

Kerry, now with the support of the Arab League, has been trying to restart direct talks between the parties to clear away obstacles to establishing an independent Palestinian state — the so-called "two state solution." But talks have been stalemated since 2010.

Since then, revolutions have ousted leaders in some Arab countries, including Israel's most important regional peace-treaty partner, Egypt, and a savage civil war has broken out in Syria on Israel's northeast border, prompting limited Israeli military action and the possibility of more to come. But even as new fighting and political change transform the region, issues dividing Israelis and Palestinians remained seemingly as problematic as ever.

A Region Divided

Israel, with 7.7 million predominantly Jewish inhabitants, sits on the eastern Mediterranean coast and borders Egypt, Jordan, Syria and Lebanon. The 4.5 million mostly Muslim inhabitants of the Palestinian territories live in the West Bank, located on the western side of the Jordan River, and the Gaza Strip, a 25-mile-long sliver of land seven miles wide along Israel's southern coast.

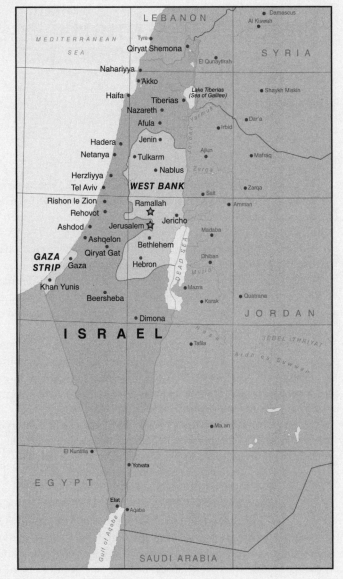

Source: CIA, *The World Factbook*

The Palestinian Authority (PA) has partial control of the West Bank, a 2,263-square-mile territory known to right-wing Israelis by its biblical names of Judea and Samaria.[3] The United Nations General Assembly late last year approved the authority's request to accept "Palestine" — previously called the "Palestinian Territories" — as a non-member state in the U.N. (The United States cast one of nine "no" votes). Google this year followed suit, using "Palestine" on its search page for both the West Bank and the Gaza Strip, a Palestinian enclave geographically separate from the West Bank and controlled by a political party (Hamas) at odds with the PA.[4]

Still, reality overwhelms symbolism, some Palestinians say. West Bank and Gaza Palestinians are citizens only of the Palestinian Authority, which is not a sovereign state. Entry into Israel is forbidden from Gaza, and West Bank Palestinians need permits to cross into Israel, including East Jerusalem, which the Palestinians claim and which contains sites sacred to Muslims, Jews and Christians.[5]

"We now have a one-state solution," says Rashid Khalidi, a historian and professor of Arab studies at Columbia University. "If it doesn't have control or authority, it's not a state. You can call it subjugation."

Aaron David Miller, a former U.S. diplomat specializing for decades in the Israeli-Palestinian conflict, concludes that peace —"peace in the sense of what we have with the Canadians, what the French have with Germans" — is out of reach for now.

Miller, now the vice president for new initiatives at the Woodrow Wilson International Center for Scholars, a

Washington think tank, argues that the Obama administration, despite Kerry's efforts, isn't as committed as some of its predecessors to brokering an accord. And he questions the capacity of Israeli and Palestinian leaders. "Do they have the credibility and authority to make the existential decisions that are necessary?"

The issues to be resolved include establishing the borders of Israel and a Palestinian state; deciding whether (or how many) Palestinians or their descendants who left or were forced out of today's Israel when it became a nation in 1948 should have the right to return permanently; and determining whether East Jerusalem should remain part of Israel.

Palestinians and some Israelis argue that although the Israeli government officially favors Palestinian statehood, Israel's real aim is continued expansion of Jewish settlements in the West Bank. Israeli government supporters argue that Palestinians in reality want a single state encompassing all of historic Palestine: Israel and the occupied territories. In other words, the end of Israel as a Jewish state.

Israel exists within part of historic Palestine, a name bestowed by the Roman Empire to replace the name Judea, after savagely repressing a Jewish rebellion there in the first century.[6] Beginning in the late 1800s, Jews fleeing vicious European and Russian anti-Semitism and seeking to re-establish the homeland built a major presence, amid an uneasy and sometimes violent coexistence with Arabs living there. (The term Palestinians to describe Arab residents came into use in the 1950s.) [7]

Israel declared statehood in 1948 under a U.N. resolution dividing Palestine between Jews and Arabs. Israel defeated invading Arab nations who opposed Israel's creation, establishing borders that didn't include any of the territory now at issue. That land fell to Israel after the

Global Views of Israel Largely Unfavorable

In 11 countries and the Palestinian territories, the United States was the only country where a majority had positive views of Israel. More people in only two countries — the United States and Russia — had a more positive than negative view of Israel. Views were especially unfavorable in predominantly Muslim countries.

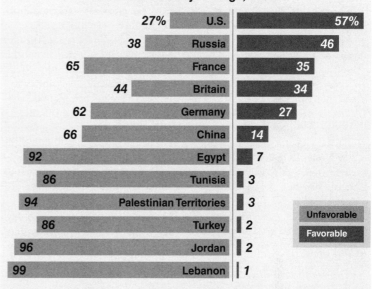

Israel Favorability Ratings, 2013*

Country	Unfavorable	Favorable
U.S.	27%	57%
Russia	38	46
France	65	35
Britain	44	34
Germany	62	27
China	66	14
Egypt	92	7
Tunisia	86	3
Palestinian Territories	94	3
Turkey	86	2
Jordan	96	2
Lebanon	99	1

* Percentages not shown for respondents who declined to answer.

Source: "Despite Their Wide Differences, Many Israelis and Palestinians Want Bigger Role for Obama in Resolving Conflict," Pew Research Center, May 9, 2013, www.pewglobal.org/2013/05/09/despite-their-wide-differences many-israelis-and-palestinians-want-bigger-role-for-obama-in-resolving-conflict/

Six-Day War of 1967, in which Israel pre-empted an attack by Syria and Egypt.

Since the early 1970s, when Israelis in significant numbers began to build settlements in the West Bank, mostly for reasons of religious ideology, the Jewish population there has grown from about 1,200 to about 360,000 today. Another 195,000 have settled in or near predominantly Palestinian East Jerusalem.[8]

In principle, 67 percent of Israelis said in two December surveys that they support an independent, demilitarized Palestine next door to Israel. Yet Palestinian statehood emerged as only a background issue in Israel's national election the following month,

Obama's Posture on Israel Draws Praise, Criticism

President rejects blanket support for Israeli policies.

It would be difficult to imagine the remark being made about any other U.S. ally: "The world must never see any daylight between our two nations," Republican candidate Mitt Romney said during the 2012 presidential campaign.[1]

Romney was charging his opponent, President Obama, with downgrading the U.S.-Israel relationship. The president reportedly had told Jewish leaders in 2009 that the George W. Bush administration's Israel policy had failed. "There was no space between us and Israel," *The Washington Post* quoted Obama as saying, "and what did we get from that? When there is no daylight, Israel just sits on the sidelines, and that erodes our credibility with the Arab states."[2]

In the end, Romney's attempt to portray any criticism of Israeli policies as weakening of support for a longtime ally didn't carry the day with voters, including Jewish voters. In fact, while Obama's relations with Israeli Prime Minister Benjamin Netanyahu were once distinctly chilly, many specialists say Obama has maintained the extraordinary closeness with Israel that has characterized U.S. foreign policy for decades.

Israel's military strength "derives in good part from the bipartisan support that the Congress . . . [and] successive administrations, both Republican and Democrat, have provided" Israel over many decades, Martin Indyk, vice president of the Brookings Institution think tank, told a House Foreign Affairs subcommittee in September. Indyk was U.S. ambassador to Israel in the Clinton administration.[3]

Indeed, since World War II, Israel has received more U.S. foreign aid — about $118 billion, mostly in military assistance — than any other country.[4]

Critics argue that the relationship is a one-way street. But the United States gets plenty in return, argues an influential think tank, the Washington Institute on Near East Policy, including military cooperation, information-technology, pharmaceutical research and agricultural technology. "Israel is a small country that punches way above its weight in a number of areas," two staff members wrote last year, "enabling it to make important contributions to various U.S. national security, economic and global foreign policy objectives."[5]

On the diplomatic front, Obama and his recent predecessors have all backed — with varying degrees of intensity — creation of a Palestinian state alongside Israel. But Obama has been criticized both for being too distant from Israel, and — from those who criticize the closeness of the U.S.-Israel relationship — for not pressuring Israel to come to terms with the Palestinians.

"Obama's failure . . . to slow the expansion of settlements has made it clear that the United States will never be a truly honest broker," Stephen Walt, a professor of international affairs at Harvard's Kennedy School of Government, said in April.[6]

Walt co-authored a 2007 book that blamed the "Israel lobby" for dominating U.S. policy, sparking accusations that the authors were perpetrating anti-Semitic stereotypes of vast Jewish influence on public affairs. "The Israel lobby in this book is an invincible juggernaut," journalist Jeffrey Goldberg — himself a critic of some organizations that lobby for Israel — wrote in *The New Republic*, stating the book's premise as "the belief that America supports Israel only because the pro-Israel lobby forces it to do so."[7]

Walt is unbending. During the April meeting, he accused Israel backers of suppressing criticism of Israel. "These zealots used these tactics because they know that a more open discussion might cause Americans to question the special relationship and to conclude that a more normal relationship would be better for everyone."[8]

Both opponents and supporters of the "no daylight" school of U.S.-Israel relations often make the same assumption: that supporting Israel means adopting a go-slow approach toward Palestinian statehood.

In fact, wrote Jeremy Ben-Ami, president of J Street, a U.S. lobbying organization that describes itself as pro-Israel and pro-peace, "When it comes to Israel, Jewish Americans are notably moderate in their views." He cited a poll showing that 82 percent of American Jews support a two-state solution, and 76 percent want Obama to propose a peace plan.[9]

As Ben-Ami noted, Romney's Israel policy failed to convince most American Jewish voters. Seventy percent of them picked Obama, said a pollster for J Street. And Jews favored by a 53-31 margin Obama's approach of calling for Palestinian statehood while maintaining support for Israel.[10]

Still, Jews make up only 2 percent of the voting population. Romney's stance on Israel was also aimed at the white evangelical population, who tend to fervently and uncritically support Israel, in part because of a religious belief that Jewish sovereignty throughout the holy land is a prelude to the second coming of Christ. A Romney campaign trip to Israel last July was seen as proving the candidate's closeness to Israel. Indeed, white evangelicals went overwhelmingly for Romney, 79 percent versus 21 percent.[11]

Obama, in his post-re-election trip to Israel in May, made a point of rejecting the across-the-board support for any Israeli policy that Romney and other Republicans had advocated. "Politically, given the strong bipartisan support for Israel in America, the easiest thing for me to do would be to put this issue aside — just express unconditional support for whatever Israel decides to do," Obama said in a widely applauded speech in Jerusalem.[12]

But, he argued to Israelis, a two-state solution was not only essential to Israel's security, but the right thing to do toward Palestinians. "Look at the world through their eyes," he said. "It is not fair that a Palestinian child cannot grow up in a state of their own. Living their entire lives with the presence of a foreign army that controls the movements not just of those young people but their parents, their grandparents, every single day."[13]

— Peter Katel

President Obama walks with Israeli President Shimon Peres, right, and Prime Minister Benjamin Netanyahu, after laying a wreath at the grave of Zionist leader Theodor Herzl in Jerusalem, on March 22, 2013, during Obama's trip to Israel and the occupied territories.

[1]"Transcript: Mitt Romney Remarks at Virginia Military Institute," *The New York Times*, Oct. 8, 2012, www.nytimes.com/2012/10/09/us/politics/mitt-romney-remarks-at-virginia-military-institute.html?pagewanted=all.

[2]Scott Wilson, "Where Obama failed on forging peace in the Middle East," *The Washington Post*, July 14, 2012, www.washingtonpost.com/politics/obama-searches-for-middle-east-peace/2012/07/14/gJQAQQiKIW_story.html.

[3]"Hearing of the Middle East and South Asia Subcommittee of the House Foreign Affairs Committee," Federal News Service, Sept. 20, 2012.

[4]Jeremy M. Sharp, "U.S. Foreign Aid to Israel," Congressional Research Service, April 11, 2013, summary page, www.fas.org/sgp/crs/mideast/RL33222.pdf.

[5]Michael Eisenstadt and David Pollock, "Asset Test: How the United States Benefits from Its Alliance With Israel," Washington Institute for Near East Policy, September, 2012, p. XIV, www.washingtoninstitute.org/policy-analysis/view/asset-test-how-the-united-states-benefits-from-its-alliance-with-israel.

[6]"The Future of Israel and Palestine — Expanding the Debate," Middle East Policy Council conference, April 25, 2013, Federal News Service.

[7]Jeffrey Goldberg, "The Usual Suspect," *The New Republic*, Oct. 8, 2007, www.newrepublic.com/article/the-usual-suspect.

[8]"The Future of Israel and Palestine. . . ," *op. cit.*

[9]Jeremy Ben-Ami, "America's Jewish Vote," *The New York Times*, Nov. 12, 2012, www.nytimes.com/2012/11/13/opinion/americas-jewish-vote.html.

[10]"The Candidates on the Israeli-Palestinian Conflict," Council on Foreign Relations, Oct. 31, 2012, www.cfr.org/israel/candidates-israeli-palestinian-conflict/p26801#p1.

[11]"How the Faithful Voted: 2012 Preliminary Analysis," Pew Forum on Religion & Public Life, Nov. 7, 2012, www.pewforum.org/Politics-and-Elections/How-the-Faithful-Voted-2012-Preliminary-Exit-Poll-Analysis.aspx; Nick Tate, "Jewish voters: By the numbers," Reuters, July 24, 2012, www.reuters.com/article/2012/07/24/us-usa-campaign-jewish-vote-numbers-idUSBRE86N05Z20120724; Maeve Reston and Paul Richter, "Romney camp hopes Israel trip secures evangelical, Jewish votes," *Los Angeles Times*, July 29, 2012, http://articles.latimes.com/2012/jul/29/nation/la-na-romney-israel-20120729; David D. Kirkpatrick, "For Evangelicals, Supporting Israel Is 'God's Foreign Policy,'" *The New York Times*, Nov. 14, 2006, www.nytimes.com/2006/11/14/washington/14israel.html?pagewanted=all.

[12]"Remarks of President Barack Obama," Jerusalem International Convention Center, March 21, 2013, www.whitehouse.gov/the-press-office/2013/03/21/remarks-president-barack-obama-people-israel.

[13]*Ibid.*

Most Palestinians Pessimistic About Peace

Only 14 percent of Palestinians believe Israel and an independent Palestinian state could coexist peacefully, compared with 50 percent of Israelis. And nearly half of Palestinians believe armed struggle is the best way to achieve statehood.

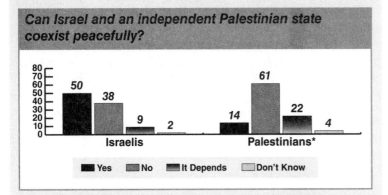

Can Israel and an independent Palestinian state coexist peacefully?

■ Yes ■ No ■ It Depends □ Don't Know

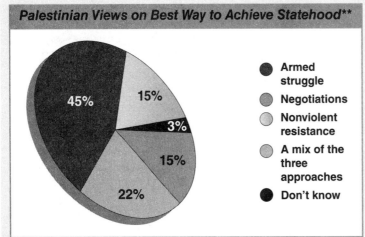

Palestinian Views on Best Way to Achieve Statehood**

- ● Armed struggle — 45%
- ● Negotiations — 22%
- ● Nonviolent resistance — 15%
- ● A mix of the three approaches — 15%
- ● Don't know — 3%

* Figures do not total 100% because of rounding.

** Pollsters interviewed only Palestinians living in the occupied territories.

Source: "Despite Their Wide Differences, Many Israelis and Palestinians Want Bigger Role for Obama in Resolving Conflict," Pew Research Center, May 9, 2013, www.pewglobal.org/2013/05/09/despite-their-wide-differences-many-israelis-and-palestinians-want-bigger-role-for-obama-in-resolving-conflict/

two-state advocate and Finance Minister Yair Lapid, a supporter.[9]

Dahlia Scheindlin, a Tel Aviv-based political analyst specializing in public opinion surveys, says the new lineup signifies that this government "doesn't see the Israeli-Palestinian issue as a problem: 'Yes, we have a fundamental disagreement on how the government will work on the Israeli-Palestinian problem, but who cares?'"

Indeed, Deputy Defense Minister Dany Danon — a member of Netanyahu's conservative Likud Party — told *The Times of Israel* that if there were a move to promote a two-state solution, "you will see forces blocking it within the [Likud] party and the government."[10]

Netanyahu's office immediately told *The Times* that Danon's comments "do not represent the position of Prime Minister Benjamin Netanyahu and the government of Israel."[11]

On the Palestinian side, Mahmoud Abbas, president of the Palestinian Authority, which would be Israel's formal negotiating partner, says talks cannot start until Israel stops expanding settlements. "The Obama administration wants us to resume negotiations in order to establish a sustainable state," a senior Palestinian official told *Haaretz*, an important left-of-center Israeli newspaper, "but in parallel Israel keeps building in the settlements and cutting the ground out from under the Palestinians' feet and anyone who seeks an agreement. We can't discuss a state we are going to establish on land on which settlements are being built."[12]

Some Israelis agree. Peace Now, the leading Israeli advocacy group for ending the occupation of the territories, said in early June that government figures show construction starts on new housing units in Israeli

which yielded a government deeply divided over Palestinian statehood. Cabinet members include Prime Minister Benjamin Netanyahu, seen by many as lukewarm at best about a Palestinian state; Trade Minister Naftali Bennett, an avowed opponent of Palestinian statehood; Justice Minister Tzipi Livni, a strong

settlements reached a seven-year high of 265 during the first quarter of 2013. "Any government committed to peace would not allow nor continue to build settlements," the organization said.[13]

Apart from the standoff with Israel, the Palestinian national movement itself is split. Abbas has appointed a new prime minister, who runs the Palestinian Authority's day-to-day activities, after the former longtime premier resigned in April, criticizing Palestinians' disunity. Indeed, in Gaza — the other Palestinian population center besides the West Bank — the government is run by Hamas, an Islamist party that does not consider Israel a legitimate nation.[14]

Views of Israel in Gaza remain colored by two Israeli military operations there, the latest last November, prompted by rockets and mortars fired from Gaza into Israel. An eight-day Israeli air campaign left 167 Palestinians dead, including 62 fighters, according to B'Tselem, the Israeli Information Center for Human Rights in the Occupied territories. Palestinians killed six Israelis, four of them civilians.[15]

In both the West Bank and Gaza, 45 percent of Palestinians view armed struggle as the best way to achieve statehood, with 15 percent favoring negotiations and 15 percent nonviolent resistance, according to a Pew Research survey released in May.[16]

That position accompanies deep pessimism among Palestinians about statehood prospects. A poll in March by the widely respected Palestinian Centre for Policy and Survey Research, based in the West Bank capital of Ramallah, showed that 46 percent of Palestinians in the West Bank considered Israeli withdrawal to 1967 borders and establishment of a Palestinian state as the most important Palestinian goal, but 59 percent believed that Israel wants to annex the entire West Bank and expel Arabs.[17]

Hussein Ibish, senior fellow at the pro-statehood American Task Force on Palestine, argues that Palestinian support for a two-state plan depends on confidence. "If people believed it was plausible," he says, "there would be even stronger numbers."

As policymakers and politicians continue to seek a solution to the Israeli-Palestinian conflict, here are some of the questions they are debating:

Is a two-state solution possible?

The idea of dividing historic Palestine into one state for Jews and one for Palestinians is slightly older than the state of Israel. A U.N. commission proposed in 1948 what was then called "partition" as a way to settle the irreconcilable claims to the same land by two peoples.

The entire Arab world rejected the plan in favor of trying to destroy the fledgling state militarily. Though the attempt failed, Palestinian organizations and Arab governments rejected the two-state idea for decades because it conceded the existence of Israel.

After 1967, a minority of Israeli politicians favored two states but were outnumbered by those wanting to hold onto the territories. Some advocated keeping the land until a new arrangement could be negotiated, while others claimed the territories were an inherent part of Israel that should never be relinquished.

But in the early 1990s, the first Intifada — Palestinian uprising — led some Israeli and Palestinian leaders to conclude that the status quo was unsustainable. Secret negotiations led to a plan for limited Palestinian autonomy as a possible first step toward statehood. That vision was set out in the 1993 Oslo Declaration of Principles, known as the Oslo Accords, the first agreement negotiated directly by Israelis and Palestinians.

But 20 years later, only one state is standing. Even to those who favor it, the two-state solution appears to a growing number of experts as, at best, an extremely unlikely outcome.

"The chances are very slim," says Aziz Abu Sarah, a Palestinian who divides his time between Jerusalem and greater Washington, where he is co-executive director of the Center for World Religions, Diplomacy and Conflict Resolution at George Mason University in Fairfax, Va. "People are getting angry, frustrated. After 20 years of negotiations, it makes sense that people think that way."

Sarah argues that a major reason a Palestinian state has not been established is that Israel has no pressing reason to withdraw from the territories. "If I was the Israeli prime minister, what would make me change my mind?" he asks rhetorically. "Even though there is a price to pay for the occupation, you have free land to farm, you have the Jordan River. So what is the incentive for the Israeli leader to change the status quo?"

Settlers argue that no incentive for Palestinian statehood exists on either side. "I think it never was possible," says Dani Dayan, former director of the Yesha Council (Council of Israeli Communities in Judea and Samaria) and now a spokesman for the predominantly religious movement. "We see ourselves as returning home," says Dayan, who is part of the movement's secular minority. "They [Palestinians] see us — and from their perspective I can understand it completely — as a 19th-century colonialist movement. Between these two genuine narratives, you will never reach a point that reconciles, because it does not exist."

Dayan believes Palestinian leaders don't really want two states. "I think their aspiration is the disappearance of the state of Israel," he says. "I respect their aspirations, but they are not going to be fulfilled."

From the opposite side of the Israeli political spectrum, Scheindlin, the Tel Aviv-based public-opinion researcher and analyst, says the growing current of world opinion against the Israeli occupation has only limited effect in Israel. "The Israeli political system suffers from short-term thinking," she says, "and Israeli society tends to lock down into quite provincial, almost parochial, thinking."

But the major obstacle to a two-state deal on the Israeli side is physical, Scheindlin argues. Increasingly, she and others say, Israeli public-works projects run through land that would become part of the Palestinian state. "The infrastructure . . . that supports settlements keeps expanding," she says. "That kind of stuff isn't going away. Systems of control are still encroaching on the Palestinians' sense of control of their areas."

Still, optimists do exist, even if their numbers are reduced. "Settlements, infrastructural and topographic and demographic changes — all these are political decisions made by the state of Israel for political reasons," says Ibish, of the American Task Force on Palestine. "Anything done for political reasons can be undone for reasons of state." He cites the 2005 Israeli withdrawal from Gaza.

Above all, Ibish says, the two-state plan remains viable because Israel has no other options. "Nothing else ends the conflict except for the two-state outcome," he says. "What are they going to do, short of this? I've never heard a plausible explanation. The status quo can drag on, but it is not a long-term, tenable and viable state of affairs."

Is the United States indispensable to an agreement between Israel and Palestinian authorities?

Since World War II the United States has been intimately involved with Israel and its neighbors. One key

measure: Since 1948, Israel and Egypt have been the No. 1 and No. 2 recipients, respectively, of U.S. foreign aid, with $118 billion going to Israel and nearly $72 billion to Egypt.[18]

The United States also played a key role in all but two attempts to resolve conflicts between Israel and neighboring countries or the Palestinians.[19] For example, Secretary of State Henry Kissinger and President Jimmy Carter helped to set the stage — during and after the 1967 Six-Day War, when Israel won the West Bank, Gaza and other territory — for the historic 1978 Camp David Accords, a peace treaty between Egypt and Israel. Then came attempts to broker agreements between Israel and the Palestinians — in Madrid, at Camp David and in Wye, Md. The only efforts in which Americans didn't participate were Israeli-Palestinian talks in 1993 that produced the Oslo Accords (although they were signed on the White House lawn), and in the negotiations leading to a 1994 Israel-Jordan peace treaty.

Deep and continuing U.S. involvement is necessary because "without peace, and with recurring conflict, Americans' resources are drained and our diplomatic strengths are dissipated by chasing cease-fires and temporary fixes," wrote a team of diplomatic and scholarly veterans of U.S.-promoted Israeli-Palestinian peace efforts.[20]

Aaron David Miller, a former State Department official who participated in Arab-Israeli peace efforts between 1985 and 2003, added a practical note. The close ties between the United States and Israel — reflected in the magnitude of foreign aid, the perception of Israel as the most reliable U.S. ally in a volatile region and strong bipartisan political support — make Washington the go-to place for all countries and organizations that want Israel influenced in one direction or another.[21] "It is our capacity to gain Israel's confidence and trust, which allows us to cajole and pressure, that makes us a compelling and attractive mediator," Miller wrote.[22]

But Miller adds in an interview that even the United States can't resolve the Arab-Israeli conflict single-handedly. "I really do believe that if an American president saw this as a priority, and if he had either an Israeli or a Palestinian leader who had capacity and vision, they could find a basis for cooperation," he says.

Such a regional figure "would have to be a bold, almost visionary, leader," Miller says, which he doesn't see right now. Egyptian President Anwar Sadat and Israeli Prime Minister Yitzhak Rabin, largely responsible for two of the major peace agreements in the region, were assassinated by compatriots who condemned them as traitors. But Miller says even with today's dim prospects for a definitive peace agreement, "We have a role to play, even if it's on life support."

Others see U.S.-Israel ties in a less favorable light. "We are bankrolling a process that has killed the two-state solution," historian Khalidi told NPR, citing what he calls a reality that contradicts official U.S. rhetoric — massive and longstanding U.S. military and political support for Israeli occupation. "Do we want American weapons to be used . . . to kill people in Palestine?"

Nevertheless, Khalidi says in an interview that he does not view the United States as the single biggest obstacle to peace. Others, he says, include "poor Palestinian leadership; an inability on the part of many Palestinians to see how violence is harmful to the cause; and the lack of a sane tactic to reach public opinion in Israel and the United States."

At the same time, Khalidi argues, "Israelis are living in an unreal world, thinking that there are no consequences for policies that they don't really believe are justified. I don't think they're fully aware of what their policies actually consist of in the occupied territories. Or if they are, other things apparently override that."

The Oslo Accords gave the Palestinian Authority control of about 38 percent of the West Bank ("Areas A and B" — with shared control of Area B), Israel has military authority in Area C, where Palestinians and Israelis maintain a tense coexistence, with Palestinians subject to military checkpoints, military trials if arrested in demonstrations and disputes over land and water rights.[23]

For Dayan, who says he deplores conditions under which West Bank Palestinians live, American influence could only be useful if the United States abandons its support for a two-state solution, which he views as an illusion. Instead, he urges the United States to back his idea for removing or lessening restrictions on Palestinians, which he said would also benefit settlers. "We can, we should, improve lives of all people living here," he says. "The right to live is most important — along with freedom of movement, expression. American involvement would be essential to persuade Palestinians and Israelis" to adopt this approach.

Yet, the traditional view of U.S. indispensability still holds among those who dismiss as fantasy Dayan's idea that Palestinians would accept second-class political status indefinitely. "There has to be a broker or a guarantor, somebody to hold the parties accountable to what they agreed to," says Ibish of the American Task Force on Palestine. "There is nobody else who wants the job, and the Israelis won't accept anyone else."

Ibish even sees an advantage to what is, from a Palestinian perspective, a U.S. tilt toward Israel. "Israelis obviously look to Americans as a friend but also a protector," he says. "Palestinians had to get used to these uncomfortable realities, but realized that the Americans are necessary to deliver the Israelis. To end the occupation, they need the U.S. to be on board with that."

Are the settlements the biggest obstacle to an agreement?

Israeli settlements in the West Bank and in East Jerusalem, now home to more than 500,000 Jewish residents, signify Israeli control of land that both Palestinians and some Israelis see as their rightful homeland.[24]

The settlements inspire supporters and opponents as few other issues. "Our right to this land is undisputable and incontestable," Michael Freund, a former aide to Prime Minister Netanyahu, wrote this year in *The Jerusalem Post*.[25]

"The entire world oppose[s] settlements and say[s] they are illegal," because they are on land that should be within a Palestinian state, Palestinian Authority President Mahmoud Abbas said in a December meeting with leaders of Fatah, the West Bank ruling party.[26]

The settlements also provide a setting for clashes between Israelis and Palestinians. Statistics on settler-on-Palestinian attacks range widely. The Washington-based Jerusalem Fund, a pro-Palestinian advocacy group, reported 3,700 incidents in 2004-2011, including 17 deaths and more than 775 injuries. The U.N. Office for the Coordination of Humanitarian Affairs in the West Bank reported three Palestinians killed by settlers and 183 injured in 2011.[27] As for Palestinian attacks on Israelis, B'Tselem, a leading Israeli human-rights organization, reports 20 Israeli deaths since 2009, the most recent in April, when a hitchhiking settler was fatally stabbed.[28]

But violence by settlers is increasingly worrying both the Israeli authorities and many settlers themselves. Most

AFP/Getty Images/Abbas Momani

Palestinians climb Israel's controversial security barrier on June, 7, 2013, during clashes with Israeli soldiers after a protest against the wall and Israeli settlements, such as Hashmonaim (background). Israelis began building the 450-mile wall between Israel and much of the West Bank in 2000 after the second Intifada began. Palestinian villagers bitterly complain that the wall cuts them off from their fields. Israelis say it has virtually eliminated attacks on civilians inside Israel.

freeze settlement expansion before negotiations resumed, and Palestinians refused to accept a definition of Israel as a Jewish state.[31]

Nevertheless, U.S. efforts to push for a settlement freeze and the U.N. vote on Palestinian membership reflect an international consensus that Israel is more committed to preserving settlements than to resuming peace talks.

Yet Israelis have agreed to major concessions on the settlements, argues Alex Safian, associate director at the Boston-based Committee for Accuracy in Middle East Reporting in America, which monitors perceived anti-Israel bias and inaccuracy in the news media. "The vast majority of settlers live in large settlements adjacent to the line" between Israel and the territories," he says. "In a peace treaty, there would be consolidation."

That is, Safian says, "One could certainly envision settlers from more farflung settlements moving to these others." Hence, "Settlements do not make an agreement impossible. That idea is a red herring."

Nevertheless, says Ibish, events of the 1990s after the Oslo agreement made Palestinians view settlements as a gauge of Israeli sincerity. "What Palestinians thought would happen was the end of the occupation everywhere in the occupied territories except for Jerusalem, settlements and military bases," he says. Instead, "the number of settlers doubled. Anything else that looks like a holding pattern brings back those memories."

Because the settlements have been constantly growing, Ibish says, they are the major obstacle. The territory on which a Palestinian state would exist "keeps getting gobbled up" by settlements and associated infrastructure, he says. "From the Palestinian point of view, settlements are about borders —'If we're going to have a state, why are you building 25 kilometers into it?'"

Many Israelis view the settlement issue through a different lens, Ibish adds. "For the Israeli government," he says, "settlements are about the security of the Jewish state, the security of Jewish Israelis."

But settler leader Dayan says settlements are an obstacle "only if you assume that a Palestinian state will not be able to assimilate an ethnic minority. If they can't assimilate, they shouldn't have a state."

notable have been attacks on Palestinians and Palestinian property committed under the name "price tag," meaning payback, by those who reject Israeli relinquishment of any occupied territory. Justice Minister Livni has advocated defining "price tag" assailants as terrorists. Israel's "security cabinet" rejected that idea in mid-June but authorized tougher action against "price tag" groups.[29]

Those attacks follow years of Israeli-Palestinian negotiations, mostly with U.S. participation, which have included proposals from Israel that would allow it to trade Israeli territory for "settlement blocs" — large subdivisions just over the line between Israel and the territories. Negotiators discussed plans along these lines in 2000, 2001 and as recently as 2008.[30] Attempts to revive talks in 2010 broke down when Israel refused to accept a U.S.-backed Palestinian demand that Israel

But Dayan's argument goes deeper, citing Palestinians' past rejection of a two-state solution. "When one side accepts partition and the other side attacks in order to prevent partition by force, partition becomes an unjust solution," he says. "Partition after aggression is a reward for aggression."

However, Israelis who favor a two-state solution don't all see settlements as the biggest problem. Among the bigger ones are security installations and procedures, including Israel's de facto military authority over the entire West Bank, Scheindlin says. "Israel has convinced itself that its security depends on that," she says. "That is going to be harder to uproot."

She adds that not all problems lie on the Israeli side, noting public opinion surveys showing that the pro-negotiation Palestinian Authority had a bare majority of support in contrast to Hamas, which opposes Israel's existence. (She spoke before release of the Pew survey showing major support for armed struggle.) "The fact that there is a real disagreement over the legitimacy of who represents the [Palestinian] people politically creates a very unstable situation," she says.

BACKGROUND

Early Clashes

Israel — or Judea, as it was called at the time — was the original homeland of the Jewish people. In 70 A.D., after the Romans destroyed the temple in Jerusalem that symbolized Jewish sovereignty, there were more Jews living elsewhere in the Mediterranean world than in Judea. Eventually, many emigrated to Western and Eastern Europe.[32]

In the 1880s, Russian Jews pioneered early Zionist emigration to Palestine at a time of growing anti-Semitism in the czarist empire. In 1897, Viennese journalist and activist Theodor Herzl launched a larger-scale drive for Jews to move to Palestine by organizing the international Zionist movement, based in Basel, Switzerland. These early efforts nearly quadrupled the Jewish population of Palestine, from 23,000 in 1882 to about 85,000 in 1914.

The Zionists argued that Jewish survival depended on establishing a Jewish homeland. At the time, Palestine and other Arab lands belonged to the Ottoman Empire, based in Istanbul, Turkey. During World War I, the empire

collapsed, and Britain and France divided up its Arab possessions, with Palestine reserved for the British.

Zionist leaders lobbied the British to endorse their project. In 1917, the British issued the single most important sentence in modern Middle Eastern history: "His Majesty's Government view with favor the establishment in Palestine of a national home for the Jewish People and will use their best endeavors to facilitate the achievement of this object, it being clearly understood that nothing shall be done which may prejudice the civil and religious rights of existing non-Jewish communities in Palestine or the rights and political status enjoyed by Jews in any other country," Foreign Secretary Arthur James Balfour wrote.[33] Arabs came to see the so-called Balfour Declaration as a betrayal of Arab Palestinians' rights to their homeland.

Jewish emigration to Palestine escalated between the two world wars as anti-Semitism mushroomed throughout Europe, pushed to genocidal extremes by Adolf Hitler's Nazi regime. Despite efforts at peaceful coexistence, Jewish-Palestinian relations steadily worsened.

In 1936, Palestinian Arabs launched a three-year revolt against British rule and Zionist ascendancy. British forces crushed the uprising, killing up to 6,000 Palestinian activists.[34] The revolt also was marked by deadly attacks on Arab civilians by units of the Irgun,* the armed wing of the Zionist "revisionist" movement. Irgun opposed the defense-only doctrine of the Haganah, the major Jewish militia.

As the clash between two peoples in one land intensified, the Jewish population rose from 175,000 in 1931 to 460,000 in 1939.[35]

Partition Fails

With the revolt ending, Britain issued a "white paper" designed to pacify the Arab Palestinians, promising independence within 10 years. It called for limits on Jewish immigration so an Arab majority would exist at independence.[36] The policy remained in effect until the end of World War II.

As the world began learning the full scope of the Nazis' efforts to exterminate Europe's Jews, Haganah defied the

---

*The full name is Irgun Zvai Leumi, meaning National Military Organization. It advocated Jewish statehood, regardless of Arab interests, throughout all of historic Palestine; Prime Minister Netanyahu's Likud Party grew out of the Irgun.

Encouraged by President Bill Clinton, Palestine Liberation Organization leader Yasser Arafat, right, and Israeli Prime Minister Yitzhak Rabin shake hands publicly for the first time on Sept. 13, 1993, after Israel and the PLO signed the landmark Oslo Accords. The agreement was designed to lead to Palestinian autonomy through a two-state solution to the Israeli-Palestinian conflict. A right-wing Israeli settler assassinated Rabin not long afterward for signing the accord.

British and smuggled shiploads of refugees into Palestine. After Jewish militias launched an anti-British campaign, Britain in 1947 turned the Palestine issue over to the United Nations.

A U.N. commission recommended splitting the region into Jewish and Arab states, with Jews inhabiting 55 percent of the territory and Arabs 45 percent. The two populations would share Jerusalem and Bethlehem under international supervision.

Arab nations opposed the plan, but on Nov. 29, 1947, the U.N. General Assembly voted 33-13, with 10 abstentions, for partition.

Both Jews and Arabs saw the vote as a prelude to Jewish statehood. Civil war broke out immediately, ending in defeat for Palestinian forces. Some 100,000 Palestinians fled to other Middle Eastern cities and to the predominantly Arab areas known as the West Bank and Gaza. Some had been forced or pressured to leave.

On May 14, after the last British official departed, the Zionist General Council declared Israeli statehood. Eleven minutes after the announcement, President Harry S. Truman recognized Israel, a move seen as vital to assuring international legitimacy.

The next day Egyptian, Syrian, Iraqi and Jordanian armies invaded Israel, joined later by forces from other Arab countries. Yet, the invaders soon were outnumbered by the newly formed Israel Defense Force (IDF), which fielded 108,000 troops by the end of 1948. They were better trained and well-armed, thanks to weapons purchases in Europe and the United States.

By the end of the conflict, which Israelis call the War of Independence and Palestinians call the Nakba (catastrophe), Israel remained an independent nation and up to 860,000 Palestinians had fled or been forced out of the country.[37] Israeli historian Benny Morris chronicles several expulsions reported in official Israeli files at the time. But, he concludes — countering some other historians — that Israeli leadership did not mount a large-scale, systematic expulsion of Arabs, who now constitute about 20 percent of Israel's population.[38]

After defeating its major enemy, Egypt, Israel ended up with the coastal enclave known as the Gaza Strip, and the two countries signed an armistice in 1949. The other invading countries followed suit.[39]

These agreements, which weren't official peace treaties, effectively created Israel's first borders — the so-called "green line," including the division of Jerusalem between Israel and Jordan. Jordan held on to the territory stretching north, south and east of Jerusalem to the Jordan River — known as the West Bank of the Jordan.

In the Arab world, Israel's victory was followed by deadly anti-Jewish violence in Libya, Syria, Lebanon, Egypt and elsewhere. The Egyptian and Iraqi governments suspended Jews' civil rights, imprisoning thousands. Up to 600,000 Jews fled from Arab countries — from land their families had owned for centuries — many headed for Israel.

Short Wars

The 1948 borders held until 1967, when the Six-Day War redrew Israel's map and made the Palestinians' future an enduring issue.

The war followed 18 months of rising tension between Israel and its two biggest neighbors, Syria and Egypt. Syria was home to Fatah, an acronym for the Palestinian National Liberation Movement led by then little-known Yasser Arafat, who later became the political and military leader of the Palestine Liberation Organization (PLO).

On June 5, Egypt was preparing to invade Israel through the Sinai Desert, but Israeli warplanes destroyed virtually all of Egypt's air force while it was still on the

CHRONOLOGY

1947-1968 *United Nations creates Jewish and Palestinian states.*

1947 U.N. approves "partition" of British-occupied Palestine into Jewish and Arab states; Palestinian Arabs reject the plan but are defeated in civil war with Jewish militia.

1948 Zionist leaders declare Israeli statehood after British depart. . . . Arab states invade Israel, which defeats them. . . . Up to 860,000 Palestinians flee Israel.

1949 Armistice agreements with Arab nations divide Jerusalem into Israeli and Jordanian territory and make the West Bank part of Jordan.

1967 In Six-Day War, Israeli troops conquer Jordanian part of Jerusalem, the West Bank, Sinai Desert and Gaza Strip. . . . U.N. Security Council calls for Israel to withdraw troops from occupied territories.

1968 Israeli cabinet endorses settlers moving into occupied territory near Jerusalem.

1973-1993 *More war, an Egypt-Israel peace treaty and a Palestinian uprising eventually force Israelis and Palestinians into negotiations.*

1973 Syria and Egypt launch surprise attack on Israel on Yom Kippur holiday; Israel eventually repels them.

1977 Egyptian President Anwar Sadat stuns world by traveling to Jerusalem and urging peace.

1978 Camp David Accords lead to Egypt-Israel peace treaty.

1981 Egyptian extremists assassinate Sadat for making peace with Israel.

1982 Israel invades Lebanon to dislodge Palestine Liberation Organization (PLO). . . . Up to 3,500 people are massacred in Palestinian refugee camps in Beirut by Israel's Lebanese Christian allies.

1987 Palestinians in West Bank begin six-year uprising (Intifada) against Israeli occupation.

1991 Palestinian and Israeli negotiators meet secretly in Oslo, Norway.

1993 Israeli Prime Minister Yitzhak Rabin and PLO leader Yasser Arafat appear on White House lawn with President Bill Clinton to sign Oslo Accords, designed to lead to two-state solution.

1995-Present *Peace attempts continue, but chances of two-state solution appear dim.*

1995 Israeli settler assassinates Rabin in retaliation for signing Oslo Accords.

2000 Israeli-Palestinian negotiations at Camp David fail to advance Palestinian statehood. . . . Second Intifada begins in Israel.

2004 Arafat dies.

2005 "Second Intifada" ends, after deaths of 3,000 Palestinians and 1,000 Israeli civilians and security personnel. . . . Israel withdraws from Gaza Strip, dismantles settlements.

2006 Islamist Hamas, which rejects Israel's legitimacy, wins parliamentary elections in Gaza (2006); West Bank ruling party Fatah refuses to cede power, provoking civil war. Hamas wins.

2008-2009 Rocket attacks from Gaza prompt major Israeli military operation that kills up to 1,100 Palestinian civilians.

2010 Israeli Prime Minister Ehud Olmert and Palestinian leader Mahmoud Abbas nearly reach two-state deal. . . . No new talks held after Olmert successor Benjamin Netanyahu refuses moratorium on West Bank settlements.

2011 Egyptian President Hosni Mubarak forced out in Arab Spring uprising, prompting Israeli worries about future of Egypt-Israel peace treaty.

2012 U.N. accepts Palestine as nonmember state.

2013 President Obama visits Israel and West Bank and urges compromise. . . . Arab League backs Israeli-Palestinian peace accord that includes land swaps.

Boycott Targets Israel's Palestinian Policy

Campaign of divestment, sanctions has had only limited success.

The news made headlines worldwide. In May, renowned British physicist Stephen Hawking canceled plans to attend a conference in Jerusalem hosted by Israeli President Shimon Peres.

"I have received a number of emails from Palestinian academics," Hawking wrote to the conference organizers. "They are unanimous that I should respect the boycott."[1]

By "boycott," Hawking meant campaigns in Europe and the United States calling for economic and cultural isolation of Israel. The efforts — known as "Boycott, Divestment, Sanctions" (BDS) — have been underway for more than a decade.

In June, U.S. singer-pianist Alicia Keys' announcement that she would stick to plans to perform in Tel Aviv on July 4 prompted calls urging her to follow the example of others who shun Israel. "It would grieve me to know you are putting yourself in danger (soul danger) by performing in an apartheid country," writer Alice Walker said in an open letter to Keys.[2]

Boycott advocates are especially active on college campuses and in churches. "BDS fundamentally calls on all peace-loving U.S. citizens to fulfill their profound moral obligation to desist from complicity in Israel's system of oppression against the Palestinian people, which takes the form of occupation, colonization and apartheid," Omar Barghouti, a co-founder of the boycott movement and the Palestinian Campaign for the Academic and Cultural Boycott of Israel, wrote in February.[3]

Counter-boycott movements charge that the movement has goals far beyond changing Israeli policy toward Palestinians. "Boycott activists try to delegitimize and demonize Israel," says Stand With Us, a Los Angeles-based Israel advocacy organization. "They call for boycotts to . . . isolate and cripple the Jewish state."[4]

The publicity that BDS has focused on the Israeli-Palestinian issue may represent success in itself. But boycott victories are scarce on the economic front. Israel's economy has been expanding steadily for most of the past 10 years, according to the World Bank.[5]

Google, which pleased Palestinian statehood backers by adopting the term "Palestine" for the West Bank, is nonetheless poised to boost Israel's economy in a big way. In early June, Google planned to spend a reported $1 billion-plus to buy Waze, an Israeli mapping software firm, whose developers would keep working from Israel.[6]

A coalition of European nongovernmental organization backs a boycott variant:

Refusal to buy outdoor furniture, baked goods and other products made in Israeli settlements in West Bank territory that Palestinians claim for a future state. However, an effort in the European Union to require products made in Israeli settlements to carry labels of origin reportedly was postponed after U.S. diplomats said the move would damage peace efforts.[7]

In the United States, the Presbyterian Church (U.S.A.) voted narrowly last year not to cut off investments in firms linked to Israeli occupation of the West Bank. Attempts to pressure U.S. colleges and universities to cut off investments in firms doing business with Israel have not scored any victories, though some student governments — most recently, at the University of California, Berkeley — have called for divestment from firms linked to Israeli activities in the West Bank.[8]

BDS campaigners in 2010 greeted as a major success a decision by DePaul University in Chicago to quit cafeteria sales of Sabra brand hummus, which is partly owned by an Israeli company that provides financial support to an Israeli army combat unit. Princeton students that year defeated a resolution to boycott Sabra. And DePaul's administration in 2011 reinstated Sabra-brand hummus.[9]

Entertainers have become the public face of the boycott movement. Last December, singer Stevie Wonder canceled a Los Angeles performance at a fundraiser for Friends of the Israel Defense Force. Roger Waters, the former bass player for the rock band Pink Floyd and a leading boycott campaigner, said he had helped persuade Wonder.[10] In 2010, singers Elvis Costello and the late Gil Scott-Heron, as well as guitarist Santana, canceled concerts in Israel.[11]

The BDS drive began in 2001, when a conference of nongovernmental organizations in Durban, South Africa, called for isolating Israel as "an apartheid state."[12]

Three years later, Palestinian academics in the West Bank capital of Ramallah launched a more precisely targeted "Palestinian Campaign for the Academic & Cultural Boycott of Israel."[13]

And in 2005, a wider range of Palestinian organizations called for "Boycott, Divestment and Sanctions" to force Israeli compliance with demands including the return of all Palestinian refugees to their homes in present-day Israel.[14]

Anti-BDS campaigners call the return proposal a veiled bid to eliminate Israel. If all Palestinian refugees — defined by U.N. agencies as including all descendants of the original refugees — returned, they say, Israel would no longer be a Jewish state. Under the U.N. definition, the total refugee population is 5 million.[15]

In Europe, where the BDS movement runs stronger than in the United States, teachers' unions in Ireland and Britain have voted to boycott Israeli academic institutions. British parliamentarian and anti-Israel campaigner George Galloway made that concept personal last February, walking out of an Oxford University debate concerning the West Bank upon learning his opponent was Israeli. "I don't recognize Israel," he said, "and I don't debate with Israelis."[16]

— Peter Katel

A Palestinian BDS advocate demonstrates on June 8, 2013, near the Jewish settlement of Bat Ayin and the West Bank village of Surif, west of Hebron.

AFP/Getty Images/Hazem Bader

[1] Quoted in Harriet Sherwood and Matthew Kalman, "Furore deepens over Stephen Hawking's Israel boycott," *The Guardian*, May 8, 2013, www .guardian.co.uk/science/2013/may/08/hawking-israel-boycott-furore.

[2] Quoted in Dave Itzkoff, "Despite Protests, Alicia Keys Says She Will Perform in Tel Aviv," *The New York Times*, May 31, 2013, http://arts beat.blogs.nytimes.com/2013/05/31/despite-protests-alicia-keys-says-she-will-perform-in-tel-aviv/.

[3] Omar Barghouti, "The BDS movement explained," *New York Daily News*, Feb. 25, 2013, www.nydailynews.com/opinion/boycott-israel-article-1.1271226?pgno=1#ixzz2TUJQMXpV; and Anshel Pfeffer, "Academic boycotter to study in Tel Aviv," *Jewish Chronicle*, April 23, 2009, www.thejc.com/news/israel-news/academic-boycotter-study-tel-aviv; Letter, president Zvi Galil, Tel Aviv University, May 3, 2009, http://israel-academia-monitor.com/index.php?type=large_advic&advice_id=7064&page_data%5Bid%5D=174&cookie_lang=en.

[4] "BDS, a Hostile Campaign," Stand With Us, undated, www.standwi thus.com/bds/.

[5] "GDP growth (annual %)," World Bank, http://data.worldbank.org/indicator/NY.GDP.MKTP.KD.ZG/countries/1W-IL?display=graph.

[6] Liz Gannes, "Google Officially Buys Waze in a $1 Billion-Plus Deal, Will Keep It Independent," *All Things D*, June 11, 2013, http://allth ingsd.com/20130611/google-officially-closes-waze-deal-will-keep-it-independent/.

[7] Quoted in Herb Keinon, "EU: No intention to boycott products from settlements," *Jerusalem Post*, Dec. 7, 2012, www.jpost.com/Diplomacy-and-Politics/EU-No-intention-to-boycott-settlement-products; "EU's trade balance with Israel," European Union, April 26, 2013, http:// trade.ec.europa.eu/doclib/docs/2006/september/tradoc_113402.pdf; Barak Ravid, "After U.S. request, EU delays decision to label products from Israeli settlements," *Haaretz*, May 19, 2013, www.haaretz.com/news/diplomacy-defense/after-u-s-request-eu-delays-decision-to-label-products-from-israeli-settlements.premium-1.524644.

[8] "ASUC Passes Divestment Resolution For Second Time," Students for Justice in Palestine at UC Berkeley, April 18, 2013, http://calsjp .org/?tag=bds; Laurie Goodstein, "In Close Vote, Presbyterian Church Rejects Divesting in Firms That Aid Israeli Occupation," *The New York Times*, July 6, 2012, www.nytimes.com/2012/07/06/us/presbyterian-church-wont-divest-in-firms-aiding-occupation.html.

[9] Marcy Oster, "Chickpea pick: DePaul administration backs Sabra hummus," Jewish Telegraphic Agency, May 24, 2011, www.jta

.org/2011/05/24/news-opinion/united-states/chickpea-pick-depaul-administration-backs-sabra-hummus; Tamar Lewin, "New Subject of Debate on Mideast: Hummus," *The New York Times*, Dec. 3, 2010, www.nytimes.com/2010/12/04/education/04hummus.html; Sami Kishawi, "DePaul 'divests' from Israeli hummus product," 16 Minutes to Palestine, Nov. 19, 2010, http://smpalestine.com/2010/11/19/depaul-divests-from-israeli-hummus-product/.

[10] Quoted in "Stevie Wonder cancels show at Israel Defense Forces fundraiser," Reuters, Nov. 30, 2012; Danny Shea, "Roger Water on Israel Boycott: 'I Am Considering My Position,' " *The Huffington Post*, April 16, 2013, www.huffingtonpost.com/2013/04/16/roger-waters-on-israel-bo_n_3093070.html; Jon Blistein, "Roger Waters Calls for Boycott of Israel," *Rolling Stone*, March 20, 2013, www.rollingstone .com/music/news/roger-waters-calls-for-boycott-of-israel-20130320.

[11] "Rocker Costello cancels Israel gig," AFP, May 18, 2010, www .google.com/hostednews/afp/article/ALeqM5hWsCcwapYWCe PCfoGx9QpWl74hVA.

[12] "NGO Forum Declaration," World Conference Against Racism, Sept. 3, 2001, http://i-p-o.org/racism-ngo-decl.htm.

[13] "Call for Academic and Cultural Boycott of Israel," July 6, 2004, http://pacbi.org/etemplate.php?id=869.

[14] "Palestinian Civil Society Call for BDS," BDS Movement, July 9, 2005, www.bdsmovement.net/call.

[15] "Who are Palestine refugees?," United Nations Relief and Works Agency or Palestine Refugees in the Near East, undated, www.unrwa .org/etemplate.php?id=86.

[16] Lucy Sherriff, "British MP abandons debate with Israeli student," *The Huffington Post*, Feb. 21, 2013, www.huffingtonpost.co.uk/2013/02/21/anti-semitic-george-galloway-oxford-debate-israeli-student _n_2731009.html; "Irish union official: Israel boycott passed without debate," *The Jerusalem Post*, April 19, 2013, www.jpost.com/Jewish-World/Jewish-Features/Irish-official-Israel-boycott-passed-without-debate-310356; Alan Cowell, "British Academics' Union Endorses Israel Boycott," *The New York Times*, May 31, 2007, www.nytimes .com/2007/05/31/world/europe/31britain.html.

Wide Divide Separates Israelis, Palestinians

While Israel's economy has been growing, the Palestinian territories of the West Bank and Gaza continue to suffer economically. Israel has an estimated per capita GDP of $32,200, compared to $2,900 in the territories. Israel's unemployment rate is about 6 percent versus more than 20 percent in the West Bank and Gaza. Israel's government has also been more stable. Benjamin Netanyahu, Israeli prime minister from 1996 to 1999, reassumed the post in 2009. The Palestinian Authority, which governs the West Bank, recently appointed Rami Hamdallah as its prime minister. The Gaza Strip is controlled by the militant Islamist group Hamas, but the Palestinian Authority has disputed its legitimacy.

Israel

Population: 7.7 million (2013 est.)
Type of government: parliamentary democracy
Head of government: Benjamin Netanyahu (since 2009)
Legislative branch: Knesset, 120 seats, political parties are elected by popular vote and assigned seats on a proportional basis
Religions: Judaism 76%, Islam 17%, Christianity and other 7%
GDP per capita: $32,200 (2012 est.)
Unemployment rate: 6.3% (2012 est.)
Major industries: high-technology products, wood and paper products, food and beverage, metals and chemical products, plastics, textiles

West Bank

Population: 2.7 million (2013 est.)
Type of government: Palestinian Authority, interim self-government body
Prime minister: Rami Hamdallah (since June 2013)
Legislative branch: Palestinian Legislative Council, 132 members elected from 16 electoral districts in the West Bank and Gaza
Religions: Islam 75%, Judaism 17% (Israeli settlers), Christianity and other 8%
GDP per capita: $2,900 (2008 est.)
Unemployment rate: 23% (2012 est.)
Major industries: small-scale manufacturing, quarrying, textiles, soap

Gaza Strip

Population: 1.8 million (2013 est.)
Type of government: Hamas, militant Sunni Islamic organization (disputed by Palestinian Authority)
Prime minister of Hamas: Ismail Haniya (disputed by Palestinian Authority)
Legislative branch: Palestinian Legislative Council, 132 members elected from 16 electoral districts in the West Bank and Gaza
Religions: Islam 99%, Christianity 1%
GDP per capita: $2,900 (2008 est.)
Unemployment rate: 30% (2012 est.)
Major industries: textiles, food processing, furniture

Sources: The World Factbook, Central Intelligence Agency, 2013, https://www.cia.gov/library/publications/the-world-factbook/index.html; Freedom House, www.freedomhouse.org

Golan Heights from Syria and took the Sinai from Egypt.

After that victory, Israel found itself a majority-Jewish country of 2.7 million ruling 1.4 million Palestinians in the West Bank and Gaza. Israeli politicians considered several options for dealing with the Palestinians, including deporting them to Iraq or Morocco, granting them limited political autonomy and turning the West Bank and its inhabitants back to Jordan. The government settled on occupation, at least temporarily. As for Jerusalem, the vast majority of Israelis wanted to keep the entire city.

Some Israelis had long seen Judea and Samaria as an integral part of Israel. After the war, they began planning to settle the area. Foreshadowing future opposition, a top government lawyer concluded in September, 1967, that Israeli settlements in the occupied territories would violate international law.

That same month, the Israeli cabinet approved opening a Jewish a settlement in Etzion, south of Jerusalem, the site of a Jewish community destroyed in 1948.

International opinion opposed the occupation drive from the beginning. In late 1967 the U.N. Security Council approved Resolution 242, which calls for "withdrawal of Israel armed forces from territories occupied in the recent conflict" as well as formal peace treaties and recognized national boundaries and a "just settlement of the refugee problem."[40]

According to the U.N., there are 5 million Palestinian refugees — including all descendants of the original refugees (who numbered either 750,000 or 860,000, according to different U.N. agencies) who lost their homes in 1948. Of these, 1.4 million live in camps — poor urban neighborhoods in

ground. Jordan then joined the war, but ended up losing the West Bank and East Jerusalem. Israel also seized the

Jordan, Lebanon, Syria, Gaza and the West Bank. Recently, the Syrian civil war has forced tens of thousands of Palestinians from Syria to Palestinian refugee enclaves in Lebanon.[41]

Six years after the Six-Day War, Egypt and Syria launched a surprise attack against Israel on Oct. 6, 1973, coinciding that year with Yom Kippur (Day of Atonement), the holiest day in the Jewish religious calendar.[42] The attackers were trying to regain territory lost in 1967 — for Syria, the Golan Heights, and for Egypt, the Sinai Peninsula.

But Israel, aided by an emergency U.S. arms shipment (in response to Soviet arms airlifted to Egypt and Syria) counterattacked and advanced to within artillery range of Damascus and Cairo.[43]

The Yom Kippur War marked the start of permanent U.S. participation in peacemaking efforts in Israel, although U.S. presidents and diplomats had been closely involved with Israel and its conflicts since its inception.

Early Peace Process

Secretary of State Kissinger helped negotiate an end to the Yom Kippur War. Syria and Israel settled on a cease-fire — in effect to this day. Egypt and Israel broke precedent by holding direct talks, leading to the 1978 Camp David Accords, shepherded by President Carter. That deal made possible a 1979 Egypt-Israel peace treaty, the first between the Jewish state and any of its neighbors. Under the treaty, Israel returned the Sinai Peninsula to Egypt in 1982.

The key figure in the peace deal was Sadat, then president of Egypt. He had electrified the world in 1977 when he flew to Jerusalem and told Israel's parliament, the Knesset, that he wanted peace. However, the treaty enraged Egyptian Islamist extremists, who assassinated Sadat in 1981.[44]

Later, American diplomats helped broker Israel's second peace treaty — with Jordan in 1994.[45] But left undone was another of the Camp David agreements: a plan to enforce "the legitimate rights of the Palestinian people and their just requirements."[46]

Instead, Israelis continued building settlements in the occupied territories. From 1967, when the first West Bank settlement was established, through the mid-1970s, the settler population in the West Bank and Gaza reached as high as 11,000.[47]

Then settlement-building accelerated, in defiant response to a 1975 U.N. General Assembly resolution holding that "Zionism is a form of racism and racial discrimination." The resolution, repealed in 1991, intensified Israelis' distrust of the U.N. and its agencies.[48]

In 1977, Israelis voted out the mainstay Labor Party and elected a government dominated by the Likud Party, an outgrowth of the Irgun, and headed by that organization's former leader, Menachem Begin. Although Labor had begun and maintained the occupation, Likud explicitly held that the territories were inherently part of Israel.

In 1982, as conflict with the PLO — the major Palestinian political-military group — intensified, Israel invaded Lebanon to eradicate a major PLO presence there. In Beirut, Israeli forces sealed off two adjoining Palestinian refugee camps, Sabra and Shatila, which also housed a large population of Lebanese Shiite Muslims. Aided by Israel's sealing of the camps, Israel's Lebanese Christian militia allies massacred up to 3,500 refugees, including women and children. The incident remains a rallying cry for opponents of Israel and Israeli human-rights activists.[49]

An official Israeli commission judged the government and its military indirectly responsible. Defense Minister Ariel Sharon was forced to quit. Israeli documents declassified in 2012, one historian says, show U.S. failure to pressure the Israeli government to protect the lives of camp residents.[50]

Uprisings

Until late 1987, Israel fought its major conflicts with external enemies. That year, Palestinians in the occupied territories began to rebel, confronting Israeli troops with stones and barricades. Although tensions had been building, the immediate spark was the death of four Palestinians near Gaza in an auto accident caused by an Israeli civilian truck driver.

During the ensuing six-year Intifada (uprising), and the seven years that followed, Israeli security forces killed 1,376 Palestinians in the occupied territories, and Palestinians killed 185 Israeli civilians and soldiers, according to the Israeli Information Center for Human Rights in the Occupied Territories (B'Tselem).[51]

To stop the bloodshed, Israeli and Palestinian negotiators began meeting secretly in Oslo, Norway, in 1991, culminating in the Oslo Declaration of Principles of 1993. In what would become an iconic moment, PLO Chairman

A relative of a Palestinian (pictured) who died in an Israeli prison mourns during his funeral in the West Bank village of Saair on Feb. 25, 2013. Palestinian civilians arrested in the West Bank, often during protests, are subject to military trials and detention.

Arafat and Israeli Prime Minister Rabin — a former general and defense minister — signed the agreement on the White House lawn on Sept. 13, 1993, with President Clinton as witness.[52]

The agreement was designed to lead to Palestinian statehood. Provisions called for PLO recognition of Israel and Israeli acceptance of the PLO as Palestinian representative, phased Israeli withdrawal from parts of the West Bank and complete withdrawal from Gaza. Palestinians would elect a proto-government, the Palestinian Authority, to rule territory that Israel evacuated. After those confidence-building measures, talks could begin in five years on the big issues — future borders of the two states and the status of Jerusalem and the settlements.[53]

Oslo infuriated the growing settler movement. A fanatical member assassinated Rabin in Tel Aviv in 1995. A series of interim agreements in the Oslo framework saw Israeli withdrawals from parts of the West Bank. But a meeting at Camp David in 2000 failed to produce a definitive two-state solution.

In the wake of that breakdown, armed Palestinian organizations launched the "Second Intifada," which began after a provocative visit by former Defense Minister Sharon to a Jerusalem site that contains places holy to both Jews and Muslims. The conflict, which lasted until 2005, cost hundreds of lives. Palestinian suicide bombers and other attackers killed 649 Israeli civilians and 301 security personnel; and Israeli forces killed 3,189 Palestinians,

according to B'Tselem (whose figures don't distinguish between Palestinian combatants and noncombatants).[54]

One consequences of the second uprising was the construction of a wall between Israel and parts of the West Bank. The start of the intifada probably also helped get the formerly disgraced Sharon elected prime minister in 2001.

The insurgency ended after the 2004 death of Palestine Liberation Organization leader Arafat, the election of pro-negotiation Mahmoud Abbas as Palestinian Authority president, and a truce agreement between Sharon and Abbas. And in 2005 Israel withdrew from Gaza, ending a military presence there and evacuating 8,600 Israeli settlers from that enclave.[55]

Gaza voters then elected parliamentary representatives from Hamas, the militant Islamist organization that — unlike the Palestinian Authority — rejected Israel's right to exist. But the authority rejected the Gaza results, leading to a mini-civil war in Gaza that Hamas won in 2007. Thus, the Palestinian population was split in two both politically and geographically.[56]

Before the Gaza withdrawal, the George W. Bush administration had launched a so-called road map to Israeli-Palestinian peace. Abbas accepted the plan, but Israeli Prime Minister Sharon called for additional measures banning Palestinian violence. The plan died.[57]

In late December 2008, less than a month before Bush left office, Israel attacked Hamas in Gaza, in response to rocket attacks from there into southern Israel. The 22-day operation, which ended two days before President Obama's inauguration, cost at least 1,166 Palestinian lives, 709 of them "terror operatives," according to the Israeli Defense Force. B'Tselem put the Palestinian death toll at 1,385, while the Palestinian Centre for Human Rights estimated 1,419 Palestinian deaths, more than 1,100 of them defined as civilians.[58]

After Obama took office in 2009, he delivered a major speech in Cairo on U.S relations with the Muslim world. In the course of the talk, he spoke of "daily humiliations . . . that come with occupation" and called the Palestinian situation "intolerable."[59]

Despite the speech, peace efforts remained stalled, so the Palestinian Authority began to seek U.N. recognition of Palestine as a way to restart the statehood process. Last November, by a 138-9 vote, the General Assembly voted to grant "non-member observer state" status to Palestine.

Given the U.N.'s history of support for Palestinians against Israel, the lopsided vote was no surprise. Neither was the U.S. "no" vote. A divide appeared among Western European nations, however, where the Israeli-Palestinian conflict is a major political issue. France, Italy and Spain supported the resolution; Britain and Germany abstained. But Britain accompanied its action with a strong call for the Obama administration to kick-start the two-state negotiations.[60]

CURRENT SITUATION

Trouble at the Top

The Palestinian Authority (PA) is now led by a new prime minister, Rami Hamdallah, a career university professor and administrator with no political experience. He replaces Salam Fayyad, an economist who resigned in April after serving since 2007.

Fayyad, a former International Monetary Fund official who earned his doctorate from the University of Texas and also had served as Palestinian Authority finance minister, let loose with harsh criticism of Palestine's government after announcing his resignation.

"It is incredible that the fate of the Palestinian people has been in the hands of leaders so entirely casual, so guided by spur-of-the-moment decisions, without seriousness," Fayyad told Roger Cohen, a columnist for *The New York Times*. "We don't strategize, we cut deals in a tactical way and we hold ourselves hostage to our own rhetoric."[61]

Westerners had seen Fayyad as the key to professionalizing and modernizing the Palestinian Authority. The authority's ruling party, Fatah, the largest political grouping within the PLO, had fought Israel for years with violence rather than talking points.[62]

Hamas, the ruling party in Gaza, welcomed Fayyad's departure. Fayyad had helped the PA "protect the Zionist occupation and U.S. interests," Hamas spokesman Fawzi Barhoum said.[63]

With those words, Hamas indicated that a unity government with the PA, which Fayyad had long advocated, may not be in sight.[64]

Still, unifying the West Bank and Gaza by repairing the Fatah-Hamas split remains at the top of the Palestinian agenda. The newly appointed Hamdallah is expected to be an interim official, pending negotiations to form a unity government that would organize presidential and parliamentary elections in the West Bank and Gaza.[65]

Unifying the West Bank and Gaza might theoretically strengthen the Palestinian position in talks with Israel. However, Netanyahu is continuing to refuse to negotiate with Hamas, which opposes Israel's existence. Justice Minister Livni, a strong two-state advocate, agrees. Thus, if Palestinians formed a unity government, talks would be impossible.

"If Hamas is behind the government, that's a nonstarter," Mark Regev, Netanyahu's spokesman, told the *National Journal*.[66]

Fatah and Hamas agreed at a meeting in Cairo in May on steps toward forming an interim unity government and holding elections.[67]

However, the split remains deep. After Hamdallah was appointed, Hamas called the new West Bank government "illegal." Instead of working to form the agreed-upon unity government, "The Fatah leadership is willing to maintain and prolong the state of disagreement" between the two parties, Hamas said in a statement.[68]

New Peace Proposal

In trying times for peace optimists, a new two-state plan, touted as the Arab world's attempt to craft an accord, is drawing praise from the United States, the Palestinian Authority and some Israeli politicians. Applause has not been universal, however. Netanyahu is skeptical; one Hamas leader dismissed it outright.

Further complicating the picture, the late-April proposal by the League of Arab States, the major organization of Middle Eastern countries, coincides with rising tension in the region over the Syrian civil war.[69]

Hezbollah, the Lebanese Shiite political party and armed force with which Israel fought a 34-day war in 2006, is sending fighters to Syria to aid the Shiite government of dictator Bashar Assad. Until now, Hezbollah has fought only Israel, but the group is closely allied to Iran — Assad's major regional ally and Israel's primary foreign foe. On the other side in the Syrian civil war, anti-Assad forces, mostly from Syria's Sunni majority, are receiving arms and other aid from Saudi Arabia and Qatar — key Sunni-dominated countries involved in the revived peace plan.[70]

The key item in the late-April peace proposal is support for land swaps to compensate for territory occupied

Getty Images/Uriel Sinai

A costumed little girl watches as Israeli soldiers prepare to stand guard during a Purim parade at the West Bank Israeli settlement of Havat Gilad on Feb. 22, 2013. Many observers view the Israeli settlements in the West Bank as a major obstacle to peace between Israel and the Palestinians. Some 2.7 million mostly Muslim inhabitants live in the West Bank.

by Israeli "settlement blocs" that lie across the potential border between Israel and the West Bank.[71] An earlier version of the peace plan, proposed by Saudi Arabia in 2002, didn't include the land swaps. Palestinians and their Arab supporters generally rejected swaps at the time because they were seen as effectively allowing Israel's borders to extend beyond the line that existed before Israel took over the West Bank, East Jerusalem and Gaza in 1967.[72]

In late April, Secretary of State Kerry promoted the plan in a joint appearance with Sheikh Hamad bin Jassim bin Jabr Al Thani, prime minister of Qatar, who said the initiative would allow for "joint justice and peace between the Palestinian and the Israeli, and stability in the Middle East."[73]

If Israel and the Palestinians reached an agreement, league members said, they would sign their own peace deals with Israel.[74]

Netanyahu responded to the Arab League announcement by reiterating his argument that the stalemate is not about land and borders. "The Palestinian lack of will to recognize Israel as the national state of the Jewish people is the root of the conflict," Netanyahu told officials of Israel's foreign ministry, according to *The Washington Post*.

Nevertheless, Israeli Justice Minister Livni met with Kerry in Rome to express support for Kerry's efforts to

use the proposal to restart Israeli-Palestinian talks. "I believe that what you are doing here will create hope in the region, because some of us lost hope," she said. "And I do believe that having the meeting with the Arab League and having the statement come from [Al Thani] after the meeting was very good news, because there's the need for the support of the Arab states."[75]

It was "very important for us that peace with the Palestinians means also peace with the Arab world," she added.

The Palestinian Authority's chief negotiator, Saab Erekat, said the new proposal was consistent with the PA's approval of the land-swap idea.

However, Khalid Mashaal, the Qatar-based leader of Hamas, rejected land trades, saying they weaken the Palestinian cause. The main goal of the Arab peace plan, he said, is to allow Israel's economic integration with the region.[76]

OUTLOOK

Looming Questions

In recent decades, the Middle East has seen sudden, dramatic change and failures of vision. Among the former: Egyptian President Sadat's surprise trip to Jerusalem in 1977. Among the latter: Arab nations' belief in 1948 that they could eradicate Israel; and the belief of several Israeli leaders after 1967 that Palestinians would settle for Israeli control of the West Bank in return for higher living standards.[77]

More recently, some worry about the security of Israel's northern and southern borders after a revolution in Egypt overthrew dictator Hosni Mubarak — credited with honoring his country's peace treaty with Israel — and the Syrian civil war has spilled over into Lebanon. In early May, Israeli air attacks on Syria destroyed what sources said were Iranian missiles being delivered to Hezbollah fighters in Syria.[78]

"These strikes formed an unusually visible episode in an ongoing, usually clandestine, war being undertaken by Israel to reduce the threat posed by Iran and its various assets in the region," Jonathan Spyer, a senior research fellow at the Gloria Center, an Israeli think tank with a strong security focus, wrote in mid-May.[79]

In recent years, Prime Minister Netanyahu repeatedly has posed as a possibly imminent necessity American or

AT ISSUE

Should Google designate the West Bank as "Palestine"?

YES
Aziz Abu Sarah
Co-Executive Director, Center for World Religions, Diplomacy and Conflict Resolution, George Mason University

Written for *CQ Researcher*, June 2013

Why was Google's decision to recognize Palestine as a state the right thing to do? Of course, Google is not an international body with the power to name countries and define their status and boundaries. The United Nations has the right to legitimize states. Historically, the opinions of opposing countries in conflict with newly legitimated states are relevant to the discussion.

However, if a U.N. resolution is passed, those objections are typically disregarded. Google's decision to acknowledge Palestine as a state was a mere acceptance of the U.N.'s decision. Google does not have the authority to make this change on its own. It is simply following the U.N.'s lead.

Google defines itself as an international company that respects international law and human rights with the motto "don't be evil." It runs businesses in many countries and depends on international law to protect its operations and provide rules and guidelines on the best practices and standards. If Google does not accept the U.N.'s decisions, it would be in clear defiance of the international community and the legitimacy of the United Nations.

If every company were to choose for itself what is or is not a state, we would have anarchy and become unable to function in a globalized world.

For example, Google recognized Kosovo after it declared its independence in 2008 and gained the support of many states, despite opposition from Russia and Serbia. This decision hinges on the Hague Court's decision that Kosovo's independence did not violate international law, an action far less determinant than the U.N.'s current position on Palestine.

Israel's decision to fight Google over its recognition of a Palestinian state is disheartening, because it urges Google to ignore decisions made by the United Nations. How could Israel dispute Google's recognition of a U.N. decision, when a decision by the same international body legitimized its existence in 1948? International law is a two-way street; Israel must accept the U.N.'s decisions even when it does not agree.

This opposition from Israel ignores the connections between the recognition of a Palestinian state and the acceptance of an Israeli state. The U.N.'s acknowledgment of the 1967 borders for Palestine legitimizes Israel as a state as well. It should be remembered that the Palestine Liberation Organization has recognized Israel since 1993.

It is time that Israel and other nations recognize Palestine in return, assuming that Israel is still interested in a two-state solution.

NO
Alex Safian
Associate Director, Committee for Accuracy in Middle East Reporting in America

Written for *CQ Researcher*, June 2013

Google's decision to change its Palestinian search page to read "Palestine" rather than "Palestinian Territories" can only harm the cause of peace. Google's justification — that it is just following the U.N.'s lead — is wrongheaded and inconsistent.

The Israelis and the Palestinians have signed numerous agreements since 1993, all witnessed by other countries. Many of these agreements require that all differences between the parties be settled by direct negotiations and, as the Sharm el-Sheikh Memorandum states, "neither side shall initiate or take any step that will change the status of the West Bank and the Gaza Strip." (In return for such Palestinian promises, Israel made tangible concessions, such as the creation of the Palestinian Authority and giving up of control of land).

The Palestinians' appeal to the U.N. General Assembly to upgrade their status to "Observer State," implying U.N. recognition of Palestinian statehood, violated both their solemn promise to negotiate differences directly with Israel and their agreement not to take any steps to change the status of the West Bank and Gaza.

Such violations by the Palestinians call into question the value of any future agreements between the parties, thereby making a negotiated peace that much harder to achieve.

Moreover, many countries that witnessed the prior agreements backed the Palestinian move at the U.N, despite the fact that it violated the very agreements they had promised to support. This calls those promises into question and also makes peace that much harder to achieve.

And not just peace between the Israelis and the Palestinians. How can any country involved in difficult international negotiations trust that such agreements will have any meaning if the terms can be so easily cast aside?

Google's decision to reward this illegal and unilateral action by the Palestinians only compounds the problems.

Google's logic is also lacking because the U.N. does not determine statehood. For decades Taiwan rather than China held the "China" seat at the U.N. Obviously, China's nonmembership in the U.N. did not mean it wasn't a state. Similarly, after Taiwan was expelled from the U.N. in favor of China, Taiwan was still a sovereign state.

By the way, Taiwan's Google search page says "Taiwan," not "the non-country of Taiwan" or something similar. So Google apparently does not always follow U.N. usage.

The bottom line is that peace will come only through honest negotiations between the parties, not through unilateral appeals to the U.N. or even to Google.

Israeli bombing of nuclear sites in Iran, claiming the Iranian government is developing a nuclear weapon, which Iran denies. Most recently, Netanyahu said Iran's nuclear development project had not yet reached a danger point.[80]

Whatever happens with Iran or Israel's other neighbors, Israelis and Palestinians must decide whether and how to transform their relationship into one between two neighboring states.

Safian of the Committee for Accuracy in Middle East Reporting in America says a major change in the status quo is unlikely. "We're going to muddle along," he says. "I don't see a Palestinian Sadat who is going to arise and change things. I wouldn't be surprised if there is more violence in the next 10 years. It would be pollyannaish to think otherwise."

George Mason's Sarah says if the Palestinians change their demand from statehood to full civil and political rights, they would be "putting Israel in a corner." The message, he says, would be: " 'I want my rights as a human being.' That moves closer to the South African model" of a fight for equality.

The civil rights argument reflects a point made by Israeli opponents of the occupation — that Israel can best assure the continued Jewish character of Israel by relinquishing the occupied territories and working toward Palestinian statehood.

Otherwise, says analyst Scheindlin, "It could be that Palestinians sacrifice their national representation and the title of state in return for actual political rights, and Israel sacrifices its Jewish majority."

The worst outcome, she says, would be that Palestinians remain stateless and without full equality. "That would be a real disaster," she says. "It would be a major misreading of history to expect people to live like that, to wish away their national identity. It hasn't worked anywhere in the world."

Dayan of the settlers' council contends the idea of Palestinian statehood has failed the test of time. "The political conflict between Israel and the Palestinians is a zero-sum game," he says, with Israel the winner.

But, he adds, "The human conflict is not. When a Palestinian is humiliated, I gain nothing. When an Israeli is killed, they gain nothing. If we understand this, Israelis and Palestinians, that will start a process that could be beneficial, but now we are stuck with the attempt to solve the big problem, and the big problem has no solution."

Columbia University's Khalidi disagrees. "I don't think the status quo is sustainable," he says, but adds, "I don't know how long it might take" to end.

The solution, he says, is uncomplicated. "Just give us our rights. We're a nation, we're a people. We don't want military occupation. We don't want to be treated like second-class citizens. A lot of Israeli right-wing politicians take that as a threat. Of course, the threat is their own laws and occupation."

For the immediate future, says former diplomat Miller, the status quo may continue, but at a cost. "Israelis will keep their state," he says, "but the Palestinians and Arabs will never let them continue enjoying it."

NOTES

1. Mark Landler, "Obama Urges Young Israelis to Lead the Push for Peace," *The New York Times*, March 21, 2013, www.nytimes.com/2013/03/22/world/middleeast/gaza-militants-fire-rockets-as-obama-visits.html?pagewanted=all.

2. "John Kerry, Remarks at the American Jewish Committee Global Forum," U.S. Department of State (transcript), June 3, 2013, www.state.gov/secretary/remarks/2013/06/210236.htm.

3. "Military-Strategic Aspects of West Bank Topography for Israel's Defense," Defensible Borders for a Lasting Peace, Jerusalem Center for Public Affairs, 2005, www.defensibleborders.org/apx1.htm.

4. Barak David, *et al.*, "In historic vote, Palestine becomes non-member UN state with observer status," *Haaretz*, Nov. 30, 2012, www.haaretz.com/news/diplomacy-defense/in-historic-vote-palestine-becomes-non-member-un-state-with-observer-status-1.481531; Dan Williams, "Israel says Google's 'Palestine' page harms peace hopes," Reuters, May 6, 2013, www.reuters.com/article/2013/05/06/us-palestinians-israel-google-idUSBRE94509V20130506.

5. "Freedom in the World 2013 — West Bank," Freedom House, undated, www.freedomhouse.org/report/freedom-world/2013/west-bank.

6. Martin Goodman, *Rome and Jerusalem: The Clash of Ancient Civilizations* (2007), p. 471.

7. Rashid Khalidi, *Palestinian Identity: The Construction of Modern National Consciousness* (1997), Kindle edition.

8. "Judea and Samaria — It's Jewish, It's Vital, It's Realistic," YESHA Council —The Jewish Communities of Judea, Samaria and Gush Katif, Jan. 1, 2012, p. 2, www.myesha.org.il/_Uploads/dbsAttached-Files/hoveretweb.pdf; Amy Teibel, "Settler population surges 18% under Netanyahu," *The Times of Israel*, July 10, 2012, www.timesofisrael.com/ settler-population-surges-18-under-netanyahu; "Land Expropriation and Settlement Statistics," B'Tselem —The Israeli Information Center for Human Rights in the Occupied Territories, April 22, 2013, www.btselem.org/settlements/statistics; "International Fact-Finding Mission on Israeli Settlements in the Occupied Palestinian Territory," U.N. Office of the High Commissioner for Human Rights, undated, www.ohchr.org/EN/HRBodies/ HRC/RegularSessions/Session19/Pages/Israeli SettlementsInTheOPT.aspx; "Israeli Settlement Population 1972-2006," Foundation for Middle East Peace, undated, www.fmep.org/settlement_info/set tlement-info-and-tables/stats-data/israeli-settler-pop ulation-1972-2006.

9. Aron Heller and Josef Federman, "Israel Election 2013: Prime Minister Benjamin Netanyahu Scrambles to Keep His Job," The Associated Press (*The Huffington Post*), Jan. 23, 2013, www.huffing tonpost.com/2013/01/23/israel-election-2013-re sults-benjamin-netanyahu_n_2531995.html; Jodi Rudoren, "Israelis Form Government Days Before Obama Visit," *The New York Times*, March 15, 2013, www.nytimes.com/2013/03/16/world/mid dleeast/israeli-leaders-form-new-government-com plicating-peace-process.html; Jodi Rudoren, "Israel: Deal Gives Netanyahu Rival Palestinian Portfolio," *The New York Times*, Feb. 19, 2013, www.nytimes .com/2013/02/20/world/middleeast/deal-gives-pal estinian-portfolio-to-netanyahu-rival-tzipi-livni. html; "PM inks coalition deals with Bennett, Lapid," *The Jerusalem Post*, March 15, 2013, www.jpost .com/Diplomacy-and-Politics/Bayit-Yehudi-and-Likud-Beytenu-sign-coalition-agreement; Jodi Rudoren, "Fresh Israeli Face Plays Down Dimming of Political Star," *The New York Times*, May 19, 2013, www.nytimes.com/2013/05/20/world/mid dleeast/fresh-israeli-face-plays-down-political-decline.html.

10. Quoted in Raphael Ahren, "Deputy defense minister: This government will block any two-state deal," *The Times of Israel*, June 6, 2013, www.timesofisrael .com/deputy-defense-minister-this-government-will-block-any-peace-deal.

11. Quoted in Raphael Ahren, "PMO, distancing itself from deputy minister's comments, says government wants two-state solution," *The Times of Israel*, June 8, 2013, www.timesofisrael.com/pmo-urgently-dis tancing-itself-from-deputy-ministers-comments-says-government-wants-two-solution.

12. Quoted in Jack Khoury and Amira Hass, "Abbas to Obama: Israel talks only in exchange for settlement freeze, release of prisoners," *Haaretz*, March 22, 2013, www.haaretz.com/news/obama-visits-israel/ abbas-to-obama-israel-talks-only-in-exchange-for-settlement-freeze-release-of-prisoners.premium-1.511369.

13. "Construction Starts in Settlements Reach 7 Year High," Americans for Peace Now, June 10, 2013, http://peacenow.org/entries/construction_starts_in_ settlements_reach_7_year_high#.Ubd-ARbv0Rk.

14. Ben Birnbaum, "The End of the Two-State Solution," *The New Republic*, March 11, 2013, www.newrepublic.com/article/112617/israel-pales tine-and-end-two-state-solution.

15. "B'Tselem's findings: Harm to civilians significantly higher in the second half of Operation Pillar of Defense," B'Tselem —The Israeli Information Center for Human Rights in the Occupied Territories, May 8, 2013, www.btselem.org/press_ releases/20130509_pillar_of_defense_report; Batsheva Sobelman, "Israeli army clears itself in Gaza War," *Los Angeles Times*, April 23, 2009, p. A25.

16. "Despite Their Wide Differences, Many Israelis and Palestinians Want Bigger Role for Obama in Resolving Conflict," Global Attitudes Project, Pew Research Center, May 9, 2013, www.pewglobal.org/ files/2013/05/Pew-Global-Attitudes-Israeli-Palestinian-Conflict-FINAL-May-9-2013.pdf.

17. "Palestinian Public Opinion Poll No. (47)," Palestinian Centre for Policy and Survey Research, March 28-30, 2013, www.pcpsr.org/survey/polls/2013/p47e.html#head5.

18. Jeremy M. Sharp, "U.S. Foreign Aid to Israel," Congressional Research Service, April 11, 2013, p. 26, www.fas.org/sgp/crs/mideast/RL33222.pdf; Jeremy M. Sharp, "Egypt: Background and U.S. Relations," Congressional Research Service, pp. 7-8, www.fas.org/sgp/crs/mideast/RL33003.pdf.

19. David Aaron Miller, *The Much Too Promised Land: America's Elusive Search for Arab-Israeli Peace* (2009), p. 29; Daniel C. Kurtzer, *et al.*, *The Peace Puzzle: America's Quest for Arab-Israeli Peace, 1989-2011* (2013), pp. 17-20.

20. *Ibid.*, p. 269.

21. "Hearing of the Middle East and North Africa Subcommittee of the House Foreign Affairs Committee —The Fatah-Hamas Reconciliation: Threatening Peace Prospects," Federal News Service, Feb. 5, 2013; Jim Zanotti, "Israel: Background and U.S. Relations," Congressional Research Service, Summary and p. 10, http://assets.opencrs.com/rpts/RL33476_20121107.pdf.

22. Miller, *op. cit.*, p. 375.

23. "West Bank," Freedom House, *op. cit.*; "Area C Humanitarian Response Plan Fact Sheet," United Nations Office for the Coordination of Humanitarian Affairs, occupied Palestinian territory, August 2010, www.ochaopt.org/documents/ocha_opt_area_c_humanitarian_response_plan_fact_sheet_2010_09_03_english.pdf.

24. "Judea and Samaria — It's Jewish, It's Vital, It's Realistic," *op. cit.*; Teibel, *op. cit.*; "Land Expropriation and Settlement Statistics," *op. cit.*; "International Fact-Finding Mission on Israeli Settlements in the Occupied Palestinian Territory," *op. cit.*

25. "Fundamentally Freund: The case for Judea and Samaria," *The Jerusalem Post*, Feb. 18, 2013, www.jpost.com/Opinion/Columnists/Fundamentally-Freund-The-case-for-Judea-and-Samaria.

26. "Abbas says E1 Settlement Project will Never Happen," Palestinian News & Info Agency, Dec. 22, 2012, www.wafa.ps/english/index.php?action=detail&id=21377.

27. Yousef Munayyer, "When Settlers Attack," The Jerusalem Fund for Education and Community Development," p. 6, www.thejerusalemfund.org/ht/a/GetDocumentAction/i/32678; "Israeli Settler Violence in the West Bank," U.N. Office for the Coordination of Humanitarian Affairs, occupied Palestinian territory, December 2011, www.ochaopt.org/documents/ocha_opt_settler_violence_Fact Sheet_October_2011_english.pdf.

28. "Attacks on Israeli civilians by Palestinians, Israeli civilian killed in stabbing attack, northern West Bank," B'Tselem, The Israeli Information Center for Human Rights in the Occupied Territories, April 30, 2013, www.btselem.org/israeli_civilians/20130430_israeli_civilian_stabbed_to_death_by_palestinian.

29. Chaim Levinson, "Israel's state prosecutor: No real benefit in saying 'price tag' perpetrators are terrorists," *Haaretz*, June 2, 2013, www.haaretz.com/news/national/israel-s-state-prosecutor-no-real-benefit-in-saying-price-tag-perpetrators-are-terrorists.premium-1.527277. Barak Ravid, "Netanyahu: Price tag attacks cannot be compared to Hamas terror," *Haaretz*, June 17, 2013, www.haaretz.com/news/diplomacy-defense/netanyahu-price-tag-attacks-cannot-be-compared-to-hamas-terror.premium-1.530205.

30. Deborah Sontag, "Quest for Mideast Peace: How and Why It Failed," *The New York Times*, July 26, 2001, p. A1; Michael Hirsh, "Clinton to Arafat: It's All Your Fault," *Newsweek*, June 26, 2001, www.thedailybeast.com/newsweek/2001/06/26/clinton-to-arafat-it-s-all-your-fault.html; Birnbaum, *op. cit.*

31. Mark Landler, "U.S. Drops Bid To Sway Israel On Settlements," *The New York Times*, Dec. 8, 2010, www.nytimes.com/2010/12/08/world/middleeast/08diplo.html?_r=0; Edmund Sanders, "Mideast talks' defining debate," *Los Angeles Times*, Oct. 19, 2010, p. 1.

32. Goodman, *op. cit.*; Walter Laqueur, *A History of Zionism* (1972), pp. 41-42, 213. Except where otherwise noted, this subsection is drawn from Laqueur.

33. Quoted in Benny Morris, *1948: The First Arab-Israeli War* (2008), p. 9.

34. *Ibid.*, pp. 20-21.

35. Laqueur, *op. cit.*

36. Except where otherwise noted, this subsection is drawn from Morris, *ibid.*

37. Khalidi, *op. cit.*, Chapter 5. Also see "Frequently Asked Questions — United Nations Relief and Works Agency for Palestine Refugees in the Near East," UNRWA, undated, www.unrwa.org/etem plate.php?id=87. Note: The UNRWA count is of Palestinians who lost their homes in the period 1946-1948.

38. Morris, *op. cit.*, pp. 407-410; Glenn Frankel, "Creation Myths," *The Washington Post*, June 1, 2008, p. BW01.

39. Except where otherwise indicated, this subsection is drawn from Tom Segev, *1967: Israel, the War, and the Year That Transformed the Middle East* (2007); and Gershom Gorenberg, *Accidental Empire: Israel and the Birth of the Settlements, 1967-1977* (2006).

40. "Resolution 242 of 22 November 1967," United Nations Security Council, http://unispal.un.org/unispal.nsf/0/7D35E1F729DF491C8525 6EE700686136.

41. "Palestine refugees," United Nations Relief and Works Agency for Palestine Refugees in the Near East, undated, www.unrwa.org/etemplate .php?id=86; Sari Hanafi, "Governing Palestinian Refugee Camps in the Arab East: Governmentalities in Search of Legitimacy," American University of Beirut, October 2010, Introduction, http://burawoy .berkeley.edu/Public%20Sociology,%20Live/Hanafi/ Hanafi.Governing%20Refugee%20Camps.pdf; Josh Wood, "Palestinian Refugees Flee Syria to Find Poor Conditions in Lebanese Camps," *The New York Times*, www.nytimes.com/2013/05/30/world/mid dleeast/palestinian-refugees-flee-syria-to-find-poor-conditions-in-lebanese-camps.html?pagewanted=all.

42. Miller, *op. cit.*

43. Gorenberg, *op. cit.*

44. Kurtzer, *et al.*, *op. cit.*; Caryle Murphy, *Passion For Islam* (2002), pp. 61-63.

45. Kurtzer, *et al.*, *ibid.*, pp. 77-78.

46. "A Framework for Peace in the Middle East Agreed at Camp David," Camp David Meeting on the Middle East, Sept. 17, 1978, Anwar Sadat Archives, University of Maryland, http://sadat.umd.edu/ archives/summits/AACK%20Camp%20David%20 Framework%209.17.78.pdf.

47. Gorenberg, *op. cit.* (Kindle edition, no page number); "Settlement Populations in the Occupied Territories, 1972-2000," Foundation for Middle East Peace, undated, www.fmep.org/settlement_info/ settlement-info-and-tables/stats-data/settlement-populations-in-the-occupied-territories-1972-2000; "Land and Settlements," Palestinian Academic Society for the Study of International Affairs, in "Index of Palestine Facts," 2006, www.passia.org/pal estine_facts/pdf/pdf2006/6-Land-Settlements.pdf.

48. Quoted in Gorenberg, *op. cit.*; Paul Lewis, "U.N. Repeals Its '75 Resolution Equating Zionism With Racism," *The New York Times*, Dec. 17, 1991, www .nytimes.com/1991/12/17/world/un-repeals-its-75-resolution-equating-zionism-with-racism.html. www.nytimes.com/1991/12/17/world/un-repeals-its-75-resolution-equating-zionism-with-racism .html.

49. Thomas Friedman, *From Beirut to Jerusalem* (1989), pp. 161-164; Habib Battah, "Remembering the Sabra-Shatila massacre," Al Jazeera, Sept. 16, 2012, www.aljazeera.com/indepth/features/2012 /09/201291672947917214.html; Ellen Siegel, "A letter to the IDF soldiers at Sabra and Shatila," *+972*, Sept. 14, 2012, http://972mag.com/a-letter-to-the-idf-soldiers-at-sabra-and-shatila/55847.

50. Yaacov Lozowick, "Secrets From Israel's Archives," *Tablet*, Feb. 21, 2013, www.tabletmag.com/jewish-news-and-politics/124809/secrets-from-israels-archives?all=1; Seth Anziska, "A Preventable Massacre," *The New York Times*, Sept. 16, 2012, www.nytimes .com/2012/09/17/opinion/a-preventable-massacre .html?pagewanted=all&_r=0; William A. Orme Jr., "The Sharon Victory: Man in the News," *The New York Times*, Feb. 7, 2001, www.nytimes.com/2001 /02/07/world/the-sharon-victory-man-in-the-news-warrior-who-confounds-ariel-sharon.html.

51. "Fatalities in the first Intifada," B'Tselem, The Israeli Information Center for Human Rights in the Occupied Territories," undated, www.btselem.org/ statistics/first_intifada_tables; Howard Sachar, "The First Intifada," *My Jewish Learning*, undated, www .myjewishlearning.com/israel/History/1980-2000/ Intifada_I.shtml?p=1; Sonja Karkar, "The first intifada 20 years later," *The Electronic Intifada*, Dec. 10, 2007, http://electronicintifada.net/content/first-intifada-20-years-later/7251.

52. Kurtzer, *et al.*, *op. cit.*, pp. 35-58; "Oslo Accord," in "Shattered Dreams of Peace," PBS, June 2002, www.pbs.org/wgbh/pages/frontline/shows/oslo/ negotiations/.

53. *Ibid.*

54. "Intifada toll 2000-2005," BBC (reporting B'Tselem statistics), Feb. 8, 2005, http://newsvote.bbc.co .uk/mpapps/pagetools/print/news.bbc.co.uk/2/hi/ middle_east/3694350.stm.

55. "Second Intifada Timeline," Jerusalem Media and Communication Centre, undated, www.jmcc.org/ fastfactspag.aspx?tname=88; Daniel Byman and Natan Sachs, "The Rise of Settler Terrorism," *Foreign Affairs*, Aug. 14, 2012, www.foreignaffairs.com/ articles/137825/daniel-byman-and-natan-sachs/the-rise-of-settler-terrorism?page=show.

56. Steven Erlanger, "Hamas Seizes Broad Control In Gaza Strip," *The New York Times*, June 14, 2007, www.nytimes.com/2007/06/14/world/ middleeast/14mideast.html; Mark Joseph Stern, "How Did Hamas Come to Power in Gaza?" *Slate*, Nov. 19, 2012, www.slate.com/articles/news_ and_politics/explainer/2012/11/hamas_in_gaza_ how_the_organization_beat_fatah_and_took_con trol_of_the_gaza.html.

57. Kurtzer, *et al.*, *op. cit.*, pp. 174-177, 189-190.

58. Yaakov Lappin, "IDF releases Cast Lead casualty numbers," *The Jerusalm Post*, March 26, 2009, www.jpost .com/Israel/IDF-releases-Cast-Lead-casualty-numbers; "27 Dec. '09: One and a Half Million People Imprisoned," B'Tselem — Israeli Information Center for Human Rights in the Occupied Territories, Dec. 27, 2009, www.btselem.org/gaza_strip/20091227_a_ year_to_castlead_operation; "3 Years After Operation Cast Lead," Palestinian Centre for Human Rights, Dec. 27, 2011, www.pchrgaza.org/portal/en/index .php?option=com_content&view=article&id=7979:3-years-after-operation-cast-lead-justice-has-been-com prehensively-denied-pchr-release-23-narratives-docu menting-the-experience-of-victims-&catid=36:pchrpre ssreleases&Itemid=194.

59. Quoted in Jeff Zeleny and Alan Cowell, "Addressing Muslims, Obama Pushes Mideast Peace," *The New York Times*, June 4, 2009, www.nytimes .com/2009/06/05/world/middleeast/05prexy.html.

60. Colum Lynch and Joel Greenberg, "U.N. votes to recognize Palestine as 'non-member observer state,'" *The Washington Post*, Nov. 30, 2012, http://articles. washingtonpost.com/2012-11-29/world/3558 4628_1_palestinian-statehood-observer-state-mid dle-east-peace-talks.

61. Roger Cohen, "Fayyad Steps Down, Not Out," *The New York Times*, May 3, 2013, www.nytimes .com/2013/05/04/opinion/global/Roger-Cohen-Fayyad-Steps-Down-Not-Out.html?pagewanted =all.

62. James Bennet, "The Radical Bean Counter," *The New York Times Magazine*, May 25, 2003, p. 36, www.nytimes.com/2003/05/25/magazine/25 PALESTINIAN.html.

63. Quoted in Joel Greenberg, "Palestinian prime minister, Salam Fayyad, resigns," *The Washington Post*, April 13, 2013, http://articles.washingtonpost .com/2013-04-13/world/38510031_1_fatah-pales tinian-authority-palestinian-economy.

64. Richard Boudreaux, "A top Palestinian keen on institution-building," *Los Angeles Times*, June 23, 2009, p. A13.

65. Maher Abukhater and Edmund Sanders, "Palestinian Authority picks Rami Hamdallah as prime minister," *Los Angeles Times*, June 2, 2013, http://articles .latimes.com/2013/jun/02/world/la-fg-palestinian-premier-20130603.

66. Quoted in Michael Hirsh, "Israel: No Peace Conference With Hamas," *National Journal*, May 29, 2013, www.nationaljournal.com/nationalsecurity/ israel-no-peace-conference-with-hamas-20110607; Tamara Zieve, "Livni: Israel can't reach peace deal

with Hamas," *The Jerusalem Post*, May 18, 2013, www.jpost.com/Diplomacy-and-Politics/Livni-No-chance-Israel-can-reach-peace-deal-with-Hamas-313558.

67. Isabel Kershner, "Palestinian Authority Selects Professor to Be Next Premier," *The New York Times*, June 3, 2013, www.nytimes.com/2013/06/03/world/middleeast/president-of-palestinian-authority-appoints-next-premier.html.

68. Quoted in Abeer Ayyoub, "Gaza Factions Denounce Hamdallah Appointment," *Al-Monitor Palestine Pulse*, June 5, 2013, www.al-monitor.com/pulse/originals/2013/06/hamdallah-palestinian-authority-hamas.html.

69. Anne Barnard, "By Inserting Itself Into Syrian War, Hezbollah Makes Dramatic Gamble," *The New York Times*, May 27, 2013, www.nytimes.com/2013/05/28/world/middleeast/by-inserting-itself-into-syrian-war-hezbollah-makes-historic-gamble.html?pagewanted=all.

70. Amena Bakr and Mariam Karouny, "Qatar, allies tighten coordination of arms flows to Syria," Reuters, May 14, 2013, www.reuters.com/article/2013/05/14/us-syria-qatar-support-idUSBRE94D0GT20130514. For background, see Leda Hartman, "Islamic Sectarianism," *CQ Global Researcher*, Aug. 7, 2012, pp. 353-376.

71. Adiv Sterman, *et al.*, "Israel and Palestinians closing in on resumed peace talks," *The Times of Israel*, May 1, 2013, www.timesofisrael.com/israel-and-palestinians-closing-in-on-resumed-peace-talks.

72. Zvika Krieger, "Lost Moments: The Arab Peace Initiative, 10 Years Later," *The Atlantic*, March 29, 2012, www.theatlantic.com/international/archive/2012/03/lost-moments-the-arab-peace-initiative-10-years-later/255231; Larisa Epatko, "Lands Swaps Key to 1967 Israeli-Palestinian Border Issue," PBS NewsHour, May 24, 2011, www.pbs.org/newshour/rundown/2011/05/1967-borders.html.

73. "Remarks with Qatari Prime Minister Sheikh Hamad bin Jassim bin Jabr Al Thani After Meeting with Arab League Officials," State Department, April 29, 2013, www.state.gov/secretary/remarks/2013/04/208544.htm.

74. *Ibid.*

75. "Remarks with Israeli Justice Minister Tzipi Livni Before Their Meeting," State Department, May 8, 2013, www.state.gov/secretary/remarks/2013/05/209135.htm.

76. "Mashaal rejects land swap with Israel," *Ma'an*, May 8, 2013, www.maannews.net/eng/ViewDetails.aspx?ID=591380.

77. Gorenberg, *op. cit.* (Kindle edition).

78. Anne Barnard, *et al.*, "Israel Targeted Iranian Missiles in Syria Attack," *The New York Times*, May 4, 2013, www.nytimes.com/2013/05/05/world/middleeast/israel-syria.html?pagewanted=all.

79. Jonathan Spyer, "The Lesser of Syria's Evils," *Tablet Magazine*, May 14, 2013, www.tabletmag.com/jewish-news-and-politics/132203/the-lesser-of-syrias-evils.

80. "Netanyahu says Iran hasn't crossed nuclear 'red line,'" Reuters, April 29, 2013, www.reuters.com/article/2013/04/29/us-iran-nuclear-israel-idUSBRE93S0IQ20130429.

BIBLIOGRAPHY

Selected Sources
Books

Gorenberg, Gershom, *The Accidental Empire: Israel and the Birth of the Settlements, 1967-1977*, **Times Books, 2006.**
A U.S.-born Israeli journalist chronicles the confused beginning of the settlement drive in the West Bank and Gaza.

Khalidi, Rashid, *Brokers of Deceit: How the US Has Undermined Peace in the Middle East*, **Beacon Press, 2013.**
A professor of Middle East history concludes that U.S. regional diplomacy has enabled the growth of Israeli settlements.

Miller, David Aaron, *The Much Too Promised Land: America's Elusive Search for Arab-Israeli Peace*, **Bantam, 2009.**
In a personal chronicle of his quarter-century as a State Department peace negotiator, Miller ponders why success has been elusive.

Morris, Benny, *1948: The First Arab-Israeli War*, Yale University Press, 2008.
One of Israel's best-known historians offers a meticulous reconstruction of Israel's first war.

Articles

Ehrenreich, Ben, "Is This Where the Third Intifada Will Start?," *The New York Times Magazine*, March 15, 2013, www.nytimes.com/2013/03/17/magazine/is-this-where-the-third-intifada-will-start.html?pagewanted=all.
A freelance journalist reports on a West Bank Palestinian village's nonviolent resistance of occupation.

Goldberg, Jeffrey, "An Interview With Jeremy Ben-Ami on Settlements, Beinart, Obama, the Whole Nine Yards," *The Atlantic*, March 23, 2012, www.theatlantic.com/politics/archive/2012/03/an-interview-with-jeremy-ben-ami-on-settlements-beinart-obama-the-whole-nine-yards/254918/.
A prominent U.S. journalist on Israeli affairs speaks with the founder of a pro-Israel advocacy group that demands intensified peace efforts.

Kais, Roi, "Syrian opposition conflicted over alleged Israeli strike," *Ynet News*, May 6, 2013, www.ynetnews.com/articles/0,7340,L-4376836,00.html.
An Israeli news site reports on support for Israeli airstrikes in Syria by some anti-Israel Arab opinion leaders.

Ravid, Barak and Chaim Levinson, "Netanyahu's top security adviser: Settlements impede Western support of Israel," *Haaretz*, Feb. 7, 2013, www.haaretz.com/news/diplomacy-defense/netanyahu-s-top-security-adviser-settlements-impede-western-support-of-israel.premium-1.501940.
A left-of-center Israeli daily reports on high-level Israeli government worries about the international reaction to West Bank settlement construction.

Kenner, David, "We Are Not Fanatic Killers," *FP-Foreign Policy*, May 14, 2013, www.foreignpolicy.com/articles/2013/05/14/exclusive_interview_khaled_meshaal_hamas_syria_israel_gaza?page=0,1.
The newly re-elected Hamas leader argues he doesn't oppose talks with Israel in principle but reiterates a policy of armed resistance and dismisses the latest peace effort.

Kuttab, Daoud, "Analysis: Salam Fayyad doomed by Israeli and Palestinian enemies alike," *Ma'an News Agency*, April 18, 2013, www.maannews.net/eng/ViewDetails.aspx?ID=587200.
A prominent Palestinian journalist argues that the Palestinian Authority prime minister's resignation was the result of Israeli intransigence, Palestinian political conflicts and U.S. retaliation for a Palestinian diplomatic move in the U.N.

Remnick, David, "The Party Faithful," *The New Yorker*, Jan. 21, 2013, www.newyorker.com/reporting/2013/01/21/130121fa_fact_remnick.
The editor of *The New Yorker* explores the growth of the Israeli right wing.

Shehadeh, Raja, "The Nakba, Then and Now," IHT Global Opinion, *International Herald Tribune* (*The New York Times*), Oct. 16, 2012, http://latitude.blogs.nytimes.com/2012/10/16/the-nakba-then-and-now/.
A Palestinian lawyer writes of efforts in Israel to present the Palestinian side of events surrounding Israel's independence war.

Zieve, Tamara, "Livni: Israel can't reach peace deal with Hamas," *Jerusalem Post*, May 18, 2013, www.jpost.com/Diplomacy-and-Politics/Livni-No-chance-Israel-can-reach-peace-deal-with-Hamas-313558.
Israel's justice minister, known as a strong Palestinian statehood supporter, says no accord is possible with an organization that violently opposes Israel's legitimacy.

Reports

Sharp, Jeremy M., "U.S. Foreign Aid to Israel," Congressional Research Service, April 11, 2013, www.fas.org/sgp/crs/mideast/RL33222.pdf.
Congress' nonpartisan research arm presents a detailed accounting of U.S. support for Israel, much of it in the form of military aid, and Israelis exports of advanced military technology to the United States.

Shikaki, Khalil, "The future of Israel-Palestine: a one-state reality in the making," Norwegian Peacebuilding Resource Centre, May 2012, www.pcpsr.org/strategic/occasionalpapers/futureofisraelpalestine.pdf.
The director of the Palestinian Center for Policy and Survey Research takes a downbeat look at the possibilities of a two-state solution and recommends steps to keep hopes of Palestinian statehood alive.

For More Information

American Israel Public Affairs Committee; 202-639-5200; www.aipac.org. The leading pro-Israel advocacy organization in the United States; provides information designed to make the case for continued strong U.S. support.

American Task Force on Palestine, 1634 Eye St., N.W., Washington, DC 20006; 202-887-0177; www.americantask force.org. Pro-Palestinian statehood organization that condemns all violence against civilians by any side; maintains library of documents on statehood.

+972 Magazine, http://972mag.com. Web-based Israeli magazine opposed to Israeli occupation; publishes analysis and news by Israeli and Palestinian journalists and activists.

Committee for Accuracy in Middle East Reporting in America; 617-789-3672; www.camera.org. Based in the Boston area, dedicated to correcting what it judges to be errors showing anti-Israel bias in the news media.

J Street, P.O. Box 66073, Washington, DC 20035; 202-596-5207; www.jstreet.org. Strong advocate of Palestinian statehood from pro-Israel perspective.

Palestinian Center for Policy and Survey Research, Off Irsal Street, P.O. Box 76, Ramallah; Tel: 011-972-2-296-4933; www.pcpsr.org. West Bank-based think tank that publishes detailed public opinion polls and analysis.

Washington Institute for Near East Policy, 1828 L St., N.W., Suite 1050, Washington, DC 20036; 202-452-0650; www.washingtoninstitute.org. Think tank with heavy representation of former U.S. diplomats; publishes detailed analyses of latest developments.

3

The Iraq War: 10 Years Later

Peter Katel

Iraqi Sunnis chant anti-government slogans against Prime Minister Nouri al-Maliki's Shiite-dominated administration during a mass street demonstration in Baghdad on Feb. 8, 2013. American combat troops pulled out of Iraq in December 2011, but religious and ethnic tensions continue to plague Iraq, with bombings and shootings a persistent part of the political landscape.

AFP/Getty Images/Ahmad al-Rubaye

From *CQ Researcher*, March 1, 2013.

A decade after the United States invaded Iraq, American combat troops are gone from the country, and Iraq no longer dominates U.S. public life as it did for much of the 2000s. Yet fiery debates over the war and its aftermath continue to smolder: Was the war worth the deaths of 4,475 U.S. troops and more than $800 billion — so far — in American resources?[1] And did President Obama make the right call by not pressing harder to keep U.S. troops in Iraq?

Backers of the war, launched by the George W. Bush administration 10 years ago this month, insist it was necessary. "I am not apologetic about my advocacy for the war," says Michael Rubin, a resident scholar at the conservative American Enterprise Institute who worked in the Pentagon and Baghdad as a member of the Bush administration during the war. Rubin casts Iraq favorably as moving toward a state of "messy democracy" after decades of repression under former dictator Saddam Hussein.

But others see today's Iraq in a far dimmer light. Paul Pillar, who emerged as a war critic after retiring as a senior Central Intelligence Agency (CIA) analyst, says Iraq's elected government is "moving quite a bit toward authoritarianism." And he contends the war brought about one of the very dangers the Bush administration said it was trying to eradicate: the presence of al Qaeda terrorists in Iraq. "There was no al Qaeda in Iraq" before the war, Pillar says, "and now there is."

Although debates that dominated the buildup and early days of the war were resolved when Iraq was found not to possess weapons of mass destruction (WMDs), current debate over the war focuses

Iraq and Iran Share a Common Religious View

Iraq and neighboring Iran are the only Muslim countries with predominantly Shiite populations led by Shiites, who represent 15 percent of the world's 1.6 billion Muslims. The tiny Persian Gulf kingdom of Bahrain — the only other Muslim country with a majority-Shiite population — is ruled by Sunni sheiks. Lebanon and Yemen have mixed Sunni-Shiite populations. In majority-Sunni Syria, Sunni insurgents have been waging a two-year civil war against the regime of President Bashar al-Assad, a member of the Alawite sect, an offshoot of Shiism. Islam's Sunni-Shiite split developed in the 7th century over who should succeed the Prophet Muhammad. Sunnis believed the best qualified leader should succeed him, while Shiites believed Muhammad's blood descendants were his rightful successors.

Branches of Islam in the Middle East

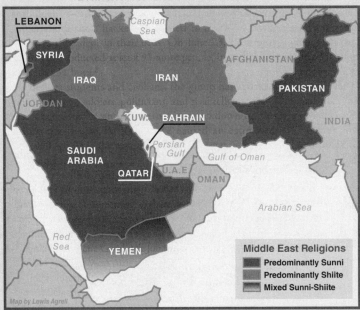

Source: John R. Bradley, "The Ancient Loathing Between Sunnis and Shi'ites Is Threatening to Tear Apart the Muslim World," *Daily Mail*, March 2011, www.dailymail.co.uk/debate/article-1367435/Middle-East-unrest-Sunni-Shiite-conflict-threatens-tear-Muslim-world-apart.html

on Obama's handling of the conflict's end. When the last U.S. combat troops left Iraq in December 2011, Obama, who won the White House as the anti-Iraq War candidate when the conflict was a hot political issue, said he had fulfilled his pledge to end the war, "responsibly" and that "a new day is upon us."[2]

However, some critics say toppling the Hussein dictatorship has altered the balance of power among the region's rival Sunni- and Shiite-dominated nations and driven Iraq — formerly led by Sunnis — into the arms of neighboring Iran, a Shiite-run theocracy that its mostly Sunni neighbors and the international community want to keep from acquiring nuclear weapons.

Iran and the United States have been at odds since 1979, and Obama has led an international campaign to toughen trade sanctions against Iran. He vowed in February to "do what is necessary to prevent them from getting a nuclear weapon," indicating that military action is not off the table.[3] But some critics say Obama gave up the chance to blunt Iran's power in the region by failing to convince the new Iraqi government to accept a continuing U.S. military presence in Iraq after 2011.

"We failed to take advantage of the surge," says Peter Mansoor, a retired Army colonel. Mansoor served as executive officer to Gen. David Petraeus, commander of U.S. and allied forces in Iraq during the so-called surge — when Bush controversially boosted U.S. troop levels in Iraq by 20,000. "I get the sense we don't have any leverage," says Mansoor.

As a result, Obama may have made it harder to curb Iran's nuclear ambitions, critics say, and given Iraqi Prime Minister Nouri al-Maliki more reason to rely on a country ruled by fellow conservative Shiites. "I think Maliki would say, 'I'm going to put my bets on my Iranian neighbor,'" says Mansoor, now a professor of military history at Ohio State University's Mershon Center for International Security Studies.

Al-Maliki has reason to feel comforted by the presence of a friendly neighbor. Iraq is suffering a continuing plague of suicide and vehicle bomb attacks — al Qaeda trademarks. At least 150 people died in such attacks so far this year, either individually or in groups targeted by bombers. Individual victims included a member of Iraq's parliament.[4]

Optimists point out that the violence, though persistent, remains at a level far below what it was in 2007, when the surge began. The move was aimed at suppressing escalating violence and preparing the government to assume responsibility for the country's security. For the United States, the surge sharply reduced American casualties in Iraq and paved the way for the withdrawal of U.S. forces.[5]

Some experts say Obama was correct in ending the military presence because the surge succeeded. Douglas Ollivant, an Army veteran of the war who also served as Iraq director on the National Security Council during the Bush and Obama administrations, says, "When you overthrow a state and start to rebuild, it's going to be a job of decades." Ollivant, currently a senior national security fellow at the New American Foundation think tank, says Iraq today "is what victory in one of these operations looks like — and it's not very pretty."

But others, including some who share Ollivant's on-the-ground experience, see the picture getting uglier. "The war is not over," says Lt. Col. Joel Rayburn, an Army intelligence officer who served in Iraq and is now a research associate at the National Defense University's Institute for National Strategic Studies in Washington.

Last year, he notes, about 4,500 civilians died violently in Iraq, 400 more than the year before.[6] That is a far cry from the nearly 27,000 civilians who died violently at the peak of the war — the 12 months that ended in March 2007.[7] But Rayburn still argues that today's level of violence "meets the textbook definition of civil war." And, he adds, "It will be higher this year, mark my words."

Even at its lower level, the violence reflects the religious and ethnic divisions that marked the Iraq War and

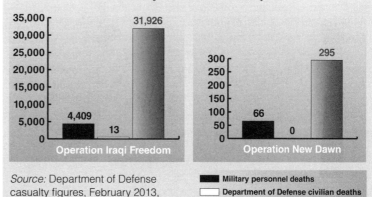

Nearly 4,500 U.S. Military Personnel Killed in Iraq

More than 4,400 U.S. military personnel died and nearly 32,000 were injured in Operation Iraqi Freedom, the U.S. combat mission in Iraq. An additional 66 died and nearly 300 were injured in a sequel mission, Operation New Dawn. It ran from September 2010 until Dec. 15, 2011, and focused on training and advising Iraqi security forces. A small number of U.S. military personnel remain in Iraq.

U.S. Military Casualties in Iraq War

Operation Iraqi Freedom: 4,409 military personnel deaths; 13 Department of Defense civilian deaths; 31,926 military personnel wounded in action

Operation New Dawn: 66 military personnel deaths; 0 Department of Defense civilian deaths; 295 military personnel wounded in action

Source: Department of Defense casualty figures, February 2013, www.defense.gov/news/casualty.pdf

■ Military personnel deaths
□ Department of Defense civilian deaths
▨ Military personnel wounded in action

continue to fester. Victims of the mass-casualty suicide bombings this year largely fell into three categories: civilian Shiites; police officers of the Shiite-dominated government; and Sunni militia who had once fought the U.S. occupation and Iraqi government but gave up their insurgency and turned against al Qaeda.[8]

In pre-invasion Iraq, Shiites were relegated to second-class status. Iraq's ruling Baath Party, along with top military and security officials, was dominated by members of the Sunni branch of Islam, Hussein among them. (Hussein's regime was secular. The new Iraq is non-sectarian in principle, with freedom of religion and women's equal rights guaranteed, but Shiite religious leaders have powerful though informal influence on government).[9]

When American military officers realized that some Sunni insurgents were growing hostile to al Qaeda, the United States adopted a counterinsurgency strategy aimed at turning the Sunni fighters into U.S. allies and full-fledged participants in building the new Iraq.

Whether that realignment survives the U.S. withdrawal is not clear. American officials poured enormous effort into persuading Iraqis to make their new

Civilian Deaths Track Course of War

Estimates of Iraqi civilian deaths vary widely, depending on the organization collecting the data and the nature and circumstances of the fatalities. Iraq Body Count, a British organization that cross-checks media reports with hospital and morgue records, government reports and other information, estimates that 122,000 Iraqi civilians have died since 2003 as a result of the U.S.-led military intervention in Iraq. Some deaths stemmed from direct military action, while others were the result of terror attacks or sectarian violence. Deaths peaked in 2006 as violence between Sunni and Shiite factions escalated, then declined sharply after additional U.S. troops were deployed in what was called the "surge." Civilian deaths have edged up during the past two years but remain far below the 2006 peak.

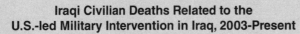

Iraqi Civilian Deaths Related to the U.S.-led Military Intervention in Iraq, 2003-Present

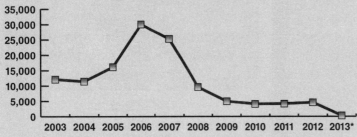

* 265, through Jan. 31

Source: "Documented Civilian Deaths From Violence," Iraq Body Count, February 2013, www.iraqbodycount.org/database/

minority, who had also refused to turn him over.

Though tensions and conflicts between and within the country's sects and ethnic groups (which include small populations of Turkmen and Christians) loom large in Iraq, they had gotten little official notice during the U.S. buildup to war.

Instead, debate centered on intelligence reports that Iraq was storing weapons of mass destruction (WMDs), attempting to acquire nuclear arms and, in the wake of the 2001 terrorist attacks on the United States, possibly harboring links to al Qaeda. "We don't want the smoking gun to be a mushroom cloud," National Security Adviser (later Secretary of State) Condoleezza Rice said in 2002, representing the Bush administration doctrine that the post-9/11 world didn't allow the United States to require 100 percent certainty before taking military action against a potential threat.[12]

But even before the Iraq invasion's one-year anniversary, exhaustive on-the-ground searches discredited the information about WMDs and nuclear weapons. And Pillar — the intelligence community's top Middle East analyst in 2000-2005 — rocked Washington after retiring in 2006 when he said that spy agencies' WMD information had not been as definitive as the administration claimed when it launched the war.

"Intelligence was misused publicly to justify decisions already made," Pillar wrote.[13]

Specifically, some CIA analysts had expressed considerable skepticism about Hussein's alleged al Qaeda links — skepticism later validated by the Senate Select Committee on Intelligence — but Bush administration officials had declared the connections a reality that added to the Iraq regime's perceived danger to Americans.[14]

Once U.S. troops, with some help from Britain and other allies, had toppled the dictatorship, post-invasion problems upended Bush administration forecasts of a quick war and a peaceful transition to democracy. "There

government represent the country's religious and ethnic diversity. Accordingly, Prime Minister al-Maliki is Shiite, Vice President Tariq al-Hashimi is Sunni and President Jalal Talabani is a Kurd (a Muslim people for whom their non-Arab ethnicity is more key to their identity than religious affiliation).

Talabani suffered a stroke in December and is being treated in Germany.[10] Al-Hashimi fled the country in 2011 after al-Maliki accused him of commanding a death squad that assassinated government officials and police officers. Al-Hashimi was later sentenced to death in absentia and now lives in Turkey, a majority-Sunni country that has refused to extradite him. In Iraq, Sunnis saw the case as part of an anti-Sunni campaign by al-Maliki.[11]

In another reflection of ethno-religious tensions, al-Hashimi had earlier taken up refuge in a semi-autonomous northern region that is home to the country's Kurdish

is no plan for an extended occupation in Iraq," Richard N. Perle, a longtime invasion advocate who chaired the advisory Defense Policy Board, said shortly before the war began. He predicted a warm welcome from Iraqis grateful for the toppling of the dictator.[15]

As policymakers, military planners and national security officials look back on the war and ponder Iraq's future, here are some of the questions they are debating:

Did the mission succeed?

Forty-two days after the invasion of Iraq, President Bush stood on the deck of the *USS Abraham Lincoln* beneath an enormous banner reading "Mission Accomplished." Bush never uttered those words. But what he did say to the assembled aircraft carrier crew and to the military in general delivered the same message: "In the battle of Iraq, the United States and our allies have prevailed. . . . Because of you, our nation is more secure. Because of you, the tyrant has fallen, and Iraq is free."[16]

Only months later, combat was intensifying for U.S. troops, and the war's original main objective — securing Iraq's alleged weapons of mass destruction — had proved groundless. In response, the Bush administration said the war's major goal was to build democracy in a country emerging from decades of vicious dictatorship rooted in deep ethnic and religious divides.

"Let freedom reign!" Bush wrote on the note informing him, in June 2004, that the United States had formally passed sovereignty to a newly formed Iraqi interim government.[17]

The remodeling of the U.S. campaign in Iraq came on the heels of conclusive evidence that Iraq didn't have WMDs or factories to make them. Vice President Richard

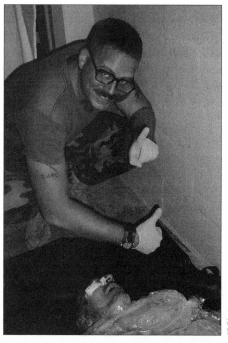

Cpl. Charles A. Graner Jr., a U.S. Army reservist, poses next to a detainee who died during interrogation in late 2003 at Abu Ghraib prison in Baghdad, Iraq. Similar photos surfaced along with revelations that American troops at the prison had tortured and humiliated Iraqi prisoners, causing a worldwide uproar. Graner was convicted of prisoner abuse and served more than six years of a 10-year sentence.

AP Photo

B. Cheney also had insisted that the Hussein regime had colluded with the 9/11 plotters, but CIA and FBI analysts disputed that conclusion and the Senate Select Committee on Intelligence upheld the analysts in a massive 2004 report on pre-war intelligence.[18]

Bush insisted that he had made the right decision based on intelligence reports he had before the war. But even as he and his administration shifted their focus to instilling democracy in Iraq, a Sunni insurgency against both U.S. forces and Shiites, aided by al Qaeda, was already under way. Meanwhile, Shiite militias, aided by Iran, were organizing to fight the occupation and the Sunnis, and the Kurdish population was solidifying control of an autonomous region in northern Iraq.[19]

During the ensuing years — which were marked by the surge, parliamentary elections and the 2011 U.S. troop withdrawal — the American public's focus on Iraq gradually receded. But among those with military connections or special interests in foreign affairs, the debate over the war's mission has never ended.

The consensus is that Iraq is not a democracy today, though there is disagreement as to whether it is heading in a democratic or dictatorial direction. Freedom House, a nonpartisan U.S. nonprofit that evaluates the state of democracy around the world, classifies Iraq as "not free." Elections were honest, the organization said, but "political participation and decision-making . . . remain seriously impaired by sectarian and insurgent violence, widespread corruption and the influence of foreign powers."[20]

Pillar, the retired CIA analyst, argues that the U.S. campaign was close to a complete failure. "There is no

Iraq War Tab Approaches $1 Trillion — At Least

The nonpartisan Congressional Research Service (CRS) estimated the cost of the Iraq War through March 2011 at $806 billion. The Obama administration withdrew remaining U.S. troops from Iraq in December 2011, but a small contingent of U.S. advisers remained to train Iraqi forces. The war's costs grew sharply from 2006 through 2008 as sectarian violence in Iraq peaked. Some experts say the war's total cost may exceed $1 trillion as veterans require future medical care. Others say the conflict's impact on the U.S. economy could drive the total cost to $3 trillion or higher.

Estimates for U.S. Funding for Iraq War, FY2003-FY2013

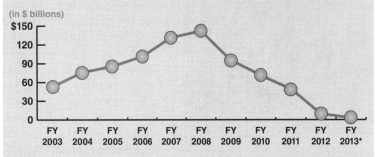

* Budget request

Sources: Amy Belasco, "The Cost of Iraq, Afghanistan, and Other Global War on Terror Operations Since 9/11," Congressional Research Service, March 2011, p. 3, www.fas.org/sgp/crs/natsec/RL33110.pdf; 2012 and 2013 figures are from Department of Defense.

conceivable way in which a balance sheet on the Iraq War can consider it a net plus," he says. Noting Iran's growing influence in Iraq, he says, "We achieved nothing and in some ways hurt ourselves."

The one concession that Pillar makes to the pro-war argument centers on the brutality of Hussein's regime, which was notorious for atrocities such as 1974 and 1987-'88 massacres of Kurds, which included the use of napalm and poison gas. At least 50,000 people, and perhaps as many as 150,000, died in the second of these campaigns.[21] "The current Iraq regime isn't as brutal as Saddam was," he says.

But Rubin, of the American Enterprise Institute, argues that "we were somewhat successful in building democracy" in Iraq. "Iraqi democracy ain't pretty but it's certainly better than Syria's or Egypt's."

He maintains that Hussein was planning to rebuild Iraq's stock of WMD's, such as the gases used on the Kurds, when pre-war international economic sanctions against the regime collapsed. Hussein, in Rubin's view, remained a regional and global security threat as long as he remained in power.

Rubin echoes the consensus that planning for a post-Hussein Iraq suffered from a fundamental flaw: "No one had an idea of what the U.S. goal would be until after war began," he says. Even so, the Bush administration from the beginning acted with the intention of planting a democratic government in Iraq, he contends. The administration, he says, had answered a resounding "no" to a crucial pre-war question: "If you remove Saddam Hussein, do you just replace him with his sons or another general?"

Yet James F. Jeffrey, U.S. ambassador to Iraq in 2010-12 and a senior diplomat in Baghdad during the Bush administration, says the Bush administration was overly optimistic that it could transform Iraq into an egalitarian state. "The theory that we could create Norway or Poland in the Middle East and [that] the region would become pro-Western or democratic — it didn't turn out that way."

Jeffrey, now a distinguished visiting fellow at the Washington Institute, a think tank on Middle Eastern affairs, rejects the view that the United States exacerbated Iraq's ethnic and sectarian problems. The Sunni-Shiite divide existed long before the invasion, he notes. And armed jihadists are active throughout the region. Still, he says, "It might have made more sense to look for an option where we would have toppled Saddam and asked the U.N. to come in and try to set up a process but not overthrow the entire political structure."

But Iraqi-American Zainab al-Suwaij views the U.S. approach as a success, especially given the contrast between the Hussein era and the present. "People are not afraid any more to speak out about things they don't like," says al-Suwaij, executive director of the American Islamic Congress, which is teaching peaceful conflict resolution in Iraq under a State Department contract. "Before, you cannot even mention Saddam's name and cannot express your feelings and your religious identity."

Al-Suwaij, who travels to Iraq every six weeks and fought in a 1991 Shiite uprising in southern Iraq that followed the defeat of Iraq in the brief Persian Gulf War, acknowledges that conditions remain difficult.

"People talk about corruption and say that basic services are not there," she says. "But at the end of the day, we know that Saddam is not there. They don't want to go back to Saddam's time."

Did the war boost Iran's regional and global power?

An irony of the Iraq War was that it was launched by an administration that viewed Iran as part of a so-called axis of evil. Yet the war changed Iraq and Iran from hostile to friendly neighbors, if not allies.

That change stems above all from the toppling of Hussein, a sworn enemy of the Islamic Republic of Iran. Hussein, who after the 1979 Iranian revolution saw the newly established Shiite regime as a mortal threat to his rule, launched a bloody, eight-year war against Iran in 1980. An estimated 1.5 million people on both sides were killed or wounded.[22]

The war, which involved the use of chemical weapons by both sides, and the hostility that persisted afterward had elements of religious conflict, deeply rooted historical enmity between Arab Iraqis and Persian Iranians and geopolitical rivalry between the two oil powers.[23]

Notably, Prime Minister al-Maliki's career demonstrates the complexities of ties between Iran, whose theocratic government is overseen by conservative Shiite religious authorities, and the Shiites who make up the dominant political force in Iraq, which has a secular government.

Al-Maliki, a member of the Dawa Shiite party that was outlawed during the Hussein dictatorship, dodged arrest by fleeing to Iran in 1979. He helped direct

Troop Levels Peaked During 'Surge'

The number of U.S. military personnel in Iraq was highest in 2007 when 20,000 extra troops were sent in as part of the "surge," designed to quell rising sectarian violence. Troop levels dropped significantly in 2010, as the United States ended its combat mission and focused more on security and counterterrorism. All U.S. troops except for about 200 military advisers and trainers left Iraq in December, 2011.

(No. of troops)

U.S. Military Personnel in Iraq, November 2003-November 2011

Sources: Amy Belasco, "The Cost of Iraq, Afghanistan, and Other Global War on Terror Operations Since 9/11," Congressional Research Service, March 2011, pp. 44-45, www.fas.org/sgp/crs/natsec/RL33110.pdf; Department of Defense

clandestine operations against Hussein's regime from there, but clashed with Iranian officials whom he considered too meddlesome. By one account, he refused orders to work against Iraq on behalf of an enemy country during the Iran-Iraq War and departed Iran for Syria.[24]

For all its complications, the new Iran-Iraq relationship has given Iran considerable military as well as political influence in Iraq. During U.S. military involvement in Iraq, American officials tracked a deadly form of improvised explosive device (IED) — one to which even tanks were vulnerable — to factories in Iran. The Americans also found a series of political and military connections between Iran and Iraqi militia and political leaders.[25]

Today, although Iran's influence on Iraq is evident, experts disagree on how deep it runs.

Not surprisingly, some of the gloomiest views come from Iraqi Sunnis. "In the United States, if you ask anyone, they say, 'We did not give Iraq to Iran,'" says Najim Abed al-Jabouri, a research fellow at the National Defense University's Near East South Asia Center for Strategic Studies in Washington. "But the truth is that the United States gave Iraq to Iran. All the Arab countries now do not like Iraq because they think Iraq is part of Iran."

Iran exerts influence within Iraq's security forces and in the economies of Shiite cities in southern Iraq, says al-Jabouri, a former mayor of the Iraqi city of Tal Afr who was granted refuge in the United States after his close cooperation with the U.S. military during the war's counterinsurgency phase.[26] Ordinary Iraqis, Shiites as well as Sunnis, are alarmed, al-Jabouri says. "The Sunni people hate Iran so much — you cannot imagine," he says, "but I have many friends in the Shia area who do not like the influence of Iran in those cities. We know they [Iranians] hate the Arabs."

Nevertheless, given the centuries of rivalry between Arab and Persian empires in the Middle East, some non-Iraqi experts question the extent of Iranian authority in Arab Iraq, despite the shared religious affiliation of the country's majority populations. "I do not believe that the Iranians are suddenly super-powerful," says Joost Hiltermann, former Middle East program director of the International Crisis Group, a conflict-resolution advocacy group based in Brussels. "They have influence. When it comes to the prime minister, they may not be able to say who it should be, but they can say who it shouldn't be."

At the same time, says Hiltermann, now the Crisis Group's chief operating officer, the United States has maintained some level of influence as well. "Iraqis are balancing between Iran and the United States and even Turkey," he says. "Their loyalty is not to anyone. I like that; they ought to be independent and not have terms dictated by anyone."

Nevertheless, says Rayburn of the National War College, Iran — though it doesn't enjoy undisputed power in Iraq — has a vested interest in keeping its neighbor politically divided. "For the Iranians, the best outcome is an Iraqi government that is friendly, weak and divided among factions over whom the Iranians have some influence or control," he says.

In that state of affairs, Rayburn says, Iran becomes the deciding voice when disputes arise within the Iraqi political class. Iranian officials, he says, ensured that al-Maliki retained the post of prime minister only with the support of Shiite political parties, despite his earlier attempt to put some distance between himself and those groups. "It was an Iranian victory to force him to go to the other Shia parties," Rayburn says.

But some Middle East experts argue that Iran's gain from the Iraq War shouldn't be seen as permanent. For now, says Ollivant, the former National Security Council Iraq director, Iran "absolutely" gained from Iraqi regime change. "Saddam Hussein was part of the league of Sunni states aligned against Iran," he says.

Iraq's elected secular government, he points out, challenges the Iranian regime in a way that Hussein did not. "The existence of the Iraqi state is an existential challenge to Iranian government legitimacy," he says. "Iranian [citizens] can look across the border and say, 'It doesn't have to be this way. [The Iraqis] are not under sanctions, the people vote and their government is not run by clerics.'"

Did the war weaken the U.S. economy?

As soon as the first signs of the U.S. economic crisis appeared in 2008, economists and others began debating what role the costly Iraq War, along with the war in Afghanistan — which began in 2001 — might have played in damaging the American economy. Since then, the debate has broadened to include the overall effects of the two wars — such as long term health care for thousands of injured veterans along with related security and military costs — on U.S. economic health.

As of the end of fiscal 2011, according to the most recent detailed accounting by the nonpartisan Congressional Research Service, since Sept. 11, 2001, the United States has spent $1.28 trillion on the so-called war on terror. That includes $806 billion for the Iraq War, plus the cost of the war in Afghanistan and $29 billion for security upgrades at military bases around the world and $6 billion in unallocated funds.[27]

But some experts say other spending on war-related programs significantly raised the overall cost. Another part of the war-funding picture is the fact that the Bush administration had won a major tax cut from Congress in 2001, two years before the war began, reducing federal revenues by $1.6 trillion over 10 years.[28] There was no effort to raise taxes to fight the war.

For the same 10-year period, the Eisenhower Study Group at Brown University's Watson Institute for International Studies arrived at a total of at least $3.2 trillion, which includes not just the cost of the war but war-related spending by the State Department and the

U.S. Agency for International Development, which oversee nation-building programs in Iraq and Afghanistan, as well as domestic anti-terrorism costs.[29] By 2013, estimates Linda J. Bilmes, a senior lecturer in public policy at Harvard's Kennedy School of Government who was part of the Eisenhower Study Group, spending on the wars has reached $2 trillion in direct expenses. But the economic effects of the conflicts will be felt for decades, she says.

"What is certainly true is that the United States has much less wiggle room in terms of spending on other things because of legacy costs of the wars," says Bilmes, who was assistant secretary of commerce in the Clinton administration. Those costs include a soaring budget for the Department of Veterans Affairs (from $50 billion in 2001 to $140 billion requested this year). The costs also include maintenance of the $750 million U.S. embassy in Baghdad, the world's biggest diplomatic outpost.[30]

Bilmes, who has been collaborating on studies of war costs with Nobel Prize-winning economist Joseph Stiglitz of Columbia University, also argues that the Iraq War helped set the stage for the housing market crash that set off the 2007-2008 recession, spurred in part by a huge increase in oil prices. Petroleum prices skyrocketed from $25-$30 a barrel in 2003 to as much as $150 a barrel in 2008. Oil-producing Iraq is located in a region that's central to world petroleum shipping, so war there typically triggers fears of supply disruption.[31] Bilmes says when the Federal Reserve sought to keep interest rates low to compensate for the oil-price spike, the low rates led to rampant speculation in housing, creating a bubble that helped spark the economic crisis.

But some Iraq War critics as well as supporters take issue with that idea.

Another Nobel laureate economist, Paul Krugman, wrote that higher oil prices caused by the war did slow down the economy. "Overall, though," the Princeton professor and *New York Times* columnist added, "the story of America's economic difficulties is about the bursting housing bubble, not the war."[32]

And some war supporters view economy-based critiques as attempts to devise new reasons to oppose the invasion. "You can't have an *a la carte* menu of everything you're blaming on it," says Rubin of the American Enterprise Institute. "If it's a mortgage crisis, it's a mortgage crisis."

Members of the U.S. Army's 3rd Infantry Regiment, known as The Old Guard, carry the flag-draped coffin of Army Pfc. Dylan J. Johnson of Tulsa, Okla., during burial services in Arlington National Cemetery in Arlington, Va., on Aug. 9, 2011. Johnson was among the 4,475 American military personnel killed in Iraq since the war began in 2003.

Rubin acknowledges that war costs added to the federal deficit. "That is something we will pay for down the line in debt payments, but it was not the immediate cause of the recession."

Sterling Jensen, a senior research associate at the Near East South Asia Center and a former interpreter and analyst in Iraq, also disputes the view that war spending helped bring on the recession. On the contrary, he says, the war may have delayed the crash via government spending that benefited government contractors, including himself. "What got us in the recession was mortgages," he says.

Jensen advances another economics-based argument — that the war in time will prove to have been worth the spending. The "Arab Spring" uprisings in the Middle East, a revolutionary series of popular protests in the region that began in December 2010, promise to provide political stability that could reduce U.S. security spending, he contends.[33]

And, Jensen adds, "If Iraq is able in five years to produce 5 million barrels a day, that will lower world oil prices, with the net effect that the U.S. economy will be doing better. And that buys time for the United States for renewable energy."

But if the region remains tumultuous, even increased oil output may not lower oil prices. Jeffrey, of the

Washington Institute, argues that the hopes for a political transformation of the Middle East weren't substantial enough to have justified a debt-financed war. "If you are allowed to fund a war on debt," he says, "then you can fund other things on debt. The war was a bad symbol of that kind of thinking."

As for hopes for a more stable and peaceful Middle East — as important as oil output is in keeping oil prices low — Jeffrey says, "The war was seen by some . . . as a good thing — that we would be able to transform a region that badly needs transformation. I don't think we can affect the region, and I don't think we did affect it by invading Iraq."

BACKGROUND

The Buildup

The idea of toppling Hussein by invading Iraq had been circulating in Washington since the end of the 42-day Persian Gulf War. In that conflict, President George H. W. Bush — father of President George W. Bush — assembled a massive, U.S.-led international military force to drive Iraqi forces from Kuwait, which Iraq had invaded and occupied.[34]

Bush decided against extending the war to force Hussein from power, fearing the regional effects of a U.S.-led regime change. He hoped the Persian Gulf War would encourage the Iraqi military to do the job.[35]

But when, in the immediate aftermath of the war, Shiites in southern Iraq and Kurds in northern Iraq rose up against Hussein, the United States withheld aid to the rebels, in part because the administration feared that the Shiites would secede from Iraq, which would benefit Iran. Hussein's forces crushed the Iraqi rebels.[36]

In response, the United Nations in March 1991 authorized a "no-fly zone" for Iraqi warplanes in the north and south, enforced by the United States and its allies. Meanwhile, trade sanctions against Iraq on oil exports and imports of militarily useful goods, authorized by the U.N. after Iraq's invasion of Kuwait, remained in place.[37]

These measures did not prevent Hussein from amassing WMDs, argued Washington conservatives who wanted the Clinton administration to do more than try to slowly erode Hussein's rule by maintaining the no-fly zones and sanctions.[38]

The call for toppling Hussein enjoyed a far more sympathetic reception in the George W. Bush administration, which began in early 2001. Bush already saw Hussein as a long-range threat. And his deputy defense secretary, Paul Wolfowitz, was one of the leading advocates of toppling Hussein.[39]

Still, the Bush administration had no immediate plans to invade Iraq. The Sept. 11 terrorist attacks on the United States immediately changed things. In its aftermath, questions arose (later confirmed) about whether the administration had downplayed accurate warnings that al Qaeda was planning an attack within the United States. After the 9/11 attacks, officials depicted Hussein as a danger that the United States could not ignore.[40]

Nearly a year after 9/11, the invasion plan surfaced in a Sept. 8, 2002, article in *The New York Times.* It cited unnamed Bush administration officials as saying Iraq was searching for nuclear bomb materials.[41] Iraq had had a nuclear weapons program before the 1991 Persian Gulf War, but it was dismantled after discovery by international nonproliferation inspectors.[42]

A series of other episodes in 2002 made clear that the administration was planning war. In his State of the Union address that year, Bush declared that Iraq, together with Iran and North Korea, formed an "axis of evil."[43]

In June 2002, Bush told the graduating class at the U.S. Military Academy at West Point: "If we wait for threats to fully materialize, we will have waited too long."[44]

And in August, Vice President Cheney declared that Hussein was on the verge of obtaining nuclear weapons. "The risks of inaction," he said, "are greater than the risks of action."[45]

By October, Congress had authorized the president to "use the armed forces of the United States as he determines to be necessary and appropriate . . . against the continuing threat posed by Iraq."[46] Intelligence agencies supported the belief that Hussein had non-nuclear chemical and biological WMDs, but they debated whether Iraq was trying to acquire nuclear weapons. Intelligence analysts were even more skeptical that the Iraqi dictatorship had ties to al Qaeda and the Sept. 11 plot.[47]

Skeptics attempted their own public and private information campaign against an Iraq War. Heavyweight Republican foreign policy establishment figures including Brent Scowcroft, a former national security adviser in the

H. W. Bush administration, argued that an invasion would dangerously destabilize the entire region.[48]

Invasion

A related fear among some senior military commanders was that the invasion plan supervised by Defense Secretary Donald Rumsfeld provided only sketchily for what the United States would do in Iraq after overthrowing the regime.[49]

Rumsfeld opposed use of the military for "nation-building" and claimed that military doctrine calling for massive deployment of troops was outmoded.

When the invasion plan was ready, the administration sent Secretary of State Colin Powell to the United Nations in February 2003 to argue that Hussein was violating U.N. resolutions on possession of WMDs and on building nuclear weapons.

On March 18, Bush used the same information to explicitly set the stage for war. He delivered an ultimatum to Hussein and his two sons to leave Iraq within 48 hours. "Their refusal to do so will result in military conflict commenced at a time of our choosing," Bush said.[50]

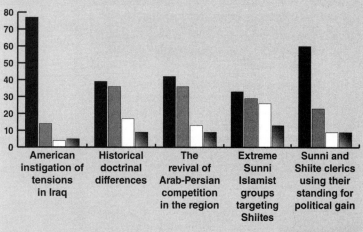

Muslims Say U.S. Worsened Sunni-Shiite Divide

More than three-quarters of Muslims surveyed in the Middle East blamed American "instigation of tensions" in Iraq for exacerbating the Sunni-Shiite divide in the Middle East. Another significant factor was the age-old rivalry between Saudi Arabia, a Sunni Arab nation, and Iran, a country of Shiite Persians.

To what extent do you blame these factors for the Sunni-Shiite conflict?

Extent factor is to blame
■ A lot
▨ A little
□ Not at all
■ Don't know

Source: "This House Believes That the Sunni-Shia Conflict Is Damaging Islam's Reputation As a Religion of Peace," Doha Debates, April 2008, clients.squareeye.net/uploads/doha/polling/shia_sunni.pdf; a total of 993 people from throughout the region responded to the survey.

The military plan initially called for the major phase of the campaign to start at dawn with a ground invasion. A British contingent was part of the force, and small groups from a handful of other nations later joined the occupation, becoming part of what was called a "multinational coalition" despite the United States' overwhelming dominance of the operation.

As Army and Marines troops in tanks and Humvees raced to Baghdad, they were prepared for attacks by Iraqi forces using chemical and biological weapons. But shortly before the invasion, Hussein told his top commanders that Iraq didn't have WMDs — a disclosure they found surprising, given his past use of chemical weapons and his determination to retain power. But he foresaw a short war that would end with his remaining in power, as in 1991. For that reason — also contradicting U.S.

expectations — Hussein had not ordered a "scorched-earth" strategy of destroying Iraq's oilfields.

As the invasion began at dawn on March 21 (March 20 in Washington) U.S. troops ran into deadly opposition not only from the Iraqi Army but from well-armed and highly trained foes in civilian garb and vehicles, the *fedayeen* (Arabic for guerrillas). Hussein had formed the paramilitary corps in 1994, setting up a nationwide network of weapons and ammunition depots and safe houses. U.S. spy agencies hadn't known.

Nevertheless, the U.S. military still had the air and ground firepower to reach its objectives. "Shock and awe" was the term used by invasion commander Gen. Tommy Franks to describe how massive air assaults on key targets in Baghdad during the early days of the war would overwhelm the enemy.

Reuters/Goran Tomasevic

The first U.S. Marines entered downtown Baghdad on April 9, 2003, and some marked the event by pulling down an iconic statue of Saddam Hussein. However, the fight for Baghdad — and all of Iraq — was only beginning.

On April 9, the first U.S. forces entered downtown Baghdad. Symbolizing the event, a soldier used a cable on a tank retriever — a heavy-duty towing vehicle — to pull down a statue of Hussein in downtown Baghdad. But the fight for Baghdad, and all of Iraq, was only beginning.

With the U.S. troop presence in Baghdad understrength for an occupation, and with the Bush administration still planning a quick exit, crowds of Baghdadis descended on government offices and museums and took everything they could lay their hands on — from office furniture to plumbing fixtures to antiquities. U.S. troops, with no orders to do police work, looked on.

TV cameras captured the scenes, leading to questions in Washington about collapsing public order. "Stuff happens," Rumsfeld responded. "Freedom's untidy, and free people are free to make mistakes and commit crimes and do bad things. They're also free to live their lives and do wonderful things, and that's what's going to happen here."[51]

Insurgency and Politics

Meanwhile, seeds of violent rebellion were sprouting in both the Sunni and Shiite communities.[52]

The trend was less surprising among the Sunnis, Hussein's branch of Islam.

But Sunni resistance might not have turned so deadly had it not been for two major U.S. actions, according

to some experts. The Americans ordered the total elimination of the Iraqi army; and a "de-Baathification" order banned senior Baath Party members from future public employment.

The orders reflected an assumption that all military commanders and party members were hard-core Hussein loyalists. In fact, many were people who had managed to survive the dictatorship by playing along.

Sunni insurgents struck their first major blows in August 2003. The most significant was a truck-bomb attack on the newly opened U.N. headquarters building. Among the 22 people killed was the mission chief. In response, the U.N. cut back its Iraq operation to a token presence.

As the insurgents organized, jihadists poured in from other countries.

One of the insurgents' most notorious acts was the killing of four U.S. security contractors in Fallujah in early 2004. Two of the men's bodies were hung from a bridge. A major Army and Marine force later that year retook the city, with high death tolls on both sides: 70 Marines and 2,175 insurgents.[53]

By then, the Bush administration and U.S. intelligence agencies had suffered a devastating blow to their credibility. In October 2003, the leader of the search for WMDs, David Kay, reported that inspectors had found nothing thus far. Three months later he announced that Iraq had no WMDs and that pre-war intelligence — which he acknowledged having believed — had been wrong. Kay's successor reinforced that conclusion in 2004.[54]

Even as insurgencies by Sunnis and al-Qaeda-linked jihadists grew, some Iraqi Shiites were also fighting the Americans, led by Muqtada al-Sadr, son of a revered religious figure believed to have been killed by the Hussein regime. The younger al-Sadr, whose base of support lay in poor Shiite communities in Baghdad and southern Iraq, preached violent resistance to the occupation.

Al-Sadr's Mahdi Army militia launched at least three uprisings against U.S. forces in 2004 and 2006, leading American officials to target him for capture or death. But because of the depth of his political support among some of the country's majority population, the Americans agreed to drop him as a target in return for a cease-fire from his militia.[55]

Meanwhile, U.S. officials from President Bush on down plunged into the inner workings of Iraqi politics, hoping

CHRONOLOGY

2002-2005 *President George W. Bush orders invasion of Iraq to topple Saddam Hussein and seize reported weapons of mass destruction (WMDs).*

September 2002 U.S. officials report Iraq is developing nuclear weapons. . . . In U.N. speech, Bush calls Iraq a threat because of human rights violations and production of biological and long-range weapons.

March 7, 2003 Chief U.N. weapons inspector says there is no evidence of Iraqi WMDs.

March 17-21, 2003 Bush gives Hussein and his two sons 48 hours to leave Iraq, which they ignore. . . . Bush orders invasion of Iraq, which begins March 21 (March 20 in the United States).

April 9, 2003 U.S. soldiers topple statue of Hussein in central Baghdad.

May 22, 2003 U.S. disbands Iraqi army, bans high-ranking members of former ruling Baath Party from government jobs.

Dec. 14, 2003 The fugitive Hussein apprehended in underground hiding place in his home region, near Tikrit.

April 2004 *The New Yorker* and CBS' "60 Minutes II" detail abuse at Abu Ghraib prison in Iraq.

Jan. 12, 2005 White House announces end of WMD search.

Jan. 30, 2005 Iraqi citizens vote in first transitional National Assembly election since occupation; few Sunnis vote.

Oct. 15, 2005 Iraqi voters approve new constitution.

2006-2008 *Sunni-Shiite conflicts intensify into civil war, prompting Bush to reinforce troop levels.*

Jan. 20, 2006 Preliminary results of first postwar parliamentary elections show that Shiite party alliance has won. Political activist Nouri al-Maliki will form government as prime minister.

November-December, 2006 Iraqi court sentences Hussein to death for crimes against humanity. . . . Hussein hanged.

Jan. 10, 2007 Bush announces "surge" of at least 20,000 additional troops.

Jan. 12, 2008 Iraqi Parliament passes bill permitting former Baath Party members to return to their government jobs.

July 2008 Last of "surge" brigades withdrawn from Iraq.

December 2008 U.S. and allied casualties for the year are down by nearly one-third from 2007; civilian deaths decline to about 9,000 from about 25,000 in 2007.

2009-Present *President Obama, who won election as anti-Iraq War candidate, oversees final U.S. withdrawal from Iraq as sectarian violence continues.*

Feb. 27, 2009 Obama announces withdrawal of most U.S. troops by Aug. 31, 2010, and all troops by Dec. 31, 2011.

June 30, 2009 U.S. troops leave cities and towns in Iraq; responsibility for security formally passed to Iraqi military.

March 7, 2010 In new parliamentary elections, secular party bloc wins narrowly but lacks majority. . . . After nine months of political maneuvering, al-Maliki forms a governing coalition.

Dec. 18, 2011 Last U.S. troops leave Iraq, except for 200 military advisers.

September 2012 Sunni Vice President Tariq al-Hashimi sentenced to death in absentia on grounds he organized political assassinations; from refuge in Istanbul he denies charges.

December 2012 Civilian death toll for the year rises to 4,600, from 4,100 in 2011.

January 2013 Bombings and individual shootings kill 265 civilians and police officers. . . . Defense secretary nominee Chuck Hagel clashes with Republican Sen. John McCain, R-Ariz., over impact of the Iraq surge, which Hagel had opposed.

February 2013 Car bombs in Shiite neighborhoods in Baghdad kill at least 21.

March 20, 2013 Ten-year anniversary of U.S.-led invasion of Iraq.

Iraq Conflict Was a Costly Learning Experience

"War should be the last resort, not the first."

All wars hold bitter lessons. For the men and women who planned and fought the Iraq war, the first lesson may have been that the civilians to whom they reported didn't always know as much as they thought they did.

"The early Bush administration had a belief in American military power and its ability to do things that was not necessarily misplaced — that you could rely on American military power to topple foreign leaders relatively quickly," says retired Army Col. Peter Mansoor. "In this high-tech war," he added, summarizing the view that prevailed at the time, "we could go around the world and get rid of evil-doers and replace them with someone more to our liking."

The years of heavy combat that followed the Iraq invasion made plain to the Americans doing the fighting, however, that toppling even a widely hated dictator doesn't guarantee overall success, says Mansoor, a professor of military history at Ohio State University. He commanded a tank brigade early in the U.S. occupation and later served as executive officer to Gen. David Petraeus during the 2007-2008 surge.

Some of the career officers who helped plan the war echo his view. Throughout the conflict, the military found itself doing the kind of nation-building that the Bush administration initially said wouldn't be necessary. Only Saddam Hussein's removal would be needed to assure a peaceful future, Bush administration officials said.

The split between military brass and the administration's Pentagon leadership burst into public view even before the war started. In February 2003, Gen. Eric Shinseki, then Army chief of staff, told the Senate Armed Services Committee that "something on the order of several hundred thousand soldiers" would be needed to occupy Iraq and keep the country from descending into a civil war between rival ethnic groups. Shinseki pointed to his experience in the 1990s as a commander of the U.S.-led peacekeeping force in Bosnia, where a war between Serbs and Bosnian Muslims had claimed more than 97,000 lives, 65 percent of them Muslims — 8,000 of whom were killed in a single episode of what the U.N. war crimes tribunal defined as genocide.[1]

But two key civilian architects of the Iraq war — Defense Secretary Donald Rumsfeld and Deputy Secretary Paul Wolfowitz — dismissed Shinseki's warnings. "Wildly off the mark," Wolfowitz declared shortly before the U.S.-led invasion of Iraq. Unlike Bosnia, he said, Iraq had suffered no history of ethnic conflicts.[2]

As events turned out, U.S. troops found themselves fighting a heavily ethnic and sectarian war in Iraq. The conflict continues today on a smaller scale. Their experiences led to yet another lesson of the Iraq conflict: that applying overwhelming force, until then the standard U.S. military doctrine, wasn't always the best strategy. Instead, Petraeus and other commanders worked to break the bond between Iraqi insurgents and the general population, using such "counterinsurgency" tactics as improving the economy and opening schools.[3]

Petraeus' strategy — known in pre-Iraq days as "Military Operations Other Than War," or "Moot-Wah" — wasn't

to further the stated U.S. goal of helping to build a stable democracy.

Administration plans were hampered, however, by shocking revelations by investigative reporter Seymour Hersh of *The New Yorker* and CBS News that U.S. troops had tortured and humiliated prisoners at Abu Ghraib Prison. Photos taken by some of the military guards for their own amusement illustrated the article, which caused a worldwide uproar and made "Abu Ghraib" a synonym for inhumane treatment of prisoners.[56]

Nevertheless, the Bush administration continued its new nation-building strategy. In June 2004, the United States formally handed over national sovereignty to a caretaker government appointed by the United Nations, with American officials also heavily involved.

The country's first elections, to choose an assembly to draft a constitution, were held in January 2005. Though the vote was peaceful, it failed politically, since most Sunnis boycotted the polls.[57]

widely endorsed then. The prevailing Army view, writes Fred Kaplan, author of a new book on the counterinsurgency debate, was that "real men don't do moot-wah."[4]

Counterinsurgency, by most accounts, proved the best approach when Petraeus applied it nationwide in Iraq during the surge. But it may have been oversold as a solution in Iraq, Kaplan argued in *Foreign Affairs* magazine. The strategy worked in sectors where Sunnis turned against al Qaeda, but it failed to persuade many Iraqis that the country's post-invasion government was legitimate, he wrote.

"Counterinsurgency is a technique, not a grand strategy," Kaplan wrote. It is unlikely to become the prevailing U.S. military doctrine, given its failed application in Afghanistan, where conditions favor the insurgents, he argued. "No one could make it work in Afghanistan."[5]

Whatever strategy guides commanders, their troops still get killed and wounded. In Iraq, where a small number of U.S. military personnel remain, 4,475 service members died between the 2003 invasion and early February 2013, and 32,220 were wounded in action.[6] (U.S. military operations ceased on Dec. 15, 2011, but about 200 military advisers remain in Iraq.)

Combined with injuries from the war in Afghanistan, casualties as of last December 7 included 253,330 traumatic brain injuries — 6,476 of them classified as "severe or penetrating" — and 1,715 amputations.[7] In addition, both wars left 103,792 deployed service members with diagnoses of post-traumatic stress disorder (PTSD).[8]

Yet, despite the Iraq war's legacy of carnage and loss, Mansoor argues that today's Army has little in common with the U.S. military that fought America's last drawn-out conflict, the war in Vietnam.

As in Iraq, the Vietnam War also saw divisions between field commanders and Washington officials, as well a debate within the military about counterinsurgency versus massive firepower. But "after Vietnam," Mansoor says, "the Army became a hollow force." By contrast, he says, the post-Iraq War military is stronger than it was in 2003, when the invasion began.

"Now that the frequency of overseas tours has diminished, people are restoring their health in mind, body and spirit," Mansoor says. And from the standpoint of military readiness, "the Army is full of combat-experienced veterans," he says. "You can't create that in any other way than going to war."

Even so, the collapse of the Iraq War's original justification — to prevent the use of weapons of mass destruction, which turned out not to exist — reinforced another lesson, Mansoor says: "War should be the last resort, not the first."

— *Peter Katel*

[1] Quoted in "Army chief: Force to occupy Iraq massive," The Associated Press (*USA Today*), Feb. 25, 2003, http://usatoday30.usatoday.com/news/world/iraq/2003-02-25-iraq-us_x.htm; "Bosnia war dead figure announced," BBC News, June 21, 2007, http://news.bbc.co.uk/2/hi/europe/6228152.stm; Marlise Simons, "Court Convicts a Bosnia Serb General of Genocide," *The New York Times*, Dec. 12, 2012, www.nytimes.com/2012/12/13/world/europe/zdravko-tolimir-former-commander-of-bosnian-serb-army-is-convicted-of-genocide.html.

[2] Quoted in Eric Schmitt, "Pentagon Contradicts General On Iraq Occupation Force's Size," *The New York Times*, Feb. 28, 2003, p. A1.

[3] Fred Kaplan, *The Insurgents: David Petraeus and the Plot to Change the American Way of War* (2013).

[4] Fred Kaplan, "The End of the Age of Petraeus," *Foreign Affairs*, January-February 2013, www.foreignaffairs.com/print/135904.

[5] *Ibid.*

[6] Hannah Fischer, "U.S. Military Casualty Statistics: Operation New Dawn, Operation Iraqi Freedom, and Operation Enduring Freedom," Congressional Research Service, Feb. 5, 2013, p. 5, www.fas.org/sgp/crs/natsec/RS22452.pdf.

[7] *Ibid.*, pp. 8-9.

[8] *Ibid.*, p. 6.

Subsequent votes in 2005 — to ratify the constitution and form a parliament and cabinet — were preceded by intense U.S. efforts to ensure that Sunnis weren't excluded from the political process. In the December 2005 elections to form a government, Sunnis did vote in big numbers.

But negotiations in early 2006 among parties and coalitions with the highest vote totals resulted in formation of a government headed by al-Maliki, a Shiite with a long record of resistance to Hussein and seen as allied to Shiite militias — including al-Sadr's — that were killing Sunni opponents.[58]

Surge and Departure

Despite Bush administration hopes, sectarian violence worsened even as Iraq's elected government got up and running.[59]

The 2003 capture of Hussein in an underground hiding place had not weakened the Sunni insurgency. Neither had his trial and execution by hanging three years later, surrounded by guards chanting al-Sadr's name.

Al Qaeda in Iraq, capitalizing on Sunni fears of the new Shiite-led government, enjoyed support in western, majority-Sunni provinces. A precisely targeted U.S. airstrike killed a top foreign jihadist leader, Abu Musab al-Zarqawi, a Jordanian, in June 2006, but it did not cripple the organization, as officials had hoped.[60]

Meanwhile, government security forces in Baghdad were actively cooperating with Shiite militias in killing Sunnis living in mixed neighborhoods. A classified CIA analysis summed up the situation in two words: "civil war."[61]

The Bush administration was receiving conflicting advice on how the military should respond. One school of thought was that boosting U.S. troop strength would reduce the violence.

Bush was persuaded. In January 2007, he announced that he was ordering five brigades, more than 20,000 troops, to Iraq.[62] "To step back now would force a collapse of the Iraqi government, tear that country apart and result in mass killings on an unimaginable scale," he said.[63]

Bush also appointed Gen. Petraeus, a veteran of the invasion and first phase of the occupation, as Iraq's new military commander for Iraq. Petraeus was also the U.S. military's leading advocate of counterinsurgency — the strategy of using both political and military action to defeat popular uprisings. During his first stint in Iraq, Petraeus had used that approach in the majority-Sunni area around the city of Mosul.[64]

Counterinsurgency seemed well-suited to developments in western Iraq, where Sunni tribes were abandoning their alliance with al Qaeda. The Sunnis resented the jihadists' suicide bombing campaign against Shiites and Americans; their practice of forcing families to hand over their daughters as wives for al-Qaeda fighters; and

Iraqi Prime Minister Nouri al-Maliki (right), a Shiite, greets Iranian President Mahmoud Ahmadinejad (left) in 2009 during al-Maliki's fourth visit to the Shiite-led country since taking office in 2006. Critics say the withdrawal of U.S. combat troops from Iraq risks allowing Iran to increase its influence in Iraq. The backdrop for the debate is the international community's attempt to curb Iran's nuclear ambitions.

their extremist religious rules — such as prohibiting smoking — enforced by violence.[65]

In 2006, Sunnis in the city of Ramadi announced the Anbar (Province) Awakening, in which Sunnis organized against al Qaeda and accepted U.S. help toward that goal. The following year, Petraeus ordered a variant of that approach, in which Sunnis who organized into paramilitary units dubbed the Sons of Iraq were paid by the U.S.-led military.[66]

As the Sunni threat to Shiites diminished, Americans encouraged the al-Maliki government to support suppression of Shiite militias in Baghdad and the southern city of Basra. In 2008, the prime minister agreed, leading some Americans to hope that he had changed his attitude toward those groups, to some of which he had longstanding ties. The surge officially ended in July 2008.

During the last year of the Bush administration, Iraq and the United States signed a "Status of Forces Agreement" under which U.S. troops would pull out of Iraqi cities by June 30, 2009, and leave Iraq entirely by the end of 2011.

U.S. officials assumed that the incoming Obama administration, which took over in January 2009, would negotiate a deal with al-Maliki to keep a military force of some size in the country.

But neither side was eager for a troop deal. Negotiations ended about two months before the final U.S. contingent pulled out in December 2011, when the Iraqis refused to grant legal immunity to U.S. troops, which the Obama administration defined as an ironclad condition for a continuing military presence.

The last 500 U.S. troops deployed in Iraq drove out in a convoy on Dec. 18, 2011. As they neared the Iraqi border, Sgt. First Class Rodolfo Ruiz told his men: "Hey guys, you made it."[67]

CURRENT SITUATION

Bombs and Repression

Religious and ethnic differences continue to play out violently in the new Iraq, with bombings and shootings a regular part of the political landscape.

In recent months, mass-casualty suicide bombings have targeted Shiites and Sunni enemies of al Qaeda. Among them were a series of bombings aimed at Shiite Muslim pilgrims in January that killed nearly 60 people; an attack on a funeral in a community of Turkmen (a minority ethnic group) that killed about 35 people; a suicide car-bomb attack on a police headquarters in the northern city of Kirkuk in early February that killed at least 36; and a series of car bombs in late February that killed at least 21 people in Shiite neighborhoods of Baghdad.[68]

"The latest evidence suggests that the country remains in a state of low-level war little changed since early 2009, with a 'background' level of everyday armed violence punctuated by occasional larger-scale attacks designed to kill many people at once," Iraq Body Count, a British-based group that tracks casualties, said in early 2013.[69]

Suicide bombings — attributed to al Qaeda-linked jihadists — capture most attention. But some analysts point to killings and repression by the Shiite-dominated government, citing the case of Vice President al-Hashimi, who was tried in absentia. "They rounded up his body-guards and tortured one to death and used confessions to sentence him [al-Hashimi] to death," says Army intelligence officer Rayburn, describing a trend of growing repression.

Human Rights Watch, a New York-based advocacy organization, said photos and other evidence suggested the guard had been tortured. Iraq's Supreme Judicial Council denied the torture accusation, made by al-Hashimi himself, saying the guard died of natural causes while in custody.[70]

Overall, Human Rights Watch concluded in a report last year: "Iraqi security forces arbitrarily conducted mass arrests and tortured detainees to extract confessions with little or no evidence of wrongdoing."[71]

Following the al-Hashimi case, 10 bodyguards of Finance Minister Rafe al-Essawi, also a Sunni, were arrested on terrorism charges, and many Sunnis viewed the arrests

> ## "No one had an idea of what the U.S. goal would be until after the war began."
>
> — *Michael Rubin,*
> *Resident scholar,*
> *American Enterprise Institute;*
> *Former adviser (2002-2004) at the*
> *Pentagon and in Baghdad*

as a prelude to criminal charges against al-Essawi.[72] In response, Sunnis mobilized.

"This is targeting all the Sunnis," Sunni leader Sheik Hamid Ahmed told a demonstration of 2,000 in Fallujah. "It was Hashimi first. Essawi now. Who knows who it will be next? The conspiracy against the Sunnis will never stop. We will not keep silent for this."[73]

Nevertheless, some anti-Maliki demonstrators in Fallujah in the Sunni heartland, say they are not motivated by sectarianism. Indeed, *The Washington Post* reported that some Shiite leaders, including militia leader al-Sadr, have sympathized with Sunni protesters.[74]

To add to the Sunnis' danger, a branch of al Qaeda is pressuring them to disavow the Shiite-led government of the "new Iraq." A cousin of al-Essawi — parliamentarian Efan al-Essawi — was assassinated in January in a suicide bombing carried out by Al Qaeda in Mesopotamia (the ancient Greek name for Iraq). The terrorist group called the parliamentarian a "criminal infidel" because of his membership in the Awakening movement.[75]

And an Iranian-supported Shiite militia that boasts of its wartime attacks on U.S. troops is shifting to a militant political role, with the support of al-Maliki. Asaib Ahl al-Haq — the League of the Righteous, sees Iran's cleric-dominated government as a model for Iraq. "If a majority votes for it, why not?" a league leader told *The Washington Post*.[76]

But Ollivant of the New America Foundation says the country is not fracturing irreparably along religious and ethnic lines, which it would have done if the surge and counterinsurgency strategy had not defeated the Sunni insurgency. "The Sunnis in 2004-2005-2006 tried to overthrow the state and failed," he says. "For a group that

Doors Close on Iraqis Who Aided U.S.

Advocates say thousands in peril as visa applications pile up.

Najim Abed al-Jabouri knows how lucky he is. The former mayor of Tal Afar collaborated with top U.S. military commanders during the most lethal years of the Iraq War. So when the American drawdown began in 2008 and al-Jabouri's options narrowed, his high-placed friends helped him reach safety in the United States.

As a top leader of the anti-al Qaeda Sunni Awakening, al-Jabouri was a big jihadist target. He also was unpopular with Iraq's new government because he'd served as a brigadier general under toppled dictator Saddam Hussein. "Many American officers knew very well that after they left Iraq, the government will fire me from my position, and I would be good hunting for al Qaeda," al-Jabouri says.

But the vast majority of the tens of thousands of Iraqis who worked for American military and civilian agencies as interpreters and helpers during the war never came in contact with American generals or ambassadors who could offer protection.

As a result, hundreds of Iraqis — at least — have been killed because of their work for the United States. Thousands more are exposed to danger after applying for special U.S. visas because the approval process under both the George W. Bush and Obama administrations moves at what critics say is a glacial pace. "The U.S. government did not stand behind everyone who worked with them," al-Jabouri says from his office at the Near East South Asia Center for Strategic Studies at the National Defense University in Washington. "Many interpreters staying in Iraq are in a very dangerous situation."

So dangerous, in fact, that many have not survived. For example, an ex-interpreter for the U.S. Agency for International Development (AID) who was trying desperately to get a U.S. visa was kidnapped, tortured and beheaded last June while his application was going through a slow-motion review process, says Kirk W. Johnson, who served with the agency in Fallujah in 2005.

Johnson founded and directs the List Project to Resettle Iraqi Allies, a nonprofit organization that works to help Iraqis reach safety in the United States. Johnson was working with the former U.S. AID interpreter when the man was killed, and he has tried to help thousands of others. "What has happened [in post-war Iraq] is a slow trickle of decapitations or an assassination here and there — never enough to focus attention, but they're happening," he says.

Working for U.S. and allied forces was dangerous for Iraqis even when foreign troops were on the ground. In 2003-2008, one contracting firm registered 360 interpreters killed, some after being tortured. (Some of the dead were non-Iraqis.) And in a notorious 2006 episode in the southern city of Basra, 17 Iraqi interpreters and other aides to the British forces occupying that region were kidnapped from a bus and murdered. A senior Iraqi police official later was accused of complicity.[1]

Johnson, aided by a small staff and volunteer lawyers, has managed to help about 1,500 Iraqis and their families reach the United States. But the list of people who have asked for help is thousands long. "When we submitted an application on behalf of an Iraqi interpreter a few months ago," Johnson says, "we were told by Embassy Baghdad that unless they expedite a case, their current expected wait time is two years for the very first interview — not for arriving in the United States, but for an interview."

That process applies to asylum applications under the longstanding U.S. refugee program, the standard path for those fleeing persecution because of politics, race, nationality, religion or membership in a social group. As for obtaining a "Special Immigrant Visa" under a 2007 law designed specifically to aid Iraqi and Afghan interpreters and other helpers, prospects appear hopeless. Since January 2012, no special visas have been issued, and the program is scheduled to end Sept. 30.[2]

The late Sen. Ted Kennedy sponsored the bill creating the five-year program. It authorized 5,000 special visas a year for Iraqi employees and contractors of the U.S. government and their families. "America owes an immense debt of gratitude to these Iraqis," Kennedy said. "They've supported our effort, saved American lives and are clearly at great risk because of it."[3]

Johnson, who had started the List Project the previous year, says passage of the legislation seemed to be a definitive win. "At the time, my list was only 1,000 names long," he says, "and Kennedy had just blasted open 25,000 visa slots."

As of January 31, about 8,300 of the special visas had been granted, and — under the separate, long-established refugee program — about 80,000 refugee visas were granted since fiscal 2007 began.[4] The latter number is relatively large, but Johnson says it appears to include only a small number of former interpreters and other direct allies and may include many Iraqis who had applied for visas after having fled to nearby countries during the Hussein dictatorship.

The dangers facing citizens of a country who help foreign troops is an old story in warfare. It is an also an old story for the United States. In 2005, the Al Jazeera network broadcast notorious film footage of Vietnamese who were seen as having some U.S. connections trying desperately to reach departing American helicopters during the final U.S. withdrawal from Vietnam in 1975. "The message for Iraqis working with Americans was clear," journalist George Packer wrote in *The New Yorker*.[5]

President Obama's 2009 inauguration aroused hope among Iraqi refugee advocates because during a major campaign speech on Iraq in 2007 Obama had slammed the Bush administration for abandoning Iraqi allies. "The Iraqis who stood with America — the interpreters, embassy workers, subcontractors — are targeted for assassination," he said. "And yet our doors are shut. . . . That's not how we treat our friends."[6]

But Johnson notes that Obama has not accelerated the Iraqi visa process. In fact, a recent terrorism case involving two Iraqi refugees has prompted a wave of congressional concern about Iraqis seeking refuge in the United States, delaying the immigration process even more.

In January, a recently arrived Iraqi refugee was sentenced to life in federal prison and another refugee to 40 years. Both had pleaded guilty in Bowling Green, Ky., to supporting a foreign terrorist organization and to lying in their U.S. admission documents. Both were admitted under the standard refugee program, and neither had worked for U.S. forces, but the repercussions of the case affected all Iraqis seeking to enter the United States.[7]

Both had been anti-American insurgents in Iraq. But a fingerprint from one on an Iraqi roadside bomb was discovered only after the men were already in the United States and were suspects in the terrorism case.[8]

"It is imperative that the interagency security screening process for all refugees be formidable and credible," Rep. Patrick Meehan, R-Pa., told a panel of government witnesses last December at a hearing of the House Homeland Security Committee's Counterterrorism and Intelligence Subcommittee.[9]

For government employees weighing Iraqis' visa applications, Johnson says, the lesson is clear. "The fewer Iraqis, the fewer Muslims, the fewer Arabs you sign your name on

Najim Abed al-Jabouri — a former mayor of a town in Iraq — cooperated with top U.S. military commanders during the anti-al Qaeda Sunni Awakening. Although he has successfully immigrated to the United States, tens of thousands of Iraqis who worked for American military and civilian agencies during the Iraq War have run into bureaucratic hurdles.

Near East South Asia Center for Strategic Studies

a visa for," he says, "the more you're doing your job."

But that attitude carries its own risks, given the inevitable need for bilingual local allies in future conflicts, he argues. "I don't know why anyone thinks we'll be able to recruit people in future wars," he says. "We're obviously not done fighting."

— *Peter Katel*

[1]Thomas Harding, "British troops in Basra seize 'rogue' police officers," *Daily Telegraph* (London), Dec. 23, 2006, p. 14; T. Christian Miller, "Foreign Interpreters Hurt in Battle Find U.S. Insurance Benefits Wanting," *ProPublica*, Dec. 18, 2009, www.propublica.org/article/iraqi-translators-denied-promised-health-care-1218; T. Christian Miller, "Chart: Iraqi Translators, a Casualty List," *ProPublica*, Dec. 18, 2009, www.propublica.org/article/chart-iraqi-translators-a-casualty-list.

[2]"FY 2013 Arrivals Sorted by Nationality by Month," Department of State, Bureau of Population, Refugees, and Migration," State Department, Refugee Processing Center Reports, Cumulative Arrivals by State for Refugee and SIV — Iraqi, www.wrapsnet.org/Reports/AdmissionsArrivals/tabid/211/Default.aspx.

[3]Quoted in Helene Cooper, "U.S. Officials Admit Delays in Issuing Visas to Iraqis," *The New York Times*, July 24, 2007, p. A10; "USCIS Announces New Special Immigrant Visa for Certain Iraqi Nationals Who Worked for the U.S. Government," U.S. Citizenship and Immigration Services, July 9, 2008, www.uscis.gov/portal/site/uscis/menuitem.5af9bb9591 9f35e66f614176543f6d1a/?vgnextoid=91b661ccdc20b110VgnVCM1 000004718190aRCRD&vgnextchannel=68439c7755cb9010VgnVC M10000045f3d6a1RCRD.

[4]"Refugee and Special Immigrant Visa, as of 31-January-2013," Department of State, Bureau of Population, Refugees, and Migration," State Department, Cumulative Arrivals for Refugee and SIV — Iraqi," www.wrapsnet.org/Reports/AdmissionsArrivals/tabid/211/Default .aspx.

[5]George Packer, "Betrayed: The Iraqis who trusted America the most," *The New Yorker*, March 26, 2007, www.newyorker.com/reporting/2007/03/26/070326fa_fact_packer?currentPage=all.

[6]Barack Obama, "Remarks in Clinton, Iowa: 'Turning the Page in Iraq,' Sept. 12, 2007," The American Presidency Project, www.presidency .ucsb.edu/ws/index.php?pid=77011; for video excerpt, Beth Murphy, "Forgotten in Iraq," Op-Doc, *The New York Times*, Dec. 5, 2012, www .nytimes.com/2012/12/06/opinion/forgotten-in-iraq.html.

[7]Andrew Wolfson, "2 Iraqi terrorists sentenced," *The Courier-Journal* (Louisville, Ky.), Jan. 30, 2013, p. B1.

[8]Brian Bennett, "Security checks redone on Iraqis in U.S.," *Los Angeles Times*, July 19, 2011, p. A1.

[9]"Rep. Patrick Meehan Holds a Hearing on Terrorists and Refugee Programs," CQ Transcriptions, Dec. 4, 2012.

Iraq War Coverage From the *CQ Researcher* Archives

For background on Iraq, see the following CQ Researcher reports:

Mary H. Cooper, "Iraq and Beyond: Post Cold-War Military Choices," Nov. 16, 1990, pp. 649-664, library.cqpress.com/cqresearcher/cqresrre1990111600.

Patrick G. Marshall, "Calculating the Costs of the Gulf War," March 15, 1991, pp. 145-155, library.cqpress.com/cqresearcher/cqresrre1991031500.

David Masci, "Confronting Iraq," Oct. 4, 2002, pp. 793-816, library.cqpress.com/cqresearcher/cqresrre2002100400.

David Masci, "Rebuilding Iraq," July 25, 2003, pp. 625-648, library.cqpress.com/cqresearcher/cqresrre2003072500.

William Triplett, "Treatment of Veterans," Nov. 19, 2004, pp. 973-996, library.cqpress.com/cqresearcher/cqresrre2004111900.

Pamela M. Prah, "War in Iraq," Oct. 21, 2005, pp. 881-908, library.cqpress.com/cqresearcher/cqresrre2005102100.

Peter Katel, "New Strategy in Iraq," Feb. 23, 2007, pp. 169-192, library.cqpress.com/cqresearcher/cqresrre2007022300.

Peter Katel, "Wounded Veterans," Aug. 31, 2007, pp. 697-720, library.cqpress.com/cqresearcher/cqresrre2007083100.

Peter Katel, "U.S. Policy on Iran," Nov. 16, 2007, pp. 961-984, library.cqpress.com/cqresearcher/cqresrre2007111600.

Peter Katel, "Cost of the Iraq War," April 25, 2008, pp. 361-384, library.cqpress.com/cqresearcher/cqresrre2008042500.

Peter Katel, "Rise in Counterinsurgency," Sept. 5, 2008, pp. 697-720, library.cqpress.com/cqresearcher/cqresrre2008090500.

Peter Katel, "Caring for Veterans," April 23, 2010, pp. 361-384, library.cqpress.com/cqresearcher/cqresrre2010042300.

Peter Katel, "America at War," July 23, 2010, updated Aug. 13, 2010, pp. 605-628, library.cqpress.com/cqresearcher/cqresrre2010072300.

Kenneth Jost, "Unrest in the Arab World," Feb. 1, 2013, pp. 105-132, library.cqpress.com/cqresearcher/cqresrre2013020100.

tried to overthrow the state and failed, they have it just about as good as it gets."

Continuing U.S. Debate

The war in Iraq may be over for the United States, but American politicians are still arguing fiercely over who among them was right or wrong when the big decisions were made.

A confirmation hearing for Obama's defense secretary nominee, former Republican Sen. Chuck Hagel of Nebraska, provided the most recent stage for the conflicts to play out.

Among Hagel's toughest critics was fellow Republican Sen. John McCain of Arizona. "Were you correct or incorrect when you said that the surge would be the most dangerous foreign policy blunder in this country since Vietnam?" McCain asked during a sharp exchange. "Were you correct or incorrect?"[77]

After refusing to give a yes-or-no answer, Hagel said he'd let history decide. And he added, "As to the comment I made about the most dangerous foreign policy decision since Vietnam — [it] was about not just the surge but the overall war of choice going into Iraq." McCain retorted: "I think history has already made a judgment about the surge, sir, and you're on the wrong side of it."[78]

Democrats aiming to bolster Hagel made a point of portraying his skepticism about the war as prescient. Sen. Bill Nelson, D-Fla., said of himself, "This senator was one of many that voted for the authorization to go into Iraq, and as it turns out, [with] the lessons of history, we were given incorrect information as a justification for going into Iraq. We were told by the secretary of defense,

Is Iraqi Prime Minister Nouri al-Maliki becoming a dictator?

YES Joel D. Rayburn
Lt. Col., U.S. Army;
Research Fellow, National War College

NO Douglas Ollivant
Senior Vice President,
Mantid International; Senior Fellow,
New America Foundation

Written for *CQ Researcher*, March 2013

What a long way Nouri al-Maliki has traveled since National Security Adviser Stephen Hadley questioned in 2006 whether he was strong enough to confront his most malignant political rivals. Today no one worries that al-Maliki might not be strong enough. Over the past six years he has pulled all the levers of state power to himself.

On paper, Iraq is a democracy, with a presidency, premiership, judiciary and ministries accountable to a parliament. Also on paper, al-Maliki is the head of a coalition government, sharing power with all the other major Iraqi parties.

In practice, the presidency is virtually powerless (especially with President Jalal Talabani sidelined by a stroke), the judiciary is an extension of the executive, the parliament is marginalized and the ministries answer directly to al-Maliki's office. Iraq is not governed as a democracy, but ruled as a regime.

Al-Maliki controls the Iraqi military through his military advisers. He runs the vast intelligence apparatus through his national security adviser. He has racked up one favorable constitutional interpretation after another from his ally, the chief justice, who ruled that only the prime minister, not the legislative branch, could initiate legislation. Outside official channels, al-Maliki's son Ahmed commands the guards who physically control the Green Zone, Iraq's seat of government.

Policy decisions are taken not by the coalition government, but by al-Maliki and a small "politburo"-style group of party allies.

The United States bequeathed Iraq a political system of checks and balances, but they no longer exist. There are no institutional checks on al-Maliki's power, only political ones. If al-Maliki's hand is stayed, it is only because of the street power wielded by his chief opponents: the Sadrists, the Kurdistan Regional Government of Massoud Barzani and the Iraqi Sunnis who have taken to the streets in tens of thousands to call for al-Maliki's ouster.

There are plenty of grievances for these groups to leverage. The al-Maliki government cannot meet Iraqis' expectations for services and security, and they are growing angrier about it by the month. Iraqis now speak of a potential "Iraq Spring."

Iraqis don't seem to care very much about whether Americans are willing to call al-Maliki a dictator. They know what he is, and their patience is wearing thin.

Rayburn served in Iraq and Afghanistan. His opinions do not represent those of the Defense Department.

Written for *CQ Researcher*, March 2013

Prime Minister Nouri al-Maliki has perhaps the world's toughest job: administering a country just emerging from 20 years of war and sanctions, capped by a decade of occupation and civil war. He was elected by a Shiite constituency that acutely feels its oppression, both historical and recent. But he must also accommodate the interests of the (formerly ruling) minority Sunni sect, along with nearly unbridled autonomy aspirations of a third ethno-sectarian group — the Kurds. The challenges for democratic governance are without precedent.

Continuing terrorist attacks challenge the government's legitimacy and demand the forceful and legitimate use of state power to protect the people. Al-Qaeda in Iraq continually tries to reboot the 2005-2008 civil war, though without success.

In addition, al-Maliki's administration suffers from three handicaps. First, government instruments are immature, and an ambiguous constitution allows divergent interpretations. Second, ongoing corruption — from petty to grand — remaining from prior governments continues to undermine progress. Finally, the "national unity" government formed in 2010 puts key ministries under the control of parties seeking to undermine al-Maliki.

In this environment, al-Maliki has wielded executive power forcefully. While this is customary in all parliamentary systems, the nascent government and ever-present threat of terrorism accentuates this need.

He has not been perfect in all of his choices. But no leader is. Whether one agrees or disagrees with the actions of an elected government, acting forcefully to overcome uncertainty, inertia and friction does not a dictator make.

There is plenty of bad news coming out of Iraq. But Iraq has made great strides. It now pumps well over 3 million barrels of oil per day, infrastructure projects are beginning to mature and Iraq is beginning to assert its place in the region, building paths for reasonable compromise and advancement.

With a remarkably open election process, al-Maliki must answer to all of Iraq in the spring of 2014. His opponents have been vocal in their opposition, as is their democratic right. But that al-Maliki is so openly branded a "dictator" by his opposition is in itself testimony to democratic tolerance. Regardless of who wins in the coming elections, he will be, by definition, no dictator.

Nor is the incumbent.

Ollivant served as a Director for Iraq at the National Security Council, 2008-'09, after two military tours in Baghdad.

by the secretary of state, by the national security adviser and the director of the CIA that there were weapons of mass destruction in Iraq."[79]

Hagel also had voted for the 2002 authorization for war — but with extreme reluctance. "Imposing democracy through force in Iraq is a roll of the dice," Hagel, a combat veteran of the Vietnam War, had said in a Senate floor speech. "A democratic effort cannot be maintained without building durable Iraqi political institutions and developing a regional and international commitment to Iraq's reconstruction. No small task. . . . In authorizing the use of force against Iraq, we are at the beginning of a road that has no clear end."[80]

Hagel's clear skepticism had hardened into opposition by the time the Bush administration decided on the surge. Congress had no direct power to block the escalation, but Hagel co-authored a resolution opposing the move and voted for legislation designed to set a deadline for troop withdrawal.[81]

Given an opening by Nelson to further explain his position on the surge, Hagel did so by alluding indirectly to his own wartime experience, during which he suffered severe wounds. "I always ask the question, 'Is this going to be worth the sacrifice?'" Hagel said. "We lost almost 1,200 dead Americans during that surge, and thousands of wounded. . . . I'm not certain that it was required."[82]

OUTLOOK

Sectarian Strife

Iraq analysts differ as sharply in their forecasts of the short-term future of the country and its neighbors as they do about virtually every other aspect of the war and its effects.

Pillar, the former CIA analyst, argues that the war heightened religious conflict. "There will be continued high levels of sectarian strife that the war unleashed directly in Iraq," he says. "We see the spillover effects in Syria today."

Jihadist extremism, he says, is likely to remain more of a danger than it would have if the United States had never invaded Iraq. "The worst of the negative vibrations that have generated more anti-Americanism have subsided now that we are actually out of Iraq," he says. "Nevertheless, it takes a long time for those sorts of waves to disperse.

We will still be hearing more than we would have about Americans being out to kill Muslims and occupy their lands and steal their resources."

Al-Suwaij of the National Islamic Council sees Iraqis adapting to democratic political culture. "I don't think people will ever be quiet if a dictator comes," she says. "They are not going to accept that someone does to them what Saddam has done. It's a huge change."

Nevertheless, she says, some of Iraq's neighbors, including Iran, Turkey and Saudi Arabia, may each have an interest in keeping Iraq unstable. "So I am optimistic," she says, "but at the same time very cautious."

Al-Jabouri, the former Tal Afr mayor now at the National Defense University, expresses a different version of restrained optimism. "If Maliki does not stay in power, and [if] many leaders of the Shia parties work together like Iraqis with the Sunni and Kurds, we are going to establish democracy in Iraq," he says. But if al-Maliki remains at the helm, "Iraq will become three states" — for Shiites, Sunnis and Kurds.

As for what the Bush administration had hoped would become an example of democracy for the entire Middle East, former ambassador Jeffrey says, "The region is going to be much as it is now and as it was 10 years ago — dysfunctional, full of violence, full of dictators." Moreover, he says, oil-producing Iraq will play a critical role in supplying U.S. energy needs.

Jeffrey adds, "All our efforts to keep on an unhappy but livable trajectory, as opposed to allowing things to slip totally out of control, will slip out of control if Iran gets nuclear weapons."

Hiltermann of the International Crisis Group shares the view that U.S. or Israeli military action against Iran would shake up the entire region, including Iran's neighbor Iraq — in unpredictable ways. The outcome of the Syrian rebellion is another wild card, he says. Otherwise, "Iraq muddles along," he says. "It will become more autocratic."

The sense of Iraq as one nation is eroding, Hiltermann says. Hussein's dictatorship "was a Mafia regime but a secular regime that held the country together. People did have a sense of Iraq identity until 2004-2005," he says. "Now you have a Shiite-run Iraq."

Army intelligence officer Rayburn sketches out a possible effect on Iraq of the ongoing uprising in neighboring Syria. "Say that al Qaeda in Iraq begins to control territory in Syria and that territory becomes a terrorist sanctuary from which they can launch attacks back into Iraq," he says. In that case, the United States might have to consider a military response, he says.

Rayburn does see a democratic culture taking hold in Iraq. "My fear is that they're going to have to go through another round of war" before rising sectarian tensions fade, he says. "Then we'll see how this next generation will do, but it would be hard to conceive of them doing worse."

Jensen of the Near East South Asia Center argues that the Maliki government's autocratic tendencies won't fully take hold. "Because of the freedom of journalism, the government will never have a monopoly on the narrative. They'd have to use complete brute force, and if they do, there will be consequences both from the United States and within Iraq. Iraqis don't want another dictator."

NOTES

1. Hannah Fischer, "U.S. Military Casualty Statistics: Operation New Dawn, Operation Iraqi Freedom, and Operation Enduring Freedom," Congressional Research Service, p. 11, www.fas.org/sgp/crs/natsec/RS22452.pdf; Amy Belasco, "The Cost of Iraq, Afghanistan, and Other Global War on Terror Operations Since 9/11," Congressional Research Service, p. 3, www.fas.org/sgp/crs/natsec/RL33110.pdf.

2. Tim Arango and Michael S. Schmidt, "Last Convoy of American Troops Leaves Iraq," *The New York Times*, Dec. 18, 2011, www.nytimes.com/2011/12/19/world/middleeast/last-convoy-of-american-troops-leaves-iraq.html?pagewanted=all; "Remarks by President Obama and Prime Minister al-Maliki of Iraq in a Joint Press Conference," The White House, Dec. 12, 2011, www.whitehouse.gov/the-press-office/2011/12/12/remarks-president-obama-and-prime-minister-al-maliki-iraq-joint-press-co.

3. "Obama's 2013 State of the Union Address," *The New York Times*, Feb. 12, 2013, www.nytimes.com/2013/02/13/us/politics/obamas-2013-state-of-the-union-address.html?pagewanted=all; "Obama: U.N. sanctions 'unmistakable message' to Iran," Reuters, June 9, 2010, www.reuters.com/article/2010/06/09/us-nuclear-iran-obama-idUSTRE6584LE20100609.

4. "Iraq bomb: Many dead in Shia mosque in Tuz Khurmato," BBC, Jan. 23, 2013, www.bbc.co.uk/news/world-middle-east-21166755; Duraid Adnan, "Burst of Iraq Violence Amid Political Crisis," *The New York Times*, Jan. 22, 2013, www.nytimes.com/2013/01/23/world/middleeast/iraq-bombing-Al-Qaeda-in-Mesopotamia-.html; "Suicide bomber kills 27 Shi'ite pilgrims in Iraq," Reuters, Jan. 3, 2013, http://uk.reuters.com/article/2013/01/03/uk-iraq-violence-idUKBRE9020E820130103; Yasir Ghazi, "Dozens Die in Attack on Police in Iraqi City," *The New York Times*, Feb. 3, 2013, www.nytimes.com/2013/02/04/world/middleeast/suicide-attack-kills-dozens-in-northern-iraq.html; "Suicide bomber ills 22 in attack on Iraq militia," Reuters, Feb. 4, 2013, www.reuters.com/article/2013/02/04/us-iraq-violence-idUSBRE91308T20130204?feedType=RSS&feedName=topNews&utm_source=feedburner&utm_medium=feed&utm_campaign=Feed%3A+reuters%2FtopNews+%28News+%2F+US+%2F+Top+News%29&utm_content=Google+Feedfetcher; Duraid Adnan, "Blasts in Baghdad's Shiite Neighborhoods Kill 21," *The New York Times*, Feb. 17, 2013, www.nytimes.com/2013/02/18/world/middleeast/baghdad-bomb-blasts.html?_r=0.

5. Amy Belasco, "Troop Levels in the Afghan and Iraq Wars, FY 2001-FY 2012: Cost and Other Potential Issues," Congressional Research Service, Summary page, July 2, 2009, www.fas.org/sgp/crs/natsec/R40682.pdf.

6. "Iraqi deaths from violence in 2012," Iraq Body Count, Jan. 1, 2013, www.iraqbodycount.org/analysis/numbers/2012/.

7. *Ibid.*

8. For background, see Leda Hartman, "Islamic Sectarianism," *CQ Global Researcher*, Aug. 7, 2012, pp. 353-376.

9. Anthony Shadid, "A Shiite Schism On Clerical Rule," *The Washington Post*, July 17, 2009, p. A8; "Freedom in the World, 2012, Iraq," Freedom House, www.freedomhouse.org/report/freedom-world/2012/iraq.

10. Duraid Adnan and Christine Hauser, "Iraqi Prime Minister Faces More Calls for Resignation," *The New York Times*, Jan. 4, 2013, www.nytimes .com/2013/01/05/world/middleeast/iraqi-prime-min ister-faces-more-calls-for-resignation.html?ref=tariq alhashimi; "Turkey: Iraqi Vice President Will Not Be Sent Back," Reuters (*The New York Times*), Sept. 11, 2012, www.nytimes.com/2012/09/12/world/europe/ turkey-iraqi-vice-president-will-not-be-sent-back .html?ref=tariqalhashimi; Jack Healy, "Arrest Order for Sunni Leader in Iraq Opens New Rift," *The New York Times*, Dec, 19, 2011, www.nytimes.com/2011/12/20/ world/middleeast/iraqi-government-accuses-top-offi cial-in-assassinations.html?pagewanted=all.

11. Nayla Razzouk, "Iraq President Talabani's Stroke May Fuel Ethnic Tensions," Bloomberg, Dec. 20, 2012, www.bloomberg.com/news/2012-12-18/ iraqi-president-jalal-talabani-hospitalized-due-to-stroke.html.

12. Quoted in "Top Bush officials push case against Saddam," CNN, Sept. 8, 2002, http://articles.cnn .com/2002-09-08/politics/iraq.debate_1_nuclear-weapons-top-nuclear-scientists-aluminum-tubes?_ s=PM:ALLPOLITICS.

13. Quoted in Walter Pincus, "Ex-CIA Official Faults Use of Data on Iraq," *The Washington Post*, Feb. 10, 2006, www.washingtonpost.com/wp-dyn/content/ article/2006/02/09/AR2006020902418_pf.html.

14. Michael R. Gordon and Bernard E. Trainor, *Cobra II: The Inside Story of the Invasion and Occupation of Iraq* (2007), pp. 145-146; "Report of the Senate Select Committee on Intelligence on the U.S. Intelligence Community's Prewar Intelligence Assessments on Iraq," U.S. Senate, July 9, 2004, pp. 60-112, http://intelligence.senate.gov/108301 .pdf.

15. Quoted in Gordon and Trainor, *op. cit.*, p. 193.

16. "Bush makes historic speech aboard warship," CNN (transcript), May 1, 2003, http://articles.cnn.com/ 2003-05-01/us/bush.transcript_1_general-franks-major-combat-allies?_s=PM:US; Thomas E. Ricks, *Fiasco: The American Military Adventure in Iraq* (2006), p. 145.

17. Quoted in *ibid.*, Ricks, p. 390.

18. "Report of the Senate Select Committee on Intelligence on the U.S Intelligence Community's Prewar Intelligence Assessments on Iraq," *op. cit.*

19. Michael R. Gordon and Bernard E. Trainor, *The Endgame* (2012), pp. 99-106.

20. "Freedom in the World, 2012, Iraq" *op. cit.*

21. Paul von Zielbauer, "Kurds Tell of Gas Attacks by Hussein's Military," *The New York Times*, Aug. 23, 2006, www.nytimes.com/2006/08/23/world/ middleeast/23iraq.html; Samir al-Khalil (later republished under his real name, Kanan Makiya), *Republic of Fear: The Inside Story of Saddam's Iraq* (1990), pp. 22-24.

22. "Iran-Iraq War," GlobalSecurity.org, updated Nov. 7, 2011, www.globalsecurity.org/military/ world/war/iran-iraq.htm.

23. "CW Use in Iran-Iraq War," CIA (Federation of American Scientists release), July 9, 1996, www.fas .org/irp/gulf/cia/960702/72566_01.htm.

24. "Nouri Kamil al-Maliki," GlobalSecurity.org, updated Sept. 7, 2011, www.globalsecurity.org/mili tary/world/iraq/maliki.htm.

25. Gordon and Trainor, *The Endgame, op. cit.*: pp. 316-318; pp. 351-368.

26. *Ibid.*, pp. 168-169.

27. Belasco, "The Cost of Iraq, Afghanistan, and Other Global War on Terror Operations Since 9/11," *op. cit.*, pp. 1-3.

28. Glenn Kessler, "Why the Bush tax cuts were enacted," *The Washington Post*, Dec. 19, 2012, www .washingtonpost.com/blogs/fact-checker/post/his tory-lesson-why-the-bush-tax-cuts-were-enacted /2012/12/19/55a93ac6-4a1d-11e2-ad54-580638 ede391_blog.html.

29. "Estimated Dollar Costs of Wars," Costs of War, Eisenhower Research Group, Brown University, June 2011, http://costsofwar.org.

30. Tim Arango, "U.S. Planning to Slash Iraq Embassy Staff by as Much as Half," *The New York Times*, Feb. 7, 2012, www.nytimes.com/2012/02/08/world/ middleeast/united-states-planning-to-slash-iraq-embassy-staff-by-half.html.

31. "OECD Factbook 2011-2012: Economic, Environmental and Social Statistics," Organisation for Economic Co-operation and Development, undated, www.oecd-ilibrary.org/sites/factbook-2011-en/06/02/03/index.html;jsessionid=1gp3pg5q2xxjb.epsilon?contentType=/ns/Chapter,/ns/StatisticalPublication&itemId=/content/chapter/factbook-2011-54-en&containerItemId=/content/serial/18147364&accessItemIds=&mimeType=text/html.

32. Paul Krugman, "An Iraq recession?" The Conscience of a Liberal (blog), *The New York Times*, Jan. 29, 2008, http://krugman.blogs.nytimes.com/2008/01/29/an-iraq-recession/.

33. For background, see Kenneth Jost, "Unrest in the Arab World," *CQ Researcher*, Feb. 1, 2013, pp. 105-132; and Roland Flamini, "Turmoil in the Arab World," *CQ Global Researcher*, May 3, 2011, pp. 209-236.

34. For background, see Patrick G. Marshall, "Calculating the Costs of the Gulf War," *Editorial Research Reports*, March 15, 1991, pp. 145-155; available at *CQ Researcher Plus Archive*.

35. Gordon and Trainor, *Cobra II, op. cit.*, pp. 12-13.

36. *Ibid.*; Gordon and Trainor, *The Endgame, op. cit.*, p. 5.

37. John A. Tirpak, "Legacy of the Air Blockades," airforce-magazine.com, February 2003, www.airforce-magazine.com/MagazineArchive/Pages/2003/February%202003/0203legacy.aspx; "Iraq: No Fly Zones," Ministry of Defence (U.K.), Nov. 6, 2009, www.iraqinquiry.org.uk/media/38010/mod-no-fly-zone-r1.pdf/; Kenneth Katzman and Christopher M. Blanchard, "Iraq: Oil-For-Food Program, Illicit Trade, and Investigations," Congressional Research Service, June 14, 2005, pp. 1-5, www.fas.org/sgp/crs/mideast/RL30472.pdf.

38. Thomas E. Ricks, *Fiasco: The American Military Adventure in Iraq* (2006), pp. 20, 23.

39. Gordon and Trainor, *Cobra II, op. cit.*, p. 15.

40. *Ibid.*, pp. 17-19; Scott Shane, "'01 Memo to Rice Warned of Qaeda and Offered Plan," *The New York Times*, Feb. 12, 2005, www.nytimes.com/2005/02/12/politics/12clarke.html.

41. Michael R. Gordon and Judith Miller, "Threats and Responses: The Iraqis; U.S. Says Hussein Intensifies Quest For A-Bomb Parts," *The New York Times*, Sept. 8, 2002, www.nytimes.com/2002/09/08/world/threats-responses-iraqis-us-says-hussein-intensifies-quest-for-bomb-parts.html?pagewanted=all&src=pm.

42. "Iraq 'ended nuclear aims in 1991,'" BBC, Aug. 11, 2004, http://news.bbc.co.uk/2/hi/middle_east/3556714.stm; "Iraqi Nuclear Weapons," Federation of American Scientists, updated May 31, 2012, www.fas.org/nuke/guide/iraq/nuke/program.htm.

43. Gordon and Trainor, *op. cit., Cobra II*, pp. 40-41.

44. "Text of Bush's Speech at West Point," *The New York Times*, June 1, 2002, www.nytimes.com/2002/06/01/international/02PTEX-WEB.html?pagewanted=all; Gordon and Trainor, *Cobra II, ibid.*, p. 72.

45. Quoted in Ricks, *op. cit.*, p. 49.

46. Quoted in *ibid.*, p. 63.

47. Gordon and Trainor, *op. cit., Cobra II*, pp. 140-149.

48. *Ibid.*, pp. 47-48.

49. Except where otherwise indicated, this subsection is drawn from Gordon and Trainor, *Cobra II, op. cit.*

50. "Bush ultimatum to Saddam: Text," BBC News, March 18, 2003, http://news.bbc.co.uk/2/hi/americas/2859269.stm.

51. Quoted in Ricks, *op. cit.*, p. 136.

52. Except where otherwise indicated, this subsection is drawn from Ricks, *op. cit.*

53. "Official: Al-Zarqawi may be in Fallujah," CNN, June 17, 2004, http://articles.cnn.com/2004-06-16/world/iraq.main_1_al-zarqawi-qaeda-rocket-attack?_s=PM:WORLD; Gordon and Trainor, *The Endgame, op. cit.*, pp. 56-64, 115-120.

54. Brian Knowlton, " 'We were almost all wrong,' inspector says," *The New York Times*, Jan. 29, 2004, www.nytimes.com/2004/01/29/news/29iht-kay_ed3_.html; "What Inspectors Saw, and Didn't See," *The New York Times*, Oct. 3, 2003, www.nytimes.com/2003/10/03/international/middleeast/03WTEX.html; David E. Sanger, "A Doctrine Under Pressure: Pre-emption Is Redefined," *The New York*

Times, Oct. 11, 2004, www.nytimes.com/2004/10/11/politics/11preempt.html.

55. Bill Roggio, "Sadr threatens new uprising; Iraqi and US forces press attack," *Long War Journal*, April 20, 2008, www.longwarjournal.org/archives/2008/04/sadr_threatens_new_u.php.

56. Seymour M. Hersh, "Torture at Abu Ghraib," *The New Yorker*, May 10, 2004, www.newyorker.com/archive/2004/05/10/040510fa_fact.

57. Kenneth Katzman, "Iraq: Elections, Government, and Constitution," Congressional Research Service, Nov. 20, 2006, http://fpc.state.gov/documents/organization/76838.pdf.

58. *Ibid.*

59. Except where otherwise noted, this subsection is drawn from Gordon and Trainor, *The Endgame*, *op. cit.*

60. John F. Burns, "U.S. Strike Hits Insurgent at Safehouse," *The New York Times*, June 8, 2006, www.nytimes.com/2006/06/08/world/middleeast/08cnd-iraq.html?pagewanted=all.

61. Quoted in Gordon and Trainor, *The Endgame*, *op. cit.*, p. 295.

62. "Operational Unit Diagrams," U.S. Army, undated, www.army.mil/info/organization/unitsandcommands/oud/.

63. "President Bush Addresses Nation on Iraq War," CQ Transcripts Wire, Jan. 10, 2007, www.washingtonpost.com/wp-dyn/content/article/2007/01/10/AR2007011002208.html.

64. "Insurgents' Hoped To Change Military From Within," NPR, Jan. 24, 2013, www.npr.org/2013/01/24/169990594/insurgents-hoped-to-change-military-from-within.

65. Najim Abed al-Jabouri and Sterling Jensen, "The Iraqi and AQI Roles in the Sunni Awakening," *Prism* (National Defense University), December 2012, www.ndu.edu/press/lib/images/prism2-1/Prism_3-18_Al-Jabouri_Jensen.pdf.

66. *Ibid.*; Greg Bruno, "Finding a Place for the 'Sons of Iraq,'" Council on Foreign Relations, Jan. 9, 2009, www.cfr.org/iraq/finding-place-sons-iraq/p16088.

67. Quoted in Joseph Logan, "Last U.S. troops leave Iraq, ending war," Reuters, Dec. 18, 2011, www.reuters.com/article/2011/12/18/us-iraq-withdrawal-idUSTRE7BH03320111218.

68. "Bombs in Iraq Kill 36, Mostly Shiite Pilgrims," The Associated Press (*USA Today*), Jan. 17, 2013, www.usatoday.com/story/news/world/2013/01/17/iraq-car-bomb/1841467/; www.nytimes.com/2013/01/24/world/middleeast/funeral-bombing-in-northern-iraq-kills-at-least-35-mourners.html; Yasir Ghazi, "Dozens Die in Attack on Police in Iraqi City," *The New York Times*, Feb. 3, 2013, www.nytimes.com/2013/02/04/world/middleeast/suicide-attack-kills-dozens-in-northern-iraq.html; Duraid Adnan, "Blasts in Baghdad's Shiite Neighborhoods Kill 21," *The New York Times*, Feb. 17, 2013, www.nytimes.com/2013/02/18/world/middleeast/baghdad-bomb-blasts.html?_r=0.

69. "Civilian deaths in 2012 compared to recent years," Iraq Body Count, Jan. 1, 2013, www.iraqbodycount.org/analysis/numbers/2012/.

70. "Iraq's judiciary denies Hashemi bodyguard tortured," Reuters, March 22, 2012, http://uk.reuters.com/article/2012/03/22/uk-iraq-hashemi-bodyguard-idUKBRE82L1BR20120322; "Iraq: Investigate Death of VP's Bodyguard," Human Rights Watch, March 23, 2012, www.hrw.org/news/2012/03/23/iraq-investigate-death-of-v-p-s-bodyguard-custody.

71. "Iraq: A Broken Justice System," Human Rights Watch, Jan. 31, 2013, www.hrw.org/news/2013/01/31/iraq-broken-justice-system.

72. Duraid Adnan and Tim Arango, "Arrest of a Sunni Minister's Bodyguards Prompts Protests in Iraq," *The New York Times*, Dec. 21, 2012, www.nytimes.com/2012/12/22/world/middleeast/arrest-of-al-essawis-bodyguards-prompts-protests-in-iraq.html.

73. Quoted in *ibid.*

74. Liz Sly, "Arab Spring-style protests take hold in Iraq," *The Washington Post*, Feb. 8, 2013, http://articles.washingtonpost.com/2013-02-08/world/36986802_1_sunni-minister-protest-organizers-maliki.

75. Quoted in Duraid Adnan, "Burst of Iraq Violence Amid Political Crisis," *The New York Times*, Jan. 22, 2013, www.nytimes.com/2013/01/23/world/middleeast/iraq-bombing-Al-Qaeda-in-Mesopotamia.html.

76. Quoted in Liz Sly, "Iranian-backed militant group in Iraq is recasting itself as a political player," *The*

Washington Post, Feb. 18, 2013, www.washington
post.com/world/middle_east/iranian-backed-mili
tant-group-in-iraq-is-recasting-itself-as-a-political-
player/2013/02/18/b0154204-77bb-11e2-b1
02-948929030e64_story.html.

77. "Hearing of the Senate Armed Services Committee,"
transcript, Federal News Service, Jan. 13, 2013.

78. *Ibid.*

79. *Ibid.*

80. Quoted in Charles P. Pierce, "Chuck Hagel on the
Iraq War," Politics blog, *Esquire*, Jan. 8, 2013, www
.esquire.com/blogs/politics/chuck-hagel-
iraq-2002-010813.

81. Noam N. Levey, "Senate retains Iraq war timeline,"
Los Angeles Times, March 28, 2007, p. A1; Jonathan
Weisman, "Bipartisan Senate Measure Confronts
Bush Over Iraq," *The Washington Post*, Jan. 18, 2007,
p. A1.

82. "Hearing of the Senate Armed Services Committee,"
op. cit.

BIBLIOGRAPHY

Selected Sources

Books

Gordon, Michael R., and Bernard E. Trainor, *Cobra
II: The Inside Story of the Invasion and Occupation of
Iraq*, Vintage, 2007.
The chief military correspondent for The New York Times
(Gordon) and a retired Marine general chronicle the Iraq
invasion and first phase of the occupation.

Gordon, Michael R., and Bernard E. Trainor, *The
Endgame: The Inside Story of the Struggle for Iraq, From
George W. Bush to Barack Obama*, Pantheon, 2012.
An equally detailed sequel to *Cobra II* covers the Iraq civil
war, the surge and U.S. disengagement.

Johnson, Kirk W., *To Be a Friend Is Fatal: A Story
From the Aftermath of America at War*, Scribner,
2013 (available July).
The founder of an advocacy group for Iraqis tells of their
attempts to gain U.S. refuge in order to save their lives.

Mansoor, Peter, R., *Baghdad at Sunrise: A Brigade
Commander's War in Iraq*, Yale, 2008.

The early days of the war as seen by a colonel — now a
professor of military history — who was in the thick of
the action.

Ricks, Thomas E., *Fiasco: The American Military
Adventure in Iraq*, Penguin, 2006.
A former military correspondent for *The Washington Post*
writes critically and skeptically of the buildup to war and
the conflict's first phase.

Articles

Bowman, Tom, "As the Iraq War Ends, Reassessing
the Surge," NPR, Dec. 16, 2011, www.npr.org/
2011/12/16/143832121/as-the-iraq-war-ends-reas
sessing-the-u-s-surge.
A Pentagon correspondent reports on the debate over
whether a U.S. troop buildup and counterinsurgency
strategy turned the tide in Iraq.

Cooper, Helene, and Thom Shanker, "U.S. Embraces
a Low-Key Response to Turmoil in Iraq," *The New
York Times*, Dec. 24, 2011, www.nytimes
.com/2011/12/25/world/middleeast/us-loses-lever
age-in-iraq-now-that-troops-are-out.html?page
wanted=all.
Reporters provide early coverage of the Obama
administration's policy of leaving Iraqis to settle conflicts
themselves.

Kaplan, Fred, "The End of the Age of Petraeus,"
Foreign Affairs, January-February 2013, www.for
eignaffairs.com/articles/138459/fred-kaplan/the-
end-of-the-age-of-petraeus.
A veteran national security writer examines counterinsurgency strategy as a solution in guerrilla wars.

Miller, T. Christian, "U.S. Insurance Firm Neglects
Survivors of Iraqi Translators, May Face Criminal
Charges," *ProPublica*, May 23, 2011, www.pro
publica.org/article/us-insurance-firm-neglects-survi
vors-of-iraqi-translators-may-face-criminal.
In cooperation with the *Los Angeles Times*, an online
investigative journalism organization reports on a criminal
investigation into apparent failure to compensate survivors of Iraqis killed while acting as interpreters for the
U.S. government.

Sly, Liz, "Arab Spring-style protests take hold in
Iraq," *The Washington Post*, Feb. 8, 2013, www.wash
ingtonpost.com/world/middle_east/arab-spring

-style-protests-take-hold-in-iraq/2013/02/08/
f875ef7e-715f-11e2-b3f3-b263d708ca37_story.html.
A Mideast correspondent covers growing political and
social discontent in Iraq and the government's response.

Visser, Reidar, "An Unstable, Divided Land," *The*
New York Times, **Dec. 15, 2011, www.nytimes**
.com/2011/12/16/opinion/an-unstable-divided-land
.html.
The Obama administration misjudged the nature of
Iraqi sectarian and ethnic conflicts, thereby worsening
them, a Norwegian expert on Iraq argues.

Reports

Fischer, Hannah, "U.S. Military Casualty Statistics:
Operation New Dawn, Operation Iraqi Freedom, and
Operation Enduring Freedom," Congressional
Research Service, Feb. 5, 2013, www.fas.org/sgp/crs/
natsec/RS22452.pdf.
Congress' nonpartisan research service has assembled the
most up-to-date statistics on casualties in Iraq and
Afghanistan.

Harrison, Todd, "The Impact of the Wars in Iraq and
Afghanistan on the US Military's Plans, Programs
and Budgets," Center for Strategic and Budgetary
Assessments, August 2009, www.csbaonline.org/pub
lications/2009/08/impact-of-iraq-afghanistan-war-
on-militarys-plans/2/.
As the United States was winding down its presence in
Iraq, an experienced analyst assessed the effects of both
the Iraq war and the Afghanistan conflict on the armed
services.

Mason, R. Chuck, "U.S.-Iraq Withdrawal/Status of
Forces Agreement: Issues for Congressional
Oversight," Congressional Research Service, July 13,
2009, www.fas.org/sgp/crs/natsec/R40011.pdf.
The intricacies of U.S.-Iraq relations in the war's final
U.S. phase are laid out clearly in a research report for
Congress.

For More Information

American Enterprise Institute, 1150 17th St., N.W.,
Washington, DC 20036; 202-862-5800; www.aei.org/search/
Iraq. Conservative think tank that is home to several architects and advocates of the Iraq war; regularly posts commentary and analysis on Iraq.

Brookings Institution, 1775 Massachusetts Ave., N.W.,
Washington, DC 20036; 202-797-6000; www.brookings
.edu/research/topics/iraq. Centrist think tank that publishes
analyses and opinion pieces on Iraq.

Institute for the Study of War, 1400 16th St., N.W., Suite
515, Washington, DC 20036; 202-293-5550; www.under
standingwar.org. Think tank founded by an advocate of the
Iraq surge; publishes weekly updates on Iraq in addition to
analyses of conditions there.

Iraq Body Count, P.O. Box 65019, Highbury Delivery
Office, Hamilton Park, London N5 9BG, United Kingdom;
www.iraqbodycount.org. Nonprofit group that bases constantly updated casualty statistics on cross-checked media

reports, hospital and morgue records, government reports
and information from nongovernmental organizations.

The List Project to Resettle Iraqi Allies, The List Project, P.O. Box 66533, Washington, DC 20035; 888-895-
5782; http://thelistproject.org. Nonprofit group founded
in 2006 that publicizes the plight of interpreters and
others facing mortal danger because of their work for the
U.S. military and civilian agencies and works to get them
U.S. visas.

New America Foundation, 1899 L St., N.W., Suite 400,
Washington, DC 20036; 202-986-2700; http://newamerica
.net. Fellows and staff members of the liberal think tank
publish analysis and commentary.

The Washington Institute (formerly, Washington Institute
for Near East Policy), 1828 L St., N.W., Suite 1050,
Washington DC 20036; 202-452-0650; www.washingtonin
stitute.org. Analyses from the specialized think tank tends
to treat Iraq in a regional context.

Analysts at the National Cybersecurity and Communications Integration Center in Arlington, Va., prepare for Cyber Storm III, a sweeping cybersecurity exercise, on Sept. 24, 2010. Some experts say a hostile country could bring the United States to a virtual standstill without firing a shot. In 2011, the number of cyber-attacks on U.S. government and private-sector websites jumped 20 percent from 2010.

From *CQ Researcher*, February 15, 2013.

4

Improving Cybersecurity

Roland Flamini

S ervices on McLean, Va.-based Capital One bank's website were blocked for more than a day in January after self-proclaimed Islamist hackers put the site out of action. A Middle Eastern protest group calling itself al-Qassam Cyber Fighters claimed responsibility — as it had for a string of cyber-attacks over the previous five months on U.S. financial institutions, including Bank of America, JPMorgan Chase, Wells Fargo and U.S. Bank.[1]

As usual, the hackers stole neither money nor confidential information. Instead, they flooded the website with e-mails to keep customers from being able to log on. Their aim: to pressure the United States to remove from YouTube a 13-minute video depicting the Prophet Mohammed in an unfavorable light. The low-budget film, "Innocence of Muslims," was made by a Los Angeles-based Egyptian, Nakoula Busseley Nakoula, a convicted embezzler, and it sparked anti-U.S. protests across the Muslim world.

But U.S. intelligence officials say Iran sponsored the bank attacks as part of an emerging cyberwar between the United States and Iran's religious leaders, although both Iran and al-Qassam denied that Iran was involved.[2]

The United States also blamed Iran for an August 2012 cyber-attack on Saudi Aramco that destroyed much of the data stored in the computers of the world's biggest oil producer, leaving behind the image of a burning American flag. The attack caused so much damage that up to 30,000 computers were compromised and had to be replaced.[3] During the past decade, cyber "war" has been about preserving the integrity of the Internet against continuous attempts to corrupt, subvert or censor it.

83

'Phishing' Is Most Common Security Breach

Phishing, or trying to acquire personal or other information by posing as a trustworthy entity — usually through e-mail — accounted for more than half of security breaches and other suspicious online activity reported in fiscal 2011 to the Department of Homeland Security. The reports came from state and federal government agencies, individuals and businesses.

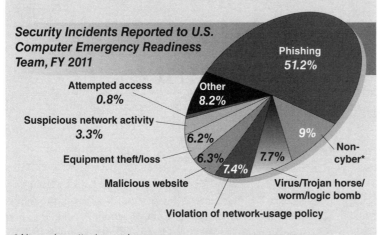

Security Incidents Reported to U.S. Computer Emergency Readiness Team, FY 2011

Phishing 51.2%

Other 8.2%

Attempted access 0.8%

Suspicious network activity 3.3%

6.2%

Equipment theft/loss 6.3%

7.4%

Malicious website

9%

Non-cyber*

7.7%

Virus/Trojan horse/ worm/logic bomb

Violation of network-usage policy

Non-cyber attacks, such as tampering with hardware, do not take place in cyberspace.

Figures do not total 100 because of rounding.

Source: "Fiscal Year 2011: Report to Congress on the Implementation of the Federal Information Security Management Act of 2002," Office of Management and Budget, March 2012, www.whitehouse.gov/sites/default/files/omb /assets/egov_docs/fy11_fisma.pdf

Just as the atomic bomb led to a nuclear arms race in the second half of the 20th century, nations are now locked in a new race to develop cyberweapons — and the technology to protect against them. Cyberwarriors across the globe constantly probe online for military and industrial secrets. Meanwhile, criminal-justice systems worldwide are fighting a complex, cross-border war against cybercriminals in which individual thieves and organized criminal enterprises steal money, intellectual property and personal records, such as credit card information. A third group, known as hacktivists, defaces the websites of institutions and organizations whose ideas they oppose.[4]

However, nailing down the attacker's identity, and often the purpose and nature of the threat, can be tricky. For instance, both Russia and China have consistently denied allegations of engaging in cyber-espionage,

making it hard to distinguish between, for instance, industrial espionage aimed at giving a foreign military manufacturer a leg up on international competitive bidding and espionage by a hostile government for military purposes.

In 2011, the number of cyberattacks on U.S. government and private-sector sites jumped 20 percent from 2010, but exact numbers remain elusive, according to U.S. Army Gen. Keith Alexander, head of the Defense Department's new Cyber Command and a key figure in the government's efforts to protect America from cyberattacks. According to Alexander, for every company that reports being hacked, another 100 don't even realize their systems have been invaded. He called the loss of industrial information and intellectual property "the greatest transfer of wealth in history."[5]

Alexander also said the wealth transfer reached $1 trillion worldwide in 2008, but the figure has been widely dismissed as grossly exaggerated. By comparison, the U.S. gross domestic product in 2012 was $15.9 trillion.[6] Alexander said U.S. companies lose $250 billion a year to criminal hackers, but that, too, has been challenged by other cybercrime experts.[7]

"We have very little idea of the size of cybercrime losses," wrote two Microsoft researchers. Most cybercrime statistics are "wholly unreliable" because of "absurdly bad statistical methods," they said.[8]

Still, many experts agree the threat is both real and large — real enough for the Obama administration to have made cybersecurity a top priority.

In October 2012, Defense Secretary Leon Panetta warned that unless the United States better defends its infrastructure — its power lines, transportation links, computer networks and other vital systems — the country could face a "cyber Pearl Harbor," referring to Japan's surprise air attack on the U.S. naval base in Hawaii that killed 2,402 people and sank or damaged 16 ships on Dec. 7, 1941.

"An aggressor nation or extremist group could use these kinds of cyber tools to gain control of critical switches," Panetta said. "They could derail passenger trains . . . , contaminate the water supply in major cities or shut down the power grid across the country."[9]

In January, Homeland Security Secretary Janet Napolitano cautioned that a "cyber 9/11" as devastating as last year's deadly Hurricane Sandy, which caused major power failures and other havoc in the Northeast, could happen "imminently." She said protective steps should be taken to "mitigate" the extent of the damage.[10]

According to reports, the annual National Intelligence Estimate warns that sustained economic espionage is chipping away at the country's economic competitiveness. Sources quoted in media stories identified France, Israel and Russia as well as China as the main aggressors in seeking economic intelligence. The reports come at a time when the Obama administration is making a determined effort to increase awareness of the need to address cyberthreats.[11]

Such dire warnings by senior government officials have been accompanied by pressure for Congress to pass the Obama administration's proposed new cybersecurity legislation. About 40 bills and resolutions addressing the issue have been stalled in Congress, partly because of political gridlock and also because many business and privacy groups oppose many of the measures. Business groups call the proposals government overreach, while privacy groups fear the measures could lead to government eavesdropping. Congress last adopted cybersecurity legislation in 2002.[12]

Major Cyber-Attacks, 1982-2013

1982 — The CIA uses a so-called logic bomb — computer code that causes software to malfunction — to cause a section of the trans-Siberian pipeline to explode after accusing the KGB of having stolen the pipeline's software technology from Canada. Several ex-KGB officials later attribute the explosion to poor construction, not an attack by the CIA.

1988 — Cornell University graduate student Robert Morris Jr. creates a computer worm that infects more than 600,000 computers at military, academic and medical facilities. He becomes the first to be convicted under the Computer Fraud and Abuse Act.

1998 — U.S. officials discover a two-year pattern of hacking, called "Moonlight Maze," of computers at the Pentagon, NASA, Energy Department and research universities. Officials trace the hacking to computers in Russia, but Russia denies involvement.

2004 — Sandia National Laboratory employee Shawn Carpenter discovers a three-year series of attacks on military and government-contractor systems that results in intelligence leaks. The attacks, called "Titan Rain," leave behind a series of "zombified" machines that make future attacks easier. Investigators suspect hackers in the Chinese military.

2004 — MyDoom e-mail worm infects 100 million Microsoft Windows systems worldwide and causes an estimated $39 billion in damage. The creator of the worm, which resurfaced in 2009, is unknown but believed to be Russian.

2007 — A pro-Kremlin group is blamed for shutting down Estonian government networks amid the country's dispute with Russia over the controversial relocation of a Soviet World War II memorial statue within Estonia.

2008 — A corrupt flash drive, infected by an unspecified foreign intelligence agency, is inserted into a U.S. military laptop and compromises sensitive information stored in military networks. The U.S. Cyber Command, responsible for protecting the military's computer systems, is created in response to the attack.

2009 — Unknown spies hack Pentagon systems and steal designs for the $300 billion Joint Strike Fighter project.

2010 — Stuxnet malware, designed by the United States and Israel, infects an Iranian nuclear facility, destroying 1,000 centrifuges.

2012 — In an unsuccessful attempt to halt Saudi oil production, Cutting Sword of Justice, a hacker group with ties to Iran, claims responsibility for infecting 30,000 computers belonging to Saudi oil supplier Aramco with the "Shamoon" virus. Partly in response to the attack, the Pentagon increases personnel for Cyber Command.

2012 — "Hacktivist" group Anonymous shuts down Swedish government websites to protest possible extradition of WikiLeaks founder Julian Assange to Sweden.

2012 — The FBI, with help from Facebook, arrests 10 members of an international cybercrime ring that the FBI says infected 11 million computers and caused $850 million in damages.

2012-2013 — Islamist hacker group al-Qassam Cyber Fighters launches denial-of-service attacks on websites of Bank of America, Capital One, Chase and other major banks to pressure the United States to remove the controversial "Innocence of Muslims" film from the Internet.

Sources: "Significant Cyber Incidents Since 2006," Center for Strategic and International Studies, January 2013, csis.org/files/publication/ 130206_Significant_Cyber_Incidents_Since_2006.pdf; various news reports

Legislation co-sponsored last year by Sen. Joseph I. Lieberman, I-Conn., included many of the Obama administration's cyberproposals and also would have established voluntary cybersecurity standards for U.S. businesses. The Senate killed the measure largely because of opposition from Republicans and the U.S. Chamber of Commerce, the nation's largest business lobby. Congress last adopted cybersecurity legislation in 2002.

The most recent proposal — the Cybersecurity Act of 2012, co-sponsored by Sens. Susan Collins, R-Maine, and Joseph I. Lieberman, I-Conn. — included much of the Obama administration's recommendations and would have established voluntary cybersecurity standards for U.S. businesses. The Senate killed the measure twice — once in the summer and again in November — largely because Republicans and the U.S. Chamber of Commerce, the nation's largest business lobby, opposed it.

The measure "would have put a federal agent inside most . . . businesses' data centers," says Jody Westby, a leading cybersecurity consultant and adjunct professor at the Georgia Institute of Technology, who doesn't oppose some form of regulation but was critical of the proposal.

The fact that any company that signed up for the government's protective measures would have come under the surveillance of the Department of Homeland Security's cybersecurity division raised privacy issues. Homeland Security uses a network intrusion system called Einstein to monitor all federal agency networks for potential attacks. But, according to an analysis prepared for Congress, the system "raises significant privacy implications, a concern shared by the Department of Homeland Security (DHS), interest groups, academia, and the general public." DHS has developed

some measures to minimize these concerns, but there are still objections.[13]

Such legislation also would inevitably lag behind evolving cyberthreats, opponents say, because the bureaucracy would not move quickly enough to stay abreast of ever-changing cyber developments.

In the absence of legislation, President Obama in February issued his long-expected executive order enabling the DHS and the National Security Agency (NSA) to share with the private sector unclassified "reports of cyberthreats to the U.S. homeland that identify a specific targeted entity" — and even classified information in the case of threats to critical infrastructure companies.

The 38-page order includes specific instructions on protecting privacy when the information flow goes the other way and companies share information about their customers with the government. The NSA's chief privacy officer and its officer of civil rights and civil liberties are specifically charged with supervising the privacy implications. The order also urges companies to "benefit from a competitive market for [cybersecurity] services and products."[14]

Civil liberties groups gave Obama's order conditional approval but said they would want to see how it would work in practice. The order "rightly focuses on cybersecurity solutions that don't negatively impact civil liberties," said Michelle Richardson, legislative counsel at the American Civil Liberties Union.

Obama's action came in for criticism from House Republicans even before it was issued. Sen. Charles R. Grassley, R-Iowa, said Obama was going down "a dangerous road" in circumventing the legislative process. House Intelligence Committee Chairman Mike Rogers, R-Mich., and C.A. Dutch Ruppersberger, D-Md., were due to re-introduce the Cyber Intelligence Sharing and Protection Act (CISPA), which passed the House in the last Congress but failed to gain support in the Senate.[15]

Cybercriminals who break into online accounts and steal money and identities are no less a concern than state-sponsored attackers. Cybercrime should be addressed with more determination, says Westby. Currently, cybertheft is "the perfect crime," she says, because few law enforcement officers work on the issue, so when security experts seek help from authorities, the police are "too stretched" to be of much assistance.

Moreover, she says, only about 50 countries worldwide have harmonized their cybercrime laws, and bilateral extradition agreements are slow and archaic — taking months to execute "when minutes matter."

Cybercriminals exploit such territorial differences. "It is not uncommon for a cybercriminal to reside in one country, have drop zones or caches in several countries and attack victims using a 'botnet' consisting of . . . computers spread around the globe" infected with malicious software, Westby says. The Federal Bureau of Investigation (FBI) — aided by Facebook — recently broke up a major operation that reflected the global dimensions of cybercrime. The 10 arrested ring members were from Bosnia, Croatia, Macedonia, New Zealand, Peru, the United Kingdom and the United States. In one of the largest cybercrime hauls in history, the group had infected 11 million computers worldwide and stolen more than $850 million.[16]

In another case, reported this month, software producer Microsoft and Symantec, an information-security firm, reportedly disrupted a global cybercrime ring that was secretly controlling hundreds of thousands of individuals' computers in an operation known as the Bamital Botnet.[17] It used a "click fraud" scheme, which is the fraudulent use of pay-per-click online advertising.

Time is of the essence in fighting cybercrime, says veteran cybersecurity specialist J. Thomas Malatesta, chief operating officer of Ziklag Systems, a Washington, D.C.-based mobile and wireless security company. "The technology just keeps getting better and better, and we're always trying to keep up with the bad guys," he says. "The threat is compounded because it has moved into mobile phones, and every time people access apps the potential to import malware [malicious software] is huge."

While cybercrime can damage individual and corporate bank accounts, cyber-espionage can potentially undermine the economy. Cyberspies who steal intellectual property so foreign companies can produce U.S.-designed goods more cheaply can cost millions of American jobs as well as American companies millions of dollars, according to a 2011 report from the Office of the National Counterintelligence Executive, part of a federal office that focuses on foreign threats and espionage damage.

The report said China and Russia were trying to build up their economies using pilfered industrial secrets.

The Chinese "are the world's most active and persistent perpetrators of economic espionage," the report said. And Russian intelligence sources "are conducting a range of activities to collect economic information and technology from U.S. targets."[18]

Chinese hackers represent a serious and "increasingly potent" concern for companies and government agencies with potentially sensitive data, said the U.S.-China Economic and Security Review Commission, the congressional watchdog on bilateral trade with China and its security implications.[19]

In another recent incident, several leading American news organizations reportedly were hacked by the Chinese after publishing stories about high-level corruption and vast wealth accumulated by relatives of top Chinese leaders.[20]

But cyber-espionage can also be a two-way street. Two years ago the United States teamed up with Israel to infect computers at an Iranian nuclear facility with a malignant program called Stuxnet. The virus destroyed 1,000 of its 5,000 centrifuges, causing delays in Iran's controversial uranium enrichment program.[21] Although the secret attack did not derail the program, Stuxnet was a game changer, because it served notice that the United States had the technology and will to retaliate against cyber-attacks.

As policymakers and security specialists debate whether cyber-attacks threaten national security, here are some of the questions being asked:

Are doomsday cyberwar scenarios exaggerated?

In his best-selling 2010 book *Cyber War*, former White House anti-terrorism and cybersecurity adviser Richard A. Clarke maintained that it would take an enemy only 15 minutes to create chaos across the United States by crippling communications networks and the power grid. In his "Judgment Day" scenario, hackers would shut down or disable networks in the Pentagon, air traffic control towers, industrial plants and railway systems, causing train and plane crashes, cutting off water supplies, crippling the banking system and plunging the nation into darkness.

A recent cybersecurity report, prepared with the participation of the U.S. Naval War College, quotes U.S. intelligence officials as saying that "Russian and Chinese hackers are already hacking into U.S. electricity networks and inserting malware that they could later activate (i.e., in a future conflict with the United States) to shut down the electric grid."[22] President Obama echoed some of those same concerns in a July op-ed in *The Wall Street Journal*, in which he urged the Senate to pass the Collins-Lieberman bill. "It would be the height of irresponsibility to leave a digital back door wide open to our cyber-adversaries," the president warned.[23]

Another form of attack — creating "digital wildfires" by spreading false information through the Internet — could create public panic that could cause economic damage, according to the 2013 "Global Risks" report of the World Economic Forum, a major annual gathering of world financial leaders in Davos, Switzerland. "Our hyper-connected world could also enable the rapid viral spread of information that is either intentionally or unintentionally misleading or provocative, with serious consequences," the report said.[24]

Still, some experts doubt both the likelihood and impact of a large-scale cyber-attack. Their doubts are based partly on the Cold War concept of "mutually assured destruction," in which the devastating power of weapons held by adversaries discouraged their use and helped to prevent nuclear conflict.

"I tend to think the threat [of wide-scale cyber-attack] is overstated," says Paul Rosenzweig, a visiting fellow at the Center for Legal and Judicial Studies at the conservative Heritage Foundation, which has criticized Obama's approach to cybersecurity. "Would the Chinese want to do it? They could, but we would then turn off Beijing. It's a small possibility as an adjunct to a real-life kinetic

Federal Agencies Report Huge Rise in Attacks

Security breaches and suspicious online activities at federal agencies jumped 12-fold from 2005 to 2011, according to the Department of Homeland Security.

Security Incidents Reported by Federal Agencies to the U.S. Computer Emergency Readiness Team, Department of Homeland Security, FY 2005 and FY 2011

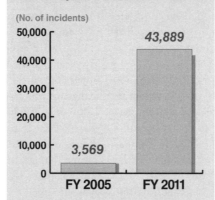

(No. of incidents)

Sources: "Fiscal Year 2007: Report to Congress on Implementation of the Federal Information Security Management Act of 2002," Office of Management and Budget, 2008, p. 10, www.whitehouse.gov/sites/default/files/omb/assets/omb/inforeg/reports/2007_fisma_report.pdf; "Fiscal Year 2011: Report to Congress on the Implementation of the Federal Information Security Management Act of 2002," Office of Management and Budget, March 2012, p. 17, www.whitehouse.gov/sites/default/files/omb/assets/egov_docs/fy11_fisma.pdf

war. But an independent cyberwar is not happening."

Rosenzweig calls talk of a cyber-attack on infrastructure a scare tactic. For some people, "there's value in enhancing a threat because it could lead to more government regulation," he says.

Larry Clinton, president of the Internet Security Alliance, a trade association of cybersecurity companies, believes a Chinese attack would be economically counterproductive. "Why would the Chinese want to destabilize the U.S. economy by taking down our electric grid?" he argues. "China owns half our debt, and destabilizing our economy would destabilize China's economy."

And Jerry Brito, director of the Technology Policy Program at George Mason University, wrote, "There is no evidence that anyone has ever died as a result of a cyber-attack. And the evidence of cyber-attacks causing physical destruction are limited to very subtle and targeted attacks — like the Stuxnet worm that affected Iran's nuclear enrichment program, likely carried out by the United States."[25]

James Lewis, a cybersecurity specialist at the Center for Strategic and International Studies (CSIS), a think tank in Washington, contended that Obama's "digital back door" is actually many back doors. He argued that the national security threat to the U.S. infrastructure from cyber-attacks is oversimplified and "overstated." Critical infrastructures, especially in large economies, are "distributed, diverse, redundant and self-healing," he wrote, "rendering them less vulnerable to attack. In all cases, cyber-attacks are less effective and less disruptive than physical attacks."[26]

Lewis does not rule out the possibility of a major cyberattack, but he is skeptical about its strategic value. "If you are China or Iran, blacking out the East Coast for a week may not be much good and might actually escalate any conflict in harmful ways," he says in an e-mail. "I still don't believe in cyber catastrophes, but that doesn't mean we should accept being largely defenseless."

Should the U.S. government impose cybersecurity standards on the private sector?

In defending his proposed cybersecurity law last year, Lieberman warned that 87 percent of small and medium-size businesses are unprotected and "don't even have written cybersecurity policies." Nevertheless, the Senate twice defeated the Collins-Lieberman proposal, even though it only called for voluntary cybersecurity standards for companies.

Obama's executive order does not mandate security standards for privately owned companies that oversee the country's national infrastructure, which the president calls, "a strategic national asset." It instructs the Department of Homeland Security and other federal agencies to inform the private sector of any cyberthreats against them in a timely manner. But the president's critics still favor self-regulation by the private sector over government involvement.

"A regulatory approach is wrong for cybersecurity," says the Heritage Foundation's Rosenzweig, who says he prefers that the private sector agree to its own set of rules. In addition, he says regulations would "likely harm innovation" because the government would in effect be dictating which security measures should be developed, "to the detriment of perhaps better solutions."

Rosenzweig believes it would be a short step from voluntary regulations to mandatory rules. He argues that the private sector would be trapped into costly security measures. Besides, he contends, it would not be wise to establish public standards "because the bad guys will know what they have to beat."

Raphael Mudge, founder of the security firm Strategic Cyber, voiced similar reservations. "I've got these regulatory issues," he said at a recent cybersecurity conference. "What's going to bite me if I invite the government in?"[27]

The increased-cost argument was borne out by a Bloomberg report that said it would cost $344.6 million

Mark Fabro, a training consultant for the Department of Homeland Security, explains how computer networks can be exploited at a cybersecurity defense facility at the Idaho National Laboratory in Idaho Falls, on Sept. 29, 2011. The average computer system is infected by a virus for 416 days before being detected, according to a recent study by the Virginia cyberprotection firm Mandiant.

REUTERS/Jim Urquhar

a year for a utility and energy company to install and maintain cybersecurity technology that could repel 95 percent of cyber-attacks.[28]

The business community favors something akin to the Cyber Intelligence Sharing and Protection Act, passed by the Republican-controlled House in 2011 but never sent to the Senate, where the Democratic majority favored a different measure. The House bill focused on allowing companies to exchange threat information with each other and with the government "without the threat of frivolous lawsuits, public disclosure and more regulation," said Ann M. Beauchesne, vice president of the Chamber of Commerce's National Security and Emergency Preparedness Department.

"Policymakers should not complicate or duplicate existing industry security standards with mandates and bureaucracies, even if couched in language that would mischaracterize these standards as 'voluntary,' " Beauchesne said last October.[29]

But Obama, who threatened to veto the House measures, argued in his *Wall Street Journal* article that "simply sharing more information is not enough. Ultimately, this is about security gaps that have to be filled."[30]

Obama's view has considerable support in the cybersecurity community. "We need legislation for the primary reason that our adversaries are hitting us very, very hard," says Malatesta of Ziklag Systems. "It's very painful for companies and other entities to have information stolen seven days a week, and there needs to be some kind of baseline. But in essence, getting everybody to think the same is like herding cats."

Allan Friedman, who follows cybersecurity at the Brookings Institution think tank in Washington, agrees regulation is probably needed but says it should be minimal. "We probably need minimum standards of security for the private sector, especially to defend against fraud and espionage," he says. But any regulation "runs counter to the Internet's origins of being a medium of free expression."

Ironically, while the Obama administration was pushing American businesses to accept cybersecurity regulations, U.S. policymakers at the U.N.-sponsored World Conference on International Telecommunications in Dubai refused — along with delegates from several European countries — to endorse a new global telecommunications treaty that included some Internet issues. The United States said including the Internet in a long-standing international agreement on radio and telecommunications treaty opened the door to government regulation and potential censorship of the Internet.[31]

Should the United Nations regulate the Internet?

Currently, the Internet is lightly regulated by three national and international entities.

The Internet Corporation for Assigned Names and Numbers (ICANN), an independent institution created in 1998 under contract to the U.S. Department of Commerce, runs the URL address system. The Internet Engineering Task Force, a semiformal group of leading computer scientists, oversees standards and protocols. Web design is an ongoing process conducted by the World Wide Web Consortium (W3C), an independent international group with offices around the world.

Although all three organizations operate primarily through consensus, on most issues American corporations and groups — such as Google, Microsoft and various Internet lobbying associations — have had the strongest influence.

"It's not much of a stretch to say the Internet works as well as it does precisely because it has managed to stay largely immune from interference and oversight from traditional governments — slow moving, expensive,

partisan government," wrote Larry Downes, an Internet industry analyst.[32]

While the United States and most of Europe staunchly defend the Internet's independence, governments — especially those without a strong free-speech tradition — increasingly seek to control the Internet. For instance, China, Russia, Tajikistan and Uzbekistan want the U.N. General Assembly to adopt what they have termed the International Code of Conduct for Information Security. "Laws are necessary to keep the virtual world in order," declared the *China Daily*. "In this age of globalization, free flow of information is precious, but not without obeying laws."[33]

Beijing would clearly welcome an internationally sanctioned regulatory structure to control its 538 million Internet users, as would Moscow.[34] And some U.S. experts also believe global accords are needed to combat cybercrime.

"There has to be some international agreement because otherwise everything will fall apart," says Westby of the Georgia Institute of Technology. For instance, she says, it's urgent to speed up the extradition process for transferring criminals from one country to another to stand trial. "The existing framework for getting assistance internationally is archaic."

However, the Heritage Foundation's Rosenzweig is skeptical about international agreements. "The U.S. will abide by the rules, and the others will honor them in the breach," he says.

In December, the International Telecommunications Union (ITU) — a 150-year-old organization that coordinates global telephone intercommunication and is now a U.N. agency — held a conference in Dubai to update its latest regulations, which were adopted in 1988 before the huge popularity of cell phones and the advent of the Internet. However, the United States and some other Western nations refused to ratify the revised treaty because it gave the ITU a role in managing the Internet. For example, U.S. negotiators said, a provision allowing the ITU to regulate spam would open the way to controlling content.

"The Internet has given the world unimaginable economic and social benefit during these past 24 years. All without U.N. regulation," declared Terry Kramer, a high-tech business executive who led the U.S. delegation. "We candidly cannot support an ITU treaty that is inconsistent with the multistakeholder model of Internet governance."[35]

The U.K. and Canada also refused to sign the treaty, as did several European countries, but the pact was nevertheless adopted, 89-55. Because it is nonbinding, Kramer shrugged off the fact that the treaty will go into effect in 2015.

Opponents of U.N. involvement portrayed the vote as an American victory. "Good news everyone: The United Nations didn't take over the Internet!" declared one writer. After 12 days of debate, "absolutely nothing is different, at least if you live in the United States."[36]

Others aren't so sure. Because Russia and China voted for the treaty, along with many developing African and Latin American countries, some fear that the resulting division could undermine the role that a fast, universally accessible Internet plays in the growth of the global economy. The U.K.-based *Financial Times* said the result "raises the prospect of a split in the international community pursuing different objectives, potentially undermining the power of the Internet to spur global economic growth."[37]

The Economist magazine, also based in the U.K., called the dispute over the new Internet regulatory system "a new Cold War."

BACKGROUND

Early Cyber-Attacks

The word "hacker" predates computers. It once meant someone incompetent at work. The word is now fixed in computer-speak to describe someone who breaks into a system illegally.

Newsweek is credited with first using the word "hackers" in that context in a September 1983 story titled "Beware: Hackers at Play," which described the FBI arrest of the Milwaukee 414s, a group of young hackers accused of breaking into more than 60 computers, including those at the Los Alamos National Laboratory and the Memorial Sloan-Kettering Cancer Center. Although group members were released without charges, the incident focused public attention on computer crime.[38]

The 1983 movie "WarGames," a box office hit in which a high school student hacks into the computer system of the North American Aerospace Defense

Robert Morris Jr. leaves Federal Court in Syracuse, N.Y., on Jan. 22, 1990. The Cornell University computer science student created malware that infected more than 600,000 computers at American military, academic and medical research facilities. He was convicted and sentenced to three years of community service and fined $10,000.

Command in Colorado Springs, Colo., inevitably triggered an increase in hacker activity — and raised fears of an accidental launch of America's intercontinental ballistic missiles (ICBMs).

By 1984, concern about the criminal dimension to the newly developed Internet was strong enough that Congress passed the Computer Fraud and Abuse Act (CFAA), the first legislation making it a crime to break into computer systems. But the law lacked teeth. For one thing, it didn't cover juveniles. Also, it required proof that a computer had been accessed without authorization, effectively blocking cases involving employees. The legislation also did not criminalize cases where the suspect did not tamper with the data, which effectively meant data stored on a computer could be viewed by a hacker without penalty.

The act was used in 1988 to prosecute Robert Morris Jr., a Cornell University computer science student who created the Morris "worm," an early piece of malware that infected more than 600,000 computers at military, academic and medical research facilities across the country. Morris was convicted and sentenced to three years of probation and 400 hours of community service and fined $10,000 plus the cost of his supervision.[39]

In 1987 President Ronald Reagan signed the Computer Security Act, a tougher law that required security guidelines for federal computer systems but limited the Pentagon's role in cybersecurity to matters of national defense.

C H R O N O L O G Y

1990s *Concern about cybersecurity is debated in U.S. political, economic and military spheres.*

1995 Two movies, "The Net" and "Hackers," reflect rising public perception of cybersecurity threats.

1996 CIA Director John Deutsch tells Congress that foreign organized crime is behind cyber-attacks on the U.S. private sector.

2000-2010 *Cyber-attacks increase in scope and frequency, mostly by China, Russia and Iran. Little progress is made in developing defensive safeguards.*

2000 "I Love You" self-replicating worm spreads quickly through the Internet. Disguised as an e-mail message, it infects millions of Windows computers causing them to malfunction. By 2002, the worm will have earned the world record as the most virulent at that time. Its creator, a hacker in the Philippines, is arrested but later released because the country has no laws against malware.

2002 In response to the 9/11 terrorist attacks, President George W. Bush announces formation of the Department of Homeland Security, which combines several border protection and law enforcement entities (Sept. 20). The new department — along with the FBI and Defense Department — helps to monitor U.S. cybersecurity.

2007 Hackers penetrate Defense Secretary Robert Gates' unclassified e-mail system. . . . Attacks on other U.S. government computer systems result in the theft of 10-20 terabytes of files — more data than in the Library of Congress.

2008 Bush establishes the Comprehensive National Cybersecurity Initiative (CNCI), a program to protect federal computer systems and operations (Jan. 20). . . . *Newsweek* reports that hackers stole foreign policy information from the presidential campaign computers of Sens. Barack Obama and John McCain; computer experts on the Obama team suspect Russia or China. . . . A foreign intelligence agent infects several thousand computers used by the Tampa-based U.S. Central Command, which oversees U.S. forces in Iraq and Afghanistan; the Pentagon calls it "the most significant breach of U.S. military computers ever" (Nov. 6).

2009 Newly inaugurated President Obama orders a 60-day, comprehensive review of U.S. cybersecurity policy and development of a strategy to secure America's digital infrastructure (Feb. 10). . . . Hackers in China hit Google and up to 34 other U.S. companies, stealing significant technological secrets (Dec. 29).

2010 United States and Israel attack Iran's nuclear plant at Natanz with the virulent Stuxnet cyberworm and destroy 1,000 of the facility's 5,000 centrifuges.

2011-Present *Rising concern over cyber-attacks results in more than three dozen cybersecurity bills being introduced in Congress, but none is enacted due to partisan disagreements.*

Jan. 1, 2011 Annual survey of more than U.S. 600 companies says cyber-attacks cost them a total of $73.8 million in 2010 — down from $237 million the previous year, reflecting beefed up cybersecurity and an amended definition of intrusions. . . . President Obama sends proposed legislation to Congress requiring private companies providing critical infrastructure, such as water and power, to protect their online systems from hackers. It is never adopted.

2012 U.S. House of Representatives passes Cyber Intelligence Sharing and Protection Act, which would make sharing information about cybersecurity easier for the government and private sector (April 26), but the Senate fails to vote on it. . . . Gen. Keith Alexander, director of the National Security Agency, says cyber thieves have stolen an estimated $1 trillion, calling it "the greatest transfer of wealth in history." Most experts consider the figure inflated.

2013 Pentagon announces a fivefold increase in its cybersecurity personnel in order to face growing cyberthreats and to be able to strike back at attackers. . . . *The New York Times* says Chinese hackers penetrated its computers, stealing passwords and staff e-mail exchanges. *The Washington Post* reports hacking is constant hazard with all Beijing-based media.

Still, in passing the Computer Security Act Congress rejected the Reagan administration's vision of the law, which was to put the Pentagon in charge of cybersecurity for both the public and private sectors. That left the CFAA as the template for most future cybercrime legislation over the next three decades.

In 1994, for example, the CFAA was amended to stiffen the sentences of those who transmitted malicious code, or malcode, such as computer viruses or worms. Two years later the National Information Infrastructure Protection Act extended CFAA further, allowing prosecution of anyone viewing computer information without authorization, regardless of whether it was for financial gain. Also in 1994, the Communications Assistance for Law Enforcement Act required Internet service providers to allow law enforcement officers to keep individuals under electronic surveillance.

The 2002 Cyber Security Enhancement Act, passed soon after the Sept. 11 terrorist attacks, gave law enforcement officials greater access — without a warrant — to personal data stored by Internet service providers. The Federal Information Security Management Act, also passed in 2002, established requirements for protecting government information technology systems and data.

Those were the last major cybersecurity measures enacted by Congress despite the introduction of numerous proposals over the past decade, including more than 40 measures just in the last Congress. In May 2011, the Obama administration sent a package of legislative proposals to Congress. That package, wrote Rita Tehan, an information research specialist at the Congressional Research Service, gave "the federal government new authority to ensure that corporations that own the assets most critical for the nation's security and economic prosperity are adequately addressing the risks posed by cybersecurity threats."[40]

Obama and members of his administration lobbied heavily in favor of the bill. In his *Wall Street Journal* op-ed urging the Senate to adopt it, Obama wrote, "Foreign governments, criminal syndicates and lone individuals are probing our financial, energy and public safety systems every day."[41] Differing views about the role of government led to the measure's defeat, however. Thus, the president issued his executive order calling on infrastructure companies to voluntarily adopt a minimum set of government-created security standards.[42]

Cyber-Espionage

In 1998, officials discovered that over a three-year period data had been stolen from computers at NASA, the Defense and Energy departments and several weapons laboratories. The source of the attacks, dubbed the "Moonlight Maze," was never proved, but the Russian government was suspected, making the attack the first likely case of state-sponsored hacking — cyberespionage — against another country.[43]

In January 2000, the Clinton administration released its cybersecurity strategy, which took a tough stand on investigating and responding to foreign and domestic cyberattacks. However, the document faded away after civil libertarians and privacy groups criticized it as intrusive and an attempt to drastically expand government surveillance of the nation's communications network.

In 2004, hackers stole information from military laboratories, NASA, the World Bank, Lockheed Martin — a major defense contractor — and the Lockheed Martin-operated Sandia National Laboratories, a contractor in New Mexico for the U.S. Department of Energy's National Nuclear Security Administration. Shawn Carpenter, a computer specialist at Sandia, tracked the attackers to a government research facility in China's Guangdong Province. Code-named "Titan Rain," the attacks are considered some of the most destructive yet detected. As often happens, few details of the attack were revealed, but press reports said a great deal of computerized information was stolen and damaged.[44]

In 2005, hackers penetrated the database of the Federal Deposit Insurance Corp. — a federal banking agency — taking the Social Security numbers, salary data and other personal information of some 6,000 current and former agency employees.

Then in 2007, the unclassified e-mail account of then-Secretary of Defense Robert Gates was hacked, and in 2008 thousands of computers at the U.S. Central Command in Tampa, Fla., were infected with a virus. In 2009, cyber spies hacked into the Pentagon computer system and stole information concerning the $300 billion Joint Strike Fighter project — the Defense Department's costliest weapons program ever.[45]

According to Microsoft, attacks on defense agencies quadrupled between 2006 and 2009, while attempts to penetrate federal civilian agencies jumped from 20,000 in

How Internet Activists Overcome Censorship

The Chinese have a word for it: Fanqiang

In war-torn Syria, where the regime of Bashar Assad has shut down the Internet, as many as 40,000 people still manage to access Facebook, Twitter and other social networks, thanks to software supplied by the West.[1]

One censorship-evading program, Psiphon, — was created at the University of Toronto with help from the U.S. Department of State.[2] Psiphon is "the iPod of circumvention. It works very simply," says Rafal Rohozinski, who headed its development. "All it exists to do is to give you access to blocked content." Once the user quits the site, he says, Psiphon leaves no trace of the visit.

Psiphon and similar software reflect the diametrically opposed challenges cybersecurity poses to governments: Authoritarian regimes want to control citizens' access to the Internet; democratic governments — and especially the United States — are committed to keeping it open to all.

In February 2011, Secretary of State Hillary Rodham Clinton called the Internet "the public space of the 21st century" and said "the United States continues to help people in oppressive Internet environments get around filters, stay one step ahead of the censors, the hackers and the thugs who beat them up or imprison them for what they say online."[3] The State Department supports the training of Internet activists and organizes online public awareness campaigns about censorship and surveillance.[4]

Since 2008, Congress has allotted $95 million to the State Department for global Internet-freedom efforts; the department has requested $27.5 million for 2013.[5]

China, with 538 million Internet users — more than the United States, Japan, the United Kingdom and Germany combined — is a prime target of U.S. circumvention efforts. But so are some other countries that routinely block access to websites, such as Iran, North Korea, Saudi Arabia and Myanmar (Burma). For a while during the 2011 upheavals in Egypt, the government of deposed President Hosni Mubarak shut off the Internet to prevent dissident groups from coordinating plans.

Keeping the Internet uncensored is a continuous cat-and-mouse game in which programmers offer penetration tools either free or at nominal cost to tech-savvy bloggers and students across the globe, from Beijing to Riyadh.

Such "proxy" software allows locked-out citizens to — as the Chinese put it — *fanqiang*, or "scale the wall." That wall is better known as the "Great Firewall," the unofficial name of China's Golden Shield Project, its online censorship system.

U.S.-based members of the Falun Gong, a controversial religious sect that is persecuted in China, developed the anti-censorship tool Freegate, which uses a collection of portals called Dynaweb to evade government blocking. If a portal detects an attempt to block information, users are

2008 to 30,000 in 2009. At least 100 foreign intelligence agencies "have sought to break into U.S. computer networks," according to Microsoft.[46]

The number of attempted hacks into the Defense Department's 15,000 networks has grown exponentially since 2005, when the Pentagon reportedly logged more than 79,000 attempted intrusions.[47] By July 2011, they were occurring "thousands of times a day," according to then-Deputy Secretary of Defense William Lynn.[48]

In the 2008 presidential race, not even the candidates were immune from hacking. Both the Obama and McCain campaigns said they were hacked, allegedly by China. A Chinese embassy spokesman denied the charge, calling it

"unwarranted, irresponsible and misleading and intentionally fabricated to fan China-threat sensations."[49] In November 2002, President Bush signed legislation establishing the Department of Homeland Security, consolidating 22 separate government agencies charged with, among other things, securing the country's borders and preventing future 9/11-style attacks.

The measure called for establishment of a National Cyber Security Center within DHS charged with tightening security in federal agencies. Among other approaches, the department was to decrease the number of government Internet connections in order to reduce entry points for cyber-intruders. The department was shifted to another portal, a process that continues until the information reaches its destination.

To compensate for its limited Internet access, China offers its Web users homegrown alternatives that it can control, such as Baidu, China's answer to Google, and Tencent, the country's dominant portal for instant messaging and social networking. Rebecca MacKinnon, a specialist on China's Internet and a senior fellow at the New America Foundation, a liberal think tank, says about 5 percent of Chinese Internet users take advantage of proxy software to overcome China's Web censorship. Besides activists, journalists and some academics, however, most Chinese are only vaguely aware that the Internet is censored in China, she says, and choose Chinese software out of loyalty to a national product.

But China's Internet censorship takes surprising turns, as many observers have noted, sometimes with amusement. When Chen Guangcheng, a blind Chinese human rights activist, sought asylum in the U.S. Embassy in Beijing, the story was headline news worldwide, but not in China.

To prevent average Chinese people from finding out, the authorities promptly blocked such obvious search terms as Guangcheng's name, initials and hometown. However, taking

Besides academics, journalists and human rights activists like Chen Guangcheng, most Chinese are only vaguely aware that the Internet is censored in China.

AFP/Getty Images/Saul Loeb

no chances — and aware of the worldwide popularity of U.S. movies — they even blocked access to the poignant 1994 prison movie "The Shawshank Redemption," about an innocent man unjustly imprisoned for life.

— *Roland Flamini*

[1] Matthew Braga, "Canadian encryption software beats Syrian regime's censors," *The Globe and Mail*, July 16, 2012, www.theglobeandmail.com/technology/tech-news/c1anadian-encryption-software-beats-syrian-regimes-censors/article4418613/. For background on the Syrian conflict, see Kenneth Jost, "Unrest in the Arab World," *CQ Researcher*, Feb. 1, 2013, pp. 105-132; and Roland Flamini, "Turmoil in the Arab World," *CQ Global Researcher*, May 3, 2011, pp. 209-236. For background on social networking, see Marcia Clemmitt, "Social Media Explosion," *CQ Researcher*, Jan. 25, 2013, pp. 81-104, and Marcia Clemmitt, "Social Networking," *CQ Researcher*, Sept. 17, 2010, pp. 749-772.

[2] Braga, *op. cit.*

[3] Dominic Rushe, "U.S. to spend $30m to break Web censorship in repressive regimes such as China and Iran," *The Guardian*, May 11, 2011, www.guardian.co.uk/world/2011/may/11/us-30m-fighting-internet-censorship.

[4] Rebecca MacKinnon, "The Shawshank Prevention," *Foreign Policy*, May 2, 2012, www.foreignpolicy.com/articles/2012/05/02shawshank_prevention.

[5] Thomas Lum, *et al.*, "China, Internet Freedom, and U.S. Policy," Congressional Research Service, July 13, 2012, www.fas.org/sgp/crs/row/R42601.pdf.

given overall responsibility for overseeing cybersecurity in the private sector when the need arose.

The Department of Homeland Security, working with the National Institute of Standards and Technology (NIST) and the Office of Management and Budget (OMB), is responsible for defending all "dot gov" websites. DHS says the Cyber Security Center coordinates operations of the six federal cyber centers, including those of the FBI and the Department of Homeland Security's Office of Intelligence and Analysis. The U.S. Cyber Command, created in 2010, is responsible for protecting the military's computer systems. In January, however, Pentagon officials said they planned to expand the force fivefold to extend

its defensive posture to a retaliatory capability against foreign cyber-adversaries.[50] In interviews, officials said the national mission teams would operate against targets overseas.

'Hactivist' Headaches

Hackers with a cause — or "hacktivists" — target both government and private computer networks. Since 2010, the notorious hacktivist group Anonymous has attacked targets ranging from the Syrian regime to Sony, the big entertainment and electronics corporation. One of the group's most high-profile campaigns went after opponents of the 2010 release by Wikileaks editor Julian

Easter Eggs, Honeypots and Botnets

Cyberspeak is a language of its own.

Like every other type of technology, cybersecurity has its own jargon. Sometimes referred to as cyberspeak, high-tech experts use it describe what they do and what kind of threats they face trying to keep cyberspace safe. Here are some of the most commonly used terms:

- **Black hat/white hat** — Just like old Hollywood Westerns, the cyberworld has good guys and bad guys. The black hats are hackers who penetrate computer systems to destroy or steal files. The white hats are hackers, too, but they ride to the rescue, testing website security and warning of potential breaches.
- **Botnet** — A network of computers controlled by cybercriminals using malicious software.
- **DoS (denial of service) attack** — An attack designed to shut down a website by flooding it with traffic, causing it to crash. A DDoS (distributed denial of service) attack utilizes multiple machines to launch a denial of service attack.
- **Drive-by download** — A computer program — often a virus — that copies itself onto someone's computer without their knowledge while that person is visiting a website or viewing an HTML e-mail message.
- **Easter Egg** — Computer code hidden within an application that can be triggered by a certain action.

- **Firewall** — Software or hardware that monitors information coming from the Internet and blocks or allows it, depending on the user's settings.
- **Honeypot** — An isolated and monitored computer, data or network site that attracts and traps invading malware — malicious software — in order to detect or counteract unauthorized use of a computer system.
- **Malware** — Any harmful, malicious software that can attack a computer, such as viruses, worms and Trojan horses.
- **Munging** — Disguising an e-mail address so it is blocked from spam programs looking for e-mail addresses. Munging also refers to manipulating data to change its final form.
- **Trojan horse, virus, worm** — A destructive software program that masquerades as a legitimate application. Once downloaded it can either introduce a virus or create access for malicious users to steal information.
- **Zero day attack** — An attack on a software vulnerability that has been discovered but has not yet been repaired. Often this occurs when hackers discover a vulnerability before the software's creators have found it.

— Roland Flamini

Assange of thousands of U.S. State Department cables.[51] For example, after the Swedish government sought to extradite Assange in connection with an alleged rape, Anonymous brought down the Swedish attorney general's computer system. The rape charge was seen by Wikileaks supporters as a trumped-up attempt to discredit Assange and has since been dropped.

In mid-January of last year, parts of the Justice Department's website were hacked, along with the sites of several entertainment companies, shortly after federal officials shut down Megaupload.com, charging that the file-sharing site violated anti-piracy laws by allowing users to illegally access movies and music. Anonymous claimed responsibility. Separately, the Energy Department electronics network also was hacked in mid-January 2013. The identity of the hackers was unclear. The agency said no classified data were compromised.[52]

In 2010, Google and more than 30 other U.S. companies doing business in China were collectively robbed of secret technological data. The attacks had originated in China, even as the regime imposed new regulations on Google that the Internet search engine said amounted to censorship.

Secretary of State Hillary Rodham Clinton sharply criticized such tactics. "Countries that restrict free access to information or violate basic rights of Internet users risk walling themselves off from the progress of the next century."[53] The State Department has intensified its program to devise software to circumvent cybercensorship in tightly controlled regimes such as China and Iran.

CURRENT SITUATION

Chinese Espionage

China continues to conduct pervasive cyber-attacks to collect information from U.S. military, government and corporate sites — primarily oil, gas and other energy companies — according to a series of U.S. government reports.[54]

The Chinese "are the world's most active and persistent perpetrators of economic espionage," said a report from the U.S. Office of the National Counterintelligence Executive. "Chinese attempts to collect U.S. technological and economic information will continue at a high level and will represent a growing and persistent threat to U.S. economic security."[55]

When the computer system at the White House Military Office was penetrated on Sept. 30, 2012, media reports linked the hackers to the Chinese government, although the White House did not mention Chinese involvement. Still, defense officials say Pentagon sites continue to be targeted by Chinese hackers. "Their level of effort against the Department of Defense is constant," said Rear Admiral Samuel Cox, head of Naval Intelligence.[56]

Since 2005, successive annual reports to Congress by the U.S.-China Economic and Security Review Commission have detailed Chinese intrusions demonstrating the "patience and calculated nature" of the threat.[57] In 2009 the commission said China was "conducting a long-term, sophisticated, computer network exploitation campaign" using "access to high-end software development resources . . . and an ability to sustain activities inside targeted networks, sometimes over a period of months."[58]

Experts have identified three groups of Chinese hackers — those directly under government control, those at universities and quasi-government agencies and freelance "patriotic" hackers, who are permitted to function as long as their targets are American or European. The intruders are using customized tools provided by Chinese "black hat" programmers — individuals who support illegal hacking. "The depth of resources necessary" for such attacks, the report said, "is difficult at best without some type of state sponsorship."[59]

So far, the identities of the Chinese hackers who recently breached American media organizations' computers are unknown. *The New York Times*, Bloomberg News, *The Wall Street Journal* and *The Washington Post* said their reporters' e-mails and files had been attacked by hackers traced to China. *The Times* last fall had reported extensively on its months-long investigation of relatives of Prime Minister Wen Jiabao, who accumulated nearly $3 billion in wealth during his leadership. *The Times* said its security experts had found "digital evidence that Chinese hackers, using methods that some consultants have associated with the Chinese military in the past, breached *The Times*'s network."[60] Bloomberg earlier had reported that the extended family of Vice President Xi Jinping, scheduled to become president in March, had accumulated assets worth hundreds of millions of dollars.[61]

The Post and *The Journal*, which have not been investigating Chinese leaders' finances, said cyber-attacks on their computers appeared to target the e-mails and files of reporters covering sensitive Chinese political issues.[62]

The Chinese government consistently denies any involvement in hacking, and a succession of senior American officials has tried unsuccessfully to engage their Chinese counterparts on the issue.

"China does not have a monolithic, coordinated policy approach to cybersecurity," contrary to U.S. perceptions, according to an analysis last year by the University of California Institute of Global Conflict and Cooperation in conjunction with the U.S. Naval War College. Creating a coherent national policy would be impossible, the report said, because a tangle of regulatory institutions and often-contradictory policy directives plagues China's industrial and commercial sectors. In addition, public and private sectors often pursue incompatible interests, and policy coordination is stymied by "a fractious network of military, intelligence and other state entities involved in cyber policy and activity," it continued.[63]

Chinese officials claim that foreign hackers increasingly are penetrating Chinese sites, and domestic cybercrime — involving both Chinese criminals and victims — has ballooned. A Chinese official quoted in the 2012 report said that some 8.5 million Chinese computers "were attacked by rogue programs every day" in 2011, up 48 percent from 2010.

While the figure is presumably an average, Li Yuxiao, director of the Chinese Internet Governance Research Center at Beijing's University of Posts and Telecommunications, wrote that it reflected China's insufficient emphasis on information security. "(China's) Internet technologies need further development. General public

AFP/Getty Images/Atta Kenare

An Iranian man surfs the Internet at a cafe in Tehran on Jan. 24, 2011, a day after Iran officially launched a cyberpolice unit to confront what the government said were Internet crimes and disruptive social networks. The United States has blamed Iran for a series of recent attacks on big U.S. banks as part of an emerging shadow cyberwar between the United States and Iran's religious leaders; Iran denies it was involved.

education is barely satisfactory. Further international cooperation is really needed," he said.[64]

During his last official visit to Beijing in September 2012, Defense Secretary Panetta tried to discuss cybersecurity with Chinese leaders but came away with little more than an agreement to talk again. "It's clear that they want to engage in a dialogue on this issue," Panetta said, "and I guess that's the most important thing."[65]

He saw the agreement as "the beginning of trying to perhaps be able to develop an approach to dealing with cyber issues that has some semblance of order here, as opposed to having countries basically all flying in the dark."[66]

Criminal Hacking

Today's cyber-attacks originating in Russia are more likely to be the work of criminals than spies, experts say. For example, a cybersecurity report by McAfee Labs in December warned that Russian-led hackers were planning to attack 30 American regional banks and financial institutions.[67]

The offensive is an extension of Project Blitzkrieg, a program that has stolen $5 million from banks since 2008, according to McAfee. To gain access, hackers used customer e-mails that carry out banking transactions or warn banks of suspicious activity on their accounts.[68] Russian hackers also run extortion rackets, demanding money from companies in exchange for not penetrating their systems, and volunteering — for a price — to persuade other hackers not to attack the companies.

Iranian hackers, meanwhile, are not as skilled as the Chinese or Russians, experts say, but since the Stuxnet attack the government has stepped up its hacking activity, mainly aimed at sabotage. The attack on Saudi Aramco is allegedly an example, although some experts believe the virus used was not advanced enough to have caused the amount of damage attributed to it without inside help.

Nevertheless, said a 2011 report by the Center for Strategic and International Studies, American companies "are still not prepared." While "securing cyberspace had become a critical challenge for national security . . . the new energy in the national dialogue on cybersecurity has not translated into progress," the report concluded.[69]

Currently, private computer networks are protected only by individual action and market forces. In his executive order, Obama made what administration officials called "a down payment" on a more determined national approach to defending American companies from cyber-attacks by increasing the level of information-sharing and encouraging firms to "find [cybersecurity] technology in the private sector." In his State of the Union address on Feb. 12, he urged Congress to "act as well by passing legislation to give the government a greater capacity to secure our networks and deter attacks."[70]

But opponents fear the rules' new information-sharing mechanisms will endanger trade secrets and reveal too much to the federal government, even though the White House says the government will take steps to ensure the confidentiality of shared information. "A regulatory program would likely become highly rigid in practice and thus counterproductive to effective cybersecurity — due in large part to a shift in focus from security to compliance," according to the U.S. Chamber of Commerce's Beauchesne. Furthermore, homogenizing security would just make it easier for cyber-attackers, she writes in an e-mail.

As for exchanging information, she continues, businesses need certainty that information shared with the government "will not lead to frivolous lawsuits, . . . be publicly disclosed, [or] used by officials to regulate other activities."

Should Congress enact cybersecurity legislation?

YES Jody R. Westby
Founder and CEO,
Global Cyber Risk, LLC

NO Paul Rosenzweig
Principal, Red Branch Consulting;
Senior Adviser, The Chertoff Group;
Visiting Fellow, Heritage Foundation

Written for *CQ Researcher,* February 2013

Written for *CQ Researcher,* February 2013

The real question with respect to cybersecurity is not whether Congress should enact legislation but what kind of legislation it should adopt. It is important to be practical about what Congress can realistically achieve. There will never be a perfect cybersecurity solution. Companies will never be able to prevent or counter all threats, and sometimes the bad guys will get in. But we should still try to catch them.

Today, cybercrime is the perfect crime. Cybercriminals seldom get caught. Congress can help change that in four ways.

First, few legal obstacles prevent companies from sharing cyberthreat information with the government, but many barriers block the government from sharing cyber-intelligence with the private sector. It could be that the information is classified or protected at some level; that the government is afraid of sharing information and being accused of favoring one company or industry over another, or that the information was obtained from another company or government and no mechanism exists for sharing it. Legislation could clear this path.

Second, Congress could specify what government assistance can help private entities defend against cyber-attacks and what confidentiality would be involved. Beyond an obscure provision in National Security Directive 42 regarding possible National Security Agency assistance to government contractors, a government agency (other than law enforcement) is not authorized to help a private company counter a nation state-sponsored attack. As a practical matter, no company, even a savvy communications provider, has the resources to defend against the capabilities of a nation state. Providing a government-backup capability to U.S. businesses — and doing it publicly in the form of a law — would send a powerful message to countries contemplating such attacks and encourage companies to seek government help.

Third, Congress could provide funding and U.S. leadership in advancing harmonized cybercrime laws and promoting international assistance in cybercrime investigations. Since Internet communications often hop from one country to another before delivery, cybercrime investigations often run into international legal and diplomatic roadblocks. Obtaining foreign assistance requires court filings and takes months when minutes and seconds matter before data disappear.

Fourth, Congress could facilitate a culture of cybersecurity by directing publicly listed companies to specify in Securities and Exchange Commission filings whether they have fully implemented a cybersecurity plan, policies and procedures.

Congress remains intent on passing a bill that creates a federal regulatory system for cybersecurity. That would be a mistake.

Regulation is only necessary if you think cyber vulnerabilities of our critical infrastructure (CI) are an existential threat. We would not be thinking of a new regulatory scheme just to deal with cybercrime. The entire premise of the pro-regulation argument is that our CI is vulnerable to, say, a Chinese attack. But that's not an accurate assessment of the actual risk. A Chinese cyber-attack is as unlikely as a war with China over Taiwan.

More important, regulation is an especially poor choice for a dynamic and changing environment, such as the Internet, in which performance standards we might develop today are almost certainly irrelevant to the Internet architecture that will exist in, say, three years. The mean time required for significant regulation to be developed in the United States is 18 to 24 months. In that time, network processing speeds double. Meanwhile, innovation is frozen, as everyone who develops cybersecurity solutions waits for the federal government to define the next steps necessary to meet emerging or future threats.

Even worse, the entire focus of the proposed regulatory structure is misguided. It recapitulates a Maginot Line-type mentality, in which defense is the only solution. We need guidelines on building system resiliency, and we need to plan for failure. Nor can we have much confidence in the Department of Homeland Security as a regulatory authority — its one effort in that regard, the Chemical Facility Anti-Terrorism Standards, has been a distinct failure.

Finally, the rush to federal regulation will have significant adverse effects on our international posture. What if, for example, U.S. performance standards are not consistent with, say, Canada's? Indeed, there is every reason to expect that American cybersecurity standards will be different from European standards or Asian ones — leading to a fractured network.

Worst of all, Internet freedom will suffer. Already, China argues that its regulation of the internal Chinese cyberdomain is "just like" America's use of the National Institute of Standards and Technology to set standards. We may comfortably laugh that off now, but we will have a much harder time making the public case for Internet freedom of expression if our own security standards incorporate, for instance, chilling requirements for authentication or "deep packet inspection" or surveillance technology for reading emails, chat messages and Web visits inside a network.

> **"A regulatory program would likely become highly rigid in practice and thus counterproductive to effective cybersecurity — due in large part to a shift in focus from security to compliance."**
>
> *— Ann M. Beauchesne,*
> *Vice President, National Security and*
> *Emergency Preparedness Department,*
> *U.S. Chamber of Commerce*

Even with an executive order in place, however, the administration repeatedly has said Congress needs to pass additional cybersecurity laws. Legislative reforms are needed to provide additional corporate liability protections and stiffer criminal penalties for cybercrimes and to lift limits on hiring of cybersecurity experts, said Homeland Security Secretary Napolitano.[71]

To that end, Senate Democrats last month introduced a measure calling on Congress to develop a public-private system to defend the nation's infrastructure and establish a system for sharing cyberthreat information.

House Republicans, however, said on Feb. 13 they would reintroduce a cybersecurity bill passed by the House last year. It would protect companies that share cyberthreat information and allow the government to give classified threat information to the private sector. Obama threatened to veto the House bill last year on the grounds that it wouldn't shield the nation's critical infrastructure from attacks or protect the privacy of consumer data.[72]

Meanwhile, The European Union on Feb. 7 announced draft cybersecurity regulations that could affect American companies doing business there. Under the rules, banks, stock exchanges, hospitals and transportation companies reportedly would have to adopt stringent network security standards. In addition, critical infrastructure companies would have to tell regulators about significant cyber-attacks and could even be required to disclose such breaches to the public. Companies in the United States currently must make such disclosures only if consumers' personal data is breached, but the rules differ by state.

"If and when adopted," the European rules "will be a game changer" for multinational U.S. companies,

Stewart Baker, former assistant secretary at the Department of Homeland Security, told Bloomberg News. "If companies are required to report breaches in Europe, they won't be able to avoid reporting breaches in the U.S. as well."[73]

OUTLOOK

Managing Intrusions

Computer systems will always be vulnerable, says cyber specialist Irving Lachow, director of technology and national security at the Center for a New American Security in Washington.

"You cannot prevent people from breaking in," he says. "The question is how hard you want to make them work to break in; the next question is how long it takes to detect them."

Increasingly, he said, defensive research focuses on quickly locating and controlling viruses. Because the average computer system is infected by a virus for 416 days before being detected, according to a recent study by the Virginia-based cyberprotection firm Mandiant, companies must manage intrusions after they've been detected.

"You can set up a little honeypot [a device designed to attract the attention of intruders] where you want it [the virus] to go," says Lachow. "That's where sophisticated companies are moving."

As more and more people across the globe gain access to the Internet, authoritarian governments will keep trying to manage access within their borders, experts predict. Western democracies continue to oppose U.N. passage of the proposed International Code of Conduct for Information Security, which they say would promote censorship. Sponsors contend it would establish "a multilateral, transparent and democratic" governance mechanism for the Internet while curbing dissemination of information that "incites terrorism, secessionism, extremism or undermines other countries' political, economic and social stability."[74]

Some commentators predict the Internet will be balkanized into two or more systems with different rules, as some governments attempt to control their citizens' access to social media — especially after the rift created at the Dubai telecommunication conference. Beijing, for instance, has created its so-called Great Firewall — the country's system of online restrictions — and has stepped up its targeting of virtual private networks, or VPNs, commonly used to bypass government efforts to block access to certain websites. China also has created its own hybrids of Facebook and Twitter in an effort to reduce reliance on the Internet.[75]

In the United States, few experts believe Defense Secretary Panetta's "cyber Pearl Harbor" scenario is a real threat in the foreseeable future. "We have a heterogeneous infrastructure," says Martin C. Libicki, information technology specialist at the Rand Corp., a California-based think tank. "For example, we have 20 different natural gas pipelines. It would be very difficult to take down a whole infrastructure at any one time [although] I imagine al Qaeda would like to do it. But they don't have the technical talent; and Russia and China don't act out of whims. The world would have to get darker before either think they would get an advantage by trying."

However, policy makers, diplomats and military personnel continue to debate the theoretical question of when a cyber-attack constitutes a justification to declare war, according to Catherine Lotrionte, associate director of the Institute of Law, Science and Global Security at Georgetown University. "In some circles, this discussion is going on every day," she says.

"Most of what's happening [in cyberwarfare] will not trigger the laws of conflict," she explains. "In the U.N. Charter the use of force is lawful only if you suffered an armed attack. But in cyberwarfare, what constitutes an armed attack?"

"There's no question that cyberwarfare is going to be a component of warfare into the future," says Lachow. "But there needs to be some tangible impact. China's not going to go to war to steal our stuff, but if they try to take Taiwan and they use a cyber-attack to delay our response — that's another story."

To determine whether war is justified, says Lotrionte, "the effect, scope, intention and duration of the attack" must be taken into account. "If the dams are attacked, the probable result will be flooding, but does it involve loss of life? Or, what if an attack triggers a financial crisis? How long will it last, and what if it devastates the finances of a country?"

Still, she says, "it's always going to be the policymakers who make the ultimate decision whether to listen to the lawyers and comply with what would be legal — or not."

"The character of cyberwarfare is you don't get destruction, you get disruption," says Libicki. "Really, it's a question of at what point you put your foot down."

NOTES

1. Lee Ferran, "Capital One Website Disrupted, Cyber Protesters Claim Attack," ABC News, Jan. 24, 2013, http://abcnews.go.com/blogs/headlines/2013/01/capital-one-website-disrupted-cyber-protestors-claim-attack/.

2. Steve Huff, "US Intelligence Suspects Iran of Using 'bRobots' to DDS American Banks," *BetaBeat*, Jan. 9, 2013, http://betabeat.com/2013/01/u-s-intelligence-suspects-iran-of-using-brobots-to-ddos-american-banks/.

3. Wael Mahdi, "Saudi Arabia Says Aramco Cyberattack Came from Foreign States," Bloomberg News, Dec. 9, 2012, www.bloomberg.com/news/2012-12-09/saudi-arabia-says-aramco-cyberattack-came-from-foreign-states.html.

4. For background, see Marcia Clemmitt, "Computer Hacking," *CQ Researcher*, Sept. 16, 2011, pp. 757-780.

5. "Cybersecurity at Risk," *The New York Times*, July 12, 2012, www.nytimes.com/2012/08/01/opinion/cybersecurity-at-risk.html.

6. Peter Maass and Megha Rajagopalan, "Does Cybercrime Really Cost $1 Trillion?" *Propublica*, Aug. 1, 2012, www.propublica.org/article/does-cybercrime-really-cost-1-trillion.

7. *Ibid.*

8. Dinei Florencio and Cormac Herley, "The Cybercrime Wave That Wasn't," *The New York Times*, April 15, 2012, www.nytimes.com/2012/04/15/opinion/sunday/the-cybercrime-wave-that-wasnt.html?_r=1.

9. Elisabeth Bumiller and Thom Shanker, "Panetta Warns of Dire Threat of Cyberattack on U.S.," *The New York Times*, Oct. 11, 2012, www.nytimes.com/2012/10/12/world/panetta-warns-of-dire-threat-of-cyberattack.html?pagewanted=all&_r=0.

10. Reuters, "U.S. homeland chief: cyber 9/11 could happen imminently," Yahoo News, Jan. 24, 2013,

http://news.yahoo.com/u-homeland-chief-cyber-9-11-could-happen-215436518.html.

11. Ellen Nakashima, "U.S. said to be target of massive espionage campaign," *The Washington Post*, Feb. 10, 2013, www.washingtonpost.com/world/national-security/us-said-to-be-target-of-massive-cyber-espionage-campaign/2013/02/10/7b4687d8-6fc1-11e2-aa58-243de81040ba_story.html.

12. Rita Tehan, "Cyber Security: Authoritative Reports and Sources," Congressional Research Service, Sept. 11, 2012, www.fas.org/sgp/crs/misc/R42507.pdf.

13. Edward Liu, *et al.*, "Cybersecurity: Selected Legal Issues," Congressional Research Service, April 2012, www.fas.org/sgp/crs/misc/R42409.pdf.

14. The White House, "Improving Critical Infrastructure Cybersecurity," Feb. 12, 2013, www.wired.com/images_blogs/threatlevel/2013/02/Presidents-Cybersecurity-Executive-Order.pdf.

15. Zachary Goldfarb, "Obama weighing executive action on housing, gays, and other issues," *The Washington Post*, Feb. 10, 2013, www.washingtonpost.com/politics/obama-weighing-executive-actions-on-housing-gays-and-other-issues/2013/02/10/e966cc06-7065-11e2-8b8d-e0b59a1b8e2a_story.html.

16. "Facebook helps FBI bust cybercriminals blamed for $850 million losses," Reuters, Oct. 11, 2012, www.reuters.com/article/2012/12/12/us-cybercrime-fbi-idUSBRE8BB04B20121212.

17. Jim Finkle, "Exclusive: Microsoft and Symantec disrupt cyber crime ring," Reuters, Feb. 6, 2013, http://in.reuters.com/article/2013/02/06/us-cybercrime-raid-idINBRE91515K20130206?feedType=RSS&feedName=everything&virtualBrandChannel=11709.

18. "Foreign Spies Stealing U.S. Economic Secrets in Cyberspace," Office of the Counterintelligence Executive," October 2011, www.ncix.gov/publications/reports/fecie_all/Foreign_Economic_Collection_2011.pdf.

19. "Report to Congress of the U.S.-China Economic and Security Review Commission," November 2012, www.uscc.gov/annual_report/2012/2012-Report-to-Congress.pdf.

20. Nicole Perlroth, "Washington Post Joins List of News Media Hacked by the Chinese," *The New York Times*, Feb. 1, 2013, www.nytimes.com/2013/02/02/technology/washington-posts-joins-list-of-media-hacked-by-the-chinese.html?_r=1&&pagewanted=print.

21. Gerry Smith, "U.S. Can Launch Cyber Attacks But Not Defend Against Them, Experts Say," *The Huffington Post*, June 6, 2012, www.huffingtonpost.com/2012/06/01/stuxnet-us-cyberattack_n_1562983.html.

22. "China and Cybersecurity: Political, Economic, and Strategic Dimensions," University of California Institute on Global Conflict and Cooperation, U.S. Naval War College, April 2012, www.google.com/url?sa=t&rct=j&q=&esrc=s&source=web&cd=1&ved=0CE0QFjAA&url=http%3A%2F%2Figcc.ucsd.edu%2Fassets%2F001%2F503568.pdf&ei=TTwFUdGFAeqy0QHT1oCADg&usg=AFQjCNHh8iFi8z0wt4lMj57eHDoiByKcCA&bvm=bv.41524429,d.dmQ.

23. Barack Obama, "Taking the Cyberthreat Seriously," *The Wall Street Journal*, July 19, 2012, http://online.wsj.com/article/SB10000872396390444330904577535492693044650.html.

24. "Global Risks 2013," World Economic Forum, February 2013, www3.weforum.org/docs/WEF_GlobalRisks_Report_2013.pdf.

25. Jerry Brito, "Measured Response to a Limited Threat," *The New York Times*, Oct. 17, 2012, www.nytimes.com/roomfordebate/2012/10/17/should-industry-face-more-cybersecurity-mandates/let-industry-make-a-measured-response-to-a-limited-cyber-threat.

26. James Lewis, "Assessing the Risks of Cyberterrorism, Cyberwar, and other Cyberthreats," Center for Strategic and International Studies, December 2002, http://csis.org/files/media/csis/pubs/021101_risks_of_cyberterror.pdf.

27. "Cybersecurity: A Special Report, Defenders on the Internet frontlines," *The Washington Post*, Nov. 13, 2012, p. AA4.

28. Eric Engleman and Chris Strohm, "Cybersecurity Disaster Seen in U.S. Survey Citing Spending Gaps,"

Bloomberg News, Jan. 31, 2012, www.bloomberg
.com/news/2012-01-31/cybersecurity-disaster-seen-
in-u-s-survey-citing-spending-gaps.html.

29. Ann M. Beauchesne, "More Regulation Isn't the
Answer," *The New York Times*, Oct. 18, 2012, www
.nytimes.com/roomfordebate/2012/10/17/should-
industry-face-more-cybersecurity-mandates/more-
regulation-isnt-the-answer.

30. Obama, *op. cit.*

31. See Andrew Couts, "Hooray! The UN didn't take
over the Internet after all," *Digital Trends*, Dec. 14,
2012, www.digitaltrends.com/web/the-un-didnt-
take-over-the-internet-afterall/.

32. Larry Downes, "Why is the U.N. trying to take over
the Internet?" *Forbes*, Sept. 8, 2012, www.forbes
.com/sites/larrydownes/2012/08/09/why-the-un-is-
trying-to-take-over-the-internet/.

33. "Internet should be free but regulated," *China Daily*,
Jan. 26, 2010, www.chinadaily.com.cn/opinion/
2010-01/26/content_9377190.htm.

34. "Internet World Stats," www.internetworldstats
.com/top20.htm.

35. Couts, *op. cit.*

36. *Ibid.*

37. Simeon Kerr and Daniel Thomas, "Discord follows
U.S. refusal to sign web pact," *FTonline*, Dec. 14,
2012, www.ft.com/intl/cms/s/0/fd73d4ec-4611-
11e2-b780-00144feabdc0.html.

38. William D. Marbach with Madlyn Resener, *et al.*,
"Beware: Hackers at Play," *Newsweek*, Sept. 5, 1983,
p. 42.

39. "The Robert Morris Internet Worm," http://groups
.csail.mit.edu/mac/classes/6.805/articles/morris-
worm.html.

40. Rita Tehan, "Cybersecurity: Authoritative Reports
and Resources," Congressional Research Service, Sept
11, 2012, www.fas.org/sgp/crs/misc/R42507.pdf.

41. Obama, *op. cit.*

42. Jaikumar Vijayan "Obama to issue cybersecurity
executive order this month," *Computer World*, Feb.
1, 2013, www.computerworld.com/s/article/9236
438/Obama_to_issue_cybersecurity_executive_
order_this_month.

43. Frontline, "Moonlight Maze" PBS, March 24, 2003,
www.pbs.org/wgbh/pages/frontline/shows/cyber
war/warnings/.

44. James Lewis, "Titan Rain and China," Center for
Strategic and International Studies, 2005, http://
csis.org/files/media/csis/pubs/051214_china_titan_
rain.pdf.

45. Siobhan Gorman, August Cole and Yochi Dreazen,
"Computer Spies Breach Fighter Jet Project," *The
Wall Street Journal*, Aug. 21, 2009, http://online.wsj
.com/article/SB124027491029837401.html.

46. Anita Ferrer, "Why cybersecurity is so important in
government IT (Infographic)" *FedTech*, Sept. 25,
2012, www.fedtechmagazine.com/article/2012/09/
why-cybersecurity-so-important-government-it-
infographic.

47. Peter Brookes, "Flashpoint: The Cyber Challenge,"
Armed Forces Journal, March 2008, www.armed
forcesjournal.com/2008/03/3463904.

48. David Martin, "First Look Inside the Military's
Cyber War Room," CBS, July 14, 2011, www
.cbsnews.com/8301-18563_162-20079585.html.

49. Demetri Sevastopulo, "Cyber attacks on McCain
and Obama teams 'came from China,' " FTonline,
Nov. 11, 2008, www.ft.com/intl/cms/s/0/3b400
1e2-ac6f-11dd-bf71-000077b07658.html
#axzz2KEv6M087. See also Ellen Nakashima and
John Pomfret, "China proves to be an aggressive foe
in cyberspace," *The Washington Post*, Nov. 11, 2009,
www.washingtonpost.com/wp-dyn/content/arti
cle/2009/11/10/AR2009111017588.html.

50. Ellen Nakashima, "Pentagon Approves Expansion of
Force Handling Cybersecurity," *The Washington Post*,
Jan. 28, 2013, p. A8, articles.washingtonpost
.com/2013-01-27/world/36583575_1_cyber-pro
tection-forces-cyber-command-cybersecurity.

51. For background, see Alex Kingsbury, "Government Secrecy," *CQ Researcher*, Feb. 11, 2011,
pp. 121-144.

52. Ed O'Keefe and Ian Shapira, "Justice Department
Web site inoperable after feds seize Megaupload,"
The Washington Post, Jan. 19, 2012, www.washing
tonpost.com/blogs/federal-eye/post/justice-depart
ment-web-site-goes-down-after-feds-seize-megaup

load/2012/01/19/gIQAd2GpBQ_blog.html; and Timothy Gardner, "Energy Department hacked, says no classified data was compromised," Reuters, Feb. 4, 2013, www.reuters.com/article/2013/02/04/net-us-usa-cybersecurity-doe-idUSBRE9130ZL20130204.

53. Shane McGlaun, "Hillary Clinton Delivers Speech on Internet Freedom," *Daily Tech*, Jan. 22, 2010, www.dailytech.com/article.aspx?newsid=17487.

54. Lolita C. Baldor, "Chinese Cyber Attacks on U.S. Continue Totally Unabated, Leon Panetta Complains," *The Huffington Post*, Sept. 20, 2012, www.huffingtonpost.com/2012/09/20/chinese-cyber-attacks-leon-panetta_n_1899168.html.

55. Ken Dilanian, "Fact check: Is China involved in cyber attacks?" *Los Angeles Times*, Oct. 22, 2012, http://articles.latimes.com/2012/oct/22/news/la-pn-fact-check-debate-cyber-attacks-20121022.

56. BBC: "White House confirms cyber-attack on "unclassified" system, www.bbc.co.uk/news/world-us-canada-19794745.

57. Eric M. Hutchins, *et al.*, "Intelligence Driven Computer Network Defense Informed by Analysis of Adversary Campaigns and Intrusion Kill Chains," Lockheed Martin Corp., www.lockheedmartin.com/content/dam/lockheed/data/corporate/documents/LM-White-Paper-Intel-Driven-Defense.pdf.

58. Bryan Krekel, "Capability of the People's Republic of China to Conduct Cyber Warfare and Computer Network Exploitation," U.S.-China Economic and Security Review Commission, October 2009, www.uscc.gov/researchpapers/2009/NorthropGrumman_PRC_Cyber_Paper_FINAL_Approved%20Report_16Oct2009.pdf.

59. *Ibid.*

60. Jethro Mullen, "New York Times, Wall Street Journal say Chinese hackers broke into computers," CNN, Jan. 31, 2013, www.cnn.com/2013/01/31/tech/china-nyt-hacking.

61. See David Barboza, "Billions in Hidden Riches for Family of Chinese Leader," *The New York Times*, Oct. 25, 2012, www.nytimes.com/2012/10/26/business/global/family-of-wen-jiabao-holds-a-hidden-fortune-in-china.html?pagewanted=all. Also see Jethro Mullen, "China blocks *New York Times*

website after story on leader's family wealth," CNN, Oct. 26, 2012, www.cnn.com/2012/10/26/world/asia/china-times-website-blocked/index.html.

62. Perlroth, *op. cit.*

63. "China and Cybersecurity: Political, Economic and Strategic Dimensions," University of California Institute of Global Conflict and Cooperation; U.S. Naval War College; Study of Innovation and Technology in China, April 2012, http://www-igcc.ucsd.edu/assets/001/503568.pdf.

64. *Ibid.*

65. Baldor, *op. cit.*

66. *Ibid.*

67. Dean Wilson, "McAfee warns of cyber threat to 30 U.S. banks," *VR-Zone*, Dec. 13, 2012, http://vr-zone.com/articles/mcafee-warns-of-cyber-threat-to-30-us-banks/18396.html.

68. *Ibid.*

69. James A. Lewis and others, "Cybersecurity Two Years Later," Report of the CSIS Commission on Cybersecurity for the 44th Presidency, January 2011, http://csis.org/files/publication/110128_Lewis_CybersecurityTwoYearsLater_Web.pdf.

70. Gerry Smith, "Obama's Cybersecurity Order Weaker Than Previous Proposal," *The Huffington Post*, Feb. 12, 2013, www.huffingtonpost.com/2013/02/12/obama-cybersecurity-state-of-the-union_n_2669941.html.

71. See Josh Smith, "Cybersecurity Order 'Close to Completion,'" *National Journal*, Sept. 19, 2012, www.nationaljournal.com/tech/cybersecurity-order-close-to-completion--20120919.

72. Engelman and Riley, *op. cit.*

73. *Ibid.*

74. "China, Russia and Other Countries Submit the Document of International Code of Conduct for Information Security to the United Nations," Ministry of Foreign Affairs of the People's Republic of China, Sept. 13, 2011, www.fmprc.gov.cn/eng/wjdt/wshd/t858978.htm.

75. "Great Firewall 'upgrade' hits China users," *Bangkok Times*, Dec. 21, 2012, www.bangkokpost.com/tech/computer/327350/great-firewall-upgrade-hits-china-internet-users.

BIBLIOGRAPHY

Selected Sources

Books

Bowden, Mark, *Worm: The First Digital World War*, **Atlantic Monthly Press, 2011.**
A journalist recounts how the Conficker worm infected its first computer in November 2008 and within a month had infiltrated 1.5 million computers in 195 countries, including in the British Parliament.

Brenner, Joel, *America the Vulnerable: Inside the New Threat Matrix of Digital Espionage, Crime, and Warfare*, **Penguin Press, 2011.**
A former head of counter-intelligence for the director of national intelligence and former inspector general of the National Security Agency assesses America's online vulnerabilities.

Clarke, Richard, and Robert K. Knake, *Cyberwar: The Next Threat to National Security & What to Do About It*, **Ecco Books, 2012.**
A former White House cybersecurity czar (Clarke) and a fellow at the Council on Foreign Relations (Knake) warn that cyber-attacks pose a real and crippling danger to the nation's infrastructure.

Dunn Cavelty, Myriam, *Cyber Security and Threat Politics: U.S. Efforts to Secure the Information Age*, **Rutledge, 2009.**
An expert at the Center for Security Studies in Zurich, Switzerland, traces the history of a decade of U.S. cybersecurity policy.

Mitnick, Kevin, *Ghost in the Wires: My Adventures as the World's Most Wanted Hacker*, **Little Brown, 2011.**
One of history's most elusive hackers — now a security consultant — tells his remarkable story.

Sanger, David, *Confront and Conceal: Obama's Secret Wars and Surprising Use of American Power*, **Crown, 2011.**
A senior *New York Times* journalist tells how President Obama accelerated the use of innovative cyberweapons to fight rapidly growing threats around the world; includes the story of how the United States and Israel developed and used the Stuxnet virus against Iran's nuclear-development program.

Articles

"War in the fifth dimension," *The Economist*, July 1, 2010, www.economist.com/node/16478792.
In this lead article, the U.K.-based magazine calls cyberspace the fifth dimension of war after land, sea, air and space and speculates on what cyberwar would be like.

Lieberman, Joseph, *et al.*, "Should Industry Face More Cybersecurity Mandates?" Room for Debate, *The New York Times*, Oct. 17, 2012, www.nytimes.com/roomfordebate/2012/10/17/should-industry-face-more-cybersecurity-mandates/.
A former senator and seven others involved in cybersecurity debate the pros and cons of more government regulation to protect the private sector from attacks.

O'Harrow, Robert, "Zero Day: The Threat in Cyberspace," *The Washington Post*, June 12-Dec. 25, 2012, www.washingtonpost.com/investigations/zero-day.
A seven-part series of articles by an investigative reporter examines different aspects of cybercrime, including how hackers operate and how cyber thieves find rich pickings in the health care sector.

Reports and Studies

"A Comparative Analysis of Cybersecurity Initiatives Worldwide," International Telecommunications Union, 2005, www.itu.int/osg/spu/cybersecurity/docs/Background_Paper_Comparative_Analysis_Cybersecurity_Initiatives_Worldwide.pdf.
A comparative study compiled by the U.N. telecommunications agency says "there can be no question that the Internet demands an international approach," but a global culture on cybersecurity remains out of reach because of conflicting national and regional interests.

"Cybersecurity: Selected Legal Issues," Congressional Research Service, April 20, 2012, www.fas.org/sgp/crs/misc/R42409.pdf.
A report prepared for Congress critiques some 40 proposed cybersecurity laws pending before lawmakers.

"Cybersecurity Two Years Later: a Report by the Commission on Cybersecurity for the President," January 2011, http://csis.org/files/publication/110128_Lewis_CybersecurityTwoYearsLater_Web.pdf.

The panel warns that progress on protecting the nation's infrastructure from cyberthreats had been too slow since an earlier examination of the issue in 2009.

"Special Eurobarometer 390: Cybersecurity," European Commission, July 2012, http://ec.europa .eu/public_opinion/archives/ebs/ebs_390_en.pdf.

A European Union survey of Internet usage and cybersecurity in all 27 member states shows uneven Internet usage (92 percent of the population in Denmark, 44 percent in Portugal) but a high level of awareness of the dangers of cyberterrorism and cybercrime.

For More Information

Brookings Institution, 1775 Massachusetts Ave., N.W., Washington, DC 20036; 202-797-6000; communications@brookings.edu. A centrist Washington think tank that studies a wide range of policy issues, including cybersecurity.

Federal Bureau of Investigation, Information and Technology Branch, 935 Pennsylvania Ave., N.W., Washington, DC 20535-0001; 202-324-3000; www.fbi.gov/contact-us. A Justice Department agency that investigates cyber-attacks and other federal crimes.

Information Technology Industry Council, 1101 K St., N.W., Suite 610, Washington, DC 20005; 202-707-8888; info@itic. A trade organization representing computer companies.

Security and Defence Agenda, 4, rue de Science, 1000 Brussels, Belgium; 32-2-300-2992; info@securitydefence

agency.org. Independent think tank run by two former NATO secretaries general — Javier Solana and Jaap de Hoop Scheffer — focusing on global defense and security, with special focus on cybersecurity.

US-CERT (United States Computer Emergency Readiness Team), Department of Homeland Security, DHS/US-CERT, Attn: NPPD/CS&C/NCSD/US-CERT, Maindrop 0635, 245 Murray Lane, S.W., Bldg. 410, Washington, DC 20598; 1-888-282-0870; www.us-cert.gov. Leads Department of Homeland Security's efforts to improve the nation's cybersecurity, working collaboratively with public and private sectors.

The White House, 1600 Pennsylvania Ave., N.W., Washington, DC 20500; 202-456-1111; www.whitehouse .gov/contact/submit-questions-and-comments. Invites comments and questions on cybersecurity from the public by phone, letter or e-mail.

5

Assessing the Threat from al Qaeda

Barbara Mantel

Sami Dayan, an al Qaeda leader in Yemen, was sentenced in April to 15 years in prison for his role in the 2012 assassination of a Yemeni general. Yemen-based Al Qaeda in the Arabian Peninsula (AQAP) is among four Sunni Muslim extremist groups that have sworn allegiance to al Qaeda leader Ayman al-Zawahiri. AQAP targets local, U.S. and other Western interests in the region and has attempted attacks against the United States.

From *CQ Researcher*,
June 27, 2014.

In late April, a CIA officer and a U.S. Special Operations commando shot and killed two armed men trying to kidnap them from a barbershop in Sana, the capital of Yemen. Officials later said the dead men were members of an al Qaeda-linked cell that had broken 19 inmates out of a Yemeni prison in February, tried to assassinate a German diplomat in April and killed a Frenchman in May.[1]

The barbershop shooting shines a light on America's clandestine operations in Yemen, where U.S. Special Operations troops train Yemeni counterterrorism forces and American commandos help target al Qaeda suspects for drone strikes.[2]

As of April 21, the United States had launched 94 drone attacks and 15 conventional air strikes in Yemen, most since 2009 under President Obama, according to the Washington-based New America Foundation, a think tank that tracks U.S. drone warfare. The drone and cruise missile strikes have killed between 669 and 887 militants and up to 87 civilians.[3]

"For the foreseeable future, the most direct threat to America at home and abroad remains terrorism," Obama told graduating cadets at the U.S. Military Academy at West Point last month.[4] And Yemen has become the center of the country's counterterrorism campaign, home to Al Qaeda in the Arabian Peninsula (AQAP), the Sunni Muslim extremist group and al Qaeda franchise that poses the most serious direct threat to the United States, according to counterterrorism officials.

"AQAP . . . has made repeated efforts to export terrorism to our homeland," Jeh Johnson, Secretary of Homeland Security, told

Al Qaeda Network Spans Africa, Middle East

Al Qaeda operates from bases in eastern Afghanistan and western Pakistan. Al Qaeda affiliates operate in Syria, the Arabian Peninsula, Somalia and parts of northwestern Africa. Groups that share the Islamist philosophy of al Qaeda but are not official affiliates include the Islamic State of Iraq and Greater Syria (ISIS)* and Boko Haram in Nigeria.

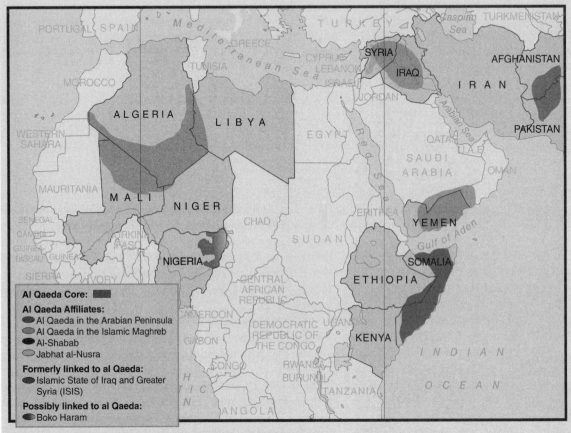

* ISIS, formerly Al Qaeda in Iraq, split off from al Qaeda in February.

Source: Colin Freeman, Barney Henderson and Mark Oliver, "Al-Qaeda map: Isis, Boko Haram and other affiliates' strongholds across Africa and Asia," The Telegraph (U.K.), June 12, 2014, http://tinyurl.com/muhhuka; "Global Terrorism Database," National Consortium for the Study of Terrorism and Responses to Terrorism, University of Maryland and the U.S. Department of Homeland Security, http://tinyurl.com/m4bfw6

Congress in May.[5] Operatives from AQAP hid bombs in printer toner cartridges being shipped aboard U.S.-bound flights in 2010, and AQAP was blamed for a suicide bomber's bungled 2009 attempt to detonate an explosive device — hidden in his underwear — aboard a Detroit-bound jet.

Al Qaeda will forever be associated in the American mind with the Sept. 11, 2001, terrorist attacks that killed 2,977 people and prompted President George W. Bush to declare war on terrorism. But today's al Qaeda is far different from the hierarchical organization that mounted the 9/11 attacks, led by Osama bin Laden operating from a safe haven in Afghanistan. Since 2004, U.S. drone strikes have killed dozens of top al Qaeda leaders hiding in neighboring Pakistan, and a U.S. Navy SEAL team killed bin Laden there in 2011.

Now experts describe a smaller, weaker, Pakistan-based al Qaeda leadership, often referred to as "al Qaeda core," operating alongside a murky far-flung network of affiliates, associates and supporters. Such groups have been attempting to control territory in northwest and eastern Africa and in Iraq, Syria and Yemen in the Middle East. They are taking advantage of the instability and civil war that emerged in some countries after the Arab Spring protest movement swept across North Africa and the Middle East in 2011, dislodging at least four dictators.[6]

These groups, which are Sunni, are also taking advantage of renewed ethnic and religious conflict stemming from the age-old struggle over which branch of Islam — Sunni or Shiite — will control the Middle East. Shiite-led Syria* and Iraq are supported by the region's major Shiite power, Iran. The rival Sunni-led governments of Saudi Arabia and the Gulf States have been supporting Sunni rebels in Syria, but not al Qaeda. Private citizens, however, have been sending money to extremists in Syria despite legal prohibitions in Saudi Arabia and Kuwait, a big source of funds.[7]

But counterterrorism experts disagree about the strength of the operational ties of the affiliates and associates to al Qaeda's core leadership, their long-term goals and whether they pose a direct threat to the West. In fact, the experts can't agree on the very nature of al Qaeda: Is it a strong terrorist network led by al Qaeda's core leadership in Pakistan, a loose network of affiliates with weakening links to core al Qaeda or more of a brand opportunistically adopted by disconnected jihadists groups?

*Syria's leaders are Alawites, a Shiite sect.

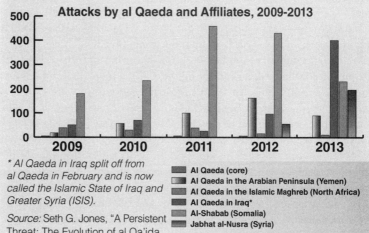

Al Qaeda Attacks Exceed 900 in 2013

Attacks by al Qaeda and its main affiliates — plus the breakaway affiliate Al Qaeda in Iraq — more than tripled from 2009 to 2013, to 929. Nearly 90 percent of the 2013 attacks were carried out by groups in Syria, Somalia and Iraq. Al Qaeda core has not launched an attack since 2012.

Attacks by al Qaeda and Affiliates, 2009-2013

* Al Qaeda in Iraq split off from al Qaeda in February and is now called the Islamic State of Iraq and Greater Syria (ISIS).

Al Qaeda (core)
Al Qaeda in the Arabian Peninsula (Yemen)
Al Qaeda in the Islamic Maghreb (North Africa)
Al Qaeda in Iraq*
Al-Shabab (Somalia)
Jabhat al-Nusra (Syria)

Source: Seth G. Jones, "A Persistent Threat: The Evolution of al Qa'ida and Other Salafi Jihadists," RAND Corp., 2014, p. 35, http://tinyurl.com/pxtkmsm

"The Defense Department, the Justice Department and the State Department each have their own definition of the problem," says Christopher Swift, a fellow at the University of Virginia's Center for National Security Law.

Yet defining and understanding al Qaeda is critical to forming policy, experts say. "We can't fight an enemy that we don't know," says Katherine Zimmerman, a senior analyst for the Critical Threats Project at the American Enterprise Institute, a Washington think tank. "We need to understand the enemy to craft a strategy to defeat it."

Most analysts agree that four al Qaeda affiliates, or franchises, are part of the network. They have sworn allegiance to Ayman al-Zawahiri, bin Laden's successor, believed to be living in Pakistan, and have been recognized by him in return. They are:

- Al Qaeda in the Arabian Peninsula, whose leader, Nasir al-Wahishi, is also Zawahiri's second-in-command at al Qaeda;
- Al-Shabab, an extremist group fighting for control of Somalia;

- Al Qaeda in the Islamic Maghreb (AQIM), which aims to overthrow the Algerian government and institute an Islamic state;
- Jabhat al-Nusra, formed two years ago to overthrow President Bashar al-Assad in Syria's bloody civil war.

Until February, the Islamic State of Iraq and Greater Syria (ISIS)* — considered one of the most ruthless jihadist groups — was officially affiliated with al Qaeda. Formerly known as Al Qaeda in Iraq, the group broadened its fight into Syria and has dramatically expanded its presence in Iraq, taking control this year of the Iraqi cities of Ramadi, Falluja, Mosul and Tikrit and currently working its way south to Baghdad. Zawahiri severed ties to the group over its brutal tactics and its refusal to obey his order to leave the Syrian theater to Jabhat al-Nusra.

While most analysts agree on which groups are al Qaeda affiliates, they disagree on which other violent jihadist groups in Pakistan, the Middle East and North Africa are al Qaeda "associates." Arguments hinge on whether one believes a group shares al Qaeda's ideology — a belief in violent jihad to create an Islamic caliphate under strict Islamic law, or sharia, extending across all Muslim lands; has strong operational ties to core al Qaeda or its sworn affiliates; and potentially threatens the West.

For instance, Zimmerman and others who define al Qaeda broadly also include an alliance of militant groups called Tehrik-e Taliban Pakistan (TTP), which is fighting the military in Pakistan's tribal territories.* "TTP has worked very closely with al Qaeda leadership and shares al Qaeda's ideology," says Zimmerman. She also includes Ansar al Din, which took control of northern Mali in 2012 but was ousted by French forces in early 2013. "It seeks to install a sharia-based government in north Mali and would permit AQIM to use the region as a base of operations."

---

*ISIS is also sometimes referred to as the Islamic State of Iraq and the Levant (ISIL), or the Islamic State of Iraq and Syria.

*The TTP, also known as the Pakistan Taliban, is not directly affiliated with the Afghan Taliban, which is fighting international coalition and Afghan security forces in Afghanistan. Both groups are on U.S. foreign terrorist lists. The five detainees recently released from Guantánamo in exchange for U.S. Sgt. Bowe Bergdahl were from the Afghan Taliban, which is not formally part of al Qaeda.

Thomas Joscelyn, a senior fellow at the Foundation for Defense of Democracies, a Washington think tank, also includes Ansar al-Sharia in Tunisia, a radical Islamist group formed in 2011 and accused of a wave of political assassinations last year. "First of all, the leaders have al Qaeda dossiers, and, second, their rhetoric is openly al Qaeda," says Joscelyn. "Third, there are reports of them working with AQIM, and their social media is littered with al Qaeda propaganda." He also includes Ansar al-Sharia in Benghazi, notorious for its role in the Sept. 11, 2012, consulate attack that killed U.S. Ambassador to Libya J. Christopher Stevens and three other Americans.

But Swift says groups like Ansar al Din have only loose opportunistic ties to al Qaeda. "If you define al Qaeda by its ideology, you will find al Qaeda everywhere, which is not a terribly helpful basis for analysis," he says. "You can share the al Qaeda ideology and not have any operational link to al Qaeda and also have very different political objectives."

"Al Qaeda is largely a brand more than a coherent organization," says Robert Grenier, chairman of ERG Partners, a consultant to private security and intelligence firms, and former head of the CIA's Counterterrorism Center. "The al Qaeda brand is still very powerful and is therefore appropriated by extremist groups which share a very similar doctrine of Islam, but operationally, those organizations, most often, have . . . only very tenuous connections with al Qaeda core."

In fact, Grenier argues that even AQIM and al-Shabab, which have sworn allegiance to al Qaeda, "operate quite independently, and their specific local agendas, although maybe working in parallel, are actually quite separate."

As the world watches the ongoing civil war in Syria and the increasingly successful insurgency in Iraq, here are some of the questions being debated by counterterrorism experts and government officials:

Is al Qaeda weaker since Osama bin Laden was killed?

U.S. drone strikes and targeted assassinations have killed bin Laden, nearly three dozen of his key lieutenants and hundreds of fighters in Pakistan. "Al Qaeda's core leadership has been degraded, limiting its ability to conduct attacks and direct its followers," said a recent U.S. State Department analysis.[8]

"The drone strikes have had a severe impact on al Qaeda core in Pakistan," says former FBI Special Agent Clint Watts, a senior fellow at the Foreign Policy Research Institute, a Philadelphia-based think tank. The strikes have "really slowed down their communications and coordination."

But al Qaeda's core should not be underestimated, says Bruce Hoffman, director of Georgetown University's Center for Security Studies. It has a defined and articulated strategy and "a deeper bench of personnel than we imagined," says Hoffman. Al Qaeda is filling key spots with Pakistanis — its media arm recently has been publishing more in Urdu, Pakistan's national language, than in Arabic — and "there still are senior commanders in al Qaeda who have fought in Afghanistan against the [Soviets in the 1980s] and have gravitas and stature," he says.

Even if al Qaeda's core is replenishing its ranks and hanging on, Zawahiri is losing control of the group's affiliates, say some analysts, citing Syria as a prime example. "In recent months, a full-scale civil war has erupted within al Qaeda," said J. M. Berger, editor of *intelwire.com*, which publishes terrorism research and analysis.[9]

When Zawahiri ordered ISIS to leave Syria and allow rival affiliate Jabhat al-Nusra to spearhead al Qaeda's fight against Syrian President al-Assad, ISIS openly defied him and continued its bloody feud with Jabhat al-Nusra. ISIS then taunted Zawahiri on social media.[10] "In Syria, Zawahiri is starting to resemble a guide more than a military commander," said Berger.[11]

Daveed Gartenstein-Ross, a senior fellow at the Foundation for Defense of Democracies, disagrees with Berger. ISIS has drawn little support from other groups, he said, while Zawahiri is supported "across the al Qaeda spectrum," including by AQAP, AQIM, al-Shabab and other militant jihadist groups and "a coterie of extremist clerics."[12]

In addition, al Qaeda's leadership is still exerting some control in Syria, according to Gartenstein-Ross, with several senior al Qaeda figures "integrated into Syrian jihadists groups at the highest level." They include founding al Qaeda member Abu Firas al-Suri and al Qaeda's former head of security for counterintelligence, Abu Wafa al-Saudi.[13]

Still, Zawahiri cannot offer the deep pockets and safe haven that bin Laden could, many analysts say. In fact, most al Qaeda affiliates raise their own money, sometimes through kidnapping for ransom, such as AQIM.

In June, ISIS allegedly stole $430 million from Iraq's central bank in Mosul, which would make it the world's richest terrorist group.[14]

While core al Qaeda may be weaker, many analysts argue that the al Qaeda network, however defined, is stronger. In fact, al Qaeda affiliates — and former affiliate ISIS — control more territory today than in 2011, when bin Laden was killed and the Arab Spring began. Al Qaeda was not in Syria or Lebanon two years ago, but now Jabhat Al-Nusra and ISIS control large swaths of northeastern Syria, and ISIS is gaining considerable territory in Iraq. And both are making inroads into Lebanon.

If other groups with looser ties to core al Qaeda are included, the amount of territory under al Qaeda's control expands. Since bin Laden's death, "we've seen al Qaeda offshoots active in Mali, Mauritania, Niger and crossing the border to stage attacks in Cameroon," says Hoffman. "They have been very adept at taking advantage of lawless border areas and ungoverned or under-governed regions."

However, al Qaeda affiliates and associated groups are often their own worst enemy, says Andrew Liepman, a senior policy analyst at the Rand Corp., a think tank in Santa Monica, Calif., and a former principal deputy director of the National Counterterrorism Center. "They overstretch, they establish brutal regulations that communities don't welcome — whether it's no drinking, no smoking, no mixing of the sexes or no education of girls," he says.

For example, he cites what happened in 2012 in the northern reaches of Mali, a moderate Muslim country in West Africa. Ansar al Din and AQIM took over large swathes of territory, but when the French went in to clear them out in early 2013, the local population applauded the French — their former colonial masters — for liberating them from the harsh tactics and rules imposed by the Islamists.

And in Somalia, al-Shabab refused Western aid during the 2011 famine in southern Somalia. "The local population thought that was ridiculous, and that, combined with a pretty aggressive campaign by Kenyan and African Union troops, pushed al-Shabab into the bush between Somalia and Kenya," he says.

However, al-Shabab remains lethal, as it demonstrated last September, when members stormed the Westgate Mall in Nairobi, Kenya, killing at least 67 people.

Guide to al Qaeda Affiliates

Four Sunni Muslim extremist groups have sworn allegiance to al Qaeda leader Ayman al-Zawahiri:

Al Qaeda in the Arabian Peninsula (AQAP): *Based in Yemen. Emerged when Yemeni and Saudi terrorists groups unified in January 2009. Targets local, U.S. and other Western interests in the Arabian Peninsula and has attempted attacks against the United States. Leader Nasir al-Wahishi is second-in-command to Zawahiri.*

Al Qaeda in the Islamic Maghreb (AQIM): *Based in Algeria. Operates in the country's coastal areas and parts of the south, as well as in Mali's northern desert regions. Founded in 1998 as a faction of Algeria's then-largest terrorist group. Algerian counterterrorism measures have reduced its ranks from more than 30,000 to fewer than 1,000. Targets local and Western interests.*

Al-Shabab: *Emerged from militant wing of Somali Council of Islamic Courts that took over most of southern Somalia in 2006. Recently weakened by Somali, Ethiopian and African Union military forces but continues lethal attacks in Somalia, Kenya and Ethiopia. Members come from disparate clans, but its senior leaders are affiliated with al Qaeda and are believed to have fought the Soviets in Afghanistan.*

Jabhat al-Nusra: *Created in January 2012 to overthrow regime of Syrian President Bashar al-Assad. Composed mostly of Syrians, but also attracts Western fighters. Controls territory in northern Syria. Islamic State of Iraq and Greater Syria (ISIS) played significant role in its founding, but the groups have engaged in a bloody feud inside Syria for the past year.*

Source: National Counterterrorism Center, www.nctc.gov.

Does al Qaeda remain a threat to the West?

Al Qaeda's core leadership has not directed a successful attack against a Western target since the 2005 bombings of the London Underground transit system and a city bus, which killed 56 people, including the four suicide bombers, and injured more than 800. But it has not stopped trying. Afghan-born American resident Najibullah Zazi, who plotted to bomb the New York City subway system on the eighth anniversary of 9/11, testified that he and two co-conspirators had trained with al Qaeda in Pakistan.

"Al Qaeda has been doing its utmost to attack the United States and has not pulled any punches," according to retired U.S. Army officer Thomas Lynch, a research fellow at the National Defense University's Institute of National Strategic Studies in Washington. However, the attacks "failed repeatedly before bin Laden's death and should be expected to continue to fail now that he is dead."[15] Lynch says a seriously degraded al Qaeda core has lost its operational capability and is no longer a global threat.

What is left are Salafi-jihadist* groups operating with local agendas from Tunisia to Pakistan, many of which have existed, in one form or another, since before al Qaeda was created, says Lynch. "They will shout 'death to America' and 'death to the West,' and some will even claim to be of al Qaeda, although many do not, but their focus is on local revolution and insurgency in Muslim countries." And they lack "the capability to mount serious catastrophic terror threats in the West," he says.

But Hoffman, at Georgetown, says that "completely disregards their statements and what they have argued is their strategy." Salafi-jihadists may be focusing on local conflicts now, but that can change in the future, he says.

If any of the world's violent jihadist groups pose a threat to the West, it is AQAP, says Watts, of the Foreign Policy Research Institute. "Its capability has, however, been degraded a bit because of the drone strikes and the leaders they have lost," he says, "and there is debate swirling about whether their master bomb maker is still alive."

Last August, the U.S. temporarily shut down 22 embassies and consulates across the Middle East and North Africa after a message was intercepted between Zawahiri and AQAP leader Nasir al-Wahishi describing a

---

*Salifists are ultraconservative fundamentalist Sunni Muslims who want to return Islam to seventh-century religious traditions.

planned terror attack.[16] Although the message did not give time and location, it was "one of the most specific and credible threats I've seen perhaps since 9/11," Rep. Michael McCaul, R-Texas, chairman of the House Homeland Security Committee, said at the time.[17]

Western security officials also worry about ISIS leader Abu Bakr al-Baghdadi. He took the reins of Al Qaeda in Iraq in 2010, when it was at a low ebb, having been marginalized after the U.S. convinced Sunni Iraqis to turn against the group. However, the 2011 withdrawal of U.S. troops from Iraq breathed new life into Baghdadi's organization, which has adroitly exploited a growing Sunni rebellion against the sectarian rule of Iraq's Shiite-led government. The recent gains by ISIS in western and northern Iraq have raised alarms that it, too, could shift its focus to the West.

"Ultimately, ISIS seeks to create an Islamic state from where they would launch a global holy war," said Theodore Karasik, research director of the Institute for Near East and Gulf Military Analysis, located in Dubai, UAE and Beirut. "Perhaps that war is now beginning as Baghdadi's ISIS eclipses Zawahiri's al-Qaeda," he said.[18]

Yet ISIS has enemies, and its split with Jabhat al-Nusra favors the West, says RAND's Liepman. "Right now they are both busy trying to overthrow the Assad regime and also killing each other," he says. For instance, in just one 10-day period in May, a reported 230 militants were killed as the two groups battled one other.[19]

However, "given that both groups have at different times sworn loyalty to bin Laden and Zawahiri, what comes with that is antipathy to the West," says Liepman. "So in the longer term, who knows?" And Hoffman says competition between the two groups could lead one or the other to mount an attack on the West to boost its prestige.

Fractures have plagued other al Qaeda affiliates, as well, including al-Shabab, whose top leadership consists of committed international jihadis linked to al Qaeda

Taliban, Al Qaeda in Iraq Killed Most in 2013

Only three of the world's 10 most violent groups that employed terrorist tactics against noncombatants in 2013 were affiliated with al Qaeda (in red). Among the 10, four were based in the Middle East, three in Asia, two in Africa and one in South America.

Groups That Committed Deadliest Terror Attacks, 2013

Group	Total Killed	No. of Attacks
Taliban (Afghanistan)	2,340	641
Al Qaeda in Iraq*	1,725	401
Boko Haram (Nigeria)	1,589	213
Tehrik-i-Taliban Pakistan	589	134
Al-Shabab (Somalia)	512	195
Communist Party of India — Maoist	190	203
Al Qaeda in the Arabian Peninsula	177	84
New People's Army (Philippines)	88	118
Revolutionary Armed Forces of Colombia	45	77
Bangsamoro Islamic Freedom Movement (Philippines)	23	34

* Al Qaeda in Iraq split off from al Qaeda in February and is now called the Islamic State of Iraq and Greater Syria (ISIS).

Source: "Annex of Statistical Information: Country Reports on Terrorism 2013," U.S. State Department, April 2014, p. 8, http://tinyurl.com/o2s263h

and local Somali militants. Their relationship has been marked by "infighting and betrayal," and "the local radicals' cooperation has been mostly opportunistic, a method of obtaining funding, arms and training for use against domestic foes," according to Bronwyn Bruton, deputy director of the Africa Center at the Atlantic Council, a Washington think tank.[20]

"My gut instinct is absolutely, no. I can't see al-Shabab launching an attack on the U.S. It's ridiculous to me," Bruton says.

Liepman also says that, despite its fiery rhetoric, AQIM's sworn allegiance to Zawahiri is a marriage of convenience for a group that is focused on forming a regional Islamist caliphate in Algeria and neighboring states. "AQIM says they buy into the global jihad, but their actions say otherwise," says Liepman. For one thing, he points out, the group is based just across the Mediterranean from Europe but has never tried to attack there.

Hoffman says he doesn't have an explanation for why AQIM has not yet struck abroad. "But al Qaeda hadn't struck in the United States either until 9/11," he warns. (The truck bomb that exploded in a World Trade Center garage on Feb. 26, 1993, killing six people and injuring more than 1,000, was not an al Qaeda operation. Mastermind Ramzi Yousef said the attack was because of U.S. support of Israel. Yousef is the nephew of Khalid Shaikh Mohammed, who funded the attack and later joined al Qaeda and allegedly planned 9/11.)

Can the United States do more to stem al Qaeda's spread?

After ISIS surprised the West in mid-June by quickly taking over key Iraqi cities, sending Iraqi soldiers deserting in disarray, President Obama scrambled to catch up. His national security staff met around the clock, Pentagon officials briefed lawmakers, and on June 19 the president announced that he would send up to 300 military advisers to help Iraq's security forces and was prepared to launch air strikes against the Sunni militants.[21]

Meanwhile, Shiite-dominated Iran sent three battalions to Iraq to defend the government of Shiite Prime Minister Nouri Kamal al-Maliki, according to Iranian officials, while ISIS — infamous for its beheadings, brutality and repressive rules in territory it controls — threatened Karbala and Hajaf, two Iraqi cities sacred to Shiites.[22]

Analysts blamed Maliki, who they say has purged the Iraqi Army of capable leaders and centralized decision making. But many also criticize Obama's hesitation to arm moderate opponents of Assad in Syria when ISIS was gaining strength there, and his inability to reach an agreement with Iraq to keep a residual presence there when U.S. soldiers pulled out in 2011. Iraq had refused to grant legal immunity to U.S. troops beyond that date.[23]

"It's hugely frustrating," said Michael D. Barbero, a retired U.S. Army lieutenant general who oversaw the training of Iraqi troops from 2009 to 2011. "We knew they had chinks in their armor, and we knew they weren't going to get better once we left. And yet we didn't try hard enough to get an agreement to keep some people there."[24]

No one knows whether a U.S. presence could have prevented the recent resurgence of ISIS in Iraq, considering the Sunni population's growing antipathy for the Maliki regime's sectarian policies. But the same critique has been leveled against Obama's more recent decision to steadily pull most U.S. troops out of Afghanistan by the end of 2016, leaving only a normal military presence at the embassy. Just under 32,000 U.S. troops remain in Afghanistan, down from a 2011 peak of 100,000. In 2015, there will be 9,800. Obama announced the Afghanistan withdrawal plans in a Rose Garden speech in late May, saying the United States had struck significant blows against al Qaeda's leadership, eliminated bin Laden, and "prevented Afghanistan from being used to launch attacks against our homeland."[25]

But others worry that chaos, and large numbers of al Qaeda, will return to Afghanistan. "We're going to risk squandering the gains that we have made, just as we did in Iraq," said retired Gen. Jack Keane, Army vice chief of staff from 1999 to 2003. "We're about to repeat the same mistake again."[26]

The rugged region between the capital Kabul and the Pakistan border is of particular concern. "Even now, an al Qaeda safe haven is emerging in northeastern Afghanistan," said Rep. Mike Rogers, R-Mich., chairman of the House Permanent Select Committee on Intelligence. "And I question whether the enemy will take further advantage of the announced timeline to renew its efforts to launch new operations."[27] Rather than a firm deadline, many analysts would like to see an open-ended drawdown, contingent on the situation on the ground.

However, not everyone agrees Afghanistan should be a high priority. "While there is some al Qaeda presence remaining in Afghanistan that we should be worried about, there is far more to worry about in Syria, Iraq and Yemen," said Calif. Rep. Adam Schiff, a Democratic member of the Intelligence committee.[28]

Obama addressed those concerns in his West Point speech the day after his Rose Garden remarks, announcing establishment of a Counterterrorism Partnerships Fund (CPF) of up to $5 billion to build counterterrorism capacity and "facilitate partner countries on the front lines."[29]

However, four similar programs have been created in the past decade. "If the performance over the past three years of Iraqi forces and the likely performance of Afghan security forces is any guide, don't expect stability, transparency, effectiveness and a lack of corruption to spring forth from the barren soil of the CPF's new partners," said Gordon Adams, a professor of international relations at American University and President Bill Clinton's senior budget official for national security.[30]

Finding reliable partners will also be a challenge for the CPF, says Bruce Riedel, director of the Washington-based

Brookings Institution's Intelligence Project and a former senior adviser to the last four U.S. presidents on South Asia and the Middle East.

"We don't want to support the Assad regime to fight al-Nusra. Somalia really has no effective government whatsoever, so who are you going to support there? We gave a lot of money to the Pakistani government, but is there really any evidence that we are getting much help in fighting al Qaeda? Pakistan hasn't arrested a senior al Qaeda figure since 2005," says Riedel.

Yemen is the poster child for U.S. training and intelligence support, says Riedel. "Building up the [counterterrorism] capability of the government of Yemen makes a lot of sense . . . but even in Yemen, you have a weak government."

Moreover, training foreign forces inside countries with weak governments can have unintended negative consequences, said Adams. "Just take the case of Mali, where a U.S.-trained captain, Amadou Sanogo, carried out a coup in 2012, leading to the disintegration of the Malian military, a nearly successful Islamic extremist revolt, and the need for foreign intervention."[31]

Last year, U.S. Special Operations troops began to instruct and equip "hundreds of handpicked commandos in Libya, Niger, Mauritania and Mali," according to *The New York Times*. "You have to make sure of who you're training," said Maj. Gen. Patrick J. Donahue II, commander of U.S. Army soldiers operating in Africa. "It can't be the standard, 'Has this guy been a terrorist or some sort of criminal?' but also, 'What are his allegiances? Is he true to the country, or is he still bound to his militia?' "[32]

BACKGROUND

The Beginning

"Al Qaeda and transnational jihad in general are primarily creatures of the Afghan war against the Soviets," wrote political scientist Fawaz Gerges in *The Rise and Fall of Al-Qaeda*.[33]

From 1979 to 1989, an unprecedented migration of young Muslim men, predominantly from the Middle East, descended on Pakistan and Afghanistan to wage jihad, or holy war, against the Soviet Union after its invasion of Afghanistan.[34]

They were inspired by the charismatic Sunni scholar Abdallah Azzam, a Jordanian of Palestinian descent. Azzam believed in the creation of a Muslim vanguard to fight and build a strict Islamic society ruled by sharia, or Islamic law. "Azzam's preaching and advocacy of jihad to defend Afghan Muslims persecuted by the Soviets reached audiences throughout the world via audio broadcasts, magazines and flyers," counterterrorism expert Watts, of the Foreign Policy Research Institute, wrote in a short history of al Qaeda.[35]

In 1984, Azzam set up the Services Bureau, a staging base in Peshawar, Pakistan, to recruit and transition Arab fighters, known as "Afghan Arabs," into training camps in Afghanistan. As a university student, Osama bin Laden, born in Saudi Arabia in the late 1950s to a Yemeni construction magnate, had heard Azzam lecture and agreed to finance his endeavor. Bin Laden also set up his own training camp in Afghanistan, called the Lion's Den. And he began to associate with Egyptian radicals, including Ayman al-Zawahiri, a surgeon, who came to Peshawar in 1986 to work for the Red Crescent Society, the Islamic version of the International Red Cross.

Zawahiri and Azzam had competing views of jihad, a rift that deepened in 1988 as the Soviets began withdrawing from Afghanistan, which soon plunged into civil war. Zawahiri proposed redirecting the Afghan Arabs against "apostate" Muslim regimes, starting with Egypt and Algeria. In 1981, Zawahiri had been arrested and charged with collaborating in the assassination of Egyptian President Anwar Sadat, who had signed an historic 1979 peace treaty with Israel. Not long after his release in 1984, Zawahiri took over leadership of Egyptian Islamic Jihad, a terrorist organization bent on installing religious rule.

Azzam opposed taking up arms against other Muslims and, instead, wanted to send the Arab Afghans to the Palestinian territories to reclaim his ancestral land from Israel.

Both camps bitterly vied for bin Laden's allegiance and money. But bin Laden did not share either of their priorities, wrote journalist Lawrence Wright in *The Looming Tower: Al-Qaeda and the Road to 9/11*. "At the time, he envisioned moving the struggle to Kashmir, the Philippines and particularly the Central Asian republics, where he could continue the jihad against the Soviet Union."[36]

In August 1988, bin Laden and a small group of associates formed a new organization called al Qaeda — Arabic for "the base" — to direct the best fighters from

CHRONOLOGY

1980s *Osama bin Laden establishes al Qaeda.*

1984 Sunni scholar Abdallah Azzam and bin Laden establish a staging base in Peshawar, Pakistan, for Arabs fighting Soviet troops in Afghanistan. . . . Future al Qaeda leader Ayman al-Zawahiri becomes leader of Egyptian Islamic Jihad.

1986 Bin Laden establishes training camp in Afghanistan for Arabs fighting Soviets troops. . . . He meets Zawahiri in Peshawar.

1988 Soviets begin withdrawing from Afghanistan. . . . Bin Laden founds al Qaeda, Arabic for "the base," to redirect foreign fighters to other Muslim countries.

1990s *Bin Laden and Zawahiri decide to target the West.*

1992 From Sudan, bin Laden masterminds an attack against U.S. soldiers in Yemen, but two tourists die instead.

1996 Bin Laden moves to Afghanistan as Taliban guest.

1998 Bin Laden, Zawahiri and others call for Muslims to kill Americans. . . . Al Qaeda bombs U.S. embassies in Kenya and Tanzania, killing 224; President Bill Clinton launches cruise missiles against al Qaeda training camp in Afghanistan but misses senior leaders.

2000-2005 *Al Qaeda strikes United States mainland; bin Laden goes into hiding. Smaller attacks in Spain and London follow.*

2000 Two al Qaeda suicide attackers ram an explosive-laden boat into the Navy destroyer *U.S.S. Cole* in Yemen, killing 17 U.S. sailors.

2001 Nearly 3,000 people are killed after 19 al Qaeda operatives fly hijacked jets into World Trade Center, Pentagon and a Pennsylvania field (Sept. 11); President George W. Bush declares a war on terror (Sept. 20); United States launches air strikes in Afghanistan (Oct. 7). . . . British al Qaeda follower Richard Reid tries to detonate a shoe bomb on a Paris to Miami flight (Dec. 22).

2002 Bin Laden escapes to Pakistan.

2003 Al Qaeda-linked groups blamed for bombings in Kenya, Saudi Arabia, Morocco and Turkey. . . . United States invades Iraq after Bush claims it is producing weapons of mass destruction.

2004 Alleged al Qaeda bombers attack four commuter trains in Madrid, killing 191 and injuring more than 1,800.

2005 Four al Qaeda-trained British citizens bomb London's Underground transit system and a bus, killing 56 people, including the four bombers, and injuring more than 700.

2009-Present *United States foils several al Qaeda attacks and kills bin Laden; al Qaeda affiliates focus on local conflicts.*

2009 Al Qaeda-trained Afghan-American Najibullah Zazi is arrested in New York for plot to bomb subways. . . . Nigerian Umar Farouk Abdulmutallab is arrested after trying to ignite an al Qaeda-supplied bomb hidden in his underwear aboard a U.S.-bound flight.

2011 U.S. Special Forces team kills bin Laden in Abbottabad, Pakistan. . . . Civilian protests against authoritarian rulers spread from Tunisia to the Middle East; anti-government demonstrations in Syria morph into a sectarian civil war.

2013 Al Qaeda affiliate al-Shabab storms Nairobi's Westgate Mall, killing at least 67. . . . To date, U.S. drone strikes in Pakistan have killed roughly three dozen key al Qaeda lieutenants and nearly 300 lower-level militants.

2014 Zawahiri cuts ties with the Islamic State of Iraq and Greater Syria (ISIS) for its brutal tactics and for battling another al Qaeda branch in Syria's civil war. . . . U.S. drone strikes in Yemen have killed up to 887 militants linked to Al Qaeda in the Arabian Peninsula (AQAP) and up to 87 civilians. . . . ISIS forces in Iraq take control of Mosul and Tikrit; Iraq declares a state of emergency (June). . . . Obama sends the first of 300 military advisers to Iraq and is considering air strikes against ISIS.

among the Afghan Arabs. "But it was still unclear what the organization would do or where it would go after the jihad [in Afghanistan]. Perhaps bin Laden himself didn't know," wrote Wright. "Notably, the United States was not yet on anyone's list."[37]

Global Jihad Emerges

In 1989, Azzam was killed by unknown assassins, and bin Laden returned to Saudi Arabia. In 1990 he proposed that the Saudi government allow him to use Arab veterans of the Afghan conflict — now scattered across Pakistan, Afghanistan and the Middle East — to fight Iraq, which had invaded Kuwait and threatened Saudi Arabia. The government refused, and bin Laden watched, enraged, as American troops established bases in the Saudi kingdom to protect it and expel the Iraqis from Kuwait. He soon came to see the United States as an occupying force of nonbelievers in the Arabian peninsula, home to Mecca, Islam's holiest city.

In 1992, Sudan's new Islamist-backed government invited bin Laden to move there, hoping he would invest in the country's development. Bin Laden quickly built an empire of factories and farming estates. But American troops remained in Saudi Arabia, overseeing the ceasefire with Iraq and, equally galling to bin Laden, using his ancestral home of Yemen as a stopover on their way to famine-plagued Somalia to protect U.N. aid workers from local militias.

"After all the plans al Qaeda had nurtured to spread an Islamist revolution, it was America that appeared to be waxing in influence across the region," said Wright.[38] In late December, 1992, two bombs exploded at hotels in Aden, Yemen, targeting U.S. troops. Bin Laden would claim credit for the attack, in which two Austrian tourists died, but no soldiers.

With the Yemeni attacks, "a new vision of al Qaeda was born" as a global terrorist organization, wrote Wright. "America was the only power capable of blocking the restoration of the ancient Islamic caliphate, and it would have to be confronted and defeated."[39]

In October, 1993, 18 U.S. soldiers were killed in Mogadishu, the capital of Somalia, in an incident that ended with shocking images of dead, naked American troops being dragged through the streets and their bodies burned by local insurgents. In 1996, the U.S. initiated a grand jury investigation of bin Laden's role in the "Blackhawk Down" incident, and the FBI and the CIA created a joint operation to track him down.

Meanwhile, under international pressure, Sudan expelled bin Laden, who settled in Afghanistan in 1996 as a guest of the Taliban, which had recently seized control of Kabul and implemented strict Islamic law. Zawahiri joined him in the late 1990s and officially merged Egyptian Islamic Jihad with al Qaeda.

In February 1998, bin Laden, Zawahiri and other radical jihadists declared that killing "Americans and their allies — civilians and military — is an individual duty for every Muslim who can do it in any country in which it is possible to do it." Their main complaints against the United States were: the presence of U.S. troops in the Arabian Peninsula; their fear that the United States was intent on destroying the Muslim people of Iraq through economic sanctions; and its support of Israel and corrupt dictatorships in the Middle East and North Africa.[40]

The call to arms drew a new generation of young fighters — from Europe, North Africa and the Middle East — to train with al Qaeda in Afghanistan. And it signaled a shift in Zawahiri's strategy from attacking apostate and pro-Western Muslim rulers to attacking the West.

By that time, the number of intelligence reports on al Qaeda plots was growing, but "few in the United State's government were listening," wrote terrorism analyst Seth G. Jones in *Hunting in the Shadows: The Pursuit of al Qa'ida Since 9/11.* "It took gruesome terrorist attacks to spur the government to move against bin Laden and Zawahiri."[41]

On Aug. 7, 1998, al Qaeda operatives bombed the U.S. embassies in Nairobi, Kenya, and Dar es Salaam, Tanzania, killing 224 people and injuring more than 4,500. President Bill Clinton responded by launching a cruise missile strike against a suspected al Qaeda training camp in Afghanistan, but neither bin Laden nor senior al Qaeda leaders were killed.

The embassy bombings "had a profound impact on U.S. counterterrorism efforts," wrote Jones. The CIA established a special unit to plan operations against bin Laden and put a covert team in Afghanistan.[42] But bin Laden and Zawahiri eluded capture, and on Oct. 12, 2000, two al Qaeda suicide attackers rammed an explosives-laden boat into the Navy destroyer *U.S.S. Cole* in the Port of Aden, Yemen, killing 17 U.S. sailors.

The United States did not respond militarily, and al Qaeda operative Khalid Sheikh Mohammed, with bin

Al Qaeda Seeks Weapons of Mass Destruction

While intent on attacks, the group lacks know-how, experts say.

Al Qaeda's interest in developing and using weapons of mass destruction (WMDs) dates back to the 1990s. During that decade, al Qaeda tried to purchase uranium for nuclear weapons, established a biowarfare laboratory in Afghanistan to develop weaponized anthrax and undertook a separate project to produce ricin and other chemical-warfare agents.[1]

"Those efforts were seriously disrupted by the U.S. invasion [of Afghanistan], but I don't think that al Qaeda or its affiliates and associates have completely abandoned the desire for these weapons," says Bruce Hoffman, director of Georgetown University's Center for Security Studies.

In 2003, al Qaeda put out a fatwa — an opinion handed down by an Islamic scholar — justifying the use of weapons of mass destruction. "And in 2008, Ayman al-Zawahiri" — al Qaeda's second-in-command at the time — "wrote a book and explained why WMD was still important," says Rolf Mowatt-Larssen, a senior fellow at Harvard University's Belfer Center for Science and International Affairs and a former director of intelligence and counterintelligence at the U.S. Department of Energy. Commentaries and statements from al Qaeda's core — its Pakistan-based leadership — since then suggest that "the goal is the same," he says.

But the focus of al Qaeda's core leadership and that of its affiliates diverge, says Mowatt-Larssen. Al Qaeda's core "recognizes that at the very high end there are two options: a nuclear event or a large-scale biological weapon, like anthrax," Mowatt-Larssen says. The affiliates are more interested in mid- and low-level events, such as a chemical attack on a rival's territory or an assassination using cyanide, "in order to get rid of rivals and start panic," he says.

But al Qaeda and its affiliates have not succeeded, as far as is known publicly, in effectively using weapons of mass destruction. Hoffman and Mowatt-Larssen point to several reasons for that.

First, such weapons, especially nuclear or biological ones, are difficult to develop and use. "It is really hard to get nuclear material," says Mowatt-Larssen. "There is some on the black market, but there may not be enough for terrorists to build a viable nuclear device."

Even if terrorists were about to acquire enough nuclear material, Hoffman points out, the terrorists would then "have to design a bomb and figure out how to trigger it. The technological and scientific hurdles are tremendous, and I would think that they would be insurmountable without state support."

Biological weapons are difficult to fabricate and difficult to disseminate effectively, says Hoffman. "I believe the Japanese cult Aum Shinrikyo had at least on nine occasions tried to use biological weapons, and it didn't succeed," he says. "And that's why they turned to chemical weapons and

---

Laden's blessing, continued to plan an attack on the U.S. homeland, which bin Laden believed would force the United States to pull out of the Middle East and lead to the establishment of conservative Islamic regimes. Mohammed, a Pakistani citizen, was captured by the CIA and Pakistan intelligence in Pakistan in 2003 and is awaiting trial at the Guantánamo Bay military prison, accused of masterminding 9/11.

Retreat to Pakistan

Nine days after 9/11, President George W. Bush declared a "war on terror" and demanded that the Taliban turn over bin Laden and al Qaeda leaders.[43] Bin Laden "was confident that the United States would respond to the attacks in New York and Washington only with cruise missile strikes, as it had done three years earlier," wrote journalist Peter Bergen in *Manhunt: The Ten Year Search for Bin Laden from 9/11 to Abbottabad.*[44]

But the U.S. response was quick and fierce. Within a week, Congress granted Bush authority to use force against any "nations, organizations, or persons" involved in the 9/11 attack or that "harbored" those responsible. On Oct. 7, Bush launched air strikes in Afghanistan, and by early December, the Taliban was ousted and bin Laden and al Qaeda's core members had retreated to the Afghan mountains, where they battled U.S. and British Special Forces. Rather than pushing the United States out of Muslim lands, 9/11 had invited an invasion.[45]

sarin." The group captured worldwide attention in 1995 when it released sarin, a nerve agent, onto Tokyo subway cars, killing 12 people.

"What is the most likely WMD that al Qaeda might get its hands on? In my view: chemical," says Hoffman. "But still, you need to have a lot of it to have an effect; you've got to have a way to deliver it; it can dissipate; and you have to protect yourself."

When Tamil Tiger insurgents used chlorine gas to attack a Sri Lankan armed forces base in 1990, Hoffman explained, the wind changed direction and blew the gas back at the Tigers, who had to abort the attack. [2] And during the height of the Iraq War in 2006, Al Qaeda in Iraq used chlorine gas in its bombs, but while the explosions killed people, "the chlorine itself didn't really harm anyone," says Hoffman.

Besides finding it difficult to obtain destructive materials, al Qaeda hasn't succeeded at deploying a WMD because U.S. drone strikes have seriously degraded al Qaeda's core leadership, and security officials have been effective at preventing attacks, says Mowatt-Larssen. For example, a police raid of a London apartment in 2003 found castor oil beans — the raw material for ricin — along with production equipment and recipes for ricin, botulinum and other poisons. Two years later, a British court found a suspected al Qaeda operative arrested in connection with the raid guilty of plotting to spread ricin in public areas of the United Kingdom.[3] A year ago, Iraq said it had captured an al Qaeda cell that planned to produce mustard gas and other poisons for attacks in Iraq, Europe and the United States.[4]

In addition, while al Qaeda and its affiliates are expert in conventional weapons, they may not have personnel with expertise in chemical, biological or nuclear weapons, Hoffman says. However, the civil war in Syria could change that equation, he says. In a deal brokered by the United States and Russia in the wake of a deadly chemical attack on civilians, allegedly by the regime of Syrian President Bashar al-Assad, Assad agreed to allow Syria's chemical weapons stockpiles to be destroyed, which the United Nations announced on June 23 had been accomplished.

"What is worrisome is that veterans of the Syrian Army's chemical corps might find their way into al Qaeda's ranks in Syria and provide that expertise and knowledge," says Hoffman.

"I think it would be hardest for [al Qaeda and its affiliates] to use WMD's against the United States. I believe it is certainly becoming more of a problem in the Middle East," he says.

— *Barbara Mantel*

---

[1]Bruce Hoffman, "Low-Tech Terrorism," *The National Interest*, March-April 2014, p. 3, tinyurl.com/lgd4age.

[2]*Ibid.*

[3]"Killer jailed over poison plot," BBC News, April 13, 2005, http://news.bbc.co.uk/2/hi/uk_news/4433709.stm.

[4]"Iraq says captures al Qaeda chemical gas team," Reuters, June 1, 2013, http://articles.chicagotribune.com/2013-06-01/news/sns-rt-us-iraq-violence-chemicalsbre9500cg-20130601_1_mustard-gas-iraqi-kurdish-chlorine-gas.

In February, bin Laden and some associates slipped into Pakistan, where many hid in the relative anonymity of the bustling city of Karachi and set about rebuilding al Qaeda. But after Pakistan and the United States captured several key operatives in the next several years — including 9/11 planner Mohammed — al Qaeda's leaders retreated to northern Pakistan's lawless tribal regions, where they set up training camps, albeit on a smaller scale than in Afghanistan. Bin Laden's whereabouts were unknown.

Meanwhile, bombings of Western targets in North Africa, Europe and the Middle East demonstrated al Qaeda's reach. In some cases, governments blamed al Qaeda directly, such as for the May 12, 2003, bombings

in the Saudi capital Riyadh, which killed 35 people. In other incidents, violent jihadist groups with suspected connections to al Qaeda either claimed responsibility or were blamed. Analysts still disagree about whether al Qaeda directed the March 11, 2004, bombing of commuter trains in Madrid, which killed 191 people and left at least 1,800 injured, or whether the dozens of men arrested, mostly Moroccan, were only tenuously linked to al Qaeda.

Al Qaeda's link to the July 7, 2005, bombings of the London Underground and a city bus is much clearer: The four British citizens, three of Pakistani descent, who detonated the bombs had trained at al Qaeda's camps in Pakistan. The explosions — the deadliest terrorist attack

Is Boko Haram Aligned with al Qaeda?

"They are boys who . . . rape women, kill children and steal from the population."

Boko Haram caught the world's attention when it kidnapped 276 schoolgirls from a remote northern Nigerian village on April 14. But the brutal Islamist insurgency has been terrorizing northeastern Nigeria and nearby border areas for years.

Since 2009, Boko Haram has killed an estimated 6,500 people, according to Bronwyn Bruton, deputy director of the Africa Center at the Atlantic Council, a Washington think tank.[1] In a particularly horrific attack in February, the group — whose name, loosely translated from the local Hausa language, means "Western education is forbidden" — attacked a secondary school in northeastern Nigeria and shot, hacked or burned to death 59 boys, many as they slept in their beds. On June 23, the group reportedly abducted at least 91 more people, including 60 girls and 31 boys.[2]

Besides students and civilians, the group has attacked police officers, soldiers, politicians, and rival religious leaders. Their attacks, and a government crackdown on the group that began in 2009, have caused an estimated 250,000 people in the region to flee their homes in the past 10 months.[3]

Last month Nigerian officials met in Paris with representatives from neighboring Chad, Cameroon, Niger and Benin to forge an agreement to share intelligence and coordinate patrol and rescue efforts in the border areas where Boko Haram operates. At a news conference after the meeting, Nigerian President Goodluck Jonathan called Boko Haram the "al Qaeda of West Africa."[4]

He is not alone in tying Boko Haram to al Qaeda. Last November, the State Department declared Boko Haram a foreign terrorist organization with "links to al-Qa'ida in the Islamic Maghreb (AQIM)."[5]

Yet some analysts say the al Qaeda label is misleading. "It is very much in President Jonathan's interest to say Boko Haram is part of the international terror movement because it then gives him a claim on international resources," says John Campbell, former U.S. ambassador to Nigeria (2004-2007) and author of *Nigeria: Dancing on the Brink*.

While the group issues statements supporting al Qaeda's goals, Boko Haram's focus is strictly local, and the organizations have no formal ties, Campbell says. "I don't doubt that you have members of Boko Haram who have talked to people who claim to be part of al-Shabab or al Qaeda in the Islamic Maghreb," he says, but Boko Haram "is a different kind of creature."

Its violence is too unfocused and brutal even for al Qaeda, says Bruton, who calls Boko Haram an African rebel group. "Al Qaeda's violence is very strategic. They use violence to send a very careful political message, whereas African rebel groups tend to be really predatory," said Bruton. Members of African rebel groups like Boko Haram "are young boys who do drugs, they are not educated . . . and they are especially known to rape women, to kill children, to steal from the local population." Al Qaeda's leaders would worry that such behavior would sully its brand, she said.[6]

Other analysts, however, agree with the State Department's assessment. "Al Qaeda affiliates' purpose is to handle local affairs," says Jacob Zenn, an analyst of African and Eurasian Affairs for The Jamestown Foundation, a Washington-based think tank. For example, "Al Qaeda in the Islamic Maghreb does mostly attacks in Algeria. Boko Haram attacks in Nigeria." Zenn calls Boko Haram a "clandestine" al Qaeda affiliate, because they haven't yet "formalized the connection to the world."

The United States, France, Britain and Israel have sent special forces and intelligence operatives to help search for the kidnapped girls, although U.S. actions are constrained by prohibitions on direct military assistance to any foreign military unit that has violated human rights. "Since 2009, the Nigerian military has been widely accused by local witnesses and human rights groups of killing thousands of people — many of them innocent civilians — in its efforts to destroy Boko Haram," said Bruton."[7]

in British history — killed 56 people, including the four suicide bombers, and injured more than 700.[46]

Unbeknown to the CIA, that same year bin Laden moved into a walled compound in Abbottabad, Pakistan, and began relying on a few select couriers to communicate with others in the al Qaeda leadership and beyond, including al Qaeda in Iraq, which was created after the United States invaded Iraq in 2003.

Boko Haram was created in 2002 in the northeastern Nigerian state of Borno by Islamist cleric Mohammed Yusuf, whom the government executed in 2009 after an armed uprising in the region. "From sermons and statements, you can say their goal is the establishment of God's kingdom on Earth through justice for the poor, achieved through the rigorous application of Islamic law, or sharia," says Campbell. The group has been unclear, however, as to whether it wants sharia law imposed nationwide or only in Nigeria's predominantly Muslim northern states, he adds.

After the government crackdown in 2009, Boko Haram splintered into several groups and became increasingly radical and brutal. The group's putative leader now is Yusuf acolyte Abubakar Shekau. Boko Haram "is a symptom of decades of failed government and elite delinquency finally ripening into social chaos," said Nigerian analyst and blogger Chris Ngwodo.[8]

While analysts disagree on Boko Haram's ties to al Qaeda, they agree that a growing Western presence in Nigeria could push the group into the arms of international jihadists. Last month, says Campbell, a northern Nigerian religious leader warned that if Western troops get involved in the fight against Boko Haram, it would "lead to an influx of foreign fighters into northern Nigeria in support of Boko Haram."

To eliminate the threat from Boko Haram, says Campbell, the Nigerian government should halt human rights abuses by its military and police, reduce government corruption and reduce the stark differences that have historically existed between the predominantly Muslim north and the mostly Christian south. For example, he points out, fewer than 20 percent of northern Nigerian women can read and write, compared to more than 80 percent in the south. "You are really asking for a country to transform itself, and that is usually hard for countries to do," says Campbell.

— *Barbara Mantel*

AFP/Getty Images/Pius Utomi Ekpei

A woman rallies in Lagos, Nigeria, for the release of 287 Nigerian schoolgirls captured by Boko Haram on April 14. Thought by some to be linked to al Qaeda, the brutal group reportedly abducted at least 91 more youths on June 23.

[1]"Bronwyn Bruton on Boko Haram," Atlantic Council, May 29, 2014, http://tinyurl.com/qh88yk2.

[2]Robyn Dixon, "Nigeria kidnapping: 60 girls and women, 31 boys said to be abducted," *Los Angeles Times*, June 24, 2014, http://tinyurl.com/koaafel.

[3]Ishaan Tharoor, "MAP: What Boko Haram is doing to Nigeria," *The Washington Post*, June 5, 2014, http://tinyurl.com/ku4dynn.

[4]John Irish and Elizabeth Pineau, "West Africa leaders vow to wage 'total war' on Boko Haram," Reuters, May 17, 2014, http://tinyurl.com/lzgw7nt.

[5]"Terrorist Designations of Boko Haram and Ansaru," U.S. Department of State, Nov. 13, 2013, http://tinyurl.com/m7mmky6.

[6]"Bronwyn Bruton on Boko Haram," *op. cit.*

[7]Bronwyn Bruton, "Intelbrief: Nigeria: The Limits of US Assistance," Atlantic Council, May 13, 2014, http://tinyurl.com/lerd7p7.

[8]Mohammed Aly Sergie and Toni Johnson, "Terrorist Groups: Boko Haram," Council on Foreign Relations, May 5, 2014, http://tinyurl.com/q4yvapy.

Bin Laden was initially "ecstatic about the opportunities that the 2003 American invasion presented to establish an al Qaeda affiliate in the Arab heartland," wrote Bergen. But by 2005, "he had grown increasingly worried about the brutal tactics of al-Qaeda in Iraq." The group blew up Shia mosques, killed fellow Sunnis, and its leader — Abu Musab al-Zarqawi — posted online the gruesome videos of hostage beheadings. Bin Laden worried that

AP Photo

AFP/Getty Images/Ali al-Saadi

Battle for Iraq

In a photo released by the Islamic State of Iraq and Greater Syria (ISIS), militants appear to be leading away captured Iraqi soldiers dressed in plain clothes on June 14. (Top) The militants' claims that they later executed 1,700 soldiers could not be independently verified. In the sectarian conflict in Iraq, the former al Qaeda affiliate has captured several major cities and in late June appeared to be closing in on Baghdad. Also on June 14, Shiites in Baghdad (bottom) pledged to join Iraqi security forces in the fight against ISIS. The Sunni-Shiite battle over Iraq and neighboring Syria reflects a 1,000-year-old conflict between the two Muslim sects and is seen by many analysts as a proxy battle to determine whether Shiite-dominated Iran or Sunni-led Saudi Arabia will dominate the Arab world.

Zarqawi was harming the al Qaeda brand and publicly apologized for Zarqawi's behavior after U.S. air strikes killed him in 2006.[47]

Bin Laden was also disappointed in al Qaeda trainees' failed attempts to carry out attacks in the United States, thwarted partly by America's post-9/11 intelligence and security apparatus and partly by the trainees' own bungling.

In early September 2009, Najibullah Zazi, an Afghan-American trained by al Qaeda in Pakistan, traveled from Denver to detonate bombs in the subways of New York. But he was arrested by the FBI, which had him under surveillance. On Christmas Day the same year, Nigerian Umar Farouk Abdulmutallab tried unsuccessfully to ignite a bomb hidden in his underwear as his Amsterdam-to-Detroit flight was about to land. He told investigators he had acquired the device in Yemen, home of AQAP.[48]

After those attempts, President Obama intensified the U.S. drone campaign in Pakistan, begun by President George W. Bush, and extended it to Yemen. By 2014, the controversial drone strikes — which international rights groups complained were killing innocent civilians and alienating the local population — had killed dozens of key al Qaeda lieutenants, including propagandist Anwar al-Awlaki, a U.S. citizen in Yemen, and hundreds in the middle ranks.[49]

Arab Spring

After a nearly decade-long manhunt, on May 1, 2011, a U.S. Navy SEAL team killed bin Laden at his Abbottabad compound. "The death of bin Laden marks the most significant achievement to date in our nation's effort to defeat al Qaeda," President Obama told the nation. "His death does not mark the end of our effort. There's no doubt that al Qaeda will continue to pursue attacks against us."[50] Six weeks later, al Qaeda appointed Zawahiri as bin Laden's successor.

Bin Laden's death was soon eclipsed by the momentous events of the Arab Spring, which began five months earlier with peaceful protests in Tunisia and spread across North Africa and the Middle East. A combination of civilian protests, internal military intervention and, in the case of Libya, rebel fighting and Western military help, toppled dictators in Tunisia, Egypt, Libya and Yemen, seeming to undercut bin Laden's claim that attacking America was a necessary prelude to dislodging dictatorial regimes. Initially, at least, "al Qaeda's leaders, foot soldiers, and ideas played no role," wrote Bergen.[51]

But al Qaeda thrives where there is chaos, and the early promise of the Arab Spring has faded. While Tunisia adopted a new constitution in January and is transitioning to democracy, fighting among rival militias and a renegade general's attempted coup is pushing Libya toward

AT ISSUE

Is the threat posed by former Guantánamo detainees exaggerated?

YES Bailey Cahall
Policy Analyst, International Security Program, New America Foundation

Written for *CQ Researcher*, June 2014

The May 31 release of U.S. Army Sgt. Bowe Bergdahl in exchange for five former senior Taliban officials being held at the U.S. detention facility at Guantánamo Bay, Cuba, has renewed the debate over how many former detainees end up returning to the battlefield. Days after Bergdahl's release, Sen. John McCain, R-Ariz., told Fox News that 30 percent of the released detainees "have already gone back into the fight," a figure that has been repeated by a number of other sources. But this number is a misleading conflation of the U.S. government's own estimates.

The Office of the Director of National Intelligence (ODNI) — which releases an unclassified summary report about the recidivism rates of former detainees every six months — said in January that 104 (17 percent) of the 614 detainees released from the prison have engaged in "terrorist activities," and 74 (12 percent) are suspected of doing so. Yet it is impossible to assess the validity of these numbers because the U.S. government has not publicly released the names of any of these detainees since 2009.

But even if the numbers were correctly parsed, the phrase "terrorist activities" adds to the confusion. In the public sphere, these are treated as if they were all attacks, but the ODNI combines planning and conducting attacks with financing terrorist operations and facilitating the movement of people involved in such activities.

While none of these are good, some are certainly worse than others. There is a scale to the level of threat these activities pose, but commentators act as if they are absolutes.

To be sure, some former Guantánamo detainees are quite dangerous. For example, Said Ali al-Shiri, who was transferred to Saudi Arabia in 2007, cofounded Al Qaeda in the Arabian Peninsula in 2009. And Abdullah Ghulam Rasoul emerged as a top Taliban commander after being transferred to Afghanistan and subsequently released in 2007.

Yet the men who were transferred from Guantánamo in exchange for Bergdahl are not being released freely into Afghan society. They must first spend a year in Qatar, a rich and efficient police state, and they have been banned from travel during that time.

Assuming that ban holds, by the time they are able to return to Afghanistan, there will no longer be a U.S. combat presence in the country, minimizing any potential threat they might pose to American soldiers there.

NO Daveed Gartenstein-Ross
Senior Fellow, Foundation for Defense of Democracies

Written for *CQ Researcher*, June 2014

In considering whether detainees released from Guantánamo Bay pose a real threat, the debate over recidivism rates is somewhat beside the point. Enemy combatants are detained during wars because of concern that, if released, they will return to the fight. So it's worth examining the impact released detainees have had, as revealed in militant propaganda, credible media accounts and the work of scholars. It's no exaggeration to say Guantánamo detainees have had an impact on tens of thousands of lives since their release.

Former detainees have played prominent leadership roles in Islamist groups. In South Asia, they served as the Taliban's chief military commander, led Taliban forces in southern Afghanistan, served as the shadow governor in Uruzgan province and commanded thousands of fighters in Pakistan's Waziristan region. Former detainees served as the deputy commander of Al Qaeda in the Arabian Peninsula (AQAP) and as an AQAP operational commander (Othman Ahmed al-Ghamdi) and religious leader (Ibrahim al-Rubaish). A former detainee leads Ansar al-Sharia in Derna, Libya.

Detainees have been involved in numerous attacks since their release. They have orchestrated attacks against coalition forces in Afghanistan, directed a hotel bombing in Islamabad, participated in attacks in the Caucasus region and blew up a gas pipeline in Russia's Tatarstan republic. They carried out a suicide bombing in Iraq (13 dead) and oversaw a 2007 suicide attack in Pakistan (31 dead). Former detainees masterminded or participated in the kidnapping of a Saudi diplomat in 2012 and two Chinese engineers in Pakistan in 2004.

In addition, released detainees have found their way to the Syrian battlefield and served as foot soldiers or operatives in Afghanistan, Pakistan, Saudi Arabia and Yemen.

Other former detainees are involved in terrorist recruitment. This month Spanish authorities arrested Lahcen Ikasrrien for running a cell that provided fighters to the Islamic State of Iraq and Greater Syria, and others have been charged with recruitment or facilitation elsewhere.

There are serious policy questions about detention of nonstate actors. Unlike state-to-state conflict, such enemies rarely wear a uniform, and conflicts may last far longer when nonstate actors are involved. But these questions must be separated from questions of fact. Many released detainees do not return to militancy. But those who do have already had a significant impact.

civil war. Yemen's new president is battling separatist forces, and Egypt's military recently ousted a democratically elected, religiously conservative government. Anti-government demonstrations in Syria degenerated into a civil war, and the violence is spilling into Lebanon, Jordan and Iraq, where a renewed Sunni insurgency is fighting the Shiite-led government. Al Qaeda's formal affiliates, loosely tied associates and professed supporters have inserted themselves into each of these conflicts.

In January, Director of National Intelligence James Clapper told the Senate Select Committee on Intelligence that he expected worse to come: "In the three years since the outbreak of the Arab Spring, a few states have made halting progress in their transitions away from authoritarian rule. Nevertheless, political uncertainty and violence will probably increase across the region in 2014 as the toppling of leaders and weakening of regimes have unleashed ethnic and sectarian rivalries that are propagating destabilizing violence."[52]

CURRENT SITUATION

Foreign Fighters in Syria

On a Saturday afternoon in late May, a man entered the Jewish Museum in Brussels and shot and killed two Israeli tourists with a .38-caliber revolver. He then pulled an assault rifle from a black bag and killed a French museum volunteer and wounded a Belgian man.[53]

French authorities later arrested a suspect, 29-year-old Frenchman Mehdi Nemmouche, during a routine customs check as he arrived in France by bus. Officials said he had travelled to Syria last year to fight with the Islamic State of Iraq and Greater Syria (ISIS).[54]

The killings are likely the first by a European citizen returning from the Syrian conflict, according to European officials, although they could not say what role, if any, ISIS played in the attack or whether Nemmouche was motivated by his experience in Syria.[55] Nevertheless, his arrest underscores Western governments' warnings that some of the thousands of foreign fighters flowing into Syria — where many are thought to connect with ISIS or the al Qaeda affiliate Jabhat al-Nusra — could pose a terrorist threat once they return home.

"This raises concerns that radicalized individuals with extremist contacts and battlefield experience could either return to their home countries to commit violence at their own initiative, or participate in an al Qaeda-directed plot aimed at Western targets outside Syria," Matthew Olsen, director of the National Counterterrorism Center, told Congress.[56]

Since late 2011, as many as 12,000 citizens or residents from more than 80 countries have gone to Syria to fight the Assad regime, according to some analysts. "These numbers are unprecedented," says Aaron Zelin, a fellow at the Washington Institute for Near East Policy, whose own "best guesstimate" is more like 9,000. "It is unlike anything we've seen before" in Afghanistan, Iraq, Somalia or other places where foreigners have joined violent jihadist insurgencies.

About 100 foreign fighters in Syria are from the United States, and 2,000 to 3,000 are from Western Europe, the second-largest source after Arab countries, such as Tunisia, Saudi Arabia and Morocco.

Several factors explain why foreign Muslims are attracted to the Syrian war, experts say. "Obviously the biggest driver is the fact that the Assad regime is slaughtering innocent people," says Zelin, "and they view it as a religious duty to help out their brothers and sisters being killed." Syria also is relatively easy to reach.

In addition, the extremist groups, especially ISIS, are using social media extensively to lure recruits. Foreign fighters are drawn to ISIS and Jabhat al-Nusra because the groups "tend to be more inclusive, better organized and better financed than their more moderate counterparts," said Richard Barrett, senior vice president at The Soufan Group, a New York-based security consultancy. Concentrated in the north and the east, the extremists also are the first groups many foreigners meet after crossing the Turkish and Iraqi borders.[57]

Threat in the West

Not every foreigner fighting in Syria is a potential domestic terrorist. Some may choose never to return home; others will be killed. In May, a Florida man, Moner Mohammad Abusalha, possibly became the first American suicide bomber in Syria, according to the U.S. State Department. Abusalha had spent two months training with Jabhat al-Nusra.[58]

Most Western fighters who do return will never engage in domestic terrorism, if past experience is any guide, according to Thomas Hegghammer a researcher at the

Norwegian Defense Research Establishment in Oslo. Hegghammer studied about 1,000 jihadists from North America, Western Europe and Australia who fought abroad between 1990 and 2010. "My data, with all its limitations, indicate that no more than one in nine foreign fighters returned to perpetrate attacks in the West," he wrote.[59] Still, extrapolating from that rate, "That is potentially 300 or more people who have gone to Syria who could be involved in attempted attacks in the West," says Zelin.

Experts say it is exceedingly difficult to determine which foreign fighters will return to become domestic terrorists. In the case of Syria, there is no uniform profile of foreign fighters, let alone those who might return home bent on violence, says Zelin. While most are young Muslim men, he says, they include converts and those born into Muslim families; immigrants and those who are European-born; and people who are poor and middle class. Education levels vary as well, says Zelin.

In addition, Western intelligence agencies have few resources in Syria to track their citizens or residents. "It's a bit of a black hole," said a U.S. counterterrorism official.[60] And back home, "most states lack the resources to identify and monitor more than a few returning fighters," said Barrett.

But even countries with generous resources are becoming overwhelmed. By the end of April, the number of people in France under surveillance was growing, "and the security forces were feeling the strain," according to Barrett.[61] With far fewer American fighters in Syria, the U.S. government might have an easier time monitoring. Last month the FBI announced it had formed a special team to identify and investigate such individuals.

Some Western nations are turning to families and friends for clues. France is setting up a network of telephone hotlines and counseling centers for family, friends and community members to report radicalized young men, and Germany is considering such a system as well.

Countries also are taking legal measures. Last month, the United States designated Jabhat al-Nusra a terrorist organization — ISIS, under its former name of Al Qaeda in Iraq, has been on the terrorist list for years — allowing anyone who fights with them to be prosecuted for knowingly providing "material support or resources" to the group.[62]

In the past year, three American citizens or permanent residents have been arrested at U.S. airports or near the Canadian border for allegedly trying to leave the country to join Jabhat al-Nusra or another al Qaeda splinter group. All have pleaded not guilty or denied the charges. Another American, Sinh Vinh Ngo Nguyen of Southern California, pleaded guilty last year to "attempting to provide weapons training to al Qaeda" after fighting alongside Jabhat al-Nusra in 2012.[63]

Britain has begun detaining returnees from Syria. Last month, Mashudur Choudhury, 31, became the first Briton convicted of preparing for a terrorist act after returning from fighting in Syria.[64] France has begun to arrest people for plotting terrorism as they try to make their way to Syria, leading some defense lawyers to claim civil liberties are being violated.

"In France all they have done is to purchase a ticket; it is impossible to foresee who will leave for the purpose of carrying out terrorism," said lawyer Pierre de Combles de Nayves.[65]

Middle East Spillover

Most foreign fighters in Syria are from predominantly Muslim countries. "I definitely think that we will see those who survive Syria and return to Saudi Arabia or Jordan or elsewhere in the region create new groups or join existing radical jihadist movements," says Riedel of the Brookings Institution, "and they will not only have the skill set acquired from having fought on battlefields, they will also have a lot of prestige as veterans of jihad."

Spillover is already occurring: The ranks of two al Qaeda-linked groups in Lebanon, Jabhat al-Nusra and the Abdullah Azzam Brigades, are filling with rebel fighters from Syria and have taken responsibility for a string of suicide attacks aimed at Hezbollah, a Lebanese Shiite Muslim political party and militant group that supports the Assad regime.

"Al Qaeda in Lebanon are like these beads," said Omar Bakri Fostok, a radical Sunni preacher based in Tripoli, pulling on a string of prayer beads. "There were individuals, but they have always lacked the thread that holds them together. They were not organized. That is now changing."[66]

In Iraq, the ISIS resurgence over the last three years is partially due to "access to a steady flow of both weapons and fighters from Syria," the National Counterterrorism Center's Olsen told Congress.[67]

In Saudi Arabia, King Abdullah decreed in February that citizens who fight in conflicts abroad will face three to 20 years in prison upon returning home. Early last month, Saudi Arabia detained 62 suspected Islamic militants with reported ties to al Qaeda groups in Syria and Yemen. They represent the largest group accused of Islamist militancy in Saudi Arabia for at least two years.[68]

Jordan has recently criminalized "joining or attempting to join armed or terrorist groups, or recruiting or attempting to recruit people" to join such groups. "Let's be frank," says Riedel. "Saudi Arabia, Jordan and Egypt are police states, and they're going to go after anyone who is coming home from this in the manner that a police state does. They're just going to round people up and put them in jail."

Some governments are taking less punitive approaches. For instance, Tunisia has established an amnesty program to integrate into society individuals who have gone to Syria but have not killed anyone. Morocco is considering a similar program. And Saudi Arabia is considering expanding its system of rehabilitation centers serving the thousands it arrested during the last wave of al Qaeda attacks in the kingdom in the mid-2000s.[69]

OUTLOOK

Improving Governance

Development is the key to countering al Qaeda and Salafi-jihadist groups, says the Atlantic Council's Bruton. For example, in Nigeria, "If the U.S. can go in and build roads, build schools, speak out against Nigerian human rights abuses and be seen as a neutral party interested in resolving legitimate grievances, that would be very helpful," she says.

"Simply by improving local governance we would start to roll back where al Qaeda is able to operate," says Zimmerman of the American Enterprise Institute. "Granted, this is broad, difficult and ill-defined, but it is what is missing." For example, when the Yemeni government clears out AQAP forces from an area, "it then needs to provide basic services — food, water, shelter," with Western help, if necessary, says Zimmerman "The Yemeni government doesn't provide much to the population, which is one reason why the population is not very loyal to the government."

Without that kind of Western strategy, "I see a very strong al Qaeda," says Zimmerman. She sees a broad

sectarian war between Sunnis and Shiites across Syria and Iraq, with al Qaeda as major player; AQAP continuing along its current path; al-Shabab developing further into an East African group; and al Qaeda's resurgence in Pakistan as the United States pulls out of Afghanistan. "And, frankly, if al Qaeda moves into Afghanistan, Pakistan is not going to be pursuing it," she says.

However, Watts of the Foreign Policy Research Institute cautions that the West should not try to help develop government institutions and civil society, often called "nation building."

"I don't see how that helps us in counterterrorism," says Watts. "Mostly it creates weak democracies that become safe havens for groups like al Qaeda, which is what we're seeing in Anbar Province in Iraq."

As for ISIS' relentless advance in Iraq, he sees the group replacing al Qaeda's core leadership as the global leader of jihad, at least in the short run, especially if AQAP leader Wahishi shifts his loyalty to ISIS. But as the Iraqi Shiites, aided by the Iranians and with some Western support, repel ISIS, Watts predicts, an entirely different scenario will emerge, especially as infighting continues between ISIS and al Qaeda leadership in Pakistan.

"Al Qaeda affiliates and regional upstarts may find little incentive to hitch their group to a volatile global jihadi alliance that would only erode their local popular support without bringing in outside resources, operational capability or ideological clarity," according to Watts.[70]

Over the longer term, he says, al Qaeda affiliates and jihadi groups "would remain only very loosely connected to one another."

"Al Qaeda is being forced to change by counterterrorism pressure and by regional events," says Liepman of the Rand Corp. And the two most important events are the civil war in Syria and the upheaval in Iraq, he says. "The next couple of years will be both unstable and unpredictable for the jihadist universe, primarily because of the instability in both Syria and Iraq."

NOTES

1. Shuaib Almosawa and Eric Schmitt, "2 Yemenis Shot by Americans are Linked to Qaeda Cell," *The New York Times*, May 10, 2014, http://tinyurl.com/lvaxdf8.

2. *Ibid.*

3. "Drone Wars Yemen: Analysis," New America Foundation, April 21, 2014, http://tinyurl.com/kaxev54.

4. "Remarks by the President at the United States Military Academy Commencement Ceremony," The White House, May 28, 2014, http://tinyurl.com/o7l87wf.

5. "Testimony by Jeh Johnson, Secretary of Homeland Security," House Judiciary Committee Hearing: Oversight of the United States Department of Homeland Security, May 29, 2014, http://tinyurl.com/mwx5zen.

6. For background, see Kenneth Jost, "Unrest in the Arab World," *CQ Researcher*, Feb. 1, 2013, pp. 105-132; and Roland Flamini, "Turmoil in the Arab World," *CQ Researcher*, May 3, 2011, pp. 209-236.

7. Ben Gilbert, "Saudi Arabia walks a fine line in backing Syrian rebellion," Aljazeera America, Jan. 20, 2014, http://tinyurl.com/jwewou. For background, see Leda Hartman, "Islamic Sectarianism," *CQ Researcher*, Aug. 7, 2012, pp. 353-376.

8. "Country Reports on Terrorism 2013 — Executive Summary," U.S. Department of State, April 2014, p. 5, http://tinyurl.com/oe6wder.

9. J. M. Berger, "Debate: Is al-Qaeda a global terror threat or a local military menace?" *The Globe and Mail*, May 28, 2014, http://tinyurl.com/ohzpza2.

10. "Discord in the ranks of Al Qaeda as leader is slammed over Syria," The Associated Press, May 12, 2014, http://tinyurl.com/kvtuvdo.

11. J. M. Berger, "War on Error," *Foreign Policy*, Feb. 5, 2014, http://tinyurl.com/pbv522w.

12. Daveed Gartenstein-Ross, "Debate: Is al-Qaeda a global terror threat or a local military menace?" *The Globe and Mail*, May 28, 2014, http://tinyurl.com/ohzpza2.

13. *Ibid.*

14. Terrence McCoy, "ISIS just stole $425 million, Iraqi governor says, and became the 'world's richest terrorist group,' " *The Washington Post*, June 12, 2014, http://tinyurl.com/ljyq933.

15. Thomas Lynch, "It's Not About Al-Qaeda Anymore," *War On the Rocks*, Nov. 26, 2013, http://tinyurl.com/qhmgmwb.

16. Oren Dorell and David Jackson, "Details Emerge on al-Qaeda link to embassy closures," *USA Today*, Aug. 5, 2013, http://tinyurl.com/q4q6wrp.

17. Barbara Starr, *et al.*, "Intercepted al Qaeda message led to shuttering embassies, consulates," CNN, Aug. 4, 2013, http://tinyurl.com/lt9jo2w.

18. Terrence McCoy, "How ISIS leader Abu Bakr al-Baghdadi became the world's most powerful jihadist leader," *The Washington Post*, June 11, 2014, http://tinyurl.com/n44z5l7.

19. "Al Qaeda splinter group moves to take eastern Syrian city," Reuters, May 11, 2014, http://tinyurl.com/qdej88q.

20. Bronwyn Bruton, "The Real Reason al-Shabab Attacked a Mall in Kenya," *Defense One*, Sept. 24, 2013, http://tinyurl.com/oelke4h.

21. Mark Landler and Michael Gordon, "U.S. to Send Up to 300 Military Advisers to Iraq," *The New York Times*, June 20, 2014, http://tinyurl.com/pybqkhe.

22. Farnaz Fassihi, *et al.*, "Iraq Scrambles to Defend Baghdad," *The Wall Street Journal*, June 13, 2014, http://tinyurl.com/k7nm5w5.

23. Kevin Sullivan and Greg Jaffe, "Collapse of Iraqi army a failure for nation's premier and for U.S. military," *The Washington Post*, June 12, 2013, http://tinyurl.com/olw2dly.

24. *Ibid.*

25. "Statement by the President on Afghanistan — Rose Garden," The White House, May 27, 2014, http://tinyurl.com/ma33ne7.

26. "How realistic is Obama's new Afghanistan timeline?" PBS Newshour, May 27, 2014, http://tinyurl.com/ppswx3y.

27. Eli Lake, "As Obama Draws Down, Al Qaeda Grows in Afghanistan," *The Daily Beast*, May 29, 2014, http://tinyurl.com/o4qmert.

28. *Ibid.*

29. "Remarks by the President," *op. cit.*

30. Gordon Adams, "Obama's Big, New Counter-terrorism Plan is a Hot Mess," *Foreign Policy*, May 30, 2014, http://tinyurl.com/mnccc2v.

31. *Ibid.*

32. Eric Schmitt, "U.S. Training Elite Antiterror Troops in Four African Nations," *The New York Times*, May 26, 2014, http://tinyurl.com/opv335n.

33. Fawaz A. Gerges, *The Rise and Fall of Al-Qaeda* (2011), p. 34.

34. For background, see Thomas J. Billitteri, "Afghanistan Dilemma," *CQ Researcher*, Aug. 7, 2009, pp. 669-692.

35. Clint Watts, "The Three Versions of Al Qaeda: A Primer," Foreign Policy Research Institute, December 2013, http://tinyurl.com/p5qnz6b.

36. Lawrence Wright, *The Looming Tower: Al-Qaeda and the Road to 9/11* (2007), p. 150.

37. *Ibid.*, pp. 150, 152.

38. *Ibid.*, p. 193.

39. *Ibid.*, pp. 198-199.

40. Seth G. Jones, *Hunting in the Shadows: The Pursuit of Al Qa'ida Since 9/11* (2012), p. 46.

41. *Ibid.*, p. 47.

42. *Ibid.*, pp. 48-49.

43. President Bush Speech to a Joint Session of Congress, Sept. 20, 2001, http://tinyurl.com/3btzktw.

44. Peter L. Bergen, *Manhunt: The Ten-Year Search for Bin Laden from 9/11 to Abbottabad* (2012), p. 23.

45. For background, see Kenneth Jost, "Rebuilding Afghanistan," *CQ Researcher*, Dec. 21, 2001, pp. 1041-1064; and David Masci and Kenneth Jost, "War on Terrorism," *CQ Researcher*, Oct. 12, 2001, pp. 817-848.

46. Bergen, *op. cit.*, p. 68; Global Terrorism Database, National Consortium for the Study of Terrorism and Responses to Terrorism, http://tinyurl.com/p5b49ee.

47. Bergen, *ibid.*, pp. 138-139.

48. *Ibid.*, pp. 117-118.

49. For background, see Thomas J. Billitteri, "Drone Warfare," *CQ Researcher*, Aug. 6, 2010, pp. 653-676.

50. "President Obama's Speech on Osama Bin Laden," *Discovery News*, Feb. 11, 2013, http://tinyurl.com/o6mtsgl.

51. Bergen, *op. cit.*, p. 259.

52. James R. Clapper, "Statement for the Record: Worldwide Threat Assessment of the US Intelligence Community," Senate Select Committee on Intelligence, Jan. 29, 2014, p. 12, http://tinyurl.com/omy462h.

53. Scott Sayare, "Suspect Held in Jewish Museum Killings," *The New York Times*, June 1, 2014, http://tinyurl.com/karok85.

54. *Ibid.*

55. *Ibid.*

56. Matthew Olsen testimony, Senate Foreign Relations Committee Hearing: "Extremism and Sectarianism in Syria, Iraq and Lebanon," March 6, 2014, p. 3, http://tinyurl.com/mobzrpj.

57. Richard Barrett, "Foreign Fighters in Syria," The Soufan Group, June 2014, p. 25, http://tinyurl.com/ncv7erx.

58. Mark Mazzetti, *et al.*, "Suicide Bomber Is Identified as a Florida Man," *The New York Times*, May 31, 2014, http://tinyurl.com/kxw4vut.

59. Thomas Hegghammer, "Should I Stay or Should I Go? Explaining Variation in Western Jihadists' Choice between Domestic and Foreign Fighting," *American Political Science Review*, February 2013, p. 10, http://tinyurl.com/oagxzwe.

60. Greg Miller, *et al.*, "American suicide bomber in Syria raises fears for U.S.," *The Washington Post*, June 2, 2014, http://tinyurl.com/p3b2r59.

61. Barrett, *op. cit.*

62. "Foreign Terrorist Organizations," U.S. Department of State, http://tinyurl.com/d9s57hn.

63. Peter Bergen, "Americans dying for al Qaeda," CNN, June 2, 2014, http://tinyurl.com/mzaep4l.

64. Kimiko De Freytas-Tamura, "Foreign Jihadis Fighting in Syria Pose Risk in West," *The New York Times*, May 30, 2014, http://tinyurl.com/n7dl558.

65. Alissa J. Rubin, "Fearing Converts to Terrorism, France Intercepts Citizens Bound for Syria," *The New York Times*, June 3, 2014, http://tinyurl.com/ke6a67j.

66. Loveday Morris, "Al-Qaeda builds networks in Lebanon as security slips" *The Washington Post*, March 18, 2014, http://tinyurl.com/l7svldp.

67. Olsen, *op. cit.*

68. Rania El Gamal and Yara Bayoumy, "Saudi Arabia says uncovers al Qaeda cell plotting attacks," Reuters, May 6, 2014, http://tinyurl.com/ko52fez.

69. Aaron Y. Zelin and Jonathan Prohov, "The Foreign Policy Essay: Proactive Measures — Countering the Returnee Threat," *LawFare* (blog), May 18, 2014, http://tinyurl.com/n4qu5rv.

70. Clint Watts, "ISIS's Rise After al Qaeda's House of Cards," Foreign Policy Research Institute, March 22, 2014, http://tinyurl.com/mgoghvk.

BIBLIOGRAPHY

Selected Sources

Books

Bergen, Peter L., *Manhunt: The Ten-Year Search for Bin Laden from 9/11 to Abbottabad*, Crown, 2012.
CNN's national security analyst traces the hunt for al Qaeda leader Osama bin Laden.

Gerges, Fawaz A., *The Rise and Fall of Al-Qaeda*, Oxford University Press, 2011.
A professor at the London School of Economics chronicles al Qaeda's emergence from local jihadist movements and its subsequent decentralization.

Jones, Seth G., *Hunting in the Shadows: The Pursuit of Al Qa'ida Since 9/11*, W.W. Norton, 2012.
A senior RAND Corp. analyst chronicles the fight against al Qaeda.

Wright, Lawrence, *The Looming Tower: Al-Qaeda and the Road to 9/11*, Vintage Books, 2007.
A journalist explains the growth of Islamic fundamentalism, al Qaeda's rise and the intelligence failures that culminated in the 9/11 terrorist attacks in the United States.

Articles

"Discord in the ranks of Al Qaeda as leader is slammed over Syria," The Associated Press, May 12, 2014, http://tinyurl.com/kvtuvdo.
A breakaway al Qaeda affiliate strongly criticizes al Qaeda's leader Ayman al-Zawahiri for siding with rival Jabhat al-Nusra.

Almosawa, Shuaib, and Eric Schmitt, "2 Yemenis Shot by Americans are Linked to Qaeda Cell," *The New York Times*, May 10, 2014, http://tinyurl.com/lvaxdf8.
The two Yemeni men shot dead trying to kidnap two American Embassy employees in Yemen were part of an al Qaeda cell.

De Freytas-Tamura, Kimiko, "Foreign Jihadis Fighting in Syria Pose Risk in West," *The New York Times*, May 30, 2014, http://tinyurl.com/n7dl558.
Thousands of Westerners have gone to fight with radical Islamist groups in Syria, raising concerns that some may return home trained to commit violent attacks.

Gilbert, Ben, "Saudi Arabia walks a fine line in backing Syrian rebellion," Aljazeera America, Jan. 20, 2014, http://tinyurl.com/ljwewou.
Saudi Arabia forbids citizens from fighting abroad or sending money to support extremist groups in Syria, but many send funds anyway, using bank accounts in Kuwait.

Landler, Mark, and Michael R. Gordon, "Obama Orders 300 Advisors to Iraq," *The New York Times*, June 20, 2014, http://tinyurl.com/pybqkhe.
The president will deploy military advisers to help Iraqi security forces and is prepared to launch air strikes against Sunni militants.

Miller, Greg, *et al.*, "American suicide bomber in Syria raises fears for U.S.," *The Washington Post*, June 2, 2014, http://tinyurl.com/p3b2r59.
U.S. counterterrorism officials were caught unawares when a Floridian exploded a suicide bomb in Syria.

Sayare, Scott, "Suspect Held in Jewish Museum Killings," *The New York Times*, June 2, 2014, http://tinyurl.com/karok85.
A Frenchman accused of killing three people at a Brussels museum had fought with radical Islamist fighters in Syria.

Sullivan, Kevin, and Greg Jaffe, "Collapse of Iraqi army a failure for nation's premier and for U.S.

military," *The Washington Post*, June 12, 2014, http://tinyurl.com/olw2dly.

The U.S.-trained Iraqi army suffered mass desertions as breakaway al Qaeda group advanced.

Reports and Studies

"Country Reports on Terrorism 2013 — Executive Summary," U.S. State Department, April 2014, http://tinyurl.com/oe6wder.

The government's latest review of the state of worldwide terrorism gives a region by region breakdown of violent groups.

Barrett, Richard, "Foreign Fighters in Syria," The Soufan Group, June 2014, http://tinyurl.com/ncv7erx.

A counterterrorism expert documents the flow of foreign fighters into Syria.

Hoffman, Bruce, "Low-Tech Terrorism," *The National Interest*, March-April 2014, http://tinyurl.com/lqd4aqe.

The director of Georgetown University's Center for Security Studies analyzes the weapons terrorists choose to use.

Johnson, Jeh, Testimony before House Judiciary Committee Hearing, May 29, 2014, http://tinyurl.com/mwx5zen.

The secretary of Homeland Security outlines the terror threat inside the United States.

Olsen, Matthew, "Extremism and Sectarianism in Syria, Iraq, and Lebanon," testimony before Senate Foreign Relations Committee hearing, March 6, 2014, http://tinyurl.com/mobzrpj.

The National Counterterrorism Center director analyzes growing instability in Syria, Lebanon and Iraq.

For More Information

American Enterprise Institute, 1150 17th St., N.W., Washington, DC 20036; 202-862-5800; www.aei.org. Conservative think tank focusing on government, politics, foreign policy, economics and social welfare.

Atlantic Council, 1030 15th St., N.W., 12th Floor, Washington, DC 20005; 202-463-7226; www.atlanticcouncil.org. Centrist think tank conducting research on international affairs.

Brookings Institution, 1775 Massachusetts Ave., N.W., Washington, DC 20036; 202-797-6000; www.brookings.edu. Centrist think tank researching foreign policy, global development, economics and social policy.

Bureau of Counterterrorism, U.S. Department of State, 2201 C St., N.W., Washington, DC 20520; 202-647-4000; www.state.gov/j/ct. Helps develop and coordinate counterterrorism strategies.

Foreign Policy Research Institute, 1528 Walnut St., Suite 610, Philadelphia, PA 19102; 215-732-3774; www.fpri.org. Conservative think tank focused on international issues.

National Consortium for the Study of Terrorism and Responses to Terrorism (START), 8400 Baltimore Ave., Suite 250, College Park, MD 20740; 301-405-6600; www.start.umd.edu. University-based research center on terrorism.

National Counterterrorism Center, Washington, DC 20511; www.nctc.gov. Government agency that analyzes terrorism intelligence and plans counterterrorism activities.

Rand Corp., 1776 Main St., Santa Monica, CA 90401; 310-393-0411; www.rand.org. Think tank focused on security, health, education, sustainability, growth and development.

Holding a copy of the Koran, a supporter of Egyptian President Mohammed Morsi rallies with members of the Islamist Muslim Brotherhood in Cairo on Dec. 14, 2012. The military coup that removed Morsi from office in July 2013 has been followed by a severe crackdown on the Muslim Brotherhood and other civil society organizations.

From *CQ Researcher,*
February 1, 2013.
Updated February 1, 2015.

6

Unrest in the Arab World

Kenneth Jost

Four years after a Tunisian fruit peddler helped give birth to political reform movements through much of the Arab world, Tunisians went to the polls in December 2014 in the North African country's first free and fair presidential election. With 3 million votes cast, Tunisians gave a 55 percent majority to Beji Caid Essebsi, a secularist and reform-minded veteran of the country's previous authoritarian regime, over Moncef Marzouki, the incumbent and favorite candidate of supporters of the country's leading Islamist political party, Ennahda.

The presidential election continued a process of democratization in Tunisia marked by the peaceful election of a constituent assembly in 2011 and the drafting of a new constitution called liberal and progressive by Western observers and human rights groups. Marzouki promptly conceded the election and vowed to work for political stability.

A month later, negotiations over the new government were still unresolved, but Tunisia's advances earned it a rating of "free" from the U.S.–based human rights group Freedom House in its annual survey. Tunisia was the first Arab county to win that rating since Lebanon had been deemed free in the early 1970s before the outbreak of its protracted civil war.

Tunisia was the only bright spot in the Arab world in Freedom House's report, which gave "partly free" ratings to three of the Arab countries in the Middle East and North Africa and called 12 others "not free." Saudi Arabia and Syria, wracked by a four-year-long civil war, were both rated among the "worst of the worst" countries

Freedom Continues to Elude Arab World

Revolutions and popular unrest across much of the Arab world have yet to lead to full democracy and individual rights in any of the region's countries. Only one country is rated as "free," and three others as "partly free," by the international human rights group Freedom House. Furthermore, only Qatar and the United Arab Emirates have achieved even a middling score on political corruption by Transparency International, a Berlin-based anticorruption advocacy group.

Arab Countries' Mixed Responses to Prodemocracy Protests

Country Type; head of government	Population	GDP per capita	Freedom House freedom rating, 2014	Transparency International corruption score, 2013 (0 to 100, with 0 being the most corrupt)
Algeria	38.8 million	$7,500	Not free	36
Republic; independent from France since 1962. Prime Minister Abdelmalek Sellal in power since September 2012.				
Bahrain	1.3 million	$29,800	Not free	49
Constitutional monarchy; independent from U.K. since 1971. King Hamad bin Isa Al Khalifa in power since 1999.				
Egypt	86.9 million	$6,600	Not free	37
Republic; British protectorate until 1922. Longtime president Hosni Mubarak deposed in February 2011; Mohammed Morsi elected president in June 2012 with support of Muslim Brotherhood, ousted by military coup in July 2013; military chief Abdel Fattah el-Sisi elected president June 2014.				
Iraq	33.6 million	$7,100	Not free	16
Parliamentary democracy; independent from British administration since 1932 as part of a League of Nations mandate. Prime Minister: Nouri al-Maliki, elected in 2006, resigned in August 2014, succeeded by Haider al-Abadi in move for more inclusive government.				
Jordan	7.9 million	$6,100	Not free	49
Constitutional monarchy; independent from British mandate since 1946. King Abdullah II in power since 1999.				
Kuwait	2.7 million	$42,100	Partly free	44
Constitutional emirate; independent from U.K. since 1961. The emir, Sheik Sabah Al Ahmed Al Sabah, has been in power since 2006.				
Lebanon	5.9 million	$15,800	Partly free	27
Republic; independent from French administration since 1943 as part of a League of Nations mandate. Tammam Salam, elected prime minister February 2014, serves as acting president after Parliament unable to fill post in six ballots.				

Country Type; head of government	Population	GDP per capita	Freedom House freedom rating, 2014	Transparency International corruption score, 2013 (0 to 100, with 0 being the most corrupt)
Libya	6.2 million	$11,300	Not free	18
Political reforms instituted after deposition and death of ruler Moammar Gadhafi, but country now in civil war between military and Islamist supporters of former General National Congress; Abdullah al-Thinni chosen interim prime minister in March 2014, but election ruled unconstitutional in November 2014.				
Morocco	33.0 million	$5,500	Partly free	39
Constitutional monarchy; independent from France since 1956. King Mohammed VI in power since 1999.				
Oman	3.2 million	$29,800	Not free	45
Monarchy; independent since mid-1700s following Portuguese and Persian rule. Sultan Qaboos bin Said al-Said in power since 1970.				
Qatar	2.1 million	$102,100	Not free	69
Emirate; independent from U.K. since 1971. Ruled by al Thani family since mid-1800s.				
Saudi Arabia	27.3 million	$31,300	Not free	49
Monarchy; founded in 1932 after several attempts to unify the Arabian Peninsula. King Salman succeeded to throne Jan. 23, 2015, after death of his half-brother Abdullah bin Abdul Aziz Al-Saud.				
Syria	18.0 million	$5,100	Not free	20
Authoritarian regime; French mandate until 1946. President Bashar Assad's family in power since 1970.				
Tunisia	10.9 million	$9,900	Free	40
Republic; independent from France since 1956. Beiji Caid Essebsi elected president in December 2014.				
United Arab Emirates	5.6 million	$29,900	Not free	70
Federation with some powers reserved for member emirates; independent from U.K. since 1971. President: Sheik Khalifa bin Zayed Al Nahyan, in power since 2004.				
Yemen	26.1 million	$2,500	Not free	19
Republic; independent from Ottoman Empire since 1918. South Yemen unified with North Yemen in 1990. Pro-American president Abed Rabbo Mansour Hadi resigned on Jan. 22, 2015, after Shiite Houthi rebel control gained control of capital city.				

Sources: "Corruption Perceptions Index 2014," Transparency International, December 2014, www.transparency.org/whatwedo/publications/P30#1; "Freedom in the World 2015," Freedom House, January 2015, https://freedomhouse.org/sites/default/files/01152015_FIW_2015_final.pdf; The World Factbook, Central Intelligence Agency, January 2015, www.cia.gov/library/publications/the-world-factbook/index.html.

worldwide on the group's scale of political and legal rights.*

"The news is almost all pretty gloomy," Arch Puddington, the group's research director, said as the report was unveiled in Washington on Jan. 27. The report notes that some of the countries that adopted political reforms in the early days of the so-called Arab Spring are moving backward in terms of democratization.

As a prime example, Egypt, the Arab world's most populous country, was criticized for "a return to autocracy" and "a crackdown on all forms of dissent" four years after the ouster of the longtime president Hosni Mubarak. The report also saw backsliding on reform in other countries, including Iraq and its Persian Gulf island neighbor Bahrain. Reforms in Libya and Yemen had given away as each descended into civil wars.[1]

---

*This report does not detail events and conditions in Iraq, which are covered in a separate report. It also does not encompass these six members of the League of Arab States: Comoros, Djibouti, Mauritania, Palestinian National Authority, Somalia, and Sudan.

Timeline: The Syrian Civil War

2011

March 15-16	Demonstrators demand release of political prisoners; at least 20 protesters die as demonstrations widen in following weeks. 20 protesters die as demonstrations widen in following weeks.
April 21	President Bashar Assad lifts state of emergency, releases political prisoners; security forces kill 72 protesters.
July 29	Some security forces refuse to fire on protesters; defectors form Free Syrian Army.
Aug. 3	Syrian tanks move into Hama, killing at least 45 protesters.
Aug. 23	U.N. Human Rights Council condemns Syrian government's response to protests; opposition forms National Council of Syria, demands Assad's removal from office.
Nov. 12	Arab League suspends Syria's membership.

2012

February-March	Syrian forces begin shelling of Homs; hundreds killed.
March 21	Peace plan presented to U.N. Security Council by Arab League is championed by special envoy Kofi Annan and accepted by Russia, China; Assad accepts plan, then reneges.
April	U.N. observers enter Syria to monitor progress of Annan plan; U.N. suspends monitoring after deaths of women, children.
May 10	Two car bombs kill 55 people outside military intelligence building in Damascus; ceasefire nullified as government continues shelling cities.
June 22	Syrian forces shoot down Turkish fighter jet; fighting later crosses Turkish border.
Aug. 2	Annan resigns as special envoy amid escalating violence.
Oct. 2	U.N. reports that 300,000 refugees have fled Syria.
Nov. 29	Syrian government shuts down Internet, telephone service; launches major offensive surrounding Damascus; U.S. delivers 2,000 communication kits to rebel forces.
Dec. 11	Obama says U.S. will recognize Syrian rebels as legitimate government; U.S. designates Jabhat al-Nusra, an Islamist militia backing Syrian rebels, as terrorist organization.
Dec. 22	Syrian military forces begin using Scud missiles against rebels.

2013

Jan. 1	U.N. puts death toll at 60,000.
Jan. 6	Assad, in Damascus, vows to remain in office, continue fight against "criminals," "terrorists," and "foreign influences."
Jan. 17	Homs massacre kills 106 people; U.K.–based Syrian Observatory for Human Rights blames pro-Assad forces.
Jan. 21	Syrian National Coalition (SNC) fails to agree on transitional government.
Feb. 6-7	Insurgents attack military checkpoints, other targets in central Damascus, outskirts.
March 13	Amnesty International accuses both sides of war crimes.
March 19	Chemical weapons are believed to have been used in Aleppo; government, rebels swap accusations for blame.

"Very briefly, the Arab Spring continues to stall," says Seth Jones, associate director for the RAND Corp.'s International Security and Defense Policy Center in Washington. "I see fewer democracies and democratic shifts than I saw before."

"There's been a real backsliding," says Cole Bockenfeld, director of advocacy for the Washington-based Project on Middle East Democracy. "A lot of the optimism has receded as countries have reverted to a more authoritarian model and other countries have fallen into armed conflict."

The downbeat assessments contrast with the once-ebullient reaction to the Arab Spring, the succession of antigovernment protests and demonstrations in North Africa and the Middle East that began in Tunisia in December 2010. Within a two-month span, the "Arab street" — the oft-used metaphor for disaffected Arabs shut out of the political process — forced Tunisia's longtime president Zine El Abidine Ben Ali to flee the country and Egypt's Mubarak to step down after almost 30 years as president. By August 2011, a popular uprising in Libya, aided by military support from the United States and some NATO allies, had toppled the longtime dictator Moammar Gadhafi.

The protests spread to other countries, from monarchical Morocco in the west to the Gulf state monarchies and emirates in the east. Four years later, the political atmosphere has changed in much of the Arab world, but the pace of change has slowed or even been reversed.

Historian James Gelvin, a professor at UCLA and author of a compact overview *The Arab Uprisings*, agrees that the initial optimism about reform has proved to have been misplaced. But he contends that political conditions have changed and will continue to change. "Things have been going on since

1980, and they're continuing to go on," he says.

Despite Gelvin's view, the uprisings of the last four years caught most observers by surprise, according to U.S. scholars Mark Haas and David Lesch. In their book *The Arab Spring*, published in November 2012, they said that the waves of democratization that swept across Latin America, Eastern Europe, and Central Asia during the late 20th century were unfelt in the Arab world except for a short-lived and largely abortive "Arab spring" of 2005.[2]

Yet Haas, a political scientist at Duquesne University in Pittsburgh, and Lesch, a historian at Trinity University in San Antonio, acknowledged that conditions were ripe for revolutionary uprisings in the Middle East. They noted in particular the anger and frustration felt by the Arab world's disproportionately young populations as the global economic crisis of 2008 raised prices and drove up unemployment in much of the region.[3]

Economic pressures are increasing in early 2015 as the region feels the impact of the worldwide decline in oil prices, engineered in part by a decision by the region's leading oil producer, Saudi Arabia, to increase output. With oil prices falling by roughly half to around $50 a barrel or below, reduced revenues are creating economic problems for Saudi Arabia, for its regional rival Iran, and for such other major Arab oil producers as Iraq, the United Arab Emirates, and Kuwait.[4]

Meanwhile, political reform is taking a back seat in the heart of the Middle East to counterterrorism because of the rise of the jihadist group that styles itself the Islamic State. Proclaiming a mission to adopt an Islamic caliphate in the region, ISIS — the most common acronym for the organization — now effectively controls big swaths of territory in Syria and Iraq.*

April 11	Syrian military is accused of massacre in Sanamayn between Damascus and Daraa; more than 60 reportedly killed.
April 25	White House says it believes Syria has used chemical weapons.
April 29	Syrian prime minister escapes car-bomb assassination attempt.
May 7	U.S., Russia announce plans to seek international conference on civil war.
May 15	U.N. General Assembly calls for political transition to end civil war.
June 26	Syrian Observatory for Human Rights estimates deaths in civil war at 100,000.
Aug. 31	Obama asks Congress to authorize missile strike against Syria to retaliate for use of chemical weapons; request draws opposition from lawmakers, public.
Sept. 14	U.S., Russia agree on deal for Syria to dismantle chemical weapons; threatened missile strikes called off.
November–December	Syrian forces gain grounds in and around Damascus; rebels also on defensive in Aleppo.
2014	
Jan. 18	Syrian opposition agrees to join U.N.–brokered talks in Geneva; talks held Jan. 22–31; second session begins Feb. 10.
Feb. 4	U.S. intelligence chief James Clapper says Assad has "strengthened" hold on power.
Feb. 15	Geneva talks end in impasse; no plans to reconvene.
March 13	Syrian diplomat rejects U.N. mediator Lakhdar Brahimi's objection to plans for presidential election.
Late March	Deaths in civil war near 150,000; 9 million Syrians displaced from homes; 5.5 million children said to need aid.
May 31	Brahimi steps down as U.N. mediator.
June 4	Assad wins new seven-year term, with 88.7 percent of vote.
June 23	Syria hands over last of chemical weapons.
Sept. 11	Obama authorizes air strikes targeting ISIS inside Syria; government attacks on rebels seen to increase after U.S. move.
October	Jordan, Lebanon set restrictions on refugees.
December	Syrian Observatory for Human Rights puts death toll at 202,000.
2015	
January	Assad voices confidence in long interview with U.S. journalist (Jan. 20) . . . U.N. secretary general Ban Ki-moon says civilian casualties mount, humanitarian aid hampered (Jan. 23) . . . Talks in Moscow between government, some opposition representatives: no visible results (Jan. 26–29).

Source: Compiled from various news sources

ISIS has an explicitly anti-American and anti-Western ideology and uses brutal tactics exemplified by the video-taped beheadings of hostages from the United States, the

United Kingdom, and Japan. President Obama delivered a televised address from the White House on Sept. 10, 2014, in which he vowed to "degrade and ultimately destroy" ISIS.[5]

Experts say the focus on ISIS is turning U.S. policy in the region away from political reform. "U.S. policy has been very narrowly confined to counterterrorism, not political reform," says Jones.

"The administration has backed off its support for democratization in the region," says Bockenfeld. "It's a return to a pre-2011 strategy: a short-term focus on working with authoritarian allies that will cooperate with the United States in a broad counterterrorism strategy but without a long-term focus on how to address extremism in these societies."

ISIS's control of Syrian territory further complicates the already dim prospects for a political solution to the country's nearly five-year-old civil war, which has claimed more than 200,000 lives. The longtime strongman president Bashar al-Assad has defied early predictions that he would be forced to leave office. Today, he appears increasingly confident of political survival in a multisided struggle among his regime, ISIS, the al Qaeda-backed jihadist group Jabhat al Nusra, and a weak grouping of Western-style liberal democrats.

Tunisia offers the only example of a country that is succeeding in transcending the factors that complicate moves toward democratization, such as ethnic and tribal rivalries and the sectarian divisions between the Sunni and Shia branches of Islam. The Freedom House report credits Tunisia with having adopted a "progressive constitution" in January 2014 that was followed by "well-regarded" parliamentary and presidential elections later in the year.

The moderate Islamist political party Ennahda was the leading vote getter in Tunisia's elections for a

---

*The acronym ISIS is short for Islamic State in Iraq and Syria; the U.S. government generally has been using ISIL, short for Islamic State in Iraq and the Levant — incorporating the old Western term for the Mideast. In Arabic, the group's name is Al-Dawla Al-Islamiya fi al-Iraq wa al-Sham, or the Islamic State of Iraq and al-Sham, which incorporates an Arabic term for the region from Egypt east to Iraq.

Constituent Assembly in October 2011. The party's secretary-general went on to serve as prime minister at the head of a coalition government with a center-left secular party and a prolabor party.

Ennahda stepped aside for the final vote on the new constitution and adopted a neutral stance in the presidential balloting in December 2014 that was won by Essebi, an aged veteran of the former regime. "In the end, the different political forces in the country made important compromises that have enabled the country to move forward," says Puddington. But negotiations for the formation of a new government were proving to be difficult in the new year, with Ennahda excluded from a new coalition. "It's very fragile," Puddington remarks. "It could move in a wrong direction."

As the world continues to watch the complex political, social, and economic developments in the strategically important region, here are some of the questions being debated:

Has the Arab Spring stalled?

The Arab Spring claimed its most important victim in February 2011 when massive protests in Cairo's Tahrir Square and the port city of Alexandria forced Mubarak out of office. Four years later, however, Egypt is again led by a former general, and the government again allows little room for political opposition or dissent.

Egypt's new president, Abdel Fattah el-Sisi, has effectively led the country since engineering the military coup that toppled the elected Muslim Brotherhood government in July 2013. After resigning his position as defense minister, Sisi ran for president and won with 92 percent of the vote in a May 2014 election that was boycotted by supporters of the now-banned Muslim Brotherhood.

The Freedom House report calls Sisi's government "a ruthless dictatorship" that has returned to "autocratic rule." Jeremy Pressman, an associate professor and director of Middle East studies at the University of Connecticut in Storrs, agrees. "Egypt looks like a country just like it was before the Arab Spring," he says.

Well before the Egyptian coup, the efforts at political reform in the Arab world had already been stunted in most of the region. In Bahrain, for example, the U.S.–backed government responded to the so-called Pearl Revolution of February 2011 by firing on unarmed protesters, killing 7 and wounding at least 200 others.

Four years later, the Sunni monarchy still holds tight power over the country's Shiite majority, thanks in part to military help from its Sunni-ruled neighbor Saudi Arabia. Freedom House faults Bahrain's government for its "unwillingness to address long-standing grievances among the majority Shiite community about the drawing of electoral districts and the possibility of fair representation."

The other Gulf monarchies, including Oman and the United Arab Emirates, have responded to reform efforts with what Freedom House called in its 2014 report "bitter resistance." In other countries, including Jordan and Kuwait, governments successfully tamped down discontent with modest political reforms that left the underlying power structures unchanged.

The winds of political reform have reached Saudi Arabia hardly at all, according to experts. "I don't see prospects for change," says Gelvin, the UCLA professor. The kingdom is reforming its government under a new monarch, King Salman, following the Jan. 23 death of his half-brother King Abdullah at the age of 90. The new king is 79.

Toby Jones, a Mideast expert and associate professor of history at Rutgers University in Camden, N.J., sees "token" signs of a generational change in other positions but no likelihood of significant reform. "Saudi Arabia is not about to become a moderate or reformed political order," he says.

In Egypt, the Arab Spring ushered in the first competitive election for president since Mubarak's rise to power in 1981. Mohammed Morsi, leader of the Muslim Brotherhood, was elected in June 2012 with just under 52 percent of the vote in a contest with Mubarak's last prime minister. Morsi's government lost public confidence, however, as it failed to turn Egypt's faltering economy around.

Sisi's government has entrenched itself in power with what Freedom House calls "a relentless campaign to roll back the gains of the Arab Spring." In a withering critique, the report says that 1,300 political detainees have been given death sentences in "drumhead trials," the media has been "bent into submission," human

rights organizations have been "suppressed," and domestic critics — "both secular and Islamist" — have been "arrested or forced into exile."

Economics could be the regime's Achilles heel, however, according to Andrew Tabler, a senior fellow with the Washington Institute for Near East Policy. "In places like Egypt, you have to make jobs, put bread on the table," says Tabler. "The Brotherhood was unable to do that. We'll see if the Sisi government is better able to do it."

Pressman notes that Sisi also faces a "major internal threat" in the form of an Islamist insurgency concentrated in the Sinai Peninsula. And he questions whether Egyptians will, in effect, return to the street despite the government's repressive policies. "Once the population has a taste of its ability to change political leadership, it's hard to forget that," he says.

Puddington says that popular uprisings in the region faltered in the face of a political culture unconducive to democracy. "In the Arab world, you have forces that wanted democracy to fail and a political culture that was not used to the necessity of compromise and discussion," he says.

But Paul Salem, director of the Arab Transitions Initiative at the Washington-based Middle East Institute, sees a regionwide shift in public attitudes toward political accountability and competitive elections. "This paradigm shift is throughout the region," says Salem, a Harvard-educated dual citizen of Lebanon and the United States, "and will be with us for the next generation."

Do Islamic groups pose a threat to political reform in the Arab world?

In the first of the post–Arab Spring elections, Tunisians gave the lion's share of their ballots for a new Constituent Assembly to the moderate Islamist party Ennahda. The only religious party on the ballot, Ennahda — which means "renaissance" in Arabic — garnered about 41 percent of the valid votes. Two major liberal secularist parties shared about 25 percent of the vote, with the rest scattered among more than a dozen other parties.

As the votes were still being counted, Marzouki, leader of the second-place Congress for the Republic, sought

Syria at a Glance

Government

President Bashar Assad — Leader of Syria and regional secretary of the Arab Socialist Ba'ath Party. Elected in 2000 in unopposed referendum and initially seen as a potential reformer. Heavily criticized for human-rights violations and political corruption.

Minister of Defense General Fahd Jassem al-Freij — Appointed in July 2012 after assassination of predecessor; Assad has divided al-Freij's power among various commanders.

Syrian army — Land force estimated at 280,000 at outbreak of war; with tens of thousands of defections, size now estimated as low as 110,000.

Opposition

Free Syrian Army (FSA) — Formed in July 2011 by Syrian Army defectors. Estimated force of 100,000 soldiers with basic military training; has grown from a select group of defectors along the Turkish border to a broader group of insurgent civilians and military groups. Many rebels have adopted the FSA name.

Colonel Abd al-Ilah al-Bashir — Syrian Army defector appointed in February 2014 to lead Free Syrian Army; previous leadership called "ineffective."

National Coalition for Syrian Revolutionary and Opposition Forces (Syrian National Coalition) — Formed in November 2012 as an inclusive leadership council now with 114 members. Aims to replace Assad's regime and become international representative for Syria, but internal divisions have presented problems in forming a government. Supports the FSA. Recognized by many countries as representative of Syrian people.

Syrian National Council (SNC) — Coalition of several opposition groups dominated by Sunni Muslim majority. Military bureau coordinates activity for the Damascus Declaration for Democratic Change, the Muslim Brotherhood, Syrian Revolution General Commission, and Kurdish and tribal factions.

National Coordination Committee for Democratic Change — Comprises 13 leftist and three additional Kurdish political parties, plus an assortment of independent and youth activists. Calls for a withdrawal of military from streets, an end to military attacks against nonviolent protests, and the release of all political prisoners. Favors economic sanctions on Assad as a means of applying international pressure. Rejects foreign military intervention.

Jabhat al-Nusra — Salafi Jihadist rebel group with links to al Qaeda; has gained popular support in recent months. Worked with FSA factions to carry out attacks and large-scale bombings in the past year. The United States designated it a terrorist organization.

Ahrar al-Sham battalion — Rebel group composed of conservative Salafist and Islamist groups; has close ties to Jabhat al-Nusra. Has drawn attention from other, more radical rebel groups in Syrian rebel front.

Sources: "Guide to the Syrian opposition," BBC, Nov. 12, 2012, www.bbc.co.uk/news/world-middle-east-15798218; "Structure of SNC," Syrian National Council, www.syriancouncil.org/en/structure/structure.html; Elizabeth O'Bagy, "Middle East Security Report 6: Jihad in Syria," Institute for the Study of War, September 2012, www.understandingwar.org/report/jihad- syria; Khaled Yacoub Oweis, "Syria's army weakened by growing desertions," Reuters, Jan. 13, 2012, www.reuters.com/article/2012/01/13/us-syria-defections-idUSTRE80C2IV20120113; Samia Nakhoul and Khaled Yacoub Oweis, "World Powers Recognise Syrian Opposition Coalition," Reuters, December 2012, www.reuters.com/article/2012/12/12/us-syria-crisis-draft- idUSBRE8BB0DC2012 1212; Yelena Suponina, "Free Syrian Army's Riad al-Asaad: Political resolution of the crisis in Syria is impossible," Voice of Russia, Aug. 9, 2012, english.ruvr.ru/2012_08_09/Political-resolution-on-the-crisis-in-Syria-is-impossible/.

— Compiled by Ethan McLeod and Darrell Dela Rosa

to play down the importance of sectarian divisions. The veteran human rights activist said the election had a clear message for other countries: "Avoid anything like being for a civil war between secularists and Islamists."[6]

Eight months later, Islamists again scored a victory when Egyptians elected Morsi, candidate of the Muslim Brotherhood–backed Freedom and Justice Party. Morsi pledged to choose a prime minister from outside the

Brotherhood and to include at least one Christian and one woman in his cabinet.

Experts see no surprises in the Islamists' success at the polls. With their superior political organization, Islamist parties are bound to be "the most powerful actors in the new regimes, at least in the short run," scholars Lesch and Haas wrote in their overview.[7]

Political Islam "is the one ideology that has roots with the people," says Joshua Landis, an associate professor of international studies at the University of Oklahoma in Norman and director of the school's Center for Middle Eastern Studies. "Secularists are a distinct minority."

For much of the 20th century, Islamist organizations such as the Muslim Brotherhood advocated violence as a political tactic. But the groups saw the popular uprisings as opening up new opportunities through the political system. "It doesn't mean that Islamist organizations are going to be completely prodemocracy and human rights," Gelvin says. "But opportunities opened for them to participate in democratic government."

The sectarian division within Islam between Sunnis and Shiites is also an important factor in the ongoing political developments and the geopolitical rivalry between Shiite Iran and Sunni countries, including Saudi Arabia. "It has become the most important political fault line in the Middle East over the last decade and a half," says Rutgers professor Toby Jones. "It's only gotten worse every year."

Jones says the Sunni/Shi'a divide is a product less of history than of current politics. "Muslims have lived in various stages of harmony or conflict" through history, he says. Today, he says weak states are using sectarianism for domestic and geopolitical objectives and, in the process, making the divide "a terrible political issue" for people in the region.

Bockenfeld with the Project on Middle East Democracy agrees that sectarian divisions have become more pronounced as authoritarian governments collapsed. "Different models of identity came to the fore," he explains.

As one example, Bockenfeld points to Iraq, where the Shiite-dominated government of former prime minister Nouri al-Maliki was widely criticized for countenancing attacks on majority Sunnis by Shiite militias. Maliki agreed to resign in August 2014, but Bockenfeld says the new government has not yet instituted major reforms to bridge the sectarian divide.

Seth Jones, the RAND expert, emphasizes that Islam itself is not an inevitable hurdle to democracy. He points to Turkey, Afghanistan, and Iraq as Islamic-majority countries with established democratic institutions. The jihadist groups that argue against democracy on the ground that religious authority is superseded do not speak for all Muslims, he says.

In Egypt, Morsi helped push through a constitution approved by voters in December 2012 that declared Islam the state religion and Sharia the source of law but guaranteed freedom of worship to Christians and Jews as well. Morsi was ousted over political and economic, not religious, issues. The new constitution adopted in January 2014 with the military government's backing bans religious-based parties but carries over provisions on Islam as the state religion and Sharia as the source of law.

In Tunisia, a new constitution ratified in late January 2014 also specifies Islam as Tunisia's religion. At the urging of liberal parties, however, it includes no reference to Islamic law and guarantees that Tunisia will be a civil state with freedom of religion.[8]

In the meantime, however, the rise of ISIS shows the risk of an Islamist organization coming to power with explicitly antidemocratic and sectarian policies. "Will it become more pluralistic?" Toby Jones asks rhetorically. "The jury is still out."

Can a stable political solution be found in Syria?

With a bloody civil war about to enter its fifth year, Syrian president Assad displayed nothing but confidence and few regrets as he met with a U.S. journalist in January 2015. In a 6,000-word interview with Jonathan Tepperman, managing editor of the magazine *Foreign Affairs*, Assad depicted the regime's opponents as "terrorists" and "rebels," denied loss of control of Syrian territory, and professed a willingness to accept a political solution to the conflict but only if were ratified by a popular referendum.

Writing about the interview in *The Washington Post* a few days afterward, Tepperman bluntly described Assad as "delusional." Assad "remains as unrepentant and inflexible today as he was at the start of the Syrian civil

CHRONOLOGY

2010–2011 *Arab Spring begins; autocrats ousted in Tunisia, Egypt, Libya; Syria in civil war.*

December 2010 Tunisian fruit vendor Mohamed Bouazizi sets fire to himself to protest treatment by police (Dec. 17); incident sparks nationwide riots; President Zine El Abidine Ben Ali vows to punish protesters; Bouazizi dies on Jan. 4.

January 2011 Protests break out in Algeria, Egypt, Jordan, Yemen. . . . Ben Ali flees Tunisia (Jan. 14). . . . Demonstrations in Cairo's Tahrir Square call for Egyptian President Hosni Mubarak to resign (Jan. 25).

February 2011 Mubarak resigns; military council forms interim government (Feb. 11). . . . Libyans protest arrest of activist in Benghazi (Feb. 15); protests spread; leader Moammar Gadhafi vows to stay in office. . . . Protests erupt in Bahrain (Feb. 14), Morocco (Feb. 20).

March 2011 Protests banned nationwide in Saudi Arabia (March 5). . . . U.N. Security Council authorizes no-fly zone over Libya (March 17); rebels begin to capture territory, form transitional government. . . . Syrian security forces kill several people in provincial city of Daraa protesting arrest of political prisoners (March 18); protests spread to Damascus, other cities; tanks used to quell protests. . . . President Bashar Assad orders release of political prisoners (March 25–26).

April–June 2011 Protests in Egypt demand quick transfer of power by military. . . . Assad lifts state of emergency in Syria (April 21); security forces continue crackdowns. . . . Death toll in Egypt uprising: at least 846, according to judicial panel (April 19). . . . Four protesters sentenced to death in Bahrain (April 28). . . . Death toll in Tunisia uprising: at least 300, according to U.N. investigator (May 21). . . . Yemeni President Ali Abdullah Saleh injured in rocket attack, flown to Saudi Arabia (June 4).

July–September 2011 Free Syrian Army formed by defectors (July 29). . . . Battle of Tripoli: rebels capture city; Gadhafi overthrown (Aug. 20–28). . . . Saudi King Abdullah grants women right to vote, run in municipal elections (Sept. 25).

October–December 2011 Gadhafi captured, killed (Oct. 20). . . . Moderate Islamist party Ennahda leads in

elections for Tunisian parliament (Oct. 23). . . . Sunni groups form National Salvation Council in Syria; Islamist groups refuse to join (November). . . . Saleh agrees to yield power in Yemen (Nov. 23). . . . Parliamentary elections begin in Egypt (Nov. 28); Muslim Brotherhood's Freedom and Justice Party leads after balloting concludes (Jan. 3).

2012–Present *Protests ebb; new governments take shape; Syrian civil war continues.*

January–March 2012 Syrian conflict intensifies; Russia, China block U.N. Security Council action (Feb. 4). . . . Abed Rabo Mansour Hadi elected Yemeni president in single-candidate vote (Feb. 21). . . . Egyptian parliament creates Islamist-dominated Constituent Assembly to draft new constitution; liberal lawmakers protest (March 24).

April–June 2012 Egyptian Constituent Assembly dissolved by court order (April 10). . . . Mubarak receives life sentence for role in killings of protesters (June 2); wins retrial (Jan. 13, 2013). . . . New Constituent Assembly created; critics still dissatisfied (June 12). . . . Ben Ali convicted in absentia for role in killings of protesters in Tunisia; sentenced to life (June 19). . . . Muslim Brotherhood's Mohammed Morsi elected president in Egypt (June 24).

July–September 2012 Liberal National Front Alliance leads in Libyan parliamentary elections; Islamists distant second (July 7). . . . U.S. ambassador, three others killed in attack on consulate in Benghazi (Sept. 11).

October–December 2012 Egyptian court skirts challenge to Constituent Assembly (Oct. 23). . . . Bahrain bans all protests (Oct. 30). . . . Morsi curbs judiciary's powers (Nov. 22); withdraws move under pressure (Dec. 8). . . . Draft constitution approved by Constituent Assembly (Nov. 29–30); approved by voters (Dec. 15, 22).

January–April 2013 Death toll in Syria put at 60,000 (Jan. 2); Assad vows to remain in office (Jan. 6). . . . Libyan government sharply reduces death toll estimate in civil war: 4,700 rebels killed, 2,100 missing; government losses thought comparable (Jan. 8). . . . Women named to Saudi advisory council for first time (Jan. 11). . . . New violence in Egypt marks second anniversary of revolution; military chief fears "collapse" of state (Jan. 25–29). . . . Tunisian opposition parliamentarian Chokri Belaid assassinated in Tunis (Feb. 6).

Chemical weapons believed to have been used in attack on civilians in Aleppo, Syria (March 19).

May–August 2013 Morsi removed from office; military chief Gen. Abdel Fattah el-Sisi announces move (July 3); hundreds of protesters killed in ensuing four months of violence . . . . Secular opposition leader Mohammed Brahmi assassinated in Tunis; al Qaeda-affiliated group blamed (July 25). . . . Bahrain limits political groups' contacts with foreign officials, organizations (August) . . . . President Obama says use of chemical weapons in Syria would be a "red line" for United States (Aug. 22).

September–December 2013 Syria agrees to dispose of chemical weapons (Sept. 14) . . . . Muslim Brotherhood banned in Egypt, assets confiscated (Sept. 23). . . . Morsi placed on trial (Nov. 4); proceedings adjourned.

January–March 2014 Egyptians approve new constitution in referendum (Jan. 14–15). . . . Syria, rebels convene in Geneva for U.N.-brokered talks (Jan. 22–31) . . . . Tunisia Constituent Assembly approves new constitution (Jan. 26) . . . . Morsi defiant as trial resumes (Jan. 28) . . . Syria talks end in impasse (Feb. 15). . . Ali Zaidan removed as prime minister in Libya

(March 11). . . . Syrian diplomat rejects U.N. envoy's objection to plans for presidential elections (March 13).

April–June 2014 Egyptian court sentences Muslim Brotherhood leader, 680 others to death for killing of police officer (April 28) . . . Sisi elected president in landslide in Egypt (May 26–28) . . . Assad reelected for seven-year term (June 4) . . .Islamic State of Iraq and Syria (ISIS) proclaims worldwide caliphate over Muslims (June 29).

July–September 2014 Libyan parliament meets in Tobruk, forced out of Tripoli by rival militias (Aug. 4) . . . Iraqi prime minister Maliki agrees to resign, give way to more inclusive government (Aug. 14) . . . Jailed Bahraini activist starts hunger strike to protest crackdown (late August) . . . U.S. launches air strikes against ISIS (Sept. 11).

October–December 2014 ISIS holds on to areas in Syria, Iraq . . . Nationalist party Nidaa Tounes wins 86-seat plurality in Tunisian parliament; Ennahda with 69 (Oct. 26) . . . Egyptian court throws out Mubarak's convictions for murders of demonstrators (Nov. 29) . . . Nidaa Tounes leader Essebi wins presidency in runoff (Dec. 21).

January 2015 Oil prices fall below $50 per barrel (Jan. 5) . . .Yemeni government falls to Houthi rebels (Jan. 22) . . Saudi King Abdullah dies; succeeded by half-brother King Salman (Jan. 23) . . . Tunisia rated "free" in Freedom House report (Jan. 27); talks continue in Tunis to form coalition without Ennahda, leftist Popular Front.

war four years ago," Tepperman wrote. "Assad seems to have no idea how badly the war is going, how impractical his proposals sound and how meaningless his purported overtures are."[9]

Assad's regime has lost control of one-third or more of the country, observers estimate, with a big swath controlled by ISIS in the north and east, pockets controlled by Kurds along the Turkish border and enclaves held by the al Qaeda offshoot Jabhat al Nusra in the west and south. The regime's failing grip led the then-U.N. envoy Lakhdar Brahimi to warn as long ago as fall 2013 of the likely "Somalisation" of the country.[10]

The situation has only worsened since, according to experts. "Different parts of the country are ruled by different organizations, and each of them is armed," says Pressman, the University of Connecticut professor.

Along with others, Pressman sees no possible resolution to the political and military stalemate in the near future.

The uprising in Syria caught outside observers, not to mention the Assad regime itself, totally by surprise when it broke out in spring 2011.[11] Assad, a Western-educated ophthalmologist, had been viewed as a reformer when elected president at age 37 in 2000 after his father's death. He remained well liked in Syria despite the regime's crackdown on protests before 2011, according to Lesch, the Trinity University professor who came to know Assad well while writing a biography.[12]

The regime seemed to satisfy the country's Sunni majority while also protecting the interests of the Shia minority and the Alawite community that was the elder Assad's home and the regime's political base. In addition, the initial protests in Damascus and elsewhere in early

Syrian Civil War Has Region's Highest Death Toll

Number killed exceeds 200,000; 10 million displaced

The United Nations has given up trying to count the number of people killed in Syria's three-year-old civil war because conditions on the ground are too dangerous to get an accurate figure. But the British-based Syrian Observatory for Human Rights is continuing to use its network of in-country sources to keep a daily count of the deaths, which it calculated to have reached 202,354 by December 2014.[1]

The count of "documented deaths" by the anti-Assad organization stood at 63,074 civilians as of early December, including 10,377 children. The group counted 37,324 Syrian rebel fighters killed and 22,624 non-Syrian jihadists.

On the government side, the group counted 44,237 "regular soldiers" killed and another 28,974 deaths among the paramilitary National Defense Forces. Other deaths counted included 624 members of Lebanon's Shiite Hezbollah and 2,388 proregime Shiite fighters from beyond Syria and Lebanon.

The Syrian conflict is by far the deadliest of the uprisings that rocked the Arab world over the past three years.

But the death count is in the thousands in at least three other countries — Libya, Yemen and Egypt — and in triple or double digits in two others: Tunisia and Bahrain.

- Libya's post-revolutionary government released figures in January 2013, sharply reduced from previous reports, that estimated at least 4,700 deaths on the rebel side with 2,100 missing. Government losses were thought to be similar.
- The Yemeni government estimated in March 2012 that more than 2,000 had died in the political unrest there.
- A judicial panel in Egypt in April 2011 said that 846 people had died in the political unrest there. By March 2014, the Muslim Brotherhood was estimating that more than 2,000 supporters of ousted president Mohammed Morsi had been killed in the crackdown by the postcoup military government.
- An investigative panel in Tunisia reported in May 2011 that 300 people had died in the Tunisian uprising.

2011 drew small numbers and were easily put down. But the unrest became more serious, and the crackdown turned deadly when security forces killed at least five people in the southern provincial town of Daraa on March 18, 2011, as they were protesting the arrest of schoolchildren for antigovernment graffiti.

The death toll from the conflict passed 200,000 in December 2014, according to the London-based Syrian Observatory for Human Rights. The figure included around 63,000 civilians, according to the group's director, Rami Abdel Rahman, with at least 10,000 of them children. The group counted roughly 75,000 deaths among combatants on the government's side and 60,000 or so among opposing forces.

Rahman told the French wire service *Agence France Presse* that the actual number of deaths was probably higher. "Certain areas under regime and Islamic State group control are impossible to work in freely," he remarked.[13]

The human costs are even more staggering in terms of refugees. The United Nations refugee agency counts more than 3.8 million refugees in neighboring countries and an estimated 6.5 million Syrians internally displaced.[14]

From the start of the war, Obama said that Assad has to step aside to bring the war to a close. But U.S.–backed negotiations in Geneva early in 2014 failed to produce a breakthrough. And with the rise of ISIS, the goal of Assad's removal appears to have been deemphasized in U.S. policy if not shelved altogether.

Russia, Syria's closest and longtime ally, renewed efforts to broker a diplomatic solution to the conflict in January 2015, but the four days of talks — boycotted by the Western-backed Syrian National Coalition — ended late in the month with no visible results. In advance of the talks, Assad had cast doubt on their impact. "Not every dialogue is successful," he told interviewer Tepperman.

- In Bahrain, a reform group counted 91 deaths as of January 2013, but news organizations put the death toll less exactly at more than 50.[2]

The human costs of Syria's civil war are measured not only in deaths but also in the suffering of millions of Syrians displaced by the conflict. The United Nations refugee agency — formally, the Office of the High Commissioner for Refugees — estimates that 9 million Syrians have been displaced from their homes, nearly half of the population. That figure includes 3.8 million registered as refugees — about 10 percent of them children — and another 6.5 million or more internally displaced.[3]

—Kenneth Jost

Bombs devastated Aleppo University on Jan. 15, 2013, killing at least 87 people. Nearly 150,000 people have died in Syria's civil war, with no end to the conflict in sight.

[1] "Syria death toll now exceeds 200,000: monitor," Agence France Presse, Dec. 2, 2014, http://english.alarabiya.net/en/News/middle-east/2014/12/02/Syria-death-toll-now-exceeds-200-000-monitor-.html. For daily updates on casualties, see Syrian Observatory's Facebook page: https://www.facebook.com/syriahroe.

[2] "Libyan revolution casualties lower than expected, says new government," *The Guardian*, Jan. 8, 2013, www.guardian.co.uk/world/2013/jan/08/libyan-revolution-casualties-lower-expected-government; Ahmed al-Haj, "Yemen Death Toll: Over 2,000 Killed In Uprising," The Associated Press, March 18, 2012, www.huffingtonpost.com/2012/03/19/yemen-death-toll_n_1361840.html; Almasry Ahmed, "At least 846 killed in Egypt's revolution," *Egypt Independent*, April 19, 2011, www.egyptindependent.com/news/least-846-killed-

egypt%E2%80%99s-revolution; Hamza Hendawi, "Egypt crackdown brings most arrests in decades," The Associated Press, March 16, 2014; "Tunisia: High death toll challenges claims of smooth transition," *Los Angeles Times*, May 22, 2011, latimesblogs.latimes.com/babylonbeyond/2011/05/tunisia-uprising-violence-repression-human-rights-torture-.html; "91 Killed Since 14th February 2011," Bahrain Justice and Development Movement, www.bahrainjdm.org/78-killed-since-14th-february-2011/.

[3] "Syria Regional Refugee Response," UNHCR, http://data.unhcr.org/syrianrefugees/regional.php (visited February 2015).

Freedom House paints a bleak picture of events on the ground in Syria. It found "worsening religious persecution, weakening of civil society groups and rule of law, and large-scale starvation and torture of civilians and detainees."[15]

Experts in the U.S. expect more of the same for the foreseeable future. "I don't think anyone foresees resolution in the near future," says Bockenfeld with the Project on Middle East Democracy. Gelvin agrees. "There is no light at the end of a tunnel," he says. "Syria will continue its descent into hell."

BACKGROUND

Strangers to Democracy

The Arab world knew little of freedom or democracy before or during most of the 20th century. The defeat of

the Ottoman Empire in World War I left Arab lands from Morocco to Iraq under European rule as colonies or protectorates. As Arab nations gained independence after World War II, they emerged not as democracies but as autocracies ruled by long-serving monarchs or by strongmen from the ranks of the military. The leaders used nationalist and pan-Arabist rhetoric to hold popular support even as social and economic problems festered.[16]

An Arab empire once stretched from Spain in the west to the Asian subcontinent in the east, but the Ottoman Empire displaced it by conquest in the 15th century. European colonial powers gained footholds in North Africa in the 1800s. Britain and France took over parts of the Ottoman Empire in the Middle East after their victory in World War I. Britain controlled Palestine, Transjordan, and Iraq and exercised strong influence over Egypt after unilaterally granting it nominal independence in 1922. France got the territory that became Syria and

AFP/Getty Images/STR

Refugees fleeing Syria's civil war face harsh conditions, including supply shortages, freezing temperatures, and snow, in a camp in Turkey on Jan. 9, 2013. More than 2.5 million Syrians have registered as refugees in neighboring counties, according to the U.N.'s Office of High Commissioner for Refugees; another 6.5 million Syrians have been displaced from their homes internally.

Lebanon and maintained colonial rule over Morocco, Algeria, and Tunisia. Italy controlled what was to become Libya. The Ottoman Empire had been decentralized and religiously tolerant but with no tradition of political rights. Britain and France were granted mandates by the League of Nations in order to guide the Arab nations to self-governance, but they instituted only limited reforms and installed compliant rulers who protected the Europeans' interests even as nationalism was emerging as a force. Meanwhile, Saudi Arabia was formed in 1932 as an Islamic kingdom on the Arabian peninsula, an area viewed as worthless desert until the discovery of oil later in the decade. The end of World War II brought independence for Jordan and Syria and, in 1948, the creation of the Jewish state of Israel — with unsettling consequences for the politics of the region.

The defeat of the then-seven-member Arab League in the first Arab-Israeli War (1948–1949) stoked nationalist and pan-Arabist sentiment in many of the now-independent Arab nations. In Egypt, a military coup ousted the pro-British monarchy in 1952 and created a republic that was transformed over the next four years into a one-party state led by Gamal Abdel Nasser. Nasser translated his pan-Arabist views into an agreement with Syria in 1958 to form the United Arab Republic, but the

union lasted only until 1961 as Syria chafed under the domination of its larger partner. Nasser ruled Egypt until his death in 1970; his successor, Anwar Sadat, reinstituted a multiparty system and moved away from Nasser's Arab socialism during 11 years in office until his 1981 assassination by opponents of Sadat's landmark 1979 peace agreement with Israel.

Syria, meanwhile, experienced two decades of extreme political instability after gaining independence from the French after World War II. Politics came to be dominated by the Arab Ba'ath Party (translation: "resurrection" or "renaissance"), founded by pan-Arabist Syrians in 1947. Power lay, however, not with political institutions but with the military and security establishment. Baathists divided in the 1960s into civilian- and military-oriented wings, with Air Force officer Hafez Assad — the father of Bashar — emerging as a major figure in successive coups in 1963 and 1966. As minister of defense after 1966, Assad maneuvered against the de facto leader, Salah Jadid, and then gained unchallenged power after mounting successive military coups in 1969 and 1970.

Strongman rulers came to the fore in several other countries, generally stifling any significant moves toward democracy. In Tunisia, the anticolonialist leader Habib Bourguiba became president in 1957 of what would become a single-party state; he held office until 1987, when Ben Ali engineered his removal on grounds of mental incompetency. In neighboring Libya, Gadhafi led a bloodless military coup in 1969, ousting a corruption-tainted monarchy while espousing reformist and nationalist views; he wielded power, often ruthlessly, until his death in the Libyan Revolution of 2011. In Iraq, Saddam Hussein rose through the ranks of the Ba'ath Party to become president in 1979, the beginning of a sometimes brutal, 24-year rule that ended with his ouster in the U.S.–led invasion in 2003. In Yemen, Ali Abdullah Saleh began a 33-year tenure as president in 1978 — first as president of North Yemen and, after 1990, as president of the Yemeni Arab Republic following the unification with formerly Marxist South Yemen.

Saudi Arabia gained influence in the region through its oil wealth, but political power remained consolidated in the royal family through a succession of long-serving successors to the kingdom's founder, Ibn Saud (1932–1953).

Among the Gulf states, the island sheikhdom of Bahrain took a stab at parliamentary democracy after declaring independence from Britain in 1971, but Sheikh Isa bin Salman Al Khalifa clamped down on dissent after leftists and Shiites won nearly half the seats in parliamentary elections in 1973. Elsewhere, constitutional monarchs — Jordan's King Hussein (1953–1999) and Morocco's King Hassan II (1961–1999) — dominated the political scene while instituting reforms: modest in Morocco, more extensive in Jordan.

Overall, Freedom House's survey of the 16 Arab lands from Morocco to Iraq in 1979 rated none of them as free, nine as partly free, and seven as not free.[17]

"Freedom Deficit"

Arab and Muslim countries remained impervious to the advances for political rights and civil liberties in much of the world as the 20th century ended. Repression was the order of the day in many countries — with Egypt and Syria among the worst. In Egypt, an emergency decree ordered by Mubarak after Sadat's 1981 assassination by Muslim fundamentalists remained in effect until Mubarak was forced out of office in February 2011. In Syria, Assad put down Sunni opposition to his regime with a ruthlessness best exemplified by the 1982 massacre in the city of Hama that claimed at least 10,000 lives. By 2001, Mali in West Africa was alone among the 47 majority-Muslim countries to be rated by Freedom House as free.[18]

Mubarak rose from Air Force ranks to become Sadat's vice president and then to succeed to the presidency unopposed in a referendum held a week after the slaying. He won three additional six-year terms in successive referendums, also unopposed. Mubarak called the assassination part of a plot to overthrow the government.

The emergency decree adopted after Sadat's slaying sharply limited political activity and allowed detention and imprisonment of political dissidents. As many as 30,000 people may have been held as political prisoners during the period. Parliamentary elections were held under rules favoring Mubarak's governing National Democratic Party. The Muslim Brotherhood, the largest opposition group, remained under a ban imposed in 1954. Throughout the period, Mubarak remained an important U.S. ally, even as political conditions failed to improve and evidence of personal and government-wide corruption grew.

Assad ruled Syria through a combination of guile and ruthlessness for nearly 30 years until his death in June 2000. His secularist policies — including equal rights for women — drew opposition from the Muslim Brotherhood beginning in the mid-1970s. Assad responded to the Brotherhood's attempt to take control of the west-central city of Hama in February 1982 by ordering the city shelled and having its civilian population pay the price in lives lost.

Assad's military-security apparatus crushed any incipient opposition with similar ruthlessness, including torture. But Assad also won loyalty through financial ties with Syria's business community, patronage in a bloated state sector, and tough anti-Israeli rhetoric. The United States designated Syria a state sponsor of terrorism from 1979 on but also worked to win Assad's support for, or at least acquiescence in, Arab–Israeli peace negotiations.

Hussein in Iraq and Gadhafi in Libya earned reputations as the region's other two worst dictators and biggest problems for U.S. policy. Both countries were designated state sponsors of terrorism, though Iraq was removed from the list during the 1980s when the United States supported Baghdad in its war with Iran. Both men ruled through a combination of cult-of-personality adulation and coldblooded repression of political dissent. Hussein survived Iraq's defeat by a U.S.–led coalition in the Gulf War in 1991, his stature within Iraq seemingly enhanced; he won show elections in 1995 and 2002 with 99.9 percent and 100 percent, respectively, of the vote. Gadhafi survived a retaliatory U.S. air strike on his home in April 1986 and, like Hussein later, appeared only to gain political stature at home from his successful defiance of Washington.

The rise of Islamist parties unsettled politics in several countries, resulting in repressive crackdowns — most notably in Algeria. The Algerian government's decision to cancel parliamentary elections in 1991 to thwart a potential victory by the newly formed Islamic Salvation Front touched off a decade-long civil war that may have claimed as many as 200,000 lives. In neighboring Tunisia, Ben Ali followed suit by cracking down on Islamist groups, abandoning the political liberalization of his first years in office. In Bahrain, the Shiite majority, chafing under Sunni rule and adverse economic conditions, clamored for restoration of the postindependence constitution, but the government responded by jailing

Egypt's Military Again in Charge

Sisi, coup leader, elected president in low-turnout vote

Egypt's military has had outsize influence over political affairs ever since the young colonel Gamal Abdel Nasser led the 1952 coup that ousted the pro-British monarchy and led Egypt into a one-party state. Despite three failed wars with Israel, the military has remained the country's most powerful institution ever since, with an increasing role not only in politics but also in the nation's economy.

When the Arab Spring protests erupted in Cairo and Alexandria in 2011, it was the military that pulled the plug on the presidency of Hosni Mubarak, a former military commander. And after the country's democratically elected Islamist president, Mohammed Morsi, lost public confidence, the military again flexed its muscles by removing Morsi from office, cracking down on the Muslim Brotherhood and taking control of the reins of government.

Field Marshal Abdel Fattah el-Sisi, who led the July 2013 coup while serving as Morsi's appointee as minister of defense, now holds power as the landslide winner in a presidential election held in late May 2014.

Egypt's presidency was held by military figures from 1953 through the end of Mubarak's 30-year rule. Nasser, age 34 at the time of the 1952 coup, allowed his older ally,

Muhammad Naguib, to be installed as president when the Egyptian republic was declared in July 1953. Nasser engineered Naguib's removal in 1956 and became president himself.

Nasser died in September 1970 and was succeeded by Anwar Sadat, a schoolmate in Egypt's Royal Military Academy in the late 1930s. When Sadat was assassinated in 1981, he was succeeded by Mubarak, who had been commander of the air force before becoming Sadat's vice president in 1975.

The military made a pivotal — and surprising — decision in January 2011 not to fire on the thousands of protesters demanding Mubarak's resignation, according to Bruce Rutherford, an associate professor of political science and Middle East expert at Colgate University in Hamilton, N.Y. "The senior officer corps were all Mubarak's men," Rutherford writes. "Yet at the critical moment, they showed Mubarak the door."[1]

Rutherford says the reasons for the military's decisions are not completely known. Military leaders may simply have concluded that Mubarak's days were numbered, he speculates. But they may also have feared that soldiers, drawn from the same ranks of society as the protesters,

dissidents. Meanwhile, Yemeni president Saleh held on to power despite secessionist sentiment in the south that continued after the north's victory in a brief civil war in 1994.

Freedom House contrasted political developments in the Muslim world with changes in other regions in its 2001 annual report. Despite "significant gains for democracy and freedom" in Latin America, Africa, Eastern and Central Europe, and South and East Asia, the report stated, the Muslim world "experienced a significant increase in repression."[19]

A year later, a group of Arab intellectuals convened by a United Nations agency cited what they called the Arab world's "freedom deficit" as a major factor in the region's lagging social and economic indicators.[20] The 180-page report, sponsored by the U.N. Development Programme's regional bureau for Arab states, concluded

that despite supposed acceptance of democracy and human rights in constitutions and legal codes, representative democracy was "not always genuine and sometimes absent."

Freedoms of expression and association were "frequently curtailed," the report continued, and political participation was "less advanced" than in other developing regions. The report tied political conditions to "deep and complex economic and social problems," including "high illiteracy rates," "rampant poverty," and "mounting unemployment rates." But it closed on the hopeful note that the problems could be eased with political reforms.

Warming Trends?

The Arab world felt stirrings of political change during the early years of the 21st century, but only in 2011 did popular discontent succeed in toppling regimes. Political

might have disobeyed the order. And, Rutherford suggests, the military leaders may have become disenchanted with the evident corruption under Mubarak.

Two years later, Sisi spoke for the military in explaining the coup that ousted Morsi as an effort at "national reconciliation." In a televised news conference, Sisi said the military had no interest in politics but was acting because Morsi had failed to fulfill "the hope for a national consensus."[2]

Sisi, who was born in November 1954, graduated from the Egyptian Military Academy in 1977 and rose through the ranks over the next 30 years to become head of military intelligence and a member of the Supreme Council of the Armed Forces. Morsi turned to him in August 2012 to be minister of defense, only to see Sisi turn on him a year later.

With Sisi wielding power as deputy prime minister, the military government jailed 16,000 people in the first eight months after the coup, according to figures provided by officials to the Associated Press.[3] Despite the crackdown — or perhaps because of it — Sisi became a nationally popular figure. "Sisi has combined the cunning of a spymaster with the touch of a born politician to develop an extraordinary combination of power and popularity," the *New York Times*'s Cairo correspondent David D. Kirkpatrick wrote in early 2014.[4]

State-controlled media portrayed Sisi as Egypt's next Nasser. He resigned his posts in March as he declared his candidacy for the presidency. His election was never in doubt. He won with about 22 million votes out of the relatively low total of 23 million votes cast.

Taking the oath of office on June 8, Sisi vowed to lead an "inclusive" government and paid tribute to the successive public protests that had toppled first Mubarak and then Morsi. "It is time for our great people to reap the harvest of their two revolutions," he said. But he ruled out reconciliation with individuals or groups who "resort to violence" — seemingly a reference to the banned Muslim Brotherhood.[5]

—Kenneth Jost

[1] Bruce K. Rutherford, "Egypt: The Origins and Consequences of the January 25 Uprising," in Mark L. Haas and David W. Lesch (eds.), *The Arab Spring: Change and Resistance in the Middle East* (2012), pp. 41–43.

[2] Quoted in David D. Kirkpatrick, "Egypt Army Ousts Morsi, Suspends Charter," *The New York Times*, July 4, 2013, p. A1.

[3] Hamza Hendawi, "Egypt crackdown brings most arrests in decades," The Associated Press, March 17, 2014.

[4] David D. Kirkpatrick, "Egypt's Ruler Eyes Riskier Role: The Presidency," *The New York Times*, Jan. 28, 2014, p. A1.

[5] See David D. Kirkpatrick, "At Swearing-In, Ex-General Vows 'Inclusive' Egypt," *The New York Times*, June 9, 2014, p. A4, www.nytimes.com/2014/06/09/world/middleeast/sisi-sworn-in-as-egypts-president.html.

developments unfolded against the backdrop of increased global attention on the Muslim world as the United States waged war first against the anti-American Islamist terrorist group al Qaeda in Afghanistan and then against Saddam Hussein in Iraq. Sectarian politics complicated democratization in Iraq and figured in unfolding events elsewhere, including Syria. The ouster of leaders in Tunisia, Egypt, and Libya in 2011 encouraged democratization advocates, but Syria's civil war defied resolution, and only limited reforms were instituted elsewhere.

Midway through the century's first decade, Freedom House in 2006 reported a "positive regional trajectory" for political and civil rights in the Middle East and North Africa. Among the gains cited was Lebanon's popular "Cedar Revolution," which set the stage for free elections after forcing the withdrawal of Syria's occupying troops. The report also noted competitive elections in Egypt, Iraq, and Palestine. The gains were easy to exaggerate, however. In Egypt, Mubarak won his first competitive presidential election in September 2005 with 89 percent of the vote, and the ruling National Democratic Party still commanded a two thirds majority in parliament after December balloting despite 87 seats won by Muslim Brotherhood candidates running as independents. Parliamentary elections in Iraq the same month resulted in a fragile coalition government still riven by sectarian disputes. And in balloting a month later, the hard-line organization Hamas won a majority in the Palestinian parliament.

Five years later, the Arab street wrought more significant changes, starting in Tunisia.[21] The uprising — dubbed the Jasmine Revolution in the West but not in Tunisia itself — began with the Dec. 17, 2010, self-immolation of unlicensed street vendor Mohamed

Bouazizi to protest his alleged mistreatment by police. Protests driven by unemployment and inflation as well as political repression spread through the country quickly and picked up more steam after Bouazizi's death on Jan. 4. With a nationwide strike called and the military backing the revolution, Ben Ali fled on Jan. 14 for exile in Saudi Arabia. After false starts, a transitional government with no holdovers from Ben Ali's regime scheduled elections in October. The once-banned Islamist party Ennahda won a 41 percent plurality of the vote, but the party's leader, the once-exiled Rachid Gannouchi, pledged to support democracy and human rights. Meanwhile, Ben Ali was convicted in absentia in June of embezzlement and sentenced along with his wife to 35 years' imprisonment; the next summer, a military court convicted him, again in absentia, of his role in the deaths of protesters and sentenced him to life in prison. Saudi Arabia has refused to extradite him.

Events in Egypt proceeded even more rapidly than in Tunisia, especially after "Day of Revolt" protests in Cairo and several other cities on Jan. 25, 2011. Six days later, hundreds of thousands massed in Cairo's Tahrir Square — al Jazeera estimated the crowd at 2 million — to protest Mubarak's continued rule. Mubarak tried to quiet the unrest the next day by promising reforms and pledging not to seek reelection in September, but the protests continued, with military leaders significantly pledging neutrality.

Mubarak tried again on Feb. 10 by delegating powers to his vice president, but the next day — prodded by a phone call from U.S. President Obama — Mubarak formally resigned. In parliamentary elections held between November 2011 and January 2012, the Muslim Brotherhood's Freedom and Justice Party won 47 percent of the seats; Morsi's election as president in June made him the first Islamist elected leader of an Arab state. Meanwhile, Mubarak had been convicted in June 2012 of failing to stop the killing of protesters and sentenced to life imprisonment. Morsi's ouster a year later set the stage for the military government's decision to ban the Muslim Brotherhood even as it wrote a new constitution and laid plans for new elections in 2014.

The ouster of Gadhafi in the Libyan civil war took longer and required outside military assistance. Gadhafi's intelligence chief responded to information about a planned antigovernment demonstration in February 2011 by arresting one of the leaders, Fathi Tarbel. Despite Tarbel's release shortly afterward, the Feb. 15 arrest ignited protests that spread from the eastern city of Benghazi through much of the country. Gadhafi responded with brute force, calling in foreign mercenaries to aid his own troops and air force. In March, the U.N. Security Council authorized a no-fly zone to protect civilians; NATO set up the protective zone with U.S. help. Gadhafi's fate was sealed when rebels took over the capital city of Tripoli in late August; the fallen dictator was found on Oct. 20 hiding in a culvert west of the central coastal city of Sirte and killed on the spot. The liberal National Front Alliance won 48 percent of the seats in parliamentary elections in July 2012, with the Islamic Justice and Construction Party a distant second with 10 percent of the seats.

The uprising in Syria grew from protests over the March 2011 arrest of graffiti-writing schoolboys in Daraa into full-fledged civil war. Assad responded on March 30 with promises of political reform and some economic concessions, but then with force as the unrest continued. By summer, the death toll had exceeded 1,000. Military defectors formed the Syrian Free Army in July; the next month, opponents established the National Council of Syria, which demands Assad's resignation and democratic elections. The fighting continued even as former U.N. Secretary-General Kofi Annan attempted mediation; he abandoned the effort by August 2012 in the face of mounting casualties and a flood of refugees. With high-level defections from the regime, many observers concluded that Assad's days were numbered, but he defied opponents by pledging on Jan. 6, 2013, to stay in office. He gained a measure of international credibility with the agreement in September 2013 to dispose of chemical weapons and later to join the Geneva talks, but the decision to pull out of the talks signaled Assad's continuing refusal to step aside in favor of a national-unity transition government.

Protests in the two lesser conflict zones — Yemen and Bahrain — achieved no substantial change. In Yemen, Saleh replied to protests beginning in January 2011 with a pledge not to seek reelection in 2013. With the protests continuing, Saleh was injured in a rocket attack in June and flown to Saudi Arabia for treatment. He returned in September and two months later handed over power to his deputy, Abed Rabbo Mansour Hadi, who won an uncontested presidential election in February 2012. In Bahrain, the government responded quickly to protests that began in the capital city of Manama in February 2011 by calling in help from Saudi troops the next month. The government clamped down by destroying the Pearl Monument, the focal point of the demonstrations, banning political parties, and arresting and prosecuting leading dissidents. New protests in October 2012 prompted an indefinite ban on all political gatherings; the government went further with the decision in September 2013 to ban unauthorized contacts between domestic groups and foreign officials or organizations.

CURRENT SITUATION

Egypt's Struggles

Egypt's former general-turned-president is defending his government's tough crackdown on political dissent as the regime struggles to contain an Islamist insurgency and opposition from secular democrats.

In a combative speech delivered on Egypt's Police Day, Sisi said criticism from human rights groups ignores the government's obligation to lift the country's ailing economy. "Ninety million want to eat, drink, live and be reassured for their future," Sisi said in a Jan. 20 speech before an audience packed with police officers and public figures. "I am not saying protests are rejected, never. But I am saying that we gave the issue of the protest such a space. . . . But those 90 million want to eat."[22]

Four years of unrest have taken a toll on the Egyptian economy in the form of sharp drops in tourism and foreign investment. The government has drawn down foreign exchange reserves and depended on foreign assistance from Gulf countries to finance imports. Unemployment has increased to 13 percent, and nearly one fourth of the population subsist below the poverty line.

Sisi gained power in July 2013 at the head of a military coup that took advantage of a wave of public protests against lagging economic progress under the Muslim Brotherhood government. Morsi, the former president, is now in jail and awaiting trial on charges of conspiring with foreign groups, inciting murders of political opponents and orchestrating prison breaks of political detainees. Some 500 Morsi supporters were convicted and given death sentences in a controversial

On the Hot Seat

Mohammed Morsi (top), Egypt's first democratically elected president, now faces trial after having been ousted in a military coup in July 2013. The Muslim Brotherhood-backed Morsi came under criticism for his claims of broad executive power and his government's failure to make a dent in solving the country's daunting economic problems. President Bashar Assad of Syria (bottom) appears to be tightening his grip on power as a brutal civil war enters its fourth year. Assad, whose strongman father ruled Syria for nearly 30 years before his succession in June 2000, responded to the popular uprisings in 2011 "by waging war against his own people," says Freedom House.

summary trial in March 2014, but the death sentences were later commuted to life imprisonment, and some of the convictions have been thrown out.[23]

Meanwhile, Egyptian courts have thrown out all criminal convictions against former president Mubarak in what Freedom House calls "a depressing symbol of the country's undisguised return to autocratic rule." An appeals court in Cairo threw out the last of the convictions, for embezzlement, in a public session on Jan. 13. Earlier, a court in November had upset Mubarak's conviction and life sentence for killing of antigovernment demonstrators. Mubarak, now 86, remains out of public sight in a military hospital, where he has stayed throughout the legal proceedings because of ill health.[24]

The post-revolutionary transitions in Egypt's neighbors to the west are proceeding on significantly different paths, with generally successful democratization in Tunisia but violence- and abuse-riddled chaos in Libya.

Tunisia held firm to a democratic transition despite the assassination of two liberal opposition figures in 2013 and other unrest attributed to al Qaeda-linked extremists. Parliamentary elections in October 2014 gave the secular nationalist party Nida Tunis — translated as "Call of Tunis" — 86 of 217 seats, with the moderate Islamist Ennahda gaining 69.

Essebi bested the incumbent, Ennahda-backed candidate Moncef Mazourki, in the December runoff, held after no candidate gained a majority in a first round of voting in November. Mazourki had served as interim president since his election by the Constituent Assembly in December 2011.

After the election, Essebi resigned as the head of the party that he had formed as a counter to Ennahda, vowing to be president of all Tunisians. Prime Minister Habib Essid voiced similar sentiments as he worked to form a coalition government in January. "The government will be one for all Tunisians and its task will be to realize the objectives of the revolution, which are freedom, dignity and overcoming the challenges facing the country, particularly economic development," Essid said.[25]

Nida Tunis's coalition partner the Patriotic Front holds 16 seats in the parliament, leaving the two parties shy of a working majority. Ennahda was given no cabinet positions, and the leftist Popular Front apparently walked away out of dissatisfaction with the portfolios offered. Mazourki had called for reconciliation after his defeat and formed a new movement aimed at national unity.

Meanwhile, Tunisian officials worry about the risk of spillover from the chaos and violence in its bigger neighbor Libya. Freedom House downgraded Libya's rating from "partly free" to "not free" due to what it called "the country's descent into civil war." Two rival governments now claim power: a grouping of Islamist militias claims power in the capital city of Tripoli while the internationally recognized government sits in the eastern city of Tobruk.[26]

Freedom House says the fighting between the rival camps has resulted in a "humanitarian crisis." Hundreds of civilians have been killed, and at least 120,000 have reportedly been forced from their homes. Efforts by a U.N. envoy to form a national unity government have not borne fruit.

Syria's Agonies

Syrians are continuing to suffer under a brutal civil war with Assad increasingly confident in office, ISIS and the al Qaeda-linked Nusra Front holding ground, and the Western-backed opposition largely ineffectual.

Assad claimed renewed popular support after winning nearly 89 percent of the vote in a presidential election in June 2014, the country's first multicandidate race for president since the Baath Party came to power. Assad held the election despite warnings from U.N. officials that it could hinder a possible future political settlement. The United States, European countries, and Gulf states called the election illegitimate. Voting was not held in opposition-controlled areas.

U.N. Secretary General Ban Ki-moon painted a grim picture of the war in January 2015 in his monthly report on the conflict to the U.N. Security Council.[27] Ban said that attacks with barrel bombs and explosive weapons continue in civilian neighborhoods. The Security Council called in February 2014 for an end to the use of barrel bombs in civilian areas.

The London-based Syrian Observatory for Human Rights counted 2,014 attacks by regime warplanes and helicopters in January 2015, according to a post on the group's Facebook page. The group said 271 civilians were killed and another 1,000 wounded.

Attacks in civilian areas have contributed to a humanitarian crisis of staggering proportions. Syria's population has shrunk from its prewar total of 21.5 million, as at least 3.8 million people have fled the country as refugees, according to the U.N. refugee agency's count. Ban said about 7.6 million people — roughly 40 percent of the country's remaining population of 18.7 million — are internally displaced.

Overall, the London monitoring group counted 2,683 war-related deaths in January, including 750

Should the U.S. and its allies intervene militarily in Syria?

YES Andrew Tabler
Senior Fellow, Program on Arab Politics, Washington Institute for Near East Policy; Author, In the Lion's Den: An Eyewitness Account of Washington's Battle with Syria

Written for *CQ Researcher*, February 2013

"You break it, you buy it" may have proven true for the United States in Iraq, but great powers are often forced to help clean up conflicts they did not cause but that threaten their interests. If Washington continues its "light footprint" policy of non-intervention in Syria, the American people will likely have to foot the bill for a more expensive cleanup of the spillover of the Syria conflict into neighboring states and the overall battle against international terrorism.

Every indicator of the conflict between the Alawite-dominated Assad regime and the largely Sunni opposition has taken a dramatic turn for the worse, with upwards of 65,000 killed, 30,000 missing and up to 3 million Syrians internally displaced during one of the worst Syrian winters in two decades. The Assad regime shows no sign of ending the slaughter anytime soon, increasingly deploying artillery, combat aircraft and most recently surface-to-surface missiles against the opposition. Reports quoting high-ranking U.S. government officials say the Assad regime has already loaded chemical weapons into bombs near or on regime airfields for possible deployment.

Signs are growing of a sectarian proxy war as well, with the Islamic Republic of Iran and Lebanese Hezbollah backing their fellow Shia at the Assad regime's core and Qatar, Saudi Arabia and Turkey backing their Sunni brethren in the opposition. Al Qaeda affiliates, as well as jihadists, are now among the opposition's best-armed factions.

The Obama administration has refrained from directly intervening or supporting Syria's increasingly armed opposition, based on an argument that neither would make the situation better. But allowing the conflict to continue and simply offering humanitarian and project assistance treats merely the symptoms while failing to shape a political settlement that would help cure the disease: a brutal Assad regime that was unable to reform trying to shoot one of the youngest populations in the Middle East into submission.

The Obama administration spent its first two years encouraging a treaty between the Assad regime and Israel that would take Damascus out of Iran's orbit and isolate its ally Hezbollah. While the method proved wrong, the strategic goals of containing Iranian influence in the region and keeping it from obtaining a nuclear weapon remain as valid as ever. Helping the Syrian opposition push Assad and his regime aside more quickly would help the United States and its allies achieve those objectives.

NO Brian Fishman
Counterterrorism Research Fellow, New America Foundation

Written for *CQ Researcher*, February 2013

If we learn nothing else from more than a decade of war in Iraq and Afghanistan, it must be that high hopes and good intentions help begin wars but do not help end them. Limited war in Syria is a recipe for mission creep and another long-term U.S. commitment to war in the Middle East.

That is why proposals for increased American military intervention in Syria are unconvincing. Broad-based American military action could tip the scales against the dictatorial Syrian regime but would not resolve the deep political conflicts in Syria. And more constrained proposals for military intervention would be unlikely to resolve the conflict.

The United States has many laudable goals in Syria that could plausibly justify military force: undermining an Iranian ally, eliminating a dictator, safeguarding civilians. Indeed, the United States should never hesitate to use military force when it is necessary to protect U.S. interests, but it must use military force only when the killing and dying that it implies are likely to achieve American political goals. That is not the case in Syria.

Public discussions about Syria were hyper-optimistic after the outbreak of peaceful protests against Bashar al-Assad in early 2011. Bolstered by the successes of the Arab Spring, many hoped the protests would not turn violent; they did. Observers ignored the presence of jihadis in the insurgency for months after it became clear that groups linked to al Qaeda were a major force driving the fighting. Still, today the clear split between Arab and Kurdish elements of the rebel coalition is poorly reported in the American press. And many observers have underestimated the cohesion of the Syrian regime, even as the country collapsed around it.

The situation in Syria is undoubtedly terrible. Assad's regime limps on with backing from Iran, and al Qaeda has emerged as one of the most powerful militant networks in the country. But the idea that limited military action — a no-fly zone coupled with increased military aid to rebels — will resolve these challenges is more hyper-optimism from well-intentioned people. One example: The threat will increase that Syria's chemical weapons will be used or proliferate as the regime's hold on power weakens.

Limited military force will redefine but not end the civil war in Syria and it will commit the United States to "solving" Syria politically. During the 1990s in Iraq, no-fly zones failed to destroy Saddam Hussein's regime, and military action to depose him in 2003 heralded chaos that empowered al Qaeda and Iran. Advocates of force in Syria have not offered a plausible argument for why we would do better this time.

Shiite Muslims in Malikiya, Bahrain, demonstrate against the government and in support of political prisoners on Dec. 4, 2012. Government action against protesters in Bahrain has led to an estimated 50 to 100 deaths. Besides Syria, Bahrain provides the most dramatic example of what Freedom House labels the "intransigence" exhibited by many Arab nations toward popular uprisings.

civilians. Among combatants, the group counted 742 regime soldiers and officers and proregime fighters; 877 non-Syrians with ISIS, the Nusra Front, or affiliated groups; and 285 Syrians with rebel forces. Besides the deaths from air attacks and firefights, the group also counted 61 civilian deaths due to torture in government jails; 25 deaths from bad weather, ill treatment, or lack of medical supplies; and 20 civilians executed by ISIS militants.

Humanitarian aid continues to pose daunting challenges for the U.N., donor states, and Syria's neighboring countries. The U.N. refugee agency counted 3.8 million registered refugees at the end of January 2015, roughly one fifth of them under the age of 12. Among Syria's neighbors, Lebanon has been hardest hit, with an influx of 1.1 million refugees, roughly one fourth of its prewar population. Lebanon began imposing border restrictions in January to stem the flow.

The United States and European countries are under pressure to accept more refugees for resettlement. The U.N. agency said European countries had granted 217,000 asylum applications through December 2014, with half of those going to Germany and Sweden. The United States has accepted only 330 refugees, according

to Eleanor Acer, senior director for refugee protection at Human Rights First.

The continued fighting and funding shortfalls hamper humanitarian aid to civilians still inside the country. The United States has complained that Assad's regime blocks assistance to rebel-controlled areas; the U.N. agency complained more recently of difficulties in reaching civilians in ISIS-controlled areas. The U.N. agency called for $3.7 billion in donor funds for 2014 but received only a little more than $2 billion. Food vouchers were cut in January because of the budget shortfall.

The military stalemate between Assad's regime and the multisided opposition seems to promise more fighting, more casualties, and more suffering for the Syrian people. The United States has begun air strikes against ISIS forces in Syria and in Iraq in line with Obama's pledge to destroy the militant group but create what the University of Connecticut's Pressman calls "a tacit alliance with Assad." Obama has repeatedly vowed not to put U.S. forces on the ground.

Ban told the Security Council that ISIS had suffered "heavy casualties" in fighting with Kurdish forces in December while the Nusra Front was attracting additional fighters and resources. Meanwhile, the Free Syrian Army, the military arm of the Western-backed National Syrian Council, is described as weak — "on the ropes," in one news analysis — and rebel leaders are said to be divided on political and military strategy.[28]

"Syria has collapsed into something incoherent," says Toby Jones, the Rutgers professor. "More important, Syria is no longer its own problem. It has exported some of the worst elements of the post–Arab Spring to other states," with regional powers pitted against each other. The war, he says, is "intractable. There's no end in sight."

OUTLOOK

Unfinished Spring

"It's not easy being Arab these days," the Lebanese journalist and historian Samir Kassir wrote in an evocative dissection of the Arab peoples and their political and cultural plight in 2004. He found "a deep sense of malaise" throughout the Arab world that he said would persist unless Arabs freed themselves from "a sense of powerlessness" in order to create an Arab "renaissance."[29]

AFP/Getty Images/Mohammed al-Shaikh

Kassir lived long enough to see Syria end its occupation of his country during the earlier Arab Spring of 2005 but not long enough to enjoy his country's freedom from Syrian suzerainty. He was killed by a car bomb on June 2, 2005, a still unsolved assassination that was surely carried out by Syrian agents or Lebanese surrogates.

Some five-and-a-half years later, a Tunisian fruit peddler frustrated by the petty arbitrariness of a local policewoman threw off his sense of powerlessness in a fashion so dramatic — he set himself on fire — as to inspire fellow Arabs throughout North Africa and the Middle East. This time, the Arab Spring toppled three dictators, helped ease a fourth out of office, shook strongman rulers in other countries, and helped prompt modest reforms even in countries with only minimal agitation in the Arab street. In Saudi Arabia, King Abdullah granted women the right to vote and run in municipal elections in September 2011; he followed up in January 2013 by naming 30 women to serve on the advisory Shura Council for the first time in the kingdom's history.[30]

By then, experts were already starting to tamp down expectations. Robert Malley, regional director for North Africa and the Middle East for the conflict-mediating International Conflict Group, predicted midway through the Arab Spring's second year continued struggles even in countries with changes of government: Tunisia, Egypt, and Libya.

Those countries, Malley predicted, were likely to see "the same fights, the same unfinished, unconcluded fights, between military and civilian, between Islamist and secular, among Islamists, among tribes, between regions." And in Syria, Malley forecast an "ever descending" civil war in Syria.[31]

"We shouldn't make predictions," UCLA professor Gelvin remarked as the Arab Spring marked its second anniversary early in 2013. "Nobody foresaw any of this happening, and nobody saw the paths that these rebellions were going to take."

Today, Gelvin says he is "optimistic" about democratic reform in the long run but counsels patience. "All of these demands are now embedded in the DNA of the Middle East," he says. "Over the long term, they're there, and it's very likely that in the long term they will remember again."

Other experts are more downbeat. "People are skeptical that the transition will bring the quick progress to democracy that we initially hoped for," says the Washington Institute's Tabler. "The prospects for democratization are slim, and the prospects for stability are slim." Toby Jones, the Rutgers professor, is also discouraged. "We're stuck in a post–Arab Spring malaise," he says.

The United States had no direct role in the outbreak of uprisings in the winter of 2010 to 2011 but had some influence early on by urging Mubarak to step aside in Egypt and supporting the anti-Gadhafi rebels in Libya. Since then, however, Seth Jones, the RAND expert, says the U.S. has played "a very minimal role" in seeking to encourage political reform, seemingly chastened by the difficulties of nation building encountered in Afghanistan and Iraq.

The Islamic State's emergence as a regional force to be reckoned with shifts the U.S. focus from reform to counterterrorism. A newfound appreciation in Washington for stability in the region can be seen in the silence about easing Assad from power in Syria and in what one expert called the "festival of praise" from U.S. officials for the Saudi King Abdullah after his death.

Tamara Cofman Wittes, director of the Center for Middle East policy at the Brookings Institution in Washington, says the United States is enlisting authoritarian rulers in the fight against ISIS. "There's nothing wrong with that," Wittes says, "as long as you are open about the contradictions."

With little to cheer in the region apart from Tunisia's thus-far successful moves toward democracy, the mood among policy makers, advocacy groups, and experts is far from hopeful. "The conventional wisdom is that repression and coercion has won," says Pressman, the University of Connecticut professor. But he cautions against a gloom-and-doom attitude.

"Maybe we've reacted too hard in that direction," Pressman says. "Maybe there will be some sort of opening that's more productive in the next few years in terms of giving the people a greater voice in the political system."

NOTES

1. Freedom House, "Freedom in the World 2015," Jan. 28, 2015, https://freedomhouse.org/sites/default/files/01152015_FIW_2015_final.pdf, p. 9.

2. For background, see these *CQ Global Researcher* reports: Brian Beary, "The Troubled Balkans," Aug. 21, 2012, pp. 377–400; Brian Beary, "Emerging Central Asia," Jan. 17, 2012, pp. 29–56; and Roland Flamini, "The New Latin America," March 2008, pp. 57–84, 29–56. See also these *CQ Researcher* reports by Kenneth Jost: "Russia and the Former Soviet Republics," June 17, 2005, pp. 541–564; "Democracy in Latin America," Nov. 3, 2000, pp. 881–904; "Democracy in Eastern Europe," Oct. 8, 1999; pp. 865–888; and "Democracy in Asia," July 24, 1998, pp. 625–648.

3. See Mark L. Haas and David W. Lesch (eds.), *The Arab Spring: Change and Resistance in the Middle East* (2012), pp. 3–4. For previous coverage, see Flamini, "Turmoil," *op. cit.*, pp. 209–236; Kenneth Jost and Benton Ives-Halperin, "Democracy in the Arab World," *CQ Researcher*, Jan. 30, 2004, pp. 73–100.

4. See Stanley Reed and Clifford Krauss, "Saudi Ruler Is Expected to Keep Oil Policy Intact," *The New York Times*, Jan. 24, 2015, p. B1, www.nytimes .com/2015/01/24/business/international/king-abdullahs-death-unlikely-to-upset-saudi-oil-goals-analysts-say.html.

5. See Mark Landler, "Obama Calls for Sustained Drive to Rout Militants," *The New York Times*, Sept. 11, 2014, p. A1, http://www.nytimes .com/2014/09/11/world/middleeast/obama-speech-isis.html.

6. Quoted in David D. Kirkpatrick, "Tunisia Liberals See a Vote for Change, Not Religion," *The New York Times*, Oct. 26, 2011, p. A14. See also by same author, "Tunisia: Islamist Party Wins Vote," ibid., Oct. 28, 2011, p. A13.

7. Lesch and Haas, *op. cit.*, pp. 5–6.

8. Carlotta Gall, "Three Years After Uprising, Tunisia Approves Constitution," *The New York Times*, Jan. 27, 2014, p. A5; David D. Kirkpatrick and Carlotta Gall, "Arab Neighbors Take Split Paths in Constitutions," ibid., Jan. 15, 2014, p. A1.

9. See Jonathan Tepperman, "Syria's President Speaks: A Conversation With Bashar al-Assad," January 2015, www.foreignaffairs.com/discussions/interviews/syrias-president-speaks; "I interviewed Bashar al-Assad about Syria's civil war. He's still too delusional to end it," *The Washington Post*, Jan. 31, 2015, www.wash ingtonpost.com/opinions/i-interviewed-bashar-al-assad-about-syrias-civil-war-hes-still-too-delu sional-to-end-it/2015/01/30/571671b4-a77f-11e4-a2b2-776095f393b2_story.html. The print version appeared Feb. 1 under the headline, "I met Assad. He's too delusional to make peace," p. B1.

10. See "U.N. envoy warns of 'Somalisation' of Syria," *The National*, Oct. 29, 2013, http://www.the national.ae/world/middle-east/un-envoy-warns-of-somalisation-of-syria. For an interactive graphic showing control of Syrian territory, see BBC's "Mapping the Conflict," www.bbc.com/news/world-middle-east-22798391 (visited February 2015).

11. See David W. Lesch, "The Uprising That Wasn't Supposed to Happen: Syria and the Arab Spring," in Haas and Lesch (eds.), *op. cit.*, pp. 79–96; Gelvin, *op. cit.*, pp. 100–118.

12. David W. Lesch, *The New Lion of Damascus: Bashar al-Assad and the Modern Syria* (2005).

13. "Syria death toll now exceeds 200,000: monitor," Agence France Presse, Dec. 2, 2014, http://english .alarabiya.net/en/News/middle-east/2014/12/02/Syria-death-toll-now-exceeds-200-000-monitor-.html.

14. See "Syria Regional Refugee Response," UNHCR: The U.N. Refugee Agency, http://data.unhcr.org/syrianrefugees/regional.php (visited February 2015).

15. Freedom House, op. cit., p. 10.

16. Background on the six nations most affected by the recent unrest in the Arab world (Bahrain, Egypt, Libya, Syria, Tunisia, and Yemen) drawn in part from individual chapters in Lin Noueihed and Alex Warren, *The Battle for the Arab Spring: Revolution, Counter-Revolution and the Making of a New Era* (2012). See also Gelvin, *op. cit.*; Haas and Lesch (eds.), *op. cit.*

17. Raymond D. Gastil, *Freedom in the World 1980: Political Rights and Civil Liberties* (1980), p. 26, http://books.google.com/books?id=LIvHFydpgBgC &printsec=frontcover&source=gbs_ge_summary_r &cad=0#v=onepage&q&f=false.

18. Adrian Karatnycky (ed.), *Freedom in the World 2000-2001*, www.freedomhouse.org/article/new-study-details-islamic-worlds-democracy-deficit. For coverage, see Verena Dobnik, "Annual study shows freedom gap between Islamic countries and rest of world," The Associated Press, Dec. 18, 2001.

19. Quoted in Dobnik, *op. cit.*

20. "Arab Human Development Report 2002: Creating Opportunities for Future Generations," United Nations Development Programme/Arab Fund for Social and Economic Development, www.arab-hdr.org/publications/other/ahdr/ahdr2002e.pdf. For coverage, see Barbara Crossette, "Study Warns of Stagnation in Arab Societies," *The New York Times*, July 2, 2002, p. A11; Karen DeYoung, "Arab Report Cites Development Obstacles," *The Washington Post*, July 2, 2002, p. A10.

21. For timelines in the following summaries, see www.washingtonpost.com/wp-srv/special/world/egypt-protest-timeline/index.html. See also individual chapters in Noueihed and Warren, *op. cit.*

22. See Sarah el Deeb, "Egypt's el-Sissi says protest rights secondary to stability," The Associated Press, Jan. 20, 2015. This report follows most news media in spelling the president's name Sisi.

23. See Mariam Rizik, "Egypt's Morsi accused of leaking secrets to Qatar," The Associated Press, Aug. 28, 2014; Merritt Kennedy, "Egypt court overturns 37 death sentences in criticized trial," The Associated Press, Jan. 24, 2015.

24. For coverage, see David Kirkpatrick, "Egyptian Judge Voids Mubarak's Last Standing Conviction and Orders Retrial," *The New York Times*, Jan. 14, 2015, p. A4; http://www.nytimes.com/2015/01/14/world/middleeast/hosni-mubarak-conviction-over-turned.htm. The Freedom House quote is at op. cit., p. 2.

25. Quoted in Bouazza ben Bouazza, "Tunisia announces new minority without Islamists," The Associated Press, Jan. 23, 2015.

26. See "The Arab Spring, 4 years on," The Associated Press, Dec. 7, 2014.

27. See "UN chief paints worsening picture of war in Syria," The Associated Press, Jan. 23, 2015.

28. Anne Barnard and Somini Sengupta, "U.S. Signals Shift on How to End Syrian Civil War," *The New York Times*, Jan. 20, 2015, p. A1, http://www.nytimes.com/2015/01/20/world/middleeast/us-support-for-syria-peace-plans-demonstrates-shift-in-priorities.html.

29. Samir Kassir, *Being Arab* (English translation, 2004), published same year in French as *Considerations sur le malheur arabe.* The opening sentence, quoted in text, uses the French word *facile* (easy); the translator substituted the English word "pleasant."

30. See Rashid Abul-Samh, "Saudi women on Shura Council," *Al-Ahram Weekly*, Jan. 16, 2013; Neil MacFarquhar, "Saudi Monarch Grants Women Right to Vote," *The New York Times*, Sept. 26, 2011, p. A1. For background, see Sarah Glazer, "Women's Rights," *CQ Global Researcher*, April 3, 2012, pp. 153–180.

31. "The Arab Spring: Unfinished Business," Carnegie Council on International Ethics, June 27, 2012, www.carnegiecouncil.org/studio/multimedia/20120627/index.html.

BIBLIOGRAPHY

Selected Sources
Books

Ajami, Fouad, *The Syrian Rebellion*, Hoover Institution Press, 2012.
A senior fellow at the Hoover Institution traces Syria's history from the rise of the Assad family through the current civil war. Includes source notes.

Cook, Steven A., *The Struggle for Egypt: From Nasser to Tahrir Square*, Council on Foreign Relations/Oxford University Press, 2011.
A senior fellow at the Council on Foreign Relations chronicles modern Egypt's major historical episodes, from the decline of British rule and Nasser's rise as a pan-Arab leader to the Sadat and Mubarak eras and the demonstrations at Tahrir Square that overthrew an entrenched regime. Includes detailed notes, 40-page bibliography.

Gelvin, James L., *The Arab Uprising: What Everyone Needs to Know*, Oxford University Press, 2012.

A professor of Middle East history uses a convenient question-and-answer format to explain the origins of and prospects for the current uprisings in Arab countries. Includes source notes, further readings, websites. Gelvin is also author of *The Modern Middle East: A History* (3d. ed., Oxford University Press, 2011).

Haas, Mark L., and David W. Lesch (eds.), *The Arab Spring: Change and Resistance in the Middle East*, Westview Press, 2012.
A collection of 12 essays explores the course of events in major countries affected or unaffected by the Arab uprisings and the regional and international implications of the events. Haas is an associate professor of political science at Duquesne University, Lesch a professor of Middle East history at Trinity University in Texas.

Lesch, David W., *Syria: The Fall of the House of Assad*, Yale University Press, 2012.
A professor of Middle East history at Trinity University in Texas details the gradual shift in the popular view of President Bashar Assad from hopeful reformer at the start of his tenure to repressive tyrant. Includes detailed notes.

Miller, Laurel E., et al., *Democratization in the Arab World: Prospects and Lessons from around the Globe*, RAND Corp., 2012.
Researchers from RAND Corp., a global policy think tank, compare the most recent uprisings in the Arab world with past revolutions in Europe and the Americas. Includes notes, detailed list of references.

Noueihed, Lin, and Alex Warren, *The Battle for the Arab Spring: Revolution, Counter-Revolution and the Making of a New Era*, Yale University Press, 2012.
The book explores the origins of the current Arab uprisings; the course of events in Tunisia, Egypt, Libya, Bahrain, Yemen, and Syria; and the likely nature of future Arab politics. Includes detailed notes, brief bibliography, and source list. Noueihed is a Reuters editor based in London; Warren is a director of Frontier, a Middle East and North Africa consultancy, also based in London.

Osman, Tarek, *Egypt on the Brink: From Nasser to Mubarak*, Yale University Press, 2011.
An analysis of the past five decades of Egyptian politics explains the growth of Arab nationalism in the country amid deep religious and economic divisions in the Egyptian population. Osman, whose work has appeared in numerous international news outlets, attended American University in Cairo and Bocconi University in Italy.

Articles

Berman, Sheri, "The Promise of the Arab Spring," *Foreign Affairs*, 2013, www.foreignaffairs.com/print/135730.
An associate professor of political science at Columbia University's Barnard College compares Western countries' past responses to transitioning from autocracy to democracy to the current problems faced by Arab countries with authoritarian regimes.

Jones, Seth, "The Mirage of the Arab Spring," *Foreign Affairs*, 2013, www.foreignaffairs.com/print/135731.
A senior political scientist at the RAND Corp. warns that it remains difficult for Arab countries overthrowing unpopular governments to establish political stability and therefore should not be burdened by Western pressure to form democracies.

Reports and Studies

"Freedom in the World 2015," Freedom House, January 2015, https://freedomhouse.org/sites/default/files/01152015_FIW_2015_final.pdf.
This annual report by a nongovernment organization that advocates for democracy, political freedom, and human rights ranks the status of political freedom in countries in the Middle East and North Africa.

For More Information

Carnegie Endowment for International Peace, 1779 Massachusetts Ave., N.W., Washington, DC 20036; 202-483-7600; www.ceip.org. Foreign-policy think tank promoting active international engagement by the United States and increased cooperation among nations.

Council on Foreign Relations, 58 E. 68th St., New York, NY 10065; 212-434-9400; www.cfr.org. Nonprofit think tank specializing in U.S. foreign policy and international affairs.

Freedom House, 1301 Connecticut Ave., N.W., Suite 400, Washington, DC 20036; 202-296-5101; www.freedom house.org. Publishes annual report on the status of freedom, political rights, and civil liberties worldwide.

Human Rights Watch, 350 Fifth Ave., 34th Floor, New York, NY 10118; 212-290-4700; www.hrw.org. Conducts research and advocates for human rights in the Middle East and other regions.

International Crisis Group, 149 Avenue Louise, Level 24, B-1050 Brussels, Belgium; +32-2-502-90-38; www.crisis-group.org. Nongovernmental organization committed to preventing and resolving conflict worldwide.

Middle East Institute, 1761 N St., N.W., Washington, DC 20036; 202-785-1141; www.mei.edu. Promotes a greater understanding of Middle East issues among the American public.

Project on Middle East Democracy, 1611 Connecticut Ave., N.W., Suite 300, Washington, DC 20009; 202-828-9660; www.pomed.org. Examines how democracies can develop in the Middle East and how the United States can best support the democratic process.

Washington Institute for Near East Policy, 1828 L St., N.W., Suite 1050, Washington, DC 20036; 202-452-0650; www.washingtoninstitute.org. Promotes policies that advance American interests in the Middle East.

7

Transnational Crime

Peter Katel

Pakistani sisters Zunera, 16, at left, and Shaista are hiding in Faisalabad after being held in a Dubai brothel for four years where they were forced to work as prostitutes. Zunera displays a scar left after she was shot in the leg while trying to escape. Sex traffickers and other criminal gangs have adapted to globalization and modern technology to set up networks for a wide range of criminal enterprises.

From *CQ Researcher*,
August 29, 2014.

In the last year, some 230,000 people worldwide received a star-
tling message when they turned on their computers: "Your
personal files are encrypted! . . . To obtain the private key for this
computer, which will automatically decrypt files, you need to pay
300USD/300EUR/similar amount in another currency."[1]

The scam and an associated scheme paid off: Victims handed
over an estimated $100 million for the cyber-extortion by Russian
and Ukrainian hackers.[2]

With help from Europe and other countries, U.S. authorities
pulled the plug on the "CryptoLocker" data-ransom operation.
But those behind it remain free, like other Russian hackers in
recent years.

Cyber-extortion is part of a much broader problem that the
United Nations Office on Drugs and Crime (UNODC) calls
"transnational organized crime." It includes not only cross-border
hacking but also ivory and wildlife smuggling, piracy on the open
seas, counterfeiting of high-end, name-brand products and trafficking in drugs, human organs, weapons and sex workers.

Statistics on the phenomenon are notoriously unreliable, partly
because countries define and measure transnational criminal activity differently — or don't collect data on it at all. In its latest report,
issued in 2011, the UNODC said international criminals raked in
some $2.1 trillion in illicit profits in 2009.[3] But that figure is based
on a 1998 International Monetary Fund (IMF) estimate of laundered crime profits. "There is currently no single method that
would give clear, unambiguous and indisputable results," the U.N.
agency said.

Traffickers Use Complex International Networks

Heroin trafficking routes run from Afghanistan to Europe, and cocaine travels from South America to the United States and Europe. Gun traffickers ship weapons from the United States to Mexico and from Ukraine to Africa. Traffickers in China and India supply most of Africa's counterfeit medicines, while illegal African wildlife and animal byproducts, such as ivory, travel to buyers in Southeast Asia and China.

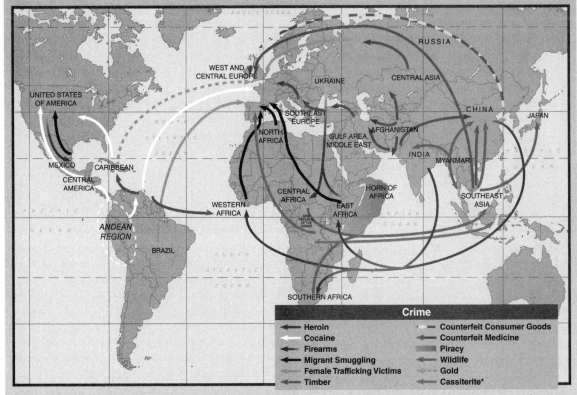

*Used to make tin. Proceeds from illegal cassiterite mining operations in the Congo are used to purchase arms for rebel groups.

Source: "The Globalization of Crime," United Nations Office on Drugs and Crime, 2010, p. 2, http://tinyurl.com/lh7okrm

Nonetheless, official assessments suggest transnational crime is overwhelming law enforcement. Such crime "poses a significant and growing threat to national and international security, with dire implications for public safety, public health, democratic institutions and economic stability across the globe," the Obama administration said in 2011.[4] "The underworld has become inextricably linked to the global economy," the UNODC said a year earlier.[5]

Some crime scholars argue, however, that transnational crime is neither new nor more of a threat than in the past. "In some ways, it was a bigger problem at earlier points in history," says Peter Andreas, a political science professor at Brown University in Providence, R.I. "In Miami in the '70s," he says, drug-money launderers "could walk into a bank with a duffel bag of cash, no questions asked."

In addition, experts say some modern developments, such as instant Internet communication and globalization, give police and prosecutors new advantages, such as the ability to trace criminals' electronic trails, as the Justice Department did to take down CryptoLocker, which was aided by a network of computers secretly infected with malware known as "Gameover Zeus."

"We succeeded in disabling Gameover Zeus and Crypto-Locker," said Deputy U.S. Attorney General James M. Cole, in part because of "strong working relationships with private industry experts and law enforcement counterparts in more than 10 countries."[6]

Still, transnational criminals today can inflict widespread damage more quickly than their predecessors. A month after the CryptoLocker plot was disrupted, another Russian hacking group reportedly captured an astonishing 1.2 billion user name-password combinations and more than 500 million email addresses.[7] Indeed, thousands of hackers, smugglers and other criminals benefit from today's Internet-enabled instantaneous global communications and the boom in international trade sparked by globalization.[8]

Meanwhile, Interpol, popularly imagined to be a sort of global super-police, is actually just a data exchange and training agency, and international treaties to control transnational crime have often been ineffective.

International agreements can prove less persuasive than profits. In Thailand, for instance, civilian and military officials profited from the trafficking of asylum seekers from Myanmar and Bangladesh — members of the Muslim Rohingya ethnic minority — for forced labor, according to a State Department annual report released in June on countries' efforts to comply with a U.N. anti-trafficking treaty.

"People died there every day," said Akram, a Rohingya rescued from a Thai rubber plantation last year. Thailand, also home to a thriving sex-worker trafficking industry, largely has not kept promises to improve anti-human trafficking enforcement, the report said.[9]

In other instances, countries may agree to cooperate in fighting global crime, but national sovereignty often trumps another country's request to have a foreign national arrested on his home turf. For instance, in July the Netherlands refused a U.S. request to extradite a former senior Venezuelan intelligence official indicted for alleged ties to Colombian drug traffickers.[10]

Moreover, the National Intelligence Council reported to Congress in 2011, "Terrorist organizations . . . are turning to criminal activities such as kidnapping for ransom to generate funding to continue their operations."[11] According to *The New York Times*, al Qaeda and close

affiliates have received at least $125 million in payments to free kidnap victims since 2008, often paid by Western European governments and sometimes disguised as aid grants.[12]

The ransom issue took on grim new urgency with the beheading — made public by a video released on Aug. 19 — of U.S. journalist James Foley by the Islamic State, often referred to as ISIS or ISIL, the jihadist army that controls parts of Syria and Iraq. Foley's kidnappers had demanded a multimillion-dollar ransom that the United States — following longstanding policy — refused to pay. But four French and two Spanish journalists had been freed earlier after their governments paid ransoms, reported journalist David Rohde of *The Atlantic* (himself a former Taliban hostage who escaped).[13]

Criminal-terrorist links clearly arouse concern. "Boko Haram has been terrorizing the Nigerian people for years, and now they're involved in this horrific case of human trafficking," said Rep. Kay Granger, R-Texas, chair of the House State, Foreign Operations and Related Programs Subcommittee, speaking of the Islamist extremist group's April kidnapping of more than 200 schoolgirls and threat to sell them.[14] "We want to hear about how the funding this subcommittee provides is being used to confront these types of issues and what is needed for the next fiscal year."[15]

Some experts want illegal corporate activities with international consequences defined as transnational crime, such as the massive sale of investment securities composed of high-risk mortgages in the 2000s — which precipitated the 2008 financial crash. "They were sold through false representation, which is a felony, and triggered a global economic crisis," says William K. Black, a professor of law and economics at the University of Missouri-Kansas City, where he teaches on white-collar crime. "It was by far one of the largest crimes in world history."[16]

But international white-collar crime is even more complicated and difficult than prosecuting other cross-border crimes, experts say. "Trying to enforce the law is a fool's game," says Jack Blum, a lawyer and early investigator of international financial crimes based in Annapolis, Md. "It takes years, it doesn't work and prosecutors generally give up."

The internationalization of financial crime reveals "fundamentally broken processes," he continues. "In the financial world, people have just purchased a version of the latest Ferrari or Lamborghini and are tooling at 200 miles an hour, and in the background you've got a couple of cops on broken rent-a-bikes trying to catch up."

Bank of America agreed on Aug. 21 to pay $16.6 billion to settle Justice Department charges of fraud in selling mortgage-backed securities. The accusations were made in a civil case, though the department did not exclude the possibility of criminal charges against individuals. However, department officials and some outside experts say proving criminal intent by executives in cases arising from the financial crash is virtually impossible.[17] The UNODC's figures on the scope of transnational crime don't include those of financial institutions allegedly acting fraudulently.

Assertions that the financial crisis stemmed from widespread cross-border law-breaking are "ideologically motivated," says Stewart Baker, a Washington lawyer and cyber-security specialist who was assistant secretary for policy in the Homeland Security Department during the George W. Bush administration. "We certainly know that transnational corporations pose special problems for international regulation, but to add those to the category of transnational crime would probably just make the category less meaningful."

As law enforcement authorities around the globe strive to arrest and prosecute international criminals, here are some of the questions academics, police and governments are debating:

Is the danger posed by transnational crime exaggerated?

The most fundamental debate concerning transnational crime is over the magnitude of the danger it represents.

It "poses a significant challenge to the United States and democratic governments and free-market economies around the world [and] a direct and immediate threat to the national security of the United States," concluded a multi-agency assessment released by the outgoing Clinton administration in December 2000.[18] That same year the U.N. General Assembly adopted a nearly identical stance.

Five years later Moisés Naím, a prominent Washington foreign-policy specialist and then-editor in chief of *Foreign Policy*, wrote in a widely cited book: "All the evidence from the illicit trade in arms, drugs, human beings, counterfeits, money laundering . . . to

say nothing of international terrorism, points us over and over to the driving force that international networks exercise in eroding the authority of states, corrupting legitimate businesses and governments and hijacking their institutions."[19]

Such alarmed tones provoked a strong counter-argument about the dangers posed by transnational crime. "What is increasing is the amount of fuss made about it and the careers built on constructing platitudes to describe it," wrote R. T. Naylor, a professor of economics at Canada's McGill University in Montreal, Quebec, a long-time scholar of illegal markets.[20]

Capitol Hill veterans such as Blum, a former staff lawyer for the Senate Antitrust Subcommittee and the Senate Foreign Relations Committee, say the grimness of some official assessments reminds him of the drug war build-up in the 1980s. "You're running a law enforcement agency, you want a budget," he says. "So you hype like crazy to make sure you have a budget."

Others share in the official alarm but acknowledge that statistics on transnational crime are unreliable for certain crimes, such as wildlife and sex trafficking. "By definition, illicit businesses don't want to be counted or sized in any kind of proper way," says Nils Gilman, associate chancellor at the University of California, Berkeley, and author of a study on black market globalization.

In one field alone — stolen art and antiquities — Interpol has estimated losses at $6 billion to $8 billion a year. "I'm extremely skeptical of all the numbers I hear," Gilman says. "The numbers are, quote-unquote, plausible, but probably because I've heard them repeated again and again."[21]

Still, cyber-crimes, he says, are genuinely new and dangerous: "The stealing of personal information is extremely disruptive and causes economic problems."

Louise I. Shelley, who directs the Terrorism, Transnational Crime and Corruption Center at George Mason University in Fairfax, Va., argues that crimes such as drug, wildlife and human trafficking clearly cause enormous damage, even if precise data is absent. "Yes, it would be better if we had data" on the many forms of illegal international activity, she says, including "data on how incredibly large the drug markets are." Citing a UNODC estimate of total transnational crime commercial volume in 2009, she said, "We don't know precisely, but we're probably talking about 7 percent of the world's trade."[22]

Yet, others say "transnational organized crime" is simply a modern term for an age-old phenomenon. "Hacking by definition is new, but it's in some ways an old crime — theft," says Brown University's Andreas. "We come up with new words to describe these things because they exist in the cyber-world."

Similarly, smuggling is an ancient crime that has increased in volume, but not necessarily as a percentage of global trade flows, says Andreas, who wrote a 2013 book on illicit trade in U.S. history.[23] "A lot of globalization is about reducing trade barriers, which in some ways has drastically reduced incentives to smuggle," he says. "The stuff that is [still] smuggled is stuff with high taxes on it, like cigarettes."

Nevertheless, even experts who see political motives behind some official characterizations of globalized crime worry that certain schemes can have grave worldwide consequences.

Blum points to "an explosion of financial crime," citing continuing damage from a long-running scam called "prime bank instrument fraud," in which people are lured to invest in nonexistent investment instruments allegedly sanctioned by major financial institutions such as the Federal Reserve or the IMF. The U.S. Treasury Department, which has posted detailed warnings about such schemes, says they have bilked individuals and organizations around the world of billions of dollars.[24]

Instrument fraud and other financial scams existed long before the Internet, Blum acknowledges. But as early as 1998, he and colleagues were warning that criminals were setting up banks online with no fixed physical address, making enforcement all but impossible.[25]

"When people commit crimes, they do not report to some international statistics agency," Blum says. "Is it much worse? What are the trends? Without hard knowledge it is hard to say. But we can sense anecdotally that, particularly in the financial area, it's out of control."

Nikos Passas, a professor of criminal justice at Northeastern University in Boston, has a more muted view. He agrees that technology has given criminals access to instant new worldwide communication, encryption and other tools that only governments used to enjoy, and that cyber-criminality can victimize large numbers of people or institutions. But, he adds, "We do not have a paradigmatic shift. We have different vulnerabilities."

AFP/Getty Images/Bima Sakti

Customs officials in Indonesia display methamphetamine that a German smuggler tried to bring into the country on Dec. 5, 2013. International enforcement has not put a major dent in the international illegal drug industry, according to the Congressional Research Service.

For instance, Passas says, criminals have also become more vulnerable, because globalization offers "different opportunities for control," such as recently revealed global communications monitoring by the U.S. National Security Agency (NSA). "The NSA has shown that. There are handles on crime; it's not like it's out of control."

Does the failure to stop drug trafficking suggest that fighting other transnational crime also will fail?

Despite decades of international anti-drug enforcement, the global illegal drug industry enjoys a steady supply of raw materials, unencumbered transportation routes and high consumer demand.

International enforcement has not put a major dent in the international illegal drug industry, the Congressional Research Service reported last year. "In 1998 . . . the United Nations committed to 'eliminating or reducing significantly' the supply of illicit drugs by 2008," the nonpartisan research agency noted last year. "In 2009, when that goal had not been accomplished, U.N. Member States agreed to recommit to achieve this goal in another decade, by 2019."[26]

Nevertheless, the prevalence of illicit drug use worldwide is "generally stable," with the total number of users "commensurate with the growth of the world population," the UNODC reported this year.[27] Although statistics on the drug trade are shaky, the agency estimates that the drug-using population ranged from as low as 162 million to as high as 324 million worldwide in 2012, or between 3.5 percent and 7 percent of the world's population.[28]

The New York-based Council on Foreign Relations said in a report last year that countries generally agree on how to define and prosecute international drug trafficking. But the "norms for law enforcement and judicial cooperation remain weak, vague or non-existent," rendering the international agreements on transnational crime essentially toothless, concluded the nonpartisan think tank.[29]

Crime specialists who favor legalizing drugs say the ineffectiveness of drug regulations proves their futility. Shrinking the drug supply through enforcement doesn't eliminate demand, they argue, and crackdowns only benefit drug traffickers. "If you succeed, what happens to the price of drugs? They go up; and profits? They go up as well — a really, really bad dynamic," says Black, of the University of Missouri-Kansas City law school. A former litigation director of the Federal Home Loan Bank Board, Black is also a former deputy director of the National Commission on Financial Institution Reform, Recovery and Enforcement, which examined the causes of the savings and loan crisis of the 1980s.

But what Black views as doomed anti-drug efforts does not necessarily mean that efforts to fight other transnational crimes will fail, he says. The United States still wields considerable global power, and financial and other crimes do not enjoy the overpowering consumer dependence on an illicit product like drugs, he says.

"We can actually create standards of conduct in areas like finance," he says. "It is hard, but . . . we know what steps to take." These include pursuing criminal prosecutions of banks that violate laws, rather than ending cases with a guilty plea and a fine, he says. In June, for instance, BNP Paribas, France's biggest bank, pleaded guilty to violating U.S. economic sanctions against Sudan and Iran and agreed to pay an $8.9 billion fine.[30]

But financial crime expert Blum says substantial differences in laws and procedures between countries pose major — and usually prohibitive — restrictions on transnational enforcement. "There is no way to compel the attendance of a witness across international borders," he says.

Technology that enabled Internet-based global banking has raced far ahead of national sovereignty laws, Blum says. "This kind of antique legal arrangement is just not working," he argues. "For all of the ways in which the Internet and the ability to wire money instantly have improved, the law enforcement side of it is nowhere.

"There are, for example, all these mutual legal-assistance treaties," he adds. "Everybody touts them. Try to use one, and see what happens." In practice, he says, countries usually give their sovereignty priority over other countries' criminal cases, regardless of treaties.

But Gilman of UC Berkeley — citing a recent U.S.-Swiss accord designed to weaken bank secrecy in Switzerland — suggests that governments trying to deal with financial problems stemming from the financial crash of 2008-09 may be about to make transnational financial crimes a higher priority. Two years ago, "I would have said no," it's not going to happen, he says. "But the United States has cracked down on bank secrecy in Switzerland to an extent I never would have imagined."

The reason is simple, Gilman says. "Governments are desperate for revenue," he explains. "That could create a shift in tolerance. If we were able to close up the holes in the global financial system, that would severely restrict all other illicit businesses, because it would be harder to launder their money."

But even if enforcement of financial crimes is getting stricter, transnational criminals remain technologically ahead of the authorities, says Douglas Farah, an investigative reporter and consultant specializing in ties between governments and organized crime in Latin America and Africa.

For instance, he says, "The Sinaloa [drug] cartel [in Mexico] and other folks have been hiring top-grade hackers. They want to know what the police are doing, and they can pay for the best," he says. "It used to be that only a few small groups could do things like high-end encryption. But now, if you look across the transnational organized crime world, there are really sophisticated Chinese, Russian and Mexican people."

As a result, Farah says, "the law enforcement and intelligence side can't really keep up."

Should the illegal activities of banks and corporations be classified as transnational crimes?

The explosion of concern about transnational crime that followed the geopolitical and economic changes of the 1990s — such as the collapse of the Soviet Union and the rise of Asian manufacturing centers — prompted arguments about how to define international law-breaking.

Should it include only hard-core crimes such as smuggling, trafficking and cyber-hacking? Or, should transnational offenses also include illegal activities by banks and corporations?

As early as the late 1980s, criminologists had begun exploring the idea of a broader definition of crime, in a "crimes of the powerful" sub-specialty, which they dubbed "state-corporate crime."[31]

The field included crimes committed by corporations on their own initiative or on orders of a government.[32] Some scholars broadened the scope of the concept to include transnational events. Passas, of Northeastern University, cites the design, operation and quality of regulation of Japan's Fukushima nuclear plant, wrecked by a 2011 earthquake and tsunami. Citing those three factors, a Japanese parliamentary investigation called the disaster "man-made." Now shuttered, the plant continues to leak radioactive water into the ocean.[33]

"If Fukushima keeps leaking . . . , you're not going to be able to eat fish in California," Passas says, citing reports of recent major leaks. But Passas concedes that, despite persistent criticism of official handling of the disaster, what may seem like criminal behavior can only be treated as such if a country has applicable laws.

Likewise, legislative bodies would have to conclude — as he has — that some financial maneuvering is criminal. "Extraordinary risk-taking with derivatives and subprime mortgages — nobody went to jail for those things," he says. "If you know what you are doing, you [can] take advantage of the legal environment. People play with definitions; some people decide that some things are going to be left out of criminal law, even very serious misconduct that has structural and systemic implications."

Karl Lallerstedt, a co-founder of Black Market Watch, a think tank in Geneva, Switzerland, that is developing ways to track illicit cross-border trade, argues that not all unethical behavior need be defined as criminal. "You are collecting toxic debt and selling it to other people," he

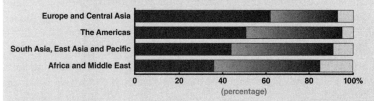

Human Trafficking Varies by Region

Sexual exploitation is the most common form of human trafficking in Europe, Central Asia and the Americas, while forced labor is more prevalent in Asia, the Pacific, Africa and the Middle East.

Victims of Human Trafficking and Exploitation (by Region and Percentage, 2007-2010)

* Includes trafficking in organs and using children as child soldiers, beggars or petty criminals or as sources of body parts for rituals and/or traditional healing.

■ Sexual exploitation
■ Forced labor
■ Other forms*

Source: "Global Report on Trafficking in Persons 2012," United Nations Office on Drugs and Crime, December 2012, p. 12, http://tinyurl.com/d99pyt7

says, differentiating between breaking criminal laws and not complying with government regulations and industry standards.

Lallerstedt is focusing on the smuggling of legal goods, such as untaxed cigarettes. Such economic crimes arouse little public indignation or law enforcement interest, despite their intersection with hard-core criminal activity, he says. "Illicit trade in normally legal goods is a low priority because it's not considered so sexy," he says. "Guns, drugs receive priority. But if the same groups are involved in multiple activities, and the same routes are being used, perhaps corrupting the same individuals to facilitate the movement of these products, [then] you have a synergy effect."

In an essay this year, Gilman of UC-Berkeley drew a deeper distinction between transnational businesspeople involved in legal transactions and transnational criminals intentionally breaking laws. The businesspeople — whom Gilman calls members of a "plutocratic insurgency" — seek to weaken government taxation and regulation, even as they enjoy government-provided services, he wrote.[34] Members of the "criminal insurgency" dodge law enforcement to provide goods and services that are quasi-legal in some places but illegal in others — such as illicit drugs.

"There are myriad connections between the two categories, but it's useful to keep them distinct," Gilman says. "Hedge fund managers aren't running drug or organ trafficking rings."

BACKGROUND

Slaves and Pirates

Experts today may debate what activities are transnational crimes, but they agree that certain activities clearly belong in the category — such as slavery, piracy and human trafficking. Yet, measured against the span of recorded history, such enterprises were legal and sometimes even government-sponsored or sanctioned — before they were prohibited.

Slavery was the norm in ancient Greece and Rome and subsequent early civilizations. And the massive Atlantic slave trade that enriched European colonial powers and shaped the futures of the United States and the Americas began as a state-sponsored enterprise, founded by the Portuguese crown in the early 1400s, during early explorations of coastal western Africa.[35]

By 1833, Britain — once a major slave-trading power — had banned slavery throughout its empire and begun efforts to ban it worldwide, with limited success. In 1845, for instance, the trafficking of slaves to the Spanish colony of Cuba was booming. Spain didn't abolish the trade until 1867; Portugal did so in 1869. European powers promised to prohibit slave-trading in their African colonies in the General Act of Brussels of 1890. But slavery and slave-trafficking were not definitively defined as international crimes until adoption of the Slavery Convention of 1926, amended in 1953.[36]

The transition from legal international activity to prohibited criminal act was even more complicated in the case of another crime whose roots date to antiquity — piracy.

For instance, during the 16th- and 17th-century wars for control of Atlantic and Caribbean trade and territory, Britain and France authorized "privateering" — the seizing of enemy vessels by naval entrepreneurs who would split the proceeds with their governments. Spain considered these robbers pirates, but some modern scholars say because the privateers attacked ships of their enemies, they were in a different category from pirates.[37]

As a young nation, the United States also authorized privateers against British vessels during the Revolutionary War and the War of 1812.[38]

But it was government-sanctioned piracy along the Barbary Coast of North Africa that led the new United States in 1794 to re-establish its navy, which had been disbanded after the American Revolution. The Ottoman provinces of Tripoli, Algiers and Tunis — known as the Barbary states — had been plundering European merchant ships in the Mediterranean Sea for centuries, demanding ransom for the crews or selling them into slavery.

After American independence, the pirates began seizing U.S. merchant ships and their crews, and for years the government paid ransom — or "tribute" — to retrieve them. But, Presidents Thomas Jefferson and James Madison went to war against the Barbary states — once in 1801-1805 and again in 1815 — eventually putting an end to the seizure of U.S. ships.[39]

Privateering was not outlawed internationally until a treaty signed in Paris in 1856. And, despite centuries-old prohibitions on piracy, it was not defined as a crime under international law until the Geneva Convention on the High Seas in 1958. Further international agreements were signed in 1992 and 1994.[40]

Trafficking in wildlife and animal parts, by contrast, was not recognized as a threat to certain animal species until the 20th century. In 1900, a convention signed in London represented the first international attempt to protect endangered species. That same year, President William McKinley signed the Lacey Act, designed with the same objective at the national level and later expanded to cover wildlife imported into the United States.[41]

The London treaty was ineffective, as were 1940 and 1968 conventions designed to protect wildlife in Latin America and Africa, respectively. Then, in 1973, 21 countries signed the sweeping Convention on International Trade in Endangered Species of Wild Fauna and Flora (CITES), which made trafficking in endangered or threatened wildlife a crime. Since then, 180 countries have signed on. But with a booming ivory trade threatening African elephants with extinction, the CITES treaty alone hasn't ensured that it is enforced everywhere.[42]

Similarly, international conventions on protecting intellectual property have not prevented a global boom in the trade of counterfeit products. International protection of patents, trademarks and copyrights dates to the 1883 Paris Convention for the Protection of Industrial Property. In addition, protection is now provided, at least legally, by the World Trade Organization's Agreement on

Trade-Related Aspects of Intellectual Property Rights, and — for strictly intellectual property matters, including patents, the U.N.'s World Intellectual Property Organization.[43]

Yet trade in counterfeit goods is thriving, projected next year to total up to $1.7 trillion, putting 2.5 million legitimate jobs at risk, according to the Paris-based International Chamber of Commerce.[44] Last year, the European Union seized about $1.04 billion worth of counterfeit goods, 12 percent of which was clothing. In the United States, an estimated $1.7 billion worth of counterfeit goods were seized in fiscal 2013, about 35 percent of which was clothing.[45]

China is by far the single biggest source of counterfeit products found in Europe and the United States: 66 percent of items seized in the EU originated in China, as did 68 percent of those found in the United States.[46] But, on paper at least, China is fully compliant with international copyright and trademark standards, embodied in the WTO agreement. But the U.S. trade representative said in 2012 that enforcement of trademark and patent protection remained spotty, marked by "the failure to impose deterrent penalties . . . sufficient to change behavior."[47]

Ironically, the United States was on the other side of the issue early in its history. The new country relied on British inventors, engineers and machine operators to copy technological breakthroughs in Britain's textile production, which had transformed a manual craft into a major industry. For the British, copying that technology was a crime. And even before America declared its independence, Britain had made it illegal for skilled British artisans and mechanics to emigrate to the United States and barred the export of textile machinery.[48]

But machines were smuggled into the United States anyway. Shortly after his inauguration, President George Washington declined personal involvement in establishing a Virginia factory — without discouraging the effort itself — using machines shipped illegally from Britain because it would constitute "a felony."

In the late 19th and early 20th centuries, transnational trafficking in human labor flourished in the United States and elsewhere, protected by corrupt low-level officials. Contractors working for U.S. mining and railroad companies brought in Chinese laborers, often using force or deception.[49] Although their employers didn't claim them

as property, the circumstances under which they entered the country and the conditions in which they lived and worked certainly qualified many of them as victims of what is now known as "human trafficking."

Among the victims were Chinese women brought in to work as prostitutes, followed by a stream of women from Europe known — in the language of the time — as "white slaves." Japanese and Mexican women also were smuggled in to work in big-city brothels. By one estimate, a New York gang made the current equivalent of $15 million in one year from trafficking women.

Prohibition

A 1920 U.S. law banning alcohol had the unintended consequence of creating a major smuggling industry to serve alcohol to American consumers.[50] By 1933, when Prohibition was repealed, a sizeable smuggling industry was concentrated along the Atlantic Coast and the Canadian side of the U.S. Northern border.

Even before Prohibition began, however, Congress had begun laying the groundwork for what would become, decades later, drug prohibition. In 1914 the Harrison Act regulated the distribution of cocaine and opiates — the most popular mood-altering substances apart from alcohol — by requiring that they be taxed and sold only by prescription. The Marihuana Tax Act of 1937 imposed further restrictions on drugs.[51]

The opiate and cocaine markets expanded, partly due to energetic efforts by traffickers from the United States and elsewhere, who developed international smuggling routes. France became a major source for legally produced opiates and cocaine that were diverted into the illegal transatlantic trade.[52]

The Comprehensive Drug Abuse Prevention and Control Act of 1970 classified drugs according to their potential for medical use and abuse.[53] The next year, President Richard M. Nixon told Congress that drug use had "assumed the dimensions of a national emergency" and declared "a war on drugs."[54]

But drug demand kept growing. By the early '70s, heroin production and smuggling routes were thriving from Turkey and then from Southeast Asia, where the U.S. government supported regional military forces that actually engaged in heroin trafficking.[55] Pakistan and Mexico also came to play ever-increasing roles in heroin trafficking. A growing U.S. appetite for marijuana, meanwhile, was

CHRONOLOGY

1790-1912 *United States creates Navy to fight piracy and extortion in North Africa. Transnational crime appears early in U.S. history as intellectual-property theft.*

1790 President George Washington condones American copying of British industrial innovations, which British consider a crime.

1801 U.S. goes to war against Barbary pirates rather than continuing to pay ransom for kidnapped Americans.

1808 Congress outlaws international trafficking of slaves to the United States, but enforcement is lax.

1912 A New York gang makes today's equivalent of $15 million smuggling foreign women for prostitution.

1920-1933 *Alcohol prohibition spurs birth of major liquor smuggling and trafficking industry.*

1920 Congress and the states adopt the 18th Amendment, prohibiting production, importation and sale of alcoholic beverages. It is repealed 13 years later.

1926 League of Nations adopts Slavery Convention to ban slavery in all forms.

1937 Marihuana Tax Act tightens restrictions on cannabis and other drugs.

1948 U.N. bans slavery and slave trade worldwide in Universal Declaration of Human Rights.

1971-1988 *U.S. sparks war on drugs, crackdown on money laundering.*

1971 President Richard M. Nixon declares "war on drugs," saying drug use has become a "national emergency."

1975 Convention on International Trade in Endangered Species goes into effect, banning international trade in species facing extinction and limiting trade in thousands of other threatened species. It has since been signed by 180 countries.

1987 "Laundering" of proceeds from booming drug smuggling and trafficking becomes huge industry.

1988 Federal money-laundering indictment against Luxembourg's Bank of Credit and Commerce International ends in landmark $14 million fine, coinciding with Senate probe of bank's involvement in asset management for dictators and terrorists.

1991-Present *Soviet Union's collapse and rise of Asian manufacturing spur global trade boom, soon to be facilitated by international digital interconnectedness.*

1991 Soviet Union collapses.

1997 An estimated 400,000 women and children from the ex-Soviet bloc and Southeast Asia are trafficked into sex trade.

2000 White House report calls international crime a direct threat to national security. . . . U.N. adopts Trafficking in Persons Protocol, the first binding international treaty specifically criminalizing human trafficking.

2003 Seventy-seven countries sign on to Kimberly Process, a certification system designed to discourage "blood diamond" trade, which finances deadly African insurgencies and terrorist activities.

2009 Russian and Ukrainian hackers are indicted for stealing more than 160 million credit-card numbers from U.S. retailers' computer systems. . . . U.N. Security Council creates a "contact group" focused on piracy of merchant vessels off Somalia.

2013 Secretary of State Hillary Rodham Clinton says booming transnational ivory trade threatens African elephants with extinction in 10 years.

2014 Justice Department announces dismantling of CryptoLocker, computer malware that encrypted victims' data, forcing them to pay an estimated $100 million worldwide to recover it. . . . African leaders at White House summit plead for more U.S. aid against elephant and rhinoceros poachers. . . . Accused Russian hacker arrested in Maldives and flown to U.S. territory. . . . Russian-based hackers steal more than 1 billion pieces of website sign-on information.

being fed not only by supplies from Mexico, the traditional source, but increasingly from Colombia, which also became a major source of cocaine.[56]

By the 1980s, the transnational illegal drug industry had grown to the point that its financial practices — especially its efforts to "launder" profits to disguise the source — had become as big an issue for policy-makers and journalists as trafficking itself.

In that period, the major overseas drug organizations, based in Colombia, wanted to repatriate dollars made in the United States back to their home countries and, in some cases, to invest some of it in the United States. Banks in Miami — considered the U.S. center of the drug trafficking industry — happily did business with clients bearing duffel bags stuffed with dollars.

In 1987 FBI agents arrested nine people in Miami and 32 others elsewhere for allegedly laundering $200 million, some of which had arrived at an FBI front company in boxes, suitcases and duffel bags in quantities of up to $2.5 million at a time. The front company had run the money through banks, which then wired it to accounts in Panama, Switzerland and Tokyo.[57]

In 1988, the issue of illegal international transactions took on a much bigger dimension after the Bank of Credit and Commerce International (BCCI) was indicted for laundering drug money. The Luxembourg-based bank had branches in many countries, including the United States.

In a plea bargain, two bank officials pleaded guilty to reduced charges, and BCCI was fined $14 million. More significantly, the Senate Terrorism, Narcotics and International Operations Subcommittee, led by then-Sen. John Kerry, D-Mass., now secretary of State, began investigating BCCI's handling of the assets of Panamanian strongman Gen. Manuel Noriega.[58]

The committee investigation and an indictment brought by famed New York City District Attorney Robert M. Morgenthau broke open the story of the bank's operations, which included systematic money laundering in several countries, the handling of assets of corrupt dictators, and financial operations on behalf of terrorist organizations. Morgenthau called the bank "one of the biggest criminal enterprises in world history."[59]

The case, which generated enormous press coverage, was the first to reveal what Kerry's panel called "the vulnerability of the world to international crime on a global scope that is beyond the current ability of governments to control."[60]

Globalized Crime

Such warnings intensified in the 1990s, as global mobility and international trade surged following the collapse of the Soviet Union in 1991 and the privatization of huge state-owned Russian industries, a process taken advantage of by insiders who grew rich from the deals. They soon became known as "oligarchs."

A highly developed criminal subculture, which had led a semi-clandestine existence under Soviet rule, flourished openly in the early post-Soviet years. But the professional criminals soon lost power to a new class in government and business.

"Government officials and powerful entrepreneurs . . . take their methods and sometimes their enforcers from the criminal world," wrote Stephen Handelman, a former correspondent for the *Toronto Star* and *Time* magazine, in 2001. Handelman wrote an early book on the rise of post-Soviet Russian organized crime.[61]

Western banks and institutions seemed untroubled, however, about doing business with the new breed of Russian enterprises, Handelman noted. In one of the early cases to grow out of such relationships, the Bank of New York in 2005 paid $38 million in fines and compensation to settle U.S. fraud and money laundering charges involving Russian funds.[62]

Whatever level of cooperation existed between Russian and American businesses, it did not extend, at least from the American point of view, to U.S.-Russia cooperation on the growing number of cyber-crime cases centered in Russia. In 2001, the FBI resorted to luring two Russian hackers, Vasily Gorshkov and Alexey Ivanov, to the United States by inviting them to fake job interviews. The two had stolen credit card numbers and other financial data, trying to extort money from the data owners to retrieve the information, and using stolen credit card numbers for purchases using PayPal. Ivanov was sentenced to four years, Gorshkov to three.[63]

Authorities also saw a sudden uptick in the number of people sold into the international sex industry, largely through networks operating from eastern and central Europe. A federal, multi-agency "International Crime Threat Assessment" concluded in 2000 that about 175,000 of the women and children brought into Europe and the United States in 1997 to serve in the sex trade were from

Investigators Examine Ancient Money-Transfer Method

"Hawala" system was once suspected in 9/11 attacks.

In the aftermath of the Sept. 11, 2001, terrorist attacks on the United States, politicians, government officials and journalists struggled to understand a new enemy and how it worked. Searchers for the key to al Qaeda's organizational techniques obeyed Washington wisdom: "Follow the money."

The hunt led many to a money-transfer system that former Deputy Treasury Secretary Stuart Eizenstat called the pipeline for a "potentially significant portion of terrorist funds into or out of the U.S.," which Secretary of State Colin Powell in 2002 called "shadowy," and the *Los Angeles Times* called "a destination point for terrorists and heroin traffickers."[1]

That system had a name that sounded suitably mysterious to Western ears —"hawala." As some experts pointed out, the system was devised centuries ago, in South Asia and the Middle East, to allow merchants and travelers to transmit money without risking robbery by carrying it with them. Similar systems were known in China as Fei-Ch'ien; in India, as Hundi; and in Thailand, as Phei Kwan.[2]

But in the post-2001 atmosphere, hawalas, more than their East Asian counterparts, came to represent a key intersection between two sets of wrongdoers who needed to move money around the globe: transnational criminals and terrorists.

The fund-transfer system seemed ideal for both sets of people. As Rand Beers, then-assistant secretary of State for international narcotics and law enforcement, told a congressional subcommittee in 2002: "Terrorists and drug traffickers use similar means to conceal profits and fund-raising. They use informal transfer systems such as 'hawala.' " He

added that they also used bulk cash smuggling and multiple bank accounts.[3]

The hawala system, which came to be used by people settling debts and by immigrants sending money home, is user-friendly. A person wanting to send money gives the cash to a nearby money-transfer agent, a "hawaldar" who may also be a merchant or shopkeeper. He, in turn, sends a message — today, by phone, fax or email — to a counterpart hawaldar near the intended recipient, perhaps in another country, who then pays the recipient. At some point, hawaldars who have done business with each other settle accounts, if one has paid out more to customers than the other.[4]

Because the system has no formal record-keeping requirements and is largely unregulated by governments, it seemed to pose obvious attractions for those who wanted their international transactions kept under the radar.

However, in 2004, the National Commission on Terrorist Attacks Upon the United States (the 9/11 Commission), reported that the attackers got their money in above-ground ways that were theoretically open to scrutiny by investigators. The attackers used wire transfers from Dubai, cash that some of them brought with them and ATM withdrawals in the United States from accounts in the United Arab Emirates. "Our investigation has uncovered no evidence that the 9/11 conspirators employed hawala as a means to move the money that funded the operation," the commission concluded.[5]

Osama bin Laden and his comrades did use hawalas in the 1990s when al Qaeda established itself in Afghanistan. But, as the commission noted, the banking system there was "antiquated and undependable."[6]

---

former Soviet-bloc countries.[64] Even more women and children were trafficked from Southeast Asia, where an estimated 225,000 women, most under 18, were sold into the sex trade in 1997.[65]

While no one disputes that sex-worker trafficking is a big industry, statistics on human trafficking of all kinds, including workers and child soldiers, for instance, are fuzzy. In 2006, the U.S. government estimated that

600,000 to 800,000 people were trafficked across international borders. But the Government Accountability Office, the federal government's accounting arm, said there were no data to support those numbers.[66]

In any case, human trafficking had been proscribed in a U.N. General Assembly convention against transnational organized crime in 2000. The treaty defined transnational organized crime as "money-laundering, corruption, illicit

Inefficient for terrorists meant inefficient for everyone else as well, pointed out experts in the hawala system — also known to academics as informal funds transfer (IFT). "Overregulation and coercive measures will not be effective," Mohammed El-Qorchi, a senior economist for the International Monetary Fund, argued in 2002, "because they might push IFT further underground. . . . They will not, in isolation, succeed in reducing the attractiveness of the hawala system. As a matter of fact, as long as there are reasons for people to prefer such systems, they will continue to exist and even expand."[7]

Nikos Passas, a professor of criminal justice at Northeastern University in Boston, who has been researching the hawala system and its counterparts since the 1990s, acknowledged that it can be used by criminals and, in principle, by violent extremists. But he said in a 2005 report to the Dutch Ministry of Justice that he had "encountered no instance of terrorist finance in the U.S. or Europe" through these informal systems. "In South Asia and Africa, there are such instances," he added, "but this is mostly because of the general use of [hawala-type systems] for all kinds of transfers and payments."[8]

Passas argued that the post-2001 focus on hawalas as potential channels for financing terrorism and crime could bring about a cure worse than the disease: a shift to more modern methods of transferring money that include gift cards, manipulation of invoices to hide transfers, use of brokerage accounts and credit and debit cards. "The problem is that even less is known" about these systems' vulnerabilities, he wrote. "Instead of increasing transparency of fund transfers and reducing crime, the authorities' efforts may produce the opposite result."[9]

Still, officials remain wary of hawalas' below-the-radar quality, even though the intense political and law enforcement focus on them has faded since the immediate post-9/11 period.

"I don't think that the notion of hawalas or of informal financial services is in and of itself problematic," Daniel Glaser, assistant Treasury secretary for terrorist financing and financial crimes, said at a panel discussion last year at the Center for Strategic and International Studies in Washington. "The problematic aspect of it is the non-transparent aspect of it, which then makes it subject to abuse by people who we wouldn't want to have access to this financial system."[10]

— Peter Katel

[1]"President George W. Bush [and others] Delivers Remarks at the Treasury Department's Financial Crimes Enforcement Network," *FDCH Political Transcripts*, Nov. 7, 2001; Josh Meyer, "Cutting Money Flow to Terrorists Proves Difficult," *Los Angeles Times*, Sept. 28, 2003, http://tinyurl.com/lh8jqey.

[2]Nikos Passas, "Demystifying Hawala," *Journal of Scandinavian Studies in Criminology and Crime Prevention*, 2006, http://tinyurl.com/lp82tj2; Mohammed El-Qorchi, "Hawala," Finance & Development, International Monetary Fund, December 2002, http://tinyurl.com/mkrhx7d.

[3]Rand Beers, "Narco-Terror: The Worldwide Connection Between Drugs and Terror," testimony to Senate Judiciary Committee, Subcommittee on Technology, Terrorism and Government Information, Federal News Service, March 13, 2002, http://tinyurl.com/k5qgu9x.

[4]*Ibid.*

[5]"The 9/11 Commission Report," National Commission on Terrorist Attacks Upon the United States, 2004, pp. 224, 237, 499, http://tinyurl.com/49xkf.

[6]*Ibid.*, p. 171.

[7]El-Qorchi, *op. cit.*

[8]Nikos Passas, "Informal Value Transfer Systems and Criminal Activities," Ministerie van Veiligheid en justitie [Ministry of Security and Justice, the Netherlands], p. 36, http://tinyurl.com/kuqxzjp.

[9]*Ibid.*, p. 38; Nikos Passas, "Informal Value Transfer Systems, Terrorism and Money Laundering," Report to the National Institute of Justice, November 2003, p. 17, http://tinyurl.com/k96bvzb.

[10]"The Center for Strategic and International Studies Holds the Global Security Forum 2013, Panel on What Role Financial Power Should Play in National Security," *CQ Transcriptions*, Nov. 5, 2013.

trafficking in endangered species of wild flora and fauna, [and] offences against cultural heritage," as well as human trafficking. It called on governments to recognize the links between international criminal activities and terrorism.[67]

Terrorism and Crime

After the Sept. 11, 2001, terrorist attacks in the United States, governments and international organizations quickly switched their anti-transnational crime efforts to focus on criminals' connections to terrorism.

Even though al Qaeda — the group behind the 9/11 attacks — had political and religious objectives, investigations showed that its logistical machinery had a structure that copied or even overlapped with transnational criminal networks. "Transnational organized crime and international terrorism increasingly share both organizational

Criminals Want Corrupt States — But Good Roads, Too

Transnational crime requires reliable global connections and banking systems.

What more could an internationally minded criminal want than a country whose government is essentially nonexistent, where a crime boss is free to conduct his business without fear of policemen's prying eyes?

A lot more, it turns out. Experts say crooks need the same basic government services — such as dependable electricity, decent roads and reliable Internet connections — as law-abiding citizens.

"The ideal locale for a transnational criminal organization is one which boasts many of the advantages of a strong, functioning state, such as modern infrastructure and communications, a banking system and enough rule of law to make life generally predictable," writes Patrick Radden Keefe, a journalist and author specializing in international crime.[1]

Fear of transnational organized crime surged during the post-Cold War period when the specter of "failed states" loomed as an international menace. In the 1990s, the breakdown of all government in Somalia, where a small-scale U.S. military intervention came to grief, seemed to represent the danger.

Failed states became a bigger concern after the Sept. 11, 2001, terrorist attacks in the United States, perpetrated by extremists hiding out in Taliban-controlled Afghanistan. As then-President George W. Bush's 2002 national security strategy document declared: "America is now threatened less by conquering states than we are by failing ones."[2]

Although armed extremism led the list of fears, crime was not far behind. By 2006, the Bush administration was warning that "weak and impoverished states and ungoverned areas" were "susceptible to exploitation by terrorists, tyrants and international criminals."[3]

Since then, though, crime experts have been drawing distinctions between collapsed or nascent states and weak ones, and weak ones with good connections to the rest of the world and those lacking such links.

For instance, barely governed states are good spots for smugglers of drugs, guns and people, Stewart M. Patrick, now director of the International Institutions and Global Governance Program at the Council on Foreign Relations think tank, wrote in 2006. "Criminal groups have become adept at exploiting weak-state capacity in conflict zones, such as Colombia or the DRC [Democratic Republic of Congo], where political authority is contested or formal institutions have collapsed."[4]

But selling products, or laundering profits, requires communications and transportation networks and functioning banks, Patrick added. Thus, "South Africa and Nigeria have become magnets for transnational and domestic organized crime," he wrote, because they have working infrastructures. "Togo has not."

Nigeria, as it happens, is ranked as shakier, overall, than Togo in this year's global ranking of "fragile states" by *Foreign Policy* magazine and the Fund for Peace, a think tank and advocacy organization favoring alternatives to armed conflict. But Nigeria comes out somewhat better than Togo in terms of the quality of its public services.[5]

How comfortable transnational criminals feel in a country also depends on the extent to which they can forge corrupt ties to law enforcement officials and politicians. This has long been an issue in some Latin American countries, and operational characteristics and at times even partner with one another," Thomas M. Sanderson, deputy director of the Center for Strategic and International Studies' Transnational Threat Initiative, wrote in 2004.[68]

In West Africa, *Washington Post* correspondent Farah had reported in November 2001 that al Qaeda was earning millions by buying diamonds from Sierra Leonean guerrillas at below-market prices and selling them in Europe.[69] Former CIA and military officials gave similar accounts to NBC News in 2005, but a State Department deputy assistant secretary said in 2006, "We have not been able to verify those reports."[70]

including the gang violence-plagued Central American nations — El Salvador, Honduras and Guatemala — the countries from which thousands of women and children have been seeking refuge by crossing the U.S. border in recent weeks. The region's gangs — with help from some corrupt police — are deeply involved in transnational drug trafficking.[6]

Trafficking relies on a thriving culture of political corruption. A former Guatemalan president, Alfonso Portillo, was sentenced in May to more than five years in a U.S. federal prison after pleading guilty to money laundering conspiracy (using U.S. banks). El Salvador's attorney general announced in June that he was investigating Defense Minister David Munguia Payes for allegedly selling military weapons to gangs, an investigation the military had tried to block. And Honduras has earned a reputation from the State Department's human rights investigators and others as a center of widespread government corruption.[7]

The three countries are grouped with a predominantly African contingent as the world's most fragile states, according to the *Foreign Policy*-Fund for Peace rankings. But they also have adequate communications and transportation networks. In fact, Honduran Foreign Minister Mireya Aguero Corrales told NPR in July, the city in her country with the highest homicide rate is also its business capital. "If you go to San Pedro Sula . . . you see a prosperous city," she said. "It's where the business centers are. Many international brand names have their maquilas [assembly plants] there."[8]

For some analysts, the attention paid to the link between fragile states and transnational crime distracts from what they see as the bigger problem of transnational criminal behavior in major institutions in wealthy countries. Swiss bankers recently told *The New York Times* about traveling to the United States to recruit clients interested in shielding their assets from the Internal Revenue Service by using Switzerland's fabled bank secrecy. Clients would use code names to call from pay phones, the bankers said. And the bankers' laptops were set up to allow easy and instant erasing of data.[9]

Author Keefe, in fact, argued that Switzerland and other tax havens had found a legal way around the issue of criminality. "In these jurisdictions, the rule of law manages to accommodate criminality," he wrote. "The corruption is written into the law itself."

— Peter Katel

[1]Patrick Radden Keefe, "The Geography of Badness: Mapping the Hubs of the Illicit Global Economy," in Michael Miklaucic and Jacqueline Brewer, eds., *Convergence: Illicit Networks and National Security in the Age of Globalization* (2013), p. 102, http://tinyurl.com/qfodcxg.

[2]Quoted in Michael J. Mazarr, "The Rise and Fall of the Failed-State Paradigm," *Foreign Affairs*, January/February, 2014, http://tinyurl.com/myoo4ds; Michael Bowden, *Black Hawk Down: A Story of Modern War* (1999).

[3]"The National Security Strategy of the United States of America," The White House, March 2006, p. 33, http://tinyurl.com/ms7unhb.

[4]Stewart M. Patrick, "Weak States and Global Threats: Fact or Fiction?" *The Washington Quarterly*, Spring 2006, p. 39, http://tinyurl.com/ljejp62.

[5]"Fragile States," *Foreign Policy*, 2014, http://tinyurl.com/m3wdvpk.

[6]Jo Tuckman, " 'Flee or die': violence drives Central America's child migrants to US border," *The Guardian*, July 9, 2014, http://tinyurl.com/k3sgahk; Steven S. Dudley, "Drug Trafficking Organizations in Central America: Transportistas, Mexican Cartels and Maras," Woodrow Wilson International Center for Scholars, University of San Diego, May 2010, http://tinyurl.com/7auevqs.

[7]"US court sentences former president of Guatemala to prison for taking bribes," The Associated Press (*The Guardian*), May 22, 2014, http://tinyurl.com/k7v9mvq; Seth Robbins, "El Salvador's Military: Arms Dealer to the Maras?" *InSight Crime*, June 16, 2014, http://tinyurl.com/q37g56b; Elisabeth Malkin, "Lawmakers Ask State Dept. to Review Support for Honduras," *The New York Times*, May 29, 2014, http://tinyurl.com/pwdg8rh.

[8]"Honduras Foreign Minister: U.S. Should Address Root Causes of Migration," NPR, July 25, 2014, http://tinyurl.com/ltmqdm5.

[9]Doreen Carvajal, "Swiss Banks' Tradition of Secrecy Clashes With Quests Abroad For Disclosure," *The New York Times*, July 8, 2014, http://tinyurl.com/nzr83u5.

However, international outrage over the trade in "blood diamonds" — diamonds trafficked to finance brutal civil wars in Liberia and Sierra Leone — led to creation in 2003 of the Kimberly Process, a system endorsed by 77 countries designed to certify diamonds as unconnected with trafficking by warring insurgents.

Meanwhile, rapid expansion of Internet connectivity and e-commerce in the early 2000s led to the parallel growth of Internet-enabled global crime. By 2005, investigators said criminal networks based in former Soviet-bloc countries, Russia above all, were deeply involved in trading bulk quantities of personal-identity information from stolen credit cards and online accounts. Experts pointed to a combination of poverty and, given a still-strong educational system, superior technological skills.[71]

As data piracy expanded, so did the ancient crime of piracy on the high seas. The first half of 2009 alone saw a total of 240 pirate attacks, most involving the hijacking of shipping vessels by Somalis operating in the Red Sea and Gulf of Aden.[72]

But international cooperation — based on common agreement that the pirates had to be stopped — made a difference. By May 2013, Somali piracy had effectively ended, without a single successful hijacking during the previous 12 months. Armed guards on ships, naval deployments by NATO, the EU, China, Russia and other countries and prosecutions of more than 1,000 pirates helped to end Somali piracy.[73]

Meanwhile, world attention had turned to high finance after the burst housing bubble precipitated a global financial crisis in 2008, when the value of investment securities backed by subprime mortgages plunged.[74] The crash prompted debate over where to draw the line between high-risk financial maneuvers involving billions of dollars and crime and vividly illustrated how interconnected the world economy had become.

CURRENT SITUATION

Arresting Russians?

The alleged leader of a hacker ring accused of reaping at least $2 million by stealing and reselling credit card information siphoned from U.S. business computer systems is awaiting trial in Seattle.[75]

Roman V. Seleznev, 30, a Russian, was grabbed in July in the Maldives, a popular Indian Ocean tourist destination, apparently by U.S. law enforcement agents. He was flown to the U.S. Pacific island territory of Guam, where a judge ordered him transferred to Seattle. He had been indicted there in 2011 for alleged bank fraud, computer hacking, identity theft and related charges. He was indicted separately in Nevada in 2012 on similar charges, and faces up to 30 years in prison.[76]

Declaring that Seleznev had been "kidnapped," the Russian foreign ministry said, "We consider this the latest unfriendly move from Washington."[77]

The arrest came only five weeks after Justice Department officials fingered another Russian as head of the CryptoLocker ransom scheme. Then, news broke of the massive theft of more than 1 billion pieces of website sign-on data — a scheme also allegedly centered in Russia.[78]

But as the circumstances of Seleznev's capture had made clear, U.S. authorities cannot count on Russia arresting alleged cyber-crooks accused of crimes in the United States.

Meanwhile, as Russian aggression in Ukraine worsened relations between the two countries, Russia in August announced that former U.S. National Security Agency analyst Edward Snowden could stay another three years in Russia. Snowden has been in Russia since 2013, when he released classified documents that revealed massive, worldwide electronic surveillance by the NSA. The Justice Department has charged him with theft and violations of the Espionage Act.[79]

But even before Snowden's Russia stay was extended, the United States had been unable to get Russian help in major hacking cases. "The FBI has tried to get cooperation, the State Department has asked for help and nothing happens," said Richard Clarke, who was special adviser for cybersecurity in the George W. Bush administration, "so law enforcement options are pretty negligible."[80]

U.S.-Russia discussions reportedly have centered on Russian and Ukrainian hackers that the Americans believe stole more than 160 million credit card numbers from Neiman Marcus and other retailers in the past seven years. A 2009 indictment in New Jersey against five of them was unsealed last year.[81] Two of the five were arrested at U.S. request while vacationing in the Netherlands in 2012.[82]

Russian police did arrest two people in June — a teenage boy and a 23-year-old man — for allegedly mounting a small-scale "ransomware" scheme targeting Apple devices.[83]

Russia is not the only country greeting U.S.-requested arrests coolly. In July, the United States had a former Venezuelan military intelligence official arrested in Aruba, a former Dutch colony in the Caribbean, 15 miles from the Venezuelan coast. U.S. indictments accused Hugo Carvajal of business ties to Colombian drug traffickers who shipped drugs to the United States via Venezuela.[84]

The Venezuelan government said Carvajal had been "kidnapped." The Dutch government, which handles

Is the transnational organized crime threat exaggerated?

YES Peter Andreas
Professor of Political Science and International Studies, Brown University

Written for *CQ Researcher*, August 2014

Illicit cross-border activities, ranging from drug trafficking to money laundering, are often lumped under the frustratingly vague term "transnational organized crime." In standard accounts, globetrotting criminals are increasingly sophisticated, organized and powerful. Governments, in contrast, are increasingly overwhelmed, outsmarted and outmaneuvered.

At first, this portrayal seems accurate. Transnational organized crime routinely defies borders, mocks laws and corrupts and sometimes violently challenges authorities. But by neglecting the past, we grossly distort our view of the present. Contrary to conventional wisdom, states have struggled with this challenge for centuries.

For the most part, transnational crime is a fuzzy new term for an old practice: smuggling. Although the speed, content, methods and organization of smuggling have varied greatly across time and place, the basic activity has not fundamentally changed. Even though the global reach of some smuggling groups has accelerated with the integration of the global economy, the image of an octopus-like network of crime syndicates that runs the underworld is fiction. Even the most sophisticated smuggling schemes tend to be defined more by fragmentation and loose, informal networks than by concentration and hierarchical organization. And no so-called drug cartel actually fits the definition of a cartel.

We are often told that the volume of organized transnational criminal activity has surged in recent decades. Of course, we have no idea how true those statistical claims are — they tend to be assertions and guesstimates rather than reliable and verifiable empirical evidence. Still, cross-border organized crime would simply have to keep pace with the illicit economy to grow at an impressive rate. But that does not necessarily mean it has increased as an overall percentage of global economic transactions. Indeed, the liberalization of trade in recent decades has sharply reduced incentives to engage in smuggling practices designed to evade taxes and tariffs, historically the backbone of illicit commerce.

The historical amnesia that too often afflicts the debate is nowhere more evident than in the depiction of our borders as increasingly overrun and overwhelmed — with the U.S.-Mexico line cited as a particularly glaring illustration. Yet, there was never a golden age of border security. Popular political calls to "regain control" of the border falsely imply that it was ever actually under control. And by historical standards, this border is in fact far more controlled than ever before.

NO Louise I. Shelley
Director, Terrorism, Transnational Crime and Corruption Center, George Mason University

Excerpted from Shelley's book, *Dirty Entanglements: Corruption, Crime and Terrorism* (Cambridge University Press, 2014)

The threat of transnational organized crime is all too real. That entangled threat of crime, corruption and terrorism now commands high-level attention because of (1) its endemic nature in many diverse regions of the world, especially in conflict regions; (2) the financial success and extensive influence of nonstate actors on governments, often by means of corruption; (3) the increasing economic role of criminals and terrorists both as employers and participants in the local and global economy; (4) the deleterious impact of crime and terrorism on communities and the political order; and (5) the incapacity of state and multinational organizations to successfully challenge transnational criminals and terrorists at the national, regional and global levels.

Contemporary illicit trade, a key component of the crime-terror relationship, is different from smuggling in previous millennia. Smuggling has existed since the dawn of history, when states began to raise revenues by imposing taxes on the movement of goods. Yet today's illicit trade carried out by criminals, terrorists and corrupt officials affects millions, if not billions, of lives by doing irreversible damage to the planet and to existing communities, whether by eliminating species or forests or spreading contagious diseases or components of weapons of mass destruction.

The future will see new kinds of dirty entanglements and groups, such as the recently established relationships between the criminal gangs of Central America and the drug cartels. State-level conflicts do not necessarily deter business relations among nonstate actors. The desire to make money in the illicit economy transcends long-term hostilities, and in the future we will continue to see such strange, strategic partnerships and new and possibly now unimaginable entanglements. In the future, identities may be more blurred.

Dirty entanglements are unfortunately on a growth trajectory. The forces contributing to their rise — including increased populations without a future, growing income inequality, increased migration and displacement, poor governance, absence of the rule of law, continuing civil unrest and conflict and climate change — show no signs of abating.

In our highly interconnected world, diverse communities must work together to counter the scourge of corruption, crime and terrorism. Unfortunately, until now, without a whole-of-society perspective, we have made little progress globally against the dirty entanglements.

matters for Aruba, decided to release Carvajal, who had a diplomatic passport.[85]

Threatened Wildlife

Transnational crime is becoming a major issue in relations between African and Asian countries and the rest of the world, as the demand for smuggled animal parts from endangered and threatened species skyrockets. Much of the increased demand, especially for elephant ivory, is being spurred by an expanding middle class in China, where carved ivory is highly prized.[86]

During a White House summit for leaders from 50 African countries in August, U.S. officials held high-level talks on how to combat the booming illegal regional trade in wildlife. "The elephants are killed in Tanzania," Tanzanian President Jakaya Kikwete said at a panel discussion with several counterparts and U.S. Interior Secretary Sally Jewell. "But the consignment [of ivory] came from Kampala, Uganda, and moved through Mombasa [Kenya's main port]. So there is definitely need for working together."[87]

The flourishing demand for ivory has devastated Africa's elephant and rhinoceros populations. Rhino horns are erroneously believed to have medicinal powers and are popular for making dagger handles in Yemen. At least 1,000 rhinos were killed last year, as were 20,000 African elephants (and 35,000 the year before), according to former Deputy Interior Secretary David J. Hayes.[88] Ivory trafficking alone is threatening African forest elephants with extinction within 10 years, then-Secretary of State Hillary Clinton said last year.[89]

The recent Washington discussions didn't yield any definitive results. However, the U.S. government has been helping African governments beef up their wildlife protection programs via training, equipment and uniforms. Still, African leaders at the summit asked for more: helicopters in Namibia, night-vision goggles in Tanzania, infrared scanners in Togo and military support in Gabon.[90]

"Well-armed, well-equipped and well-organized networks of criminals, and corrupt officials exploit porous borders and weak institutions," Obama said in February as he introduced a White House strategy to enhance enforcement of anti-wildlife trafficking laws, including diplomatic initiatives to promote international cooperation.[91]

The Justice Department also is targeting ivory and rhino horn dealers. In the past two months:

- Federal agents arrested a Canadian dealer on charges of smuggling more than $500,000 worth of both products from the United States;
- A Miami-based dealer pleaded guilty to brokering the sale of rhino horn;
- A Texas dealer pleaded guilty to conspiring to traffic horn and ivory; and
- Two men in separate cases were sentenced to 30 and 70 months, respectively, for involvement in major ivory and horn trafficking enterprises.[92]

The 70-month sentence — the longest ever in a U.S. wildlife smuggling case — was imposed on a Chinese businessman convicted of heading a smuggling enterprise that shipped $4.5 million worth of African rhino horn and ivory from the United States to China. Zhifei Li admitted he smuggled 30 rhino horns that were used to make drinking cups. Folk tradition in China and other Asian countries holds that drinking from horn cups brings good health.[93]

"If you are able to stop the market for ivory and rhino horns, definitely you will be able to save these species," Tanzanian President Kikwete said at the White House summit.[94]

OUTLOOK

Grim Future

Crime expert Blum says international financial crimes seem likely to continue to be a growth industry. "Countries are not going to cooperate" against financial crooks, he says, citing the tendencies to prize national sovereignty over other countries' criminal cases. "They're going to sign all kinds of agreements and ignore them."

And national differences on what crimes should be priorities seem likely to persist. For instance, the United Nations and several other countries define organ trafficking as illegal, but the international organ-brokering trade is prospering due to lax enforcement in many countries.[95]

Still, shifting political winds offer occasional chances to crack down on some transnational crimes, says Passas of Northeastern University. "It becomes a lot easier when old friends fall out," he says, citing the cases of former U.S. allies Panamanian strongman Noriega, Iraqi dictator Saddam Hussein, Libyan dictator Moammar Gadhafi and Egyptian dictator Hosni Mubarak. "They had all been involved for ages in corrupt financial misconduct," Passas says. "We protected them, and then they were behind bars or killed."

International politics can also complicate efforts to pressure other countries into cracking down on transnational crime. The State Department's harsh evaluation this year of Thailand's anti-human trafficking efforts led to that country's inclusion on a list of 23 countries deemed not complying with minimum standards or making significant efforts to improve. Inclusion on the list means the U.S. president can order foreign aid withheld.

But last year, Obama waived sanctions against China, Russia and Uzbekistan while imposing full sanctions on Cuba, Iran and North Korea — which already have hostile relations with the United States and receive no aid. Partial sanctions were applied to Congo, Equatorial Guinea, Eritrea, Sudan, Syria and Zimbabwe, whose relations with the U.S. are tense.

As for Thailand and other countries in its category, "You certainly wouldn't want to halt any assistance that's going specifically to increasing the capacity of our partners in those governments to fight human trafficking or to help its victims," Luis CdeBaca, the ambassador-at-large of the State Department's office that monitors and combats human trafficking, said at a June briefing.[96]

Moreover, says reporter Farah, in a post-Cold War world with two major superpowers no longer dominating international relations, crime-linked governments can more easily develop alliances without worrying about crackdowns from major powers.

Policymakers and law enforcement should focus on criminal-government ties, "especially in an age of resource constraint," Farah says, urging a focus on crime that poses major threats rather than the relatively less dangerous variety. "You have to be somewhat realistic about what is always going to be out there — handbag counterfeiting, even fairly high-end narcotrafficking."

Andreas of Brown University predicts that enforcement of laws against cyber-crime, which can victimize millions

of people and businesses at a time, will become increasingly important. "The debate used to focus primarily on the drug issue," he says. "Drugs are still quite prominent but don't monopolize the debate like they used to."

When it comes to cyber-crime, former Homeland Security official Baker argues that time is not on the criminals' side. "It is harder and harder to hide your ID consistently in cyberspace," he says. "It will be increasingly possible to ID these people."

And all high-level hackers don't enjoy ironclad protection against arrest, Baker says. They may be out of danger as long as they're in Russia or elsewhere in the old Soviet bloc, but, "The old Soviet Union is not that much fun. They will travel, and they will get busted. My hope is that we will eventually begin to weed out at least the less disciplined cyber-criminals."

In addition, cyber-tools may become a bigger part of law-enforcement's arsenal. Lallerstedt of Black Market Watch says an international agreement may soon require cigarette firms to use technology enabling them to "track and trace" every pack in order to deter smuggling, which costs governments an estimated $30 billion a year in lost cigarette tax revenue.[97]

"I'm not saying it's a magic bullet," he says. "But the further ahead you look, the more monitoring and track-and-tracing options are available."

Nevertheless, other transnational crime-watchers see much less reason for hope when looking at the big picture. Transnational criminals likely will continue reaping the benefits of inconsistent enforcement, efficient trade routes and ready markets for their goods, says Shelley of George Mason University.

"The future is grim," she says. "At the rate we're going: Goodbye rhino, goodbye elephant; welcome, trafficked people."

NOTES

1. Eric Geier, "How to rescue your PC from ransomware," *PCWorld*, Jan. 13, 2014, http://tinyurl.com/oj9myjc.

2. Matt Apuzzo, "Secret Global Strike Kills 2 Malicious Web Viruses," *The New York Times*, June 3, 2014, http://tinyurl.com/lhk254d.

3. "Estimating Illicit Financial Flows Resulting from Drug Trafficking and Other Transnational Organized Crimes," U.N. Office on Drugs and Crime, October 2011, p. 7, http://tinyurl.com/p64lrda.

4. "Transnational Organized Crime: A Growing Threat to International and National Security," in "Strategy to Combat Transnational Organized Crime," The White House, July 25, 2011, http://tinyurl.com/3t5jwtg.

5. "The Globalization of Crime: A Transnational Organized Crime Threat Assessment," U.N. Office on Drugs and Crime, 2010, p. ii, http://tinyurl.com/p64lrda.

6. "Memorandum of Law," U.S. v. Evgeniy Mikhaliovoch Bogachev, (copy on Justice Department website, undated), http://tinyurl.com/pm9zufj; "U.S. Leads Multi-National Action Against 'Gameover Zeus and 'CryptoLocker' Ransomware. . .," U.S. Justice Department, June 2, 2014, http://tinyurl.com/nbdxqoh.

7. Nicole Perlroth and David Gelles, "Russian Hackers Amass Over a Billion Passwords," *The New York Times*, Aug. 5, 2014, http://tinyurl.com/qd8ucqn.

8. For background, see the following *CQ Researchers*: John Felton, "Small Arms Trade," June 19, 2012, pp. 281-304; Robert Kiener, Human Trafficking and Slavery," Oct. 16, 2012, pp. 473-496; Sarah Glazer, "Organ Trafficking," July 19, 2011, pp. 341-366; and Peter Katel, "Mexico's Drug War," Dec. 12, 2008, pp. 1009-1032.

9. Quoted in Andrew R.C. Marshall, "Thai police target human traffickers but rescued Rohingya may face more abuse," Reuters, Feb. 13, 2014, www.reuters.com/article/2014/02/13/us-thailand-rohingya-idUSBREA1C0FB20140213. "Trafficking in Persons Report 2014," U.S. Department of State, 2014, pp. 372-376, http://tinyurl.com/kw2yz8y.

10. Tim Dees, "What Do Interpol Agents Really Do," *Slate*, July 1, 2013, http://tinyurl.com/k7mskqf; Jim Wyss, "Top Venezuela official accused in drug case averts U.S. extradition, heads back home," *The Miami Herald*, July 27, 2014, http://tinyurl.com/oeqnuxl.

11. Quoted in John Rollins and Liana Sun Wyler, "Terrorism and Transnational Crime: Foreign Policy Issues for Congress," Congressional Research Service, June 11, 2013, pp. 2-3, http://tinyurl.com/ptk4y5m.

12. Rukmini Callimachi, "Paying Ransoms, Europe Bankrolls Qaeda Terror," *The New York Times*, July 29, 2014, http://tinyurl.com/nupg66w. For background see Barbara Mantel, "Assessing the Threat from Al Qaeda," *CQ Researcher*, June 27, 2014, pp. 553-576.

13. Rukmini Callimachi, "Before Killing James Foley, ISIS Demanded Ransom from U.S.," *The New York Times*, Aug. 20, 2014, http://tinyurl.com/nf8q5tx; David Rohde. For background, see Frank Greve, "Combat Journalism," *CQ Researcher*, April 12, 2013, pp. 329-352.; David Rohde, "How the U.S. and Europe Failed James Foley," *The Atlantic*, August 2014, http://tinyurl.com/n9ojb4g.

14. Aminu Abubakar and Josh Levs, " 'I will sell them,' Boko Haram leader says of kidnapped Nigerian girls," CNN, May 6, 2014, http://tinyurl.com/lcgxyvh.

15. "Rep. Kay Granger Holds a Hearing on United States Assistance to Combat Transnational Crime Budget for F.Y. 2015," House Subcommittee on State, Foreign Operations and Related Programs, *CQ Transcriptions*, May 7, 2014.

16. For background, see Kenneth Jost, "Financial Misconduct," *CQ Researcher*, Jan. 20, 2012, pp. 53-76.

17. John Cassidy, "The Justice Department's 'War' on Wall Street: Still No Criminal Charges," *The New Yorker*, Aug. 8, 2013, http://tinyurl.com/qym7ned; Christina Rexrode and Andrew Grossman, "Record Bank of America Settlement Latest in Government Crusade," *The Wall Street Journal*, Aug. 21, 2014, http://tinyurl.com/ktlhgpa.

18. "International Crime Threat Assessment, Introduction," The White House, December 2000, http://tinyurl.com/oema9cf.

19. Moisés Naím, *Illicit: How Smugglers, Traffickers, and Copycats are Hijacking the Global Economy* (2005), Kindle edition, no page number available.

20. R. T. Naylor, *Counterfeit Crime: Criminal Profits, Terror Dollars, and Nonsense* (2014), p. 31.

21. "ICE Homeland Security Investigations: Efforts to Combat Illicit Trafficking in Stolen Art, Antiquities and Cultural Property," U.S. Department of State, press conference, Sept. 6, 2013, http://tinyurl.com/ngywyan.

22. "Transnational organized crime: the globalized illegal economy," U.N. Office on Drugs and Crime, undated, http://tinyurl.com/ko36hqa.

23. Peter Andreas, *Smuggler Nation: How Illicit Trade Made America* (2013).

24. "Prime Bank Instrument Fraud," U.S. Treasury Department, undated, http://tinyurl.com/33pjqs.

25. Jack A. Blum, *et al.*, "Financial Havens, Banking Secrecy and Money Laundering," U.N. Office on Drugs and Crime, 1998, http://tinyurl.com/mrwzdec.

26. Liana Sun Wyler, "International Drug Control Policy: Background and U.S. Responses," Congressional Research Service, Aug. 13, 2013, p. 9, http://tinyurl.com/q7dx88c.

27. *Ibid.*

28. "World Drug Report 2014," U.N. Office on Drugs and Crime, Executive Summary, p. 1, http://tinyurl.com/lsm7hgr.

29. "The Global Regime for Transnational Crime," Council on Foreign Relations, updated June 25, 2013, http://tinyurl.com/nxqt9bz.

30. Ben Protess and Jessica Silver-Greenberg, "BNP Paribas Admits Guilt and Agrees to pay $8.9 Billion Fine to U.S.," *The New York Times*, June 30, 2014, http://tinyurl.com/pp4tsn4.

31. Kris Lasslett, "A Critical Introduction to State-Corporate Crime," International State Crime Initiative, Oct. 21, 2010, http://tinyurl.com/pyf9cyb.

32. *Ibid.*

33. Quoted in Tsuyoshi Inajima, Jacob Adelman and Yuji Okada, "Fukushima Disaster Was Man-Made, Investigation Finds," Bloomberg, July 5, 2012, http://tinyurl.com/c4ju2ut; "Water leaks continue to plague No. 5 reactor at Fukushima plant," Asahi Shimbun, July 20, 2014, http://tinyurl.com/l5bp7en.

34. Nils Gilman, "The Twin Insurgency," *The American Interest*, June 15, 2014, http://tinyurl.com/qh2d3yc.

35. Hugh Thomas, *The Slave Trade: The Story of the Atlantic Slave Trade: 1440-1870* (1997), pp. 25-31; 48-67.

36. *Ibid.*, pp. 649-783, 787-790; Peter P. Hinks, *et al.*, eds., *Encyclopedia of Antislavery and Abolition* (2007), Vol. 2, pp. 502-503; "Slavery Convention," Office of the High Commissioner for Human Rights, United Nations, http://tinyurl.com/lln3u26.

37. "Counterpiracy under International Law," Geneva Academy of International Humanitarian Law and Human Rights, August 2012, p. 11, http://tinyurl.com/mfqu7as.

38. Andreas, *op. cit.*, pp. 50-56, 83-88.

39. For background, see Alan Greenblatt, "Attacking Piracy," *CQ Researcher*, Aug. 1, 2009, pp. 205-232. Also see Michael A. Palmer, "The Navy: The Continental Period, 1775-1890," Naval History and Heritage Command, http://tinyurl.com/lk5nouf.

40. "Counterpiracy under International Law," *op. cit.*, p. 11.

41. For background, see Robert Kiener, "Wildlife Smuggling," *CQ Researcher*, Oct. 1, 2010, pp. 235-262.

42. *Ibid.*; "What is CITES?" Convention on International Trade in Endangered Species of Wild Fauna and Flora," undated, http://tinyurl.com/aggl3od.

43. "WIPO — A Brief History," World Intellectual Property Organization, undated, http://tinyurl.com/kclcpc4.

44. "Estimating the global economic and social impacts of counterfeiting and piracy," International Chamber of Commerce, http://tinyurl.com/mqg8nte.

45. "Intellectual Property Seizures Statistics, Fiscal Year 2013," U.S. Customs and Border Protection, undated, http://tinyurl.com/n6wth8n; "Report on

EU customs enforcement of intellectual property rights: Results at the EU border, 2013," European Commission, 2014, http://tinyurl.com/n997qvy.

46. *Ibid.*

47. "2012 Special 301 Report," Office of the United States Trade Representative, April 2012, p. 27, http://tinyurl.com/cxywwn2.

48. Andreas, *op. cit.*, pp. 63-73.

49. Quoted in *ibid.*, p. 101.

50. See Daniel Okrent, *Last Call* (2010).

51. Steven B. Duke and Albert C. Gross, *America's Longest War: Rethinking Our Tragic Crusade Against Drugs* (1993), pp. 85-86.

52. Andreas, *op. cit.*, pp. 262-265.

53. *Ibid.*

54. Quoted in Andreas, *op. cit.*, p. 274.

55. Cornelius Friesendorf, *US Foreign Policy and the War on Drugs: Displacing the Cocaine and Heroin Industry* (2007), p. 70.

56. Andreas, *op. cit.*, pp. 275-308.

57. *Ibid.*; Leslie Maitland Werner, "Scores Arrested in Money-Laundering," *The New York Times*, June 13, 1987, http://tinyurl.com/kjmuko3.

58. Michael Wines, "Washington at Work; A Crusader Driven by Outrage," *The New York Times*, Aug. 22, 1991, http://tinyurl.com/mbq5sxe.

59. Quoted in David Sirota and Jonathan Baskin, "Follow the Money," *Washington Monthly*, September 2004, http://tinyurl.com/48edh.

60. "The BCCI Affair," Senate Foreign Relations Committee, December 1992, http://tinyurl.com/l66kb55.

61. Stephen Handelman, *Thieves in Power: The New Challenge of Corruption* (2001), http://tinyurl.com/mg4dnhb; James O. Finckenauer and Yri A. Voronin, "The Threat of Russian Organized Crime," U.S. Department of Justice, June 2001, http://tinyurl.com/qjcq49a.

62. *Ibid.*, Handelman; Timothy L. O'Brien, "Bank Settles U.S. Inquiry Into Money Laundering," *The New York Times*, Nov. 9, 2005, http://tinyurl.com/l8qnzzo.

63. "Russian Man Sentenced for Hacking into Computers in the United States," U.S. Attorney, District of Connecticut, July 25, 2003, http://tinyurl.com/p4utjal.

64. "Trafficking in Women and Children," in "International Crime Threat Assessment," *op. cit.*

65. *Ibid.*

66. "Human Trafficking: Better Data, Strategy, and Reporting Needed to Enhance U.S. Anti-trafficking Efforts Abroad," U.S. Government Accountability Office, July 18, 2006, http://tinyurl.com/8aavx4b.

67. "General Assembly resolution 55/25, United Nations Convention Against Transnational Organized Crime," Nov. 15, 2000, p. 2, http://tinyurl.com/24d4ftw.

68. Thomas M. Sanderson, "Transnational Terror and Organized Crime: Blurring the Lines," *SAIS Review*, Winter-Spring, 2004, http://tinyurl.com/qh4vor9.

69. Douglas Farah, "Al Qaeda Cash Tied to Diamond Trade," *The Washington Post*, Nov. 2, 2001, p. A1 (not online in complete form).

70. "Press Briefing on Conflict Diamonds," U.S. State Department, Dec. 5, 2006, http://tinyurl.com/o8tty5a; Chris Hansen, "Liberia's former president, a friend to terror?" Dateline NBC, July 17, 2005, http://tinyurl.com/nanml6y.

71. For background, see Peter Katel, "ID Theft," *CQ Researcher*, June 10, 2005, pp. 517-540; "Russian organised crime: The EU perspective," Library Briefing, Library of the European Parliament, March 4, 2011, http://tinyurl.com/c5momso; Alissa de Carbonell, "Ex-Soviet hackers play outsized role in cyber crime world," Reuters, Aug. 22, 2013, http://tinyurl.com/ne5hav6.

72. For background, see Alan Greenblatt, "Attacking Piracy," *CQ Researcher*, Aug. 1, 2009, pp. 205-232.

73. "No Somali pirate hijacking in nearly a year, says UN," The Associated Press (*The Guardian*), May 3, 2013, http://tinyurl.com/ppeh6xj.

74. For background, see Marcia Clemmitt, "Mortgage Crisis," *CQ Researcher*, Nov. 2, 2007, pp. 913-936.

75. "Judge won't free Russian accused of hacking in US," The Associated Press (*The Washington Post*), Aug. 1, http://tinyurl.com/pbwlodc.

76. Nicole Perlroth, "After Arrest of Accused Hacker, Russia Accuses U.S. of Kidnapping," *The New York Times* (Bits Blog), July 8, 2014, http://tinyurl.com/psufbch; "Russian National Arraigned on Indictment For Distributing Credit Card Data Belonging to Thousands of Card Holders," U.S. Attorney's Office, Western District of Washington, Aug. 8, 2014, http://tinyurl.com/onkvo97.

77. *Ibid.*

78. Perlroth and Gelles, *op. cit.*

79. Peter Finn and Sari Horwitz, "U.S. charges Snowden with espionage," *The Washington Post*, June 21, 2013, http://tinyurl.com/ke39l9k; Alec Luhn and Mark Tran, "Edward Snowden given permission to stay in Russia for three more years," *The Guardian*, Aug. 7, 2014, http://tinyurl.com/l5udg5g. For background the following *CQ Researchers* by Chuck McCutcheon: "Whistleblowers," Jan. 31, 2014, pp. 97-120, and "Government Surveillance," Aug. 30, 2013, pp. 717-740.

80. Quoted in Michael Riley, "Neiman Marcus Breach Linked to Russians Who Eluded U.S.," Bloomberg, April 6, 2014, http://tinyurl.com/kpmljn8.

81. *Ibid.*; *United States of America v. Vladimir Drinkman, et al.*, July 25, 2013, http://tinyurl.com/l3ujjrj.

82. Maud Van Gaal and David Voreacos, "Hacker Goes to Top Dutch Court in U.S. Extradition Fight," Bloomberg, May 9, 2014, http://tinyurl.com/q6xqhxv; Ted Sherman, "Russian hacker pleads not guilty, denied bail in massive data breach case," [Newark, N.J.] *Star-Ledger*, Aug. 12, 2013, http://tinyurl.com/lfepfxg.

83. Lucian Constantin, "Hackers behind iPhone ransom attacks arrested in Russia," *PCWorld*, June 10, 2014, http://tinyurl.com/qxn9lde.

84. William Neuman, "Venezuelan officers Linked to Colombian Cocaine Traffickers," *The New York Times*, July 28, 2014, http://tinyurl.com/n3o4e9t.

85. Quoted in Ray Sanchez, "Aruba releases Venezuelan ex-general wanted in U.S.," CNN, July 28, 2014, http://tinyurl.com/mq7hjfx.

86. Kiener, "Wildlife Smuggling," *op. cit.*

87. Quoted in "African leaders in Washington: How Do We Win the War on Poaching?" *The Dodo*, Aug. 7, 2014, http://tinyurl.com/kzjpwxo; Juliet Eilperin, "Obama praises U.S.-Africa summit as an 'extraordinary event,' " *The Washington Post*, Aug. 6, 2014, http://tinyurl.com/m6tdd4j.

88. David J. Hayes, "Illegal Wildlife Trafficking and the U.S.-Africa Summit," *National Geographic* (blog), Aug. 6, 2014, http://tinyurl.com/okx532k.

89. Suzanne Goldenberg, "US to destroy ivory stocks in effort to stop illegal elephant poaching," *The Guardian*, Sept. 9, 2013, http://tinyurl.com/qg5ab6e.

90. Hayes, "Illegal Wildlife Trafficking," *op. cit.*; "African Leaders in Washington," *op. cit.*

91. "National Strategy for Combating Wildlife Trafficking," The White House, February, 2014, http://tinyurl.com/mm2fw3a.

92. "Law Enforcement Stories and News Releases," U.S. Fish and Service, (varied dates), http://tinyurl.com/k4fr2dp.

93. "Ringleaders of International Rhino Smuggling Conspiracy Sentenced in New Jersey To 70 Months in Prison," U.S. Attorney's Office, District of New Jersey, May 27, 2014, http://tinyurl.com/lepnc56.

94. Quoted in "U.S.-Africa summit on wildlife poaching addresses Asian demand," Agence France-Presse (*South China Morning Post*), Aug. 7, 2014, http://tinyurl.com/kgxdn2x.

95. "Trafficking for Organ Trade," United Nations, undated, http://tinyurl.com/o7bn5hd; Kevin Sack, "Transplant Brokers in Israel Lure Desperate Kidney Patients to Costa Rica," *The New York Times*, Aug. 17, 2014, http://tinyurl.com/mldhslg.

96. "Briefing on the Trafficking in Persons Report 2014," *op. cit.*

97. Martine Geller, "Big Tobacco squares up as EU rules aim to track every cigarette," Reuters, June 18, 2014, http://tinyurl.com/m443vrf.

BIBLIOGRAPHY

Selected Sources

Books

Andreas, Peter, *Smuggler Nation: How Illegal Trade Made America*, Oxford University Press, 2013.
A Brown University political scientist concludes that transnational crime is far from a new phenomenon in the United States.

Miklaucic, Michael, and Jacqueline Brewer, eds., *Convergence: Illicit Networks and National Security in the Age of Globalization*, National Defense University Press, 2013, www.ndufoundation.org/file/pdf-test/Convergence.pdf.
National security-oriented researchers analyze ties between international criminals and religious extremists.

Naím, Moisés, *Illicit: How Smugglers, Traffickers and Counterfeiters are Hijacking the Global Economy*, Anchor Books, 2005.
The then-editor of Foreign Policy magazine argues that transnational criminals are ahead of governments and legitimate businesses in technology and trade expertise.

Naylor, R.T., *Counterfeit Crime: Criminal Profits, Terror Dollars, and Nonsense*, McGill-Queen's University Press, 2014.
A professor of economics at Montreal's McGill University who has long specialized in black markets, smuggling and money laundering questions the ideas and information underlying anti-transnational crime enforcement.

Shelley, Louise I., *Dirty Entanglements: Corruption, Crime, and Terrorism*, Cambridge University Press, 2014.
A crime scholar examines links between transnational crime and terrorist networks.

Articles

Blue, Violet, "CryptoLocker's crimewave: A trial of millions in laundered Bitcoin," *ZDNet*, Dec. 22, 2013, http://tinyurl.com/njymdlh.
A reporter for a computer security publication provides a detailed account of how hackers last year held computer users' data hostage.

Callimachi, Rukmini, "Paying Ransoms, Europe Bankrolls Qaeda," *The New York Times*, July 29, 2014, http://tinyurl.com/k8xa8az.
An investigative reporter says European governments pay hefty sums for kidnapped citizens, thus financing terrorists.

Carvajal, Doreen, "Swiss Banks' Tradition of Secrecy Clashes With Quests Abroad for Disclosure," *The New York Times*, July 8, 2014, http://tinyurl.com/nzr83u5.
Swiss bankers used techniques familiar to spies and crooks in recruiting clients interested in shielding their assets, a Europe-based correspondent reports.

Cawley, Margaret, "Phone Tap Shows US — El Salvador MS13 Connections," *InSight Crime*, Oct. 29, 2013, http://tinyurl.com/n4wlepd.
One of the major street gangs terrorizing Central America closely coordinates its activities, including extortion, with its U.S. branch, according to a website specializing in Latin American crime analysis.

Gilman, Nils, "The Twin Insurgency," *The American Interest*, June 15, 2014, http://tinyurl.com/qh2d3yc.
An associate chancellor at the University of California, Berkeley, argues that both criminals and the wealthy pressure governments in order to avoid taxes and regulation.

Perlroth, Nicole, and David Gelles, "Russian Hackers Amass Over a Billion Internet Passwords," *The New York Times*, Aug. 5, 2014, http://tinyurl.com/qas8ovb.
Technology reporters disclosed a security firm's conclusion that Russian cyber-crooks had penetrated more than 400,000 websites to steal user names and passwords.

Reports and Studies

"Comprehensive Study on Cybercrime," United Nations Office on Drugs and Crime, February 2013, http://tinyurl.com/nrxbrtl.
The world's primary anti-transnational crime monitoring agency concludes (in a report formally still in draft form) that the borderless nature of global interconnectedness is hampering anti-cybercrime enforcement.

"Elephants in the Dust: The African Elephant Crisis," United Nations Environmental Programme, *et al.*, 2013, http://tinyurl.com/qzmpntr.

Four U.N. and nongovernmental organizations report on the devastating effects of ivory trafficking on Africa's rapidly dwindling elephant population.

"Estimating Illicit Financial Flows Resulting From Drug Trafficking and Other Transnational Organized Crimes," United Nations Office on Drugs and Crime, October 2011, http://tinyurl.com/p64lrda.
The agency estimates total revenue from transnational crime, while acknowledging such statistics are problematic.

Miraglia, Paula, Rolando Ochoa and Ivan Briscoe, "Transnational organised crime and fragile states," Organization for Economic Cooperation and Development, October 2012, http://tinyurl.com/qef2zuy.
A Paris-based international economic monitoring organization says transnational crime poses grave dangers to unstable countries but argues that repressive countermeasures are unproductive.

For More Information

Black Market Watch, Geneva, Switzerland; www.blackmarketwatch.org. Think tank that is developing methods for gauging the magnitude of illicit trade.

Brookings Institution, 1775 Massachusetts Ave., N.W., Washington, DC 20036; 202-797-6000; www.brookings.edu/research/topics/crime. Think tank that studies, among other things, cyber-piracy and anti-money laundering strategies.

Insight Crime, Center for Latin American and Latino Studies, American University, 4400 Massachusetts Ave., N.W., Washington DC 20016; 202-885-6178; www.insightcrime.org. U.S. office of a Medellín, Colombia-based site that reports and analyzes Latin American crime news and trends.

Institute for Security & Development Policy, Västra finnbodavägen 2, 131 30 Nacka, Sweden; 46 (0) 8-41056960; www.isdp.eu/issues/organized-crime.html. Stockholm-based nongovernmental research center that studies transnational crime.

Terrorism, Transnational Crime and Corruption Center, George Mason University, 3351 Fairfax Dr., MS3B1, Arlington, VA 22201; 703-993-9757; http://policy-tracc.gmu.edu. Think tank that publishes research on international crime.

Transnational Threats Project, Center for Strategic and International Studies, 1616 Rhode Island Ave., N.W., Washington, DC 20036; 202-887-0200; http://csis.org/program/transnational-threats-project. National-security think tank that studies transnational crime, especially its connections to armed extremism.

United Nations Office On Drugs and Crime (UNODC), Vienna International Centre, Wagramer Strasse 5, A 1400 Vienna, Austria; 43-1-26060; www.unodoc.org. Publishes major studies on the scope and revenue of transnational crime.

8

Resurgent Russia

Brian Beary

AFP/Getty Images/Viktor Drachev

Demonstrators in Ukraine's capital, Kiev, protest on Dec. 7, 2013, after President Viktor Yanukovych backed out of a trade deal with the European Union, reportedly under pressure from Russian President Vladimir Putin. Moscow wants Ukraine to join the Eurasian Economic Union, a Russian-dominated free-trade coalition. Clashes in Ukraine between police and protesters have turned increasingly violent, and fears are mounting that the country may be on the brink of civil war. On Jan. 28, the prime minister and cabinet resigned, and restrictions on political protest imposed weeks earlier were rescinded.

From *CQ Researcher*,
February 7, 2014.
Updated January 19, 2015.

On a visit to Moldova in September, Russian Deputy Prime Minister Dmitry Rogozin did not mince words. "Energy supplies are important in the run-up to winter," he told his hosts. "I hope you won't freeze."

Rogozin's words were a veiled threat, say experts on the region, implying that if the former Soviet republic signs the major pacts that it had just negotiated with the European Union (EU), Russia might cut off its gas supply.[1]

Moldova, a small, poor country in southeastern Europe, depends heavily on Russian natural gas. Nevertheless, Moldova is refusing to cave to Russian pressure — for now. But its far bigger neighbor to the north, Ukraine, also an ex-Soviet republic, is heeding Moscow's warnings. In November 2013, Ukrainian President Viktor Yanukovych decided not to continue pursuing closer ties with the EU, just days before he was due to sign an accord with the EU at a much-heralded summit in Vilnius, Lithuania, capital of yet another ex-Soviet republic. In Ukraine, ongoing mass protests against Yanukovych's move have led to the prime minister's resignation.

Still reeling from Yanukovych's abandonment, Swedish Foreign Minister Carl Bildt, whose country is one of the 28 EU members, predicted that Ukraine's decision would lead it "not west or east, but down," adding, "it's a fairly brutal game being played" by Russia.[2]

The tug-of-war between Russia and the EU over Moldova and Ukraine has been going on since 2008, when the EU began enticing Russia's neighbors into its economic sphere via its Eastern Partnership initiative. The new program promised Eastern European countries access to Western Europe's huge market if they first made their governments more efficient, more democratic, and less corrupt.

Russia's Neighbors Lean Toward Europe or China

Several former members of the Soviet bloc say Moscow is pressuring them to join the Eurasian Economic Union (EEU), a free-trade coalition patterned after the European Union (EU) but dominated by Russia. Protests broke out in Ukraine in November after its government reneged on a commitment to sign trade pacts with the EU, reportedly after Russia pressured Ukraine to join the EEU instead. Russia denies pressuring its neighbors, but experts say the EEU is designed to keep Russia's former satellite states out of EU's economic grasp.

Economic Coalition Membership of Russia and Its Neighbors

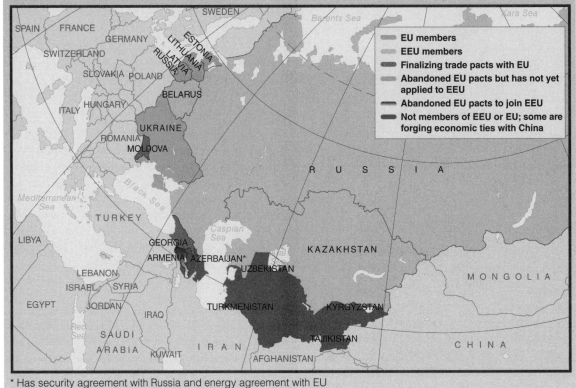

* Has security agreement with Russia and energy agreement with EU

Although the EU did not offer them full membership, it didn't exclude the possibility.

Russia was always suspicious of the Eastern Partnership but began to ramp up its opposition in late 2013, apparently after realizing that newly concluded EU trade pacts with Russia's former neighbors could pull the post-Soviet nations irrevocably into the EU's orbit. "Moscow has rediscovered the real nature of the EU: the prospect that one day Ukraine [along with the other ex-Soviet Union countries]... could begin to work its way up the rankings of corruption or doing business and,

with time, even outdistance Russia," according to Olaf Osica, director of the Centre for Eastern Studies in Warsaw, Poland.[3]

The Russians are especially wary of the EU initiative because in 2004 and 2007, 10 former Central and East European communist nations joined the EU, and many of them now have strained relations with Moscow. In fact, several of those nations are the most ardent supporters of the Eastern Partnership. And nations such as Poland and Lithuania have painful memories of Russian domination during the Cold War era. Having fought so hard for independence from Russia, they now look at Russia's economic revival and growing geopolitical activism with unease. Such strained relations are the clearest illustration of Moscow's simmering tensions with the West that are being triggered by the increasingly assertive stance that Russia is taking in its neighborhood and beyond.

Russia strongly denies that it pressures its neighbors. Alexey Drobinin, senior counselor at the Russian Embassy in Washington, says, for instance, that a recent Russian ban on imports of Moldovan wine and spirits is justified on "very hard evidence" that it's needed to protect Russian consumers from unsafe food products. "There was no political calculation involved," he says.[4]

But Moldova's government sees things differently. "This is a crucial time for my country," said Moldovan Foreign Minister Natalia Gherman. While her governing party wants to join the EU, the Communist Party — the main opposition — sides with Russia, she said. The communists prefer that Moldova reject the EU and instead join the new Russian-sponsored Eurasian Economic Union (EEU), a free-trade and economic coalition similar to the EU but which would be dominated by Russia. The pro–EU parties retained power following parliamentary elections in November 2014, with the communists and another pro-Russian party winning 46 seats, compared to 55 for the pro-Europeans parties.

Gherman dismissed the EEU as "economic and political nonsense." The EU's market of 500 million people is far bigger and better than

Russia Trails U.S., China on Growth

Russia's total output of goods and services — its gross domestic product (GDP) — and its GDP growth rate in 2013 trailed those of the United States and China. However, Russia's GDP per capita was about twice that of China's. Much of Russia's wealth comes from exports of its abundant natural gas.

Economic Data for Russia, United States, and China, 2013

GDP

(in trillions of dollars)

Russia: $2.1
U.S.: $15
China: $6.6

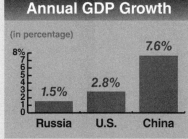

Annual GDP Growth

(in percentage)

Russia: 1.5%
U.S.: 2.8%
China: 7.6%

GDP Per Capita

(in thousands of dollars)

Russia: $14,973
U.S.: $52,839
China: $6,569

Source: "World Economic Outlook," International Monetary Fund, October 2013

anything Russia could offer with its nascent free-trade zone, she said.[5]

Gunnar Wiegand, a senior EU diplomat, said it was "regrettable" that Russia has wrongly concluded that the new EU trade pacts would harm Russian interests. "It has become almost an obsession" for Russia, said Wiegand, who negotiated many of the accords.[6]

While Russia is no longer a superpower, it remains a significant international economic force, with its strength heavily concentrated in the energy sector. It is the world's top exporter of natural gas, No. 2 in oil and No. 3 in coal.[7] In fact, the EU gets about 30 percent of its oil, gas, and coal imports from Russia. But Russia relies even more on the EU: The European Union buys about 80 percent of Russia's gas exports, 70 percent of its oil exports, and 50 percent of its coal exports.[8]

"We are more dependent on the EU than the EU is dependent on us," said Mikhail Kalugin, head of the economic section at the Russian Embassy in Washington.[9]

Beyond Europe, Russia has elevated itself from the marginal player it became after the Soviet Union collapsed in 1991 to a power that is now increasingly shaping events in geopolitical hotspots, notably the Middle East. For instance, Russia brokered a deal in September to avert a United States– and French-led military strike on Syria after Syrian leader Bashar

Russia Faces Backlash Over Immigration Policies

Millions of migrants from former Soviet republics fill low-skilled jobs.

Thousands of Russians took to the streets of Moscow in October 2013 in violent anti-immigrant protests sparked by the fatal stabbing of a Russian man by an allegedly illegal immigrant from Azerbaijan. Immigrants' stores were looted, more than a thousand rioters and 200 illegal immigrants were detained and Moscow Mayor Sergei Sobyanin called for "radical decisions" by the Russian government to address immigration policy.

Russia may no longer have a political union with its neighbors as in the Soviet era, but that has not stopped several million workers from the former Soviet republics from flocking to Russia in search of higher-paying jobs.[1]

Many ordinary Russians resent the immigrants. An opinion poll from summer 2013 found that 53 percent wanted tighter immigration laws.[2] And anti-immigrant sentiment is on the rise. For example, 70 percent oppose migrant workers taking catering jobs, up from 54 percent in 2006.[3]

But with a relatively low birth rate, a high death rate, and an unemployment rate of about 5 percent, Russia has a labor shortage. To fill jobs, it relies on labor from poorer nations in the former Soviet Union. Because of their historical ties with Russia, these workers can enter the country and find work, many without an official work permit.

Chinese employers investing in Russia have brought in thousands of Chinese workers, who, unlike Central Asian migrants, require visas to enter the country.[4]

Many Central Asian women have taken fast-food jobs that Russian students previously held. And Central Asian men from countries such as Tajikistan and Kyrgyzstan fill thousands of construction jobs. Armen Sahakyan, executive director of the Washington branch of the Eurasian Research Analysis Institute, a new Armenia-based think tank, says many workers employed to build facilities for the Winter Olympic Games in Sochi were non-Russians.

Russia also has experienced an influx of ethnic Russians from other regions, especially Central Asia. They are mainly descendants of people who emigrated there in the 1700s and 1800s, when the Russian Empire was expanding southward. When the republics where they live emerged as independent nations in the early 1990s, the new countries made their native languages, not Russian, the official tongue. This has made it harder for Russian-speaking residents to prosper — notably in government, where the native tongue is often required.[5]

Some migrants come from countries that have strained relations with Russia. A prime example is Georgia, which fought a war with Russia in 2008 over Georgia's two separatist regions, Abkhazia and South Ossetia, which Russia supports. Of a total population of 5 million Georgians, an

al-Assad allegedly launched a gas attack on his own people in the Syrian civil war, killing some 1,400.[10]

President Obama, who is reluctant to involve the United States in another military conflict, welcomed Russia's efforts.[11] But U.S.–Russian relations today are at their lowest ebb since the Cold War. In addition to supporting the EU in the struggle for Eastern Europe, the United States has condemned Russia's worsening human rights record under President Vladimir Putin, including a new law banning "homosexual propaganda." Putin also has irked Washington by giving temporary political asylum to Edward Snowden, a former National

Security Agency (NSA) contractor who last summer revealed that the NSA was conducting mass surveillance programs on U.S. and foreign citizens' phone and email records as well as on the communications of foreign heads of state.[12]

The eruption of militant Islamist violence in the Middle East following the 2011 Arab Spring uprisings — including in Syria — has spurred Russia to become more assertive in the region, given that its own southern border is a hotbed of Islamist-inspired terrorism, both inside Russia (in Chechnya and Dagestan) and in nearby countries such as Uzbekistan. And with the United

estimated 1 million work in Russia, says Archil Gegeshidze, the country's U.S. ambassador. Most went to Russia in the 1990s when the Georgian economy was failing. Many began trading agricultural products. "Georgians in Russia tend not to assimilate as easily as some other groups," Gegeshidze says. "They like to keep their ties to Georgia."

Fiona Hill, director of the Center on the United States and Europe at the Brookings Institution in Washington, sees similarities between Russia and the United States in that migrant workers in both countries tend to come from poorer regions and take manual jobs. For example, landscaping is a niche for migrants in Russia as it is for Latino migrants in the United States.

But Hill is quick to highlight one major difference. "Russia is more strategic than the U.S. in the way it uses immigration in its foreign policy," she says. For example, she says, Russia uses migrant workers' remittances — money they send back home — to advance its geopolitical goals. As petty revenge against Georgia and Moldova for aligning themselves with the European Union (EU) and NATO, Russia has threatened to block Georgians and Moldovans from using the banking system to wire money home, Hill says. Russia distrusts NATO and wants the former Soviet republics to reject the EU to join Russia's nascent free-trade zone, the Eurasian Economic Union.

Remittances from migrant workers comprise about 12 percent of Armenia's gross domestic product (GDP), Sahakyan says. Tajikistan, a small, poor former Soviet republic, has some 900,000 migrant workers in Russia. Their $3.6 billion in remittances in 2012 accounted for half of Tajikistan's GDP that year.[6]

Some Russians want immigration policies to give preference to ethnic Russians and warn that allowing so many migrants from overwhelmingly Muslim Central Asia into the country could foment Islamist terrorism.[7] But for now, economic imperatives seem to be driving Russia's immigration policy.

Russian President Vladimir Putin said in summer 2013 that immigrants from the former Soviet Union were able to assimilate. "On the whole," he said, "our policy in the migration sphere should be more flexible, certainly ensuring the rights of our indigenous citizens, but it should be more flexible so to attract labor resources at least."[8]

— *Brian Beary*

[1]"Illegal migrants may be banned from entering Russia for 10 years," Xinhua General News Service, April 4, 2013, http://en.ria.ru/russia/20130404/180446 936.html.

[2]"More than half of Russians support toughening of immigration laws in relation to citizens of CIS — research" Central Asian News Services, Aug. 15, 2013, http://bnews.kz/en/news/post/153656/.

[3]"Russians develop hard feelings towards immigrants — poll," Central Asia General Newswire, Aug. 1, 2013.

[4]Evgeny Kuzmin, "Migrant Workers Finding Opportunity in Russian Far East," Inter Press Service News Agency, Aug. 6, 2013, www.ipsnews.net/2013/08/ migrant-workers-finding-opportunity-in-russian-far-east/.

[5]See sidebar on ethnic Russians of Central Asia in Brian Beary, "Emerging Central Asia," *CQ Global Researcher,* Jan. 17, 2012, pp. 29–56.

[6]"Ratification of Russian military base deal provides Tajikistan with important security guarantees," *Jane's Intelligence Weekly,* Oct. 2, 2013.

[7]"Russian analysts: immigrants, guest workers fertile ground for radical Islamism," Interfax News Agency, May 14, 2013.

[8]"Putin says Russia needs more flexible approach to immigration," BBC Worldwide Monitoring, June 11, 2013.

States having completed the drawdown of its combat troops from Afghanistan in December 2014, Russia is boosting its military presence among its southern neighbors that flank Afghanistan, fearing that Afghanistan will again become a haven for global jihadists.[13]

Meanwhile, the world's eyes were on Russia in February 2014 when it hosted the Winter Olympic Games in the Black Sea resort town of Sochi. There were fears of terrorist attacks following suicide bombings, carried out by suspected Islamist terrorists, of a train station and trolley bus in the Russian city of Volgograd in December that killed 34 people and wounded many more.[14] President Putin ramped up security, determined to avoid any more embarrassing incidents or attacks, and the Games did proceed without incident.[15]

Russia's spotty human-rights record is also coming under scrutiny. In a not-so-subtle jab at Russia's new antigay law that equates homosexuality with pedophilia, Obama put two openly gay athletes in the delegation representing the United States in the opening ceremony on Feb. 7.[16]

Russia's relations with China, which had grown frosty during Russia's communist era, have greatly improved since they both embraced capitalism. The two giant nations are trading more manufactured goods and raw materials and have resolved longstanding border disputes.

Fiona Hill, director of the Center on the United States and Europe at the Brookings Institution think tank in Washington, says China has eclipsed Russia in industrial output and wants Russian raw materials for its manufacturing sector. China is busy increasing trade and investments in Central Asian markets that were once part of the Soviet Union, especially Turkmenistan and Uzbekistan. Kazakhstan, Kyrgyzstan, and Tajikistan, however, retain close ties to Russia as well.[17]

Meanwhile, China's economic influence in Russia's vast Siberia region is growing as Russian residents emigrate westward and China boosts its investment in the region, often bringing in Chinese migrant workers in the process. China has provided $25 billion to extend Russia's Eastern Siberia Pacific Ocean pipeline to Asia in return for guaranteed supplies of Siberian crude oil.[18]

To the south, Russia and energy-hungry India are strengthening economic ties. The two countries are collaborating on Russian projects to export liquefied natural gas to India. Russia also is selling military equipment to India, while India is selling generic pharmaceuticals to the Russians.[19]

In addition, Russia is forging closer links with Brazil, with joint projects planned on cybersecurity and space technology. Brazil also is planning to buy Russian air defense systems.[20] And in Southeast Asia, Russia is emerging as an important supplier of military goods, notably to Myanmar and Vietnam, and is an investor in offshore oil and gas exploration projects.[21]

As Russia increasingly asserts itself in its region and beyond, following are some key questions being debated.

Is Russia trying to recreate the Soviet bloc?

The Russian government strongly denies that it aims to revive the defunct Soviet Union. Drobinin at the Russian Embassy says unequivocally: "No. It is not possible to recreate what existed 25 years ago, and there is no intention to do so."

Lee Feinstein, U.S. ambassador to Poland from 2009 to 2012 and now a fellow at the German Marshall Fund of the United States, says, "Circumstances today are completely different than in Soviet times. Putin is no democrat, and he is consolidating his power, but

Russia is not a Stalinist totalitarian state. There is greater scope for individuals" — for instance, to travel and do business.

Drobinin says that since Putin was reelected president in 2012 (he was president from 2000–2008 and prime minister from 1999–2000 and 2008–2012), he has actively promoted the Eurasian Economic Union. "We see our closest neighbors as our closest partners," Drobinin says. "We treat them as equals and do not interfere in their domestic affairs."

Andrey Slepnev, trade minister at the Eurasian Economic Commission (the EEU's rule-making body), has also sought to dispel what he called an "urban legend" that "we are trying to reconstitute the Soviet Union." The EEU is an economic rather than a political initiative, Slepnev said during a 2013 visit to Washington.[22]

A Russian journalist who asks not to be named because his media outlet bars him from giving on-the-record interviews, says, "Russia does not wish to be a military superpower again. But it would like to play a bigger role in the world than it did in the 1990s," particularly in its immediate neighborhood. "Russia is behaving no differently than the U.S. does in Latin America" when Washington concludes trade agreements with countries that include provisions not directly linked to trade, he argues.

But Archil Gegeshidze, the Georgian ambassador to the United States, believes Russia goes way beyond what countries typically seek through trade agreements. He says Russia is trying to create various groupings of former Soviet republics, with Russia as the center of gravity. Whether it is the Commonwealth of Independent States (CIS), a group of nine former Soviet-bloc countries set up in the dying days of the Soviet Union to retain some form of ties among those nations, or the newer EEU initiative, "the idea is the same," and "it is always a political project."

Georgia, which was the last country to join the CIS, did so under pressure, Gegeshidze says, and formally left the CIS in 2009 shortly after a Georgia–Russia war fought over control of Georgia's secessionist regions, Abkhazia and South Ossetia. The two countries have not had diplomatic relations since then.

Asked if Russia is resurrecting its past political union with its neighbors, Brookings's Hill, a British national who has lived in Russia and speaks Russian, says, "It depends what you mean by the Soviet bloc. If you mean a rigid political and security bloc, the answer is no. But Russia does want to retain its influence in the Soviet region." For instance, she says, Russia is insisting that its neighbors not join any other economic or political bloc such as the EU Eastern Partnership. Russia argues that being part of both trading blocs simultaneously is incompatible because of how trade agreements work, such as having a common customs code.

Armen Sahakyan, founder and president of the Eurasian Research Analysis Institute, a new Armenia-based think tank, cites Russia's neighbor Belarus as evidence that Russia is not trying to create a new political union. Belarus for years has been pushing the idea of a reconfigured Soviet Union, but Putin has shown little interest in the concept, he says. "Russia wants something more similar to the EU," he says.

But Jacek Saryusz-Wolski, a Polish member of the European Parliament, believes Russia is trying to create a "closed economic union" similar to the Comecon, the Soviet trading bloc that existed during the Cold War between the Soviet Union and Central and Eastern European nations. The new EEU will be "very protectionist," with high tariffs and nontariff barriers against the rest of the world, he predicts. "But in the next stage Russia will go for a political union just like the USSR," he says.

If Russia really does intend to recreate the Soviet Union, the growing economic might of China could derail its plans. "When the Russians look eastward they are fighting a losing battle if they are fighting at all," said the late Alexandros Petersen, an adviser at the Woodrow Wilson International Center for Scholars in Washington. Petersen edited a Web forum on China's presence in Central Asia until he was killed in the Jan. 17, 2014, Taliban bombing of a Lebanese restaurant in Kabul,

Europe, China Are Key Russian Trading Partners

Despite trying to steer its neighbors away from the European Union trading alliance and into its Eurasian Economic Union, Russia remains heavily dependent on trade with Europe. Germany is Russia's second-largest supplier of imports (behind China), which totaled $314 billion in 2012. Machinery and transportation equipment, chemicals and agricultural commodities top its list of imports. The Netherlands, Germany and Italy are among the top four biggest buyers of Russian commodities, with natural gas and other fuel, metals and chemicals comprising the biggest shares of Russia's $525 billion in exports in 2012.

Russia's Top Trade Partners in 2012

Imports (Percentage share of $314 billion total)		Exports (Percentage share of $525 billion total)	
China	16.5%	Netherlands	14.6%
Germany	12.2	China	6.8
Ukraine	5.7	Germany	6.8
Japan	5.0	Italy	6.2
United States	4.9	Turkey	5.2
France	4.4	Ukraine	5.2
Italy	4.3	Belarus	4.7
South Korea	3.5	Poland	3.8
Kazakhstan	2.7	Japan	3.0
Poland	2.4	Kazakhstan	2.9
		U.K.	2.9

Source: Federal State Statistics Service of the Russian Federation

Afghanistan.[23] China is concluding multiple trade and investment deals with Kazakhstan, Kyrgyzstan, Turkmenistan, and Uzbekistan, including roads, railways, pipelines, power plants, and refineries. Such deals are "completely changing the game in the region," Petersen said.[24]

By contrast, Russian investment in Central Asia is "almost nothing," Petersen said. Leaders in Central Asia tend to prefer deals with China, he said, because China is more respectful of their sovereignty than Russia. The five Central Asian republics — Kazakhstan, Kyrgyzstan, Tajikistan, Turkmenistan, and Uzbekistan (the so-called 'Stans) — were fully integrated into the Soviet Union until its dissolution in 1991.

Is Russia helping to bring peace to the Middle East?

Russia unquestionably is taking a more active role in the major Middle Eastern conflict zones — Afghanistan,

Egypt, Iran, and Syria. But experts disagree on whether Moscow is trying to bring peace to the region.

The Russian Embassy's Drobinin insists that it is. Russia has been "very cooperative" with the United States on Syria and Iran, he says. "We have played an important role in creating the conditions to settle the issues in both cases." Russia is motivated by "our opposition to the rise of violent extremism," he adds, and while "we do not take sides" in the four-year Syrian civil war, Moscow believes the Assad regime "is a legitimate government."

Russia's pivotal role in brokering the September 2013 deal that persuaded Assad to give up his chemical weapons shows that "we have achieved something," he argues. And Russia, along with the United States, is the key mediator in the "Geneva II" peace conference that began in Switzerland that aims to end the brutal civil war in Syria, which has killed more than 200,000 people and created millions of refugees.

But Saryusz-Wolski, of the European Parliament, says the chemical weapons deal that Russia cobbled together is "a trap" that gives "a free hand to Assad to continue in power." He rejects the idea that Russia wants peace in the Middle East. Moscow's true goal is to "keep things boiling" so oil and gas prices remain high, which suits Russia because it is such a big energy supplier, he argues.

Armenian scholar Sahakyan suggests a different motivation behind Russia's support for Assad. "Russia is still a naval power and would like a base in the Mediterranean," he says. Syria's western coastline is on the Mediterranean, and Russia has maintained a naval facility in the port city of Tartus since the early 1970s. While Russia's role in the Middle East had been decreasing until recently, he adds, Russia now wants to stem its waning influence in the region.

Georgian Ambassador Gegeshidze agrees with Sahakyan that Russia's primary interest in the Middle East is neither peace nor stability but "access to the warmer seas," namely the Mediterranean Sea and Indian Ocean, which he notes has been Russia's desire since tsarist times (1547–1917).

Putin has sent mixed signals in his dealings with archenemies Iran and Israel. Despite historically having been more aligned with Iran, Putin for most of 2013 tried to improve relations with Israel, promising to support its professed right to retain nuclear weapons to deter any potential attack from Iran. But in September,

he seemed to reverse course, calling on Israel to dismantle its nuclear arsenal. The Israeli news magazine *Jerusalem Report* suggested that Putin's U-turn was him pandering to "Russia's allies in the Shi'ite axis [to] convince them to remain loyal."[25]

Many experts say Russia's opposition to Islamist militancy in the Middle East is sincere and stems from the instability generated in Russia by terrorist attacks by militants from the Caucasus region. Separatist wars in Chechnya in the 1990s caused the death, injury, or displacement of 150,000 people, including 8,000 Russians.[26] Russia has been very willing to help neighboring governments in Central Asia to suppress radical Islam — for instance, by clamping down on groups such as the Islamic Movement of Uzbekistan.

"Yes, Russia wants peace and stability in the Middle East. It does not want the blowback from the Sunni uprisings that stemmed from the Arab Spring," says Brookings's Hill. Moscow would like "strong, secular, authoritarian leaders" who serve as a "nice lid to put on" social tensions and conflicts in the region.

"They see democracy as messy and being at the root of all the problems there [in the Middle East] today," she adds. That explains why Russia has welcomed the overthrow of Egypt's democratically elected Muslim Brotherhood government in a coup last July and has been concluding new arms deals with the Egyptian military junta that deposed Mohamed Morsi, the Islamist leader.

According to Feinstein of the German Marshall Fund, Russia's role across the region has been "mixed." Sometimes, he says, Russia has been "a very clear impediment to addressing regional concerns." In Syria, Moscow has gone "from being very obstructionist to being pragmatic."

Despite the chemical weapons deal, for which Russia was widely praised by the West, during most of 2011 to 2013, Russia was strongly criticized for blocking U.N. Security Council sanctions against Assad.[27] Meanwhile, Russia has been "cooperative" in Afghanistan, Feinstein says, by providing a corridor for NATO to move troops and supplies into the war-torn country. And in Iran, Moscow "has been pragmatic so far," he says, by supporting a deal brokered by the EU in November 2013 that eased international sanctions on Iran in return for Iran suspending uranium enrichment in its nuclear program.

Russia's overall strategy, Feinstein says, is that "it wants allies to the extent that it can have them" to maintain influence globally.

Should the United States take a tougher stance with Russia?

Views are sharply divided on how the United States should respond to a Russia that is increasingly flexing its muscles on the global stage, in particular in Eastern Europe and the Middle East.

According to Sharyl Cross, a Russian foreign policy scholar and director of the Kozmetsky Center at St. Edward's University in Austin, Texas, "we should scale down our expectations" of the relationship. It is wrong to "look at everything as a new chapter in the Cold War," she said, because it remains unclear what direction Russia is actually taking.[28]

She advocated a pragmatic approach in which the two powers collaborate closely in the big regional hotspots such as the Middle East. Cooperation on defense policy is even possible, she maintained. For instance, the West "should take more seriously" former President Dmitry Medvedev's proposal for NATO and Russia to jointly conclude a pan-European Security Treaty, she said. First floated in 2008, the proposal has gained little traction in the United States.

U.S. Secretary of State John Kerry also calls for pragmatism. "Russia and the U.S. are in full agreement on a number of points" in the Syrian peace talks, he said, specifically that "there isn't a military solution." Kerry and Russian Foreign Minister Sergey Lavrov agreed that al Qaeda-linked rebel groups in Syria had no place at the "Geneva II" peace talks, which restarted in January.[29]

Armenian scholar Sahakyan says it does not make a lot of sense for the United States to get tougher with Russia. Imposing economic sanctions "would make little difference because there is so little U.S.–Russian trade," he says. On the other hand, he says, Russia can help the United States fight Islamist extremists in the Middle East.

In Europe, however, Russia has opposed NATO plans — in the works since 2009 — to install missile interceptors and radar equipment across Europe in such places as Poland and Romania, which were once part of the pro-Soviet bloc. Sahakyan says NATO should realize that "there will be a backlash" if it ignores Russia's

opposition to the NATO plan. Russia responded already, placing missiles in Kaliningrad, a small Russian region wedged between NATO member states Lithuania and Poland.[30] "I don't think taking a tougher line with Russia will achieve much," Sahakyan says.

But Saryusz-Wolski, the Polish member of the European Parliament, strongly disapproves of America's current pragmatic approach toward Russia, accusing Obama of moving "too much into the realm of *realpolitik* in dealing with Russia and away from a values-based policy." Referring to Obama's so-called strategic pivot to Asia, he says, it would be better if the United States "stopped withdrawing from Europe." However, he concedes that the prevailing view in Washington "that Europe should count on itself more… is in a way right, but it makes Europe feel less comfortable."[31]

Recent Russian military maneuvers in Europe worry Urmas Reinsalu, Estonia's minister of defense, who noted that Russia has doubled its strategic weapons in Europe during the past four years. He urged the United States to hold onto the nuclear weapons it still keeps in Belgium, Italy, the Netherlands, and Turkey as a deterrent to Russia.[32]

Georgian Ambassador Gegeshidze also is in the get-tough-with-Russia camp. "In Georgia, we have been watching Russia for centuries, and our experience prompts us to think that Russia only listens to tougher language," he says. "Russia can never be a genuine strategic partner of the U.S. because, for that, you need to share values," whereas Russia is growing increasingly authoritarian.

However, "the U.S. does not have a lot of carrots and sticks to use" with Russia because its relations are primarily security-based, rather than trade-based, says Brookings's Hill. "The only way for the U.S. to get tough with Russia is to get closer to the EU, because the EU does a huge amount of trade with Russia." The United States is negotiating a free-trade agreement with the EU, which is its biggest trade partner.[33]

Hill says the EU and United States can and should together take a tougher stance against Russia for bullying its neighbors into joining the EEU. And the United States does have at least one sanction at its disposal, she says, namely visa bans. There has been a massive increase in the number of special "government official" passports issued by the Russian government in recent years, she says. Moscow is very keen for Russians to attain visa-free travel wherever possible, so the West does have some leverage in that regard, she says.

The United States could also object to what Hill calls Russia's misuse of World Trade Organization (WTO) food safety rules to punish its neighbors by banning their products from Russian markets. For instance, shortly after Moscow banned Moldovan wine and spirits, and just days before the EU summit in Vilnius, Russia threatened to ban Polish fruit and vegetables, again on food safety grounds. Poland is one of the leading EU members supporting the free-trade deals the EU has negotiated with Georgia, Moldova, and Ukraine.[34]

Hill categorically rejects as "a complete sham" Russian officials' claims that these bans are justified on public-health grounds. Food safety standards are quite poor in Russia, she argues, citing the numerous severe bouts of food poisoning she suffered during the years she lived there.

BACKGROUND

Russia's Rise

The first Russian state, based in Kiev, the capital of modern Ukraine, emerged in the 9th century.[35] Originally a Viking settlement, Kiev was situated on a trade route from Scandinavia to Byzantium, now Istanbul.[36]

In 988 Prince Vladimir, the ruler of Kiev, adopted the Byzantine form of Christianity, planting the seed for Orthodox Christianity to become the dominant religion among Russians. Kiev developed into a major center of Christian learning in the 1000s and early 1100s. Meanwhile, two other Russian city states, Novgorod and Moscow, began to develop as economic centers.

During the Mongol invasions of Russian territories in the early 1200s, the army of Batu Khan, the grandson of Genghis Khan, plundered Kiev. The Mongols quickly established dominion over the Russians and were referred to as the Golden Horde.

During the 1300s, Moscow eclipsed Kiev as the dominant Russian principality, and in 1478, Moscow's ruler, Prince Ivan III, conquered Novgorod. Moscow grew increasingly powerful in the 1500s. Defended by semi-autonomous soldiers called Cossacks, Moscow introduced an efficient tax-collection system and instituted serfdom, a system of feudal dependency that forbade

peasants from moving away from their lord's estate. In return for protection, some land to sustain themselves, and some autonomy over their daily affairs, peasants were obliged to perform hard labor and pay taxes and were at times subject to military service.

Ivan IV, who reigned from 1533 to 1584 and was known as Ivan the Terrible, became the undisputed leader of Russia through his strong, harsh leadership and adopted the title of tsar (from the Roman word *caesar*).[37] Paranoid about plots against him, he was unusually cruel in suppressing perceived dissent, according to one historian, sending soldiers out on "black horses, each carrying a dog's head and a broom. . . to sniff out treachery and sweep it away. Supposed traitors were tortured or murdered."[38]

A series of weak leaders succeeded Ivan, with the next similarly strong tsar emerging in the late 1600s. Peter I, who became known as Peter the Great (1682–1725), captured the Baltic provinces from Sweden in 1709 at the Battle of Poltava. Peter established the most extensive diplomatic relations with European governments Russia had ever had until that point. He imported the best military technologies from Europe, established a new capital city, St. Petersburg, on the Baltic, and created Russia's first permanent army.

Catherine II (1762–1796) — known as Catherine the Great — conspired with Austria and Prussia to dismember Poland in the late 1700s, leading Russia to annex parts of modern-day Belarus, Lithuania, Poland, and Ukraine. She also instituted a new legal code that greatly improved the effectiveness of the Russian government and introduced a new system for consulting her subjects over proposed laws, in which an expanded array of social groups was involved in the process.

In 1807, a pact with French Emperor Napoleon I gave Russia control of Finland. By this time, Russia had grown into the world's largest country, stretching from the Baltic to the Black Sea and all the way to the Pacific Ocean. In the 1800s, Russia extended its territory and influence in Eastern Europe, the Caucasus, and the Balkans through various wars against the Ottoman Empire, which was slowly disintegrating. Around the same time, it gained control of the mainly ethnically Turkic peoples of Central Asia, wrenching the local mini-kingdoms called khanates from the British and Persians, a tussle referred to by historians as "the Great Game."[39] In the 1860s Russia expelled between 1 and 2 million Circassian people from their native western Caucasus.[40]

CHRONOLOGY

988–1917 *Russia emerges as the world's largest country, ruled by powerful tsars.*

988 Prince Vladimir, ruler of the Russian city state of Kiev, converts to Byzantine (Orthodox) Christianity. His conversion leads to Orthodox Christianity becoming Russia's dominant religion.

1547 The ruler of Moscow, Ivan IV, known as Ivan the Terrible, is crowned tsar, marking the culmination of Moscow's emergence as the dominant Russian power.

1703 Tsar Peter the Great establishes a new capital, St. Petersburg, on the Baltic Sea.

1917 The last tsar, Nicholas II, is deposed and later murdered as the communist Bolshevik party seizes power.

1918–1991 *Russian-dominated Soviet Union industrializes and becomes one of the world's two superpowers, along with the United States.*

1922 Union of Soviet Socialist Republics (USSR) is formed as a multiethnic, atheistic, communist state in which Russia is the largest and most powerful republic.

1928 Soviet leader Josef Stalin launches the first of several five-year plans, which transform the USSR from a mainly agricultural to a predominantly industrial country.

1945 USSR emerges as a victor in World War II, resulting in an expansion of its territory and influence in Eastern Europe. The expansion marks the onset of the Cold War, a rivalry for global dominance between the United States and USSR.

1955 Eight communist countries of Central and Eastern Europe, including the USSR, sign the Warsaw Pact military alliance, bolstering Soviet sway over the region.

1985 New Soviet leader Mikhail Gorbachev initiates a policy of greater openness called *glasnost* that encourages the Warsaw Pact nations to realign themselves westward geopolitically.

1991 USSR is dissolved after the 1989 fall of the Berlin Wall and two years of protests in former Soviet republics. Fifteen sovereign republics emerge from the former Soviet Union.

1992–2015 *After an initial period of economic and political turmoil, Russia stabilizes economically and becomes more assertive on the global stage.*

1992 Russian lawmakers privatize state-owned-enterprises, resulting in the country's rapid transformation from communism to capitalism.

1999 Vladimir Putin, a senior adviser to President Boris Yeltsin, is appointed prime minister of Russia, marking the beginning of his ascent to power.

2004 European Union (EU) and NATO expand to Russia's western border, and former communist bloc nations join the pro-Western economic and military alliance.

2008 Russian opposition to Georgia's bid to join NATO triggers a war that ends with Russia tightening control over Georgia's secessionist republics, Abkhazia and South Ossetia.

2010 Russia signs a new nuclear weapons reduction treaty, START, with the United States.

2012 Russia joins the World Trade Organization. Putin easily wins reelection as president amid accusations from international observers that the result was predetermined.

2013 Russia's relations with the EU deteriorate over EU plans to conclude free-trade and association pacts with several former Soviet republics, including Ukraine. Armenia announces it will join a Russian-sponsored customs union instead of signing a trade pact with the EU (September). To avoid a U.S.–French crackdown on Syria, Russia brokers a deal whereby Syria will give up its chemical weapons arsenal. Ukraine ditches its planned EU deal amid Western accusations of Russian intimidation (November).

2014 Russia hosts the Winter Olympics in Black Sea resort town of Sochi, casting a spotlight on the country's human rights record (February). Russia exploits power vacuum in neighboring Ukraine by annexing Crimea (March). Pro-Russian separatists in eastern Ukraine declare independent republics of Donetsk and Lugansk (April). Passenger plane shot down in eastern Ukraine, killing all 298 aboard and leading the EU and United States to impose economic sanctions on Russia (July). Russia concludes agreements with China and Mongolia aimed at forging closer economic ties (August). Russia signs peace agreement with EU and Ukraine in Minsk to end separatist conflict in eastern Ukraine (September). Falling oil prices and sanctions cause Russian ruble's value to tumble (December).

2015 Russian-led Eurasian Economic Union (EEU) enters into force with goal of reducing trade barriers among founding members Armenia, Belarus, Kazakhstan, and Russia (January 1). Russia's economy forecast to contract 3 percent year-on-year (January). Kyrgyzstan due to join EEU (May 1).

Russia Plays Leading Role in Separatist Conflicts

Moscow sees itself as a protector, but others view it differently.

When the word "separatist" is mentioned in relation to Russia, it usually conjures up the conflict with Chechnya, the predominantly Muslim republic in Russia's mountainous Caucasus region that tried unsuccessfully to secede in the 1990s.

But Russia is a pivotal player in four other so-called "frozen" separatist conflicts — in Abkhazia and South Ossetia in Georgia, Nagorno-Karabakh in Azerbaijan and Transnistria in Moldova — which remain unresolved after erupting when the Soviet Union collapsed in 1991.[1] In each case, Russia provides some support to the separatists — military, diplomatic, economic, or a combination — a thorn in the side of the countries from which the regions have seceded.

Russia was devastated to lose Azerbaijan, Georgia, Moldova, and 11 other republics when the Soviet Union was dissolved. Russia and Georgia fought a brief war in 2008, and in retaliation, Russia recognized Abkhazia and South Ossetia as independent countries in their secessionist dispute with Georgia. Russia also maintains about 1,000 troops in Transnistria, even though Russia does not share a border with Transnistria as it does with Abkhazia and South Ossetia.[2]

Georgia's U.S. ambassador, Archil Gegeshidze, says "two competing narratives" explain Russia's role in the conflicts. In the pro-Russian view, people in the breakaway republics align themselves with Russia because of their common histories, and Russia supports them as a "moral obligation," Gegeshidze says. Russia's opponents, he adds, say it "always uses these conflicts as a lever over the former Soviet republics to prevent them from jumping out of the Russian orbit."

While media reports often refer to Abkhazia and South Ossetia in one breath, Gegeshidze says they are different. Most South Ossetians speak Georgian and are culturally close to Georgians, but South Ossetia is too weak economically to be a self-sustaining country, he says. By contrast, the Abkhazians "have more choices" about whether to go it alone, he says, because their land is more fertile, they have access to the sea and Russian is the dominant language. Still, Gegeshidze says, ethnic Abkhaz control the government but are outnumbered by ethnic Armenians and Georgians in Abkhazia. So the Abkhaz are glad to have Russia's protection.

Svante Cornell, director of the Central Asia-Caucasus Institute at Johns Hopkins University in Washington, has argued that Russia uses the frozen conflicts to keep the countries within its sphere of influence.[3] For instance, Cornell pointed out that Russia has already warned that if Moldova continues to forge closer ties with the European Union against Russia's wishes, Russia would support separatists in Moldova's Transnistria region.

Russia can do the same with Nagorno-Karabakh, which is officially part of Azerbaijan but populated by ethnic Armenians who would welcome Russia's protection, Cornell said. Regional experts believe concern about the future of Nagorno-Karabakh was a major factor in Armenia's sudden decision in September 2013 to abandon

---

The completion of the Trans-Siberian Railway in 1903 boosted Russia's expanding industrial sector, which was producing a growing urban working class, from which developed socialist-oriented political parties, including the Bolsheviks and Mensheviks. A humiliating defeat for Russia in a war with newly emergent Japan in 1904 to 1905 stymied Russia's ambition of gaining influence over Korea, Chinese Manchuria, and the Far East.

That loss also helped to trigger a revolution that forced Tsar Nicholas II (1894–1917) to set up a parliament, called the Duma. During World War I (1914–1918), Russia fought on the side of France and the United Kingdom against the German-Austro-Hungarian-Turkish alliance. The Russians suffered massive casualties, leading to two revolutions in 1917 in which Nicholas was deposed and later murdered and Bolshevik leader Vladimir Lenin came to power. He established a "dictatorship of the proletariat," as advocated by the founders of Marxist political ideologies, including Karl Marx himself, laying the foundation for the multiethnic Soviet

a trade agreement negotiated with the EU and instead join the Russian-backed Eurasian Economic Union (EEU).

Armen Sahakyan, founder and executive director of the Washington office of the Eurasian Research Analysis Institute, an Armenian-based think tank, says Russia's goal in the frozen conflicts is "to preserve the status quo" because doing so allows it to retain influence. As for Georgia, Sahakyan suggests Moscow might give Abkhazia and South Ossetia back to Georgia if it agreed to join the EEU. And it could do the same with Transnistria, he says.

The key other player is the 28-member European Union. In June 2014, Georgia and Moldova defied Russia's warnings by signing comprehensive free-trade and association agreements with the EU. But it is unclear how these accords will be applied in the frozen conflicts.

Gunnar Wiegand, a senior EU diplomat, said the visa-free regime the EU is offering Moldova would apply to Moldovans living in Transnistria. And Transnistrians also would benefit from lower import tariffs under the EU trade pact, since most of Moldova's heavy industry is in Transnistria.

As for the broader question of who will govern the four regions in the long term, the stalemate has become so entrenched that the answer remains unclear. With the EU adopting its trade incentives "carrot" approach, in contrast to Moscow's "stick" approach, Russia's attraction for the region's residents remains its "hard power," while the EU's attraction remains its "soft power," Cornell says.

— *Brian Beary*

[1]For a full account of these conflicts, see Brian Beary, *Separatist Movements* (2011).

[2]David M. Herszenhorn, "Russia Putting a Strong Arm on Neighbors," *The New York Times*, Oct. 22, 2013, www.nytimes.com/2013/10/23/world/europe/russia-putting-a-strong-arm-on-neighbors.html?_r=0.

Separatist Conflicts Fester in Russia's Southwest

Russia provides some support for separatist movements in three former Soviet republics on its southwestern border near Sochi, site of this month's Winter Olympic Games. The four so-called "frozen" separatist conflicts are in Georgia, where Abkhazia and South Ossetia want to secede; Azerbaijan, where separatists are active in Nagorno-Karabakh; and Moldova, where the breakaway region of Transnistria is located.

Source: Brian Beary, various open sources online.

[3]Cornell spoke at an event titled "Pushback to Putin's Eurasian Dream? The Looming Facedown between China, the EU and Russia," at the School of Advanced International Studies, Johns Hopkins University, Washington DC, Dec. 4, 2013.

Union. Many non-Russian peoples who lived in the defunct Russian Empire tried to establish independent republics, but Lenin suppressed such moves. In 1922, they became part of the new, Russian-dominated Union of the Soviet Socialist Republics (USSR).

The Soviet Era

Lenin, who died in 1924, was succeeded by Josef Stalin, a high-ranking Georgian-born official who in 1922 had become general secretary of the Communist Party.

Stalin boosted industrial production through a series of five-year plans, which began in 1928, and forced the collectivization of farms.

When middle-class farmers from Ukraine and Kazakhstan resisted, Stalin brutally repressed them, with millions murdered or deported to labor camps in Siberia. Stalin also devised an elaborate system of keeping files on Communist Party members, which he used to devastating effect in the late 1930s, when he conducted wide-scale purges, eliminating anyone he viewed as a potential threat.

During World War II (1939–1945), the Soviets joined France, the United Kingdom, and the United States in defeating the German-Japanese alliance. Some 27 million Soviet soldiers and civilians were killed — or 14 percent of the population.[41] The war enabled Stalin to regain territories ceded to Germany in World War I, notably the three Baltic nations of Estonia, Latvia, and Lithuania, and parts of modern-day Belarus. In addition, Stalin pushed Central and Eastern European nations, including East Germany, into the Comecon economic union, as well as a military alliance, the 1955 Warsaw Pact. In 1946, Britain's former wartime prime minister, Winston Churchill, famously described the alliance as creating an "Iron Curtain" between Western Europe and the region.

The period between 1945 and the fall of the Berlin Wall in 1989 became known as the Cold War, in reference to the intense geopolitical rivalry that existed between the Soviet Union and the United States, the world's two superpowers. Among the tensest episodes were the 1948 to 1949 Berlin Airlift, in which the U.S. military flew supplies into West Berlin to foil a Soviet blockade; the 1962 Cuban Missile Crisis, in which the United States threatened war if the Soviets did not remove missiles they had placed in Cuba; and the Soviet invasion of Afghanistan in 1979, which sparked a U.S. boycott of the 1980 Moscow Olympic Games.[42]

When Stalin died in 1953, he was succeeded by Nikita Khrushchev, who denounced Stalin's extreme political repression but retained his socialist policies. Khrushchev made some economic adjustments, though, such as giving Russian families their own apartments and expanding state welfare benefits. Abroad, Khrushchev kept a firm grip on the Soviet satellite states, notably sending troops to quell an anticommunist uprising in Hungary in 1956.

After the Soviet politburo peacefully ousted Khrushchev in 1964, the new leader, Leonid Brezhnev, deployed troops to Czechoslovakia in 1968 to suppress the so-called Prague Spring, a movement to introduce democracy and liberalize personal freedom. High oil prices in the 1970s enabled Russia to maintain its status as a military superpower, but its economy stagnated, and its public finances deteriorated accordingly.

A new chapter began when Mikhail Gorbachev became the Soviet leader in 1985. He dramatically improved relations with the West, signing major disarmament treaties with President Ronald Reagan. Gorbachev adopted a so-called *glasnost* policy to allow greater freedom of speech, a policy that reverberated throughout the Warsaw Pact nations. East European countries began to throw off Soviet domination, beginning with Poland, which held partly free and fair elections in June 1989.

The toppling of the Berlin Wall in November 1989 marked the end of the Cold War as Bulgaria, Czechoslovakia, East Germany, Hungary, and Romania quickly joined Poland in abandoning communism and becoming free-market democracies. Lithuania's declaration of independence from the Soviet Union in March 1990 marked the beginning of the end of the USSR, which was officially dissolved on New Year's Eve in 1991, and all 15 Soviet republics emerged as independent countries.

Chaos and Resurgence

After the Soviet Union collapsed, Russia plunged into trauma and chaos. Economically, it embraced a model of unfettered capitalism that enriched a relative few but slashed the living standards of many ordinary Russians. Price controls were relaxed and state-owned enterprises privatized.

Russia also had to deal with an internal war in the early 1990s, when Chechnya, a southern republic in the mountainous Caucasus region, tried to secede. Russian troops eventually suppressed the uprising, but violence in the region persists.

Boris Yeltsin, Russia's president from 1991 to 1999, struggled to keep order at home while trying to build good relations with the rest of the world. In the mid-1990s, Russia, Ukraine, and the United States agreed to begin eliminating their nuclear arsenals, resulting in Ukraine becoming a nuclear weapons–free country.

Yeltsin appointed Putin as his prime minister in 1999, and Putin took over the presidency from Yeltsin in 2000. Higher oil prices in subsequent years gave Putin sufficient revenues to cement his grip on power. In addition, he placed control of the giant energy company Gazprom back in government hands, further strengthening his political power.[43] In foreign policy, Putin was far less friendly than Yeltsin toward the West. He opposed the United States–led Iraq War in 2003, the NATO-sponsored secession of Kosovo from Serbia in 2008, and the U.S. plan to install a missile defense system in Eastern Europe in the mid-2000s.

Putin also resented NATO's expansion to his doorstep in 2004, when Estonia, Latvia, and Lithuania joined the Western military alliance. In addition, he viewed with unease the European Union's expansion in 2004 and 2007, when it accepted as members eight former communist nations from Central and Eastern Europe.[44] The new EU member states were staunchly pro-American and eagerly contributed troops to the United States–led Iraq War.

Constitutionally limited to two consecutive terms, Putin handpicked his prime minister, Dmitry Medvedev, to succeed him. Medvedev was elected in March 2008 with 70 percent of the vote.[45] With a softer style, Medvedev helped to warm Russia's relations with the West. A major achievement was conclusion of a new nuclear arms reduction treaty (START) in 2010.[46]

Medvedev was aided by Obama's election as president in November 2008, especially after the Obama administration vowed to "hit the reset button" and work to improve U.S.–Russian relations. The two cooperated in combating militant Islam in Afghanistan, with Russia granting the NATO mission there access to transport corridors that allowed NATO military personnel and equipment to travel from bases in the Baltic through Russia.

During the Arab Spring uprisings in 2011, Russia chose not to veto a U.N. Security Council move to deploy a NATO military mission in Libya. That mission led to the removal from power of Libyan leader Moammar Gadhafi in the summer of 2011. Meanwhile, the United States backed Russia's bid to join the WTO, giving it enhanced access to world markets for trade and investment purposes.[47]

Tensions ran high, however, when Georgia and Ukraine made bids to join NATO, which the United States supported but Russia firmly opposed. The situation was a contributing factor in the Russia–Georgia war that erupted in summer 2008, which ended with Russia tightening its control over Georgia's two secessionist regions, Abkhazia and South Ossetia.

U.S.–Russian relations soured in 2012, as the two countries could not reconcile their competing plans to develop new missile-defense systems in Europe.

As the United States began withdrawing its troops from Afghanistan in 2011, Russia began boosting its military presence in Central Asia. For instance, in September 2012, Moscow persuaded Tajikistan to allow Russian military bases there to remain open until 2042 by extending its existing lease.[48] Putin, who had been prime minister under Medvedev, was easily reelected president for six more years in May 2012. His return to the presidency quickly led to a chilling of relations with the West, due both to Putin's more confrontational style as well as to Western criticism of his human-rights record, for instance on freedom of the press.

Russian–United States relations became further strained last summer after NSA contractor Snowden was granted political asylum in Russia after disclosing details of the NSA's mass surveillance programs of U.S. and foreign citizens.

"It's not our fault that he found himself in Russia," says the Russian Embassy's Drobinin. He insists that Moscow was legally required to examine Snowden's claim for asylum and could not send him back to the United States, since the two countries do not have an extradition treaty.

An Armenian soldier in the self-proclaimed republic of Nagorno-Karabakh guards the border with Azerbaijan near the town of Martakert. Nagorno-Karabakh is officially part of Azerbaijan but populated by ethnic Armenian separatists, who would welcome Russia's protection. Concern about the future of Nagorno-Karabakh is seen as a major factor in Armenia's sudden decision in September 2013 to abandon a trade agreement negotiated with the European Union and instead join the Russian-backed Eurasian Economic Union.

AFP/Getty Images/Karen Minasyan

Meanwhile, the atmosphere in Eastern Europe began heating up as the EU and Russia competed for influence in the region. Moldova has aligned itself more closely with the EU since 2009, when a strongly pro-Western government was elected, replacing the ruling communists. This caused tension in Moldova's relations with Moscow, especially after Russia in September 2013 banned Moldovan wine and spirits, officially due to public-health concerns.

In the fall of 2013, Ukraine became an even bigger battleground between Russia and the EU, when the EU urged Kiev to sign an association and trade agreement. However, the EU also demanded the release from prison of Ukrainian opposition leader Yulia Tymoshenko for medical treatment in Germany — something the Ukrainian government refused to do.

Meanwhile, on Sept. 3, 2013, Armenian President Serzh Sargsyan announced Armenia would join the Russian-backed EEU instead of signing trade and association pacts it had concluded with the EU.[49] The decision came as a shock: Even Armenian diplomats in Washington were blindsided by the sudden shift that occurred after conversations between Sargsyan and Putin.

CURRENT SITUATION

Tensions in Ukraine

Ukraine was plunged into turmoil when President Yanukovych refused to sign the trade and association agreements with the EU. Popular protests focused around Independence Square in Kiev snowballed after the Vilnius summit in a movement dubbed Euro-Maidan in Ukrainian, or "Euro-Square." Clashes between the police and protesters turned increasingly violent — and even militant — with widespread arrests and several deaths and beatings reported.

On Jan. 28, 2014, the prime minister and cabinet resigned, and restrictions on political protest imposed weeks earlier were rescinded.[50] Obama, in his State of the Union speech on Jan. 28, 2014, said, "In Ukraine, we stand for the principle that all people have the right to express themselves freely and peacefully, and have a say in their country's future."[51]

By contrast, media coverage in Russia of the protests characterized the demonstrators as violent rioters. Voice of Russia, the government-owned broadcaster, alleged that the protests were being spearheaded by "well-organized radical groups — mainly, football ultras, professional raiders and militants who have undergone special training."[52]

The backlash in Ukraine soured Russia's relations with the rest of Europe. An EU–Russia summit did go ahead as planned in Brussels on Jan. 28, 2014, and was attended by President Putin, EU Commission President Jose Manuel Barroso, and EU Council President Herman Van Rompuy. However, given the dire state of their relations, the meeting was confined to a working lunch between the leaders. In the postsummit press conference, President Van Rompuy said the European integration offers to Ukraine, Georgia, or Moldova were "fully compatible" with Russia's interests. Putin said, "We would most likely abolish [our] preferential measures for Ukraine if it signs the [EU] association agreement."[53]

The Russian Embassy's Drobinin insisted: "it was Ukraine's decision taken in their national interests" not to sign the EU deal and that it was "misleading" to claim that Russia exerted pressure on Kiev.

Drobinin conceded that the EU–Ukraine deal would, however, hurt Russia's economy by causing EU goods to flood duty-free into the Russian market through Ukraine after being stamped with a "Made in Ukraine" label.

But Judy Dempsey, a scholar at the Carnegie Endowment for International Peace, said "Putin is desperate to hold on to [Ukraine], knowing full well that if Ukraine goes over to the EU, Russia's own bulwarks against the EU's creeping democratic influence will crumble."[54]

The U.S. administration intensified diplomatic efforts to persuade the East European countries to align themselves with the EU. Secretary of State Kerry, for instance, visited Moldova in December 2013, and U.S. Assistant Secretary of State for European and Eurasian Affairs Victoria Nuland made numerous trips to the region.

"The United States stands with you in search of. . . the European future that you have chosen and you deserve," Nuland said, addressing the media in Kiev on Dec. 11, 2013, after meeting with Yanukovych. "It is still possible to save Ukraine's European future," and "the world is watching."[55]

The Vilnius summit debacle, where Yanukovych decided at the last minute he would not sign the trade deal with the EU, made EU leaders bolder and blunter about their feelings. EU leaders Van Rompuy and

Barroso said jointly that they "strongly disapprove of Russia's position and actions" regarding Ukraine.

The U.S. Senate responded similarly, passing a resolution on Jan. 7, 2014, referring to "Russian economic coercion" in Ukraine and urging U.S. and EU leaders "to continue working together to [move] Ukraine toward a future in the Euro-Atlantic community."[56]

Welcoming the resolution, Deputy Assistant Secretary of State Thomas Melia said, "I believe the embers that sparked the protests in late November are still burning and will not be easily extinguished."[57] Nuland, his State Department colleague, added, "There is, also, a good deal of disinformation in Russia about the effect that the EU's Eastern Partnership could have on its economy and arrangements with neighbors."[58]

Meanwhile, Georgia and Moldova, which at the Vilnius summit initialed their EU trade deals — a preliminary step before signing the accords — grew more determined than ever to conclude them despite or perhaps because of the harsh warnings from Moscow. Armenian scholar Sahakyan says Georgia and Moldova may have less to fear from Russian economic retaliation than Ukraine because they are less economically dependent on Russia.

Nevertheless, he says, heavy-handedness from Russia is "not smart" because it hurts Russia's relations with the West. Armenia's government, he points out, could still turn back to the EU if Russia does not provide it with the security guarantees it wants.

Hot Spots and Winter Games

As NATO wound down its presence in Afghanistan, Russia moved in to fill the security vacuum. Its new extended lease on a military base in Tajikistan means that 7,000

Russian troops will stay on to help the Tajiks deal with any potential militant Islamist threats. The Tajik government worries about militants crossing the porous borders it shares with Afghanistan and Pakistan.[59]

Russia also is donating $1.1 billion in military weapons to Kyrgyzstan and paying $4.5 million a year to lease the country's Kant airbase for use by the Russian military. The United States, in contrast, is closing its Kyrgyz base at the Manas Transit Center.

"The underlying political message is that Russia is a more durable security partner than the U.S.," according to *Jane's Intelligence Review,* the security magazine.[60]

Getty Images/Asahi Shimbun

Russian police officers were a major presence at the 2014 Winter Olympic Games in Sochi, Russia. Sochi lies in the Caucasus region, a hotbed of Muslim radicalism. Islamist-inspired terrorists said they planned to attack the games, although no attack took place. Russian President Vladimir Putin has firmly opposed such groups in the past.

In Syria and Iran, Russia managed to maintain a working relationship with the EU and United States, as evidenced by the Nov. 23, 2013, deal on Iran's nuclear program that the EU brokered. Carnegie Endowment for International Peace scholars Andrew Weiss and Dmitri Trenin said the United States and Russia are in an era of "purely transactional relations against the background of deep mutual mistrust" and that "this may be the 'new normal' in U.S.–Russian relations."[61]

However, tensions between NATO and Russia continued to mount on the issue of missile defense. Talks to develop a joint system, which began in 2010, became hopelessly deadlocked. Russia wants NATO's missile defense system to be operationally linked to Russia's, while NATO prefers to limit such cooperation to information sharing between the NATO and Russian command-and-control centers. NATO also is resisting Russia's demand for a legal guarantee that the NATO missile defense system would not be used against Russia.[62]

Russia's new short-range ballistic missiles deployed in Kaliningrad could theoretically be used to destroy NATO's planned radar facility and missile interceptor in neighboring Poland. The missiles have a range of about 250 miles.[63] Artis Pabriks, defense minister of Lithuania, a NATO member state that borders Kaliningrad, said, "We have followed these events for quite some time, and

Should the United States take a tougher stance with Russia?

YES Ariel Cohen
Senior Research Fellow in Russian and Eurasian Studies, Heritage Foundation

Written For *CQ Researcher*, February 2014

With the U.S. Olympic team now in Sochi and Washington engaged in intensive talks with Moscow on the Syrian cease-fire and Iran's nuclear program, this is a good time to examine the United States–Russia relationship.

The Obama administration's ballyhooed Russian "reset" was an abysmal failure. There is no shared threat assessment and no mutual understanding between the United States and Russia on how to deal with the changing geopolitical environment. Instead, Russia's anti–U.S. foreign policy tilt prevents diplomatic cooperation. Because Russia still views America as a "principal adversary" — a Cold War legacy — it wants to constrain America's diplomatic and military maneuverability.

Flush with oil cash, Putin has chosen to build up Russia's military power, launching a $700 billion rearmament program, including massive nuclear missile modernization. Meanwhile, he has nearly eliminated U.S. missile defenses in Europe. He also has successfully confronted the Bush and Obama administrations over Iran, effectively saved Syrian President Bashar al-Assad, and supported a "deal" over the future of Iran's atomic program that brings Tehran to the threshold of nuclear statehood.

Moscow wants to see U.S. power diminished in Eurasia, the Middle East, and Europe. Putin's vision includes domination over the former Soviet bloc as an independent pole in a "multipolar world." Russia's pressures on Ukraine and Georgia continue unrelentingly, aimed at bringing Kiev and Tbilisi into Moscow's fold, most likely through the Eurasian Economic Union, a post-Soviet satellite state system not unlike the Warsaw Pact.

President Obama should ask the National Security Council to conduct a bottom-up review of Russia policy. He also should strengthen ties with former Soviet bloc countries concerned about their independence, such as Azerbaijan, Georgia, Kazakhstan, Turkmenistan, Ukraine, and Uzbekistan, and provide economic advice and political-military cooperation if requested. That would be particularly timely, since the United States plans to withdraw troops from Afghanistan later this year.

Russia's intransigent foreign policy will require the administration to provide global leadership and consistent, robust pushback when U.S. interests are at stake. Disagreements over security concerns and geopolitics hinder U.S.–Russian cooperation in counterterrorism, nonproliferation, global security, and business. Moscow's anti–U.S. approach means tough times for U.S.–Russian relations. But when engaging Moscow, the United States must guard its national security interests, not engage in a self-deluding, feel-good policy exercise.

NO Armen Sahakyan
Executive Director Washington, DC Branch, Eurasian Research Analysis Institute

Written For *CQ Researcher*, February 2014

When discussing the question of taking a tougher stance with Russia, one must bear in mind two important questions. First, what is the trigger to adopt such a policy? And second, will the policy lead to any favorable outcomes for the United States?

Recently, a widely cited reason has been Russia's ambition to form the Eurasian Economic Union (EEU) by Jan. 1, 2015. It is expected to be an economic union of five former Soviet states that will break down internal trade barriers, adopt a common tariff on foreign goods and other such free-trade measures. The United States has long been a proponent of free trade and globalization, yet it is alarmed with the idea of the EEU. The U.S. motive thus becomes questionable and the adoption of a harsher policy toward the EEU would likely hurt the U.S. international image as the torchbearer on free trade. It would be wiser to further develop friendly relations with the EEU states and ensure their continued integration into the world economy.

As for the second question — whether getting tough on Russia will produce a favorable outcome — I see it as counterproductive for the United States, which needs a strong Russia in the region and should be on favorable terms with it, considering the looming pullout of U.S. and coalition forces from Afghanistan.

Russia also has key roles to play regarding the ongoing instability in Syria and the fight against terrorism. As a permanent Security Council member, Russia also is instrumental in matters affecting the entire world. Should U.S.–Russia relations deteriorate, it would be much harder to reach a consensus on a wide range of issues, further destabilizing the balance of power.

Even if we were to disregard all of those considerations, it is doubtful that a tougher policy would be effective, since the United States does not have many "buttons" that it can push to pressure Russia. Russia and the United States do not have the deepest economic ties. The same underdeveloped relations exist on many other fronts, and it is questionable whether economic or other types of pressure would yield any favorable outcomes.

A cost-benefit analysis would show that the United States will be better off by further deepening its ties with Russia, cooperating in antiterrorism and other areas, and facilitating the EEU's integration with other trading blocs, such as NAFTA, the EU, and others.

this is not a surprise for us," but added that "it creates unnecessary political tension and suspicions and reduces mutual trust because we don't see reason why Russians would need such weapons here.... I think it's just to show who is the boss in the region."[64]

In February 2014, the world spotlight turned to the southern Russian resort city of Sochi for the Winter Olympics. Russia spent $51 billion on the games, more than eight times the amount spent for the previous Winter Olympics in Vancouver, Canada.[65]

In efforts to burnish his image in the run-up to the Olympics, Putin in December 2013 released longtime jailed businessman Mikhail Khodorkovsky and two anti-Putin activists from the pop band Pussy Riot.[66]

Security was exceptionally tight at the Games, as there were fears that Islamist terrorists would strike, but the Games ultimately took place without any security incident. By the end of the year, Sochi was experiencing a new boost in tourism as the sudden fall in the Russian ruble's value on currency markets caused Russians to forego foreign travel and vacation at home instead.[67] The boost for the tourism industry was also an effort by Russians to prop up their economy after it slid into recession over the course of the year due to falling oil prices and the impact of sanctions that the EU and United States imposed in retaliation for Russia's actions in Ukraine.

Continuing Tensions

Russia is likely to continue trying to enhance its voice in major international forums. With its WTO membership sealed, Russia now has its sights set on joining the Organisation for Economic Co-operation and Development, a Paris-based coalition of 34 developed nations that works to promote democracy and free markets. In order to be allowed to join, Russia will need to prove to the members, which are almost all advanced economies, that it has a genuinely free market and open economy, one in which businesses have confidence they can come and invest in a corruption-free, legally certain environment. Given the well-documented governance problems in the country, convincing them will be no small task.[68]

Russia also is expected to consolidate its historical hold over the Arctic region.[69] Norway's defense minister, Ine Eriksen Soreide, recently said Russia's increased military activity in the Arctic was "cause for concern" and

that NATO and Russia "do not see eye to eye" over joint naval exercises in the Arctic. "Small things can spark tensions," Soreide cautioned, pointing out that Norway shared a 122-mile land border and 466-mile sea border with Russia.[70]

As for Russia's ultimate goal regarding the Eurasian Economic Union, "We want to create a common [trading] space from Lisbon to Vladivostok," says Kalugin, of the Russian Embassy in Washington. Thus, the EU is part of Russia's plan as well, with the EU's 28 member states remaining Russia's top trading partners, Kalugin stresses.

Some demographers predict that Russia eventually will lose control of Siberia as Russians continue migrating out of the area and are replaced by Chinese migrant workers. But the Russian Embassy's Drobinin disputes such predictions. "Siberia is not some kind of promised land," he says. "It is really hard to live there," given its harsh climate and remoteness.

Four former Soviet-bloc countries that are now members of the EU — Estonia, Latvia, Lithuania, and Poland — will be leading the resistance to Russia's attempts to extend its influence into its Soviet-era sphere. "We were under occupation for 50 years," said Vydas Gedvilas, the speaker of the Lithuanian Parliament. "Now we are doing everything in our power to get these countries closer to the EU."[71]

Similarly, Estonian Defense Minister Reinsalu urged NATO to keep its door open to new members and for the United States to retain a military presence in Europe.[72] The State Department's Nuland has urged the EU to leave the welcome mat out for Ukraine.[73]

Russia's recent arm twisting "will ultimately lead to disaster" in its foreign relations, predicted Stephen Blank, a senior fellow for Russia at the American Foreign Policy Council, a Washington think tank. Refusing "to recognize the sovereignty and independence" of Armenia, Georgia, Kyrgyzstan, and Ukraine makes the region "fundamentally unstable" and "under constant threat of war," Blank argued.[74]

Frederick Starr, chairman of the Central Asia-Caucasus Institute at Johns Hopkins University in Washington, called Putin's policy "an absurd replay of Alexander III's" eastward expansion of the Russian Empire in the late 1800s, which culminated in the Russian revolution of 1905.[75]

"Everything is possible — both a drift of the former Soviet [countries] toward Russia, combined with the inward collapse of its states and societies," according to Olaf Osica, director of the Warsaw-based Centre for Eastern Studies, "as well as increasing opposition by the [Eastern Partnership] countries against the Kremlin's conduct."[76]

Epilogue

Russia's relations with its neighbors and the West were already on the cusp of a major transformation when this report was first published on February 7, 2014. Since then, that process has escalated, leading to an even more radical realignment than most experts had forecast in early 2014.

The central battleground, literally and figuratively, has been Ukraine, over which there has been a dizzying deterioration in Russia's relations with the European Union and the United States. On Feb. 22, Ukraine's pro-Russian President Viktor Yanukovych, responding to weeks of increasingly violent clashes between his security forces and pro-Western protesters in Kiev, unexpectedly fled the capital and headed eastward to Russia. His departure set in motion a chain of events that culminated in the election on May 25 of a new, more pro-Western Ukrainian president, Petro Poroschenko, who took 54 percent of the vote. Whereas Yanukovych had, days before the planned ceremony, balked at signing the free-trade and association agreements with the EU following pressure from Russia, Poroschenko had no such hesitation and signed the EU accords on June 27.[77] This further alienated Russia from Ukraine by cementing Ukraine's pro-Western orientation.

Meanwhile, Russian President Vladimir Putin had used the power vacuum created by Yanukovych's sudden departure by deploying troops to capture Crimea, a province in Ukraine most of whose residents are ethnically Russian. Three days after a hastily organized referendum in Crimea in which a clear majority voted to split from Ukraine, Russia formally annexed Crimea on March 19, ignoring the protests of Ukraine's government, which denounced the move as "robbery."[78] While Russia considers its annexation of Crimea as a legally conducted act, the EU, the United States, and Ukraine refuse to recognize it. In May, pro-Russian separatists in the eastern part of Ukraine which borders Russia

declared two independent republics, Donetsk and Lugansk. Separatist militias seized control of territories there, immediately putting themselves in conflict with the Ukrainian military.[79] Disturbed by these developments and blaming them on Russia, the EU and the United States imposed visa bans and asset freezes on officials and businessmen thought to be part of Putin's inner circle.

On July 17, a Malaysia Airlines passenger plane was shot down over separatist-held territory in eastern Ukraine, killing all 298 aboard, most of whom were Dutch nationals. The EU and the United States were quick to point the finger at Russia for having aided the separatist militias who were accused of having (accidentally) shot down the plane, mistaking it for a Ukrainian military jet. The crash investigation is ongoing, the findings due to be published in summer 2015. However, the EU and the United States in late July decided to impose trade sanctions targeting Russian access to international finance, and its defense and energy sectors, each of which forms the lifeblood of the Russian economy. Moscow retaliated by imposing a ban on imports of EU and U.S. foods.[80]

In this increasingly polarized climate, many countries in Russia's vicinity felt pressured to put themselves more solidly in either the pro-Russian or the pro-Western camp. Georgia and Moldova joined Ukraine by signing trade and association agreements with the EU, which aim to integrate all three into the EU's economy. In return, these countries have pledged to push through major political reforms such as reducing corruption and making their judiciaries stronger and more independent. Three other former Soviet republics, Armenia, Belarus, and Kazakhstan, have aligned more with Russia by joining the Eurasian Economic Union (EEU), an alternative economic bloc to the EU that entered into force on January 1, 2015.[81] Russia dominates the EEU economically, accounting for 85 percent of its gross domestic product (GDP). The GDP of the four EEU members amounts to $4 trillion, which compares to China, the EU and U.S. who each have a GDP of around $18 trillion, adjusted for purchasing power.[82] The small, poor central Asian republic of Kyrgyzstan is due to join the EEU on May 1, 2015. Russia has also strengthened economic ties with its eastern neighbors, China and Mongolia, with high-level political meetings held throughout the year at which large new projects were announced. For instance, Russia and China unveiled plans to construct a high-speed rail link, and Russia has signed a $400 billion contract to supply energy-hungry China with 38 billion cubic meters of gas.[83]

President Putin's actions in Ukraine led to Russia being suspended from the Group of Eight (G8) organization of the world's largest economies. A meeting planned to take place in the Russian resort city of Sochi in June 2014 was moved to Brussels, and the G8 was reduced to the G7.[84] NATO member countries neighboring Russia, notably Estonia, Latvia, Lithuania, and Poland, pressured the United States to boost its military presence in the region, fearful that Russia had intentions of further expansionism following its successful annexation of Crimea. The United States responded by rolling out a series of actions, including providing nonlethal defense equipment to Ukraine, deploying F-16 fighter jets to Poland, and increasing the U.S. Navy's presence in the Baltic and Black Seas.[85]

The heightened geopolitical tensions had begun to bite Russia economically by the fall of 2014. On top of the sanctions imposed against it, global prices of oil plummeted, which have hurt Russia's finances severely, the government relying heavily on revenues from oil exports. Having declined steadily over the year, on Dec. 15, 2014, the Russian ruble tumbled to record lows as jittery financial markets lost confidence in its economic prospects.[86] When the International Monetary Fund released an updated global economic outlook in January, it had revised its figures for Russia sharply downward, forecasting a 3 percent contraction of the Russian economy in 2015. The news caused further slippage in the Russian currency and led one credit-rating agency to downgrade Russian government bonds to junk status.[87]

Despite the souring of Russia's relations with the West, they have continued limited cooperation in trying to restore order to the worsening security situation in the Middle East. A new challenge emerged in the summer of 2014 when an Islamist militant group, ISIS, captured large swaths of territory in Iraq and Syria, exploiting the chaos created by the four-year civil war in Syria and the chronic weakness of the government of Iraq. While both the West and Russia oppose the Islamist militants, they disagree over the future of Syria, with Russia supporting President Bashar al-Assad, while the EU and the United

States oppose him. Russia also still co-operates with the EU and the United States in the longstanding negotiations with Iran aimed at preventing Iran from building nuclear weapons. An interim agreement signed in November 2013 remains in place, although progress in implementing it has been patchy.

Summing up the past year's tumultuous events, Russian journalist Maria Lipman, a Visiting Fellow from the European Council on Foreign Relations, said "the transformation has been beyond anybody's expectation."[88] The annexation of Crimea signaled "a shift towards aggressive conservatism" in Russia, she said, while adding "it has pushed Putin farther than he probably meant to go" but "it is not within his capacity to stop, slow down, or reverse the consequences." Inside Russia, Putin's popularity ratings soared above 80 percent after the annexation. In the months since then, "society has been pushed back to overwhelming paternalism" as Russians rely on Putin for everything, she said.

NOTES

1. "Rogozin Warns Moldova on Relations," Reuters, Sept. 5, 2013, Reuters, www.themoscowtimes.com/business/article/rogozin-warns-moldova-on-relations/485526.html.

2. Foreign Minister Bildt was speaking at a conference titled "The European Union's Eastern Partnership: What to Expect at Vilnius," hosted by the Brookings Institution in Washington, DC, on Nov. 21, 2013, www.brookings.edu/events/2013/11/21-european-union-eastern-partner-ship-vilnius.

3. See Olaf Osica, "The Eastern Partnership: Life Begins after Vilnius," Center for European Analysis, Dec. 13, 2013, http://cepa.org/content/eastern-partnership-life-begins-after-vilnius.

4. T. J., "Why has Russia banned Moldovan wine?" *The Economist,* Nov. 25, 2013, www.economist.com/blogs/economist-explains/2013/11/economist-explains-18.

5. Minister Gherman was speaking at a discussion on the EU Eastern Partnership, organized by the European Institute in Washington, DC, on Sept. 18, 2013.

6. Wiegand was speaking at an event titled "The EU's Eastern Partnership in Light of Present Challenges," hosted by Johns Hopkins University in Washington, DC, Jan. 16, 2014.

7. Presentation by Mikhail Kalugin, head of economic section, Embassy of Russia to the United States, at discussion titled "Securing Northern Europe's Energy Independence: A Finnish Perspective," organized by the European Institute, Washington, DC, Dec. 19, 2013.

8. *Ibid.*

9. *Ibid.*

10. See Human Rights Watch, "Attacks on Ghou-ta," Sept. 10, 2013, www.hrw.org/node/118725/.

11. Paul Lewis, "Obama welcomes Syria chemical weapons deal but retains strikes option," *The Guardian,* Sept. 14, 2013, www.theguardian.com/world/2013/sep/14/barack-obama-syria-chemical-weapons-deal.

12. For background, see Chuck McCutcheon, "Government Surveillance," *CQ Researcher,* Aug. 30, 2013, pp. 717–740.

13. "Ratification of Russian military base deal provides Tajikistan with important security guarantees," *Jane's Intelligence Weekly,* Oct. 2, 2013, www.janes.com/article/27898/ratification-of-russian-military-base-deal-provides-tajikistan-with-important-security-guarantees.

14. "Russia: 2 suspects arrested in bombing," the Associated Press, Jan. 30, 2014, www.lasvegassun.com/news/2014/jan/30/russia-2-suspects-arrested-suicide-bombing/.

15. "Winter Olympics: Russia launches Sochi security clampdown," BBC News, www.bbc.co.uk/news/world-europe-25633632.

16. Kelly Whiteside, "Obama sends message by naming Sochi Olympic delegation," *USA Today,* Dec. 20, 2013, www.usatoday.com/story/sports/olympics/sochi/2013/12/17/white-house-sochi-olympics-delegation-to-include-gay-athlete/4051581/.

17. Brian Beary, "Emerging Central Asia," *CQ Global Researcher,* Jan. 17, 2012, pp. 29–56.

18. Helen Robertson, "Russia's energy trade with China to quadruple by 2025," *Petroleum Economist,* October 2013, www.petroleum-economist.com/Article/3258056/Russias-energy-trade-with-China-to-quadruple-by-2025.html.

19. MK & Danfes, "Putin's India Visit Furthers Indo-Russian Ties," *The Day After,* Jan. 1, 2013; also see "Indian Generic Drugmakers Pile Into Russian Market," *Business Monitor International,* March 14, 2013, www.pharmaceuticalsinsight.com/file/158892/indian-generic-drugmakers-pile-into-russian-market.html.

20. Matthew Smith, "Brazil, Russia agree to space and cyber collaboration," *Jane's Defence Industry,* Nov. 1, 2013.

21. Jon Grevatt, "Russia increases defence industrial presence in Myanmar, Vietnam," *Jane's Defence Weekly,* March 5, 2013.

22. Andrey Slepnev, minister for trade, Eurasian Economic Commission, speaking at Center for Strategic and International Studies in Washington, DC, at a discussion titled "The Future of the Eurasian Economic Union," Oct. 31, 2013.

23. On Jan. 17, 2014, Alexandros Petersen was shot dead while dining at a popular Lebanese restaurant in downtown Kabul, Afghanistan. Petersen was the victim of an anti-Western terrorist attack carried out by Taliban militants that killed 21 people.

24. Petersen was speaking at an event titled "Pushback to Putin's Eurasian Dream? The Looming Facedown between China, the EU and Russia," School for Advanced International Studies, Johns Hopkins University, Dec. 4, 2013.

25. Zvi Magen, "Putin flexes his muscles," *The Jerusalem Report,* Oct. 7, 2013, www.jpost.com/Jerusalem-Report/The-Region/Putin-flexes-his-muscles-326954.

26. David Des Roches, "Russia in the Middle East: Help or Hinderance?" *The Diplomatic Insight,* Dec. 31, 2012.

27. Rick Gladstone, "Friction at the U.N. as Russia and China Veto Another Resolution on Syria Sanctions," *The New York Times*, July 19, 2012, www.nytimes.com/2012/07/20/world/middleeast/russia-and-china-veto-un-sanctions-against-syria.html?_r=0.

28. Professor Cross spoke at the "Round Table on the NATO-Russian Relationship," Woodrow Wilson International Center for Scholars, Jan. 10, 2014.

29. "Press Availability with U.S. Secretary of State John Kerry, Russian Foreign Minister Sergey Lavrov and UN Special Representative Lakhdar Brahimi," Paris, France, Jan. 13, 2014, www.state.gov/secretary/remarks/2014/01/219604.htm.

30. "Kaliningrad: European fears over Russian missiles," BBC News, Dec. 13, 2013, www.bbc.co.uk/news/world-europe-25407284.

31. For background, see Roland Flamini, "U.S.-Europe Relations," *CQ Researcher,* March 23, 2012, pp. 277–300.

32. Reinsalu made his comments at a discussion titled "Ten Years in NATO; Twelve Years in Afghanistan: An Estonian Perspective on the Future of NATO," Center for Strategic and International Studies, Jan. 6, 2014, http://csis.org/event/ten-years-nato-twelve-years-afghanistan

33. See Brian Beary, "U.S. Trade Policy," *CQ Researcher,* Sept. 13, 2013, pp. 765–788.

34. "Russia may ban import of Polish fruits and vegetables," Voice of Russia, Nov. 16. 2013, http://voiceofrussia.com/news/2013_11_16/Russia-may-ban-import-of-Polish-fruits-and-vegetables-5949/.

35. For background on Russian history, see Kenneth Jost, "Russia and the Former Soviet Republics," *CQ Researcher,* June 17, 2005, pp. 541–564.

36. For a concise overview of Russian history, see Geoffrey Hosking, *Russian History: A Very Short Introduction* (2012).

37. See Jason McClure, "Russia in Turmoil," *CQ Researcher,* Feb. 21, 2012, pp. 81–104.

38. Hoskings, *op. cit.*, p. 22.

39. Jost, *op. cit.*

40. Walter Richmond, *The Circassian Genocide* (2013).

41. McClure, *op. cit.*

42. For background, see Roland Flamini, "Dealing With the 'New' Russia," *CQ Researcher,* June 6, 2008, pp. 481–504.

43. McClure, *op. cit.*

44. For background, see Brian Beary, "The New Europe," *CQ Global Researcher,* Aug. 1, 2007, pp. 181–210.

45. Flamini, "Dealing With the 'New' Russia," *op. cit.*

46. *Ibid.*

47. For details of Russia's WTO membership obligations, see "Office of the United States Trade Representative's Report on Russia's Implementation of the WTO Agreement," December 2013, www.ustr.gov/sites/default/files/Russia-WTO-Implementation-Report%20FINAL-12-20-13.pdf.

48. See Beary, "Emerging Central Asia," *op. cit.*

49. David M. Herszenhorn, "Russia Putting A Strong Arm On Neighbors," *The New York Times*, Oct. 23, 2013, www.nytimes.com/2013/10/23/world/europe/russia-putting-a-strong-arm-on-neighbors.html?_r=0.

50. "Ukraine's protests: Praying for peace," *The Economist,* Jan. 30, 2014, www.economist.com/news/europe/21595512-government-resigns-opposition-protesters-remain-defiantly-streets-praying.

51. "Obama's 2014 State of the Union address: transcript," ABC News, Jan. 28, 2014, www.cbsnews.com/news/obamas-2014-state-of-the-union-address-full-text/.

52. "Who is who in pro-EU protests events in Ukraine?" Voice of Russia, Jan. 30, 2014, http://voiceofrussia.com/2014_01_30/Who-is-who-in-pro-EU-protests-events-in-Ukraine-4142/.

53. Joanna Sopinska, "Expert consultations on Eastern Partnership agreements," *Europolitics,* Jan. 29, 2014.

54. Judy Dempsey, "Is This Ukraine's Turning Point?" *Carnegie Europe,* Dec. 9, 2013, http://carnegieeurope.eu/strategiceurope/?fa=53847.

55. "Remarks to the Media Following Meeting With President Yanukovych," U.S. Department of State, Dec. 11, 2013, www.state.gov/p/eur/rls/rm/2013/dec/218604.htm.

56. "S.RES.319 — Expressing support for the Ukrainian people in light of President Yanukovych's decision not to sign an Association Agreement with the European Union," U.S. Senate Resolution approved by unanimous consent on Jan. 7, 2014, http://

thomas. loc.gov/cgi-bin/query/D?c113:3:./temp/ ~c113vhuJWD::

57. Thomas O. Melia, deputy assistant secretary, Bureau of Democracy, Human Rights and Labor, statement to the Senate Foreign Relations Committee hearing on the situation in Ukraine, Jan. 15, 2014.

58. *Ibid.*

59. "Ratification of Russian military base deal provides Tajikistan with important security guarantees," *Jane's Intelligence Weekly*, Oct. 2, 2013.

60. "Neighbourhood watch: Russia's response to insecurity in Central Asia," *Jane's Intelligence Review*, Dec. 1, 2013.

61. Dmitri Trenin and Andrew S. Weiss, "Dealing With the New Normal in U.S.-Russian Relations," Carnegie Endowment for International Peace, Dec. 20, 2013, http://carnegie.ru/2013/12/20/dealing-with-new-normal-in-u.s.-russian-relations/gwto.

62. Brooks Tigner, "NATO-Russian missile defence talks deadlocked," *Jane's Defence Weekly*, Nov. 27, 2013.

63. "Russian missile deployment to Kaliningrad does not heighten war risk but will cause decline in diplomatic relations," *Jane's Intelligence Weekly*, Dec. 18, 2013.

64. Steve Gutterman, "Russia has stationed Iskander missiles in western region: reports," Reuters, Dec. 16, 2013, www.reuters.com/article/2013/12/16/us-russia-missiles-idUSBRE9BF0W020131216.

65. "Sochi: Olympic Flame in the Caucasus," teleconference, Woodrow Wilson Center for International Scholars, Washington, DC, Jan. 13, 2014.

66. Masha Gessen, "Don't be fooled by Putin," CNN, Dec. 21, 2013, www.cnn.com/2013/12/21/opinion/gessen-putin-khodorkovsky/.

67. Karoun Demirjian, "Russian economic crisis helps save Putin's post-Olympic dream at Sochi," *Washington Post*, Jan. 18, 2015, www.washingtonpost.com/world/europe/russian-economic-crisis-helps-save-putins-post-olympic-dream-at-sochi/2015/01/17/d8c7bbd8-92b1-11e4-a66f-0ca5037a597d_story.html.

68. Chris Weafer, "Russia's Path to Progress Goes Through OECD," *The Moscow Times*, Dec. 11, 2013, www.themoscowtimes.com/opinion/article/russias-path-to-progress-goes-through-oecd/491391.html#ixzz2s0B47xi9.

69. See Brian Beary, "Race for the Arctic," *CQ Global Researcher*, August 2008, pp. 213–242.

70. Soreide made her comments at a discussion titled "Writing NATO's Next Chapter: The View from Norway," Center for Strategic and International Studies, Jan. 9, 2014, http://csis.org/event/writing-natos-next-chapter.

71. Gedvilas made his remarks at a discussion on the EU's Eastern Partnership, European Institute, Sept. 18, 2013.

72. Reinsalu, *op. cit.*

73. Statement to the Senate Foreign Relations Committee hearing on the situation in Ukraine, Jan. 15, 2014.

74. Blank was speaking at a conference titled "Pushback to Putin's Eurasian Dream? The Looming Facedown between China, the EU and Russia," School of Advanced International Studies, Johns Hopkins University, Dec. 4, 2013.

75. Starr was speaking at a conference titled "Pushback to Putin's Eurasian Dream?. . ." *ibid.*

76. Osica, *op. cit.*

77. Laura Smith-Spark, Ben Brumfield and Mick Krever, "Ukraine signs EU deal that sparked months of upheaval; extends cease-fire," CNN, June 27, 2014, http://www.cnn.com/2014/06/27/world/europe/ukraine-crisis/index.html.

78. "Russia's annexation of Crimea is 'armed robbery,' says Ukrainian PM Yatsenyuk," Euronews, March 21, 2014, www.euronews.com/2014/03/21/russia-s-annexation-of-crimea-is-armed-robbery-says-ukrainian-pm-yatsenyuk.

79. Mark MacKinnon "In Ukraine, Donetsk People's Republic lurches to life," *The Globe and Mail*, May 12, 2014, www.theglobeandmail.com/news/world/in-ukraine-donetsk-peoples-republic-lurches-to-life/article18621492.

80. "Russia bans fruit, veg, meat, fish, dairy imports from EU and US," RTE News, Aug. 8, 2014, http://www.reuters.com/article/2014/08/07/

us-ukraine-crisis-russia-food-idUSKBN0G70Q1 20140807

81. Editorial, "Eurasian Economic Union Comes into Force Jan 1, Promising Benefits from Integration," *The Astana Times*, Jan. 2, 2015, www.astanatimes.com/2015/01/eurasian-economic-union-comes-force-jan-1-promising-benefits-integration.

82. International Monetary Fund's World Economic Outlook database: www.imf.org/external/ns/cs.aspx?id=28.

83. William Wan and Abigail Hauslohner "China, Russia sign $400 billion gas deal" *Washington Post*, May 21, 2014, www.washingtonpost.com/world/europe/china-russia-sign-400-billion-gas-deal/2014/05/21/364e9e74-e0de-11e3-8dcc-d6b7fede081a_story.html.

84. Julian Borger and Nicholas Watt, "G7 countries snub Putin and refuse to attend planned G8 summit in Russia," *The Guardian* (UK), March 24, 2014, www.theguardian.com/world/2014/mar/24/g7-countries-snub-putin-refuse-attend-g8-summit-russia.

85. Zachary A. Goldfarb "U.S. announces $1 billion program to boost military presence in Eastern Europe," *Washington Post*, June 3, 2014, www.washingtonpost.com/politics/us-announces-1-billion-program-to-boost-military-presence-in-eastern-europe/2014/06/03/414c0240-eb00-11e3-9f5c-9075d5508f0a_story.html.

86. Katie Lobosco, "Apple closes online store in Russia as ruble tumbles," CNN News, http://money.cnn.com/2014/12/16/news/companies/apple-russia-ruble/index.html.

87. Anna Andrianova and Ksenia Galouchko "Russia Credit Rating Is Cut to Junk by S&P for the First Time in a Decade" Bloomberg, Jan. 26, 2015, www.bloomberg.com/news/articles/2015-01-26/russia-credit-rating-cut-to-junk-by-s-p-for-first-time-in-decade.

88. **Lipman was giving a presentation titled** "Russia After Crimea: How the Dramatic Transformations of 2014 Scrapped the Achievements of Post-Soviet Development," at the George Washington University, Washington, DC, on January 29, 2015, http://elliott.gwu.edu/events-calendar#/?i=1

BIBLIOGRAPHY

Selected Sources
Books

Bullough, Oliver, *The Last Man in Russia*, Basic Books, 2013.
In a mix of travelogue, sociological study, and biography, a British journalist and author who lived for several years in Russia describes contemporary Russian society.

Hill, Fiona, and Clifford G. Gaddy, *Mr. Putin: Operative in the Kremlin*, Brookings, 2013.
A senior fellow at the Brookings Institution, a major Washington think tank, assesses Vladimir Putin's leadership of Russia.

Hosking, Geoffrey, *Russian History: A Very Short Introduction*, Oxford University Press, 2012.
An emeritus professor of Russian history at University College London provides a succinct history of Russia, from its medieval origins to contemporary events.

Judah, Ben, *Fragile Empire: How Russia Fell in and out of Love With Vladimir Putin*, 2013.
An associate fellow at the European Council on Foreign Relations sketches a revealing portrait of the Russian leader.

Mankoff, Jeffrey, *Russian Foreign Policy: The Return of Great Power Politics*, Rowman & Littlefield Publishers, 2011.
A fellow at the Center for Strategic and International Studies examines how Russian foreign policy has developed since the end of the Cold War.

Stent, Angela E., *The Limits of Partnership: U.S.–Russian Relations in the Twenty-First Century*, Princeton University Press, 2014.
The director of the Center for Eurasian, Russian, and East European Studies at Georgetown University describes U.S.–Russian relations since the collapse of the Soviet Union.

Articles

Dempsey, Judy, "Is This Ukraine's Turning Point?" Carnegie Europe, Dec. 9, 2013, http://carnegieeurope.eu/strategiceurope/?fa=53847.

A journalist and scholar assesses where Ukraine may be headed geopolitically.

Des Roches, David, "Russia in the Middle East: Help or Hindrance," *The Diplomatic Insight*, Dec. 31, 2012, pp. 19–20, http://thediplomaticinsight.com/wp-content/uploads/2013/01/december-2012-magazine.pdf.
An associate professor at the National Defense University examines Russia's role in current Middle Eastern politics.

Jones, Stephen, "Reaching the Summit: Implications of Vilnius for Georgia," The Central Asia-Caucasus Analyst, Dec. 11, 2013, http://www.cacianalyst.org/publications/analytical-articles/item/12879-reaching-the-summit-implications-of-vilnius-for-georgia.html
A professor of Russian studies at Mount Holyoke College examines the consequences of Georgia's initialing major trade and association pacts with the EU in November 2013.

Leigh, Michael, "Ukraine's Pivot to Europe?" German Marshall Fund of the United States, Nov. 13, 2013, www.realclearworld.com/articles/2013/11/13/ukraines_pivot_to_europe.html
A senior adviser to the German Marshall Fund of the United States, a nonpartisan organization that promotes trans-Atlantic cooperation, explains Ukraine's dilemma in deciding whether to align itself with Russia or Europe.

Lindberg, Todd, "A Bear in the Desert: Why did the Obama administration allow a Russian resurgence in the Middle East?" *The Weekly Standard*, July 1, 2013, www.weeklystandard.com/articles/bear-desert_736859.html.
A research fellow at the conservative Hoover Institution criticizes President Obama for allowing Russia to reassert itself in the Middle East.

Osica, Olaf, "The Eastern Partnership: Life Begins after Vilnius," Center for European Analysis, Dec. 13, 2013, http://cepa.org/content/eastern-partnership-life-begins-after-vilnius.
A director of the Centre for Eastern Studies in Warsaw urges the EU to try to keep Georgia and Moldova on their current pro-EU path.

Trenin, Dmitri, and Andrew S. Weiss, "Dealing With the New Normal in U.S.–Russian Relations," Carnegie Endowment for International Peace, Dec. 20, 2013, http://carnegie.ru/2013/12/20/dealing-with-new-normal-in-u.s.russian-relations/gwto.
Two scholars outline how Russia's U.S. relations deteriorated in 2013.

Reports and Studies

"Report on Russia's Implementation of the WTO Agreement," Office of the U.S. Trade Representative, December 2013, https://ustr.gov/sites/default/files/Russia-WTO-Implementation-Report%20FINAL-12-20-13.pdf
The U.S. agency that negotiates trade agreements reports on how Russia is complying with its obligations at the World Trade Organization, which Russia joined in 2012.

"U.S.–Russia Bilateral Presidential Commission — 2013 Joint Report," United States Department of State, December 2013, www.state.gov/documents/organization/219326.pdf.
The report describes the main areas in which the United States and Russia cooperate bilaterally.

For More Information

The Atlantic Council, 1030 15th St., N.W., 12th Floor, Washington, DC 20005; 202-778-4952; www.atlantic council.org. Think tank that promotes the trans-Atlantic relationship conducts research on defense and economic and foreign policies.

Brookings Institution, 1775 Massachusetts Ave., N.W., Washington, DC 20036; 202-797-6000; www.brookings .edu. Centrist think tank with a unit that studies relations between the United States and Europe.

Carnegie Moscow Center, 16/2 Tverskaya, Moscow 125009, Russia; +7 495-9358904; www.carnegie.ru. Division of the Washington-based Carnegie Endowment for International Peace that does research and promotes debate on post-Soviet Russia and Eurasia.

Embassy of the Russian Federation to the United States of America, 2650 Wisconsin Ave., N.W., Washington, DC 20007; 202-298-5700; www.russianembassy.org. Official representative of the Russian government in the United States.

Eurasian Economic Commission, Ul. Letnikovskaya 2, Moscow 115114, Russia; +7 495 669 2400 ext. 4117. Regulatory body of the Eurasian Economic Union; aims to develop a free-trade area in Russia and the former Soviet republics.

German Marshall Fund of the United States, 1744 R St., N.W., Washington, DC 20009; 202-683-2650; www.gmfus .org. Foundation with several Russia-specialist scholars that promotes trans-Atlantic relations.

Heritage Foundation, 214 Massachusetts Ave., N.E., Washington, DC 20002; 202546-4400; www.heritage.org. Conservative think tank that focuses in part on U.S.–Russia relations.

School of Advanced International Studies, Johns Hopkins University, Nitze Building, 1740 Massachusetts Ave., N.W., Washington, DC 20036; 202-663-5600; www.sais-jhu.edu. Foreign policy–oriented institution with expertise in the Central Asian-Caucasus region.

Woodrow Wilson Center for International Scholars, Ronald Reagan Building and International Trade Center, One Woodrow Wilson Plaza, 1300 Pennsylvania Ave., N.W., Washington, DC 20004; 202-691-4000; www.wilsoncenter .org. Think tank with longstanding interest in Russia and Eastern Europe.

Farmers in Tokyo protest Japan's participation in negotiations over the U.S.-proposed Trans-Pacific Partnership on Oct. 26, 2011. Japanese farmers say the pact would unfairly benefit U.S. exporters and allow exports of genetically modified foods. President Obama also is seeking passage of a free-trade agreement with the 28-member European Union. If passed, it would be the biggest bilateral trade pact ever, affecting 40 percent of the global economy.

From *CQ Researcher*, September 13, 2013.

9

U.S. Trade Policy

Brian Beary

For decades, the European Union (EU) banned imports of American hormone-treated beef because of concern about the safety of growth hormones to humans.

The U.S. government complained to the World Trade Organization (WTO) that the ban violated free-trade rules because the EU could not prove the hormones were harmful to consumers. The WTO agreed.

To settle the dispute, the EU said it would continue to ban imports of hormone-treated beef, but agreed to allow up to 45,000 metric tons of hormone-free U.S. beef to enter its 28 member countries duty-free each year — a special exception available only to American beef exporters. The United States then lifted retaliatory tariffs it had imposed on EU products.

Since the compromise was reached, U.S. shipments of non-hormone-treated beef to the EU have soared to $200 million this year — three times what they were before the deal was struck in 2009. The agreement, originally scheduled to expire in August, was extended last month for two more years.[1]

"The duty-free quota represents a compromise that allows U.S. beef to enter the market," says Joe Schuele, director of communications at the Denver-based U.S. Meat Export Federation, but "we still maintain that the hormone ban has no scientific basis."

Such agreements show "what we can accomplish with practical, problem-solving approaches to trade barriers," U.S. Trade Representative (USTR) Michael Froman said.[2]

Currently, American and European trade negotiators are focusing on a much bigger trade deal. On July 8, they launched talks for a

Proposed Trade Pacts Cover 40 Countries

The United States and the 28-member European Union began talks on July 8 on a comprehensive free-trade agreement, the Transatlantic Trade and Investment Partnership (TTIP). If successful, the treaty would be the largest bilateral free-trade pact in the world, affecting 40 percent of the global economy. Meanwhile, the United States and 11 Asian and Pacific Rim countries have been negotiating since 2009 on a multilateral trade pact known as the Trans-Pacific Partnership (TPP). The Obama administration says the two treaties would create American jobs and help the United States compete with China, whose state-sponsored capitalism has made it a global economic superpower.

Countries Participating in Two Major Trade Pacts

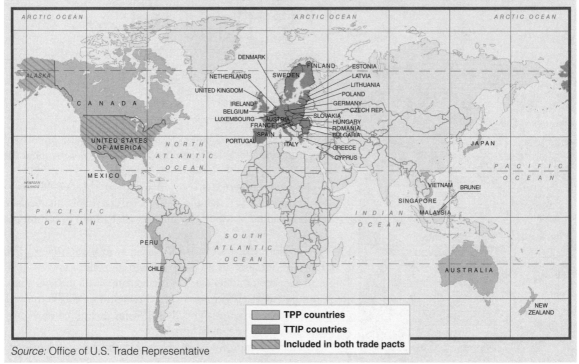

Legend:
- TPP countries
- TTIP countries
- Included in both trade pacts

Source: Office of U.S. Trade Representative

comprehensive bilateral free-trade agreement, called the Transatlantic Trade and Investment Partnership (TTIP), between the United States and the 28-member European Union. If they succeed, it would be the biggest bilateral free-trade pact ever, affecting 40 percent of the global economy. It would also breathe new life into the U.S.-Europe relationship, which has flagged as both sides have nervously eyed the faster-growing economies in Asia.[3]

Meanwhile, the United States since 2009 has been negotiating the Trans-Pacific Partnership (TPP), a multilateral trade pact among the United States and 11 Asian and Pacific nations. TPP is scheduled to be completed by

the end of this year. (The other participants are Australia, Brunei, Chile, Canada, Japan, Malaysia, Mexico, New Zealand, Peru, Singapore and Vietnam.)

President Obama has two primary motives in advancing such agreements: to create U.S. jobs by expanding exports and to steer global trade rules in ways favorable to the United States and other free-market economies. With the U.S. economy finally getting some momentum after the 2007-09 financial crisis, Obama believes the time is ripe for further market openings.

John Murphy, vice president for international affairs at the U.S. Chamber of Commerce, says 38 million

American jobs depend on trade and that "the potential to create more jobs through trade is huge."

The two sweeping trade pacts could also help the United States compete with China, whose state-sponsored capitalism has made it a global economic superpower.[4] The Chinese government's propensity to provide cheap government loans for exporters, subsidies to develop new technologies and a low currency exchange rate have private sector-dominated countries such as the United States crying foul, alleging China has created an unlevel international playing field.[5] As a result, China's state-owned enterprises distort international trade by giving unfair advantage to the subsidized firms, critics say.

Amid these developments, the 18-year-old World Trade Organization is struggling to remain relevant. The WTO was created in 1995 as the primary forum for liberalizing trade worldwide by reducing barriers to free trade and arbitrating trade disputes. But the WTO has taken a battering since its flagship project — a new round of trade negotiations launched in Doha, Qatar, in 2001 — died a slow and painful death.

As the WTO floundered, countries have rushed to conclude bilateral and regional trade deals — more than 250 since the WTO was created.[6] This year alone, accords have been completed between Canada and Jordan, Chile and Malaysia and the EU and Central America.[7]

This new "competitive liberalism" approach to trade — in which countries compete with one another to conclude the most advantageous trade deals — makes sense in today's economy, where products are assembled in multiple countries, according to Ari Van Assche, a professor of international business at HEC Montréal, a major Canadian business school. The new trade deals tackle issues such as removing restrictions on foreign investment, harmonizing regulations and scrapping tariffs on imported intermediate goods (those midway along the production process).[8]

Most Americans Back Foreign Trade

Nearly 60 percent of Americans think foreign trade will help the economy. In 2011 and 2012, as the economy struggled to recover from the recent steep recession, the public was evenly divided on trade. Views on trade have largely tracked the status of the U.S. economy over the past decade, with Americans more likely to see it as an economic opportunity from the robust mid-1990s through the early 2000s and as a threat during the worst years of the recession.

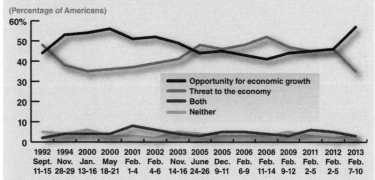

"Do you see foreign trade more as an opportunity for economic growth through increased U.S. exports or a threat to the economy from foreign imports?"

Source: "Americans Shift to More Positive View of Foreign Trade," Gallup, Feb. 28, 2013, www.gallup.com/poll/160748/americans-shift-positive-view-foreign-trade.aspx

Carla Hills, who served as U.S. trade representative for President George H. W. Bush from 1989-1993, charges that Obama did not embrace this new reality as enthusiastically as he should have in his first term. "We [the United States] were sitting on the sidelines for three years," she said. "Now we are playing catch-up, and we are choking on the issues."[9]

Obama initially was reluctant to negotiate new trade agreements, in part because of rising resentment toward such treaties that began in the 1990s. Many Americans blamed the 1994 North American Free Trade Agreement (NAFTA), which eliminated trade barriers among the U.S., Canada and Mexico, for the outsourcing of manufacturing jobs from the United States to lower-wage Mexico. That trade agreement, negotiated behind closed doors as are most trade deals, caused a surge of public anger in the United States, especially after the public learned more about its contents when Congress debated whether to ratify it or not.

A recent poll suggests Americans are more receptive to the European trade talks, with 58 percent supporting increased trade with the EU. Experts attribute that attitude to the fact that both the U.S. and EU have similar wage levels and worker protection rules, making it less likely the agreement would trigger outsourcing in either direction.[10] Public sentiment about the trans-Pacific treaty remains largely untested.[11]

In addition, experts say, the openness with which the two treaties are being negotiated could help to build public support. But that support could plummet if the new deals are seen as being cooked up secretly, NAFTA-style. Consequently, the administration threw open at least some of the doors to the talks, inviting more than 100 stakeholders, journalists and negotiators to a three-hour networking event in July 2013 at the White House Conference Center during the opening round of the trans-Atlantic talks.

Image aside, a big question still haunts the talks: Will the trade deals create jobs for Americans? In the 1950s and '60s, the U.S. economy clearly benefitted from free trade. But since then it seems that other countries — Japan in the 1970s and '80s, and China in the 1990s and 2000s — have benefitted more.

Supporters of the new agreements claim the pendulum is swinging back in favor of the United States. After a decade in decline, U.S. manufacturing is slowly reviving, with 500,000 jobs added in the past three years, compared with 5 million jobs lost between 2000 and 2009.[12]

On the downside, the U.S. trade deficit — created when imports exceed exports, usually resulting in lost domestic manufacturing jobs — has mushroomed since the 1990s, reaching $535 billion in 2012.[13]

But that figure can be misleading, noted Marc Levinson, manager for transportation and industry analysis at the nonpartisan Congressional Research Service.[14] Trade statistics are "increasingly problematic," he said, because they take insufficient account of the globalized nature of manufacturing. For example, if someone imports a computer, it counts 100 percent as an import even if it contains electronic chips patented in the United States, deriving part of its value from inside the country, he explained.

Any U.S. trade deal will have to be approved by Congress, where attitudes about trade are mixed. Rep. Ted Poe, R-Texas, said the expansion of exports expected under the trans-Pacific trade deal would be good news back home in Houston, a major export hub.

Rep. Brad Sherman, D-Calif., struck a more critical note, however. "We have been traveling this road for 20 years, and we [still] have the largest trade deficit in the world," he said, adding that "the definition of insanity is doing the same thing over and over again and expecting another result."

As lawmakers, trade negotiators, labor leaders and business executives discuss the pending trade agreements, here are some of the key questions being debated:

Will expanding free trade create jobs for Americans?

Experts generally agree free-trade agreements expand trade, but stark disagreement persists about whether that translates into more jobs at home.

Both the European and Pacific trade agreements will find "new markets for growth" of American exports, creating jobs in the United States, says Joshua Meltzer, a fellow in global economy and development at the Brookings Institution, a Washington think tank. He believes the trans-Pacific trade deal would have greater potential than the European pact to create jobs here because the Asia-Pacific markets are newer, largely unexploited territories for American companies.

Carol Guthrie, spokeswoman at the Office of the U.S. Trade Representative, estimates that each $1 billion in additional exports supports more than 5,000 jobs. The trans-Atlantic trade pact (TTIP) "will serve to expand our exports to the EU by further lowering tariffs and removing red tape and bringing our regulatory environments closer together," she says. The Pacific treaty, she says, will "increase U.S. involvement in supply chains in the competitive markets of the Asia-Pacific, lowering tariffs and creating rules to make sure that American firms and workers are not undercut or disadvantaged when doing business in the region."

The EU's trade spokesman, John Clancy, says, "It is evident that the TTIP will create jobs." He cited a study showing that €119 billion ($157 billion) is expected to be added to the EU economy just by eliminating tariff and regulatory barriers. "We are convinced the U.S.-EU trade pact will be a win-win deal in terms of jobs."[15]

Indeed, there seems to be consensus among experts that additional jobs created by the trans-Atlantic pact would benefit both economies, because they both have similar wage levels and rules for protecting workers and investors.

But Lori Wallach, director of Global Trade Watch, a program of the Washington-based consumer advocacy group Public Citizen, thinks neither agreement will help the U.S. job market. "We are replicating a model of the last 20 years that has led to our trade deficit exploding and has cost us 5 million manufacturing jobs," she says. "That's 25 percent of total U.S. manufacturing jobs."

Citing the NAFTA experience, which she believes led to a hemorrhaging of U.S. manufacturing jobs, she says today's free-trade agreements invariably bolster the rights of investors, who often are given incentives to relocate jobs abroad. In NAFTA's case, those jobs went to Canada and Mexico, she says. The agreements also will cost service-sector jobs, she says, through clauses that guarantee the free movement of data, which effectively bar countries from requiring that computer servers be located in their home territories. That leads to offshoring of engineering, actuarial and computer programming services, she says.

With average Vietnamese wages, for example, only about a third of Chinese pay levels, the offshoring problem will be especially relevant to the trans-Pacific agreement, Wallach says. She says trade accords should stop establishing dispute panels presided over by private-sector trade lawyers because such panels invariably side with investors, to the detriment of working conditions and human rights.

California Rep. Sherman said the growing trade deficit has displaced 2.8 million American jobs in recent years. In 2012, nearly two decades after NAFTA became effective, the United States ran a $31 billion goods trade deficit with Canada and a $62 billion goods trade deficit

Top U.S. Trading Partners: Canada, Mexico, China

Canada and Mexico spent more buying U.S. products in 2012 than any other countries, but the United States spent more importing goods from China and Canada than from anywhere else. The value of U.S. goods sold to the 11 countries negotiating the Trans-Pacific Partnership (TPP) trade agreement with the United States was more than five times the amount the United States sold to China in 2012.

Top U.S. Trade Partners, by Total Value of Goods,* 2012
(in $ billions)

U.S. Exports to:
Canada $292.5 • Mexico $215.9 • China $110.5 • Japan $70 • U.K. $54.8 • EU-28 $265.7 • TPP-11** $689.1

U.S. Imports from:
China $843.2 • Canada $425.6 • Mexico $323.9 • Japan $277.6 • Germany $146.4 • $1.8.7 • EU-28 $381.6 • TPP-11**

* Does not include trade in services or investments.

** Reflects totals for the 11 countries negotiating with the United States to form the Trans-Pacific Partnership trade pact. The countriesare Australia, Brunei, Chile, Canada, Japan, Malaysia, Mexico, New Zealand, Peru, Singapore and Vietnam.

Source: "Top U.S. Trade Partners," Foreign Trade Division, Census Bureau, U.S. Department of Commerce, www.trade.gov/mas/ian/build/groups/public/@tg_ian/documents/webcontent/tg_ian_003364.pdf

with Mexico, compared to a deficit before NAFTA of $10.8 billion with Canada and a surplus of $1.7 billion with Mexico.[16] And just a year after a U.S.-South Korea free-trade agreement entered into force, the United States experienced its highest-ever trade deficit with South Korea — $2.5 billion in May 2013.[17]

However, Ed Gerwin, a free-trade advocate from Third Way, a conservative Washington think tank, pointed out that oil imports, which comprise about a third of all imports, are the main contributor to the U.S. trade deficit. The United States actually runs a trade surplus in manufactured and agricultural goods, Gerwin noted.[18]

But Celeste Drake, a trade and globalization specialist at the AFL-CIO, the umbrella federation representing a large sector of U.S. organized labor, said NAFTA has cost the United States 700,000 jobs, China's accession in

2001 to the WTO cost 2.7 million U.S. jobs, and the U.S.-Korea deal 40,000 jobs, so far.[19]

"We are concerned that TPP [the Trans-Pacific Partnership] could repeat the mistakes made with NAFTA," Drake said, citing for example, Japan's refusal to open its car sector to foreign competition. To prevent negative impacts, Drake recommends inserting provisions such as retaining "buy American" government procurement regulations, opening markets only on a reciprocal basis and preventing currency manipulation.

"The U.S. cannot afford another trade agreement that hollows out our manufacturing base and adds to our substantial trade deficit," she concluded.

Can U.S. firms compete with state-owned companies?

In recent years Chinese state-owned banks have provided extremely generous loans to huge state-owned companies on terms that no commercial bank would grant. This oft-criticized practice gives Chinese companies an unfair advantage when they compete with private foreign companies in international trade, say competing companies and their governments.

And that is not a small problem: In China, the world's second-biggest economy after the United States, the government owns 37 of the largest 40 companies. Such enterprises not only benefit from cheap loans but often enjoy monopolies in their home markets, making them extremely hard for private companies to compete against in the global marketplace.

The WTO has been ill-equipped to referee disputes between countries on this issue because its rules were crafted in the 1990s, before China's meteoric rise.

"It's a real problem," U.S. Trade Representative Froman has said. While every country has some companies that are state owned or operated in some form, he said, the challenge is to prevent them from having a distorting impact on the market when they compete with private companies in selling their products or services in the international market.[20]

The Chamber of Commerce's Murphy calls the rise of state capitalism and state-owned enterprises "increasingly worrisome" and insists it be addressed in the trans-Pacific trade pact.

Robert Zoellick, former U.S. trade representative (2001-2005) and president of the World Bank (2007-2012), has suggested that the trans-Pacific pact be used as leverage on this issue, given that China is not part of the pact yet but might like to join.[21]

However, some believe complaints about state-owned companies killing off private competition are overstated.

Michael Blanding, a Boston-based investigative journalist and author, noted that the number of companies controlled or owned by governments is declining — in China, as well as in Russia, Australia, Canada, France and Japan. It is becoming more common, he wrote, for governments to keep a minority share in companies.[22]

But Heriberto Araújo and Juan Pablo Cardenal, China-based journalists who have written a book on the subject, contend that China's command-and-control industrial policy enabled it in 2012 to overtake the United States and become the world's largest trading nation (as measured by the sum of exports and imports).[23] The Chinese government also now controls oil and gas pipelines from Turkmenistan to China and from South Sudan to the Red Sea. The government-owned Chinese firm Cosco manages the main cargo terminal in Greece's largest port, Piraeus; and a Chinese sovereign wealth fund, C.I.C., has a 10 percent stake in London's Heathrow Airport.[24]

Beijing's reach even extends to the Arctic. Greenland has awarded a Chinese firm the contract to exploit its enormous mining resources — using Chinese workers who will earn less than the minimum wage — because no one else could match China's investment offer.[25]

Change may be on the horizon. Brookings' Meltzer believes China is in the process of curbing its subsidization of domestic industry. "China has a mixed economic model," he says, meaning that it is partly free-market oriented and partly state-controlled. "And Chinese officials are discussing reform to redress the imbalance created by relying too much on government investment and not enough on private consumption to grow the economy," Meltzer says.

According to the EU's Clancy, the Trans-Pacific Partnership could be a catalyst for such reform, while the U.S.-EU trade pact can also serve as "a laboratory" for how to deal with the issue. He hopes the EU and United States can "define and further develop the international rule book" on state-owned enterprises.

The first task will be to define what a state-owned enterprise is, he says, and then negotiators will have to agree on what constitutes noncompetitive behavior. As these discussions lead to common understandings, it could help the WTO develop fair rules for global trade involving state-owned and subsidized companies, he believes.

Something needs to be done, argued the AFL-CIO's Drake, because under existing trade law the United States cannot take action against a foreign state-owned enterprise that uses government subsidies to establish a factory in the United States and then produces products below the cost of a U.S. firm. For instance, she said, a Chinese state-owned company, Tianjin Pipe, recently broke ground on a $1 billion facility in Texas to produce seamless pipe to transport oil and gas.[26]

But as U.S. Sen. Jeff Flake, R-Ariz., notes, the United States provides farmers billions of dollars a year in government subsidies. In fact, he said, for the past three years the United States has spent $150 million a year subsidizing Brazilian cotton farmers to comply with a WTO ruling requiring the United States to either stop subsidizing American farmers or subsidize Brazilians farmers as well.[27]

Thus, Drake predicted, there would be "strong resistance" among the other Pacific negotiating partners to including a provision in the treaty allowing countries to enact laws aimed at blocking foreign state-owned companies from killing off domestic competition.[28]

Does expanding free trade help promote human rights and democracy?

Proponents of free trade have often argued that opening up global markets eventually leads to democracy. When a country opens up to outside manufacturers, their argument goes, prices for goods and commodities fall, leading to higher living standards. As citizens become wealthier they begin to demand greater personal freedom and push for an end to human rights abuses.

But experts disagree over what impact the European and Pacific regional trade agreements will have on human rights and democracy in the real world.

U.S.-European Pact Would Be World's Largest

The Transatlantic Trade and Investment Partnership (TTIP) between the United States and the 28-member European Union would be the biggest bilateral free-trade pact in the world, affecting 40 percent of the global economy. The Trans-Pacific Partnership (TPP) being negotiated among the United States and 11 other Asian and Pacific Rim countries would dwarf the 1994 North American Free Trade Agreement (NAFTA) among the United States, Canada and Mexico.

Comparison of Trade Pacts, by Population and GDP

Trade Agreement	No. of Countries	Population	GDP
TTIP	29	821 million	$33 trillion
TPP	12	792 million	$28 trillion
NAFTA	3	465 million	$19 trillion

Sources: Brock R. Williams, "Trans-Pacific Partnership (TPP) Countries: Comparative Trade and Economic Analysis," Congressional Research Service, June 10, 2013, p. 5; World Economic Outlook, International Monetary Fund, April 2013; CIA *World Factbook*

In the case of the European pact, it is less of an issue because the two negotiating partners represent mostly mature democracies with relatively high rankings on human rights.

Within the trans-Pacific pact, however, one of the negotiating partners is Vietnam, which regularly is accused of using child labor and paying sub-poverty wages in its textile sector, which employs 2 million people. In addition, the nongovernmental watchdog group Worker Rights Consortium has reported that some factory owners, to avoid paying maternity benefits, force female employees to sign contracts in which they agree not to become pregnant.[29] The average wage for workers in Vietnam's footwear industry is $124 a month, well below the estimated $220 it takes to buy food for a family of three; the government prosecutes those who try to form independent labor unions.[30]

"Vietnam is the dictatorship of the proletariat," said U.S. Rep. Dana Rohrabacher, a conservative Republican from California. He doubts Vietnam would become freer if the United States traded with it more, adding, "It didn't work with China."[31]

Free-trade critics such as Rohrabacher complain that China's trade-fueled economic prosperity has led to little progress toward democracy.

CNN political analyst Fareed Zakaria also pointed out recently that China's authoritarian capitalist model has enabled it to allocate money earned from its massive trade surplus for long-term domestic infrastructure projects. Were China a democracy beholden to voters, he argued, it would have had to use more of that money to subsidize consumer goods.[32]

But Brookings' Meltzer predicts that democracy will come later to China, as higher living standards brought about by increased trade gradually foment greater popular demand for freedom.

USTR spokeswoman Guthrie says the Pacific and European trade pacts will address "many trade-related priorities such as development, transparency, workers' rights and protections, environmental protection and conservation."

And the AFL-CIO's Drake noted that the United States obtained some commitments on improved labor rights in previous trade pacts and that some of those commitments have become progressively stronger. For example, she said, if U.S. negotiators use the Peruvian free-trade agreement signed in 2006 as a floor of minimum standards, the trans-Pacific pact could become a vehicle for strengthening workers' rights.[33]

However, labor rights in Mexico deteriorated after passage of NAFTA, she argued, and an action plan on labor enshrined in the 2012 U.S.-Colombia free-trade agreement "is not making much difference on the ground."[34]

Public Citizen's Wallach pinpoints another problem with free-trade agreements: They take decisions out of the hands of elected officials by locking in treaties that do not allow lawmakers to change a word. For instance, the European Parliament in July 2012 rejected an Anti-Counterfeiting Trade Agreement (ACTA), approved earlier by the WTO, because EU lawmakers were excluded from the talks. Yet, Wallach predicts that much of ACTA's substance will be inserted into the U.S.-EU trade pact.

EU trade spokesman Clancy says negotiators have learned from the ACTA experience and "the aim is to be more transparent as we work through the U.S.-EU areement. For example, the EU side has published its initial position papers on different areas, such as services and investment."

Wallach also worries that investor-state dispute settlement panels, which have been suggested for the trans-Pacific and European pacts, would have a detrimental impact on the environment and conditions for workers. Judges are replaced by trade lawyers on the panels, which rule on legal battles between governments and investors over such issues as local minimum-wage laws and bans on mining toxic chemicals.[35] Because of who presides over them, the dispute settlement panels' decisions often are skewed to favor investors over governments, argues Public Citizen, a consumer group that has compiled a database of such cases brought under NAFTA. The suits include cases filed by a tobacco manufacturer, a wind energy firm, a high-fructose corn syrup producer and a metal smelter. In the 80 documented cases, governments ended up paying $405.4 million to investors in compensation settlements for lost profits arising from local laws that restrict foreign investment.[36]

Furthermore, says Wallach, even if the investor loses a case, the government — and thus the taxpayers — ends up paying huge legal fees. As a result, sometimes the mere threat of an investor filing such a case leads a government to ditch a planned law, Wallach says.

BACKGROUND

Evolving Trade Policy

When the United States was founded, mercantilism was the prevailing trade philosophy.[37]

Conceived in Europe in the late Middle Ages, mercantilism held that exports were good because they brought gold and silver into a country, while imports were bad because they did not add value to the economy. Characterized by high import duties, mercantilism encouraged governments to control foreign trade in order to promote national security and motivated much of Europe's colonial expansion during the 16th to 18th centuries. For example, the state-sponsored Dutch East India Co., which greatly increased Dutch trade with modern-day Indonesia in the 1600s and 1700s, helped the Netherlands accumulate great wealth.

By the late 1700s, however, newer theories about free trade, developed by Scottish economic philosophers David Hume and Adam Smith, were beginning to supplant mercantilism. Hume and Smith maintained that private enterprise paved the way toward more freedom and wealth and that it was better for states if their neighbors also became wealthy trading nations. Their ideas were slowly distilled into concrete policies in the 1800s, and governments began to reduce tariffs — notably the United Kingdom repealed duties on grain imports in 1846.

The United States, from its first piece of trade legislation — the 1789 Tariff Act under which relatively mild tariffs were introduced — pursued a mixed approach on trade policy. The more industrialized North supported tariffs to promote domestic manufacturing, while the agricultural South pushed for eliminating tariffs to encourage cotton, rice and tobacco exports. The North-South split on trade helped precipitate the Civil War (1861-1865).

By the late 1800s, with U.S. industry booming, an era of high tariffs was dawning. Custom duties averaged 57 percent in 1897 and accounted for half of all federal revenues. After briefly declining in the early 1900s, tariff rates rose rapidly again during World War I (1914-18) and throughout the 1920s, when depressed farm prices created protectionist political pressures.

Throughout this period, the Republicans, the dominant party in the North, pushed protectionist measures in Congress and fought fierce battles with the more free-trade-oriented Southern Democrats. The last time Congress imposed import duties was in 1930 through the Smoot-Hawley Tariff Act, which established tariffs averaging 59 percent on some 20,000 products. Europe retaliated by raising its tariffs on U.S. products, causing world trade to decline to a third of its 1929 level.[38] This trade war helped deepen the Great Depression in the early 1930s, as U.S. exports and imports slumped to early 1900 levels.

Since that economic nadir, every American president has resisted protectionism. President Franklin Delano Roosevelt pushed the Reciprocal Trade Agreements Act through Congress in 1934, which transferred authority for setting tariff rates from Congress to the president.

During the 1930s, the United States passed important labor legislation, such as the 1935 National Labor Relations Act, which protected the right of collective bargaining, and the 1938 Fair Labor Standards Act, which forbade employment of children under 16 years of age during school hours and established a minimum wage. During World War II (1939-'45), trade flows were

South Korean Kias are unloaded in Brunswick, Ga., on, Aug. 16, 2013. While the United States continues to import toys, cars and steel from big Asian producers, it also is expanding market share in fields such as financial services, software and engineering. However, the U.S. is still running a $414 billion deficit in the amount of goods imported vs. those exported.

determined more by military alliances than by commercial factors.

Eliminating Tariffs

In 1946, as Europe and East Asia lay in ruins, the new U.S. president, Harry S. Truman, threw his weight behind an international conference convened in Geneva to expand world trade. It led to the signing of the General Agreement on Tariffs and Trade (GATT) by 23 countries on Oct. 30, 1947.

Over the next half-century, GATT helped to reduce tariffs on manufactured goods worldwide. It also established international rules imposing so-called anti-dumping duties on imports to protect domestic industries. "Dumping" is a predatory pricing policy in which manufacturers attempt

CHRONOLOGY

1776-1934 *U.S. gains independence from Great Britain, emerges as the world's leading trading nation.*

1789 U.S. Tariff Act imposes relatively mild tariffs on imports.

1846 United Kingdom repeals duties on food imports, signaling the rise of free trade.

1861 U.S. Civil War begins, pitting industrial North against agricultural South on slavery as well as divisions over trade policy.

1930 U.S. Smoot-Hawley Tariff Act imposes tariffs averaging 59 percent on 20,000 products. World trade slows, deepening the Great Depression.

1934 Reciprocal Trade Agreement Act lets president set tariff rates.

1947-1993 *World trade becomes freer as tariffs are reduced, eliminated.*

1947 Twenty-three countries sign General Agreement on Tariffs and Trade (GATT), aiming to boost trade by reducing tariffs. It eventually achieves its mission, while expanding membership.

1974 Trade Act gives president so-called fast-track authority to submit trade agreements to Congress for a single up or down vote.

1978 China's new leader, Deng Xiaoping, opens his country of some 1 billion people to world markets.

1991 After Soviet Union collapses, Russia and former communist-bloc countries embrace free-market capitalism.

1993 President Bill Clinton signs North American Free Trade Agreement (NAFTA) into law, liberalizing trade among U.S., Canada and Mexico.

1995-2008 *A backlash against free trade develops in Europe and the United States as companies outsource jobs to lower-wage economies in Asia and Latin America.*

1995 GATT is reconstituted into the World Trade Organization (WTO).

1999 At a November meeting in Seattle, WTO members fail to agree to new round of trade-liberalization talks after the city is rocked by protests by grassroots organizations. Talks finally begin in Doha, Qatar, in 2001.

2001 China joins WTO, gaining greater access to global markets, which it fully exploits to become the world's second-largest economy after the United States.

2008 The financial crisis and a deep recession create strong protectionist pressures. After years of lackluster progress, WTO's Doha Round of talks collapses.

2009-Present *Bilateral and regional free-trade pacts become more popular as the WTO fails to deliver a new world-trade agreement.*

2009 President Obama signs off on an $80 billion government bailout and restructuring package to prevent the U.S. auto industry from bankruptcy.

2010 U.S. participates in talks for a massive regional trade agreement, the Trans-Pacific Partnership, with 11 Asian and Pacific Rim nations.

2011 Congress approves free-trade agreements with Colombia, Panama and South Korea after Obama finally submits them, marking the end of a four-year gap in promoting new trade agreements.

2012 Swayed by a grassroots campaign against it, European Parliament rejects an Anti-Counterfeiting Trade Agreement (ACTA) negotiated at the WTO by a group of mostly advanced economies that includes the United States.

2013 United States and European Union begin talks on the Transatlantic Trade and Investment Partnership. . . . Japan, the world's third-largest economy, joins in the Trans-Pacific Partnership free-trade talks, scheduled to conclude in December. . . . Brazilian Roberto Azevêdo becomes the first Latin American head of the WTO.

2014 U.S.-EU trade pact scheduled to be completed in October.

to put competitors out of business by selling their products at below cost. Under GATT, trade disputes could be mediated, but there was no mechanism for enforcing GATT agreements.

Two other international institutions were conceived at the same time to help forge a more liberalized economic order: the International Monetary Fund (IMF) to regulate exchange rates and the World Bank to provide loans to developing countries.[39]

GATT made progress during "rounds" of negotiations to cut tariffs. Notable successes were the Kennedy Round (1962-1967), named after President John F. Kennedy, and the Tokyo Round (1973 to 1979).

By the late 1960s, however, protectionist sentiment was on the rise again in the United States after the stellar postwar recovery of Western Europe and Japan made them serious trade rivals, notably in the auto and steel sectors, where they were beginning to expand their exports to the United States.

Under the 1974 Trade Act, the U.S. president was granted so-called fast-track authority to conclude trade agreements and submit them to Congress for a single yea or nay vote without the possibility of amendments.

Meanwhile, communist countries — where trade with the United States was limited — watched as capitalist economies outpaced their own. Many decided they needed to adapt their economic models to avoid falling behind.

China was the first to change course, when in 1978 leader Deng Xiaoping opened the world's most populous country to global trade. Communist Vietnam began transitioning to a socialist-oriented market economy in 1986. The collapse of the Soviet Union in 1991 led Russia and the Eastern bloc countries to embrace their own versions of free-market capitalism.[40]

During the GATT Uruguay Round (1986-1994), tariffs were reduced even further, and the decision was made to transform GATT into the World Trade Organization, with the power to enforce trade agreements and settle disputes. With tariffs already at historically low levels, countries began redirecting their energies toward removing nontariff barriers, such as regulations on manufacturing standards and government subsidies.

In 1985 the United States for the first time agreed to remove all trade tariffs with another country when it signed a free-trade agreement with Israel. In 1988 a U.S.-Canada free-trade agreement sowed the seeds for NAFTA.

Adding Mexico to the pact was controversial, because many in the United States worried — which later proved warranted — that domestic manufacturing would head south of the border to take advantage of lower wages and production costs.

After a fractious debate, Congress ratified NAFTA in November 1993 by a vote of 234 to 200 in the House, and by 61-38 in the Senate. President Bill Clinton signed the measure into law on Dec. 8, 1993.[41]

Globalization Backlash

The 1990s marked the beginning of a new era of globalization characterized by an increasingly integrated global economy — spurred in part by the rapid growth of the Internet and marked by an upsurge in free trade and the free flow of capital and access to cheaper overseas labor markets. Countries in Asia and Latin America — including Chile, China, Mexico and South Korea — enjoyed robust growth, often fueled by a surge in exports.

Booming exports helped China lift nearly 600 million citizens out of poverty in the 1990s and 2000s, while extreme poverty in Vietnam fell from 64 to 17 percent between 1993 and 2008.[42]

China got another big boost in 2001, when it was allowed to join the WTO despite lingering concerns about its dismal human rights record and widespread fears that its huge pool of cheap labor would allow it to seriously undercut competitors.

Meanwhile, buoyed by NAFTA, Mexico boosted its trade with Canada eightfold, energizing its auto, electronics, aerospace and medical devices sectors.[43]

It was during this period that the word "outsourcing" entered the popular lexicon, commonly used to mean manufacturers in high-paying advanced economies shifting production to lower-wage countries such as Mexico or China. While outsourcing generated heavy criticism at home because of the job losses, defenders of globalized production stressed that it lowered prices for consumer goods, greatly benefitting low-income populations worldwide.

But anti-globalization sentiments grew as globalization increasingly became associated in the United States and Europe with job losses and backsliding in worker, consumer and environmental protections. Some companies — including major retailers such as Nike — were paying sub-poverty-level wages to overseas workers, and

Tiny Nanoparticles Have Big Trade Implications

U.S. and EU differ on labeling nanoproducts.

Tiny particles and machines — so small they are invisible to the naked eye — may trigger a dustup in U.S.-European trade relations.

Nanotechnology — the science of creating molecule-size machines and materials — involves the use of particles less than 100 nanometers long, or 80,000 times smaller than the width of a human hair.*

Nanoparticles are used in foods, beverages, toys, electrical appliances, beauty products and a wide range of other consumer and industrial products. For instance, nanotitanium makes sunscreen invisible when applied to the skin, nanocrystals enhance the clarity of liquid crystal display screens and silver ions kill microbes and control odor in washing machines.

Such nanoproducts are made by U.S. and foreign manufacturers and traded worldwide. But the United States and European Union (EU) differ on how to regulate them, presenting a dilemma for trade negotiators.

The nanotech industry has been growing rapidly, especially in the past decade. The United States has been the market leader, according to Hilary Flynn, a senior analyst at Lux Research, a Boston-based research and consultancy firm specializing in emerging technologies, with sales of nano-enabled products worldwide projected to soar to $650 billion in 2015, up from $10 billion in 2004.[1] Flynn estimates that about 540,000 U.S. manufacturing jobs depended on nanotechnology in 2010, a figure she expects to grow to 3.1 million by 2015.[2]

And Europe is catching up fast, with revenue from nano-enabled products projected to surpass the United States by 2015. The number of products containing nanomaterials sold in the European Union reached 475 in 2010,

---

* A nanometer is one-billionth of a meter.

up 300 percent from a year earlier, according to the European Consumers' Organisation, a Brussels-based group of 41 independent consumer organizations from 31 European countries.[3] Asian and Pacific countries also are beginning to develop nanotech products.

However, some scientists warn that nanotechnology poses environmental and health risks, especially for workers or consumers breathing in the tiny particles. Consumer groups want products containing nanotech ingredients regulated and labeled, even though the products themselves may already be regulated.[4] Without regulation, consumers become the industry's guinea pigs, the groups say.

"[H]undreds of products [are] on sale on the European market containing nanomaterials without any assessments . . . of the risks that these may pose to public health," said Monique Goyens, managing director of the European Consumers' Organisation. "We need to put an end to this public-safety 'Russian roulette.'"[5]

The U.S. Food and Drug Administration (FDA) regulates nano-ingredients contained in food, cosmetics and veterinary and tobacco products, while the U.S. Environmental Protection Agency (EPA) has jurisdiction over nanoproducts used in industrial chemicals and pesticides. So far, the FDA's position has been that nanoproducts do not need to be labeled.

But the European Union has been sympathetic to environmentalists' concerns. The EU embraces the "precautionary principle" under which products are kept off the market until manufacturers prove they are safe. In the United States, the approach varies depending on the sector being regulated. For industrial chemicals, for example, the regulatory burden lies with the EPA to show risk, whereas with pesticides it is up to manufacturers to show they are safe.

Beginning in July, the EU required that all nanomaterials in cosmetics be labeled. But the leading U.S. cosmetics

---

unregulated mining and dumping of toxic chemicals were harming local environments.

When the WTO met in Seattle in November 1999 to start a new round of trade liberalization talks, the city was rocked by protests organized by grassroots organizations from around the world. For a while, Seattle

resembled a battle zone: 500 protesters were arrested, and massive property damage occurred. Delegates from the WTO's 135 member countries left the city without even launching a new round of talks.

In July 2001 the G8 world economic summit in Genoa — attended by leaders of the eight largest global

industry lobby, the Personal Care Products Council, contends that such labels are an unnecessary burden on manufacturers. Because U.S.-made cosmetics have been tested and approved by the FDA, it said, there is no need to test each individual ingredient separately.

Moreover, the council's representative told a public hearing on a pending U.S.-EU free-trade pact in May that if the EU requires nano-ingredients to be labeled, it will set a precedent because when the EU makes policies, "other countries tend to replicate them."

Lynn Bergeson, a lawyer who helps U.S. companies get their nanotech innovations approved by regulators, says labeling nano-ingredients would "not necessarily impart information that is useful to the consumer who wants to know if there is an enhanced risk associated with it." Nevertheless, she notes, some U.S. nanotech companies have voluntarily labeled their products to reduce the risk of being sued in states that generally have strong consumer protection laws.

At a networking event during the U.S.-EU trade talks in July, Karen Hansen-Kuhn, international program director at the Minnesota-based Institute for Agriculture and Trade Policy, a nongovernmental group promoting sustainable farming, urged the United States to adopt the EU's precautionary principle on nanotech foods. She said some 2,000 food products contain nanoparticles, citing as an example nanotitanium, which is used in donuts as a coloring in powdered sugar coating.[6]

But Bergeson doubts the nanosector will become a new headache in trans-Atlantic trade relations. The industry is working to educate both American and European consumers on the issue, she says, and there is already some common ground between European and American regulators, such as in the pesticides sector.

Many people watching the progress on the U.S.-EU trade pact say that how the two sides handle the nanotech issue could have a major impact on the industry's development. Others say it could set the stage for future global regulation of new technologies. Hansen-Kuhn said the situation is urgent.

A technician at the nanotechnology firm temicon GmbH in Dortmund, Germany, examines a microscreen used in the medical technology and foodstuffs industries. Foods, beverages, toys, electrical appliances and beauty products containing nanoparticles are made by U.S. and foreign manufacturers and traded worldwide. U.S. and European Union regulators differ on how to ensure they are safe, however, presenting a dilemma for trade negotiators.

"More research needs to be done before this enters our food system — not after," she argued.[7]

— *Brian Beary*

[1]Hilary Flynn, "U.S. Continues to be a Nanotech Leader, but Losing Ground to EU and Emerging Economies," Powerpoint presentation, Nanotechnology Caucus Briefing, Washington, D.C., Nov. 15, 2011.

[2]*Ibid.*

[3]Sophie Petitjean, "Nanomaterials products triple," *Europolitics*, Oct. 25, 2013, www.europolitics.info//nanomaterials-products-triple-art285257-12.html. For background, see David Masci, "Nanotechnology," *CQ Researcher*, June 11, 2004, pp. 517-540.

[4]Ophélie Spanneut, "Nanomaterials: Case-by-case approach to safety assessment," *Europolitics*, Oct. 3, 2012.

[5]Petitjean, *op. cit.*

[6]Andy Behar, "Study the use of nanoparticles in food," CNN, Feb. 14, 2013, www.cnn.com/2013/02/14/opinion/behar-food-nanoparticles.

[7]Hansen-Kuhn was speaking at a stakeholders' conference on July 10, 2013, organized by the Office of the U.S. Trade Representative to coincide with the launch of the opening round of negotiations on the Transatlantic Trade and Investment Partnership in Washington, D.C.

economies — attracted 150,000 anti-globalization protesters. Italian police stormed a school where about 100 demonstrators were sleeping, leading to mass beatings even though the protesters had been peaceful. Elsewhere, police shot dead a 23-year-old protester during street clashes.[44]

Organizers held the next big WTO meeting in Doha, Qatar, a remote, autocratic state in the Persian Gulf, to make it harder for protesters to mobilize. The Doha Round of trade talks was launched in 2001, but it failed to make progress. This was less because of anti-globalization opposition, however, and more because

Will the World Trade Organization Survive?

Regional trade deals imperil the 159-nation forum, say some trade specialists.

"We're not dead yet." Michael Punke, the U.S. ambassador to the World Trade Organization (WTO), did not quite offer a ringing endorsement of the Geneva-based body in July.[1] But if the WTO is not dead, there are many who believe it to be on life support — at least as a forum for eliminating trade barriers.

The pessimism largely stems from the failure of the WTO's so-called Doha Round of talks to lower global trade barriers. The talks, which began in Doha, Qatar, in 2001, stalled in 2008. While "there is no monopoly on disappointment in the Doha Round," Punke said, "if the WTO members have not exactly shrouded themselves in glory, they have at least kept the ship afloat."

The WTO was created in 1995 as a reincarnation of the General Agreement on Tariffs and Trade (GATT), the 1947 treaty that sought to reduce trade tariffs between nations. GATT's remarkable success led to great expectations for the WTO, which has the additional power to enforce trade agreements and adjudicate disputes.

But trade liberalization efforts were spectacularly derailed when the WTO's flagship project, the Doha Round, collapsed after emerging economies such as China and India grew increasingly assertive and refused to accept the terms pushed by the more industrialized countries.

Now, the organization has decidedly downsized its ambitions for the upcoming WTO ministerial meeting, scheduled for this December in Bali, Indonesia.

According to U.S. Trade Representative Michael Froman, the question is, "Can we land a small package?" at the Bali meeting. That "package" would be composed of separate agreements designed to streamline border and customs procedures and expand trade in services and information technology products.[2] If those efforts fail, it will be "very difficult" for the WTO to move forward, Froman warned.

Recent events give little cause for optimism. With support from more than 70 countries, the WTO agreed in 1996 to abolish tariffs on information- and communication-technology products. But this summer's talks to expand that agreement to cover new products such as DVDs, video cameras and video game consoles suffered a setback, further sapping confidence in the WTO's capacity to deliver deals. Froman said he was "extremely disappointed" that the talks were suspended after China proposed excluding 106 products from the agreement's scope.

Some believe the proliferation of bilateral and regional trade agreements, forged in national capitals rather than at WTO headquarters in Geneva, further undermines the organization's authority. The latest examples are two major regional pacts currently under negotiation: the Trans-Pacific

emerging economies such as Brazil, India and China began to drive harder bargains with the United States and the EU. For example, they refused to give in to trans-Atlantic demands that they open their markets on a reciprocal basis.

Regional Pacts

The financial crisis of 2008 led to the demise of the Doha Round, as the recession that gripped the United States and Europe from late 2007 to 2009 triggered rising protectionist demands. The global appetite for a comprehensive world-trade agreement seemed to have evaporated for the time being.

Governments for the most part managed to resist resurgent protectionism, however, and the trade liberalization agenda found a new forum — or forums. Countries began signing new bilateral and regional free-trade pacts.

The EU and Asia were especially active on this front. For example, since 2000 China has sought free-trade deals with India and South Korea and finalized pacts with the ASEAN trading bloc of 10 Southeast Asian nations. In the United States, President George W. Bush had initialed free-trade agreements with Colombia, Panama, Peru and South Korea in the mid-2000s but managed to get Congress to ratify only the Peru deal before leaving office in January 2009.

Partnership, which involves the United States and 11 Asian and Pacific Rim countries, and the Transatlantic Trade and Investment Partnership between the United States and the European Union.

However, former U.S. Trade Representative Carla Hills, who negotiated the North American Free Trade Agreement (NAFTA) for President George H. W. Bush, put a more optimistic spin on the trade regionalization trend.[3] She recalled how in 1990 many in GATT were despondent when the Uruguay Round of trade liberalization talks hit a roadblock. But after the United States, Canada and Mexico agreed to the North American Free Trade Agreement (NAFTA) in December 1992 (Congress ratified it a year later), GATT negotiators were inspired to get things moving again. The Uruguay Round recovered and a deal was concluded, which led to the establishment of the WTO.

Hills suggested that regional agreements being negotiated could be partly integrated into the WTO framework. For instance, the U.S.-EU pact could adopt the WTO's dispute-settlement mechanism rather than creating its own. Hills pointed out that the WTO's dispute-adjudication panels have "put a ceiling on retaliation" by governments over perceived violations of trade rules. "If we did not have that, we would have the law of the jungle," she said.

As for Europe, America's biggest trading partner, EU trade spokesman John Clancy insists "the multilateral [i.e. WTO] route is by far our preference" in solving trade disputes. But deals negotiated outside of the WTO, he says, can become "an embryo of real international standards" that could then be transposed into a multilateral setting. Privately,

most trade officials admit that the current situation, in which dozens of free-trade pacts are being concluded by a dizzying constellation of countries, is not optimal.

But who is to say the WTO, having taken many unexpected turns in recent years, will not surprise again? On Sept. 1 Brazilian Roberto Azevêdo became its new director general, the first Latin American to head the organization. His daunting challenge: to restore the WTO's reputation as the premier venue for forging a world of freer trade.

"The WTO and the multilateral trading system are at an important crossroads," Azevêdo said in his welcome message. "The choices that the WTO's 159 members make in the coming months will determine the path we take as we set out together to strengthen and support the multilateral trading system."[4]

— *Brian Beary*

---

[1]Speech at the WTO's Trade Negotiating Committee, Office of the U.S. Trade Representative, Geneva, Switzerland, July 22, 2013, www.ustr.gov/about-us/press-office/speeches/transcripts/2013/july/amb-punke-WTO-tnc.

[2]Speech at a discussion on the U.S. trade agenda, U.S. Chamber of Commerce, Washington, D.C. July 30, 2013; www.uschamber.com/webcasts/next-steps-american-trade-agenda-2.

[3]Hills was a keynote speaker at a discussion on "A North America-European Union Free Trade Agreement?" Woodrow Wilson Center for International Scholars, July 26, 2013, www.wilsoncenter.org/event/north-america-european-union-free-trade-agreement.

[4]"Roberto Azevêdo takes over," World Trade Organisation, Sept. 1, 2013, http://wto.org/english/news_e/news13_e/dgra_13aug13_e.htm.

President Obama, responding to pressure from labor unions and other constituents within his Democratic Party, tweaked the deals with Colombia, Panama and South Korea before finally sending them to Congress. All three agreements were approved in October 2011.

Meanwhile, the U.S. share of exports to rapidly growing East Asia plummeted 42.4 percent between 2000 and 2010 as the United States fell behind other emerging and advanced economies in forging new trade agreements with countries in the region. For instance, at the same time, Russia's share of exports increased by 50 percent, Australia's by 42.7 percent and Saudi Arabia's by 28 percent.[45]

But it was not all bad news for the United States on trade. After a decade of job losses, U.S. manufacturing has been recovering since 2009, with half a million jobs added in Obama's first term.[46]

As a case in point, USTR Froman recently toured a New Balance running shoe factory in Maine, noting that "they are employing more than ever before" and "making improvements to the production process." Froman's trip was designed to showcase a major success story in this sector and to counter the oft-heard narrative about the supposed decline of American manufacturing.

Such success was a vindication of Obama's policy of enforcing trade laws more aggressively, having brought 18 trade complaints before the WTO thus far, Froman said.[47] Similarly, the Obama administration claimed credit for helping to revive the Detroit-based U.S. auto sector with an $80 billion government bailout and restructuring package for General Motors and Chrysler in 2009.[48]

CURRENT SITUATION

Declining Deficit

The generally positive trajectory in the U.S. economy continues. In early August the Obama administration announced a significant rise in exports and manufacturing output and a declining trade deficit and unemployment rate. Between May and June, the monthly trade deficit fell 22 percent, to $34.2 billion, its lowest one-month deficit since the fall of 2009. However, an imbalance between the goods and services sectors continues, with the United States running a $414 billion deficit (January to July, 2013) in the amount of goods imported vs. the amount of goods exported and a $134 billion surplus in services exported.[49] Thus, while Americans continue to import lots of toys, cars and steel from big Asian producers like China and Japan, they also are harnessing their high-skilled workforce to expand market share in fields such as financial services, software and engineering.

Meanwhile, between July and August the jobless rate fell from 7.4 percent to 7.3 percent — its lowest level since Obama took office.[50] In total, 7.5 million jobs have been created in the past 42 months, the White House has pointed out, but economists say some of the unemployment decline represents people who have simply stopped looking for work.[51]

"We're exporting more to all sorts of different countries," wrote Ryan Avent, economics correspondent for *The Economist*. The declining trade deficit "didn't come from just one set of products or one set of countries." Moreover, he said, the export surge suggests that the recovery is "sustainable," and "less based on government support . . . [or] borrowing and consumption."[52]

While U.S. economic growth picks up, China's extraordinary growth rate is beginning to taper, as rising wages cause China to lose its competitive edge, and global demand for its exports slows.[53] Even so, the latest IMF forecast says the U.S. economy will grow by nearly 2 percent in 2013, compared to almost 8 percent for China.

Trade Talks

The successful launch of U.S.-EU trade talks in July was almost thwarted by a spat over U.S. government spying. In May former National Security Agency (NSA) computer specialist Edward Snowden revealed that the United States, as part of its counter-terrorism efforts, had monitored the emails of millions of Europeans. The revelations caused consternation among EU governments and the European Parliament.[54] Historically protectionist France — which has more misgivings about the trade pact than the EU's other big economies, Germany and the U.K. — initially called for postponing the talks. Ultimately the French backed down after the Germans and British insisted that the agreed timetable be honored. The EU and United States instead set up a separate working group to discuss the data-privacy implications of the NSA spy programs.

Trade representative Froman expects the "most challenging part" of the talks to be the discussions on regulatory cooperation. There are major differences between the U.S and EU systems in this area, he noted, with U.S. standard-setting bodies mostly private-sector based, whereas in Europe they tend to be quasi-governmental.[55]

Agriculture will be one of the most sensitive sectors. U.S. producers of genetically modified (GM) food and feed hope to reduce the time it takes to get their products approved by the EU, but they are pragmatic enough to realize that expecting a complete overhaul of the EU's GM labeling and tracing laws is unrealistic. U.S. farmers also hope to stymie EU efforts to extend special protection to products such as Greek feta cheese. "Geographic indication" protection rules aim to prohibit U.S. producers from using certain geographical terms (such as "Camembert" cheese) on their labels because the American-made products are not actually made in those regions.

Audio-visual services are another hot button issue, with France particularly keen to ensure that its system of quotas, which limit the number of non-French-language movies that can be screened in cinemas and on television in France, be preserved. In talks earlier in 2013 among EU member states, Paris managed to get some reassurances to this effect. However, it remains something of a bone of contention, and the EU says it has the right to return to its member governments during negotiations to ask for its mandate to be extended to cover the audio-visual sector.[56]

Have regional and bilateral trade agreements usurped the WTO?

YES
Kent H. Hughes
Director, Program on America and the Global Economy, Woodrow Wilson International Center for Scholars

Written for *CQ Researcher*, September 2013

NO
Daniel Ikenson
Director, Herbert A. Stiefel Center for Trade Policy Studies, Cato Institute

Written for *CQ Researcher*, September 2013

The World Trade Organization (WTO) is under attack, not for what is has done but for its failure to deal with new challenges to international trade. Regional trade and bilateral trade agreements have surged as a result. Beyond specific rules, large trade imbalances, currency manipulation and significant investment incentives all demand action. There is a risk of a weakened WTO or one that becomes increasingly irrelevant to global trade.

There is promise, however, in the ability of bilateral and regional free-trade agreements to develop new governing rules for international trade that can, in turn, create a new structure for the WTO.

The current structure of trade rules is based on the assumption of competitive free markets with limited intervention by national governments. With the rise of Japan, an alternate approach to growth has arisen, often referred to as the East Asian Miracle. China is now practicing its own variant of this approach.

State-owned and state-influenced enterprises now play a significant and growing role in international trade. Currencies are kept undervalued — acting as a subsidy to exports and a barrier to imports. Generous tax and other subsidies are used to attract high-technology factories and research facilities from the United States and other advanced industrial countries. Rampant intellectual property theft, the impact of trade on the environment, labor and the distribution of the fruits of global growth all raise concerns.

Instead of attempting to fashion new rules at the 159-member WTO, small clusters of countries can work on developing rules that will eventually command global respect. The ongoing Trans-Pacific Partnership trade negotiations are exploring rules for state-owned enterprises, intellectual property and digital data and may explore the reality of undervalued currencies. The recently launched Transatlantic Trade and Investment Partnership holds out the potential for harmonizing a host of regulatory rules that could become a global, WTO-sanctioned standard.

Regional trade negotiations can be a laboratory for trade rules that will revitalize the WTO. Jagdish Bhagwati, the eminent trade economist from Columbia University, has decried the proliferation of free-trade agreements as a spaghetti bowl of international trade. Adding the experimental sauce of regional trade agreements can make that spaghetti bowl a tasty meal for a 21st-century WTO.

Since the World Trade Organization was born in 1995, multilateral negotiations to reduce trade barriers have borne no fruit, while bilateral and regional trade agreements have flourished. Some 216 such "preferential" deals have come into force since 1995, with dozens more at various stages of negotiation.

Preferential agreements — especially large ones expected to break new ground, such as the Trans-Pacific Partnership (TPP) and the Transatlantic Trade and Investment Partnership (TTIP) — may slightly reduce the WTO's profile, but they are unlikely to marginalize the institution or undermine respect for it.

The WTO's legislative (negotiating) leg may be broken, but its executive and judicial functions continue to work rather well. Despite having occasional misgivings about the WTO's various imperfections, most governments benefit from its existence, recognize its importance to the global trading system and appreciate its utility for resolving grievances. Even parties to preferential agreements — such as the United States, Canada and Mexico within the North American Free Trade Agreement (NAFTA) — continue to rely on the WTO to help resolve disputes, even though NAFTA has its own dispute-settlement mechanism. That's in part because the WTO system, with its 463 disputes-worth of jurisprudence, is — by and large — perceived as fair and objective. Moreover, WTO agreements provide rules and standards on issues such as dumping and government subsidies, which some preferential agreements, such as NAFTA, do not address.

WTO member countries account for 97 percent of the world's trade, so it is unlikely that the organization will be supplanted as the best forum for delivering liberalization to the broadest group of countries. As more preferential agreements are concluded, increasing the volume of trade subject to multiple sets of rules, standards and disciplines, the imperative of harmonizing and "multilateralizing" the best of these agreements under the WTO's roof will grow compelling. Businesses and others affected by the rules of trade frequently express preference for multilateral liberalization because, among other reasons, fewer sets of distinct rules enable greater economies of scale in production and lower administrative and compliance costs. The greater the number of noodles in the so-called spaghetti bowl, the greater the cost of compliance and accounting.

The proliferation of preferential agreements is a response to the failure of the Doha Round to deliver results. Rather than being ends in themselves, these agreements represent a competition in liberalization from which the seeds of best practices will be harvested and planted under the WTO.

In Europe, the U.S.-EU pact "is the only show in town," said Michael Geary, a fellow at the Woodrow Wilson International Center for Scholars in Washington. Dogged by a jobless rate of 11 percent, Europe sees the treaty as a way to inject growth into its stagnant economy, he said.[57]

EU and U.S. neighbors — Canada, Mexico, Switzerland and Turkey — are excluded from the talks, causing worry in those countries that the U.S.-EU deal will undo recent progress in integrating themselves into trans-Atlantic trade. Thus, when Turkish Prime Minister Recep Tayyip Erdogan visited the White House in May, he asked Obama if Turkey could join the pact. But Washington's priority is to get the U.S.-EU deal finished as soon as possible and "then we can deal with other countries," said Froman.[58]

In July the scope of the Trans-Pacific Partnership was expanded significantly when Japan, the world's third-largest economy, joined the other 11 nations at the negotiating table.[59] Some observers now speculate that China may eventually join.

In August, negotiators held their 19th round of talks in Brunei. While their goal remains to conclude a pact by the end of 2013, it is unclear how close they are to meeting this goal because they have been so tight-lipped about the finer details of the negotiations. This is causing growing alarm and anger among parliamentarians and grassroots activists. According to Maira Sutton, global policy analyst for the Electronic Frontier Foundation, a San Francisco-based advocacy group for Internet users, "heavy criticism by lawmakers, opposition leaders and civil society groups from around the world is mounting" against the deal. Sutton noted that lawmakers in Peru, Chile, New Zealand and Canada were trying to force the debate out into the open but that trade officials continued to hold secretive meetings — sometimes not even telling the stakeholders they are taking place. Her organization is concerned that the pact will tighten copyright protections and weaken data-privacy norms in ways that will be harmful to Internet users.[60]

Chinese officials have expressed interest in learning more about the pact, according to USTR spokeswoman Guthrie, and "we have been pleased to share that information." She adds that pact members "look forward to potentially expanding the platform by working with other economies that are willing to adopt TPP's commitments."

But even if the United States were to give China the green light, the other TPP participants would have to agree unanimously.

Among the TPP participants, Vietnam has been vocal in wanting to force the United States to eliminate import tariffs on footwear. Such tariffs protect the U.S. athletic footwear industry, but lower-paying Vietnamese footwear manufacturers want to compete freely in the U.S. market.[61]

Regardless of what happens with the Pacific trade pact, the Obama administration seems determined to continue pursuing China at the WTO over alleged violations of trade rules. In the latest case, the United States marked a victory on Aug. 2 when the WTO backed Washington in a case involving duties imposed by Beijing on U.S. exports of broiler chickens.

The future of U.S.-China relations may not be entirely adversarial, however. For instance, Froman seems open to concluding a bilateral investment treaty with China. Such an accord should require that foreign investors are treated the same as domestic ones, with only a few sectors, which he did not specify, excluded, he said.[62]

The Obama administration is also trying to ramp up trade links with sub-Saharan Africa. In August 2013 Froman went to Ethiopia to take part in talks aimed at updating a preferential trade arrangement called the African Growth and Opportunity Act (AGOA), first established by Congress in 2000. Set to expire in 2015, AGOA allows thousands of African-made products to enter the U.S. market duty-free. President Obama's goal is to achieve a "seamless renewal" of the agreement.[63]

Congressional Action

President Obama's plans to conclude the two trade pacts will come to nothing, of course, if Congress decides to block them.

In a recent exchange on Capitol Hill, Froman said "we stand ready to work with you to craft a bill" to renew the Trade Promotion Authority, the law giving the president fast-track authority on trade pacts, which expired in 2007.[64]

But observers say Obama will have to twist arms within his own party to secure renewal, and Democrats who still believe free-trade agreements cost U.S. jobs will probably try to extract concessions from him in return for their support. As for the Republicans, although they have backed free-trade deals in recent decades, a 2010 Pew poll showed that since Obama took office, Republicans have become less supportive of such pacts, with only 28 percent believing they are good for the United States.[65]

Congress is unlikely to renew the fast-track law unless it also extends until 2020 the Trade Adjustment Assistance Act, which provides unemployment benefits and re-training for workers adversely affected by expanded trade.

Also expected to be bundled into the fast-track package is the Generalized System of Preferences (GSP). It provided duty-free entry to American markets for up to 5,000 products from 127 developing countries, but Congress allowed the 37-year-old program to expire on July 31. Congress must decide whether the GSP should continue to apply to all developing countries, since today's top beneficiaries — India, Thailand, Brazil, Indonesia and South Africa — have all progressed from low- to middle-income countries.

Public Citizen's Wallach believes the Obama administration hopes to suppress public opposition to its trade deals in part by rebranding them. For instance, when first conceived in the 1990s, the U.S.-EU pact was called TAFTA (the Transatlantic Free Trade Area), but it has since been rechristened to avoid awkward parallels with NAFTA.

As for the Pacific pact, there have been no major opinion polls asking Americans specifically about those negotiations, according to Bruce Stokes, director of the Global Economic Program at Pew Research Center's Global Attitudes Project.[66] In fact, he noted, there has been relatively little news coverage of the trans-Pacific pact in the United States, in contrast to Japan, where it is widely publicized.

OUTLOOK

Change in China

As the two big regional trade deals draw closer to conclusion, trade is expected to become more of a hot-button issue in the United States.

"The grassroots are not buying" the administration's sales pitch about these deals creating jobs, says Public Citizen's Wallach, but "the elites of both parties are." The question, as she sees it, is how quickly lawmakers will catch up with their constituents.

Of the two deals, the trans-Pacific pact is likely to generate the most controversy. When the U.S. Senate

confirmed Froman as U.S. trade representative by a 93-4 vote in June, one of the four opposing senators was consumer-rights champion Elizabeth Warren, D-Mass. She was irked by Froman's refusal to send her a draft negotiating text of the Pacific treaty.

The AFL-CIO's Drake argued on behalf of organized labor that if the new trade deals are to avoid repeating past mistakes, U.S. negotiators must draw some red lines, including:

- Retaining "buy American" laws that allow governments to give preference to U.S. products and services when making purchases;
- Eliminating subsidies to state-owned enterprises;
- Granting market access only on a reciprocal basis; and
- Establishing rules on food and toy safety and on currency manipulation.[67]

Polls indicate the U.S.-EU treaty will be an easier sell to Congress. Support for removing all remaining tariffs on European-U.S. trade in goods stands at 48 percent. Pew's Stokes has noted, however, that "if history is any guide, inevitable frictions will erode public support as adversely affected interests complain, while those that stand to benefit are less vocal."[68]

Stokes suggests the pact is part of a U.S.-EU strategy to offset the rise of China by establishing common technical and regulatory standards that would become global business norms.[69] If the U.S.-EU agreement is concluded, it also could pave the way for an even bigger regional pact.

For instance, former trade representative Hills has called for the U.S.-EU pact to be enlarged into a North American-EU free-trade agreement, bringing Mexico and Canada on board. This "would have a lot of benefits" by building on NAFTA's success in integrating supply chains, she contended.[70] Turkey can be expected to push for something similar, given that its 1995 customs union with the EU means that it will, in any case, have to apply whatever tariff regime is agreed to under the Transatlantic Trade and Investment Partnership.

As for what will happen to state-owned enterprises in emerging economies such as China, Craig Allen, deputy assistant secretary for Asia at the U.S. International Trade Administration in the Department of Commerce, predicts "they will dramatically restructure" as the Chinese government begins to realize that the state-sponsored economic model stifles technological innovation. Allen says reforming the state-owned sector will be key to helping China escape the "middle-income trap," in which developing countries grow rapidly for a while but then hit a ceiling that keeps them a tier below advanced economies.

Meanwhile, revival in the U.S. manufacturing sector is creating optimism about future growth prospects. According to Gene Sperling, director of the National Economic Council in the Obama administration, "the wind is at our back now" as manufacturers who set up shop elsewhere in the early 2000s are returning home. "We are up 500,000 jobs," he said, adding that the administration's priorities are to modernize infrastructure, harness energy supplies and better enforce international trade rules.[71]

The administration's buoyant mood has yet to fully filter down into the general public, however, which remains anxious about the state of the economy. Asked to account for this disconnect, *The Economist*'s Avent said it was because "we're in such a deep hole, and the road out has been so long and slow that we still have a ways to go."[72]

NOTES

1. Brian Beary, "Transatlantic beef trade agreement extended," Europolitics, Aug. 28, 2013.

2. "U.S. Trade Representative Froman, Secretary of Agriculture Vilsack Announce Continued EU Market Access for American Producers of High-Quality Beef," press release, Office of the United States Trade Representative, Office of the United States Trade Representative, Aug. 1, 2013, www.ustr .gov/Froman-Vilsack-Announce-Continued-EU-Market-Access-for-American-Beef-Producers.

3. For background, see Roland Flamini, "U.S.-Europe Relations," *CQ Researcher*, March 23, 2012, pp. 277-300.

4. See "The Rise of State-Controlled Capitalism," NPR, May 17, 2010, www.npr.org/templates/story/ story.php?storyId=126835124.

5. See Jason McClure, "State Capitalism," *CQ Global Researcher*, May 15, 2012, pp. 229-256.

6. See Kemal Kirisci, "Turkey and the Transatlantic Trade and Investment Partnership: Boosting the Model Partnership with the United States," Brookings Institution, September 2013, www.brookings.edu/ research/papers/2013/09/turkey-transatlantic-trade-and-investment-partnership-kirisci.

7. For full list, see "Regional Trade Agreements Information System" (database), World Trade Organization, http://rtais.wto.org/UI/PublicAllRTAList.aspx.

8. Professor Van Assche was speaking at a conference entitled, "The Trans-Pacific Partnership: New Rules for a New Era," at the Woodrow Wilson International Center for Scholars, June 19, 2013.

9. Former USTR Carla Hills was a keynote speaker at a discussion entitled "A North America-European Union Free Trade Agreement?" at the Woodrow Wilson Center for International Scholars, July 26, 2013.

10. Bruce Stokes, "The Public Supports a Transatlantic Trade Pact — For Now," Pew Research Center, Feb. 19, 2013, www.pewglobal.org/2013/02/19/the-public-supports-a-transatlantic-trade-pact-for-now-2/.

11. Bruce Stokes, "Americans' Support for TPP Remains Untested," Pew Research Center, April 1, 2013, www.pewglobal.org/2013/04/01/americans-sup port-for-tpp-remains-untested.

12. From an introductory handout for a discussion entitled "Manufacturing U.S. Prosperity: A Policy Discussion," Brookings Institution, July 25, 2013, www.brookings.edu/events/2013/07/25-manufac turing-policy.

13. "U.S. International Trade In Goods And Services — June 2013," Bureau of Economic Analysis, U.S. Census Bureau, Aug. 6, 2013, www.census.gov/for eign-trade/Press-Release/current_press_release/ ft900.pdf.

14. Marc Levinson was a panelist at a talk, entitled "Innovating American Manufacturing: New Policies for a Stronger Economic Future," Brookings Institution, July 10, 2013.

15. For more information on the potential economic impact of TTIP, see "Transatlantic Trade and Investment Partnership: Who benefits from a free

trade deal," Global Economic Dynamics/Bertelsmann Stiftung, June 17, 2013, www.bfna.org/sites/default/files/TTIP-GED%20study%2017June%202013.pdf.

16. See U.S. Census Bureau database: www.census.gov/foreign-trade/balance/.

17. Remarks by Rep. Sherman at hearing on the Trans-Pacific Partnership negotiations, Subcommittee on Terrorism, Non-proliferation, and Trade, Committee on Foreign Affairs, U.S. House of Representatives, Aug. 1, 2013.

18. Gerwin was testifying at a hearing on the Trans-Pacific Partnership negotiations, Subcommittee on Terrorism, Non-proliferation, and Trade, Committee on Foreign Affairs, U.S. House of Representatives, Aug. 1, 2013.

19. Figures cited in Drake's written testimony to the hearing on the Trans-Pacific Partnership negotiations, Subcommittee on Terrorism, Non-proliferation, and Trade, Committee on Foreign Affairs, U.S. House of Representatives, Aug. 1, 2013.

20. USTR Froman was speaking at a discussion on the U.S. trade agenda, U.S. Chamber of Commerce, July 30, 2013.

21. Zoellick was speaking at a conference entitled, "The Trans-Pacific Partnership: New Rules for a New Era," Woodrow Wilson International Center for Scholars, June 19, 2013.

22. Michael Blanding, "What Capitalists Should Know About State-Owned Enterprises," *Forbes*, Feb. 22, 2013, www.forbes.com/sites/hbsworkingknowledge/2013/02/22/what-capitalists-should-know-about-state-owned-enterprises/.

23. "China Eclipses U.S. as Biggest Trading Nation," Bloomberg News, Feb. 10, 2013, www.bloomberg.com/news/2013-02-09/china-passes-u-s-to-become-the-world-s-biggest-trading-nation.html.

24. Heriberto Araújo and Juan Pablo Cardenal, "China's Economic Empire," *The New York Times*, June 1, 2013, www.nytimes.com/2013/06/02/opinion/sunday/chinas-economic-empire.html?pagewanted=all&_r=0.

25. *Ibid.*

26. Written testimony by Drake at hearing on the Trans-Pacific Partnership negotiations, *op. cit.*

27. Flake made his remarks at a conference hosted by the U.S. House of Representatives and organized by the Cato Institute entitled "Free Trade, Free Markets: Rating the 112th Congress," on June 19, 2013.

28. Written testimony by Drake at hearing on the Trans-Pacific Partnership negotiations, *op. cit.*

29. "Made in Vietnam: Labor Rights Violations in Vietnam's Export Manufacturing Sector," Worker Rights Consortium, May 2013, www.workersrights.org/linkeddocs/WRC_Vietnam_Briefing_Paper.pdf.

30. *Ibid.*

31. U.S. Rep. Rohrabacher was speaking at a hearing on the Trans-Pacific Partnership negotiations, Subcommittee on Terrorism, Non-proliferation, and Trade, Committee on Foreign Affairs, U.S. House of Representatives, Aug. 1, 2013.

32. Fareed Zakaria, "Fareed Zakaria GPS," CNN, July 21, 2013, http://podcasts.cnn.net/cnn/services/podcasting/audio/2013/fareed.zakaria.gps/GPS_0721_audio.mp3.

33. Testimony by Drake, *op. cit.*

34. *Ibid* (oral testimony).

35. "Investor-State Attacks on the Public Interest," Public Citizen (accessed Sept. 4, 2013), www.citizen.org/investorcases.

36. "Table of foreign investor-state cases and claims under NAFTA and other U.S. trade deals," Public Citizen, March 2013, www.citizen.org/documents/investor-state-chart1.pdf.

37. For history of trade policy, see *Trade: U.S. Policy Since 1945* (1984), pp. 31-59.

38. For background, see Mary H. Cooper, "World Trade," *CQ Researcher*, June 9, 2000, pp. 497-520.

39. Brian Hansen, "Globalization Backlash," *CQ Researcher*, Sept. 28, 2001, pp. 761-784.

40. Jason McClure, "State Capitalism," *CQ Global Researcher*, May 15, 2012, pp. 229-256.

41. Mary H. Cooper, "Rethinking NAFTA," *CQ Researcher*, June 7, 1996, pp. 481-504.

42. McClure, *op. cit.*

43. Presentation by Kenneth Smith, Trade Counselor at the Embassy of Mexico, at a discussion entitled

"A North America-European Union Free Trade Agreement?" Woodrow Wilson Center for International Scholars, July 26, 2013.

44. Hansen, *op. cit.*

45. See Ed Gerwin, "Least In The East," Third Way, January 2013, www.thirdway.org/publications/632.

46. Introductory handout, Brookings Institution, *op. cit.*

47. Froman comments were made during a discussion on the U.S. trade agenda, U.S. Chamber of Commerce, *op. cit.*

48. For background, see Thomas J. Billitteri, "Auto Industry's Future," *CQ Researcher*, Feb. 6, 2009, pp. 105-128.

49. "U.S. International Trade In Goods And Services — June 2013," *op. cit.*

50. Jeff Cox, "Jobs growth misses high hopes; unemployment rate drops to 7.3%," CNBC, Sept. 6, 2013, www.cnbc.com/id/101014110.

51. "Fact Sheet: The G-20 St. Petersburg summit," White House, Sept. 6, 2013, www.whitehouse.gov/the-press-office/2013/09/06/fact-sheet-g-20-st-petersburg-summit.

52. Linda Wertheimer, "How is The U.S. Economy Doing? Examining Latest Data," NPR, Aug. 9, 2013, www.npr.org/2013/08/09/210412620/what-do-latest-numbers-tell-us-about-u-s-economy.

53. Howard Schneider, "Inheriting a complex trade agenda," *The Washington Post*, June 22, 2013.

54. For background, see Chuck McCutcheon, "Government Surveillance," *CQ Researcher*, Aug. 30, 2013, pp. 717-740.

55. Froman comments at U.S. Chamber of Commerce, *op. cit.*

56. Howard Schneider, "Disputes threaten to bog down talks on U.S.-E.U. trade," *The Washington Post*, May 14, 2013.

57. Geary was speaking at a conference entitled "The Trans-Pacific Partnership: New Rules for a New Era," Wilson Center, June 19, 2013.

58. Froman comments at U.S. Chamber of Commerce, *op. cit.*

59. Howard Schneider, "Larger issues loom in free trade debate," *The Washington Post*, July 24, 2013.

60. Maira Sutton, "International Criticism Escalates Against TPP as Negotiations Go Further Underground," Electronic Frontier Foundation, Sept. 6, 2013, www.eff.org/deeplinks/2013/09/international-criticism-escalates-against-tpp-negotiations-go-further-underground.

61. Howard Schneider, "Evolving Obama Pushes hard for global pacts," *The Washington Post*, March 9, 2013.

62. Froman comments at U.S. Chamber of Commerce, *op. cit.*

63. "USTR Froman Looks to Next Steps in Review, Renewal of African Growth and Opportunity Act," press release, Office of the U.S. Trade Representative, Aug. 13, 2013, www.ustr.gov/Froman-Next-Steps-in-Review-Renewal-of-AGOA.

64. Froman testimony, House Ways and Means Committee, July 18, 2013.

65. "Americans Are of Two Minds on Trade: More Trade, Mostly Good; Free Trade Pacts, Not So," Pew Researcher Center, Nov. 9, 2010, www.pewresearch.org/2010/11/09/americans-are-of-two-minds-on-trade/.

66. Stokes, *op. cit.*, April 1, 2013.

67. Testimony by Drake, *op. cit.*

68. Stokes, *op. cit.*, Feb. 19, 2013.

69. Bruce Stokes, "U.S.-China Economic Relations in the Wake of the U.S. Election," Pew Research Center, Dec. 10, 2012, www.pewglobal.org/2012/12/10/u-s-china-economic-relations-in-the-wake-of-the-u-s-election.

70. Former USTR Hill, *op. cit.*

71. Sperling was the keynote speaker at a discussion entitled "Manufacturing U.S. Prosperity: A Policy Discussion," Brookings Institution, July 25, 2013.

72. Wertheimer, *op. cit.*

BIBLIOGRAPHY

Selected Sources

Books

Sheng, Hong, and Zao Nong, *China's State-Owned Enterprises: Nature, Performance and Reform*, World Scientific Publishing Co., 2013.

Two top Chinese academics from the Unirule Institute of Economics argue that China's state-owned enterprises are inefficient, have a poor record at income distribution and enjoy unfair competitive advantages.

VanGrasstek, Craig, *The History and Future of the World Trade Organization*, **WTO Publications, 2013, www.wto.org/english/res_e/booksp_e/history-wto_e.pdf.**
A trade consultant describes the origins and development of the Geneva-based World Trade Organization, including its dispute settlement rules.

Articles

Aguilar, Julián, "Twenty Years Later, Nafta Remains a Source of Tension," *The New York Times*, **Dec. 7, 2012, www.nytimes.com/2012/12/07/us/twenty-years-later-nafta-remains-a-source-of-tension.html?_r=0.**
A reporter assesses the impact the North American Free Trade Agreement (NAFTA) has had on Canada, Mexico and the United States.

Araújo, Heriberto, and Juan Pablo Cardenal, "China's Economic Empire," *The New York Times*, **June 1, 2013, www.nytimes.com/2013/06/02/opinion/sunday/chinas-economic-empire.html?pagewanted=all&_r=0.**
The authors explain how China's state-owned enterprises use their competitive advantage to gain dominance in foreign commercial markets.

Blanding, Michael, "What Capitalists Should Know About State-Owned Enterprises," *Forbes*, **Feb. 22, 2013, www.forbes.com/sites/hbsworkingknowledge/2013/02/22/what-capitalists-should-know-about-state-owned-enterprises/.**
A Boston-based writer explains the structural changes that have occurred in publicly owned companies in countries such as China and Russia that embraced capitalism relatively recently.

Petitjean, Sophie, "Nanomaterials products triple," *Europolitics*, **Oct. 25, 2010, www.europolitics.info//nanomaterials-products-triple-art285257-12.html.**
A reporter charts the increasing use of nanoingredients in products and the concern it is causing among consumer rights groups.

Reports and Studies

"Americans Are of Two Minds on Trade — More Trade, Mostly Good; Free Trade Pacts, Not So," **Pew Research Center, Nov. 9, 2010, www.pewresearch.org/2010/11/09/americans-are-of-two-minds-on-trade/.**
A leading think tank examines its survey data on what Americans think about free trade agreements.

"China 2030: Building a Modern, Harmonious, and Creative Society," **World Bank, 2013, www.worldbank.org/content/dam/Worldbank/document/China-2030-complete.pdf.**
A study by the World Bank and the Development Research Center of the Chinese State Council outlines what policies, including on trade, China needs to adopt to progress from a middle-income to a high-income nation.

"Made in Vietnam: Labor Rights Violations in Vietnam's Export Manufacturing Sector," **Worker Rights Consortium, May 2013, www.workersrights.org/linkeddocs/WRC_Vietnam_Briefing_Paper.pdf.**
An independent labor rights watchdog describes how textile factory workers in Vietnam are being exploited.

"Table of foreign investor-state cases and claims under NAFTA and other U.S. trade deals," **Public Citizen, March 2013, www.citizen.org/documents/investor-state-chart1.pdf.**
The consumer advocacy organization provides a comprehensive inventory of claims filed by corporations against governments under NAFTA's dispute settlement mechanism.

Gerwin, Ed, "Least In The East," **Third Way, January 2013, http://content.thirdway.org/publications/632/Third_Way_Policy_Memo_-_Least_In_the_East.pdf.**
A Washington think tank shows how the United States has lost a great deal of market share in Asia in the past decade as Asian and Pacific countries have forged new trade agreements with one another.

Macoubrie, Jane, "Informed Public Perceptions of Nano-technology and Trust in Government," **Woodrow Wilson International Center for Scholars/**

The Pew Charitable Trusts, September 2005, www .wilsoncenter.org/sites/default/files/macoubriere port1.pdf.
A social scientist analyzes a survey on public attitudes toward nanotechnology, finding that most American feel the benefits of nanotechnology outweigh the risks, but half didn't know what it was.

Stokes, Bruce, "Americans' Support for TPP Remains Untested," Pew Research Center, April 1, 2013, www .pewglobal.org/2013/04/01/americans-support-for-tpp-remains-untested.
A political analyst crunches the latest polling data on how Americans feel about their trade relationships with Asia's two largest economies, China and Japan.

For More Information

AFL-CIO, 815 16th St., N.W., Washington, DC 20006; 202-637-5018; www.aflcio.org. The umbrella federation for U.S. organized labor closely monitors developments in U.S. trade policy.

Brookings Institution, 1775 Massachusetts Ave., N.W., Washington, DC 20036; 202-797-6000; www.brookings .edu. An independent public policy think tank that researches trade-related topics.

Cato Institute, 1000 Massachusetts Ave., N.W., Washington, DC 20001; 202-842-0200; www.cato.org. A libertarian think tank that advocates free-market-based trade.

Delegation of the European Union to the United States, 2175 K St., N.W., Washington, DC 20037; 202-862-9500; www.euintheus.org. The Washington office of the 28-member European Union.

International Trade Administration, 1401 Constitution Ave., N.W., Washington, DC 20230; 202-482-2867; www .trade.gov. A division of the Department of Commerce that promotes trade and foreign investment and enforces trade laws and agreements.

Nanotechnology Institute (NTI), 4801 S. Broad St., Suite 200, Philadelphia, PA 19112; 215-972-6700; http://nanote chinstitute.org. A partnership between industry and academia that promotes nanotechnnology by connecting industry with university assets through its 13 member research institutions.

Public Citizen, 1600 20th St., N.W., Washington, DC 20009; 202-588-1000; www.citizen.org. A citizens' rights advocacy group whose Global Trade Watch arm opposes U.S. free-trade agreements.

U.S. Chamber of Commerce, 1615 H St., N.W., Washington, DC 20062; 202-659-6000; www.uschamber .com. Represents three million U.S. businesses and strongly supports free-trade agreements.

World Trade Organization, Centre William Rappard, Rue de Lausanne 154, CH-1211 Geneva 21, Switzerland; +41 (0)22 739 51 11; www.wto.org. A forum for governments to negotiate trade agreements and settle trade disputes.

10

Millennium Development Goals

Danielle Kurtzleben

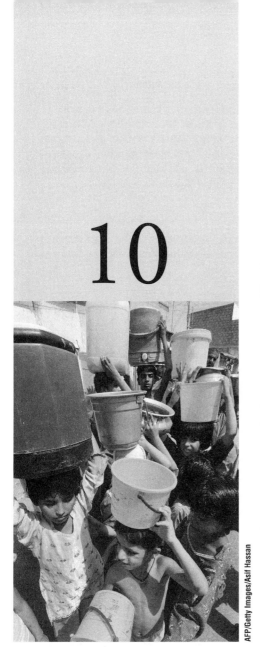

AFP/Getty Images/Asif Hassan

Pakistani children in a Karachi slum area queue up for safe drinking water from a public faucet The U.N. announced that in 2010 the world had met the MDG target of halving the proportion of people without access to safe water and sanitation, the cause of many childhood and other diseases.

From *CQ Researcher*,
September 4, 2012.
Updated January 30, 2015.

Jan Vandemoortele used to get glassy stares when he told family and friends he worked on "good governance and capacity development" at the United Nations — international development jargon for helping governments improve the lives and health of their constituents.

But after he helped craft the U.N.'s landmark Millennium Development Goals (MDGs) in 2000, he could tell people, simply, "I am working to get all girls in school and reduce maternal mortality."

That's how the former U.N. official explains the value of the framework he helped to create to boost economic growth and well-being in developing nations. The MDGs were adopted in 2001 after the U.N.'s 2000 Millennium Summit, when world leaders agreed to establish eight specific goals — with measurable targets — for reducing poverty and relieving related barriers to economic development. Each of the organization's 189 members pledged to meet the targets by 2015, with help from roughly two dozen international organizations.

Those leaders, presumably, were able to go home and succinctly explain to their neighbors and families about the good they were hoping to accomplish in the world. Now the question is whether, this year — 2015 — they'll be able to give another succinct summation: "We did it."

Judging by progress over the last 14 years, they may be able to do just that — at least on some of the goals. Two key targets — slashing by half the 1990 levels of extreme poverty and the proportion of people without access to safe drinking water — were both met by 2010, five years ahead of the 2015 deadline.[1] Girls' primary school

Progress Has Been Made, but Obstacles Remain

India and China — representing nearly half of the developing world's population — have made the most progress toward meeting the U.N.'s eight ambitious Millennium Development Goals (MDGs) by 2015, largely due to their rapid economic growth. But sub-Saharan Africa, which was far behind the rest of the developing world at the outset, has farther to go to meet the goals. Worldwide, significant strides have been made in reducing extreme poverty and making safe drinking water more accessible to all, but obstacles remain in attaining the rest of the goals: achieving universal primary education and gender equality, improving child mortality rates and maternal health, fighting HIV-AIDS, malaria, and other diseases, ensuring environmental sustainability, and creating a global partnership for development.

Progress in Achieving MDGs, as of 2011

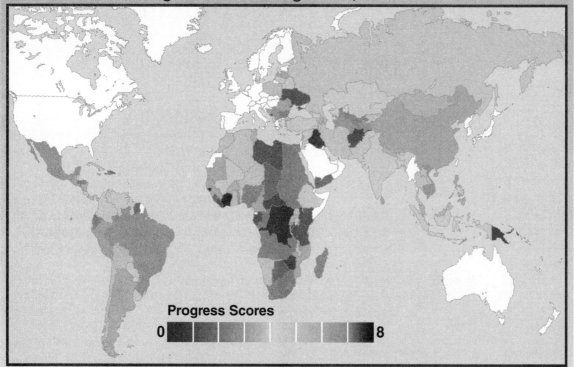

Progress Scores

0 ▬▬▬▬▬▬▬▬ 8

Source: "MDG Progress Index: Gauging Country-Level Achievements," Center for Global Development, www.cgdev.org/section/topics/poverty/mdg_scorecards. Map by Lewis Agrell

enrollment has[2] reached near-parity with boys, and the living conditions for more than 200 million slum dwellers have been ameliorated — double the target for 2020.[3]

There has been marked progress on the other goals as well. The death rates for children under age 5 fell by nearly 50 percent between 1990 and 2012.[4] And by 2012, 90 percent of children in developing nations were enrolled in primary school, up from 82 percent in 1999.[5]

"The concerted efforts of national governments, the international community, civil society and the private sector have helped expand hope and opportunity for people around the world," U.N. Secretary-General Ban Ki-moon wrote in the 2014 report on MDG progress. "But more needs to be done to accelerate progress. We need bolder and focused action where significant gaps and disparities exist."[6]

Progress has indeed been uneven, with most gains occurring in economically vibrant India and China — which together represent 46 percent of the developing world's population. Achievements in eradicating poverty and hunger, for instance, have been due largely to rapid improvements in East Asia. "Over a 25-year period, the poverty rate in East Asia fell from nearly 60 percent to under 20 percent," the U.N. noted in 2010, and by 2015, poverty rates are expected to fall to around 5 percent in China and 24 percent in India.

But sub-Saharan Africa's extreme poverty rate declined far less dramatically — from 56 percent to 48 percent — during the 20-year period between 1990 and 2010.[7] In fact, the region has experienced remarkably slow progress — even declines — on many of the targets that the world as a whole has met.

In many cases, simple tactics led to progress. For instance, eliminating primary school fees helped to boost enrollment in several African countries; setting up tent schools brought education to children in remote areas of Mongolia; and using indigenous languages helped educate Bolivian children in outlying tribal regions.[8]

Routine immunizations have helped reduce child mortality in Africa, Vietnam, and Bangladesh, and the distribution of insecticide-treated bed nets, particularly in Africa, has dramatically reduced the spread of malaria.

There have also been disappointments. Gender equality remains largely out of reach by several measurements, such as representation in classrooms, workplaces, and government, and child deaths are not declining as quickly as hoped. And although the

Most Rich Countries Miss Global Aid Target

Since 1970, developed nations have promised — and mostly failed — to provide foreign aid equivalent to at least 0.7 percent of their gross national incomes (GNI). Only five developed countries — all in Northern Europe — met the target in 2009 (bottom). Although the United States contributed far more foreign aid in total dollars than any other country in 2009 (top), it ranked 19th among the top 20 industrialized countries in the percentage of national income contributed in foreign aid.

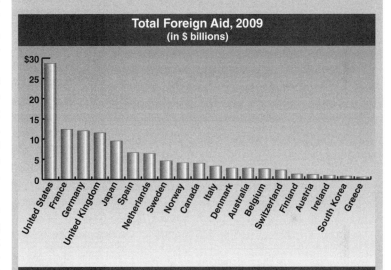

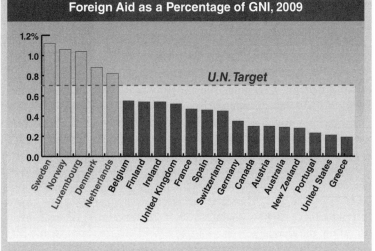

Source: "Development Aid Rose in 2009 and Most Donors Will Meet 2010 Aid Targets," Organisation for Economic Co-operation and Development, April 2010.

Tackling Poverty Using Simple Techniques

Inexpensive strategies can be keys to progress.

After years of fighting poverty through the Millennium Development Goals (MDGs), aid groups have learned new tactics for improving the lives of the world's poorest. Here are several:

Use low-cost strategies. Swooping in with lots of money and advanced technology can lead to improvements, but other methods often work better.

"The most effective health technologies are very cheap and very simple," Charles Kenny, a senior fellow at the Washington-based Center for Global Development, wrote in his 2011 book *Getting Better: Why Global Development Is Succeeding and How We Can Improve the World Even More.* For example, he noted, one third of the 10 million annual child deaths in impoverished countries could be prevented with just three inexpensive, straightforward approaches: oral rehydration therapy, breast feeding, and insecticide-treated bed nets.[1]

Even large-scale improvements to a nation's health-care system need not be massively expensive, he noted. Malaysia and Sri Lanka have virtually eliminated maternal mortality by making midwives available in rural areas. The dramatic improvement, he notes, has occurred even though spending on maternal and child health services in those countries is less than 0.4 percent of gross domestic product.[2]

Change social norms. Development is not just about aid organizations creating new institutions or services. The public also must have a genuine desire to use new programs.

More girls are attending school worldwide today not only because more schools have been opened but also because "it became normal to send girls to school," Kenny says, a cultural shift that occurred over decades.

Sanitation is another area where changing social norms provides benefits. To encourage pit latrine use and help people understand the health implications of defecating in the open, one specialist does a demonstration in which he puts excrement next to a plate of food so people can see how flies cross from one to the other.[3]

Use mobile phones. Mobile phones can open a world of economic possibilities to villagers in a developing country. "Poverty results from the lack of access to markets, to emergency health services, access to education, the ability to take advantage of government services and so on," Jeffrey Sachs, director of Columbia University's Earth Institute, told CNN in 2011. The mobile phone and IT technology can end "that kind of isolation in all its different varieties."[4]

Farmers in poor nations can use phones to find out where they can sell grain for the best price, and people can pay bills and send money to each other using cell phones, the World Bank notes.[5]

Still, mobile phones are no panacea. A recent study showed that 60 percent of the poorest one fourth of Kenyans did not use the country's mobile phone service, *Slate* reported this year. "Telecom companies have relatively little incentive to build out

maternal mortality ratio dropped by 45 percent between 1990 and 2013, "much more needs to be done."[9]

Limited women's empowerment is a major barrier to meeting some of the goals, according to Francesca Perucci, lead author of the U.N.'s 2012 MDG report. "[Gender equality] is slow to come in many settings, and then, of course, it's a big obstacle to reaching most of the other goals," she says. "Through women's empowerment you can achieve progress in other areas — child health, education, the economy."

And because women's empowerment is often difficult due to cultural norms, success is slow going. "It's not a

matter of big donor initiatives or intervention," says Perucci. "It's a much broader policy issue."

Other far-reaching issues can restrict a country's MDG progress, she notes. If a country has a deeply troubled health-care system, for instance, change can require significant political action and a long time before maternal health and child mortality will improve. In addition, she adds, maternal and child health goals haven't received as much attention in recent years as other goals have.

As the MDG deadline rapidly approaches, here are some of the questions development experts and political leaders are asking:

infrastructure, especially in poorer, rural markets," the online magazine said. Moreover, the cost of mobile phone service can be prohibitive for the poorest Kenyans, it said.[6]

Still, there is something to be said for a tool that can boost poor countries' economies and that people seek out on their own, as New York University economist and former World Bank official William Easterly pointed out in his 2006 book *The White Man's Burden: Why the West's Efforts to Aid the Rest Have Done So Much Ill and So Little Good.*

"The explosion of cell phones shows just how much poor people search for new technological opportunities, with no state intervention, with no structural adjustment or shock therapy to promote cell phones," he wrote, adding that the phones can provide services that would otherwise be "logistical nightmares in societies without good landline phones, functional postal services or adequate roads."[7]

— Danielle Kurtzleben

A South African shop owner displays her mobile phone on May 5, 2011, in a township near Cape Town. Development economists say cell phones can inexpensively increase people's access to markets, emergency health services, education, and government services. "If you had to wire up Africa with land lines for telephones, it could never have been done," says Barry Carin, a senior fellow at the Canadian think tank the Center for International Governance Innovation.

[1]Charles Kenny, *Getting Better: Why Global Development Is Succeeding and How We Can Improve the World Even More.* New York, New York: Basic Books, 2011, p. 126.

[2]*Ibid.,* pp. 126–127.

[3]"West Africa: Smoothing the Way for More Pit Latrines," IRIN [U.N. news agency], Aug. 31, 2011, http://irinnews.org/Report/93621/WEST-AFRICA-Smoothing-the-way-for-more-pit-latrines.

[4]Kevin Voigt, "Mobile Phone: Weapon Against Global Poverty," CNN, Oct. 9, 2011, http://articles.cnn.com/2011-10-09/tech/tech_mobile_mobile-phone-poverty_1_mobile-phone-cell-phone-rural-villages?_s=PM:TECH.

[5]Shanta Devarajan, "More Cell Phones than Toilets," The World Bank, April 12, 2010, http://blogs.worldbank.org/africacan/more-cell-phones-than-toilets.

[6]Jamie M. Zimmerman and Sascha Meinrath, "Mobile Phones Will Not Save the Poorest of the Poor," *Slate,* Feb. 9, 2012, www.slate.com/articles/technology/future_tense/2012/02/m_pesa_and_other_ict4d_projects_are_leaving_behind_the_developing_world_s_poorest_people_.html.

[7]William Easterly, *The White Man's Burden: Why the West's Efforts to Aid the Rest Have Done So Much Ill and So Little Good.* New York, New York: Penguin Books, 2006, pp. 103–104.

Will the goals be successful?

The answer to that question depends on how one defines "successful," say development experts.

The goals provide simple, clear numerical measurements of "success." By that definition, all of the MDG targets won't be met by 2015, particularly on health-related goals such as maternal and child mortality.

But that view obscures the fact that three of the targets — on poverty, slum conditions, and clean water — already have been met. Despite sizable hurdles, "Much has been accomplished through the concerted and focused efforts of all, saving and improving the lives of many people," the U.N. said in its 2014 MDG report.[10]

In addition, the MDGs helped focus attention on certain development problems and boosted international cooperation on important global issues, according to Sam Worthington, president and CEO of InterAction, an alliance of development nongovernmental organizations (NGOs). "The MDGs have played an essential role for the U.S. nonprofit community by organizing the billions of dollars of private giving around concrete themes and giving nonprofits targets," says Worthington.

The "concreteness" of the MDGs has been their strength, argues Vandemoortele, and having a manageable number of clear, specific goals has given the MDGs remarkable staying power. "Those are the main reasons why the MDGs are still talked about," he says. "So many things come and go, so many acronyms, and either they don't take off or after two years they are gone," he says. The MDGs "are still measurable, and we live in a world where numbers do matter."

However, others question whether setting the goals spurred the improvements in individual targets or the success was due to other factors. For instance, the first MDG was halving the proportion of people living on $1.25 or less per day. Preliminary World Bank estimates say that target was met in 2010.[11]

But the lion's share of progress toward that goal occurred in China and, to a smaller extent, India, both of which saw stunning economic growth in recent years. In those two countries alone, the number of people in extreme poverty declined by 455 million between 1990 and 2005, according to the U.N.'s 2011 MDG report.[12] Without China in the equation, the proportion of people in developing regions living on less than $1.25 per day fell only from 41 percent in 1990 to 26 percent in 2010, so the target hasn't yet been met if China is not counted.[13] In sub-Saharan Africa during the same time period, the proportion living in poverty declined modestly, from 56 to 48 percent.

"There's no causal chain whatsoever between MDGs and poverty reduction. And I say that as a fan of the MDGs and as a big cheerleader for the reduction in poverty," says Laurence Chandy, a fellow in the Global Economy and Development program at the Washington-based Brookings Institution think tank. "It was this rapid increase in economic growth in many developing countries that brought about this big reduction in poverty."

All in all, the MDG "success" question is easy to answer on a numerical, success-or-failure basis, but the picture becomes fuzzier the deeper one looks, as the Bill and Melinda Gates Foundation — whose work in areas like global health and agriculture supports MDG progress — noted in a 2011 MDG assessment.

"While the MDGs provide a helpful quantitative framework for assessing broad-based progress in development, they do not in themselves adequately capture the distribution of progress across society, the sustainability of progress over time or subjective conceptions of progress itself."[14]

Progress in achieving universal primary education presents another clear example of this phenomenon. Abolishing primary-school fees has helped spur a surge in school enrollment in sub-Saharan Africa, but how much good are those schools doing?

"Getting children into school . . . isn't very useful if they learn little or nothing once they're there," wrote Abhijit Banerjee and Esther Duflo in their 2011 book *Poor Economics*. "The Millennium Development Goals do not specify that children should learn anything in school, just that they should complete a basic cycle of education."[15]

Development experts stress that the MDGs are only a stepping-stone. Halving the poverty rate still leaves hundreds of millions in poverty. In other words, for every signpost passed, there is another in the distance for the world to strive toward — and the opportunity to ask, "What now?"

Were the goals unfair to some countries?

Countless news articles and U.N. reports have predicted that some countries — mostly in sub-Saharan Africa — would "fail" or "fall short" in meeting the MDGs. Likewise, India is "in a race against time" to achieve the MDGs by 2015, Noeleen Heyzer, executive secretary of the U.N. Economic and Social Commission for Asia and the Pacific, said in 2012.[16]

Indeed, U.N. monitoring reports show wide disparities in poverty reduction and other MDG indicators. The World Bank's 2013 report on rural–urban development and the MDGs notes that 124 out of 143 countries being monitored are making insufficient progress toward the MDG goal for reducing infant mortality, and 107 are in danger of missing the target for maternal mortality.

New York University economist William Easterly says in some cases those comparisons are unfair, particularly with regard to sub-Saharan African countries. For instance, said the former World Bank economist in a 2007 paper, by choosing 1990 as the base year for most measurements, such as the goal to halve extreme poverty rates by 2015, the MDGs set African nations up for failure.[17]

"African economic growth was very poor in the 1990s," he wrote. "Hence, it began the MDG campaign in 2000 already 'off-track' to meet the poverty goal."[18]

In addition, the method used to measure some goals meant that African nations would miss the targets, he said. Citing data from a 2005 World Bank analysis of MDG progress, Easterly pointed out that Africa was behind in reducing the share of its population without access to clean water. However, Africa would have been "catching up if it had been measured the conventional way, [using the] percent *with* access to clean water," he wrote, concluding that "the choice of *with* and *without* is arbitrary."

Aside from such technical, statistical problems with the MDGs, others say it is unfair to dwell on individual countries' progress on what were meant to be global targets. The goals "were never formulated as targets for individual countries," says Jon Lomoy, director of the Development Co-operation Directorate at the Paris-based Organisation for Economic Co-operation and Development (OECD). "They were formulated as global targets."

"The misinterpretation of the MDGs as one-size-fits-all targets has set the bar for sub-Saharan Africa countries unrealistically high," wrote former U.N. official Vandemoortele in 2009. For example, Africa has made significant progress in curbing the spread of HIV-AIDS and in putting more children in primary schools, but because many African countries have so far to go before meeting some of the goals, it is easy to ignore the successes, he wrote.[19]

If the world fails to meet the MDGs, he argued, "it's not going to be because Africa has failed, [but] because Asia has failed to contribute its fair share" toward global poverty reduction.

Still, others say, taking a country-by-country look at poverty reduction highlights those parts of the world needing the most help and which tactics are working in particular countries. In a 2000 paper setting out guidelines for creating the MDGs, then-U.N. Secretary-General Kofi Annan pointed to deeply impoverished

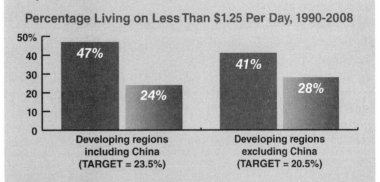

Poverty Fell, Especially in China

The first Millennium Development Goal — cutting in half the proportion of people in the developing world living in extreme poverty in 1990 — has been achieved. However, much of the progress stemmed from China's phenomenal economic growth. When China is excluded, the proportion living on less than $1.25 per day was only cut by one-third.

Percentage Living on Less Than $1.25 Per Day, 1990-2008

Developing regions including China (TARGET = 23.5%): 1990 = 47%, 2008 = 24%

Developing regions excluding China (TARGET = 20.5%): 1990 = 41%, 2008 = 28%

Source: "The Millennium Development Goals Report: 2012," United Nations, 2012, p. 6, http://www.un.org/millenniumgoals/pdf/MDG%20Report%202012.pdf

■ 1990
■ 2008

regions that desperately needed assistance, such as parts of southern Asia and sub-Saharan Africa.[20] In other words, while the goal may have been global poverty reduction, the drafters acknowledged that some had further to go than others.

Country-level measures of "success" and "failure" also can reveal a government's commitment to achieving the goals. Highly indebted countries applying for debt relief from the International Monetary Fund (IMF) must be aware of their MDG progress and submit periodic updates on their poverty-reduction strategies. While countries do not have to achieve the MDG targets to gain debt relief, they must take "ownership" of their strategies by presenting a vision of how they will reach the goals.[21]

"In terms of country-level objectives, we need to leave that much more to the country," says Lomoy. Rather than aiming for global-level goals, he says, individual nations should be allowed to shoot for their own bar, asking themselves, "What's an ambitious but still realistic target we can set for our country?"

Having country-level aspirations also helps invest smaller countries in the outcome, says Homi Kharas, former World Bank chief economist for East Asia and the Pacific and currently a senior fellow at the Brookings Institution. "If it's just a global target dominated by what happens in China, India and maybe Brazil, it's not motivating for small countries," he says.

Is the progress achieved under the goals sustainable?

While the answer to that question is "unknowable," says Barry Carin, a senior fellow at the Center for International Governance Innovation, a Canadian think tank, many trends are bolstering MDG sustainability.

For instance, innovations in science and technology are helping to achieve the health-related goals. Vaccines reduce child mortality and the spread of diseases such as diphtheria and pertussis, and scientists are working on vaccines that could halt the spread of meningitis and malaria.

Advances in communication also boost local and national economies, says Carin. "Just look at the question of connectivity and telephones," he says. "If you had to wire up Africa with land lines for telephones, it could never have been done. Now, cell phones allow everybody to be connected."

Jeffrey Sachs, a poverty expert and director of Columbia University's Earth Institute, has called cell phones "the single most transformative technology for development," noting that even a limited number of cell phones can greatly boost economic activity.

"It doesn't take more than a few phones to make a transformative difference in an area," he told the news website AllAfrica in 2008. "We're seeing small businesses develop by virtue of people having phones, being able to find clients, make purchases, get supplies."[22]

If technology were the only factor, the outlook might be sunnier. Unfortunately, the world faces significant

Big Rise in Children Attending School

The number of children not attending school dropped from more than 100 million in 1990 to just over 60 million in 2010 — a 42 percent decline. Sub-Saharan Africa has made the least progress — and Asia the most — toward the key U.N. goal of making primary education available to all by 2015.

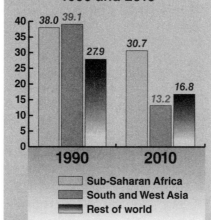

Number of Out-of-School Children by Region, 1990 and 2010

Legend:
- Sub-Saharan Africa
- South and West Asia
- Rest of world

Source: "Reaching Out-of-School Children Is Crucial for Development," United Nations Educational, Scientific and Cultural Organization, June 2012, p. 2, http://unesdoc.unesco.org/images/0021/0 02165/216519E.pdf.

problems that threaten local economies — both rich and poor.

Climate change — and the world's inaction in curbing it — is a major threat to MDG progress, says Charles Kenny, a senior fellow at the Center for Global Development, a Washington think tank. "If Bangladesh is under water in 50 years, that's going to have an effect on Bangladesh's development process," he says.

Another challenge is the ongoing economic crisis, which has brought global GDP growth to a crawl and led many wealthy countries to cut foreign aid to impoverished countries.

"The financial crisis has had a direct impact on development assistance and flows of resources to poor parts of the world," says InterAction's Worthington. Yet, he adds, "at the same time, many developing countries have continued to see significant growth."

In fact, says the Brookings Institution's Chandy, during the 2007 to 2008 recession, developing countries fared "a lot better than the West did, and there are many reasons why that might be the case." For one thing, he says, their financial markets "are much less developed" and less exposed to the problems that roiled places like Europe and the United States.

That news would likely come as cold comfort to factory workers in those countries. A 2010 study from the London-based aid organization Oxfam found that many export-dependent workers and industries in countries such as Ghana and Indonesia were devastated by the global downturn, "even when national economies seem[ed] to be weathering the storm."[23]

More recently, however, some developing countries' economies are slowing, partly because of Europe's ongoing debt crisis.[24] "Most low-income countries have held up relatively well so far, but now face intensified adverse spillover effects from the slowdown in both developed and major middle-income countries," the U.N. warned in 2013. The organization's "World Economics Situation and Prospects 2013" report noted decelerating GDP growth for low- and lower-middle-income countries in recent years.[25]

Even if many developing countries remain strong, the fate of the world's largest nation looms as a major threat for the global economy.

"Frankly, so far, the developing world has weathered the global recession comparatively well," says Kenny. "That won't go on forever. If China crashes, we're all in trouble."

Indeed, the list of clear and present dangers that could shut down MDG progress at times seems endless. Still, the question of whether progress is sustainable may largely boil down to one factor.

"A lot of it depends on growth. If you have dramatic population growth and poor economic growth, things will get worse," says Carin.

BACKGROUND

Unmet Goals

Although the U.N. formally introduced the world to the MDGs in 2001, the goals had, in fact, been decades in the making.

The world has a long, if not successful, history of setting human development targets. U.S. President Franklin D. Roosevelt, for example, crafted his own ambitious goals for fighting poverty. In his 1941 State of the Union address, he laid out "four freedoms," including "freedom from want," that he believed would be foundational to rebuilding the world after World War II.[26]

Likewise, in the U.N.'s Universal Declaration of Human Rights in 1948, the fledgling organization's 58 members agreed that human beings were entitled to 30

A Chinese woman washes clothes at a slum across from new, subsidized, government-built apartments in Shenyang, China, on March 11, 2009. Achievements in eradicating poverty and hunger — key Millennium Development Goals — have been accelerated by rapid economic growth in East Asia, where the poverty rate fell from nearly 60 percent to less than 20 percent in the past 25 years. Poverty rates in China are expected to fall to around 5 percent in 2015.

fundamental civil, political, economic, social, and cultural rights. The declaration gave birth to the Commission on Human Rights, which has promoted those rights via international treaties.[27]

At the suggestion of U.S. President John F. Kennedy, the U.N. in the 1960s declared the first "Development Decade," setting a minimum goal of 5 percent growth in aggregate national income in all less-developed countries, with developed nations contributing 1 percent of their incomes in economic aid and private investment.[28]

In a 2009 history of the MDGs, David Hulme, executive director of the Brooks World Poverty Institute at Great Britain's University of Manchester, described this period as one of "a rash of goal-setting," in which "enthusiasm to set targets ran ahead of commitment to action."[29]

When it became clear in the mid-1970s that the world would not meet the targets, the U.N. went on in 1970 and 1980 to declare its Second and Third Development Decades, which also became decades of largely unfulfilled goals.

During the Second Decade, developed nations agreed to provide 0.7 percent of their GDPs in foreign aid — a benchmark that remains in effect but that most developed countries fail to hit.

CHRONOLOGY

1960s–1980s *World experiments with development goal setting.*

1961 U.N. declares 1960s the Decade of Development, later known as the First Development Decade. Developing countries are to accelerate growth by 5 percent annually.

1970 U.N. sets 0.7 percent of gross national product as a goal for rich nations to give in foreign aid.

1971 U.N. establishes Second Development Decade, with annual GDP growth target of 6 percent for developing nations.

1973 World Bank President Robert McNamara announces goal of eradicating poverty by close of 20th century.

1981 With the Second Development Decade goals still "largely unfulfilled," U.N. establishes Third Development Decade.

1990s *World grows more optimistic in fight against poverty; holds more development summits.*

March 5–9, 1990 World Conference on Education for All in Jomtien, Thailand, establishes a goal of universal primary education by 2000.

June 3–14, 1992 At U.N. Conference on Environment and Development (the Rio Earth Summit), more than 100 heads of state agree to strive for "achieving sustainable development in the 21st century."

1995 Organisation for Economic Cooperation and Development (OECD) establishes International Development Goals (IDGs), the precursors to the Millennium Development Goals (MDGs). U.N.'s Fourth World Conference on Women in Beijing establishes 12-point Platform for Action in areas such as women's education and reproductive health.

2000s *World sets new development and antipoverty goals.*

2000 At U.N.'s Millennium Summit, 189 countries adopt Millennium Declaration, which encourages tolerance and solidarity and asserts that each individual has the right to dignity, freedom, equality, and a basic standard of living — including freedom from hunger and violence.

2001 Millennium Development Goals are formally adopted; U.N. Secretary-General Kofi Annan releases "road map" toward implementing Millennium Declaration.

March 18–22, 2002 At a summit in Monterrey, Mexico, developed nations reaffirm their commitment to giving 0.7 percent of their national incomes to poor nations.

2005 At G8 summit in Gleneagles, Scotland, developed nations agree to provide debt relief to qualifying countries (July 6–8); world leaders agree to spend additional $50 billion annually to fight poverty and reaffirm their commitment to the MDGs (Sept. 14–16).

Jan. 1, 2008 Four new MDG targets go into effect: achieving full and productive employment, universal access to reproductive health services, universal access to HIV-AIDS treatment, and reducing loss of biodiversity.

2010 At U.N. World MDG Summit in New York, leaders pledge $40 billion toward a Global Strategy for Women's and Children's Health. The first MDG target — halving the global extreme poverty rate — is met.

2012 World reaches two more targets: halving the proportion of people without access to clean drinking water and improving the lives of the world's slum dwellers. U.N. Secretary-General Ban Ki-moon names three cochairs of a high-level panel to advise on post-2015 goals: President Susilo Bam-bang Yudhoyono of Indonesia; President Ellen Johnson Sirleaf of Liberia; and Prime Minister David Cameron of the U.K. (May 9). At the Rio+20 Summit, world leaders agree to move ahead with conceptualizing sustainable development goals (SDGs) as post-2015 MDG replacements (June 20–22).

2013 World leaders attended an MDG summit in September, agreeing to redouble efforts to meet MDG goals by 2015. Pledges from countries, private-sector companies, and civil-society organizations pledged $2.5 billion to meet remaining goals.[32]

2014 In December, the UN General Assembly released a synthesis reflecting on past achievements and suggesting recommendations for the next round of MDG goals. It called for a greater understanding of individual countries' particular challenges and for the integration of new tools — including advanced technologies and private partnerships — to achieve greater success post-2015.

2015 Development leaders will meet in September to set out the next round of MGD goals. December marks the deadline for all current MDG targets.

In 1974, the United Nations resolved to establish a New International Economic Order to improve developing countries' role in international trade and narrow the gap between them and developed nations. But this, too, would be unfruitful. In 1984, the General Assembly acknowledged the lack of progress and that the targets for the decade remained unmet.[30]

During the second half of the 20th century, developing countries racked up heavy debts to both private banks and international institutions such as the World Bank and the IMF. By the early 2000s, payments on many of those debts would become larger than the indebted countries' domestic budgets for health, education and other basic needs.[31]

New Beginning

As the Cold War ended in the late 1980s, industrialized countries began to cut their foreign aid budgets, which had been used in part to curry favor in the ideological superpower struggle between communism and capitalism. Between 1985 and 1995, U.S. government spending overall rose 15 percent, but U.S. foreign aid declined by 32 percent.[33]

International development organizations, worried about cuts in aid, rallied to consider how to attack global problems.[34] The World Bank's "World Development Report 1990" and the U.N. Development Programme's (UNDP) "Human Development Report" both stressed the importance of addressing global poverty. The U.N. held four international conferences in 1990, kicking off what would be a decade of international meetings and discussions about global development.

"In the '90s, almost every year we had a summit," remembers MDG architect Vandemoortele. "We had Copenhagen. We had Cairo, reproductive health in 1994, human rights in 1993, we had settlements in 1996, a food summit in 1996."

Although the summits suggested a renewed international vigor for development, says Hulme of the Brooks World Poverty Institute, summits often have one chief outcome: hot air. "First, national ministers declare a grand goal," he says. "Subsequently this goal has some general influence on activity, but it is not systematically pursued. At the next U.N. summit or conference, the minister (or his/her successor) agrees to the same or a reduced goal for a later date."[35]

Still, the Christian relief organization World Vision described the 1990s as a time of optimism for the biggest international aid contributors. The U.S. economy, the world's largest, was humming along strongly, and two of the world's most powerful leaders, U.S. President Bill Clinton and U.K. Prime Minister Tony Blair, were beginning to work toward reducing poverty. As World Vision noted in a 2011 paper on the MDGs, the World Bank was switching its *modus operandi* in developing countries from imposing structural adjustment programs — which focused on establishing free-market economies and eliminating protectionism — toward poverty-reduction strategies.[36]

Ultimately, many of the summits helped to establish the MDG policy framework.[37]

Amid this atmosphere of hopeful global cooperation, a group of international development ministers in 1995 commissioned the OECD to predict how the next century of development would look. The organization's 1996 report, "Shaping the 21st Century," stressed the need for governments, international organizations, and financial institutions to cooperate on economic development.

More important, the report laid out six "ambitious but realizable goals," which came to be known as the International Development Goals (IDGs). They were prototypes for some of the MDGs, with many of the same aims. For example, the OECD set the goal of halving the rate of "extreme poverty" in developing countries by 2015, achieving universal primary education, making progress toward gender equality, and reducing infant and maternal mortality.

"We the Peoples"

The MDGs were born in part out of this atmosphere of goal setting and summit holding, but they were also, in former U.N. official Vandemoortele's opinion, a product of timing.

"Then came the Millennium and everyone had to do something special," he says. "The U.N., for lack of imagination called together another summit, the Millennium Summit."

In preparation, Secretary-General Annan — in an effort to help U.N. countries craft the declaration that would result from that summit, produced a report, released in early April 2000, titled "We the Peoples: The Role of the United Nations in the 21st Century." It

Do MDG Targets Mask Failure?

Critics say some goals are set too low.

Since their inception, the Millennium Development Goals (MDGs) were seen as providing strong, concrete targets for measuring progress — or lack thereof — in meeting the goals. But critics say some of the targets are set so low that the success they indicate is sometimes illusory.

For example, the first goal — halving of the proportion of people living on less than $1.25 per day — was met in 2010. However, simply boosting average earnings to $1.26 per day, or even $2 per day, still leaves a person remarkably poor.

Substantial progress also was logged in education. As measured by the MDGs, 90 percent of primary school–age children were enrolled as of 2010, and near–gender parity was achieved in primary school education in 2012.[1]

However, "Enrollment and learning are two notably different things," as Charles Kenny, a senior fellow at the Center for Global Development, wrote in his 2011 book, *Getting Better: Why Global Development Is Succeeding and How We Can Improve the World Even More.* He points to a recent survey showing that, of Indian students who had completed lower primary schooling, 31 percent could not read a simple story. Only one quarter of Ghanaian 15- to 19-year-olds scored more than 50 percent on tests of 1- or 2-digit math problems.[2]

Judging from such statistics, it's no wonder that kids in some of the poorest nations aren't learning. School days in some countries are as short as two hours.[3] In addition, just because the kids are in school doesn't mean that the teachers are. In fact, teacher absenteeism is rampant in some parts of the world. One new study found that teachers in five South African provinces were absent for more than one month in the year, or more than 20 school days.[4] A 2011 World Bank study showed that most primary school teachers in Ghana spend only 76 of 196 school days in the classroom.[5]

In other words, improving the quantity of children in the classrooms has achieved progress — statistically — toward the target. Measuring the quality of that education, however, is another story. This is just one example of the need to be careful about focusing too much on a goal and not on broader outcomes, says Homi Kharas, former chief economist in the East Asia and Pacific Region of the World Bank and currently a senior fellow at the Brookings Institution. That principle extends beyond education and to the other goals as well, he says.

He likens the link between targets and outcomes to the link between carbon dioxide (CO_2) levels and global temperature change.

AFP/Getty Images/Issouf Sanogo

Although 90 percent of primary school–age children were enrolled in schools as of 2010, experts warn that that statistic does not indicate how much the children are learning or whether there is a teacher present at all times. Above, children attend class at the Friendship Primary school in Zinder, Niger, in West Africa on June 1, 2012.

"We obviously have studies that link those two together, so it may well be that there's an intermediate target [such as CO_2 emissions] that you want to monitor," he says. "But at the end of the day, it's important to be very clear what that real outcome is" — temperature change — "so that we avoid just focusing on that one intermediate target."

— *Danielle Kurtzleben*

[1] *The Millennium Development Goals Report 2012*, United Nations, pp. 16, 20, http://mdgs.un.org/unsd/mdg/Resources/Static/Products/Progress2012/English2012.pdf.

[2] Charles Kenny, Getting Better: Why Global Development Is Succeeding and How We Can Improve the World Even More. New York, New York: Basic Books, 2011, p. 91.

[3] Larry Elliott and Decca Aitkenhead, "It's Payback Time: Don't Expect Sympathy — Lagarde to Greeks," *The Guardian*, May 25, 2012, www.guardian.co.uk/world/2012/may/25/payback-time-lagarde-greeks.

[4] Carol Paton, "SA Outdoes Poor Neighbours on Absentee Teachers," *Business Day*, May 17, 2012, www.businessday.co.za/articles/Content.aspx?id=171942.

[5] "High Teacher Absenteeism Hindering Inclusive Education in Ghana — World Bank," *Modern Ghana*, April 17, 2011, http://www.modernghana.com/news/325303/1/high-teacher-absenteeism-hindering-inclusive-educa.html.

emphasized many of the topics that would become part of the MDGs: eliminating extreme poverty, better educational and employment opportunities, promoting better health care, and combating HIV-AIDS.

In advance of the Millennium Summit, the mood was particularly ambitious, with leaders ready to make good on all of the past U.N. development shortcomings. "They kind of looked back at all these declarations and promises that were made in the past decades, and they made the mother of all declarations by summarizing the key promises the world leaders had made in terms of human development," says Vandemoortele.

However, drafting the final goals was controversial, as individuals and organizations jockeyed for their causes to be included in the MDGs. "If your goal was in the Declaration, then you could put it on the agenda at national and international meetings for years to come," wrote Hulme. "Websites buzzed, email campaigns piled up in ministers' accounts and large and small meetings were convened, especially in the rich world."[38]

Meanwhile, the goals had to have unanimous international backing — no small feat for a group of nearly 200 countries. While the process ultimately yielded eight goals, it also made for some very unhappy organizations.

For instance, Steven Sinding, director general of the International Planned Parenthood Federation in London, wrote in 2005 about the challenge of getting women's reproductive health onto the MDG agenda. At a 1994 International Conference on Population and Development in Cairo, participants agreed that women in least-developed countries needed basic reproductive rights, particularly the freedom to determine the number of children they would bear. These reproductive freedoms would be foundational for broader progress in areas such as public health, education, and the environment, Sinding says.

But not everyone supported reproductive health as a global development goal, and in the minds of some women's health advocates, politics won out over women's — and some say society's — best interests. Annan's "We the Peoples" report notably made no mention of reproductive health. The developing nations were split on the issue of reproductive health and ultimately opted to appease the more conservative member countries, said Sinding's federation.[39]

"I think the calculation of the Secretariat was, 'Let's not sacrifice the greater coherence and get involved in

International UNICEF ambassador Orlando Bloom, a British actor, visits the Kaule Community Organization in Kalika, Nepal, on Jan. 10, 2008. The UNICEF–supported organization has helped to boost school enrollment and encouraged the consumption of iodized salt, which prevents goiters. Maternal mortality and child deaths in Nepal have declined since 1996, putting the country on track to reach those two Millennium Development Goals by 2015.

these highly controversial topics,'" said Ambassador Gert Rosenthal of Guatemala, one of the Millennium Declaration's coauthors.[40]

As a result, according to women's health advocates, the issue would be ignored for 15 years on the international stage. As Sinding succinctly put it, "If you're not an MDG, you're not on the agenda."[41]

Similarly, other issues — such as economic growth and clearer targets for rich countries' assistance — did not make it into the MDGs, Hulme wrote.

Determining the numerical targets themselves was also a matter of some debate, according to Vandemoortele. Leaders eventually settled on what seemed to be a simple, diplomatic solution: The numerical goals should sustain recent development trends.

"Political leaders were asking themselves, what should be a reasonable target?" he says.

The only way to answer that question was to ask, "What have we done over the past two or three decades?"

For instance, for under–age 5 mortality, Vandemoortele explained, "We had a rate of decline of the 1970s and '80s of such a magnitude that if you extrapolate it, you would achieve a reduction of two-thirds." The same process was carried out for other targets as well. "On poverty it only says halving, because decline was much more modest in those areas."

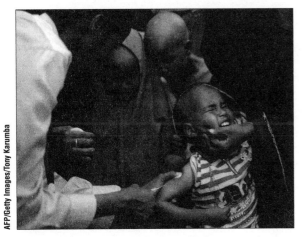

AFP/Getty Images/Tony Karumba

A young Somali refugee is vaccinated against polio and measles at the Dadaab refugee complex in northeastern Kenya on Aug. 1, 2011. Vaccines are inexpensive ways to achieve health-related MDGs worldwide. Vaccines reduce child mortality and the spread of diseases such as diphtheria and pertussis, and scientists are working on vaccines that could halt the spread of meningitis and malaria.

Following Through

But if the MDGs were simply to follow existing poverty-reduction trends, what purpose did they really serve?

Perhaps the goals' most immediate achievement was to organize international donors, recipients, and aid organizations around the MDGs as logical thematic areas of concentration. "Before the MDGs, we didn't have nicely organized communities focused on reducing malaria or increasing maternal health or decreasing infant mortality," says InterAction's Worthington.

"The shift from goals to results greatly accelerated the progress of human well-being in a number of areas," he adds. "The rapid drop in malaria happened because of this focus on results under the goals. All of these things had been happening at a certain pace, but they were accelerated once we had a set of indicators and a desire to increase results. And the goals were the frame that made that possible."

Indeed, malaria deaths, which had doubled between 1980 and 2004, reversed direction, falling from 1.8 million in 2004 to 1.2 million in 2010, largely because of the wider use of insecticide-treated mosquito nets.[42]

Developing countries, led by the IMF, also organized themselves around the new targets. They produced poverty-reduction strategy papers, updated regularly, describing the long-term structural and social policies and programs they would follow to promote overall growth and reduce poverty.[43] Although the papers force countries to assess their current and future situations, Sachs described the poverty-reduction plan process as backwards.

In his 2005 book *The End of Poverty*, Sachs outlined the typical steps in producing a policy-reduction strategy paper. "Ethiopia is told, for example, 'You can expect around $1 billion next year. Please tell us what you plan to do with that aid,'" Sachs wrote.[44]

Instead, he argued, the process should be "turned around. The first step should be to learn what the country actually needs in foreign assistance," he wrote. Then the IMF and World Bank could "go out to raise the required amount from the donors!"[45]

But obtaining the necessary aid is not easy. Donor countries have failed to meet their foreign aid commitments since before the goals were implemented. And in 2002, more than 50 heads of state signed the Monterrey Consensus, which urged developed countries to make "concrete efforts" to donate at least 0.7 percent of gross national income as foreign aid, known as official development assistance (ODA). Then again at the Gleneagles G8 Summit in 2005 in Scotland, donor countries pledged to boost ODA. But in 2013, only Norway, Luxembourg, Denmark, the United Kingdom, and Sweden hit the 0.7 mark in terms of ODA as a share of gross national income (GNI), a figure roughly comparable to GDP in many countries.[46] In 2013, the United States contributed 0.19 percent of its GNI in foreign aid.[47]

Still, since 2000, nations have taken several momentous steps forward. At Gleneagles, the G8 countries agreed to forgive the debt of highly indebted poor countries — a cause championed by Sachs, Pope John Paul II, and anti-poverty activist Bono, the lead singer of the Irish rock band U2. Under the Multilateral Debt Relief Initiative, the IMF, World Bank, and African Development Fund (a branch of the African Development Bank that provides very low-interest loans to Africa's poorest countries) would forgive 100 percent of the debt of countries with unsustainable debt burdens. But they had to first "demonstrate satisfactory performance" in macroeconomic policies, implementing a poverty-reduction strategy and managing government expenditures.[48]

So far, of 39 eligible or potentially eligible nations, 35 are receiving full debt relief, according to the IMF.[49]

Former U.N. official Vandemoortele calls debt relief a lifesaver for citizens in the world's poorest nations. "The evidence is very clear that the savings that these countries made on their national budgets were [largely] allocated to the areas that matter for reducing poverty," he says.

In 2005, member states agreed to pursue four new MDG targets to fill in gaps not addressed by the original goals: achieving full and productive employment, providing access to reproductive health and HIV-AIDS treatment, and preserving biodiversity. These four targets went into effect in January 2008. And in 2010, a $40 billion initiative on women's and children's health was implemented.

In a 2010 op-ed in *The Financial Times*, Sachs criticized the series of headline-grabbing donor meetings and promises in the 2000s as a showcase for their lack of accountability. Taken together, he said, wealthy donor countries have fallen short on every big headline pledge they made during the decade, including at:

- Monterrey in 2002, to reach 0.7 percent of GNP in development aid;
- Gleneagles in 2005, to double African aid by 2010;
- L'Aquila in 2009, to direct $22 billion over three years to raise productivity of small farmers; and
- Copenhagen in 2009, to add $30 billion over three years for climate change adaptation and mitigation.

Promises were easily made but not delivered, he said, because the commitments had no clear mechanisms for fulfillment.[50]

The economic crisis of 2008 to 2009 also threatened international aid, but the effects seem to have been muted thus far. A 2012 World Bank report notes that total disbursements by OECD donor countries increased by 4.3 percent from 2008 to 2010. The report also found that developing nations fared well by another key measure: "Despite the financial crisis . . . debt service ratios continued to fall in most developing regions."[51]

Still, the crisis delivered a blow to MDG progress on some targets. The U.N. has estimated that there were 50 million more working poor in 2011 than was projected by precrisis trends.[52] And the crisis slowed the growing share of women in nonagricultural paid employment.[53]

AFP/Getty Images/Pierre Verdy

Irish antipoverty activist and singer Bono (right), former British Prime Minister Tony Blair (center), and billionaire American philanthropist Bill Gates (left) are leading intensified efforts to reduce global poverty. In 2005, they lobbied for multilateral institutions to forgive the external debt of highly indebted poor countries so they could afford to pursue the Millennium Development Goals. Today, countries with annual per-capita incomes of $380 or less can have their debt wiped clean if they have a satisfactory poverty-reduction strategy.

Oxfam, the Christian relief organization, found that some companies in Thailand and Cambodia took advantage of the crisis to institute wage freezes, reduce work hours, or pressure workers into less-secure contracts.[54]

Interestingly, the crisis boosted progress on one goal dealing with environmental sustainability. According to the 2012 U.N. MDG report, world greenhouse gas emissions dipped slightly in 2009, from 30.2 billion to 30.1 billion metric tons, due to slowing economic activity.

CURRENT SITUATION
Mixed Progress

Although progress has been rapid and even impressive on some of the eight Millennium Development Goals, on others it has been slow. Here is a rundown on progress made thus far on key targets for each of the eight MDGs, based on the U.N.'s 2014 report on the status of the goals:[55]

- **Eradicate extreme poverty and hunger** — The first target, to cut in half the proportion of the world's inhabitants living on less than $1.25 a day, was met in 2008, driven largely by explosive economic growth in

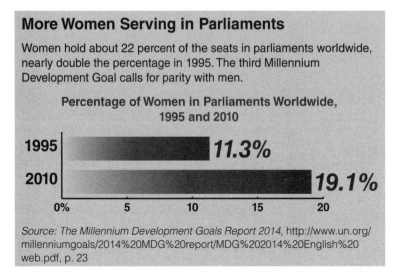

More Women Serving in Parliaments

Women hold about 22 percent of the seats in parliaments worldwide, nearly double the percentage in 1995. The third Millennium Development Goal calls for parity with men.

Percentage of Women in Parliaments Worldwide, 1995 and 2010

1995 — *11.3%*
2010 — *19.1%*

0%   5   10   15   20

Source: The Millennium Development Goals Report 2014, http://www.un.org/millenniumgoals/2014%20MDG%20report/MDG%202014%20English%20web.pdf, p. 23

Asia's emerging economies. In July 2012, the U.N. reported that "for the first time since poverty trends began to be monitored, both the number of people living in extreme poverty and the poverty rates have fallen in every developing region — including sub-Saharan Africa, where rates are highest." Another poverty-reduction target, achieving "full and productive employment and decent work for all," has been more difficult to achieve during the global economic crisis. In developing countries, a full 56 percent of employed people worked in vulnerable — informal or unpaid — situations in 2013.

• **Achieve universal primary education** — Primary enrollment in developing regions reached 90 percent by 2012, up from 82 percent in 1999. But at this rate, the goal of universal primary school enrollment will not be reached by 2015.[56] Of the 58 million children not in school, half live in conflict-prone areas, and 44 percent of those are in sub-Saharan Africa. More than half of the 61 million children who still are not in school live in sub-Saharan Africa, and 42 percent of those live in poor countries that are experiencing conflict. And being a girl is also a liability, though decreasingly so: in 1999, 58 percent of out-of-school kids were girls; by 2012, the share was 53 percent.[57]

Promote gender equality and empower women — The developing world did not eliminate gender gaps in primary and secondary education by 2005, as the U.N. had originally set out to do, but it is now within striking distance of that goal. In 2012, there were 97 girls to every 100 boys enrolled in primary school, within the three-point margin-of-error range to equal parity. However, the developing world is just shy of parity in secondary education (with 96 girls to every boy). Developing regions achieved parity in tertiary, or university, education in 2010. Another indicator for this goal — having more women in the workplace — is falling short. Worldwide, only 40 percent of nonagricultural jobs are held by women, a figure that dips as low as 19 percent in North Africa and 20 percent in Southern and Western Asia.[58]

• **Reduce child mortality rates** — Progress has been slow on reducing by two thirds the 1990 under-age-5 mortality rate of 97 deaths per 1,000 live births.[59] By 2012, under-5 deaths in developing regions had been reduced by less than one half, to 53 per 1,000, with sub-Saharan Africa making substantial progress — down from 177 in 1990 to 98 in 2012, still the world's highest.

• **Improve maternal health** — So far, the world appears likely to miss its target of reducing 1990 maternal mortality rates by three quarters by 2015. As of 2013, the rate had been reduced by less than one half, from 380 deaths per 100,000 live births to 210. As of 2008, the rate had been reduced only by about one third, from 440 deaths per 100,000 live births to 290. Progress has been slowest in the Caribbean, Oceania, southern Asia, and sub-Saharan Africa. The second target — achieving universal access to reproductive health — also remains well out of reach, largely due to low rates of contraception use, high teen pregnancy rates, and insufficient medical care for pregnant women. In 2012, only 52 percent of pregnant women in developing regions saw a doctor four or more times.[60]

• **Fight HIV-AIDS, malaria, and other diseases** — Remarkable progress has been made in halting and beginning to reverse the spread of HIV-AIDS. Between 2001 and 2012, the rate of new cases among 15- to 49-year-olds in developing regions declined from 1 in 1,000 people to just 0.6, largely due to improvement in

Have developed countries done enough to help achieve the MDGs?

YES
Jan Vandemoortele
Former Official at UNICEF and U.N. Development Program; Coarchitect of the MDGs

Written for *CQ Global Researcher*, August 2012

To further the last of the eight MDG goals — building a global development partnership — developed countries promised significant progress in four areas: debt relief, foreign aid, global governance and global trade. Despite the absence of clear, quantitative targets on these points, one can draw a proxy scorecard for their performance since 1990.

First, developed countries can rightly claim to have kept the promise on debt relief. The debt burden of the developing world has become less crippling over the past two decades. Not only has this freed money for essential services, it has also contributed to an economic revival in the developing world, where the confidence of international partners and domestic actors was undermined by excessively high debt burdens.

Second, developed countries have increased foreign aid, currently about $133 billion a year. The increase was steepest in the early 2000s, in the wake of the adoption of the MDGs. Since the mid-2000s, however, foreign aid has leveled off. Only five countries — Denmark, Luxembourg, the Netherlands, Norway, and Sweden — consistently reach the target of allocating 0.7 percent of national income to foreign aid. Most large countries spend less than 0.35 percent on foreign aid.

Third, developed countries have maintained undue influence over global institutions. This is best exemplified by the World Bank and International Monetary Fund (IMF). An unwritten rule dating to the 1940s prevails: that the former is headed by an American and the latter by a European. Still, the choice of leaders for these institutions is gradually changing in favor of women and ethnic diversity.

Finally, the global trading system and patent laws have not become more MDG friendly. The Doha round of trade negotiations remains in the doldrums, largely because developed countries try to keep the system rigged in their favor, in essence, trying to "kick away the ladder" they themselves climbed. Developed countries all used subsidies and tariffs and seldom honored patents, but they now say free trade and copyrights are essential for fostering development.

So, developed countries have contributed to MDG progress. But a partnership among equals will come about only if the MDG discourse focuses on "ideas changing minds" rather than "money changing hands." The British economist John Maynard Keynes once argued: "The power of vested interests is vastly exaggerated compared with the gradual encroachment of ideas."

NO
Gabriele Köhler
Visiting Fellow, Institute of Development Studies, Brighton, U.K.

Written for *CQ Global Researcher*, August 2012

No! For more than 50 years, developed countries have committed to transferring 0.7 percent of gross national income (GNI) to developing countries in the form of official development assistance, or foreign aid. The target was conceived by the World Council of Churches during the 1960s, when organized development cooperation was first introduced. It has been reiterated ever since and is integral to MDG goal No. 8 — building a global development partnership. It was reaffirmed at European Union and G8 summits in 2005 and at the high-level U.N. General Assembly MDG review in 2010.

Despite those commitments, the average foreign-aid-to-GNI ratio for 23 of the world's most industrialized countries in 2011 was 0.31 percent — less than half the promised rate. Only five countries complied with the target. So on the whole, the developed world has not done enough to help developing countries achieve the MDGs.

However, other measures would have a more systemic impact on MDG achievement than meeting the 0.7 threshold, such as making deep structural reforms in international trade rules and revamping the international finance system. Preferential market access for developing countries' products and services, freer intellectual property rights, freedom of migration at properly remunerated wages, and predictable international financial markets are preconditions for the MDGs to halve poverty, increase employment and decent work, and assure access to affordable food, nutrition, or medication.

Moreover, financial flows from outside cannot solve domestic structural inequities. Many low-income countries display rising income and wealth inequalities. They also have deteriorating health and education systems and tolerate exploitative work conditions and weak social-protection provisions for poverty, unemployment, childhood, and old age.

If, however, developing countries' governments would adopt a higher tax-to-gross-domestic-product (GDP) ratio and better control their expenditures, they could afford more public goods, services, and social assistance payments. In many low- and middle-income countries, taxes are only 15 percent of GDP — compared to an average of 40 percent in developed countries. More equitable tax systems could rebalance income inequality while ensuring that food price supports, education, health, water and sanitation, infrastructure, and environmental protection are generously funded. Such reforms are a precondition for equitably achieving the MDGs.

sub-Saharan Africa, where rates fell by nearly one half. Still, treatment hasn't expanded quickly enough to hit another target: universal access to HIV-AIDS treatment. As of 2012, only 30 percent of people living with HIV in developing countries were receiving antiretroviral treatment.[61]

Meanwhile, progress on many other serious diseases has been mixed. By 2012, malaria deaths declined 46 percent since 2000, largely attributable to expanded use of insecticide-treated mosquito nets. However, new diagnoses of tuberculosis in the developing world are holding steady with 8.6 million cases in 2012, though the rate of infection fell slightly from the previous year.

• **Ensure environmental sustainability** — This goal has four targets and 10 indicators covering a variety of environmental problems, some of which cannot be measured, such as integrating sustainable development principles into country policies and reversing the loss of biodiversity by 2010. According to the U.N., the world's total acreage of protected areas has increased to cover 14 percent of terrestrial and coastal marine areas by 2012, from just 8.3 percent in 1990,[62] and

HIV-AIDS patients are treated at a medical facility at a Buddhist Temple in Lopburi province, north of Bangkok, on Nov. 27, 2011. Expanded access to treatment worldwide has meant remarkable progress in halting and beginning to reverse the spread of HIV-AIDS. Between 2001 and 2010, the rate of new cases among 15- to 49-year-olds in developing regions declined by 22 percent, much of that in sub-Saharan Africa, where rates fell by nearly one third. Yet treatment hasn't expanded quickly enough to hit another MDG target: universal access to HIV-AIDS treatment. As of 2010, only 48 percent of people living with HIV in developing countries were receiving antiretroviral treatment.

more species are surviving than would have without conservation, but the gains have not been significant enough for this goal to have been declared met. However, the U.N. declared in 2012 that the world has met the goal of halving the proportion of people without access to safe water and sanitation, and 200 million slum dwellers have either improved water and sanitation access or better housing.[63]

• **Develop a global partnership for development** — The last MDG has no clear targets. Rather, it calls for improving international trade, addressing poor countries' debt, and providing access to pharmaceuticals and technology. Nevertheless, there has been some measurable progress. Development aid continues to grow, even though it has fallen as a share of donor countries' income. Least-developed countries are benefiting from preferential trade agreements, and debt-servicing ratios for those countries are trending downward. However, given the goal's vague wording, exactly what "success" will look like when it is achieved is somewhat of a mystery.

Lessons Learned

After 12 years, the world has learned several lessons about meeting the Millennium Development Goals, most important that they are interconnected. Universal primary education, for instance, implies gender equality at least in schooling.

It also has become clear that improving the lot of women can improve a country's economy and health. Likewise, the U.N. noted in its 2011 MDG progress report, growing up in rural settings, living in poor households, and having a less-educated mother all increase a child's risk of dying at a young age. And making measles vaccinations more available has helped to reduce child deaths due to measles by 78 percent since 2000.

According to former UNDP head Kemal Dervis, it is important to understand the interconnectedness of the goals in order to make sustainable progress. For instance, he points out, improving health and education in the poorest countries is critical, but economic growth is necessary to reinforce those benefits. Unfortunately, no MDG explicitly targeted economic growth.

"It is true that if you don't have a healthy and educated labor force, you're not likely to grow," says Dervis. "But, on the other hand, if you produce a lot of high school graduates and have a very good health-care system, if your financial system doesn't work, there's not enough investment." When people are then left poor and jobless, "it's difficult for the country to break out of the trap of being poor."

Others point out that the strongest MDGs were those with specific, quantifiable targets. The weakest goals were those that were less clear, said UNDP poverty practice director Selim Jahan. For instance, the last goal about developing a global partnership for development was rarely assessed because it did not have any deadlines, said the goal.

"It will be useful if, in the post-2015 period, there is an initial assessment of . . . how improvements in development cooperation . . . would positively impact other MDGs," he wrote in 2009.[64]

OUTLOOK

Future Planning

Regardless of whether the goals will be met by the end of 2015, world leaders are looking ahead to what comes next. In 2012, U.N. Secretary-General Ban Ki-moon created a high-level panel to prepare for a new set of development goals. The panel had three cochairs: Prime Minister David Cameron of the U.K., Liberian President Ellen Johnson-Sirleaf, and President Susilo Bam-bang Yudhoyono of Indonesia.

In an open letter last year, the panel had a number of recommendations.[65] It called for global leaders to begin mapping out post-2015 goals in earnest, for global partnerships to be strengthened based on frank assessments of individual responsibilities, for the implementation of long-term development plans to start now, for accountability monitoring for all stakeholders, for all leaders to take data collection seriously, and for private-sector businesses to play a bigger part as development initiatives unfold.

A synthesis report, released by the UN General Assembly in December 2014, suggested that the next round of MDGs — which will instead be called "Sustainable Development Goals," or SDGs[66] — be improved by paying closer attention to the specific conditions in each country. "Special attention was required for the most vulnerable, in particular African countries, the

least developed countries, the landlocked developing countries and the small island developing states," it said. "Particular attention should also be given to the challenges faced by middle-income countries and countries in situations of fragility and conflict."[67]

Amina J. Mohammed, Ban Ki-moon's special advisor on post-2015 development planning, agrees that the next round of goals will have to take a closer look at context. "The sustainable development agenda really looks at a broader and deeper response to the challenges that we have," she said to the UN News Centre in December. "And it takes together the economic, the social and the environmental dimensions that we have."[68]

Thangavel Palanivel, UNDP chief economist for the Asia-Pacific region, says that key issues under discussion include food security, income inequality, governance, and conflict. In addition, a high-level meeting of the U.N. General Assembly was convened in September 2013 to address a "disability-inclusive development process" to ensure that the world's disabled people, who are disproportionately poor and make up nearly 15 percent of the world's population,[69] are considered in any new development goals.[70]

While those may be admirable topics to tackle, says the Center for Global Development's Kenny, they must also be measurable so progress can be tracked, which could prove difficult. "The measure has to be agreed on by 180-odd world leaders," Kenny says. "On child mortality, everyone agrees what child mortality is. On maternal mortality, everyone agrees what maternal mortality is. On democracy, not everyone agrees what democracy is," he says. "How do you measure it on a scale of 0 to 10?"

Likewise, he notes, while some want a goal addressing failed states, countries would have to agree on the definition of a "failed" state — a label most countries would not want applied to them. As Carin, of the Center for International Governance Innovation, succinctly puts it, "What's the use of an aspirational statement like 'life should be wonderful' if you can't measure progress?"

Carin's organization has proposed 12 goal options, which include new concepts such as "universal connectivity" and "disaster reduction."[71] Likewise, the U.K.–based think tank IDP advocates a fundamental reshaping of the MDGs to make sure they are "more explicitly rights-based and participatory." For instance, the group said in an April 2012 paper, the goals should recognize countries' rights to undertake "bolder" or unorthodox policies in areas such as land reform and hunger reduction.[72]

As with the MDGs, scores of players are ready to dive in and have their voices heard in the debate over the new goals. But while having more voices yields a more comprehensive view, it could ultimately lead to a more confusing set of targets. "Ultimately, if too many threads get woven into this and the goals lose their ability to be concrete, they will no longer be effective," says Inter Action's Worthington.

Challenges notwithstanding — and with the old deadline quickly approaching — development officials are ready to enter the next phase with even higher expectations. "What we do want to see is that by the time. . . these goals and the framework is approved, the transition to the new set of goals will be one that takes the unfinished business of the MDGs to greater heights and broadens it," says Mohammed. "That we can hit the ground running."

A special summit on sustainable development will be held in New York in September of 2015, where the coming SDG agenda will be finalized.

NOTES

1. "A Fall to Cheer," *The Economist,* March 3, 2012, http://www.economist.com/node/21548963.

2. "The Millennium Development Goals Report: 2014," United Nations. http://www.un.org/millenniumgoals/2014%20MDG%20report/MDG%202014%20English%20web.pdf

3. "Millennium Development Goal Drinking Water Target Met," March 6, 2012, www.who.int/mediacentre/news/releases/2012/drinking_water_20120306/en/index.html. Also see "The Millennium Development Goals Report 2012," United Nations, http://mdgs.un.org/unsd/mdg/Resources/Static/Products/Progress2012/English2012.pdf.

4. "The Millennium Development Goals Report: 2014," United Nations; p. 24, http://www.un.org/millenniumgoals/2014%20MDG%20report/MDG%202014%20English%20web.pdf.

5. *Ibid.,* p. 26.

6. "The Millennium Development Goals Report: 2014," United Nations. http://www.un.org/millenniumgoals/2014%20MDG%20report/MDG%202014%20English%20web.pdf

7. "The Millennium Development Goals Report: 2014," United Nations; p. 8, http://www.un.org/millenniumgoals/2014%20MDG%20report/MDG%202014%20English%20web.pdf

8. "MDG Goal 2 Fact Sheet," *op. cit.*

9. "The Millennium Development Goals Report: 2014," United Nations; p. 5, http://www.un.org/millenniumgoals/2014%20MDG%20report/MDG%202014%20English%20web.pdf

10. "The Millennium Development Goals Report: 2014," United Nations; p. 5, http://www.un.org/millenniumgoals/2014%20MDG%20report/MDG%202014%20English%20web.pdf.

11. "The Millennium Development Goals Report 2012," *op. cit.,* p. 7.

12. "The Millennium Development Goals Report 2011," United Nations, p. 7, http://www.un.org/millenniumgoals/pdf/%282011_E%29%20MDG%20Report%202011_Book%20LR.pdf.

13. "The Millennium Development Goals Report: 2014," United Nations; p. 8, http://www.un.org/millenniumgoals/2014%20MDG%20report/MDG%202014%20English%20web.pdf.

14. "Mapping Progress: Evidence for a New Development Outlook," Overseas Development Institute, 2011, p. 14.

15. Abhijit Banerjee and Esther Duflo, *Poor Economics* (2011), p. 74.

16. Hari Kumar, "India in a 'Race Against Time' to Meet Millennium Goals," *The New York Times,* Feb. 22, 2012, http://india.blogs.nytimes.com/2012/02/22/india-in-a-race-against-time-to-meet-millenium-goals/.

17. William Easterly, "How the Millennium Development Goals Are Unfair to Africa," Brookings Global Economy and Development, Brookings Institution, November 2007, p. 2.

18. *Ibid.,* p. 5.

19. Jan Vandemoortele, *Taking the MDGs Beyond 2015: Hasten Slowly*, Beyond 2015.org, May 2009, p. 2, www.eadi.org/fileadmin/MDG_2015_Publications/Vandemoortele_PAPER.pdf.

20. Kofi A. Annan, "We the Peoples: The Role of the United Nations in the 21st Century," United Nations, 2000, http://www.un.org/en/events/pastevents/pdfs/We_The_Peoples.pdf.

21. "Factsheet — Poverty Reduction Strategy Papers (PRSP)," International Monetary Fund, April 19, 2012, www.imf.org/external/np/exr/facts/prsp.htm.

22. Cindy Shiner, "Africa: Cell Phones Transform Continent's Development," AllAfrica, Sept. 18, 2008, http://allafrica.com/stories/200809180986.html.

23. Duncan Green, Richard King, May Miller-Dawkins, "The Global Economic Crisis and Developing Countries: Impact and Response," January 2010, p. 9, www.iadb.org/intal/intalcdi/PE/2010/04613.pdf.

24. For background, see Sarah Glazer, "Future of the Euro," *CQ Global Researcher,* May 17, 2011, pp. 237–262.

25. World Economic Situation and Prospects 2013: Global Outlook, United Nations, 2013,pp. 1-3. http://www.un.org/ru/publications/pdfs/2013%20world%20economic%20situation%20and%20prospects.pdf

26. For background, see Peter Katel, "Ending Poverty," *CQ Researcher,* Sept. 9, 2005, pp. 733–760.

27. "A United Nations Priority: Universal Declaration of Human Rights," United Nations, www.un.org/rights/HRToday/declar.htm.

28. "UN," *Political Handbook of the World* (2012).

29. David Hulme, "The Millennium Development Goals (MDGs): A Short History of the World's Biggest Promise," Brooks World Poverty Institute, University of Manchester, September 2009, p. 8.

30. Peter Jackson, "A Prehistory of the Millennium Development Goals: Four Decades of Struggle for Development in the United Nations," *U.N. Chronicle,* Jan. 12, 2007, http://unchronicle.un.org/article/prehistory-millennium-development-goals-four-decades-struggle-development-united-nations/.

31. Katel, *op. cit.,* p. 741.

32. UN News Service Section, "UN News - At UN, World Leaders Agree To Scale Up Actions Against Poverty, Set New Development Goals". N. p., 2015. Web. http://www.un.org/apps/news/story.asp?NewsID=46002#.VP7up9LF-aJ

33. "The Politics of Poverty: Aid in the New Cold War," Christian Aid, p. 11, www.un-ngls.org/orf/politics%20of%20poverty.pdf.

34. Todd Moss, "Crying Crisis," *Foreign Policy,* Sept. 20, 2010, www.foreignpolicy.com/articles/2010/09/20/crying_crisis.

35. Hulme, *op. cit.,* p. 8.

36. "Reaching the MDGs 2.0," World Vision, September 2011, p. 3.

37. *Ibid.*

38. Hulme, *op. cit.,* p. 25.

39. "Reproductive Health and the MDGs," International Planned Parenthood Foundation, April 24, 2012, www.ippf.org/news/blogs/reproductive-health-and-mdgs.

40. *Ibid.*

41. *Ibid.*

42. Christopher J. L. Murray, *et al.*, "Global Malaria Mortality Between 1980 and 2010: A Systematic Analysis," *The Lancet,* Feb. 4, 2012, www.thelancet.com/journals/lancet/article/PIIS 0140-6736%2812%2960034-8/abstract.

43. "Factsheet — Poverty Reduction Strategy Papers (PRSP)," *op. cit.*

44. Jeffrey D. Sachs, *The End of Poverty* (2005), p. 271.

45. *Ibid.*

46. OECD Tables and Charts: http://www.oecd.org/dac/stats/documentupload/ODA%202013%20Tables%20and%20Charts%20En.pdf

47. *Ibid.*

48. "Factsheet — The Multilateral Debt Initiative," International Monetary Fund, June 26, 2012, www.imf.org/external/np/exr/facts/mdri.htm.

49. Imf.org. 'Factsheet — Debt Relief Under The Heavily Indebted Poor Countries (HIPC) Initiative'. N. p., 2015. Web. https://www.imf.org/external/np/exr/facts/hipc.htm.

50. Jeffrey Sachs, "Pool Resources and Reinvent Global Aid," *Financial Times,* Sept. 20, 2010, www.ft.com/intl/cms/s/0/4c510f34-c4fb-11df-9134-00144feab49a.html#axzz20pxJ2uiS.

51. Global Monitoring Report 2012, *op. cit.,* p. 26.

52. The Millennium Development Goals Report 2012, *op. cit.,* p. 8.

53. *Ibid.*, p. 21.

54. The Global Economic Crisis and Developing Countries, *op. cit.*, p. 5.

55. "The Millennium Development Goals Report: 2014," United Nations; p. 23, http://www.un.org/millenniumgoals/2014%20MDG%20report/MDG%202014%20English%20web.pdf

56. "The Millennium Development Goals Report: 2014," United Nations, http://www.un.org/millenniumgoals/2014%20MDG%20report/MDG%202014%20English%20web.pdf

57. "The Millennium Development Goals Report: 2014," United Nations; p. 17, http://www.un.org/millenniumgoals/2014%20MDG%20report/MDG%202014%20English%20web.pdf

58. "The Millennium Development Goals Report: 2014," United Nations; p. 21, http://www.un.org/millenniumgoals/2014%20MDG%20report/MDG%202014%20English%20web.pdf

59. *Ibid.*, p. 24.

60. *Ibid.*, p. 30.

61. *Ibid.*, p. 36.

62. "The Millennium Development Goals Report: 2014," United Nations; p. 42, http://www.un.org/millenniumgoals/2014%20MDG%20report/MDG%202014%20English%20web.pdf

63. "Fact Sheet — MDG 7," United Nations, www.un.org/millenniumgoals/environ.shtml.

64. Selim Jahan, *The Millennium Development Goals Beyond 2015* (2009), p. 5.

65. "One Year On: An Open Letter from Former Members of the UN Secretary-General's High-Level Panel of Eminent Persons on the Post-2015 Agenda," United Nations; p. 1-3, http://www.un.org/sg/management/pdf/HLP_2015_open_letter_sept_2014.pdf

66. "The Economics of Optimism," *The Economist.* N. p., 2015. 2015.http://www.economist.com/news/finance-and-economics/21640361-debate-heats-up-about-what-goals-world-should-set-itself-2030

67. 'United Nations Official Document,'. United Nations, N. p., 2015. Web. http://www.un.org/ga/search/view_doc.asp?symbol=A/69/700&Lang=E

68. 'UN News - Interview With Amina J. Mohammed, Secretary-General's Special Adviser On Post-2015 Development Planning,' UN News Service Section, N. p., 2015. Web. http://www.un.org/apps/news/newsmakers.asp?NewsID=113.

69. 'Press Statements - Message on The International Day For Persons With Disabilities,' United Nations, N. p., 2015. Web. http://www.un.org/en/ga/president/68/news/international_day_for_persons_with_disabilities2013.shtml.

70. "High-Level Meeting of the General Assembly on Disability and Development," Sept. 23, 2013, www.un.org/disabilities/default.asp?id=1590.

71. "Conference Report: Post-2015 Goals, Targets, and Indicators," Centre for International Governance Innovation, p. 5, www.cigionline.org/publications/2012/5/post-2015-goals-targets-and-indicators.

72. Gabriele Köehler *et al.,* "Human Security and the Next Generation of Comprehensive Human Development Goals," Institute of Development Studies, April 2012, pp. 5, 8.

BIBLIOGRAPHY

Selected Sources

Books

Duflo, Esther, and Abhijit Banerjee, *Poor Economics*, Public Affairs, 2010.
Two MIT economics professors examine the factors behind poverty and what to do about it, exploring everything from the minutiae (the buying habits and parenting choices of the poor) to broader systemic factors (markets and governance).

Kenny, Charles, *Getting Better*, Perseus Books, 2011.
A senior fellow at the Center for Global Development in Washington, DC, traces the giant leaps the world has

made in development, focusing on advances other than income metrics, while acknowledging that plenty more can and should be done for the world's poorest.

Sachs, Jeffrey, *The End of Poverty: Economic Possibilities for Our Time*, Penguin Books, 2006.
The director of Columbia University's Earth Institute lays out in depth a remarkable wealth of personal and statistical information on fighting poverty, plus a framework for ending it by 2025.

Easterly, William, *The White Man's Burden: Why the West's Efforts to Aid the Rest Have Done So Much Ill and So Little Good*, Penguin Books, 2007.
A New York University economist delivers a scathing rebuke to the developed world's efforts to aid the developing world, pointing out the unintended consequences of development aid.

Articles

"Reproductive Health and the MDGs," International Planned Parenthood Federation, April 24, 2012, www .ippf.org/news/blogs/reproductive-health-and-mdgs.
The federation provides a fascinating insight into the political fight to get reproductive health into the Millennium Development Goals.

"WEST AFRICA: Smoothing the way for more pit latrines," IRIN [humanitarian news and analysis], Aug. 31, 2011, http://irinnews.org/Report/93621/WEST-AFRICA-Smoothing-the-way-for-more-pit-latrines.
Aid workers talk frankly about the dirty business of changing societal attitudes toward basic sanitation.

Moss, Todd, "Crying Crisis," *Foreign Policy*, Sept. 20, 2010, http://foreignpolicy.com/2010/09/20/crying-crisis/.
A senior fellow and vice president for programs at the Center for Global Development in Washington, DC, argues that paying more attention to MDG successes instead of continually begging for aid might "strengthen the policymakers, teachers and health workers in poor countries" and inspire more aid donations.

Shiner, Cindy, "Africa: Cell Phones Transform Continent's Development," *allAfrica*, Sept. 18, 2008, http://allafrica.com/stories/200809180986.html.
In this Q and A, economist Jeffrey Sachs explains how cell phones are revolutionizing life in the world's poorest countries.

Reports and Studies

"Global Monitoring Report 2014/15: Ending Poverty and Sharing Prosperity," World Bank, 2014.
The bank's MDG monitoring report assesses progress in attaining the goals while casting a critical eye on how global economic growth, environmental degradation, and international trade play into the fight against poverty.

"The Millennium Development Goals 2014," United Nations, 2014.
The latest official U.N. reckoning of MDG progress, this comprehensive report lays out where the world started, how far it has come, and which regions are making more or less progress than others.

Annan, Kofi, "We the Peoples," United Nations, 2000.
This report set the tone for development of the Millennium Development Goals in 2000 and provides fascinating insight into the political jockeying that went into the process.

Easterly, William, "How the Millennium Development Goals Are Unfair to Africa," Brookings Global Economy and Development, 2007.
A New York University economist lays out a thorough, statistic-by-statistic analysis of how MDG measures of "success" might be unfair — particularly to sub-Saharan Africa.

Hulme, David, "The Millennium Development Goals (MDGs): A Short History of the World's Biggest Promise," University of Manchester, Brooks World Poverty Institute, September 2009.
A professor in the school of environment and development at the University of Manchester in the U.K. provides a thorough and critical chronology of how the MDGs came into being, putting them into a longer-term context of the ongoing global fight against poverty.

On the Web

La Trobe University, "Millennium Development Goals," Podcast series, 2010.
In this 20-episode series, leading experts discuss how the goals were created, the challenges to meeting them, and the future of global development targets.

For More Information

The Bill and Melinda Gates Foundation, 500 Fifth Ave., North, Seattle, WA 98102; 206-709-3100; www.gatesfoundation.org. A philanthropic organization that works on a variety of issues, including global health and development.

Center for Global Development, 1776 Massachusetts Ave., N.W., Suite 301, Washington, DC 20036; 202-416-0700; www.cgdev.org. A think tank that works to reduce global poverty and inequality.

The Earth Institute, Columbia University, 405 Low Library, #MC 4335, 535 West 116th St., New York, NY 10027; 212-854-3830; www.earth.columbia.edu. An institute, headed by famed economist Jeffrey Sachs, that seeks to address a host of global poverty issues, with a focus on sustainability.

Institute for Development Studies, Library Road, Brighton, BN1 9RE, UK; +44 1273 606261; www.ids.ac.uk. A research and educational institution that promotes social justice, sustainable growth, and ending poverty.

United Nations Development Programme, One United Nations Plaza, New York, NY 10017 USA; 212-906-5000; www.undp.org. The U.N.'s primary development organization.

World Bank, 1818 H St., N.W., Washington, DC 20433; 202-473-1000; www.worldbank.org. Provides technical and financial support to help countries boost their citizens' standards of living.

World Health Organization, Avenue Appia 20, 1211 Geneva 27, Switzerland; +41 22 791 21 11; www.who.int. A U.N. agency that works to improve global public health.

World Vision, 34834 Weyerhaeuser Way So., Federal Way, WA 98001; 888-511-6548; www.worldvision.org. A Christian humanitarian organization that fights poverty worldwide.

Voices From Abroad

GORDON BROWN

Former Prime Minister, United Kingdom

Gender equality not reached

"We know tragically it's impossible, despite all the changes, to change a situation where 350,000 mothers are dying each year from maternal mortality. It will not change quickly enough even if the figures go down, to meet that Millennium Development Goal. We know we have not achieved the Millennium Development Goal on gender equality."

This Day (Nigeria), November 2011

OLU AKEUSOLA

Provost, Michael Otedola College of Primary Education, Nigeria

Not attainable

"The MDGs are not attainable or achievable. Look, we are just deceiving ourselves in this country [Nigeria]. For over 40 years, the United Nations had said that for every nation to develop, it must accrue a minimum 25 percent annual budgetary allocation to its education sector. Malaysia gave it a trial and today it is working for them. That's why Malaysia, which gained independence with Nigeria during the same period, has outsmarted us in terms of growth and development."

Vanguard (Nigeria), August 2012

JUSTIN YIFU LIN

Chief Economist, World Bank, Lebanon

Food prices causing problems

"High and volatile food prices do not bode well for attainment of many MDGs, as they erode consumer purchasing power and prevent millions of people from escaping poverty and hunger, besides having long-term adverse impacts on health and education. Dealing with food price volatility must be a high priority, especially as nutrition has been one of the forgotten MDGs."

Daily Star (Lebanon), April 2012

India/*The National Herald*/Paresh Nath

SERGEY LAVROV

Foreign Minister, Russia

Efforts must be strengthened

"Faced with the acute crisis in the financial/economic sphere, and limited funds for international development assistance, it is a relevant and urgent task to coordinate and increase the effectiveness of international efforts in critical areas. This is necessary if we [Russia] are to achieve the timely realization of the Millennium Development Goals, which are defined in the Millennium Declaration and other fundamental documents of the United Nations."

Russian Ministry of Foreign Affairs, October 2011

KING ABDULLAH

Jordan

Jordan advancing

"Today, due to the work of thousands of Jordanians, in schools, in healthcare, in communities across the country, we are in the process of achieving many of our millennium goals. Goal two, for example, has effectively been achieved: ensuring that all children enroll in primary school and stay in school, ending youth illiteracy, and giving our students the foundation they need to advance in life."

Jordan Times, September 2010

WEN JIABAO
Premier of the State Council, China

China's commitment

"China has always responded positively to U.N. initiatives and made unremitting efforts to realize the Millennium Development Goals. China has lowered the number of people living in absolute poverty by more than 200 million since 1978, accounting for 75 percent of the number of people lifted out of poverty in developing countries. We pay attention to protecting and improving the people's livelihood by institutional means."

Xinhua News Agency (China), September 2010

GEORGE CHICOTY
State Secretary for Foreign Affairs, Angola

A reassessment

"2015 is the deadline, and so far we are assessing issues related to half of the journey and all countries are already thinking that we will have to re-assess and see how we will manage to achieve the Millennium Development Goals."

Angola Press Agency, September 2010

11

Booming Africa

Jason McLure

A young mineworker in South Kivu province in the Democratic Republic of Congo (DRC) helps to extract cassiterite and coltan, valuable minerals used to manufacture sophisticated electronics. More than 90 percent of the DRC's export income comes from diamonds, minerals, and oil, leaving the economy vulnerable to fluctuations in global prices. Many African countries are trying to become less dependent on such commodity exports.

From *CQ Researcher*,
November 20, 2012.
Updated February 3, 2015.

Getty Images/Tom Stoddart

Just over two decades ago, destitute Mozambique could have been the poster child for the economic basket case that was much of sub-Saharan Africa. More than a million people had died in a 17-year civil war, and up to a third of its 15 million people had fled their homes. With much of its farmland sown with land mines, the country had to import grain to feed itself. And the war's $15 billion cost — about seven times Mozambique's annual economic output — had virtually bankrupted the country.

Today, the Texas-sized country bordering the Indian Ocean is rising from the ashes. Newly built resorts offer $600-a-night rooms along the 1,550-mile coastline. Vast coal deposits and the discovery of natural gas reserves twice the size of Saudi Arabia's could make Mozambique one of the world's largest energy exporters in the next decade, and a new aluminum smelter is one of the biggest in the world.

Mozambique's turnaround has been mirrored across much of sub-Saharan Africa, where per capita income has risen 137 percent since 2000[1]. Six[2] of the world's 10 fastest-growing economies currently are in sub-Saharan Africa, which is projected to grow by 5.5 percent this year, compared with 3.1 percent in the United States and 1.3 percent in eurozone countries, according to the International Monetary Fund (IMF).[3]

Yet many outside of Africa still think of the continent as it was 20 years ago. As recently as 2000, *The Economist* labeled Africa "the hopeless continent." The misperception "represents... a chasm between perception and reality," said a report in 2012 from Ernst & Young, an international accounting firm.[4] "The facts tell a different story — one of reform, progress and growth."

A Continent on the Rise

In the past 20 years, 17 sub-Saharan countries are experiencing what some are calling an African Renaissance. These "emerging" countries have embraced democracy and economic reforms — such as slashing regulations, tariffs, and the cost of starting a business — and saw per-capita income rise more than 2 percent per year between 1996 and 2008, according to Steven Radelet, chief economist at the U.S. Agency for International Development. In his 2010 book *Emerging Africa,* Radelet also identified six "threshold" economies, with growth rates under 2 percent but showing signs of a turnaround. Ten oil-exporting countries have economies and politics that are heavily influenced by oil revenues, and 16 others are neither oil exporters nor considered "emerging," according to Radelet.

Economic Status of Sub-Saharan Africa

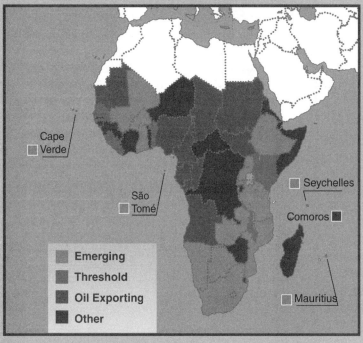

Source: Steven Radelet, *Emerging Africa: How 17 Countries Are Leading the Way* (2010). Map by Lewis Agrell.

The fruits of Africa's recent growth are visible across the continent: in the polished marble floors of the 205,000-square-foot Accra Mall, an American-style complex in Ghana's capital city featuring Apple and Nike stores and a five-screen cinema; in the high-tech, deep-water oil drilling platforms off Angola's coast; and in the sharp reductions in infant mortality in countries such as Ethiopia and Rwanda.

Analysts bullish on the continent's future see indications that sub-Saharan Africa is set for a sustained period of economic growth that could raise many of its countries to middle-income status. "Economic growth in Sub-Saharan Africa remains strong and is poised for lift-off," said a recent World Bank report.[5]

The growth is attributable in part to a boom in oil revenues stemming from increased production in petro-states such as Angola, Chad, and Equatorial Guinea. Yet, significantly, between 1996 and 2008, a star group of 17 emerging African economies produced per-capita income growth of more than 2 percent per year — and another 7 nearly reached that milestone, which economists say is a significant measure of rapidly rising living standards. None of the 24 countries were oil exporters.

"Thailand in 1960 looks a lot like Ethiopia or the Democratic Republic of Congo today," says Susan Lund, director of research at the McKinsey Global Institute, a subsidiary of the international consulting firm. "South Korea in 1965 looks like Senegal, Tanzania or Ghana. When you look backwards you think Africa could capture this potential."

And while it may seem far-fetched to compare Africa's rise to that of emerging economic giants like India, China, or Brazil, consider the following:

• Between 2010 and 2020, some 122 million young people will enter Africa's labor force, providing a massive "demographic dividend" that will give the continent a larger labor force by 2035 than any country or region, including China or India.[6] By 2040, 1.1 billion

Africans will be of working age, according to McKinsey.

- Although most of Africa is viewed as corrupt, 31 sub-Saharan nations are considered less corrupt than Russia, and 14 score better than India on Transparency International's Corruption Perceptions Index.[7]

- Africa's income per capita is greater than India's, and six sub-Saharan countries have greater income per capita than China.[8]

- While African countries are considered more difficult to do business in than other developing nations, 3 sub-Saharan countries rank ahead of Russia on the World Bank's "ease of doing business" index; 9 were ahead of Brazil and 17 ahead of India.[9]

Several changes have fueled sub-Saharan Africa's growth since the dark days of the 1970s and 1980s. First, countries across the continent have significantly improved governance and expanded democracy. Though many countries are still dominated by a single party or governed by authoritarian rulers — such as Rwanda's Paul Kagame or Uganda's Yoweri Museveni — corrupt, unaccountable despots like Zimbabwe's Robert Mugabe are an increasingly rare species. Major civil wars such as those that damaged the economies of Angola, Mozambique, and Liberia in the 1980s and 1990s have ended or quieted significantly.

"Africa has reached the point that the Scandinavians got to 100 years ago, when they decided they are tired of fighting each other and said: 'Let's put everything down and work towards a more peaceful region,'" says Ifediora Amobi, director of the African Institute for Applied Economics in Enugu, Nigeria. "More stability will translate into growth."

Africa Among Fastest-Growing Regions

Africa's gross domestic product (GDP) — a measure of economic output — grew at an average rate of 5.1 percent from 2000 to 2010, second only to emerging Asia (top). Angola, which has been exploiting its newfound oil reserves, had the world's fastest-growing GDP during the decade ending in 2010. For the current five-year period, seven of the world's fastest-growing economies (below, in red) are expected to be in Africa, with Ethiopia ranked just behind booming China and India.

Compound Annual GDP Growth by Region, 2000–2010

Region	Growth
Emerging Asia	8.6%
Africa	5.1%
Middle East	4.5%
Latin America	3.7%
Central and Eastern Europe	3.1%
World	2.8%
Developed economies	1.5%

World's Fastest-Growing Economies, by Annual Average GDP Growth

2001-2010		2011-2015	
Angola	11.1%	China	9.5%
China	10.5%	India	8.2%
Myanmar	10.3%	Ethiopia	8.1%
Nigeria	8.9%	Mozambique	7.7%
Ethiopia	8.4%	Tanzania	7.2%
Kazakhstan	8.2%	Vietnam	7.2%
Chad	7.9%	Congo	7.0%
Mozambique	7.9%	Ghana	7.0%
Cambodia	7.7%	Zambia	6.9%
Rwanda	7.6%	Nigeria	6.8%

Sources: "Africa's Impressive Growth," *The Economist*, January 2011, www .economist.com/blogs/dailychart/2011/01/daily_chart; David Fine, *et al.*, "Africa at Work: Job Creation and Inclusive Growth," McKinsey Global Institute, August 2012, p. 1, www.mckinsey.com/insights/mgi/research/ africa_europe_middle_east/africa_at_work.

Second, African central banks and finance ministries have become better economic managers. In the late 1970s and 1980s, Ghana was hit by low prices for cocoa, its main export, and high prices for oil, which it imported. The government responded by controlling consumer prices, paying artificially low prices to cocoa farmers and expanding the civil service nearly 10-fold. As a result, the budget deficit ballooned, inflation reached 120 percent, and cocoa production plummeted. Since the reversal of some of the harmful policies, Ghana's economy has become one of the strongest in Africa, with growth averaging more than 5 percent over the past 25 years.[10]

In addition, Africans have benefited enormously from technological advances, particularly in communications and information technology. The Internet provides more information — ranging from scientific research to engineering designs to financial data — than the continent's largest research libraries, and it is increasingly available, even in rural areas. Moreover, on a continent where phone service was once rare and expensive, mobile phones have become ubiquitous, even in remote areas of the Sahara Desert.

"Africa had no connectivity, and now everyone is connected by mobile phone. That has just changed things everywhere," said Jacko Maree, chief executive officer of South Africa–based Standard Bank Group.[11]

Finally, international lending institutions have forgiven many African countries' foreign debt, which has freed up government revenues to be spent on education, health care, and infrastructure. Sub-Saharan Africa's foreign debt to official creditors has fallen by about half over the last 10 years.[12]

To be sure, growth has not occurred evenly across the continent, and even some of Africa's fastest-growing economies still face corruption, inequality, and ethnic strife. Long-running conflicts continue in Somalia, South Sudan, and the Democratic Republic of Congo, discouraging foreign investment, hindering efforts to build infrastructure, and prolonging instability.

In addition, outside of South Africa and a handful of small countries such as Mauritius, nearly all sub-Saharan economies depend heavily on exports of raw materials such as oil, gas, minerals, or agricultural commodities, leaving them vulnerable to fluctuations in global prices.

"A lot of this [growth] is still being driven by natural resources," says Vijaya Ramachandran, a senior fellow at the Washington-based Center for Global Development. "Africa has not diversified into manufactured exports. It has not been able to compete with Asian countries."

Moreover, while exports of minerals, oil, and gas generate high revenues for governments, they have so far provided few jobs for Africans. Many of the jobs in these industries are filled by foreign workers trained by multinational companies. The failure to develop labor-intensive manufacturing has left many countries with high unemployment. Although the unemployment rate for the countries south of the Sahara was around 7.6 percent in 2013, only 22.6 percent of Africa's labor force is in formal, wage-paying jobs, according to the International Labor Organization. The remainder are in subsistence farming or informal trades such as hawking wares on the street — jobs the ILO describes as "vulnerable employment."[13]

"A lot of people in the West are so impressed with our growth, but in Sierra Leone a lot of the growth has come from the exploitation of iron ore," says Omotunde Johnson, Sierra Leone country director for the London-based International Growth Centre, a think tank. "The miners are all foreigners, so that is going to create a new set of problems when these African youth who are not trained and educated are not getting work."

As analysts examine Africa's economic expansion, here are some of the questions they are asking:

Can African economies diversify away from natural resource production?

Africa's recent growth has been driven largely by production of oil, gas, and minerals. The so-called extractive industries account for more than 25 percent of exports in about half of the sub-Saharan countries, and in some cases the share is much higher.[14] In Angola, oil accounts for 90 percent of export earnings and about half of total GDP.[15] In Botswana, diamonds account for about half of revenue and about 80 percent of exports.[16] In Equatorial Guinea, oil and gas make up almost 90 percent of GDP and virtually all export revenues.[17]

Between 2000 and 2009, oil production in Africa rose 24 percent. The continent now has about 10 percent of the world's oil reserves and 8 percent of its gas.[18]

But with oil prices falling to less than $50 a barrel in early 2015, the risks of relying so heavily on a single commodity have become abundantly clear; governments in Angola,[19] Nigeria,[20] and other hydrocarbon-based economies have been scrambling to enact budget cuts.

"Technology is changing rapidly, and there will be more natural resource discoveries in Africa going forward," says Ramachandran, of the Center for Global Development. "Almost all of Africa will be an oil or mineral exporter. The question is how will they manage this?"

In the past, rising natural resource earnings have not been used to lift large numbers of people out of poverty. Paradoxically, developing countries rich in natural resources generally do not perform as well economically as countries without oil, gas, or mineral wealth — a phenomenon known in economic circles as the "resource curse."[21]

"They have grown more slowly, and with greater inequality — just the opposite of what one would expect," Joseph Stiglitz, a Nobel Prize–winning economist, wrote in Britain's *The Guardian.*

"After all," he continued, "countries whose major source of revenue is natural resources can use them to finance education, health care, development and redistribution."[22]

The "resource curse" is blamed on several factors, including:

- Rapidly rising energy and mineral earnings tend to boost the value of the exporting country's currency, making foreign imported goods cheaper for the local population but making it harder for local exports of commodities or manufactured goods to compete with countries that have cheaper currencies.
- Governance may suffer as political leaders focus on capturing ballooning export revenues rather than taxing citizens for public services. Corruption abounds when a relatively small number of government officials control access to lucrative extraction licenses and contracts.
- Booms caused by high world prices often spur high levels of government spending and borrowing, which can

Poor Governance Hinders Africa's Progress

Some foreign investors are wary of investing in sub-Saharan Africa's industrialization, largely because of corruption and the lack of infrastructure. The region is the most poorly governed in the world (top) and trails the emerging BRICs (Brazil, Russia, India and China) in the development of infrastructure (bottom).

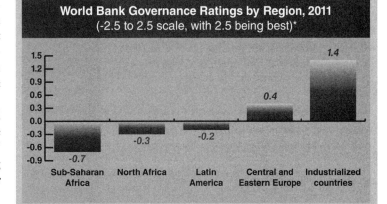

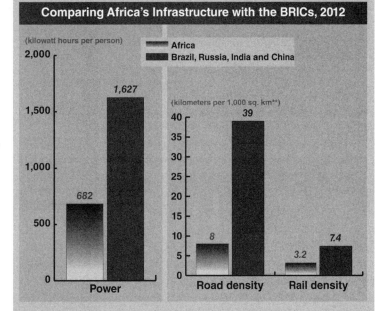

* Based on government accountability, stability, and effectiveness; regulatory and legal systems, and corruption levels

** A kilometer is about six-tenths of a mile. A square kilometer is 0.39 of a square mile.

Sources: "Is Africa About to Take Off?" *Societe Generale,* May 2011; and David Fine, et al., "Africa at Work: Job Creation and Inclusive Growth," McKinsey Global Institute, August 2012, p. 43

Miners' Strike Deepens South Africa's Woes

Vast gulf between rich and poor bedevils the economy.

Even now, exactly how the trouble started in a dusty, brush-strewn field in Marikana, South Africa, on Aug. 16, 2012 isn't entirely clear. In the end, though, the clash between about 3,000 South African police and a similar number of striking platinum miners left 44 people dead, including 34 miners.

Video of the confrontation showed police opening fire with automatic rifles after tear gas failed to disperse the crowd, some of whom were armed with clubs and spears. Police said they came under fire first and initially charged 270 strikers with murder.[1]

The charges were dropped after a public outcry, and the government has opened an official inquiry into the incident. Whatever the outcome, the clash exposed deep divisions in South Africa and frustration with a democracy that has allowed wide disparities in income to persist 18 years after the end of the country's hated apartheid government.

"Nothing, nothing, nothing has changed," a Marikana man told the BBC after the bloodshed. "Democracy is just a word like a bird flying up in the sky."

South Africa is the largest economy in sub-Saharan Africa but has one of the most unequal distributions of income anywhere in the world. The top 10 percent of the population accounts for 58 percent of income, while the bottom 50 percent earns just 8 percent.

The legacy of apartheid is seen as a major reason for the inequity, because blacks were largely denied the opportunity to gain education, land, and capital. Economic growth has averaged 3.2 percent annually since 1995, a modest rate for a middle-income country.[2] And it has not been rapid enough to resolve inequalities or quell discontent among a growing population, where unemployment stands at 25.2 percent.

The strike, which ended after the mine operator, U.K.–based Lonmin, agreed to raise wages by up to 22 percent, has served as a catalyst for other labor actions. By early October, an estimated 70,000 miners were on strike around the country, nearly a quarter of the total and a figure that included iron, gold, and coal miners. An additional 28,000 truck drivers also went on strike seeking better pay and conditions.[3]

"Down with monkey salaries — down," said Buti Manamela, president of the Young Communist League, during a march near the offices of global mining giant AngloGold Ashanti in Orkney. "Divided we fall, united we stand.... We can never achieve Nelson Mandela's rainbow nation if we are unequal in terms of wages."[4]

The actions have led some mining companies to threaten to close mines and lay off workers, dampening the outlook for an economy hit by the eurozone crisis and slowing growth in China.[5] In late September, the Moody's credit rating agency downgraded South African debt, citing the government's "reduced capacity to handle the current political and economic situation and to implement effective strategies that could place the economy on a path to faster and more inclusive growth."[6]

The move reflects doubts about President Jacob Zuma's leadership and that of his ruling African National Congress

lead to busts and debt crises when commodity prices tumble, as happened in the early 1980s in many African countries.

To enable continued growth and boost employment and productivity, African nations must expand their manufacturing and farming sectors, say analysts. But building internationally competitive industries will be a major challenge for many African nations, given their small size and lack of roads, electricity, and other infrastructure. In fact, Africa's manufacturing sector has declined as a share of the continent's gross domestic product, falling from 15.3 percent of GDP in 1990 to 10.5 percent in 2008.[23]

"Manufacturing has started on a small scale, but that has to pick up," says Johnson, the Sierra Leonean economist. "Education and training are not there. And there is a general inefficiency in investment," he says, referring to poor investment returns due to systemic problems such as low productivity, corruption, and lack of infrastructure that are "keeping a lot of investors out."

African economies are not well integrated, part of the continent's colonial legacy. Many countries on the arbitrarily divided continent are so small they cannot generate economies of scale large enough to compete globally, as China and India have been able to do, with their

(ANC), which has run the country since its transition to democracy in 1994 under President Mandela. The country's major unions have long been key allies of the ANC, but this year's strikes have largely been wildcat labor actions undertaken without the support of union leadership — and reflect the popular perception that ANC leaders are more focused on their own enrichment than improving the lives of the poor.

That perception has been buttressed by reports that the government is paying for $27 million in improvements to Zuma's private home, ostensibly to improve security. "In 1994 there were massive problems, but there was also a massive amount of hope," William Gumede, a political analyst, told *The New York Times*.[7] "Now people feel hopeless. People have lost confidence in all of these institutions they trusted will make a difference, like the unions and the ANC. The new institutions of democracy — Parliament, the courts — people have also lost confidence that those can protect them and help them."

—Jason McLure

Striking gold miners in Carletonville, South Africa, demand better pay and working conditions on Oct. 18, 2012. The placards read, "We demand 18,500 rands — silicosis the cause of death in mines" and "Don't let police get away with murder."

[1]"South Africa's Lonmin Marikana Mine Clashes Killed 34," BBC News, Aug. 17, 2012, www.bbc.co.uk/news/world-africa-19292909. See also Faith Karimi and Nkepile Mabusi, "South African Commission Probing Miners' Deaths Starts Proceedings," CNN, Oct. 1, 2012, www.cnn.com/2012/10/01/world/africa/south-africa-mine-unrest/index.html.

[2]"South Africa Economic Update: Focus on Inequality of Opportunity," World Bank, July 2012, p. vii, http://documents.worldbank.org/curated/en/ 2012/01/16561374/south-africa-economic-update-focus-inequality-opportunity.

[3]Devon Maylie, "South Africa's Labor Woes Worsen," *The Wall Street Journal*, Oct. 3, 2012, http://online.wsj.com/article/SB10000872396390443768804578034271819419406.html.

[4]Rodney Muhumuza, "Facing Pressure to End Strikes, South African Miners Find Strength in Numbers, Tough Words," The Associated Press, Oct. 4, 2012, *Calgary Herald*, www.calgaryherald.com/business/facing+pressure+strikes+SAfrican+miners+find+strength+crowd+numbers/7344234/story.html.

[5]For background, see Christopher Hack, "Euro Crisis," *CQ Researcher*, Oct. 5, 2012, pp. 841–864.

[6]"Moody's Downgrades South Africa's Government Bond Rating to Baa1; Outlook Remains Negative," Moody's Investors Service, Sept. 27, 2012, www. moodys.com/research/Moodys-downgrades-South-Africas-government-bond-rating-to-Baa1-outlook--PR_256159.

[7]Lydia Polgreen, "Upheaval Grips South Africa as Hopes for Its Workers Fade," *The New York Times*, Oct. 13, 2012, www.nytimes.com/2012/10/14/world/africa/unfulfilled-promises-are-replacing-prospects-of-a-better-life-in-south-africa.html?pagewanted=all.

billion-person domestic markets. Landlocked Burkina Faso, for instance, has a population of 17 million — slightly smaller than Florida — and few roads to connect it to neighboring economies.

And larger African nations must compete with Chinese and other highly efficient Asian manufacturers.[24] In Ethiopia, a large, landlocked country with 95 million people, it is cheaper to buy a wooden chair made in China than one made domestically, even after transportation costs are factored in. That's because Ethiopian workers manufacture 0.3 pieces per day, compared to 4.9 in China.[25]

Even South Africa has trouble competing with Asia, despite having a highly developed infrastructure and established access to export markets in Europe and elsewhere. Willie Van Straaten, a chief executive officer of South Africa's Inventec, a company that designs exercise equipment and games, says his products are made in China because the scale of its integrated manufacturing sector makes it difficult for South Africa to compete.

"A lot of your Chinese factories have got very good vendor networks around them, so they may manufacture just one-third of the product, but two-thirds will come from the vendor network around them, and those

African Workforce to Surpass All Others

Africa's working-age population is expected to exceed 1 billion by 2040, giving the continent a larger labor force than any country or region, including China or India. Experts say the burgeoning labor force will attract outside investors because of the growing consumer market they represent, but others warn that all those workers will need jobs.

Size of the Working-Age Population (ages 15 to 64), 1970–2040

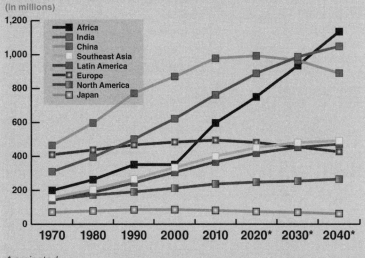

(in millions)

Legend:
- Africa
- India
- China
- Southeast Asia
- Latin America
- Europe
- North America
- Japan

* projected

Source: David Fine, *et al.,* "Africa at Work: Job Creation and Inclusive Growth," McKinsey Global Institute, August 2012, p. 13, *www.mckinsey.com/ insights/mgi/research/africa_europe_middle_east/africa_at_work.*

vendors specialize in just one item," he told the television station African Business News. "So in South Africa you have to go and manufacture almost every item at low volume which makes it very, very expensive."[26]

Some analysts say Africa's growth is not all due to commodity export earnings. Steve Radelet, chief economist at the U.S. Agency for International Development, wrote that although rising commodity prices "have helped in some cases, the turnaround in the emerging countries is not solely the result of favorable commodity prices."[27] He found that between 1980 and 2006, with the exception of nine oil-exporting countries, the ratio of the cost of imported food and other goods rose as fast as or faster than income from exports. In other words, higher prices for African exports cannot explain Africa's growth because the prices consumers paid for imports also rose.

Others say Africa has an opportunity to develop labor-intensive industries — such as horticulture, leatherworking, and textiles — especially once labor costs in China and other Asian manufacturing countries begin to rise. In Lesotho, about 37,000[28] people now work in the garment industry for companies that export textiles to the United States under the African Growth and Opportunity Act, which allows duty-free access to the U.S. market.[29]

"It's not quite as dire as you might think," says Lund of the McKinsey Global Institute. "We think the dynamics might be changing. There are two opportunities: the changing wage dynamics and higher transport costs (because of oil prices) both work against production in China."

Can Africa provide enough jobs for its fast-growing population?

Sisay Asrat, a 27-year-old from the Ethiopian town of Debre Zeit, is happy to have a job at one of the dozens of flower farms that have sprung up in her country over the past decade. Even though she is only earning a little more than a dollar a day, working in the farm's cold room packing roses to be shipped to Europe is better than having no job at all.

"There are no alternatives for those of us who don't have an education," she says. "I was dependent on my family. Now I cover my children's food, clothing, and school fees."

Generating jobs for burgeoning populations is one of the most vexing challenges facing sub-Saharan economies. The region's estimated 7.6 percent unemployment rate belies the fact that only 22.6[30] percent of the labor force has stable, wage-paying employment. From 2001 to 2012, there was only a 2.3 percentage-point drop in rates of "vulnerable employment" — a category that includes subsistence farming or other informal-sector jobs such as selling goods from market stalls and working as day laborers.[31]

"The key thing is, are people getting wage-paying employment?" says Lund of the McKinsey Global Institute. "Are they getting out of subsistence agriculture and street hawking?"

Analysts say agricultural productivity could be boosted to make farming a more stable long-term job for millions. Expanding large-scale commercial farming on uncultivated land and moving from low-value grain production to labor-intensive crops such as flower farming could add up to 14 million stable jobs in the region by 2020, according to McKinsey.

Given the strong demand for African natural resources, employment and income could be boosted by processing more of those raw goods before exporting them, analysts say. "If you add more value to the resource, then you can generate more jobs," says Ramachandran of the Center for Global Development.

For instance, Ghana and Côte d'Ivoire (Ivory Coast) together produce 60[32] percent of the world's cocoa, which can only be grown in tropical and subtropical climates.[33] Yet Switzerland and Belgium are famous for making expensive chocolates from that African cocoa. Starbucks Corp. pays Ethiopian coffee farmers as little as $1.42 per pound and sells some specialty beans — which the company roasts, grinds, and markets — for as much as $26 per pound.[34] And Africa's largest crude oil exporter, Nigeria, imports gasoline because it lacks refining capacity.[35]

African manufacturers are on pace to generate 8 million new jobs by 2020 and could add an additional 7 million over that period if governments improve infrastructure, cut unnecessary regulation, and ease access to finance. The retail sector could add up to 14 million more jobs; currently Nigeria, which had only six shopping malls for 19.5 million people in its four largest cities in 2012, according to McKinsey, is seeing a boom in retail centers with new malls planned to open soon in Delta State, Owerri, and Abuja.[36] In total, the consulting firm forecasts that the continent will add 54 million stable jobs by 2020.

Yet expanding employment comes with costs. For instance, a wave of new, large commercial farms has displaced many existing smallholders. In 2009 alone, 77 million acres of African farmland were transferred to

Changing Economies

Generating jobs for burgeoning populations is one of the most vexing challenges facing sub-Saharan governments, since only 28 percent of the region's labor force has stable, wage-paying jobs. Given the strong worldwide demand for Africa's natural resources and commodities — such as the cocoa beans being sorted by a farm worker in Côte d'Ivoire (top) — African governments want more of the continent's raw goods to be processed before they're exported, creating more domestic jobs. In Gaborone, Botswana, for instance, raw diamonds now are being sorted and polished before export (bottom).

commercial investors — many of them foreigners. Often, the land was sold out from underneath small farmers who lacked clear title to the land that their families had been tilling for generations.[37]

"All we want before they break our houses and take our fields is for them to show us the new houses where we will live, and the new fields where we will work," said Sekou Traoré, a 69-year-old villager in Mali, about plans to transfer land farmed by his family to Libyan investors.[38]

"They have to modernize agriculture, but when you modernize agriculture it's a double-edged sword because you kick out a lot of people from the agriculture sector," says Johnson, the Sierra Leonean economist.

Others say that despite Africa's recent growth, the rate of job growth is far too slow for the continent's growing workforce. While 54 million stable jobs may be added by 2020, the number of people in vulnerable employment is expected to grow by 67 million — and at current trends, the absolute number of people in "vulnerable" work will not decline until 2080.

Thus, at current rates, many African nations will have large numbers of underemployed young people, which can lead to political instability.

"The crisis of unemployment is a ticking time bomb, and if we are not careful in dealing with it we will see another Egypt and Tunisia," said Buti Manamela, secretary of South Africa's Young Communist League, referring to the legions of young people who took to the streets in 2011 and toppled Arab governments.[39]

Is Africa about to undergo an East Asia–style boom?

During the early 2000s, many sub-Saharan African governments adopted economic reforms, such as curbing deficits, privatizing banks, freeing exchange rates, and slowing inflation. The private sector expanded rapidly, fueling support for additional reforms. Growth averaged 5 percent a year during the decade before the 2007 to 2008 financial crisis but actually accelerated to 6 percent between 2006 and 2008. The growth wasn't solely attributable to oil: 22 non–oil exporters enjoyed 4 percent or higher annual growth during the decade.

"Then the global economic crisis hit, and everyone including myself panicked," says Shanta Devarajan, the Sri Lankan-born chief economist for Africa at the World Bank, "because now the payoffs for the reforms have disappeared."

In the United States and Europe, some countries took measures to stave off depression, such as nationalizing banks and expanding deficits to as high as 10 percent of gross domestic product (GDP). With the global economy in free fall and Western governments intervening to prop up ailing financial and industrial firms, it would have been understandable if African governments had

> **"The crisis of unemployment is a ticking time bomb, and if we are not careful in dealing with it we will see another Egypt and Tunisia."**
>
> **— Buti Manamela, Secretary, South Africa's Young Communist League**

run-up large budget deficits and incurred foreign debts. Instead, sub-Saharan budget deficits widened by only 2 percent of GDP in 2009, and economies continued to grow by an average of 2.8 percent, even as European and North American economies were shrinking.

By 2010, economic growth in the region had rebounded to 5.3 percent. The resilience in the face of the financial crisis indicates that even stronger growth lies ahead, says Devarajan. He predicts that the region, with the exception of fragile or failed states such as Somalia, are on the brink of a sustained economic take-off, with annual growth rates of more than 7 percent. Since the 1980s, such growth rates have been commonly associated with China, and from the 1960s to the 1990s with the East Asian "tiger" economies of South Korea, Taiwan, Hong Kong, and Singapore.

Better economic governance is not the only thing Africa shares with the East Asian tigers prior to their takeoff. Like the tigers, Africa's growth will be propelled in the coming decades by a "demographic dividend," according to some analysts.

The median age on the continent is 19, and the population's percentage of young children is expected to grow from 23 in 2010 to 38 by 2050.[40] Meanwhile, by 2035, the number of retirees and children that each worker supports, a figure known as the "dependency ratio," will fall from the highest in the world to about the same level as that in Western countries. As a result, each worker will have more disposable income to invest or spend on nonessential items.[41]

"This is what happened in East Asia in the 1970s and '80s, and if we can manage it right Africa has the demographic characteristics to experience the dividend," says Devarajan.

But others are more pessimistic about the prospects for a sustained boom, because corruption and unpredictable legal systems discourage foreign investment. "Africa is still not very good at things like corruption and efficiency of government," says Johnson, the Sierra Leonean economist. "Even some of the so-called diaspora [Africans working overseas] who might have $100,000 here and $200,000 there and together can come up with a million, even they are reluctant to go back and invest. The legal systems are awful. There are delays, there is corruption."

High transportation costs, which can be up to six times those in southern or eastern Asia, also block industrial growth in Africa. A 2009 World Bank study blamed monopolies and anticompetitive practices by trucking companies, which operate with high profit margins at the expense of other industries.[42] Reforms to prevent such problems may be adopted over time, but in the interim, they are slowing growth.

"I'm not saying they'll stand still over the next 20 years; there will be progress," says Johnson. "But when you look at the population growth, that progress will be too slow."

Others see growth being dampened in the near future by the European debt crisis and a weakening of Chinese demand for African exports like oil, copper, and coal.

Isabella Massa, a France-based researcher for the Overseas Development Institute, an international development think tank in the United Kingdom, says Europe's debt crisis will slow foreign direct investment and aid from Europe to Africa. Remittances to Nigeria from expatriate Nigerians fell by more than half in 2011, and Kenya's tourism and horticulture industries, which depend on European markets, also declined. Businesses in countries such as Angola, Rwanda, and Cameroon are receiving fewer loans from European banks as well, she adds.

"The escalation of the eurozone crisis and the fact that growth rates in the emerging BRIC [Brazil, Russia, India, and China] economies, which have been the engine of the global recovery after the financial crisis, are now slowing down making the current situation particularly worrying for African countries," says Massa.

BACKGROUND

Colonialism

Beginning in the 15th century, contact with Europeans had a profound impact on the economies of Africans. The Portuguese, English, French, and Dutch initially

Chinese workers construct a new railway near Luanda, Angola. Chinese companies have invested heavily in African mines and oil wells and have provided concessional loans to African governments to build roads, railways, and electricity plants. Thousands of Chinese workers have come to Africa in recent years to build infrastructure projects.

sought to extract gold and ivory from the continent, but by the 17th century, they had shifted their interest to a more lucrative trade: human beings.[43] Between 1600 and 1870, as many as 11.5 million Africans — mostly from Africa's western coastal states — were brought to work as slaves in North and South America.[44]

The impact of the slave trade on the region varied. The area near today's West African nations of Senegal and Gambia provided many of the slaves in the early years of the trade.[45] In the 1700s, civil wars in the area around modern-day Nigeria provided a large number of slaves, who were shipped out via ports in Benin and from British slave forts in Ghana. After the Portuguese banned the slave trade north of the equator in 1815, the trade shifted further south toward Angola and the Democratic Republic of Congo.

Bans on the slave trade in the early 19th century fueled European exploration of Africa's interior. By the late 19th century the major colonial powers — Britain, France, Belgium, Portugal and Germany — were in a "scramble for Africa," competing for huge tracts of land to secure access to natural resources such as gold and timber. In the process, they sent Christian missionaries, established large administrative bureaucracies and built railroads and other infrastructure — primarily to facilitate the export of raw materials. In the process, millions of Africans died from disease, starvation, overwork and war.[46]

CHRONOLOGY

1400s-1700s *Europeans begin trading with Africa, eventually shifting from buying gold and ivory to slaves, taking an estimated 11.5 million people from Africa and undermining local economies.*

1800s *Europeans begin colonizing Africa.*

1807 Slave trade is banned in the British Empire, but not slavery.

November 1884-January 1885 European powers meet in Berlin to establish rules for colonizing Africa; "scramble for Africa" begins.

1950s—1970s *Era of independence begins. Optimism turns to stagnation.*

1956 Substantial oil reserves are discovered in southern Nigeria.

1957 Britain grants independence to Ghana. Most British colonies become independent by 1965, including Nigeria, Uganda, Kenya, Zambia, Malawi, and Gambia.

1958 Guinea becomes independent. Most French African colonies gain independence by 1960, including Mauritania, Nigeria, Senegal, Gabon, Republic of Congo, Central African Republic, Chad, Niger, Benin, Mali, Cameroon, Togo, and Ivory Coast (now called Côte d'Ivoire).

1960 Mineral-rich Katanga province secedes from newly independent Democratic Republic of Congo with Belgium's support, sparking six years of political crisis and civil war.

1973–1979 Skyrocketing oil prices hit oil-importing African countries hard; World Bank counsels spending cuts by African governments, fueling poverty. Oil producers such as Gabon and Nigeria see revenues jump.

1980s–1990s *Heavy borrowing and economic mismanagement lead to high rates of debt; end of Cold War spurs reforms.*

1981 World Bank economists warn that many of its loans to poor countries cannot be repaid and should be canceled.

1991 Collapse of Soviet Union heralds end of Cold War and diminishing superpower support for African dictators.

1994 End of apartheid in South Africa ends international isolation of continent's largest economy.

1995 Foreign debt owed by sub-Saharan governments tops $340 billion, up from $11 billion in 1970.

1996 Chinese President Jiang Zemin visits six African countries, promising aid "without political strings." IMF and World Bank launch debt relief program for heavily-indebted poor countries.

2000s–Present *Improved economic governance along with spread of democracy and new communications technology spur growth.*

2000 United States passes African Growth and Opportunity Act, eliminating tariffs on hundreds of African products.

2005 International debt relief is expanded, freeing African governments to spend more on economic development.

2006 Forty-eight African nations attend meeting on cooperation with China in Beijing. President Hu Jintao promises to increase Sino-African trade to $100 billion by 2010.

2009 Global financial crisis slows growth in Africa, but continent avoids recessions experienced in United States and Europe. Relative isolation of African banks helps them avoid global financial contagion; continuing Chinese demand for African commodity exports helps fuel growth.

2010 Number of Africans with mobile phones tops 500 million as Internet and mobile technology spread.

2011 Oil producer South Sudan gains independence from Sudan. African oil production tops 417 million barrels per day, up from 328 million in 1991.

2012 More than 40 South African miners and police are killed during unrest over wages and benefits; anger over income inequality grows in Africa's biggest economy. Long-simmering conflicts over territory and religion kick off in northern Mali and the Central African Republic.

2013 Oil producer South Sudan erupts into bloody warfare in December, pitting the two largest ethnic groups against each other in the world's youngest country.

2014 A precipitous drop in oil prices reduces revenues for hydrocarbon-dependent countries.

The High Cost of Nigeria's Fuel Subsidy

Love of low-cost fuel costs government dearly.

Most mornings, enterprising young Africans along Togo's coastal border with Benin harvest a surprising catch: jerry cans full of fuel. Wooden boats carry the contraband gasoline on a 13-hour trip from Nigeria through the Gulf of Guinea. Then, when they are close to the coast, young men swim out with empty jerry cans and fill them with gasoline and then haul them back to shore.

The fuel is then poured into large blue barrels and distributed as far as Ghana, Mali, and Burkina Faso, where it is often sold on the street in liter liquor bottles at a steep discount from the price charged by licensed filling stations. The smuggling is profitable because fuel is heavily subsidized in Nigeria, selling for just 97 naira ($.62) per liter, or about $2.33 per gallon.[1]

Such subsidies are roundly criticized for a variety of reasons. Not only have price supports fueled the smuggling boom to other West African nations, but a disproportionate share of the subsidy benefits the wealthy and upper-middle-class Nigerians who can afford to own cars.

Moreover, the subsidy has discouraged local companies from building refineries, which has forced Africa's largest exporter of crude oil to import much of its gasoline and diesel from refineries overseas. The subsidy system also is hugely expensive and riddled with corruption. In 2011, the fuel subsidy accounted for 30 percent of government spending. In a country where more than half the population lives in poverty, the government spent $8 billion on fuel subsidies compared with $2 billion on education.[2]

Long-associated with misrule and public corruption, Nigeria in recent years has won praise from the International Monetary Fund and others for its economic management. High crude prices have helped the economy grow more than 7 percent for the past three years, and oil revenue helped cushion the economy during the 2008 global crisis. President Goodluck Jonathan's government has launched efforts to build electricity-generation plants and increase lending to small businesses and agriculture to generate employment.

The government is well aware of the costs to the economy of the subsidies. But there's a major hurdle to reducing or eliminating them: Nigerians love low-priced fuel, and for many, it's the only government benefit they see. When Jonathan attempted to end the subsidies in January, unions called a nationwide strike, and thousands of people poured into the streets of Lagos, Kano, and other cities to protest.

AFP/Getty Images/Pius Utomi Ekpei

Protesters in Lagos, Nigeria, demonstrate during a nationwide strike after the government tried to abolish decades-old fuel subsidies in January. President Goodluck Jonathan partially restored the subsidies two weeks later, citing a "near-breakdown of law and order" in parts of the country.

"The doctors are going on strike, the lawyers are not going to court, teachers are on strike, everybody is joining this because the only aspect where we feel government is in the area of subsidy," a protester told the Al Jazeera news network. "If you remove it, then the government can as well resign."[3]

Two weeks after eliminating the subsidies, Jonathan partially restored them, citing a "near-breakdown of law and order in certain parts of the country."

—Jason McLure

---

[1]Jaime Grant, "On the Road With West Africa's Fuel Smugglers," ThinkAfricaPress, March 20, 2012, http://thinkafricapress.com/economy/road-west-africa-fuel-smugglers-inevitable-spread-nigeria-fuel-crisis.

[2]Vera Songwe, "Removal of Fuel Subsidies in Nigeria: An Economic Necessity and a Political Dilemma," Brookings Institution, Jan. 10, 2012, www.brookings.edu/research/opinions/2012/01/10-fuel-subsidies-nigeria-songwe.

[3]"Nigerian Fuel Protests Turn Deadly," Al Jazeera, Jan. 10, 2012, www.aljazeera.com/news/africa/2012/01/201219132749562385.html.

In November 1884, Africa's main European coloniz-ers sought to formalize their conflicting commercial, missionary, and diplomatic efforts at a conference in Berlin.[47] At the time, the moral justification for the con-quest of Africa was underpinned by pseudoscientific ideas of European racial superiority, a desire to "civilize" technologically primitive African societies, and the hope that Europe might gain from utilizing Africa's raw materials while selling manufactured goods to its inhabitants.[48]

On the eve of World War I, Europeans ruled virtually all of sub-Saharan Africa except Ethiopia.[49] In the late 1800s, up to 10,000 independent African political and ethnic groups had been consolidated into 40 European colonies, often with scant regard to ethnic and language groups. The French colonial empire alone claimed 3.75 million square miles of African territory, an area more than 12 times the size of France.[50]

The colonial powers met with armed resistance virtu-ally everywhere and maintained authority only by pos-sessing superior arms and forming strategic alliances with traditional rulers. Financial self-sufficiency was the main goal of European colonial governments; public ser-vices such as education, sanitation, and healthcare were largely left to missionaries. European-owned companies controlled most commerce and focused on producing cash crops such as coffee, cocoa, and rubber or raw mate-rials like minerals and timber. The legacy of that com-modity-based economic model still exists in much of Africa today.

World War II had a profound, long-term impact on Africa. Nearly 400,000 Africans joined the British army, and African units helped defeat the Italians in Ethiopia and restore the rule of Emperor Haile Selassie. Africans fighting overseas also witnessed the independence move-ments in other colonies such as India and Burma, which had won pledges of self-governance from the British Crown.[51]

The war also crippled European economies and led to the rise of the United States and Soviet Union — emerg-ing superpowers that opposed colonialism. Under the 1941 Atlantic Charter between President Franklin D. Roosevelt and British Prime Minister Winston Churchill, Britain and the United States vowed to "respect the right of all peoples to choose the form of government under which they would live."[52] Anticolonialism was also a key facet of Soviet communism, which sought to replace colonial governments in Africa with procommunist nationalist ones.

Independence and Stagnation

Reform efforts by colonial administrations — ending slave labor, investing in infrastructure and social services, and offering Africans a larger governance role — were made grudgingly. Independence came to the region first in 1957, in Ghana, which had a relatively well-educated elite and plentiful cocoa, timber, and gold. By 1960, France had granted independence to most of its colonies in West and Central Africa, and by the mid-1960s, Belgium had exited its territories.

In 1963, some 32 independent African states (includ-ing those of North Africa) gathered in Ethiopia to form the Organization of African Unity (OAU), with a man-date to support the freedom of Africa's remaining colo-nies and foster continental political and economic integration.

Many of the newly independent countries faced enor-mous challenges: Some were landlocked, and most had largely illiterate and uneducated populations and lacked basic infrastructure. Independence would come later in southern Africa, where colonial or white-dominated gov-ernments ruled in Mozambique and Angola until 1975, in Zimbabwe until 1980, in Namibia until 1990, and in South Africa until 1994.

Still, economic optimism ruled in the 1960s. A lead-ing development textbook at the time foresaw Africa as having greater growth potential than East Asia, and the World Bank's top economist ranked seven African coun-tries with potential to top 7 percent annual growth rates.[53] Yet efforts at economic integration were abortive — with consequences for the continent's long-term development.

For example, Côte d'Ivoire — France's wealthiest for-mer West African colony — rejected a plan to unify with the seven other Francophone states in the region. As a result, the Ivoirians did not have to share their lucrative coffee and cocoa revenues with their poorer neighbors. The region remained divided into many small, weak states susceptible to foreign economic domination.[54]

The region's economies also were hampered by the legacy of colonial economic management. Between 1945 and 1960, as Western Europe practiced full-blown capitalism, Britain, France, and other powers shackled their colonies with wage and price controls, agricultural marketing boards, state-owned industrial companies, and other trappings of centrally planned economies.[55]

The Soviet Union influenced many postindependence African leaders in an effort to export communist ideology to the developing world. Some African leaders saw the relatively stable communist economies of 1950s Eastern Europe as good models for development. In the three decades after Ghana's independence, at least 16 countries in sub-Saharan Africa would adopt socialist policies or mold their economic systems along socialist lines, according to World Bank economist John Nellis. Yet the Soviet Union was hardly the only force pushing Africa's newly independent states away from the free market. In many countries, government ownership of resources was seen as a way to prevent an elite few from dominating the economy.

Additionally, without capital markets to finance large businesses or educated business classes to run them, African leaders as well as Western donors saw a need for governments to fill the gap. In some cases, resentment of colonial domination led to nationalization of some foreign-owned companies. Revenues from state-owned companies were considered a source of funds for building infrastructure and other parts of the economy.[56]

Foreign business interests often fueled resentment because their economic practices were viewed by some as neocolonialist. After the Democratic Republic of Congo gained independence in 1960, the copper-rich Katanga region, backed by Belgian troops and European business interests, tried to secede from the new state.[57] After two years of fighting, the effort failed, however, and the United Nations sent troops to fight on the side of the Congolese government.

In fact, conflict and bad governance played no small role in stifling economic growth. And the two problems were exacerbated by ethnic tensions and Cold War rivalry. The United States and the Soviet Union often

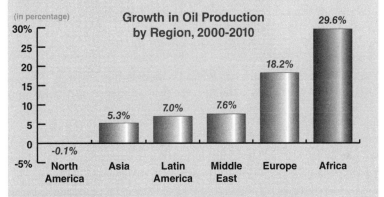

Rapid Oil Exploitation Fuels Africa's Boom

African oil production rose by about 30 percent between 2000 and 2010, faster than in any other region. The increase is due to higher global demand for oil and a surge in oil exports from Africa, which has about 10 percent of the world's reserves.

Growth in Oil Production by Region, 2000-2010
(in percentage)

- North America: -0.1%
- Asia: 5.3%
- Latin America: 7.0%
- Middle East: 7.6%
- Europe: 18.2%
- Africa: 29.6%

Source: "Oil Production," BP Statistical Review, 2012, www.bp.com/sectiongenericarticle800.do? categoryId=9037169&contentId=7068608

backed rival armed factions in sub-Saharan Africa, which helped to extend civil wars. It also led to support for authoritarian "Big Men," such as Zaire's [now the Democratic Republic of Congo (DRC)] Mobutu Sese Seko, who relied on foreign aid and support to buttress his corrupt rule rather than good governance and democracy. During the period between independence and the fall of the Berlin Wall, many of Africa's large countries experienced horrific civil wars or interstate conflicts, including Mozambique, Angola, Nigeria, DRC, Zimbabwe, Chad, Sudan, Ethiopia, Somalia, Uganda, and Tanzania. These protracted conflicts stifled investment and infrastructure development and kept living standards low.

By the 1980s, bad governance and ongoing conflicts had fueled massive external borrowing by governments and state-owned companies. Foreign debt in sub-Saharan Africa had increased from around $11 billion in 1970 to $340 billion in 1995. Many countries had borrowed heavily during a period of high interest rates in the 1970s, much of it from multilateral institutions such as the African Development Bank and IMF, but when commodity prices plummeted in the 1980s, the fall undermined their ability to repay the loans.

Often, the borrowed money was diverted for private use. For instance, the Mobutu regime in Zaire may have stashed up to $18 billion in foreign banks, a significant portion of which likely came from external loans to the government.[58] Other borrowing was used for consumption or white elephant development projects, such as the administrative capital city of Yamoussoukro, built by Côte d'Ivoire's late President Félix Houphouët-Boigny in his birthplace — complete with a $300 million Catholic basilica.

As a result, many countries found themselves in a "debt trap," in which they could not even pay the interest on their foreign debts, causing them to spiral ever higher. In oil-exporting Nigeria, for example, a disastrous four-year period of borrowing in the 1980s during a period of low world oil prices has haunted the country for more than 20 years. As late as 2003, its external debt was equivalent to 71 percent of its gross domestic product, and interest payments on government debt alone were equivalent to 7 percent of the country's entire economic output.[59]

The combined effects of corruption, conflict, poor economic policies, overborrowing, and unfair trade practices by wealthy nations — which subsidize their domestic farming and light-manufacturing industries — left sub-Saharan economies in tatters by the early 1990s.

From 1965 to 1987, as Asia's economies were growing annually by 4 percent and Latin America's by 2.1 percent, African per-capita GDP grew by only 0.6 percent. The differences in growth rates had dramatic effects over time. For instance, in 1965, Zambia's per-capita income was higher than that of South Korea. But by 1998, South Korea's was more than 17 times larger.[60]

A host of other statistics detailed the stagnation. Food production in the 1980s was 20 percent lower than in 1970, even as population soared. Per-capita incomes fell by almost 2 percent a year. Primary school enrollment declined from 79 percent to 67 percent.

By the 1990s, widespread pessimism about sub-Saharan Africa's prospects abounded. "The economic failure is undercutting a drive for political liberalization, raising ethnic rivalries to a dangerous level and forcing countries to impose politically inflammatory austerity programs, often under the dictates of Western financial institutions," John Darnton, a foreign correspondent, wrote in *The New York Times* in June 1994, as Rwanda was convulsed by a genocide that left at least 800,000 dead.

African "Renaissance"

Such gloomy assessments didn't give a full picture of some of the changes underway in sub-Saharan Africa.

After the collapse of the Soviet Union in 1991, the continent embraced economic reforms — particularly in 17 countries now classified as "emerging Africa" by Radelet, the chief USAID economist. Countries slashed regulations and tariffs and cut the costs of starting a business.[61]

Democratic reforms slowly advanced as well. After decades of struggle, South Africa's apartheid government permitted multiracial elections in 1994. And in a "second liberation," long-serving autocrats such as Benin's Mathieu Kérékou, Zambia's Kenneth Kaunda, and Malawi's "Life President" Hastings Banda were voted out of office. The number of African leaders leaving office due to coups, assassination, or other violent means declined sharply.

By the late 1990s, reforms in Radelet's 17 emerging countries — a group that excludes oil exporters — had begun to pay off. Per-capita income began to rise at more than 2 percent per year, an important threshold for sustained growth. Farm productivity in the emerging countries rose 50 percent between 1996 and 2006, and investment and trade nearly tripled.[62] Meanwhile, a series of debt-relief measures by Western banks and governments in the 1990s and early 2000s freed up cash for education, health, and infrastructure.

The political and economic gains of the late 1990s and early 2000s weren't universal. The Democratic Republic of Congo, Sudan, Sierra Leone, and Liberia spent parts of that period embroiled in horrific civil wars. Life expectancy in parts of southern Africa declined during the period amid an AIDS epidemic. A number of countries, such as Somalia, the Central African Republic, and Eritrea, remained fragile states with limited growth prospects. Others, such as Angola, the Republic of Congo, and Equatorial Guinea, enjoyed rapid increases in their GDP, fueled by oil exports and rising global petroleum prices — but the gains were not shared by the majority of the population.

Despite these setbacks, by the late 1990s, South Africa's then-Deputy President Thabo Mbeki had heralded the dawn of an "African Renaissance" built on popular government, economic growth, and poverty alleviation.[63] By 2009 the idea had gained such currency that Senegal began work on a "Monument to the African Renaissance," a 170-foot sculpture (taller than the Statue of Liberty) of a man, woman, and child meant to symbolize Africa's rise.[64]

CURRENT SITUATION

Hope and Change

With 49 countries in sub-Saharan Africa as diverse as South Africa and Somalia, it is difficult to make generalizations about the vast region. Here are overviews of African economies by subregion.

East Africa

Cars are banned on the cobblestoned streets of Lamu, a medieval stone city on Kenya's Indian Ocean coast. The town, a UNESCO World Heritage Site where tourists mingle with load-bearing donkeys and souvenir salesmen, may soon lose some of its tranquil atmosphere.

Construction began in 2012 on a $23 billion port project and oil refinery — the jewel of a new transport corridor meant to link landlocked South Sudan and Ethiopia to the sea via Kenya, which is still under construction. "I am proud to say this is one of the biggest projects that we are carrying out in Africa," Steven Ikuwa, a manager of the project, told the BBC.[65]

With economic growth of more than 7 percent from 2003 to 2008, East Africa was one of the world's fastest-growing regions prior to the global financial crisis. Growth dipped in 2009, partly due to postelection violence in 2007 to 2008 in Kenya — the region's business and transport hub — and the effects of the global slowdown. But since then, growth has bounced back, and the region is expected to grow by 6 percent in 2015.[66]

However, East Africa is marked by political instability and wide disparities in development among countries. The skyscrapers and landscaped office buildings of Kenya's capital, Nairobi, house the local offices of multinational firms such as Google, Samsung, and Pfizer. In Rwanda, the economy is roaring ahead, two decades after genocide left 800,000 people dead. Economic growth lifted more than 1 million people — nearly 10 percent of the population — out of poverty between 2006 and 2011, while Kenya's investments in an advanced fiber-optic network has attracted such companies as Visa, along with top-flight educational institutions like Carnegie Mellon University. Ethiopia is

A power plant rises near Libreville, Gabon, on Oct. 11, 2012, part of a $20 billion infrastructure plan financed in part by the country's abundant oil revenues. But critics complain that much of the country's oil wealth has been diverted to the family of President Ali Bongo, who owns dozens of houses around the world. By one estimate, the Bongo family has stolen up to 25 percent of the country's gross domestic product during its four-decade rule.

AFP/Getty Images/Steve Jordan

pushing ahead with ambitious development plans including the construction of Africa's largest hydropower plant, a railway to Djibouti, and 10 new sugar factories to turn the country into one of the world's top ten exporters of the commodity.

Meanwhile, much of Somalia had no stable central government from 1991 to 2012. A new government backed by the international community has struggled to restore order for the past three years, and investment has been deterred by an Islamist insurgency. Nevertheless, the economy has managed to stave off collapse — nine mobile phone companies compete for business, and demand in neighboring Kenya is strong for Somali exports such as meat and the widely used narcotic leaf khat, which is chewed.[67] African Union peacekeepers have captured key cities held by al-Shabaab, a radical Islamist militia, though attacks continue — and not only in Somalia. A brazen attack in Nairobi killed at least 67 people at the popular Westgate shopping mall in 2013.[68] South Sudan, which gained independence from Sudan in 2011, came away with only 100 miles of paved roads in an area larger than France.[69] But a new conflict erupted in 2013, pitting the country's two largest ethnic groups against each other in a civil war that has since killed thousands. An East African regional bloc is leading efforts to bring peace to the world's youngest country.

Central Africa

Gabonese President Ali Bongo doesn't lack for places to sleep. The president, who took power in 2009 after the death of his father Omar, owns dozens of houses around the world, including three in Beverly Hills, one on the French Riviera, and a $120 million, 14-bedroom mansion in Paris. By one estimate, the Bongo family has siphoned off as much as 25 percent of the oil exporter's gross domestic product during the family's four-decade rule.

"There's absolutely no shame," said Jack Blum, a United Nations consultant and expert on offshore banking. "The people running the country are guilty of grand theft nation."[70]

Indeed, oil has been a blessing for the leaders of Central African nations such as Gabon, Equatorial Guinea, and Chad. But, for ordinary people, it has brought fewer benefits. Wealth began flowing into Equatorial Guinea in the late 1990s as it expanded offshore oil production. Today, just 0.7 percent of its GDP is spent on education, compared to the average elsewhere in Africa of 3.9 percent, and more than half the population lacks access to basic services such as clean water and electricity.[71] The region's greatest crisis in recent years has been in the Central African Republic, where majority-Muslim fighters advanced from the country's northeast and captured several cities and towns beginning in December 2012. To this day — despite the intervention of regional troops — violence and animosity between Christians and Muslims is ongoing. The death toll has exceeded 5,000.

Amid ongoing crises in the region, Chad — home to one of Africa's most powerful militaries — has emerged as a regional power broker, despite concerns about domestic corruption and human rights abuses.

Still, there is cause for hope. The Democratic Republic of Congo, central Africa's most populous nation, is gradually recovering from two wars, the last of which officially ended in 2003. Though conflict simmers in the eastern Kivu region, the DRC's economy will

> **Oil exporter Angola grew by an average of more than 14 percent per year in 2003 to 2008. Yachts in the harbor of the capital, Luanda, must steer through garbage and debris as they come and go. A one-bedroom apartment in the center of Luanda rents for $12,000 a month, leading one British tabloid to declare it "the most expensive city in the world."**

grow by more than 7 percent this year and 8.2 percent in 2013, according to the IMF.[72] Foreign direct investment increased more than fourfold from 2010 to 2011, fueled by telecom companies seeking to expand mobile communications in the heavily populated country.[73]

Southern Africa

In 2012, the De Beers diamond consortium announced it had begun sorting rough diamonds in Botswana's capital, Gaborone, a process it had previously done in London. The move to Botswana, the world's largest producer of diamonds, transformed the southern African nation into a major gem-trading hub, with about $6 billion in gem sales annually.[74]

The shift is emblematic of Botswana's rise from being one of the world's poorest nations at independence to a middle-income nation today, with per-capita income of $15,752 in 2013.[75] Experts attribute the rise to political harmony and wise management of the country's diamond reserves. But the country is working hard to boost tourism, financial services, and other sectors in anticipation of its greatest resource running dry in two or three decades.[76]

Botswana and other southern African nations comprise sub-Saharan Africa's wealthiest region. They also are the most economically integrated, through the 15-nation free-trade bloc known as the Southern African Development Community. Their economies are closely linked with that of South Africa, the regional giant.

However, integration can also have disadvantages. South Africa's advanced economy is heavily reliant on exports to Europe. The European Union is South Africa's largest trading partner and buys one third of its

Is Africa poised for an East Asia–style economic boom?

YES

G. Pascal Zachary
Professor of Journalism, Arizona State University; author, Hotel Africa: The Politics of Escape

Written for *CQ Global Researcher*, November 2012

When I visited Ghana in June, I met dozens of former U.K. residents — well-educated offspring of Ghanaian immigrants to Britain — who'd recently returned to their ancestral home in West Africa in pursuit of better opportunities. With Britain's economy contracting and Ghana's expanding, thousands from the African diaspora are now working in Africa, in jobs and companies that need their professional skills.

What a historic reversal. Throughout much of sub-Saharan Africa, economic conditions are better than at any time in more than 50 years and have been excellent since the beginning of the 21st century. The obsession of the U.S. media and foreign-aid lobby with disaster, disease, and mayhem in Africa has long distorted the continent's image. But with commodity prices high, low levels of debt by global standards, expanding domestic markets, and near-record levels of foreign investment, Africa's economic strength is impossible to dismiss.

From 2000 to 2010, 6 of the world's 10 fastest-growing countries were in sub-Saharan Africa: Angola, Nigeria, Ethiopia, Chad, Mozambique, and Rwanda. In 8 of the past 10 years, sub-Saharan Africa has grown faster than Asia. While many of the region's growth stars rely in part on oil exports, Ethiopia — which has no oil — saw its economy grow 7.5 percent in 2011. In 2012, the International Monetary Fund expects Africa to grow at 6 percent — about the same as Asia.

And Africa's boom is benefiting a broad swath of African society — reversing the continent's brain drain, reducing rural poverty, enabling governments to broaden access to free education, and improving Africans' technological sophistication.

Will the boom continue? With robust commodity prices, tangible productivity gains due to the mobile communications revolution, and the fledgling expansion of African agriculture, the answer is surely yes. Meanwhile, an astonishing 50 percent of Africa's under-25 population is fueling household formation and growth in personal consumption unmatched in the world.

The problems aren't those touted by Afro-pessimists: that Africa remains dependent on imported goods, corruption flourishes, and women are unempowered. While these concerns are considerable, they coexist with an Africa that's generating wealth at an unprecedented rate. The challenge for African leaders is no longer coping with the scourge of scarcity but rather managing prosperity by reducing inequality and expanding opportunity, especially for women. The big political question is how to ensure that all Africans benefit from the boom.

NO

Omotunde E. G. Johnson
Sierra Leone Country Director, International Growth Centre London

Written for *CQ Global Researcher*, November 2012

If Africa is to embark on an East Asian–style economic takeoff, it needs drastic improvement in economic governance and management. This in turn requires much better leadership and cooperation than exists at the present time. The prospect of this happening in the near future is not good.

African countries now face three overarching policy challenges: raising investment, boosting the efficiency of investment, and increasing technological change and innovation. To do that, African citizens must be willing and able to design and implement appropriate economic policies.

As everyone knows, investment — in equipment, research and development, and education and training — is good for growth. Such investment, relative to domestic product, is currently low in Africa, on average, compared to what Asian countries were able to attain during their years of rapid growth, as well as today.

The efficiency of investment in Africa is low by world standards — a symptom of underlying factors, such as government inefficiency, low education and training, poor operation of markets, weak institutions (rules), corruption, and political instability.

The policy failings in Africa come mainly from weaknesses in governance arrangements (rules, processes, and organization) which in turn come from weaknesses in leadership and cooperation. The role of institutions in the development process has come to be greatly appreciated over several decades now. Institutions are rules governing behavior in human interaction. But institutions are themselves outcomes of cooperation. In other words, they are elements of the order that cooperation brings about. Hence, countries succeed in the development process when they are able to cooperate to bring about appropriate political, legal, and social institutions that favor economic development and growth.

To embark on an East Asian–style economic takeoff, African countries need more cooperation. Trust and self-interest will play major roles in bringing that about. Leadership is also crucial. The vast majority of African countries can benefit from transforming leadership at all levels: political, civil society, and business.

In building institutions, legitimation processes matter. Indeed, one of the operational requirements for institutions to be effective is legitimacy. Institutions that are not legitimated by the populace at large will not be willingly obeyed and promoted by the people; there will be no sense of loyalty to the institutions.

manufacturing exports — making South Africa vulnerable to the eurozone crisis, as Europe's slowing economies buy fewer South African goods.[77]

Fortunately, strong demand from Asia has helped counteract some of the slowing demand in Europe. In 2013, South Africa reported more than $23 billion in bilateral trade with China, up 32 percent from the year before,[78] although the South African goods China buys are different from those exported to the European Union.

"While South Africa's export profile to Europe is fairly balanced, the same cannot be said for China and other large emerging market partners," said Simon Freemantle, an economist with Johannesburg-based Standard Bank.[79] In 2011, 90 percent of South Africa's exports to China were made up of commodities, he says.

Strong demand for commodities has fueled growth elsewhere in southern Africa. New oil exporter Angola grew by more than 14 percent per year on average between 2003 and 2008. Its economy slowed during the downturn, when oil prices fell, but is expected to grow again by 5.5 percent this year.[80] The rest of the country's economy has struggled to keep up with the tide of petrodollars pouring in. Yachts in Luanda's harbor must steer through garbage and debris as they come and go. A one-bedroom apartment in the center of the capital rents for $12,000 a month, leading one British tabloid to declare it "the most expensive city in the world."[81]

Meanwhile, Zimbabwe's economy is slowly recovering from a spectacular swoon, when it shrank by half between 1998 and 2008 after President Robert Mugabe began seizing land, mainly from white farmers, and held onto power through violence-riddled elections. The United States and Europe responded with sanctions, further crippling the economy.

After a national unity government was forged in 2009 between Mugabe's ruling party and the opposition, the economy began slowly growing. Zimbabwe dropped its devalued currency and replaced it with the dollar. But growth has been stunted by a government directive in 2011 that all foreign-owned companies cede 51 percent ownership to black Zimbabweans.[82] This year the economy is projected to grow by 4.5 percent, according to the IMF. The 91-year-old Mugabe remains president, though he is in frail health.

West Africa

Niger is among the world's poorest countries, ranking last of 187 nations on the U.N.'s 2014 Human Development Index. One in eight children dies before age 5, and 60 percent of the population lives in poverty, according to the World Bank.

Yet shoots of hope are sprouting. The country's economy expanded by 11.1 percent in 2012 on higher production of uranium from the country's mines and the beginning of its first oil production and is projected to grow by 5.9 percent this year.[83] Foreign aid and government efforts have helped increase life expectancy from 42 in 1992 to 58 in 2012, while the percentage of children in primary school has risen to 71 percent, from 50 percent one decade ago.[84]

Niger's growth is emblematic of a transformation underway in West Africa. The region's economy grew by an estimated 7.4 percent last year,[85] led by strong growth in regional powers Nigeria and Ghana and a rebound in Côte d'Ivoire following a decade of political instability and civil war. Oil discoveries in the Gulf of Guinea, which stretches from Ghana to Sierra Leone, also have boosted growth expectations. Nigeria, which became the continent's largest economy after a rebasing of GDP in 2014, had been the region's only major oil exporter until 2007, when U.K.–based Tullow Oil made a large discovery in Ghana.

"What you've had since then was an increasing number of finds showing that there are oil systems in the region," British oil analyst John Marks told a reporter after the announcement of discoveries off Sierra Leone and Liberia. "Announcements like this will only raise the excitement."[86]

Political instability continues to pose risks for growth, however. In Mali, soldiers ousted the democratically elected president in 2012, and radical Islamists took control of the northern part of the country, where they instituted Islamic law before being ousted by regional and French forces.[87] The region remains volatile, as it sits on the peripheries of the largely lawless Sahel. Nigeria has also suffered from ongoing violence perpetrated by Boko Haram, an Islamist group rooted in the country's northwest. The group made headlines in 2014 for a mass kidnapping of more than 200 schoolgirls from the town of Chibok and again for a 2015 massacre in the town of Baga that killed hundreds — and possibly thousands — of people.[88]

But the biggest threat to the region came in 2014 when ebola, a communicable and often-fatal virus, wreaked havoc across Sierra Leone, Guinea, and Liberia, in the most deadly surge of the disease ever recorded. The death toll has exceeded 8,000, due in large part to inadequate health-care services that enabled the disease to spread.[89]

OUTLOOK

Chinese Challenges

As sub-Saharan African countries strive for an East Asian–style transformation in the coming decades, much will depend on their relationship with the world's most important emerging economy: China. Africa's trade with China has risen from $10 billion in 2000 to $198.5 billion in 2012.[90,91]

In addition, Chinese companies have invested heavily in African mines and oil wells and have provided concessional loans to African governments to build roads, railways, and electricity plants. "Their investment ideas are backed by finance," says Ifediora Amobi, director of the Nigeria-based African Institute for Applied Economics. "Even when the Chinese say we'll come build it and put it together, it still is a good model for most countries."

Chinese companies have provided African governments with an alternative to foreign aid and multinational corporations. The competition has allowed African governments to strike better deals than they otherwise would have obtained, say some experts.

"You're finding the big Chinese state-owned companies competing very aggressively on the continent," said Maree of South Africa's Standard Bank, which is 20 percent owned by a Chinese state bank. "Our view is that generally China has been a huge force for good and for growth and development in Africa."[92]

Others see the relationship as carrying risks as well as rewards. Even on concessional terms, African governments could risk being overburdened by debt. In addition, China's authoritarian government's willingness to do business with unsavory regimes such as Zimbabwe and Sudan can undermine needed governance reforms, says Massa, the France-based economist for the Overseas Development Institute.

The Chinese economic juggernaut is a challenge for Africa as its economies seek liftoff in a more competitive global economy than other emerging countries faced in previous decades. "The East Asian countries didn't have to face competition from China," says the World Bank's Devarajan. "China didn't have a China to compete with in global markets."

Others worry that China will continue to dominate manufacturing — discouraging the development of African manufacturing — and that Africans aren't benefiting enough from the commodities-for-infrastructure deals with Chinese firms. "The stream of cheap Chinese exports to Africa may reduce incentives for African firms to build productive capacity or make their products less competitive in foreign markets," says Massa. "Finally, there is a risk that African countries endowed with natural resources are seeing their resources drain slowly away without profiting enough from Chinese deals."

The lack of strong growth in high-employment industries such as manufacturing will lead to deepening political tensions and instability in countries with growing numbers of underemployed and "vulnerable" employed people, says Johnson, the Sierra Leonean economist. Such instability will make it difficult for many countries to enjoy the sustained period of growth needed to improve living standards.

"What will change is the nature of the conflict," he adds. "Right now a lot of conflict is for control of the state. The fight [in the future] will be over jobs and income."

Africa's wealthiest economies may be able to avoid such an outcome, says Lund of McKinsey. "For the most diversified economies you are seeing this tipping point," she says. "But then for the rest of the African countries, they're in the opposite situation, where the number of vulnerable [people] employed will continue to grow."

Others see the challenges to industrialization for African nations — small size, lack of regional integration, and poor infrastructure — as major stumbling blocks. Natural resource wealth may also prove a hindrance if revenue management does not improve. As Chinese labor costs rise, rival developing nations, such as India, could emerge as the next low-cost center of manufacturing.

"I would find it hard to envision" an East Asia–style takeoff for Africa, says Ramachandran of the Center for Global Development. "The Asian cost advantage will still be significant. Ten years from now I can see better management of resources that could translate into more service [jobs] and back-office operations."

The fact that hundreds of millions of workers in sub-Saharan Africa will still be doing subsistence agriculture or other vulnerable types of work in the decades to come does not necessarily mean their economies will not attain annual rates of 8 percent growth or more, says Devarajan.

"We have to accept the fact that even under the best of circumstances, a large number are going to go into the informal sector," he says. "So we have to acknowledge that rather than fight it. Informal is normal, at least for the next 20 years. Then we should ask the question about how we can improve their productivity."

Devarajan predicts that by 2025, all of sub-Saharan Africa, except fragile states such as the DRC, Somalia, and South Sudan, will be middle-income countries with per-capita income above $5,000. Development will no longer be measured by the percentage of children completing primary school but secondary education and college. Some sub-Saharan countries, in his view, may even become "manufacturing powerhouses."

"In 2025 it will look like what East Asia looks like today," he says.

NOTES

1. "World Bank Data: GDP per Capita (Current U.S. Dollars)," http://data.worldbank.org/indicator/NY .GDP.PCAP.CD.

2. "World Economic Outlook 2014," IMF, October 2014, http://www.imf.org/external/pubs/ft/ weo/2014/02/.

3. "World Economic Outlook 2014," IMF, October 2014, http://www.imf.org/external/pubs/ft/ weo/2014/02/.

4. "Building Bridges: Ernst & Young's Attractiveness Survey 2012: Africa," Ernst & Young, www.ey.com/ ZA/en/Issues/Business-environment/2012-Africa-attractiveness-survey.

5. "Africa Poised for Faster Growth in Spite of Volatile Global Economy," World Bank, April 2012, http:// www.worldbank.org/en/news/press-release/2012/04/ 18/africa-poised-for-faster-growth-in-spite-of-volatile-global-economy-new-world-bank-report.

6. "Africa at Work: Job Creation and Inclusive Growth," McKinsey Global Institute, 2012, www .mckinsey.com/insights/mgi/research/africa_ europe_middle_east/africa_at_work.

7. "2014 Corruption Perceptions Index," Transparency International, 2014, http://cpi.transparency.org/ cpi2014/results/.

8. "GNI Per Capita Ranking, Atlas Method and PPP based," World Bank, 2014, http://data.worldbank.org/ data-catalog/GNI-per-capita-Atlas-and-PPP-table.

9. "Doing Business 2014: Economy Rankings," World Bank, June 2014, http://www.doingbusiness.org/ rankings.

10. "The Economic Rise of Mozambique," Al Jazeera English, Aug. 18, 2012, www.aljazeera.com/pro grammes/countingthecost/2012/08/ 201281714 514039254.html.

11. Radelet, *op. cit.,* p. 96.

12. *Regional Economic Outlook: Sub-Saharan Africa,* IMF, April 2014, p. 90, http://www.imf.org/exter nal/pubs/ft/reo/2014/afr/eng/sreo0414.pdf.

13. *Global Employment Trends, 2014,* International Labor Organization, 2014. pp. 19, 68, http://www .ilo.org/wcmsp5/groups/public/—dgreports/— dcomm/—publ/documents/publication/ wcms_233953.pdf.

14. Data on oil exports from U.S. Energy Information Administration database, www.eia.gov/countries/. See also "Democratic Republic of Congo," *RevenueWatch,* www.revenuewatch.org/countries/ africa/democratic-republic-congo/overview.

15. "Angola's Economy set to slow as oil prices collapse," Joe Brock, Reuters, Jan. 29, 2015, http://www .reuters.com/article/2015/01/29/angola-economy-idUSL6N0V645F20150129.

16. "As diamond mines decline, Botswana searches for new way to shine," Ryan Lenora Brown, *Christian Science Monitor,* http://www.csmonitor.com/World/ Africa/2014/1027/As-diamond-mines-decline-Botswana-searches-for-new-way-to-shine.

17. *Equatorial Guinea 2014,* African Development Bank, 2014, p. 2, http://www.africaneconomicout-look.org/fileadmin/uploads/aeo/2014/PDF/CN_ Long_EN/Guine_equatoriale_EN.pdf.

18. For background, see Jennifer Weeks, "The Resource Curse," *CQ Global Researcher,* Dec. 20, 2011, pp. 597–622.

19. "Angola's Economy set to slow as oil prices collapse," Joe Brock, Reuters, Jan. 29, 2015, http://www.reuters.com/article/2015/01/29/angola-economy-idUSL6N0V645F20150129.

20. "Nigeria Budget-Cut Threat Falls Short As Oil Prices Drop," Bloomberg, Nov. 2104, http://www.bloomberg.com/news/articles/2014-11-18/nigeria-budget-cut-pledge-falls-short-as-oil-prices-drop.

21. Joseph Stiglitz, "Africa's Natural Resources Can Be a Blessing, Not an Economic Curse," *The Guardian,* Aug. 6, 2012, www.guardian.co.uk/business/economics-blog/2012/aug/06/africa-natural-resources-economic-curse.

22. *Economic Development in Africa: 2011*, United Nations Conference on Trade and Development, July 11, 2011, http://unctad.org/en/docs/aldcafrica2011_en.pdf.

23. For background, see Karen Foerstel, "China in Africa," *CQ Global Researcher,* Jan. 1, 2008, pp. 1–26.

24. "Africa at Work: Job Creation and Inclusive Growth," *op. cit.,* p. 34.

25. "South Africa: Challenges in Manufacturing," *African Business News,* Nov. 9, 2011, www.youtube.com/watch?v=hGxlz89ADd8.

26. Radelet, *op. cit.,* p. 44.

27. Caswell Tlali, "U.S. Saves 40,000 Jobs in Lesotho," *Sunday Express* (Lesotho), Aug. 5, 2012, http://sundayexpress.co.ls/?p=7152.

28. "Industry: Growth in textiles and clothing plays central role in jobs creation," Jonathan Clayton, *Financial Times*, April 18, 2013, http://www.ft.com/intl/cms/s/0/fa4d7476-9b98-11e2-8485-00144feabdc0.html.

29. Tlali.

30. *Global Employment Trends, 2014*, International Labor Organization, 2014, pp. 19, 68, 69, http://www.ilo.org/wcmsp5/groups/public/—dgreports/—dcomm/—publ/documents/publication/wcms_233953.pdf

31. *Global Employment Trends, 2014*, International Labor Organization, 2014, p. 68, http://www.ilo.org/wcmsp5/groups/public/—dgreports/—dcomm/—publ/documents/publication/wcms_233953.pdf.

32. "Bitter Sweets: Could Ebola affect global chocolate supplies?" Bruce Kennedy, CBS Money Watch, Oct. 8, 2014, http://www.cbsnews.com/news/bitter-sweets-could-ebola-affect-global-chocolate-supplies/.

33. Isis Almeida, "Ghana, Ivory Coast's Cocoa Areas Seen Getting Improved Rainfall," Bloomberg News, Sept. 13, 2012, www.bloomberg.com/news/2012-09-13/ghana-ivory-coast-s-cocoa-areas-seen-getting-improved-rainfall.html.

34. Marianne Stigset, "Yirgacheffe Has Starbucks' Number in Coffee Brand Row (Update 1)," Bloomberg, April 17, 2008, www.bloomberg.com/apps/news?pid=newsarchive&sid=aLB6drYEOTF8&refer=home.

35. Jessica Donati, "Nigerian Fuel Shortages Loom as Suppliers Drop Out," Reuters, June 1, 2012, www.reuters.com/article/2012/06/01/nigeria-fuel-subsidies-idUSL5E8GV9WI20120601.

36. "Retail soars as more shopping malls berth in Nigeria," Anne Agbaje, Business Day, Nov. 7, 2014, http://businessdayonline.com/2014/11/retail-soars-as-more-shopping-malls-berth-in-nigeria.

37. For background, see Jina Moore, "Resolving Land Disputes," *CQ Global Researcher,* Sept. 6, 2011, pp. 421–446.

38. Neil MacFarquhar, "African Farmers Displaced as Investors Move In," *The New York Times,* Dec. 21, 2010, www.nytimes.com/2010/12/22/world/africa/22mali.html?pagewanted=all.

39. "Unemployment a 'Ticking Time Bomb," *The Times* (South Africa), May 27, 2012, www.timeslive.co.za/local/2012/05/27/unemployment-a-ticking-time-bomb-ycl. For background, see Roland Flamini, "Turmoil in the Arab World," *CQ Global Researcher,* May 3, 2011, pp. 209–236.

40. "Attitudes About Aging: A Global Perspective in Major Regions of the World," Pew Research Center, Jan. 30, 2014, http://www.pewglobal.org/2014/

01/30/chapter-3-aging-in-major-regions-of-the-world-2010-to-2050/.

41. "Africa at Work," *op. cit.*, p. 2.

42. Supee Teravaninthorn and Gael Raballand, *Transport Prices and Costs in Africa: A Review of the International Corridors*, World Bank, 2009, www.infrastructurea frica.org/system/files/WP14_Transportprices.pdf.

43. Basil Davidson, *The African Past* (1964), pp. 176–177.

44. Philip Curtin, *The Atlantic Slave Trade: A Census* (1969).

45. Roland Oliver and Michael Crowder (eds.), *The Cambridge Encyclopedia of Africa* (1981), pp. 146–148.

46. Foerstel, *op. cit.*

47. Thomas Pakenham, *The Scramble for Africa: White Man's Conquest of the Dark Continent from 1876 to 1912* (1991), pp. 239–255.

48. Jason McLure, "Sub-Saharan Democracy," *CQ Global Researcher*, Feb. 15, 2011, pp. 92–94.

49. Parts of South Africa were under independent white rule at the time. Liberia, established as a homeland for freed U.S. slaves in the 1840s, was functionally a U.S. protectorate despite being granted independence.

50. Martin Meredith, *The Fate of Africa* (2005), p. 2.

51. *Ibid.*, p. 8.

52. "The Atlantic Charter," Aug. 14, 1941, U.S. National Archives, www.archives.gov/education/les sons/fdr-churchill/images/atlantic-charter.gif.

53. William Easterly and Ross Levine, *Africa's Growth Tragedy: Policies and Ethnic Divisions*, World Bank Policy Research Working Paper, August 1995, http://papers.ssrn.com/sol3/papers.cfm?abstract_id=569226.

54. Meredith, *op. cit.*, p. 64.

55. John R. Nellis, "Public Enterprises in Sub-Saharan Africa," *World Bank Discussion Paper,* 1986.

56. For background, see J. McChesney, "Privatization: Third World Moves Slowly," *Editorial Research Reports,* 1988, available at *CQ Researcher Plus Archive.*

57. Oliver and Crowder, *op. cit.,* p. 260.

58. "Debt Sustainability: Oasis or Mirage," United Nations Conference on Trade and Development, 2004, pp. 5–16, http://archive.unctad.org/Templates/WebFlyer.asp?intItemID=3246&lang=1.

59. "The Burden of Debt," PBS Online News-hour, July 2003, www.pbs.org/newshour/bb/africa/nigeria/debt.html.

60. Malcolm McPherson, *Restarting and Sustaining Growth and Development in Africa: A Framework for Improving Productivity*, U.S. Agency for International Development, http//:pdf.usaid.gov/pdf_docs/pnack931.pdf.

61. Radelet, *op. cit.,* pp. 71–79.

62. *Ibid.,* pp. 27–38.

63. Thabo Mbeki, "The African Renaissance: South Africa and the World," Speech at the United Nations University in Japan, April 9, 1998, http://archive.unu.edu/unupress/mbeki.html.

64. "Dakar's African Renaissance Monument Project Has Detractors," Voice of America, Nov. 1, 2009, www.voanews.com/content/a-13-2008-08-22-vo a64/405373.html.

65. "Lamu Port Project Launched for South Sudan and Ethiopia," BBC News, March 2, 2012, www.bbc.co.uk/news/world-africa-17231889.

66. "African Economic Outlook 2014: Eastern African Countries," African Development Bank, 2012, www.africaneconomicoutlook.org/en/countries/.

67. Damina Zane, "Somalia: 20 Years of Anarchy," BBC News, Jan. 26, 2011, www.bbc.co.uk/news/world-africa-12278628.

68. Lucas Barasa, "Kibaki Commends Kenyan Forces Over Kismayo Victory," *Daily Nation* (Kenya) Sept. 28, 2012, www.nation.co.ke/News/Kibaki+commen ds+KDF+over+Kismayu+victory/-/1056/1520274/-/10jb9e2z/-/index.html.

69. "One-Year Old South Sudan: Potential to Be Harnessed," NPR, July 9, 2012, www.npr.org/2012/07/09/156491044/1-year-old-south-sudan-potential-to-be-harnessed.

70. Brian Ross and Anna Schecter, "Obama Invites Ali Bongo to White House," ABC News, June 8, 2011, http://abcnews.go.com/Blotter/obama-invites-ali-bongo-white-house/story?id=13791159#.UGYPwhiy83Q.

71. Joseph Kraus and Jonathan Hershon St. Jean, "Equatorial Guinea No Place to Hold a Human Rights Summit," *The Guardian,* Aug. 24, 2012, www.guardian.co.uk/global-development/poverty-matters/2012/aug/24/equatorial-guinea-human-rights-summit.

72. "DR Congo Economic Growth Seen at 8.2 Percent in 2013 — IMF," Reuters, Sept. 28, 2013, http://af.reuters.com/article/commoditiesNews/idAFL5E8KS75820120928. For background, see Josh Kron, "Conflict in Congo," *CQ Global Researcher,* April 5, 2011, pp. 157–182.

73. "African Economic Outlook 2012: Central African Countries," African Development Bank, 2012, www.africaneconomicoutlook.org/en/countries/.

74. "As diamond mines decline, Botswana searches for new way to shine," Ryan Lenora Brown, *Christian Science Monitor*, http://www.csmonitor.com/World/Africa/2014/1027/As-diamond-mines-decline-Botswana-searches-for-new-way-to-shine

75. "World Bank Data: GDP per Capita," 2014, data.worldbank.org/indicator/NY.GDP.PCAP.CD.

76. "As diamond mines decline, Botswana searches for new way to shine," Ryan Lenora Brown, *Christian Science Monitor*, http://www.csmonitor.com/World/Africa/2014/1027/As-diamond-mines-decline-Botswana-searches-for-new-way-to-shine.

77. "South Africa Urges G20 Summit to Tackle Eurozone Crisis," Xinhua, June 17, 2012, http://news.xinhuanet.com/english/world/2012-06/18/c_123295579.htm.

78. "Bilateral trade with China on the increase," Linda Ensor, BDLive, March 2014, http://www.bdlive.co.za/business/trade/2014/03/12/bilateral-trade-with-china-on-the-increase.

79. "South Africa Must Protect Competitive Advantages as BRICs Build Ties With Africa," Standard Bank, March 29, 2012, www.standard bank.com/Article.aspx?id=-177&src=m2012_34385466.

80. *Regional Economic Outlook: Sub-Saharan Africa,* IMF, April 2014, p. 90, http://www.imf.org/external/pubs/ft/reo/2014/afr/eng/sreo0414.pdf.

81. Barbara Jones, "Luanda: The Capital of Angola, the Most Expensive City in the World," *The Daily Mail,* Aug. 4, 2012, www.dailymail.co.uk/news/article-2183616/Luanda-The-capital-Angola-expensive-city-world.html.

82. "Zimplats Happens," *The Economist,* March 17, 2012, www.economist.com/node/21550289.

83. *Regional Economic Outlook: Sub-Saharan Africa,* IMF, April 2014, p. 90, http://www.imf.org/external/pubs/ft/reo/2014/afr/eng/sreo0414.pdf.

84. World Bank Data, Data.worldbank.org/country/niger.

85. "Measuring the Pulse of Transformation in West Africa," African Development Bank, Nov. 2014, http://www.afdb.org/en/blogs/measuring-the-pulse-of-economic-transformation-in-west-africa/.

86. Alphonso Toweh and Simon Akam, "UPDATE 2 — New Discoveries Raise West African Oil Hopes," Reuters, Feb. 21, 2012, http://af.reuters.com/article/liberiaNews/idAFL5E8DL1DE20120221?sp=true.

87. "Northern Mali Islamists Reopen Schools With Girls in Back," The Associated Press, Sept. 28, 2012, www.usatoday.com/story/news/world/2012/09/28/mali-islam-women/1600117/.

88. "Boko Haram Attack: What Happened in Baga?" Thomas Fessy. BBC News, February 2, 2015, http://www.bbc.com/news/world-africa-30987043.

89. "WHO: Ebola Virus Death Toll in West Africa Reaches 8,289," Itar-Tass, January 10, 2015, http://itar-tass.com/en/world/770594.

90. "8 Facts about China's Investments in Africa," Brookings Institute, May 2014, http://www.brookings.edu/blogs/brookings-now/posts/2014/05/8-facts-about-china-investment-in-africa.

91. "Africa and China's Growing Partnership," Africa Progress Panel, April 2012, www.africaprogresspanel.org/index.php/download_file/view/1754.

92. Al Jazeera English, *op. cit.*

BIBLIOGRAPHY

Selected Sources
Books

Ayittey, George, *Africa Unchained: The Blueprint for Africa's Future,* Palgrave MacMillan, 2006.

A prominent Ghanaian economist is unsparing in his criticism of modern African governance, 50 years after the end of colonialism. Freeing African economies from their governments' shackles would raise living standards for the continent's poorest, he argues.

Easterly, William, *The White Man's Burden: Why the West's Efforts to Aid the Rest Have Done So Much Ill and So Little Good*, Oxford University Press, 2007.
In this seminal critique, a development economist examines why the tens of billions in aid spent in the past 50 years have done so little to alleviate poverty in the world's poorest nations. Easterly was fired by the World Bank for his earlier critiques of the ineffectiveness of Western aid.

Mahajan, Vijay, *Africa Rising: How 900 Million African Consumers Offer More Than You Think*, Pearson Education Inc., 2011.
A marketing professor offers a detailed argument for greater private-sector investment in Africa. Mahajan says the continent is richer than most people outside Africa realize, and its rapidly growing population is the next big market for multinational companies.

Miguel, Edward, *Africa's Turn?* Massachusetts Institute of Technology, 2009.
A University of California economist argues that the end to major civil wars and trade with China has bolstered African growth, though the continent still faces threats from climate change and fragile states. Nine guest experts also critique his narrative of African growth.

Radelet, Steven, *Emerging Africa: How 17 Countries Are Leading the Way*, Center for Global Development, 2009.
Now the top economist for the U.S. Agency for International Development, Radelet says that since 1995, a group of 17 African countries has plowed ahead economically without the benefit of oil. From South Africa to Tanzania to Ghana, these countries are raising living standards due to better governance, improved technology, and international debt relief.

Articles

Fox, Killian, "Africa's Mobile Economic Revolution," *The Guardian*, July 23, 2011.

From mobile banking to dissemination of agricultural prices, the rapid spread of mobile technology in Africa is revolutionizing the continent's economies.

French, Howard, "The Next Asia Is Africa: Inside the Continent's Rapid Economic Growth," *The Atlantic*, May 21, 2012.
A former *New York Times* Africa correspondent travels to Zambia to see how African societies are changing as they grow wealthier.

Grant, Jaime, "On the Road With West Africa's Fuel Smugglers," ThinkAfricaPress, March 20, 2012.
The trade in smuggled fuel from Nigeria has led to the creation of what the author calls "micro-petro-states" in Benin and Togo, where local officials and enterprising teenagers alike profit from sneaking subsidized Nigerian gasoline into other West African countries.

Smith, David, "Wikileaks Cables: Shell's Grip on Nigerian State Revealed," *The Guardian*, Dec. 8, 2010.
Royal Dutch Shell's top executive in Nigeria, where the company produces about 800,000 barrels of oil per day, told U.S. officials the company had placed company loyalists in relevant ministries within the Nigerian government so the company could keep tabs on its deliberations.

Straziuso, Jason, "Unexpected: Africa's Hotel Boom," The Associated Press, Oct. 1, 2012.
Marriott, Hilton, and Radisson are scrambling to build hotels on a continent they have long ignored. The hotel boom is a symbol of the growth of African trade and wealth.

Reports and Studies

"Africa at Work: Job Creation and Inclusive Growth," McKinsey Global Institute, August 2012.
Africa's recent growth record is good, but the continent will have to produce many more salaried jobs to reduce the share of its fast-growing population that remains in subsistence agriculture and other vulnerable forms of employment.

"African Economic Outlook: 2012," African Development Bank, Organisation for Economic Cooperation and Development, U.N. Development Program and U.N. Economic Commission for Africa (joint publication), 2012.

The annual publication synthesizes economic statistics and forecasts from a range of international agencies to describe the current and future economies of Africa.

"Building Bridges Africa: 2012 Attractiveness Survey," Ernst & Young, 2012.

Many international businesses have outdated perceptions of Africa's economies, leaving many opportunities for investment on the continent as yet unexplored. To accelerate growth, however, African governments must invest more in roads, ports, electricity generation, and other infrastructure.

For More Information

African Economic Research Consortium, P.O. Box 62882 00200, Nairobi, Kenya; +254 20 2734150; www .aercafrica.org. Researches management of sub-Saharan economies.

African Institute for Applied Economics, 54 Nza St., Independence Layout, Enugu, Nigeria; +234 706 209 3690; www.aiaenigeria.org. Think tank that provides research and policy advice with a West African focus.

African Union, P.O. Box 3243, Addis Ababa, Ethiopia; +251 11 551 77 00; www.africa-union.org. Mediates election disputes and seeks economic and political cooperation among 53 member nations.

Center for Global Development, 1800 Massachusetts Ave., N.W., Third Floor, Washington, DC 20036; www.cgdev .org. Independent think tank studying aid effectiveness,

education, globalization, health, migration, and trade in developing nations.

McKinsey Global Institute, 1200 19th St., N.W., Suite 1000, Washington, DC 20036; 202-662-3100; www.mck insey.com/insights/mgi. International economics research arm of the McKinsey consulting firm.

Overseas Development Institute, 203 Blackfriars Road, London SE1 8NJ, United Kingdom; +44 20 7922 0300; www.odi.org.uk. A leading think tank that seeks to shape policy on economic development and poverty alleviation in the developing world.

South African Institute of International Affairs, P.O. Box 31596, Braamfontein 2017, South Africa; +27 11 339 2154, www.saiia.org. Think tank that studies African governance, parliamentary performance, and natural resources governance.

Voices From Abroad

BEN SEAGER-SCOTT

Analyst, Bestinvest, England

Economic potential

"The continent sits on huge natural resources and has a young and growing population, which can drive demand as economic development progresses. Major problems remain over governmental integrity and political interventions, as well as the lack of infrastructure, both of which are vital for supporting economic growth."

Daily Telegraph (England), April 2012

MTHULI NCUBE

Vice President, African Development Bank, Tunisia

Unacceptable stagnation

"The continent is experiencing jobless growth. That is an unacceptable reality on a continent with such an impressive pool of youth, talent and creativity."

New Times (Rwanda), May 2012

KAIHRIN TRUMPEIMANN

Executive manager, DAV Professional Placement Group, South Africa

The search continues

"African companies are battling to find suitably qualified people who are the cream of the crop in their chosen fields. They are actively recruiting these skills internationally — and that includes South Africa."

Sunday Times (South Africa), October 2012

CLIFFORD SACKS

CEO, Renaissance Capital, South Africa

The next success story

"The emerging markets, and Africa in particular, are attracting unprecedented attention as capital shifts

The Khaleej Times/UAE/Paresh Nath

from developed to growth markets. With the highest concentration of fast-growing economies, Africa will be the investment success story of the next decade."

Accra Mail (Ghana), May 2012

RICHARD JENKINS

Chair, Black Creek Investment Management, Canada

Questions remain

"The big question is if I'm going to invest in South Africa and deal with some of the economic and political issues there, and I'm going to buy a gold mining stock, why wouldn't I own one in Australia or Canada instead?"

Financial Post (Canada,) July 2012

NOEL DE VILLIERS

CEO, Open Africa, South Africa

Unleashing potential

"We don't just need new jobs. We need new kinds of jobs in new niches innate to the indigenous potential of South Africa's people and assets.... New niches for new products in new markets have to be found, and these should be aligned with our indigenous skills and strengths. We have to invent new Africa-sourced products, and fast."

Sunday Times (South Africa), March 2012

PETER ESELE

President General, Trade Union Congress, Nigeria

Jobs for a growing population

"[African] governments at all levels should embark on core principles that can create the much-needed business environment for our indigenous companies to thrive and generate employment opportunities for the teeming populace."

This Day (Nigeria), June 2012

ANTHONY JONGWE

Principal Consultant, Global Workforce Solutions, Zimbabwe

The youth opportunity

"With over 40 percent of the population below 15 years, Africa is by far the continent with the largest global youthful population. Sixty percent of Africa's population is below 24 years. If managed well, this demographic represents Africa's best development asset over the coming decades."

Financial Gazette (Zimbabwe), February 2012

ROB DAVIES

Trade and Industry Minister, South Africa

The next frontier

"It's widely and increasingly recognised that Africa is the next growth frontier. The whole world is being battered by the headwinds of the global economic crisis and (also) battered by the headwinds from the slowdown in Asia."

Weekend Post (South Africa), August 2012

12

U.S. Global Engagement

Peter Katel

A girl is carried to safety in Aleppo, Syria, after being wounded by a reported barrel bomb dropped by government forces on April 27, 2014. At least 150,000 people — one-third of them civilians — have been killed in the three years of fighting between government forces and the rebels seeking to unseat President Bashar al-Assad. President Obama backed off military action against Assad after he agreed to destroy his chemical weapons.

AFP/Getty Images/Zein al-Rifai

From *CQ Researcher*, May 16, 2014.

In May, yet another foreign official came to Washington to act out a time-honored ritual: pleading for help in overthrowing a hated dictatorship.

This time the supplicant was Munzer Akbik, chief of staff in the Opposition Coalition seeking to depose Syrian President Bashar al-Assad. Although the rebels have received some U.S. weapons, they want more.[1]

"There is a wide range of sophisticated weaponry that can make a difference on the ground, [such as] missiles, the anti-aircraft, anti-tank missiles and maybe some kind of guided weaponry and heavy artillery," Akbik said.[2]

In the 1980s, Afghans fighting a Soviet invasion, Nicaraguans opposing a left-wing government and Bosnians facing assault by Serbian forces all came to Washington with similar requests.[3] Four decades earlier, as Nazi Germany bombed London, British Prime Minister Winston Churchill was unable to visit Washington personally, but he still pleaded successfully for help getting U.S. weapons, despite Americans' resistance to entering World War II prior to Japan's 1941 attack on Pearl Harbor.[4]

Akbik came to Washington at a time of multiple foreign crises: Pro-Russian separatists are fighting Ukrainians over territory; a rapidly militarizing China is asserting claims to lands held by neighbors; and the U.S. and several other nations are attempting to limit Iran's nuclear development.

As the world's economic and military superpower, the United States engages overseas in those regions and others in many ways — diplomatically, economically, militarily — and does so for many reasons, including opposing its foes, supporting its allies, protecting its

Unrest Spreads in Ukraine

Ukrainian troops and pro-Russian protesters have clashed in eastern and southwest Ukraine. Russia annexed the Crimean Peninsula in southern Ukraine in March.

George W. Bush administration. "But I don't think anybody recently has done a good job of explaining to the American public why it is that the Russia action in Crimea matters," says Jeffrey, now a distinguished visiting fellow at the Washington Institute for Near East Policy. "There is a serious public education case to be done here."

In fact, the administration is also wary of the public mood as it confronts pressure to intervene, treaty responsibilities to allies, humanitarian obligations and its own caution about military action. "America must not succumb to the temptation to turn inward," Defense Secretary Chuck Hagel said in a speech in Chicago in early May, likening public opinion now to antiwar sentiment before World War II. "We are a great nation because we engage in the world."[6]

Still, the Obama administration has generally emphasized diplomacy. The United States and some allies eased sanctions on Iran last year to encourage negotiations with its longtime foe. The negotiations — which included Russia and China — are continuing. They aim to ensure that Iran develops nuclear capabilities for peaceful purposes only. But President Obama's Iran diplomacy faces constant, deep-seated skepticism by a key U.S. ally, Israel. That attitude was reflected in March when overwhelming bipartisan majorities in the House (394 members) and Senate (83) signed letters demanding crippling sanctions against Iran if the negotiations fail.[7] (Secretary of State John F. Kerry's most recent attempt to broker peace between Israel and the Palestinians collapsed in late April.[8])

The administration also avails itself of harder-edged forms of overseas engagement. Asian allies' worries over China's military expansion — its military budget is due to grow by 12.2 percent this year — have sparked U.S. plans to send additional forces to the region.[9] To deal with the crisis in Ukraine, the administration has imposed selective sanctions against some Russian oligarchs and companies.

Engagement can also include small-scale intervention. In early May, Obama sent U.S. law enforcement and military experts to Nigeria to help find almost 300

economic self-interest and providing humanitarian assistance. But Americans are increasingly unhappy at the prospect of more U.S. involvement in foreign crises.

A *Wall Street Journal*/NBC poll in April found that nearly half (47 percent) of respondents want the United States to be less active internationally — a much higher share than in previous years. The Pew Research Center, in a survey released late last year, found "the most lopsided balance in favor of the U.S. 'minding its own business' " since the question was first asked in 1964 — 52 percent of respondents.[5]

Some foreign-policy experts welcome the public skepticism. It matches their own rejection of the doctrine of American "exceptionalism" as justification for intervention. "What nation doesn't think it is exceptional?," asks Melvin Goodman, a former CIA and State Department analyst of Soviet affairs who now directs the National Security Project at the liberal Center for International Policy in Washington. "We've carried too much of the international burden."

Other, more hawkish, experts argue that the public, though understandably wary after more than a decade of war in Iraq and Afghanistan, should be persuaded to support some actions overseas. "Americans are gun-shy about military action," says James F. Jeffrey, a former U.S. ambassador to Iraq in the Obama administration, who also served in the National Security Council in the

Nigerian schoolgirls kidnapped by a brutal Islamist militia, Boko Haram.[10]

Neither that action nor the others has aroused U.S. public opposition. What Americans do clearly oppose is major military action. The problem is "intervention fatigue," say two staff members at the Council on Foreign Relations, a New York-based think tank stemming from the Iraq and Afghan wars.[11]

Obama cited that factor in pushing back against critics who call his foreign policy too timid. "Most of the foreign policy commentators that have questioned our policies would go headlong into a bunch of military adventures that the American people had no interest in participating in and would not advance our core security interests," he told reporters during an April tour of Asia.[12]

Obama himself saw his attempt at limited military action in the Middle East turn out badly. American airstrikes in 2011 were critical to toppling Moammar Gadhafi, a move that Obama justified at the time as a moral imperative, saying he refused "to wait for images of slaughter and mass graves." But jockeying for power after the U.S.-aided overthrow of the Libyan dictator left al Qaeda-influenced militias in a strong position — strong enough to attack the U.S. Consulate in Benghazi and kill Ambassador J. Christopher Stevens and three security guards.[13]

Last year, after having warned the Syrian regime not to cross a "red line" by using chemical weapons, Obama considered and then rejected a Syria airstrike, following what U.S. and United Nations officials in August 2013 called convincing evidence of a chemical attack that the United States said killed more than 1,400 people, including children. All told, at least 150,000 people have been killed in the Syrian War.[14]

In the wake of that chastening experience, Obama not only turned away from military action against the Syrian government but then teamed up with Russia to try to solve at least the chemical-weapons element of the Syrian crisis. Although Russia is Syria's major ally and single biggest arms supplier, it agreed with the United States in

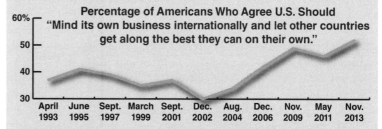

Most Want U.S. to "Mind Its Own Business"

Fifty-two percent of Americans agree that the U.S. should "mind its own business internationally." The proportion of Americans favoring less involvement in other countries' foreign affairs has grown by 22 percentage points since 2002.

Percentage of Americans Who Agree U.S. Should "Mind its own business internationally and let other countries get along the best they can on their own."

Source: "America's Place in the World 2013," Pew Research Center, Dec. 3, 2013, p. 107, http://tinyurl.com/lz3mh2y (The September 2001 survey was conducted before the 9/11 attacks.)

September that Syria should surrender all its chemical weapons for destruction.[15]

Some critics say that Obama's retreat from military action in Syria amounted to giving Russian President Vladimir V. Putin a green light in Ukraine. David Adesnik, a visiting scholar at the conservative American Enterprise Institute, a Washington think tank, argues a modified version of that critique, noting that Russia had behaved aggressively under Obama's predecessor George W. Bush, and that Obama had tried for a "reset" to prompt warmer relations with Russia.[16] "That was a big mistake," he says, but "Syria didn't have a salutary effect" on Putin's calculations of U.S. steadfastness.

The Ukraine crisis has America's Eastern European allies growing increasingly nervous about Russia's territorial intentions.

In a show of strength aimed at Russia, 600 U.S. paratroopers have begun training with Eastern European forces, and a dozen F-16 fighter jets have been deployed to Poland. The military exercises involve fellow members of the North Atlantic Treaty Organization (NATO), a military alliance the United States helped form at the start of the Cold War to deter Soviet aggression in Europe.[17]

Ukraine, a former Soviet republic that has been an independent nation since 1991, borders Russia. Since last year, Ukraine has been torn between Ukrainians who want to deepen ties to Europe and those who want to solidify ties with Russia. This spring, Russia annexed the Crimean Peninsula. The country's east has become a battleground for pro-Russian separatists, at least some of them Soviet or Russian military veterans, and the Western-oriented government.[18]

Those who fear a revival of Soviet territorial ambition have been wary ever since Putin first became Russia's president in 2000. A former Soviet intelligence officer, he has never retracted what many interpret as a sign of nostalgia for the days of Soviet power — his often-quoted view, in a 2005 speech, that "the collapse of the Soviet Union was a major geopolitical disaster of the century."[19]

Historical echoes are sounding in the United States as well. The top Republican interventionist, Sen. John McCain, R-Ariz., calls for supplying weapons to Ukraine. And he has denounced the administration policy on Syria, demanding military action, but short of "boots on the ground." McCain argued, "Our policies should be determined by the realities of the moment, not by today's isolationism dictated by the past."[20]

As foreign-policy experts watch the latest developments in Ukraine, Syria, Asia and elsewhere, these are some of the issues they are debating:

Should the U.S. military intervene in Ukraine?

With its Cold War echoes, the U.S.-Russia confrontation over Ukraine may offer the clearest test of Americans' attitudes toward U.S. intervention in international crises, and whether economic and diplomatic approaches are sufficient, or military engagement is called for. In confronting Russia, the United States is opposing the former command center of the old Soviet empire, and at the same time trying to reassure Eastern European allies that once were ruled by Soviet puppet governments.

Since the 1990s and early 2000s, those countries, including Ukraine's biggest neighbor to the west, Poland, have been members of NATO, which was born in the Cold War, and pledged to the mutual defense of any member that comes under attack.[21] American forces are participating in NATO exercises in Poland and other ex-Soviet neighbors. The Obama administration so far has drawn the line at supplying arms to Ukraine or taking direct military action.[22]

But the administration, in addition to leveling sanctions at some Russians, has agreed to provide $1 billion in loan guarantees to Ukraine.[23] Those are in addition to

a $17 billion loan from the International Monetary Fund, of which the United States is a major member, and $15 billion in other financing from the United States and other sources.[24]

The aid bolsters pro-Western Ukrainians in their demands for closer ties to Europe — demands that led them to oust elected President Viktor Yanukovych early this year. He had rejected a previously agreed upon trade agreement with the European Union that would have oriented Ukraine's economy toward Europe rather than Russia.[25] Protesters also called for better government and denounced corruption by Yanukovych and his cronies.[26]

After Yanukovych vacated the presidency, Putin supported efforts in Crimea (part of Russia until 1954) to secede from Ukraine. He then promoted annexation of Crimea.[27]

Then the Crimea scenario appeared to start replaying in eastern Ukraine, where ties to Russia are believed strong. Talks in Geneva between U.S. Secretary of State Kerry, Russian Foreign Minister Sergey Lavrov and representatives of Ukraine and the European Union yielded an agreement to de-escalate, but pro-Western and pro-Russian groups struggling in the streets of Ukraine ignored the deal.[28]

In early May, Obama made clear that he rejects any military intervention in Ukraine. "We want to see a diplomatic resolution to the situation in Ukraine," he said at a White House press conference with German Chancellor Angela Merkel. "But we've also been clear that if the Russian leadership does not change course, it will face increasing costs as well as growing isolation — diplomatic and economic."[29]

Andrew J. Bacevich, a professor of international relations and security studies at Boston University who is a West Point graduate and retired Army colonel, says the administration's measured approach properly reflects the importance of the current Ukraine clash to U.S. national-security priorities. "The classic definition of a vital interest is: Is it a place or an issue you are willing to die for?," he says. "I think the American people would probably have some doubts there."

Adesnik at the American Enterprise Institute argues that survey data about U.S. public opinion on global engagement show more nuance than skeptics acknowledge. "There's a lot of contradictory evidence," he says, acknowledging the support for the go-it-alone approach but pointing out that Americans also want their country to remain a superpower. He cites Pew survey numbers that show 56 percent of respondents believe the United States should remain the sole military superpower while 72 percent support a shared global leadership role for the United States.[30]

Adesnik also acknowledges that the public opposes military action that would place troops at risk. "But the best way to stay out of war is to indicate you're not afraid of war," he adds. "American behavior — always reaching out to your enemies — did contribute to Putin's behavior. It led him to think that Obama is always going to resort to that."

But Stephen F. Cohen, a historian of the Soviet Union and emeritus professor at Princeton and New York University, argues that debates among foreign-policy specialists over Obama's approach to the Ukraine crisis fail to take into account details of the Russia-Ukraine conflict, including the ouster of elected president Yanukovych. "The government in Kiev hasn't got a shred of legitimacy," he says. "It came to power by overthrowing a constitutionally elected president, though he may have been a very bad guy."

Between the toppling of a pro-Russian president and the expansion of NATO in Russia's neighborhood beginning in the 1990s, Cohen argues, Putin has a case for worrying about encirclement. Between that Russian case and U.S. fears of Russian aggression toward NATO allies, Cohen says, "That is where you sit down and negotiate."

If the U.S. reduces its global involvement, will China and Russia step in?

Behind demands or pleas for a more aggressive, military-oriented response to the crises in Ukraine and Syria — and whatever future conflicts may emerge — is concern that the United States may lose the superpower status it has held since World War II and the preeminent global position it has occupied since the fall of the Soviet Union in 1991. Russia's actions in Ukraine, its key roles in the Syria chemical-weapons deal and Iran nuclear negotiations, as well as China's economic might and its recent territorial aggressiveness, are amplifying concerns about U.S. global strength.

Putin is likely to continue to resist a geopolitical order in which U.S.-dominated NATO extends to Russia's borders. In 2007, he said in what observers interpreted as

a jab at the United States: "There are those who would like to build a unipolar world, who would themselves like to rule all of humanity."[31]

Significantly, given Moscow's insistence on dangers to ethnic Russians in Ukraine, in his 2005 speech calling the Soviet collapse disastrous, Putin said that when the empire fell, "Tens of millions of our co-citizens and compatriots found themselves outside Russian territory."[32]

By April of this year, Russian Foreign Minister Lavrov picked up the theme, warning that Russian citizens would treat any attack on Russian-speakers in Eastern Ukraine as an attack on Russia.[33]

At that time, Obama was beginning a tour of Asia that grew out of his policy of shoring up U.S. allies over what is seen as a long-term military and political challenge by China. "There's a widely held view in the region that the U.S.-China relationship is tipping toward being much more confrontational," Bonnie S. Glaser, a senior adviser for Asia at the Center for Strategic and International Studies, told Bloomberg News.[34]

The confluence of the Russia and Asia events underlined the concerns of some experts that a diminishing U.S. presence in global affairs would be replaced by China or Russia or the two together.

But even some of those most alarmed at what they see as U.S. disengagement draw clear distinctions between Russia and China and their potential for expanding their presence. "Russia is not really interested in or really integrated into the outside world," says former U.S. Ambassador to Iraq Jeffrey of the Washington Institute for Near East Policy. "China is different — very integrated into the outside world." But Russia, otherwise economically disconnected, is a vital supplier of petroleum to Europe.

China may be connected, but it is not indispensable, because its economy centers on manufacturing, which can be done elsewhere, argues Bruce Jones, director of the International Order and Strategy Project at the centrist Brookings Institution think tank. "The threat to American leadership is greatly exaggerated," he says. "In the next 10 or 15 years, the Chinese economy will be as large as the United States' but not as influential."

As for Russia, Jones says, it arouses no global allegiance, especially among its fellow members of the so-called BRICS countries (Brazil, Russia, India, China, South Africa). "The notion that Russia is leading some

Russia, U.S. Are Biggest Military Spenders

Russia spent 4.5 percent of its gross domestic product (GDP) on its military in 2012, while U.S. expenditures were slightly lower. In total, however, the $645.7 billion U.S. military budget that year was 11 times Russia's and six times China's.

Military Expenditures as Percentage of GDP, 2012

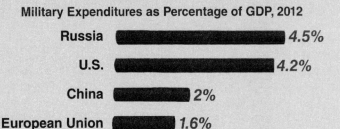

Russia	4.5%
U.S.	4.2%
China	2%
European Union	1.6%

Source: "Military expenditure (% of GDP)," World Bank, http://tinyurl.com/mckxvjq

anti-American coalition in the BRICS is facile," he says. "China is not about to be led; India is not about to be led."

But other global-engagement partisans argue that possible new threats from old Cold War foes have more to do with U.S. withdrawal than with Russian or Chinese muscle-flexing. "There is more danger that there will be no leader," says Adesnik of the American Enterprise Institute. "Imagine what the sanctions effort on Iran would be without the United States to take the lead. Other countries only get convinced to sign up when the United States says, 'We are going to lead.'"

Adesnik does agree with the skeptics who question the leadership capabilities of America's two big rivals. "No one wants to be led by China and Russia," he says. "They are not at the forefront of solving problems."

But Goodman at the Center for International Policy argues that the Obama administration's "pivot" to Asia amounts to a direct challenge to China in the form of Cold War-style containment. "That is what China fears. We have more subtle reminders available than to announce a pivot."

Still, Goodman says, little chance exists of a Russia-China alliance against the United States. "There is too much mutual suspicion along that 6,000-kilometer border."[35]

Is the post-Cold War vision of the U.S. as the "indispensable nation" still valid?

As secretary of State in the Clinton administration, Madeleine Albright in 1998 coined what has become

a favored description among global engagement partisans of America's place in the world: the "indispensable nation."

At the time, the administration was preparing for possible military action against Iraqi dictator Saddam Hussein, to enforce a United Nations resolution that he relinquish weapons of mass destruction. Asked by host Matt Lauer on the NBC "Today" show what she would tell the parents of U.S. military personnel "being asked to clean up a mess for the rest of the world," Albright said:

"But if we have to use force, it is because we are America; we are the indispensable nation. We stand tall and we see further than other countries into the future, and we see the danger here to all of us. I know that the American men and women in uniform are always prepared to sacrifice for freedom, democracy and the American way of life."[36]

When she spoke, the Soviet Union's collapse had ended the Cold War, NATO had begun expanding to countries of the former Soviet empire, the administration had intervened in Bosnia and was about to press for NATO airstrikes on Serbia. The United States had also grappled with issues of post-Cold War engagement in other parts of the world. In 1990-91, President George H. W. Bush had assembled a multinational alliance to reverse an Iraqi invasion of Kuwait, a key world oil supplier. But in 1994, the United States took no action to stop the genocide in Rwanda, a moral failure for which President Bill Clinton eventually took responsibility.

In 2003, just months after the start of the Iraq War, President George W. Bush lauded the United States as the exemplar of democratic government: "It is no accident that the rise of so many democracies took place in a time when the world's most influential nation was itself a democracy."[37]

But in 2011, when Obama was announcing the downshifting of the U.S. campaign in Afghanistan, he captured what seemed to be the public mood after years of war: "America, it is time to focus on nation-building here at home."[38]

The otherwise hawkish former U.S. Ambassador to Iraq Jeffrey summarizes that mood, shared by Obama,

Americans in general, and himself: "Never, ever try to change the internal situation in a country by putting thousands of ground troops in."

However, he contends, the reality is that the United States is indeed indispensable. Americans should understand that the nation's seemingly inexhaustible supply of cheap imported goods grows out of U.S. power. "We're the world's reserve currency; people pour money into this country," he says. "These things all flow from the U.S. position in the world."

Ted Galen Carpenter, a senior fellow for defense and foreign policy studies at the conservative-libertarian Cato Institute, responds that U.S. economic power is being eroded by the very military strength that "indispensability" advocates champion. "We're in severe danger of draining the strength of the economy to preserve all of these commitments in the world," he says.

In any event, Carpenter argues, the entire indispensability concept amounts to "national narcissism." The reality, he says, is that the idea of one indispensable nation no longer fits global reality. "The world is becoming more multipolar economically and militarily," he says, "and this notion of the indispensable nation is becoming obsolete."

But Jones at Brookings argues that the growing power of other nations doesn't change the fact that "we have far greater power and influence than any actor out there." Those who reject this view "underestimate American power and overestimate the challenge posed by rising powers," he says.

Still, historian Cohen says, the indispensability doctrine is so deeply ingrained in the diplomatic corps, and in the schools that train Foreign Service officers, that it may be ineradicable. "That is the orthodoxy," he says, "An alternative point of view hasn't existed, so far in my adult lifetime, partly because of the Cold War, when you could argue that America was indispensable."

The American Enterprise Institute's Adesnik says that despite assumptions that Americans are now deeply anti-interventionist, "Public opinion rides the roller coaster of events."

Citizens now may not be in favor of intervention, he says, but, "Americans will respond much more vigorously when the perception of a threat is clear, and they have leaders who hold that America must take a leading role."

BACKGROUND

Isolationism Defeated

The United States grew slowly into its global superpower role. President Thomas Jefferson, in his 1801 inaugural speech, famously called for "honest friendship with all nations, entangling alliances with none." Nonetheless, the young nation expanded across the continent, and later into the Caribbean and Pacific, claiming Puerto Rico and the Philippines as possessions in 1898.[39]

But World War I, which began in 1914, called for judgments far more complicated than those involved in claiming new territory. On one side, Britain and France had deep ties to the United States. But sympathy for Germany ran strong among German-Americans and Irish-Americans (the latter because Germany was fighting arch-enemy Britain). American public opinion turned against Germany with publication of the "Zimmermann telegram," in which a German diplomat proposed returning formerly Mexican U.S. territory to Mexico in return for Mexico backing Germany.[40] The U.S. entered the war in 1917.

Twenty years after World War I ended in 1918, Americans were again debating whether to intervene in Europe. The period leading up to the forced U.S. entry into World War II in 1941 was marked by a fierce fight between President Franklin D. Roosevelt and anti-interventionists from right and left. Roosevelt himself took pains to avoid publicly declaring himself in favor of intervention until the war in Europe was well under way.[41]

U.S. debate intensified after Germany began the war by invading Poland in 1939, prompting Britain and France — allies of Poland — to declare war on Germany.

About two months later, a *Fortune* magazine poll of Americans found only 20 percent of respondents favored aid to European democracies.

An especially vocal group, the America First Committee, called for U.S. neutrality. America First's star spokesman was Charles Lindbergh, the aviator who had made the first solo trans-Atlantic flight. He was one of the country's best-known and most admired figures. He was also an open admirer of Nazi Germany and its anti-Semitism.

America First was resolutely anti-communist. But the U.S. Communist Party also opposed intervention, in obedience to orders from Moscow. Soviet Premier Josef Stalin and German Chancellor and Nazi Party leader

AFP/Getty Images/Gerard Malie

West Berliners watch East German border guards demolishing a section of the Berlin Wall on Nov. 11, 1989, to open a link between East and West Berlin. Erected in 1961 by communist East Germany, the wall became a symbol of Cold War hostility between the East and West. The dramatic tear-down of the wall by Berliners from both East and West Berlin presaged the implosion of the Soviet Union two years later.

Adolf Hitler had signed a non-aggression pact in 1939, under which Germany and the Soviet Union divided Poland and the Soviet Union took over the Baltic states.[42] Hitler was able to go to war with Poland, France and Great Britain without having to worry — for the time being — about fighting the Soviet Union, too.

Between April and June 1940, Germany invaded and occupied France, Belgium, the Netherlands, Norway and Denmark. Seeing German aggression as likely to erode isolationist sentiment, Roosevelt unveiled his interventionist intentions. It was a "delusion," he said in a 1940 speech, to believe that the United States could be "a lone island in a world dominated by the philosophy of force."[43]

The war took a turn when Germany betrayed its nonaggression pact and invaded the Soviet Union in June 1941. In the United States, Communist opposition to intervention ended immediately, and party members became the fiercest of hawks. The Japanese bombing of Pearl Harbor on Dec. 7, 1941, ended debate among the other anti-interventionists. Isolationism became a discredited, fringe ideology.

Cold War

The post-World War II era was marked by a bipartisan consensus among U.S. and allied leaders that U.S. action on behalf of friendly governments or against unfriendly ones was a good thing.[44]

Friendly governments were those that sided with the United States against the Soviet Union. A third category of "nonaligned" countries, including India, maintained ties with both sides.[45] Because the big Cold War players all had nuclear weapons that could destroy one another, they did not battle directly — a restraining mechanism called "mutual assured destruction."[46]

A U.S. doctrine called "containment" also shaped Cold War policy. It called for "counterforce" against the Soviet Union in the form of diplomacy and covert action, instead of war. The doctrine was formulated, though not under that name, in 1946 by George F. Kennan, then the No. 2 diplomat in the U.S. Embassy in Moscow. "If situations are properly handled," Kennan wrote, "there need be no prestige-engaging showdowns."[47]

Instead, the opposing sides faced off in proxy wars and coups in smaller countries. Soviet dictator Stalin had started off after World War II by installing puppet regimes throughout Central and Eastern Europe, as well as the eastern half of Germany. These moves followed tacit recognition of Soviet preeminence in that region in the closing months of the war by the three major wartime allies, the United States, Great Britain and the Soviet Union. Roosevelt, Stalin and British Prime Minister Winston Churchill sealed that pact during a historic meeting at the Crimean resort of Yalta.[48]

By 1949, relations between the Soviet Union and the West had deteriorated to the point that the United States and 11 major allies formed NATO to resist Soviet expansion. The Soviet bloc in turn formalized its military and political ties through the 1955 Warsaw Pact.[49]

From the U.S. side, much of the early Cold War involved secret operations by the then-new Central Intelligence Agency (CIA), formed in 1947. These operations included:

• The 1953 overthrow of Iran's elected prime minister, Mohammed Mossadeq, on the ground that he could pave the way for a Soviet takeover of the oil-rich country.[50]

• The 1954 toppling of the elected government of President Jacobo Arbenz of Guatemala, whom the United States considered a communist sympathizer.

• Involvement in the overthrow and execution of the elected prime minister of Congo, Patrice Lumumba, whom the United States considered a communist dupe.

• A failed 1961 attempt to overthrow Cuba's Soviet-allied prime minister, Fidel Castro, which ended in defeat at the island's Bay of Pigs.

In the same year as the Cuba disaster, the Soviet-allied government of East Germany — then a separate country — erected a concrete wall separating the eastern and western sectors of Berlin. The Berlin Wall became a symbol of East-West hostility.[51]

The most dangerous moment in the Cold War came in 1962, after the United States learned that Soviet nuclear missiles had been shipped to Cuba. Negotiations between President John F. Kennedy and Soviet leader Nikita S. Khrushchev averted catastrophic nuclear conflict.[52]

Meanwhile, U.S. military advisers had been working with the government of South Vietnam since 1955 in an effort to strengthen South Vietnam, then a separate nation, against North Vietnam, a communist ally of the Soviet Union and China. U.S. involvement was based on what President Dwight D. Eisenhower in 1954 called the "'falling domino' principle" — that North Vietnamese victory would lead to communist victories elsewhere in Southeast Asia.[53]

In 1964, a confrontation between U.S. warships and North Vietnamese vessels in the Tonkin Gulf led President Lyndon B. Johnson to order U.S. combat forces into Vietnam. By the time U.S. military operations ceased in 1973, 2.7 million U.S. military personnel had served in Vietnam.[54]

The war polarized the United States for the rest of the 1960s and the early '70s, and its effects arguably still influence America's global stance. There were huge anti-war demonstrations, a wave of resistance to the military draft and a political debate that tore apart the Democratic Party in 1968. Among those marked by the conflict were Sen. McCain, a Navy pilot held prisoner by North Vietnam for more than five years, and Secretary of State Kerry, a Navy veteran who became a leader of Vietnam Veterans Against the War.[55]

In 1973, following years of U.S. negotiations with the North Vietnamese, the United States withdrew military forces. Two years later, North Vietnam defeated the U.S.-allied government. The war had cost the lives of more than 58,000 American military personnel and between 1.5 million and 3.8 million Vietnamese troops and civilians.[56]

Beginning in 1979, a series of upheavals in the Middle East and Latin America opened a new era of U.S. engagement. The Iranian revolution of 1979 toppled Mohammad Reza Shah Pahlavi, a longtime U.S. ally. An Islamist government hostile to the West in general and the United States in particular took power.

That same year, the Soviet Union invaded neighboring Afghanistan to prop up a friendly government, and Nicaraguan revolutionaries aided by Cuba overthrew President Anastasio Somoza, recently abandoned as a U.S. ally. The revolutionary government in turn eventually was opposed by right-wing guerrillas, known as contras. In neighboring El Salvador, a war between the government and a left-wing guerrilla army soon intensified.[57]

With the Cold War still very much in progress, the Reagan administration (1981-89) responded to these events both openly and covertly with military and intelligence operations. In Afghanistan, the administration expanded a Carter administration CIA program to aid guerrilla forces opposing the Soviet invaders. (The Soviets withdrew in defeat in 1989.) Meanwhile, the CIA aided the contras, and U.S. military advisers assisted the Salvadoran army.

Intense political debate over Nicaragua led to a congressional ban on assistance to the contras. But U.S. Marine Lt. Col. Oliver North, a National Security Council staffer, helped devise a plan in which the United States sold weapons to Iran in return for the release of U.S. hostages held by pro-Iranian forces in Lebanon. Then, profit from the arms deal was funneled to the contras.[58]

The scheme, known as Iran-Contra, blew up into the Reagan administration's worst scandal. North was indicted for lying to Congress and trying to destroy evidence. He was convicted on three counts in 1989 and sentenced to two years probation.[59]

Soviet Collapse

The Soviet empire began imploding in the late 1980s. The dramatic tear-down of the Berlin Wall by Berliners from both east and west in 1989 symbolized the process. Germany was reunited the following year.[60] The Soviet Union formally dissolved in 1991.

The end of the Cold War, which had defined U.S. foreign policy for decades, led to a search for a new guiding principle. President George H. W. Bush in 1990 and 1991 laid out a vision of a "new world order" in which

CHRONOLOGY

1939-1962 *World War II is followed by decades-long Cold War.*

1939 World War II begins in Europe; only 20 percent of Americans favor aiding European democracies.

1941 United States enters World War II after Japan bombs Pearl Harbor; war lasts until 1945.

1949 United States joins 11 other countries to form North Atlantic Treaty Organization (NATO).

1961 CIA-sponsored invasion of Cuba at Bay of Pigs aimed at toppling regime of Fidel Castro turns into debacle. . . . Soviet satellite East Germany erects Berlin Wall.

1962 Conflict over Soviet nuclear missiles in Cuba leads United States and Soviet Union to brink of nuclear war.

1964-1985 *U.S. divided over military involvement in Vietnam; upheaval shakes Middle East, Latin America.*

1964 President Lyndon Johnson orders U.S. combat forces into South Vietnam.

1973 Peace talks with North Vietnam lead to U.S. military withdrawal. . . . Chilean military, encouraged by CIA, overthrows left-leaning president.

1979 Iranian revolution topples U.S.-backed Shah and installs religious regime hostile to United States. . . . Soviet Union invades Afghanistan. . . . Leftist Nicaraguan rebels overthrow government.

1985 Reagan administration aides begin scheme known as Iran-Contra to sell arms to Iran in return for freeing of U.S. hostages held in Lebanon, with profit to be used for U.S. aid to Nicaraguan rebels fighting left-wing government.

1989-1999 *Soviet Union falls, ending Cold War and touching off new round of global conflicts.*

1989 East Germany scraps travel restrictions on its citizens, leading to fall of Berlin Wall.

1991 Soviet Union dissolves.

1992 Yugoslavia falls apart along ethnic and religious lines, sparking armed conflict over Serbian attempt to hold onto breakaway Bosnia.

1995 NATO intervenes in Bosnia; peace talks held in Dayton, Ohio, end conflict.

1997 Three former Soviet Bloc members including Poland join NATO, a move Russia sees as hostile.

1999 Prompted by United States, NATO launches air campaign against Serbia over its actions in breakaway Kosovo province.

2001-Present *Terrorists attack United States; turmoil wracks Middle East, Eastern Europe.*

2001 Sept. 11 terrorist attacks prompt calls for aggressive U.S. response.

2003 George W. Bush administration launches war to overthrow Iraqi dictator Saddam Hussein.

2011 Syrian revolt begins . . . Libyan uprising begins. . . . President Obama orders airstrikes against Libyan government, aiding rebel victory.

2012 U.S. Ambassador J. Christopher Stevens and three embassy staffers killed by armed militants in Benghazi, Libya. . . . Obama declares that Syrian government use of chemical weapons would mark a "red line."

2013 Syria uses chemical weapons against civilians; Obama backs off military action. . . . Administration makes deal with Russia to remove chemical arms from Syria. . . . Ukrainian citizens protest President's Viktor Yanukovych's rejection of European Union trade deal.

2014 Ukrainian uprising topples president. . . . Russia supports Crimea secession from Ukraine, then annexes Crimea. . . . U.S. contributes troops to NATO exercises to reassure Russia's Eastern European neighbors. . . . Obama administration begins supplying some Syrian rebels with weapons. . . . Pro-Russian separatists effectively take over much of eastern Ukraine.

"the rule of the law, not the law of the jungle, governs the conduct of nations."[61]

Despite hopes, the end of the Cold War did not bring global peace.[62]

Shortly before the Soviet collapse, Iraqi dictator Saddam Hussein in 1990 invaded the tiny oil kingdom of Kuwait. In response — and to protect world oil power Saudi Arabia — Bush assembled a 670,000-strong military alliance of 39 countries dominated by the United States, which contributed 425,000 personnel.[63]

The Persian Gulf War lasted less than three months. Because the war was brief, and because the United States was not acting alone and was fighting a tyrant, no major antiwar movement developed. The war ended with the rout of Iraqi troops from Kuwait, but Bush did not try to topple Hussein. The United States encouraged Shiite and Kurdish Iraqis who rose up against Hussein at war's end, but they got no U.S. aid, and many were slaughtered or fled Iraq.[64]

A subsequent crisis in Europe provoked intense debate about the extent of U.S. involvement overseas. After the collapse of the Soviet Union, Yugoslavia (which had been made up of modern-day Croatia, Montenegro, Serbia, Slovenia, Bosnia and Herzegovina, and Macedonia) disintegrated. The region fell into war and what was called "ethnic cleansing" — the removal, accompanied by massacres, of ethnic or religious minorities from areas claimed by a majority population.

The conflict centered on Bosnia. In 1992 Muslim Bosnians and Croats voted for independence, but Serbia wanted to keep Bosnia. Bosnian Serbs besieged Sarajevo, a historic city defended by Muslims. Serb artillery attacks, sniper killings and a food blockade drew world attention and prompted some U.S. public figures to denounce U.S. inaction.

The U.N. sent a protective force, which set up so-called safe havens for Muslims, including one in the Bosnian village of Srebrenica. But in 1995, Serb forces overran the village, after U.N. troops were overwhelmed. More than 7,000 Muslim men were massacred. No slaughter on such a scale had taken place in Europe since World War II.

U.S. experience engaging — or not — in other nations influenced the American reaction. Srebrenica followed the horrific 1994 genocide in Rwanda, which the United States and other nations didn't try to stop; members of the Hutu ethnic majority slaughtered hundreds of thousands of members of the Tutsi ethnic group.[65] Clinton later acknowledged his administration's non-reaction to Rwanda as a failure.[66]

Among the reasons analysts have pointed to for the Clinton administration's failure to intervene in Rwanda was a 1993 military catastrophe during a raid by U.S. special-operations forces during a humanitarian mission to Somalia.[67] The mission, chronicled in the book and film "Black Hawk Down," ended in 18 American deaths. Video of a dead American being dragged through the streets of Mogadishu seemed to illustrate the dangers of humanitarian operations in violent environments.[68] But Samantha Power, then a journalist and now the U.S. ambassador to the U.N., rejected this reasoning in a detailed, scathing account of the U.S. failure to act in Rwanda.[69]

Finally jolted into action by the Srebrenica massacre, the Clinton administration helped launch a NATO bombing campaign against Serb forces. After Clinton pressured Serbia to sign a peace deal, in late 1995 he ordered 20,000 U.S. troops to Bosnia to join a NATO peacekeeping force. To do so, he overcame strong congressional resistance, especially but not exclusively among Republicans. Opponents questioned the U.S. national interest in bringing peace to the Balkans.[70]

In 1999, another phase of the Balkan crisis erupted over Kosovo, a Serbian province with an ethnic Albanian majority population. NATO, dominated by its senior member, the United States, began an air campaign of more than five months against Serbian forces, including bombing the Serbian capital, Belgrade.

The United States also took military action in 1998 with cruise missile attacks in Afghanistan and Sudan. The targets were said to be linked to terrorist leader Osama bin Laden, who had just orchestrated deadly bombings of U.S. embassies in Tanzania and Kenya. His network, al Qaeda, had not yet become universally known.[71]

Major Wars

The Sept. 11 attacks on the United States by al Qaeda operatives opened a period in which the United States moved beyond small-scale, limited military operations to full-fledged global war against Muslim jihadists.

But unlike the short Persian Gulf War, the wars in Afghanistan (2001 to the present) and Iraq (2003-2011) ran

U.S. Weighs Interests of Allies

Saudis speak out about Syria; Europeans worry about Ukraine.

Managing international friends and allies may be harder than being commander in chief of the world's biggest military machine.

Take Saudi Arabia, a major American ally. Twenty-four years ago, the United States assembled an enormous multinational military force, in large part to protect Saudi Arabia — successfully — from attack by Iraqi dictator Saddam Hussein, who had invaded neighboring Kuwait.

But last year, the Saudi monarchy was so furious at the United States and other world powers for not intervening in Syria that the kingdom refused a seat on the United Nations Security Council. "Allowing the ruling regime in Syria to kill and burn its people by the chemical weapons, while the world stands idly . . . is also irrefutable evidence and proof of the inability of the Security Council to carry out its duties and responsibilities," the Saudi government said in announcing its move.[1]

The Saudis are both a world oil power and a center of the majority Sunni branch of Islam. Fellow Sunnis are the bulk of the rebel militias fighting the Syrian government, which is controlled by members of the minority Alawite Muslim sect, a splinter group of the Shiite branch of Islam.

If the Saudis were trying to make sure that President Obama got the message to step up aid to the Syrian rebels, they succeeded. In March, Obama traveled to Riyadh, the Saudi capital, where he personally told Saudi King Abdullah that the United States remained determined to back non-jihadist forces among the Syrian rebels.[2]

Weeks later, Harakat Hazm ("Movement of Steadfastness"), a Syrian rebel formation of 5,000 fighters that the United States considers moderate, received the first shipment of U.S. BGM-71 antitank missiles.[3]

While the Syrian civil war forces the administration to weigh the dangers of supplying advanced weaponry that could fall into the hands of anti-Western extremists against the need to maintain ties with Saudi Arabia, Obama faces equally tough choices involving America's European allies in the Ukraine crisis.

For one thing, the European Union (EU) is divided over how aggressively to hit back at Russia over its actions in Ukraine. Consequently, EU sanctions have been more limited than American measures. In Germany, Europe's economic powerhouse, the business establishment is openly opposing tougher EU sanctions.

Germany has more companies doing business with Russia — about 6,200 firms — than the rest of the EU combined, and it depends on Russia for about one-third of its gas and oil.[4] All in all, the 28 EU countries did 267.5 billion euros ($371.8 billion) worth of trade with Russia in 2012, the latest figures available. European countries import 84 percent of Russia's oil exports and about 76 percent of Russia's natural gas. They export 123 billion euros ($192.7 billion) worth of goods to Russia.[5]

"There's no question that Germany's economic interests would be best served by avoiding sanctions," Klaus-Jürgen Gern, an economist at a German think tank, the Kiel Institute for the World Economy, told *The Wall Street Journal.*[6]

German Chancellor Angela Merkel, appearing in Washington with Obama in early May, has so far maintained unity with Obama while delaying stronger economic measures against Russia. At a joint press conference, she said that if Russia disrupts a Ukrainian election scheduled for May 25, "We will not have a choice but to move forward with additional, more severe sanctions."[7]

She added that among EU countries "some are more vulnerable than others to potential Russia retaliation."[8]

Poland, a fellow EU member, also gets about 30 percent of its gas from Russia, but it takes a tougher line toward the Russians. "Russia needs our money more than we need its gas," Foreign Minister Radoslaw Sikorski told *The Washington Post.*[9]

Poland, whose history as a Soviet satellite is still fresh in the minds of Sikorski and other leaders, played a major part in demanding and receiving U.S. military reassurance in the form of NATO military exercises on Polish soil that began in April. Poland had sent troops to back the United States in Afghanistan and Iraq, Sikorski reminded *Foreign Policy* magazine. "Now we feel it's payback time."[10]

In Asia, Obama is carrying out another balancing act — protecting the interests of friendly and allied countries while not alarming the region's giant, China. "We're not interested in containing China," Obama said in April. He was on a trip promoting the administration's "pivot to Asia" — reassurances to Asian countries worried about signs of Chinese expansionism, such as claims to non-Chinese territory as well as to sovereignty in air and coastal zones.[11]

To reassure China's neighbors, Obama signed a pact with the Philippines allowing greater access to its military bases by U.S. troops, ships and aircraft. Previously, the administration began deploying 2,500 Marines to Australia. And the first of four new U.S. coastal warships assigned to patrol Pacific waters near China has begun its mission.[12]

Although the deployments send a clear message of support for Asian allies dealing with territorial disputes, Obama added that the message isn't meant provocatively. "My hope is, is that at some point we're going to be able to work cooperatively with China as well," he said in Manila, "because our goal here is simply to make sure that everybody is operating in a peaceful, responsible fashion."[13]

— Peter Katel

President Obama and German Chancellor Angela Merkel hold a news conference at the White House on May 2, 2014. Merkel said if Russia disrupts a Ukrainian election scheduled for May 25, Germany would impose "more servere sanctions."

[1] Quoted in Robert F. Worth, "Saudi Arabia Rejects U.N. Security Council Seat in Protest Move," *The New York Times*, Oct. 18, 2013, http://tinyurl.com/m2rkubz.

[2] Michael D. Shear and Michael R. Gordon, "Obama Offers Assurance to Saudis on Syria Stance," *The New York Times*, March 28, 2014, http://tinyurl.com/ll3augt.

[3] Liz Sly, "Syrian rebels who received first U.S. missiles of war see shipment as 'an important first step,'" *The Washington Post*, April 27, 2014, http://tinyurl.com/ljavuxj.

[4] Matthew Karnitschnig, "German Businesses Urge Halt on Sanctions Against Russia," *The Wall Street Journal*, May 1, 2014, http://tinyurl.com/khedgms.

[5] "Russia's trade ties with Europe," BBC, March 4, 2014, http://tinyurl.com/mlw8ddl; "Russia, trade," European Commission, updated Nov. 19, 2013, http://tinyurl.com/oufrlx7.

[6] Quoted in Karnitschnig, *op. cit.*

[7] "Full Transcript: Obama, Merkel Press Conference," *The Wall Street Journal*, May 2, 2014, http://tinyurl.com/l6nzk82.

[8] *Ibid.*

[9] Lally Weymouth, "Talking with Poland's foreign minister about the Ukraine crisis and Russia's next moves," *The Washington Post*, April 18, 2014, http://tinyurl.com/kqmk9kd.

[10] Quoted in Michael Weiss, "Can Radek Sikorski Save Europe?" *Foreign Policy*, April 30, 2014, http://tinyurl.com/mk3nk28.

[11] Quoted in Mark Landler, "On a Trip That Avoids Beijing, Obama Keeps His Eye on China," *The New York Times*, April 26, 2014, http://tinyurl.com/mzcv753; Ian Johnson, "The China Challenge," *New York Review of Books*, May 8, 2014, http://tinyurl.com/q7cymxu.

[12] Matt Siegel, "As Part of Pact, U.S. Marines Arrive in Australia, in China's Strategic Backyard," *The New York Times*, April 4, 2012, http://tinyurl.com/879fnxs; Kirk Spitzer, "New Warship Gives U.S. Pivot Some Punch," *Time*, March 21, 2013, http://tinyurl.com/nz72fq7. For background, see Reed Karaim, "China Today," *CQ Researcher*, April 4, 2014, pp. 289-312.

[13] "Remarks by President Obama and President Benigno Aquino III," transcript, The White House, April 28, 2014, http://tinyurl.com/qg75rpo.

Probable GOP Candidates Debate Intervention

"The most interesting debate is in the Republican Party."

Foreign policy arguments among potential candidates in the 2016 Republican presidential primary largely amount to feints and jabs, with no full-scale fights. But the debate among Republicans concerning interventionism overshadows any foreign policy argument among Democrats, at least so far.

Republicans all express varying degrees of opposition to the Democratic Obama administration's foreign policy. Arizona Sen. John McCain, the most outspoken critic, has charged the administration with running "a feckless foreign policy where nobody believes in America's strength anymore." And Sen. Lindsey Graham of South Carolina called Obama a "weak and indecisive president that invites aggression."[1]

Nevertheless, McCain already lost a presidential election in 2008, and Graham is not on any list of expected Republican presidential contenders. Among potential candidates, Kentucky Sen. Rand Paul stands in the middle of the Republican foreign policy argument. The political heir to his libertarian father, former Rep. Ron Paul, R-Texas, the younger Paul does not embrace McCain-Graham style hawkishness. But he also has been trying to distance himself somewhat from his father's hard-line stand against involvement in almost any foreign conflict.

Notably, in an opinion piece in *The Washington Post* in April, Paul sought to explain a 2012 vote of his concerning Iran. Paul had cast the lone vote against a Senate resolution opposing "any United States policy that would rely on efforts to contain a nuclear weapons-capable Iran." That is, the resolution opposed any U.S. acceptance of Iran possessing or being able to make nuclear weapons.[2]

In his op-ed, he wrote, "I am not for containment in Iran." He added that his 2012 vote had been misunderstood. "It is . . . dumb, dangerous and foolhardy to announce in advance how we would react to any nation that obtains nuclear weapons. Real foreign policy is made in the middle, with nuance; in the gray area of

diplomacy, engagement and reluctantly, if necessary, military action."[3]

The Republican often mentioned as Paul's opposite on foreign affairs, Sen. Marco Rubio of Florida, criticizes the Obama administration for, in effect, overdoing nuance and diplomacy. "One lesson we should take from the current crisis in Ukraine is that when authoritarian regimes sense weakness and opportunity they will exploit it," Rubio wrote in *Foreign Policy* magazine.[4]

Between Rubio and Paul, some conservative foreign policy strategists leave no doubt whom they favor. "On one hand you have Rubio, who embraces the model of American leadership that has sustained global peace," Danielle Pletka, vice president of foreign and defense studies at the conservative American Enterprise Institute, told *National Journal.* "And then you have Rand Paul who wants to spend less money to do less with the world. I see this as a genuine competition of ideas."[5]

Pletka is a member of the Committee on the Present Danger, an advocacy group from the Republican neoconservative wing that was founded in the Cold War and now is devoted to promoting antiterrorism policy.[6]

Paul has derided the neoconservatives, who provided much of the ideological and bureaucratic thrust for the post-Sept. 11 campaigns in Afghanistan and Iraq.[7] In Paul's words: "To this crowd, anyone who doesn't clamor first for the military option is somehow an isolationist. The irony is that the crowd that claims they want to engage often opposes diplomatic engagement."[8]

Veteran public opinion analyst Andrew Kohut, founding director of the Pew Research Center, has argued that the public is not demanding foreign policy aggressiveness. "The GOP's difficulty with exploiting public discontent with Obama's handling of foreign policy," he wrote, "is that the president's unwillingness to be more assertive in Syria or Ukraine reflects the public's mood — including Republicans."[9]

James F. Jeffrey, a former ambassador in the Obama administration who also served in President George W. Bush's National Security Council, argued that Republicans still need "a policy of activism that doesn't immediately default to the neocons," who held sway during the Bush administration. He added, "Between George W. Bush and Rand Paul, more and more Republicans are saying Rand Paul."

Writing in early 2013, before Rand Paul had made much of an impression, Daniel W. Drezner, a professor of international politics at Tufts University's Fletcher School of Law and Diplomacy, argued even more strongly that the neoconservatives had done major damage to the GOP. "Since the knee-jerk Republican response has been to call for military action anywhere and everywhere trouble breaks out," he wrote, "the American people have tuned out the GOP's alarmist rhetoric."[10]

On the Democratic side, the top potential nominee so far is also the leader in foreign policy experience among presidential hopefuls in both parties. Former Secretary of State Hillary Rodham Clinton has been characterized by some left-liberals as a hawk, having supported stepping up the U.S. campaign in Afghanistan, using airstrikes in Syria and intervening in Libya.

Foreign policy expert Stephen F. Cohen, a historian of the Soviet Union and an emeritus professor at New York and Princeton universities, points to a lack of diplomacy in a recent statement by Clinton likening Russian President Vladimir V. Putin's insistence on protecting the rights of ethnic Russians in other countries to Adolf Hitler's pre–World War II strategy of using the defense of ethnic Germans as a pretext for war.[11]

"She says he's like Hitler," Cohen says, asking how Clinton would able to meet with Putin after a comment so insulting.

Still, Cohen says, "The most interesting debate is in the Republican Party, with Rand Paul trying to move into the mainstream with his less interventionist perspective."

— *Peter Katel*

Sen. Rand Paul, R-Ky., left, has distanced himself from hardline stands against foreign involvement. Sen. Marco Rubio, R-Fla., at right, claims the Obama administration is overdoing nuance and diplomacy.

[3]Rand Paul, "Where I stand on containing Iran," *The Washington Post*, April 15, 2014, http://tinyurl.com/nh8f8yq.

[4]Marco Rubio, "I Come Bearing . . . Reassurance," *Foreign Policy*, April 24, 2014, http://tinyurl.com/lfuvny9.

[5]Beth Reinhard and Ben Terris, "The GOP's Identity Crisis: Marco Rubio Versus Rand Paul," *National Journal*, March 15, 2013, http://tinyurl.com/pyapllr.

[6]"Committee on the Present Danger," http://tinyurl.com/m68l9r5.

[7]James Mann, *Rise of the Vulcans: The History of Bush's War Cabinet* (2004).

[8]David Adesnik, "Rand Paul bravely attacks a battalion of straw-men," American Enterprise Institute, Jan. 17, 2014, http://tinyurl.com/ozpabbv.

[9]Andrew Kohut, "Is Attacking Obama's Foreign Policy a Winning Strategy?," *Politico*, April 29, 2014, http://tinyurl.com/oldw6ke.

[10]Daniel W. Drezner, "Rebooting Republican Foreign Policy," *Foreign Affairs*, January-February 2013, www.cfr.org/world/rebooting-republican-foreign-policy/p29717.

[1]Michael Hirsh, "The GOP's Foreign Policy Problem," *National Journal*, March 6, 2014, http://tinyurl.com/kvj4qeg.

[2]Ben Brumfield and Ted Barrett, "U.S. Senate votes to fund the federal government, strengthens resolve on Iran," CNN, Sept. 22, 2012, http://tinyurl.com/loklnps.

[11]Philip Rucker, "Hillary Clinton's Putin-Hitler comments draw rebukes as she wades into Ukraine conflict," *The Washington Post*, March 5, 2014, www.washingtonpost.com/politics/hillary-clintons-putin-hitler-comments-draw-rebukes-as-she-wades-into-ukraine-conflict/2014/03/05/31a748d8-a486-11e3-84d4-e59b1709222c_story.html.

long and cost thousands of lives. More than 4,400 American and civilian defense employees died in Iraq, and more than 2,317 in Afghanistan and nearby countries.[72]

The United States originally went to war in Afghanistan to topple the Muslim fundamentalist Taliban government, which was hosting al Qaeda — a move that enjoyed widespread post-9/11 public support. The war in Iraq was launched to overthrow Hussein and seize what were said to be his nuclear and chemical weapons. After these weapons were determined not to exist, the war became a campaign to establish a democratic government — a development that President George W. Bush said would encourage democracy throughout the Middle East.[73]

As casualties mounted, so did opposition, though not to anti-Vietnam War levels. One reason may have been that young men did not face the military draft, which had been abolished in 1973.[74] Nonetheless, ending the Iraq war was one of the major planks in Obama's successful 2008 presidential campaign.

After the U.S. withdrawal from Iraq, conflict between the country's Shiite-majority government, established with U.S. help, and members of the Sunni minority, including jihadists, intensified. The Shiites and the Sunnis are the two major branches of Islam, and relations between them remain contentious in the Middle East.[75]

The Afghan War, which began first, did not yield a definitive victory over the Taliban, which became a guerrilla army after it was removed from the government. Jihadist attacks elsewhere continued, and al Qaeda remains a feared terrorist network.[76] Indeed, Muslim extremists now have a new field of battle in Syria.

During the ensuing pro-democracy surge in the Middle East known as the "Arab Spring," Libyans rose up in 2011 against the 42-year dictatorship of Moammar Gadhafi.[77] Obama, urged on by Libyan and American supporters of the revolt, and acting under authority of a U.N. resolution, ordered a U.S. air campaign that established a no-fly zone over Libya — grounding its air force — and attacked some government forces. "Operation Odyssey Dawn" assured the revolution's success eight months after it began.[78]

Although the Libya operation seemed at first to show the positive results of small-scale intervention, it was followed by a jihadist attack on the U.S. consulate in Benghazi in 2012 that killed Ambassador J. Christopher Stevens and three other Americans.[79]

CURRENT SITUATION

Sanctioning Putin

Eastern Ukrainian cities remain a battleground between pro-Russia and pro-Ukrainian government forces. But with events moving at a dizzying pace, Ukrainians and foreign observers alike are trying to decode statements by Russian President Putin that seem to indicate a willingness to tamp down the potential for all-out war.

In early May, Putin announced that he would pull back an invasion-ready force of 40,000 Russian troops, plus warplanes, that had been stationed on the Russian side of the border. NATO and officials of the provisional Ukrainian government in Kiev were not taking the statement at face value.[80]

Nevertheless, Putin did strike a tone different from his previous belligerence. "I simply believe that if we want to find a long-term solution to the crisis in Ukraine, open, honest and equal dialogue is the only possible option," he said at a Kremlin press conference.[81]

One immediate question was the practical effect of a May 11 referendum in two eastern Ukrainian provinces, which pro-Russians announced as showing overwhelming support for autonomy from the Ukrainian government in Kiev. Another was whether the Kiev government would be able to hold a nationwide presidential election on May 25.[82]

While debate continues on whether the United States and its allies should intervene militarily, the Obama administration and the European Union are expanding the list of individuals and companies targeted by economic sanctions.[83] "The goal is to change [Putin's] calculus with respect to how the current actions that he's engaging in in Ukraine could have an adverse impact on the Russian economy over the long haul," Obama said in late April.[84] The United States has frozen assets, banned commerce and imposed other sanctions against numerous Russian politicians, companies and business figures.

Whatever the long-range effect of sanctions, so far they seem of no consequence on the ground in eastern Ukraine. Pro-Russia separatists have taken over a series of towns and cities, and the country's acting president acknowledged in late April that the provisional government's security services have been "helpless" against these groups, which U.S. officials say are controlled by Russian special forces.[85]

Is the Obama administration responding effectively to the Ukraine crisis?

YES — John Kerry
Secretary of State

NO — Sen. John McCain, R-Ariz.
Member, Senate Foreign Relations Committee

Excerpted from Senate Foreign Relations Committee hearing, April 8, 2014

What we see from Russia is an illegal and illegitimate effort to destabilize a sovereign state and create a contrived crisis with paid operatives across an international boundary.

Our preference, and the preference of our friends and allies, is de-escalation and a diplomatic solution. But Russia should not for a single solitary second mistake the expression of that preference as an unwillingness to do what is necessary to stop any violation of the international order.

At NATO last week, and in all of my conversations of the past weeks, it is clear that the United States and our closest partners are united in this effort, despite the costs, and willing to put in effect tough new sanctions on those orchestrating this action and on key sectors of the Russian economy in energy, banking, mining. They are all on the table. And President Obama has already signed an executive order to implement these actions if Russia does not end its pressure and aggression on Ukraine.

It must be the reality that the United States and our allies will not hesitate to use 21st century tools to hold Russia accountable for 19th century behavior. It doesn't have to be this way. But it will be this way if Russia continues down this provocative path.

We have made it clear that Russia needs to take concrete steps to disavow separatist actions in eastern Ukraine, pull back its forces outside the country, which they say they have begun to do with the movement of one battalion, and demonstrate that they are prepared to come to these discussions, to do what is necessary to de-escalate.

So, Russia has a choice: to work with the international community to help build an independent Ukraine that could be a bridge between East and West, not the object of a tug of war, that could meet the hopes and aspirations of all Ukrainians. Or, they could face greater isolation and pay the costs for their failure, to see that the world is not a zero-sum game.

His [Putin's] oligarchs are not able to travel to various places. They're losing money. The ruble has gone down 7 percent. There's an impact in Europe. I think [Putin has] had a massive change in public opinion in Ukraine. People who once felt better about Russia don't today. He has united many Ukrainians, even those who are Russian-speaking, against Russia.

Excerpted from Senate Foreign Relations Committee hearing, April 8, 2014

My hero, Teddy Roosevelt, used to say talk softly, but carry a big stick. What [the Obama administration is] doing is talking strongly and carrying a very small stick, in fact, a twig.

What has been done so far as a result of the Russian dismemberment of Ukraine in violation of a treaty that they signed in return for the nuclear inventory of Ukraine, which was then the third largest nuclear power? Some individual sanctions, some diplomatic sanctions, a suspension — not removal from the G-8. And, now, more threats to come.

I predicted that Putin would go into Crimea because he couldn't bear to give up Sevastopol, because he is what he is.

And I am now very concerned, because of our lack of response, whether he will foment discontent in the manner which he is now, which will then demand autonomy for parts of eastern Ukraine.

And when a foreign minister of Russia lies to your face, once, twice, three, four times, I would be reluctant to take his word for anything.

So, here we are with Ukraine being destabilized, a part of it dismembered, and we won't give them defensive weapons.

We don't want to provoke? We don't want to provoke Vladimir Putin by giving these people the ability to defend themselves after their country has been dismembered and there is provocations going on? That, I say to you, is the logic of appeasement.

I want to know, and I think the American people should know, and maybe most importantly, the people of Ukraine should know why won't we give them some defensive weapons when they're facing another invasion, not the first, but another invasion of their country. It is just beyond logic.

When we don't give people assistance to defend themselves, then it — just as the Syrian decision — it reverberates throughout the entire world. I would like to know why it is not at least under serious consideration to give them some defensive weapons.

[The administration's] view of what the Ukrainians need is vastly different from what the Ukrainians think they need, which is a sovereign right to try to defend themselves, which is something that we have done historically, helping people who are struggling against overwhelming odds.

Sanctions by the European Union have been kept minimal, to avoid hurting some of its members' considerable business ties with Russia, including imports of Russian oil and natural gas.[86] The EU in March and April imposed visa bans and asset freezes on 48 Russian politicians and military commanders.

EU sanctions haven't included business figures or companies. "Some EU countries may have been reluctant to do so given the important economic ties many EU countries have with such persons and institutions," the nonpartisan Congressional Research Service reported in March.[87]

Speaking more bluntly, an unnamed senior European official told *The Wall Street Journal*: "There's still a lot of nervousness in Europe about heading in that direction. They don't want to burn bridges with the Kremlin."[88]

From the Russian side, Putin and his officials shrugged off the punitive actions. "Sanctions are not effective in the contemporary world and are not bringing the desired outcome," Putin said in April.[89]

U.S. political debate on sanctions has been sparse so far. In April, some Republicans on the Senate Foreign Relations Committee expressed skepticism to Kerry about the measures' effectiveness. "They mocked our last set of sanctions," said Sen. Ron Johnson, R-Wis.[90]

Kerry disputed that, adding, "I think it's clear that we have huge capacity to have an impact. . . . [Russians] are not incapable of analyzing America's capacity here with respect to banking and finance and movement of people."[91]

Meanwhile, McCain was the only committee member to advocate arming the Ukrainians.

Obama appears committed to managing the crisis so that it doesn't lead to full-scale confrontation. *The New York Times* reported that the president has told visitors privately that Ukraine is not a big issue for most Americans.[92]

A late-April survey by Pew and *USA Today* found that 53 percent of respondents supported stepping up economic and diplomatic sanctions against Russia. But 62 percent opposed sending arms to the Ukrainian government.[93]

Syria: Ballots and Bombs

With war ravaging his country, Syrian President Assad is preparing for a June 3 election — or something resembling an election — that he is universally expected to win overwhelmingly.

When he stood for election to his second term in 2007, Assad was the sole candidate. Official results showed him winning 97.29 percent of the vote. He first became president after his father, Hafez Assad, died in 2000. Between father and son, the Assads have ruled Syria since 1979.[94]

This time, Assad will be one of seven contenders, but none of the others is believed to stand a chance. Election law requires candidates to have lived in Syria continuously for 10 years, effectively barring exiled oppositionists.[95]

As the election nears, the Obama administration has stepped up its controlled efforts to aid some of the rebels fighting the Assad government. Obama has in recent months defined Syria policy in humanitarian terms as "helping the Syrian people" facing the "repressive regime" of Assad.[96]

Nevertheless, Obama has not backed off his refusal to send in U.S. troops or take other direct military action. "America is not the world's policeman," he said in September. "Terrible things happen across the globe, and it is beyond our means to right every wrong."[97]

Together with Saudi Arabia, the administration has shipped a small number of advanced anti-tank missiles to rebel militias deemed "moderate," *The Wall Street Journal* reported in April. In the context of the Syrian war, moderate means not commanded by Islamist extremists.[98]

The new arms reportedly represent a test to determine whether the recipients can be trusted with anti-aircraft weapons, which they have long demanded. American officials have been reluctant, because of the potential danger to civilian aircraft. But events such as the bombing of a school by Syrian government aircraft in the city of Aleppo — killing at least 17 students and two teachers — have ratcheted up the pressure on the administration.[99]

Speaking early last year, before the chemical weapons deal with Russia, Obama cited the practical and even moral "limitations" on U.S. action. "What offers the best prospect of a stable post-Assad regime?" he asked. "And how do I weigh tens of thousands who've been killed in Syria versus the tens of thousands who are currently being killed in the Congo?"[100]

Decades of civil war in Congo have cost millions of lives. Last year, the U.N. formed its first offensive military force, allied with the Congolese government military, to fight rebels.[101]

The Syrian civil war began more than three years ago, after Assad ordered his military to crush anti-government demonstrations. By now, the armed opposition reportedly consists of as many as 1,000 groups of varied sizes, made up of an estimated 100,000 fighters, representing a wide variety of religious and political views.[102]

Complications involved in determining which opposition groups the United States should support begin with the presence of a strong religious aspect to the Syrian war. Assad and his top supporters belong to the Alawite religious minority, an Islamic sect with an ancestral tie to Shiism. Sunnis, the majority sect of Islam, make up the backbone of the anti-Assad forces.[103]

Some rebels are supported by Sunni militants and al Qaeda-linked extremists who represent an extremist Sunni fringe. The government in turn is relying in part on the highly organized and combat-ready Hezbollah ("Party of God") militia from Lebanon. The Iranian-supported Shiite force has fought two wars with Israel, previously its main enemy.[104]

In addition, Assad government forces receive weapons and fighters directly from Iran, the target of longstanding U.S. and international efforts to curb its nuclear-development program. These are shipped by aircraft that pass through Iraqi airspace. To complicate the situation further, Iraq's Shiite-majority government, which has extensive ties to Iran, was installed with the help of the U.S. government during the war to topple Sunni dictator Saddam Hussein. Speaking to *The New Yorker* magazine, Iraqi Prime Minister Nouri al-Maliki defined the Syrian war as a conflict between Assad and al Qaeda, with the former preferable to the latter. "There is no more moderate opposition in Syria," he said.[105]

The administration, though cautious about which groups to aid, does not agree. Nevertheless, a persistent criticism of the administration's Syria policy is that there was a missed chance to help rebels early in the war. "We had an opportunity before the fundamentalists," says former CIA and State Department analyst Goodman. "We had a humanitarian obligation from the outset."

However, he acknowledges, there was no public support. Referring to Obama's cancellation of airstrikes in favor of negotiating the chemical-weapons deal, Goodman

said the president "marched right up to the brink and looked behind him and there was no one behind him."

OUTLOOK
Cautious Posture

The future of Ukraine and of relations with Russia, the outcome of the Syrian civil war, and the possibility of a definitive Iranian nuclear agreement remain highly uncertain, but some analysts argue that Americans' aversion to major military operations abroad is likely to continue.

"The American public, because of Iraq and Afghanistan, has been shocked into an isolationist mentality," says former ambassador Jeffrey.

But others say the American public is not categorically opposed to U.S. involvement in global affairs. "As frustrated as the public is with foreign policy, it isn't ready to abandon internationalism or to embrace unilateralism," said a Council on Foreign Relations analysis that accompanies the 2013 Pew survey.[106]

The analysis cited 72 percent support for shared world leadership, and 56 percent approval of the United States maintaining military supremacy. Nevertheless, Pew found support for going alone (38 percent) higher than at any time in nearly 50 years, except for 2009, when 44 percent supported that view.[107]

A major unknown is how the public would respond to a major attack against the United States or against U.S. interests abroad. The overwhelming support for a military response after the Sept. 11 attacks points to one possibility.

Sudden, catastrophic events aside, how public officials analyze the present can affect the course they set for U.S. policy. Carpenter of the Cato Institute, for one, argues that politicians ignore the strength of anti-interventionist public opinion at their peril. "If you continue to defy public opinion in the long term, that is likely to have political consequences," he says, adding, "In this case I think the public is correct."

Some argue that public caution about interventionism is well-founded. "This is the hundredth anniversary of World War I," says Bacevich of Boston University, pointing to a conflict that participants thought would be over in a matter of months. "The lesson of that is that once control is lost, it is difficult to restore order."

NOTES

1. Michael R. Gordon and Eric Schmitt, "Rebels to Ask for Antiaircraft Missiles," *The New York Times*, May 7, 2014, http://tinyurl.com/nhpm3zm.

2. *Ibid.*

3. Bernard Gwertzman, "Afghans Put Case Before All Forums," *The New York Times*, June 19, 1986, http://tinyurl.com/o45wea9; Norman Kempster, "Bosnian Leaders brings Arms Plea to U.S.," *Los Angeles Times*, Jan. 31, 1995, p. A4.

4. "Lend-Lease and Military Aid to the Allies in the Early Years of World War II," U.S. Department of State, Office of the Historian, undated, http://tinyurl.com/ln4d573.

5. "Public Sees U.S. Power Declining as Support for Global Engagement Slips: America's Place in the World 2013," Pew Research Center, Dec. 3, 2013, pp. 5, 20, 39, http://tinyurl.com/lz3mh2y; Janet Hook, "Americans Want to Pull Back From World Stage, Poll Finds," *The Wall Street Journal*, April 30, 2014, http://tinyurl.com/nst3umr.

6. "Secretary of Defense Chuck Hagel, Chicago Council on Global Affairs," U.S. Department of Defense, May 6, 2014, http://tinyurl.com/pcyb6bw.

7. Rebecca Shabad, "Congress fires warning shot at Iran," *The Hill*, March 18, 2014, http://tinyurl.com/myr8rlo; Robert J. Einhorn, "Preventing a Nuclear-Armed Iran: Requirements for Comprehensive Nuclear Agreement," Brookings Institution, March 2014, pp. 1-2, http://tinyurl.com/m689brf; Dan Roberts, "Obama admits Israel has good reason for skepticism over Iran nuclear deal," *The Guardian*, Nov. 24, 2013, http://tinyurl.com/nk7uxpb.

8. William Booth and Ruth Eglash, "Kerry's nine-month quest for Middle East peace ends in failure," *The Washington Post*, April 29, 2014, http://tinyurl.com/k2vpju3.

9. David J. Lynch, "China Challenges Obama's Asia Pivot With Rapid Military Buildup," Bloomberg, April 22, 2014, http://tinyurl.com/lkumsre.

10. Pamela Constable, "White House to send specialists to help recover abducted Nigerian schoolgirls," *The Washington Post*, May 6, 2014, http://tinyurl.com/nxwsbpb.

11. "Public Sees U.S. Power Declining," *op. cit.*, pp. 52-54.

12. "Remarks by President Obama and President Benigno Aquino III of the Philippines in Joint Press Conference," The White House, April 28, 2014, http://tinyurl.com/qg75rpo.

13. Mimi Hall, "Obama cites 'responsibility' of U.S. in Libya intervention," *USA Today*, March 28, 2011, http://tinyurl.com/ocafhb9; David D. Kirkpatrick, "A Deadly Mix in Benghazi," *The New York Times*, Dec. 28, 2013, http://tinyurl.com/lqeqtyv.

14. Joby Warrick, "More than 1,400 killed in Syrian chemical weapons attack, U.S. says," *The Washington Post*, Aug. 30, 2013, http://tinyurl.com/ksj2lc2. "Syria chemical attack: What we know," BBC, Sept. 24, 2013, www.bbc.com/news/world-middle-east-23927399. Reuters, April 1, 2014, www.reuters.com/article/2014/04/01/us-syria-crisis-toll-idUSBREA300YX2014041.

15. Michael R. Gordon, "U.S. and Russia Reach to Destroy Syria's Chemical Arsenal," *The New York Times*, Sept. 14, 2013, http://tinyurl.com/nytjlha; "Russia in the Syrian Conflict," *Russian Analytical Digest*, June 10, 2013, pp. 8-9, http://tinyurl.com/oxgp83m.

16. Mark Silva, "Obama's Russian Reset Lost in Putin's Translations," Bloomberg, April 3, 2014, http://tinyurl.com/pk4a5s6.

17. Sgt. A. M. LaVey, "173rd paratroopers arrive in Poland, Baltics for unscheduled exercises," *Army.mil*, April 30, 2014, http://tinyurl.com/lbx9oej; Griff Witte, "After Russian moves in Ukraine Eastern Europe shudders, NATO to increase presence," *The Washington Post*, April 18, 2014, http://tinyurl.com/msbuwlz; for background, see Roland Flamini, "Future of NATO," *CQ Researcher*, Jan. 1, 2009, pp. 1-26.

18. C. J. Chivers and Noah Sneider, "Behind the Masks in Ukraine, Many Faces of Rebellion," *The New York Times*, May 3, 2014, http://tinyurl.com/kreeybb; for background, see Brian Beary,

"Resurgent Russia," *CQ Researcher*, Feb. 7, 2014, pp. 121-144.

19. "Annual Address to the Federal Assembly of the Russian Federation," President of Russia, April 25, 2005, http://tinyurl.com/ns5c6k4.

20. "Remarks by Sen. John McCain on Mass Atrocities in Syria as World Commemorates Anniversary of Rwandan Genocide," Official Website of U.S. Sen. John McCain, April 10, 2014, http://tinyurl.com/oxcpv5y; Sangwon Yoon,. Sangwon Yoon, "Losing Syrian Rebels Press in Washington for Better Arms," Bloomberg, May6, 2014, http://tinyurl.com/lu9dk6v. Sean Sullivan, "McCain: Obama would face impeachment if he puts 'boots on the ground' in Syria," *The Washington Post*, Sept. 6, 2013, www.washingtonpost.com/blogs/post-politics/wp/2013/09/06/mccain-obama-would-face-impeachment-if-he-puts-boots-on-the-ground-in-syria.

21. "Collective defence," North Atlantic Treaty Organization, undated, http://tinyurl.com/co3p5vp.

22. Adam Entous, "U.S. Balks at Ukraine Military-Aid Request," *The Wall Street Journal*, March 13, 2014, http://tinyurl.com/mqcj9cu.

23. "Treasury Secretary Lew Announces Signing of $1 Billion Loan Guarantee Agreement for Ukraine," U.S. Department of State, April 14, 2014, http://tinyurl.com/o9pjq6f.

24. Michael R. Gordon, "Kerry Takes Offer of Aid to Ukraine and Pushes Back Against Russian Claims," *The New York Times*, March 4, 2014, http://tinyurl.com/n34e4jv; Ian Talley, "IMF Approves $17 Billion Emergency Aid for Ukraine's Economy," *The Wall Street Journal*, April 30, 2014, http://tinyurl.com/mrgnpb6.

25. Ian Traynor and Oksana Grytsenko, "Ukraine suspends talks on EU trade pact as Putin wins tug of war," *The Guardian*, Nov. 21, 2013, http://tinyurl.com/mmxpjgs; "Why is Ukraine in turmoil?," BBC News, Feb. 22, 2014, http://tinyurl.com/pxrf62y.

26. Kathy Lally, "Mansion was only a fixer-upper, Yanukovych says," *The Washington Post*, Feb. 28, 2014, http://tinyurl.com/l4twebj.

27. Henry Chu and Sergei L. Loiko, "Tensions escalate as Russia presses claim for Ukraine's Crimea," *Los Angeles Times*, March 7, 2014, http://tinyurl.com/nhbuooy.

28. Julian Borger and Alec Luhn, "Ukraine crisis: Geneva talks produce agreement on defusing conflict," *The Guardian*, April 17, 2014, http://tinyurl.com/p774zod; Thomas Grove and Aleksander Vasovic, "New Russia sanctions threats as Ukraine stalemate goes on," Reuters, April 18, 2014, http://tinyurl.com/lv8s2sc.

29. "Remarks by President Obama and German Chancellor Merkel in Joint Press Conference," The White House, May 2, 2014, http://tinyurl.com/kd7ggec.

30. "Public Sees U.S. Power Declining. . .," *op. cit.*, pp. 19, 22.

31. Chris Baldwin, "Putin says Russia threatened by 'unipolar world,' " Reuters, Nov. 5, 2007, http://tinyurl.com/lpw7d3t.

32. "Annual Address to the Federal Assembly of the Russian Federation," *op. cit.*

33. Jay Solomon and Andrey Ostroukh, "Russia's Foreign Minister Sergei Lavrov Warns Ukraine," *The Wall Street Journal*, April 24, 2014, http://tinyurl.com/m8k3vb3.

34. David J. Lynch, "China Challenges Obama's Asia Pivot With Rapid Military Buildup," Bloomberg, April 22, 2014, http://tinyurl.com/kc9gh4k.

35. For background, see Reed Karaim, "China Today," *CQ Researcher*, April 4, 2014, pp. 289-312.

36. "Transcript: Albright Interview on NBC-TV," USIS Washington File, Feb. 19, 1998, http://tinyurl.com/oeyqz2d.

37. "Remarks by President George W. Bush at the 20th Anniversary of the National Endowment for Democracy," National Endowment for Democracy, Nov. 6, 2003, http://tinyurl.com/4r62tdv.

38. Scott Wilson, "Obama announces plan to bring home 33,000 'surge' troops from Afghanistan," *The Washington Post*, June 22, 2011, http://tinyurl.com/6xpdnka.

39. David A. Lake, *Entangling Relations: American Foreign Policy in its Century* (1999), p. 3; Thomas

Jefferson, "Inaugural Address," The American Presidency Project, March 4, 1801, http://tinyurl.com/p38qgqq.

40. Justus D. Doenecke, *Nothing Less Than War: New History of America's Entry into World War I* (2011), pp. 1-18; 195-196; 149; 276; "Zimmermann Telegram," Our Documents, National Archives, http://tinyurl.com/ofnks2z.

41. Except where otherwise noted, this subsection is drawn from Susan Dunn, *1940: FDR, Willkie, Lindbergh, Hitler — the Election amid the Storm* (2013).

42. "German-Soviet Pact," United States Holocaust Memorial Museum, updated June 10, 2013, http://tinyurl.com/8gs6efm.

43. Franklin Delano Roosevelt, "'Stab in the Back' Speech," Miller Center, University of Virginia, June 10, 1940, http://tinyurl.com/q3z48v8.

44. Except where otherwise noted, this subsection is drawn from Tim Weiner, *A Legacy of Ashes: The History of the CIA* (2008).

45. "The India-Pakistan War of 1965," U.S. Department of State, Office of the Historian, undated, http://tinyurl.com/kbboxbl; "Bandung Conference (Asian-African Conference), 1955," U.S. Department of State, Office of the Historian, undated, http://tinyurl.com/mapu3jl.

46. Robert Jervis, "The Dustbin of History: Mutual Assured Destruction," *Foreign Policy*, Nov. 1, 2002, http://tinyurl.com/pv9cp2q.

47. Tim Weiner and Barbara Crossette, "George F. Kennan Dies at 101; Leading Strategist of Cold War," *The New York Times*, March 18, 2005, http://tinyurl.com/q8eg9g9; "Kennan and Containment, 1947," U.S. Department of State, Office of the Historian, undated, http://tinyurl.com/o6qqj3q; George Kennan, "Telegram . . . to the Secretary of State," Feb. 22, 1946, http://tinyurl.com/mw4k3nq.

48. "The Yalta Conference, 1945," U.S. Department of State, Office of the Historian, undated, http://tinyurl.com/mwuxwgu.

49. The NATO founding countries were: Belgium, Canada, Denmark, France, Iceland, Italy, Luxembourg, the Netherlands, Norway, Portugal, the United Kingdom, United States; "Member countries," North Atlantic Treaty Organization, undated, http://tinyurl.com/muurlsu; "A Short History of NATO," North Atlantic Treaty Organization, undated, http://tinyurl.com/knxknrh; "1955: Communist states sign Warsaw Pact," BBC, http://tinyurl.com/ywdx7o; "The Warsaw Security Pact," May 14, 1955, Avalon Project, Yale Law School, http://tinyurl.com/men7dor.

50. Weiner, *op. cit.*, pp. 92-105.

51. Frederick Taylor, "The Berlin Wall: A Secret History," *History Today*, February 2007, http://tinyurl.com/muqkgfy.

52. "The Cuban Missile Crisis: The 40th Anniversary," National Security Archive, The George Washington University, undated, http://tinyurl.com/p2wml5p.

53. "The Quotable Quotes of President Dwight D. Eisenhower," Eisenhower National Historic Site, undated, http://tinyurl.com/laxv8hb; "The Domino Theory," GlobalSecurity.org, undated, http://tinyurl.com/9v283vh.

54. Marc Selverstone and David Coleman, "Gulf of Tonkin, 1964: Perspectives from the Lyndon Johnson and National Military Command Center Tape," Miller Center, University of Virginia, undated, http://tinyurl.com/kgek74h; Andrew Gelman, "How Many Vietnam Veterans Are Still Alive?," *The New York Times*, March 25, 2013, http://tinyurl.com/qckaec4.

55. Michael Kranish, "With antiwar role, high visibility," *The Boston Globe*, June 17, 2003, http://tinyurl.com/flfx; "John Kerry Then: Hear Kerry's Historic 1971 Testimony Against the Vietnam War," Democracy Now!, Feb. 20, 2004, http://tinyurl.com/yl2gd4l; Todd Gitlin, *The Sixties: Years of Hope, Days of Rage* (1987).

56. John Tirman, "Why do we ignore the civilians killed in American wars?," *The Washington Post*, Jan. 6, 2012, http://tinyurl.com/7cwuq8h, www.archives.gov/research/military/vietnam-war/casualty-statistics.html.

57. Kate Doyle and Emily Willard, "'Learn from History,' 31st Anniversary of the Assassination of

Archbishop Romero," National Security Archive, March 23, 2011, http://tinyurl.com/ky8npps.

58. "The Iran-Contra Affair," American Experience, WGBH, undated, http://tinyurl.com/3djty9z.

59. "Final Report on the Independent Counsel for Iran/Contra Matters," U.S. Court of Appeals, Chapt. 2, Aug. 4, 1993, http://tinyurl.com/5eee9.

60. Klaus Dahmann, "Fall of the Berlin Wall and Reunification (1989-1990)," *Deutsche Welle*, April 22, 2013, http://tinyurl.com/qe6axmk.

61. "George H. W. Bush — Foreign Affairs," Miller Center, University of Virginia, undated, http://tinyurl.com/l6evb78.

62. Archie Brown, "Reform, Coup and Collapse: The End of the Soviet State,: BBC, updated Feb. 17, 2011, http://tinyurl.com/6zxyv88.

63. "Gulf War Fast Facts," CNN, Sept. 15, 2013, http://tinyurl.com/mxjdmww.

64. Chronology, Gulf War, (drawn from Rick Atkinson, *Crusade: The Untold Story of the Persian Gulf War* (1993), Frontline, PBS, undated, http://tinyurl.com/d8w3jxf; Thomas E. Ricks, Fiasco: *The American Military Adventure in Iraq* (2006), pp. 5-6; "No-fly zones: The legal position," BBC, Feb. 19, 2001, http://tinyurl.com/btbrxlt.

65. "Rwanda: How the genocide happened," BBC, Dec. 18, 2008, http://tinyurl.com/yksb33z.

66. Samantha Power, "Bystanders to Genocide," *The Atlantic*, Sept. 1, 2001, http://tinyurl.com/lduvwob.

67. Walter Clarke and Jeffrey Herbst, "Somalia and the Future of Humanitarian Intervention," *Foreign Affairs*, March/April 1996, http://tinyurl.com/kaet69a.

68. Mark Bowden, *Black Hawk Down* (1999).

69. Power, *op. cit.*

70. "Balkan Accord: The Address; Clinton Lays Out his Case for U.S. Troops in Balkans," *The New York Times*, Nov. 28, 1995, http://tinyurl.com/ks55323; Katherine Q. Seelye, "Balkan Accord: In Congress," *The New York Times*, Dec. 14, 1995, http://tinyurl.com/mtje8zk.

71. James Bennet, "U.S. Cruise Missiles Strike Sudan and Afghan Tarets Tied to Terrorist Network," *The New York Times*, Aug. 21, 1998, http://tinyurl.com/k22kecs.

72. "Operation Iraqi Freedom . . . Operation Enduring Freedom, U.S. Casualty Status," updated May 9, 2014, http://tinyurl.com/29va4fp; Matt Spetalnick, "Obama, Karzai accelerate end of U.S. combat role in Afghanistan," Reuters, Jan. 12, 2013, http://tinyurl.com/b3ks34e; Michael Holmes, "Inside Iraq: Two years after U.S. withdrawal, are things worse than ever?," CNN, Jan. 15, 2014, http://tinyurl.com/o5btyxs.

73. "Remarks by President George W. Bush at the 20th Anniversary of the National Endowment for Democracy," National Endowment for Democracy, Nov. 6, 2003, http://tinyurl.com/4r62tdv.

74. Sanford Gottlieb, "The Anti-Iraq War Movement is a Far Cry From Vietnam," Pacific News Service, Sept. 21, 2005, http://tinyurl.com/ljbq957; David Crary, "Iraq and Vietnam: Contrasting Protests," The Associated Press, March, 21, 2007, http://tinyurl.com/oxnfkd3; Andrew Glass, "U.S. military draft ends, Jan. 27, 1973," *Politico*, Jan. 27, 2012, http://tinyurl.com/o74rs26.

75. For background, see Leda Hartman, "Islamic Sectarianism," *CQ Researcher*, Aug. 7, 2012, pp. 353-376.

76. For background, see Peter Katel, "The Iraq War: 10 Years Later," *CQ Researcher*, March 1, 2013, pp. 205-232.

77. Ian Black, "Barack Obama, the Arab Spring and a series of unforeseen events," *The Guardian*, Oct. 21, 2012, http://tinyurl.com/my8zqqt.

78. Adam Nossiter and Kareem Fahim, "Revolution Won, Top Libyan Official Vows a New and More Pious State," *The New York Times*, Oct. 23, 2011, http://tinyurl.com/c7c9vwm; Jeremiah Gertler, "Operation Odyssey Dawn (Libya): Background and Issues for Congress," Congressional Research Service, March 30, 2011, http://tinyurl.com/6draa8z.

79. Kirkpatrick, *op. cit.*

80. C. J. Chivers and David M. Herszenhorn, "Separatists in Ukraine Vow to Proceed With

Autonomy Vote," *The New York Times*, May 8, 2014, http://tinyurl.com/kem4bm5.

81. Neil MacFarquhar, "Putin Announces Pullback From Ukraine Border," *The New York Times*, May 7, 2014, http://tinyurl.com/l2x8nyb.

82. Chivers and Herszenhorn, *op. cit.* Andrew E. Kramer and Alan Cowell, "Ukraine Authorities Dismiss Referendums as 'Farce,'" *The New York Times*, May 12, 2014, www.nytimes.com/2014/05/13/world/europe/ukraine.html?hp&_r=0.

83. MacFarquhar, *op. cit.*

84. "Remarks by President Obama and President Benigno Aquino III. . .," *op. cit.*

85. Alison Smale and Andrew Roth, "Ukrainian Says That Militias Won the East," *The New York Times*, April 30, 2014, http://tinyurl.com/kuwjsdk.

86. Jay Solomon, William Mauldin and Colleen McCain Nelson, "U.S., Europe Impose New Sanctions on Russia," *The Wall Street Journal*, April 29, 2014, http://tinyurl.com/ln2l78g.

87. Steven Woehrel, "Ukraine: Current Issues and U.S. Policy," Congressional Research Service, May 8, 2014, p. 7, http://tinyurl.com/pbcw576; Ilya Arkhipov and Anton Doroshev, "U.S. Sanctions Will Unite Russian Elite, Putin Aide Says," *Bloomberg Businessweek*, April 28, 2014, http://tinyurl.com/mvjj5x2.

88. Jay Solomon, *et al.*, *op. cit.*

89. Arkhipov and Doroshev, *op. cit.*

90. "Hearing of the Senate Foreign Relations Committee," www.foreign.senate.gov/imo/media/doc/04%2008%202014,%20International%20Affairs%20Budget1.pdf.

91. *Ibid.*

92. Peter Baker, "In Cold War Echo, Obama Strategy Writes Off Putin," *The New York Times*, April 19, 2014, http://tinyurl.com/lqka2jx.

93. "Bipartisan Support for Increased U.S. Sanctions against Russia," Pew Research Center, April 28, 2014, http://tinyurl.com/kzr7ndm.

94. "Syrians Vote For Assad in Uncontested Referendum," The Associated Press, May 28,

2007, http://tinyurl.com/npcwke4; "Hafez al-Assad, obituary," *The Guardian*, June 14, 2000, http://tinyurl.com/m8qqdhz.

95. Dominic Evans, "Assad seeks re-election as Syria war rages," Reuters, April 28, 2014, http://tinyurl.com/pcbj95h.

96. "Remarks by President Obama and President Benigno Aquino III. . .," *op. cit.*; "Full Transcript: President Obama's Sept. 10 speech on Syria," *The Washington Post*, Sept. 10, 2013, http://tinyurl.com/ns5njac.

97. *Ibid.* (Obama speech)

98. Ellen Knickmeyer, Maria Abi-Habib, Adam Entous, "Advanced U.S. Weapons Flow to Syrian Rebels," *The Wall Street Journal*, April 18, 2014, http://tinyurl.com/m5lz3wt.

99. Anne Barnard and Hwaida Saad, "Children's Art at Syria School, and Then a Bomb," *The New York Times*, April 30, 2014, http://tinyurl.com/k9l37u8; Ben Hubbard, "Syrian Election Announced; Rebels Report New Weapons," *The New York Times*, April 21, 2014, http://tinyurl.com/kffs2ms.

100. Franklin Foer and Chris Hughes, "Barack Obama Is Not Pleased," *The New Republic*, Jan. 27, 2013, http://tinyurl.com/bkc5eev.

101. Jonathan Saruk, "Africa's deadliest war enters new phase,: *USA Today*, Aug. 21, 2013, http://tinyurl.com/kdgzcbe; "Measuring Mortality in the Democratic Republic of Congo," International Rescue Committee, 2007, http://tinyurl.com/mju56np.

102. Liam Stack, "In Slap at Syria, Turkey Shelters Anti-Assad Fighters," *The New York Times*, Oct. 27, 2011, http://tinyurl.com/3b35yhn; "Syria crisis: Guide to armed and political opposition," BBC, Dec. 13, 2013, http://tinyurl.com/ms45abz.

103. Martin Chulov and Mona Mahmood, "Syrian Sunnis fear Assad regime wants to 'ethnically cleanse' Alawite heartland," The Guardian, July 22, 2013, http://tinyurl.com/kytqyd8; "The sectarian divisions in Syria's violent uprising," CBC News, July 19, 2012, http://tinyurl.com/k2svd4w; for background, see Leda Hartman, "Islamic Sectarianism," *CQ Researcher*, Aug. 7, 2012, pp. 353-376.

104. Mona Alami, "Hezbollah takes lead in pounding Syrian rebels," *USA Today*, Feb. 27, 2014, http://tinyurl.com/pwyex8s; Alison Smale, "Flow of Westerners to Syria Prompts Security Concerns," *The New York Times*, Jan. 15, 2014, http://tinyurl.com/pzno7bx.

105. Dexter Filkins, "What We Left Behind," *The New Yorker*, April 28, 2014, http://tinyurl.com/mo2lo23.

106. "Public Sees U.S. Power Declining. . .," *op. cit.*, pp. 6, 52-54.

107. *Ibid.*, pp. 18, 21.

BIBLIOGRAPHY

Books

Bacevich, Andrew J., *The Limits of Power: The End of American Exceptionalism*, Holt Paperbacks, 2009.
A Boston University political scientist and former Army colonel warns that the deep-seated American belief in global superiority is disastrous.

Gaddis, John Lewis, *The Cold War: A New History*, Penguin Books, 2006.
A Yale University historian considered the leading scholar of the Cold War distills his past work into a narrative account of the entire period.

Jones, Bruce, *Still Ours to Lead: America, Rising Powers, and the Tension Between Rivalry and Restraint*, Brookings Institution Press, 2014.
The decline in U.S. influence following the 2008 financial crisis shouldn't be confused with total eclipse, argues a foreign-policy specialist at the centrist think tank, who writes that the United States is in "a category of one."

Lesch, David W., *Syria: The Fall of the House of Assad*, Yale University Press, 2013.
The United States is far more limited in what it can do to bring peace to Syria than many foreign-policy experts believe, argues a Trinity University historian who met repeatedly with Assad earlier in his rule.

Weiner, Tim, *Legacy of Ashes: The History of the CIA*, Anchor, 2008.
A *New York Times* national security correspondent recounts the Cold War's numerous cloak-and-dagger battles.

Articles

Bendavid, Naftali, "Syria Making Good Progress in Chemical Weapons Removal," *The Wall Street Journal*, April 25, 2014, http://tinyurl.com/kuc6lw9.
Even amid war and rising tensions with Russia — a key architect of the Syria chemical weapons deal — removal of the weapons is proceeding well.

Cohen, Stephen F., "Cold War Again: Who's Responsible?" *The Nation*, April 1, 2014, http://tinyurl.com/ouyhq9n.
A leading critic of U.S. policy toward Russia argues that current tensions grow out of post-Cold War NATO expansion, not any territorial ambitions by Russian President Vladimir Putin.

Costigliola, Frank, "What Would Kennan Say to Obama?" *The New York Times*, Feb. 27, 2014, http://tinyurl.com/kmc8wco.
The late George F. Kennan, once the leading U.S. Cold War strategist, would warn President Obama against maintaining the role of world policeman and advise him that aggressive measures against a foe can lead to war, writes a University of Connecticut professor who edited Kennan's diaries.

Fisher, Max, "American isolationism just hit a 50-year high. Why that matters," *The Washington Post*, Dec. 4, 2013, http://tinyurl.com/ldb26uf.
A foreign-policy blogger argues that results of a survey showing public disengagement from international affairs represent a powerful trend among Americans.

Kaplan, Fred, "Eastern Promises," *Slate*, April 23, 2014, http://tinyurl.com/n435xp6.
President Obama's attempt to refocus U.S. foreign policy on Asia is a good idea, a journalist specializing in national security writes, but presidential plans don't dictate the course of events, in this case the Ukraine crisis.

Landler, Mark, "On a Trip That Avoids Beijing, Obama Keeps His Eye on China," *The New York Times*, April 26, 2014, http://tinyurl.com/nv8zht4.
Obama's trip to Asia was also marked by the balancing of neighbors' fears of China with the U.S. need to maintain a working relationship with the Asian giant.

Sorokin, Vladimir, "Let the Past Collapse on Time!" *New York Review of Books*, May 8, 2014, http://tiny url.com/ondzqbf.

A novelist who was a dissident in Soviet times and who remains in Moscow writes that the end of communism in Russia did not vanquish Soviet-style rule.

Reports

"Oral Update of the independent international commission of inquiry on the Syrian Arab Republic," *U.N. Human Rights Council*, March 18, 2014, www.ohchr .org/Documents/HRBodies/HRCouncil/CoISyria/ OralUpdate18March2014.pdf.

The UN commission recounts the most blatant and shocking human-rights violations committed during a horrific civil war now in its fourth year.

"Public Sees U.S. Power Declining as Support for Global Engagement Slips," Pew Research Center, Dec. 3, 2013, http://tinyurl.com/pqfsrre.

The most comprehensive survey to date on U.S. public opinion concerning global engagement, which tracks shifts in American attitudes toward the world over decades, is sparking interest in the foreign-policy and political communities.

Woehrel, Steven, "Ukraine: Current Issues and U.S. Policy," Congressional Research Service, May 8, 2014, www.fas.org/sgp/crs/row/RL33460.pdf.

A Europe specialist in Congress' nonpartisan research arm reports on the most recent developments in Ukraine, and Congressional response to date.

For More Information

American Enterprise Institute, 1150 17th St., N.W., Washington, DC 20036; 202-862-5800; www.aei.org/policy/ foreign-and-defense-policy/. Conservative Washington think tank that includes interventionist-oriented scholars and analysts.

Brookings Institution, 1775 Massachusetts Ave., N.W., Washington, DC 20036; 202-797-6105; www.brookings .edu. A centrist research and advocacy center with a foreign affairs wing that studies international economic and human rights issues.

Carnegie Endowment for International Peace, 1779 Massachusetts Ave., N.W., Washington, DC 20036; 202-483-7600; www.carnegieendowment.org. Longtime centrist

institution that maintains satellite offices in Beirut, Moscow, Brussels and elsewhere.

Cato Institute, 1000 Massachusetts Ave., N.W., Washington, DC 20001; 202-842-0200; www.cato.org. Libertarian think tank that opposes military solutions to problems.

Center for International Policy, 2000 M St., N.W., Suite 720, Washington, DC 20036; 202-232-3317; www.ciponline .org. Liberal think tank that advocates demilitarization and action against human-rights abuse.

Council on Foreign Relations, 58 E. 68th St., New York, NY 10065; 212-434-9400; cfr.org. A foreign-policy think tank including former senior diplomats.

13

Free Speech at Risk

Alan Greenblatt

Egyptian political satirist Bassem Youssef arrives at the public prosecutor's office in Cairo on March 31. Police questioned Youssef for allegedly insulting President Mohammed Morsi and Islam. The government filed charges against hundreds of Egyptian journalists but dropped them earlier this month. Free-speech advocates worry that journalists, bloggers and democracy supporters worldwide are being intimidated into silence.

From *CQ Researcher*, April 26, 2013.

It wasn't an April Fool's joke. On April 1, "Daily Show" host Jon Stewart defended Egyptian political satirist Bassem Youssef, who had undergone police questioning for allegedly insulting President Mohammed Morsi and Islam.

"That's illegal? Seriously? That's illegal in Egypt?" Stewart said on his Comedy Central show. "Because if insulting the president and Islam were a jailable offense here, Fox News go bye-bye."

Stewart was kidding, but Youssef's case has drawn attention from free-speech advocates who worry Egypt's nascent democracy is according no more respect toward freedom of expression than the regime it replaced.

The U.S. Embassy in Cairo, which had linked to Stewart's broadcast on its Twitter feed, temporarily shut down the feed after Egyptian authorities objected to it. Egypt's nascent government also has filed charges against hundreds of journalists, although Morsi asked that they all be dropped earlier this month.

Concerns are widespread that commentators, journalists, bloggers — and, yes, even comedians — are being intimidated into silence. And not just in Egypt.

Free speech, once seen as close to an absolute right in some countries, is beginning to conflict with other values, such as security, the protection of children and the desire not to offend religious sensibilities, not just in the Middle East but in much of the world, including Western Europe.

In many cases, freedom of speech is losing. "Free speech is dying in the Western world," asserts Jonathan Turley, a George Washington University law professor. "The decline of free speech has come not

319

Democracies Enjoy the Most Press Freedom

Democracies such as Finland, Norway and the Netherlands have the most press freedom, while authoritarian regimes such as Turkmenistan, North Korea and Eritrea have the least, according to Reporters Without Borders' 2012 index of global press freedom. European and Islamic governments have enacted or considered new press restrictions after a recent phone-hacking scandal in Britain and Western media outlets' irreverent images of the Prophet Muhammad triggered deadly protests by Muslims. Myanmar (formerly Burma), which recently enacted democratic reforms, has reached its greatest level of press freedom ever, the report said.

Press Freedom Worldwide, 2013

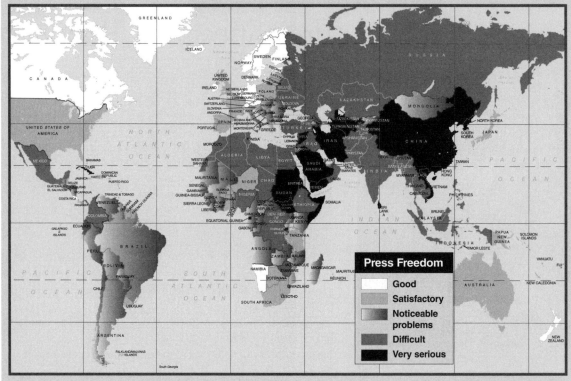

Source: "Freedom of the Press Worldwide in 2013," Reporters Without Borders, http://fr.rsf.org/IMG/jpg/2013-carte-liberte-presse_1900.jpg

from any single blow but rather from thousands of paper cuts of well-intentioned exceptions designed to maintain social harmony."[1]

In an era when words and images can be transmitted around the world instantaneously by anyone with a cell phone, even some American academics argue that an absolutist view of First Amendment protections couldn't be expected to prevail. Several made that case after protests broke out in several Muslim countries last

September over an American-made video uploaded to YouTube defamed the Prophet Muhammad.

Even the administration of President Obama, who defended the nation's free-speech traditions at the United Nations in the wake of video backlash, supports a proposed U.N. resolution to create an international standard to restrict some anti-religious speech. And, under Obama, the Justice Department has prosecuted a record number of government employees who have leaked sensitive documents, discouraging potential whistleblowers from exposing government waste, fraud or abuse.[2]

"Wherever you look, you see legislation or other measures seeking to reassert state control over speech and the means of speech," says John Kampfner, author of the 2010 book *Freedom for Sale.*

In the United Kingdom and Australia, government ministers last month proposed that media outlets be governed by new regulatory bodies with statutory authority, although they ran into opposition. Two years ago, a new media law in Hungary created a regulatory council with wide-ranging powers to grant licenses to media outlets and assess content in a way that Human Rights Watch says compromises press freedom.[3]

"Not only is legislation such as this bad in and of itself, but it is crucial in sending a green light to authoritarians who use these kind of measures by Western states to say, whenever they are criticized by the West, 'Hey, you guys do the same,'" says Kampfner, former CEO of Index on Censorship, a London-based nonprofit group that fights censorship.

Some observers have hoped the growth of social media and other technologies that spread information faster and more widely than previously thought possible could act as an automatic bulwark protecting freedom of expression. "The best example of the impact of technology on free speech is to look at the Arab Spring," says Dan Wallach, a computer scientist at Rice University, referring to the series of upheavals starting in 2011 that led to the fall of autocratic leaders in Tunisia, Egypt, Yemen and Libya.[4]

But as studies by Wallach and many others show, countries such as China and Iran are building new firewalls to block sensitive information and track dissidents. "The pattern seems to be that governments that fear mass movements on the street have realized that they might want to be able to shut off all Internet communications in the country and have started building the infrastructure that enables them to do that," said Andrew McLaughlin, a former White House adviser on technology.[5]

In January, a French court ordered Twitter to help identify people who had tweeted racist or anti-Semitic remarks, or face fines of 1,000 euros (about $1,300) per day. The San Francisco-based company refused to comply, citing First Amendment protections for free speech.[6]

But even as Twitter appeals the French court order, the microblogging site in October blocked the account of a neo-Nazi group called Besseres Hannover, or Better Hanover, which had been charged with inciting racial hatred. Twitter said it was the first time it had used

Number of Journalists Killed on the Rise

Seventy journalists were killed in 2012, nearly half of them murdered, a 43 percent increase from 2011. A total of 232 journalists were imprisoned in 2012, the highest number since the Committee to Protect Journalists began keeping track in 1990. Experts say a select group of countries has fueled the increase by cracking down on criticism of government policies.

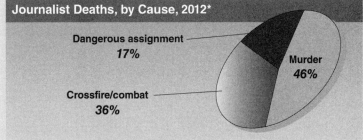

Journalist Deaths, by Cause, 2012*

Dangerous assignment **17%**

Crossfire/combat **36%**

Murder **46%**

* Figures do not total 100 because of rounding.

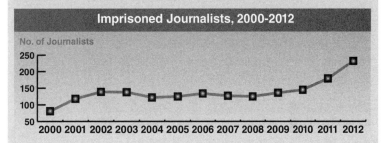

Imprisoned Journalists, 2000-2012

No. of Journalists

Source: "Attacks on the Press," Committee to Protect Journalists, 2013, www.cpj.org/attacks/

AFP/Getty Images/Attila Kisbenedek

A free-speech activist in Budapest, Hungary, protests against a new media law on March 15, 2011. The law set up a regulatory council with wide control over media outlets and content, a power that Human Rights Watch says compromises press freedom. Pictured on the poster is the revered poet of Hungary's 1848-1849 revolution, Sandor Petofi.

"There have been attempts to pass so-called religious-sensibility laws, which are, in fact, a way of curbing press freedom and expression," says Robert Mahoney, director of the Committee to Protect Journalists, a New York-based nonprofit group that promotes press freedom.

In one widely covered case, three members of the Russian punk rock band Pussy Riot were found guilty of hooliganism motivated by religious hatred last year. They had been arrested in March after a performance in Moscow's main cathedral, in which they profanely called for the Virgin Mary to protect Russia against Vladimir Putin, who was returned to the presidency soon after the performance. The three were sentenced to two years in a prison colony, but one member was released on probation before being sent to prison.[8] In more open societies, laws meant to protect against hate speech, Holocaust denial and offenses against religious sensibilities also can end up limiting what people can talk and write about.

Free-speech laws traditionally have been about the protection of unpopular and provocative expression. Popular and uncontroversial opinions usually need no protection. But in recent years, free-speech protections have been fading away.

"The new restrictions are forcing people to meet the demands of the lowest common denominator of accepted speech," Turley contends.

As people monitor the health of free expression around the globe, here are some of the questions they're debating:

Has technology made speech freer?

As Arab protesters took to the streets — and the Internet — in 2011 in countries such as Tunisia and Egypt, everyone from commentators for serious foreign-policy journals to "The Daily Show" asked whether the world was witnessing a "Twitter revolution."

Social-media sites such as Twitter and Facebook were used by activists both as organizing tools and as a means of communication with the outside world.

"Tunisians got an alternative picture from Facebook, which remained uncensored through the protests, and they communicated events to the rest of the world by posting videos to YouTube and Dailymotion," Ethan Zuckerman, a researcher at Harvard University's Berkman Center for Internet and Society, wrote in 2011. "It's likely that news of demonstrations in other parts of

technology to monitor and withhold content based on a given country's concerns and laws.

Meanwhile, government arrests of journalists and mob attacks against them are on the rise. Journalists are being arrested more often than in previous years in countries such as Russia and Turkey, and in 2012, mobs attacked journalists in Mali and Canada — among other countries — for what the protesters perceived as their blasphemous coverage of Islam. Blasphemy prosecutions have become more common, especially in predominantly Islamic countries such as Pakistan, where blasphemy laws apply only to comments about Islam or Muhammad, not to derogatory comments about Christianity, Judaism or other world religions.[7]

the country disseminated online helped others conclude that it was time to take to the streets."[9]

Unquestionably, new-media tools make it easier for activists to spread their messages farther and faster than was conceivable during the days of the mimeograph machine, or even the fax. "What's happening with new technology is that it's making publication of these stories easier, and they're reaching a bigger audience," says Mahoney, the Committee to Protect Journalists deputy director.

"Twenty years ago, you'd struggle to get published in a local newspaper," Mahoney says. "Now, as a journalist, you've got far more platforms open to you, and you can get it out."

And not just journalists. From Libya and Iran to Syria and Myanmar, activists and average citizens are able to disseminate text, images and video all over the world, ensuring that their voices can be heard even at moments when regimes are violently cracking down on them.

Social media and other technological tools have become so omnipresent that former Rep. Tom Perriello, D-Va., worries that people become addicted to the online dialogue rather than reaching out to broader populations. "My pet peeve is that people think that social media can replace traditional organizing," says Perriello, President of the Center for American Progress Action Fund, part of a liberal think tank in Washington.

And even free-speech advocates readily admit that, in a broader sense, technology can be a two-edged sword. "Suddenly, you have the ability to reach people all over the world and communicate in ways that you never could before, and that's wonderful," says Eva Galperin, global policy analyst with the Electronic Frontier Foundation (EFF), a San Francisco-based group that promotes an unrestricted Internet. "But it also allows government surveillance on a scale that was never before possible."

Journalists find that their e-mail accounts have been hacked by "state-sponsored attackers" in countries such as China and Myanmar.[10] Mobile phones become surveillance devices.

"Modern information technologies such as the Internet and mobile phones . . . magnify the uniqueness of individuals, further enhancing the traditional challenges to privacy," according to a recent study by researchers from MIT and other universities that exposed the ease of tracking individual cellphone users. "Mobility

data contains the approximate whereabouts of individuals and can be used to reconstruct individuals' movements across space and time."[11]

Authoritarian regimes also use technology to access dissidents' computers, installing malware that tracks their movements online, according to Galperin. "It records all of their keystrokes and can use the microphones and cameras on the computers, circumventing all attempts to use encryption," she says.

It's not just dictatorships. Galperin notes that EFF's longstanding lawsuit against the National Security Agency for using warrantless wiretaps in the United States is "now old enough to go to school." And many of the surveillance tools used by authoritarian regimes are made by U.S. companies, she points out.

In the United Kingdom, in response to a phone-hacking scandal that has led to government investigations and a national debate about press abuses, a communications data bill has been proposed by Home Secretary Theresa May to require Internet service providers and mobile phone services to collect and retain data on user activity. The measure is "designed to give the state blanket rights to look at e-mails and IMs [instant messages] and requires all companies to retain the data for a year and hand it over [to the government]," says Kampfner, the former editor of *New Statesman* magazine. "It was halted a few months ago, but will be reintroduced this year."

Iran, which saw its own "Twitter revolution" during a spasm of post-election protests in 2009, has attempted to keep a "Halal Internet," free of unclean influences and information from the outside world.

In March, Iran's Ministry of Information and Communications Technology blocked software used by millions of Iranians to bypass the state's elaborate Internet filtering system. "A collection of illegal virtual private networks, or VPNs, was successfully closed off by the ministry, making visits to websites deemed immoral or politically dangerous — like Facebook and Whitehouse.gov — nearly impossible," *The New York Times* reported.[12]

Governments and Internet users are engaged in an unending game of cat and mouse, Kampfner says, with each trying to advance technology in ways that gives its side the upper hand.

"There's something called Tor, an open-source project that aims to break through all those barriers, whether in

Blasphemy Laws Proliferate

Videos and cartoons mocking the Muslim Prophet Muhammad have prompted many countries to enact strict anti-blasphemy laws. Christians and Muslims have used the laws to prosecute people seen as insulting religion. Blasphemy laws in Muslim countries usually refer only to defaming Islam, and punishments can include the death penalty. Many cases involve comments or videos posted on social media such as Twitter and YouTube.

Examples of Recent Blasphemy Cases

Country	Law
Austria	Prohibits disparaging a religious object, society or doctrine. *On Dec. 11, 2010, Helmut Griese, 63, was convicted for offending his Muslim neighbor by yodeling while mowing his lawn; the neighbor claimed Griese was imitating the Muslim call to prayer. On Jan. 22, 2009, politician Susanne Winter was fined $24,000 for saying Muhammad was a pedophile because he had a 9-year-old wife.*
India	Allows up to three years in prison for insulting religion or religious beliefs. *On April 21, 2012, the Catholic Church filed a complaint against Sanal Edamaruku, the founder of the reason-based organization Rationalist International, after he exposed a "miracle" by showing water from a statue of Jesus was coming from a leaky drain. On Nov. 19, 2012, college student Shaheen Dhada and a friend were arrested for complaining on Facebook that Mumbai had been shut down for the funeral of the leader of the Hindu nationalist party.*
Iran	Bars criticism of Islam or deviation from the ruling Islamic standards. *Web designer Saeed Malekpour, 35, a Canadian, served four years on death row in Iran for "insulting Islam." He was arrested while visiting his dying father in Iran in 2008 because a photo-sharing program he created while in Canada was used by others to download pornography. The death sentence was suspended in 2012 after Malekpour "repented."*
Netherlands	Penalizes "scornful blasphemy" that insults religious feelings. *On March 19, 2008, Dutch cartoonist Gregorius Nekschot was arrested for insulting Muslims in his drawings. On Jan. 21, 2009, politician Geert Wilders was put on trial because his film "Fitna" compared Islam and Nazism. He was acquitted.*
Pakistan	Bans blasphemy, including defiling the Quran and making remarks against the Prophet Muhammad. *In 2011 the governor of Punjab and the minister for minority affairs were assassinated because they opposed the country's blasphemy laws. On June 22, 2011, 29-year-old Larkana resident Abdul Sattar was sentenced to death and fined $1,000 for sending text messages and blaspheming the Quran, Muhammad and other Islamic figures during a phone conversation.*
United Kingdom	Prohibits "hate speech" against religious groups. *On March 4, 2010, philosophy tutor Harry Taylor was sentenced to six months in prison, 100 hours of community service and fined €250 ($337 at the time) for leaving anti-Christian and anti-Islam cartoons in an airport prayer room.*

Source: International Humanist and Ethical Union, December 2012

But as many commentators have noted, free speech online depends not only on government policies and court rulings, but on private companies such as Twitter, Facebook and Google. Increasingly, these companies are being called on to block posts by terrorists and unpopular or banned political parties.

"At the end of the day, the private networks are not in any way accountable if they choose to censor or prevent individuals from accessing services," says Katherine Maher, director of strategy and communications for Access, a New York-based digital-rights group.

"The Internet is not something different," Maher says. "It is just an extension of the area in which we live."

Should religious sensibilities be allowed to limit free expression?

When an assassin's bullet narrowly missed the head of Lars Hedegaard, suspicion immediately fell on Muslims, since Hedegaard, a former newspaper editor in Denmark, has been an anti-Islam polemicist.

But a number of Danish Muslims condemned the February attack and rose to defend Hedegaard. "We Muslims have to find a new way of reacting," said Qaiser Najeeb, a Dane whose father had emigrated from Afghanistan. "We don't defend Hedegaard's views but do defend his right to speak. He can say what he wants."[13]

For free-speech advocates, it was a refreshing reaction — particularly in a country where Muslim sensitivities have run high since the 2006 publication of cartoons caricaturing the Prophet Muhammad in a Danish newspaper.

"For those, like me, who look upon free speech as a fundamental good, no degree of cultural or religious

China or Iran or anywhere else," says Wallach, the computer scientist at Rice University. "Tor keeps getting more and more clever about hiding what they're doing, and regimes like Iran get more and more clever about blocking them regardless."

discomfort can be reason for censorship," writes British journalist and author Kenan Malik. "There is no free speech without the ability to offend religious and cultural sensibilities."[14]

In recent years, a growing number of people around the globe have been prosecuted on charges of blasphemy or offending cultural sensibilities through hate speech. According to the International Humanist and Ethical Union (IHEU), only three people were arrested for committing blasphemy via social media between 2007 and 2011, but more than a dozen such arrests occurred in 10 countries last year.[15]

Turkish pianist Fazil Say, for instance, was given a suspended sentence of 10 months in jail on April 15 for posting tweets considered blasphemous, while Gamal Abdou Massoud, a 17-year-old Egyptian, was sentenced to three years for posting blasphemous cartoons on Facebook.

"When 21st-century technology collides with medieval blasphemy laws, it seems to be atheists who are getting hurt, as more of them go to prison for sharing their personal beliefs via social media," says Matt Cherry, editor of the IHEU report.

In Pakistan, those accused of blasphemy often fall victim to violence — before they even get their day in court. — Dozens have been killed after being charged with blasphemy over the past 20 years. Last November, a mob burned Farooqi Girls' High School in Lahore after a teacher assigned homework that supposedly contained derogatory references to Muhammad.

"Repeating the blasphemy under Pakistan law is seen as blasphemy in itself," says Padraig Reidy, news editor for the Index on Censorship. "You have these bizarre cases where evidence is barely given but people are sentenced to death."

Even criticizing Pakistan's blasphemy law can be dangerous. Sherry Rehman, the Pakistani ambassador to the United States, has received death threats since calling for changes in the law, while two like-minded politicians have been assassinated.[16]

In Pakistan, free speech is pretty much limited to those hanging around cafes and literary festivals, says Huma Yusuf, a columnist for the Pakistani newspaper *Dawn.* "The threat of blasphemy — a crime that carries the death penalty — has stifled public discourse," she writes.[17]

Indians protest against the American-made anti-Muslim video "Innocence of Muslims" in Kolkata on Oct. 5, 2012. The film incited a wave of anti-U.S. violence in Libya, Egypt and other countries across the Muslim world. Speaking at the United Nations after the protests, President Obama explained that such films could not be banned in the United States because of the U.S. Constitution's free-speech rights.

YouTube has been blocked throughout Pakistan since September, when an anti-Muslim video was uploaded to the site. Thousands of other websites also have been blocked, allegedly for containing pornographic or blasphemous content. "In truth, most had published material criticizing the state," according to Yusuf.

In counties such as Pakistan and Egypt, the line between blasphemy laws designed to protect against religious offense and those meant to punish minorities and stifle dissent is highly porous. "There have been attempts to protect religious sensibility which are in fact a way of curbing press freedom and expression," says Mahoney, of the Committee to Protect Journalists.

In the West, worries about offending religious and cultural sensibilities have sometimes trumped free-speech concerns. "Denigration of religious beliefs is never acceptable," Australian Prime Minister Julia Gillard stated before the United Nations in September. "Our tolerance must never extend to tolerating religious hatred."[18]

Gillard emphasized her disdain for speech that incites hatred and violence, which has become a common concern among Western politicians. "Western governments seem to be sending the message that free-speech rights will not protect you" when it comes to hate speech, writes Turley, the George Washington University law professor.[19]

Hate speech is intended to incite discrimination or violence against members of a particular national, racial or ethnic group, writes Aryeh Neier, a former top official with the American Civil Liberties Union, Human Rights Watch and the Open Society Institute.

But, Neier notes, "It is important to differentiate blasphemy from hate speech. The proclivity of some elsewhere to react violently to what they consider blasphemous cannot be the criterion for imposing limits on free expression in the U.S., the United Kingdom, Denmark or the Netherlands (or anywhere else)."[20]

In recent months, the human rights group American Freedom Defense Initiative (AFDI) has been running anti-Muslim ads on public transportation systems around the United States. Posters that appeared on San Francisco buses last month, for example, included a picture of Osama bin Laden and a made-up quote from "Hamas MTV" that said, "Killing Jews is worship that brings us closer to Allah."

After New York's Metropolitan Transit Authority tried to block the ads last summer, Federal District Judge Paul A. Engelmayer ruled that the agency had violated AFDI's First Amendment rights.

"Not only did [he] rule that the ads should be 'afforded the highest level of protection under the First Amendment,' he went on to offer some eye-opening examples," writes *San Francisco Chronicle* columnist C. W. Nevius. "Engelmayer said an ad could accuse a private citizen of being a child abuser. Or, he suggested, it could say, 'Fat people are slobs' or 'Blondes are bimbos' and still be protected."[21]

Rather than put up a legal fight, San Francisco's Municipal Railway decided to put up peace posters of its own and donate the AFDI's advertising fee to the city's Human Rights Commission.

Should the United States promote free speech abroad?

Because of the First Amendment and the history of its interpretation, the United States has what comes closest to absolute protection of free speech of any country on Earth. And many believe free expression is not only essential to democracy but a value Americans should help export to other countries.

At a 2011 Internet freedom conference in The Hague, then-Secretary of State Hillary Rodham Clinton said,

"The United States will be making the case for an open Internet in our work worldwide.

"The right to express one's views, practice one's faith, peacefully assemble with others to pursue political or social change — these are all rights to which all human beings are entitled, whether they choose to exercise them in a city square or an Internet chat room," Clinton said. "And just as we have worked together since the last century to secure these rights in the material world, we must work together in this century to secure them in cyberspace."[22]

But the right to free expression that is taken for granted in the United States is not shared around the world. Some people — including some Americans — worry that the United States risks offending governments and citizens in other nations by preserving free-speech rights — including the right to racist and blasphemous speech — above nearly every other consideration.

Such voices have been prominent when Americans have exercised their free-speech rights in ways that offend others. Threats to burn the Quran — as well as actual Quran burnings — by Florida pastor Terry Jones led to deadly riots in the Muslim world in 2010 and 2011. Last fall, video portions from an anti-Muslim film called "Innocence of Muslims" triggered riots in several predominantly Muslim nations.

Speaking to the United Nations two weeks later, President Obama explained that the U.S. government could not ban such a video because of free-speech rights enshrined in the U.S. Constitution.

"Americans have fought and died around the globe to protect the right of all people to express their views, even views that we profoundly disagree with," Obama said. "We do not do so because we support hateful speech, but because our founders understood that without such protections, the capacity of each individual to express their own views and practice their own faith may be threatened."[23]

But Obama noted that modern technology means "anyone with a cellphone can spread offensive views around the world with the click of a button."

While reality, some commentators said it was foolish to expect other nations to understand the American right to unbridled speech. "While the First Amendment right to free expression is important, it is also important to remember that other countries and cultures do not have to understand or respect our right," Anthea Butler, a University of Pennsylvania religious studies professor, wrote in *USA Today*.[24]

Americans must remember that "our First Amendment values are not universal," cautioned Eric Posner, a University of Chicago law professor.

"Americans need to learn that the rest of the world — and not just Muslims — see no sense in the First Amendment," Posner wrote in *Slate*. "Even other Western nations take a more circumspect position on freedom of expression than we do, realizing that often free speech must yield to other values and the need for order. Our own history suggests that they might have a point."[25]

Access' Maher, who has consulted on technology issues with the World Bank and UNICEF, notes that even other Western nations tend to hold free-speech rights less dear, viewing them within a context not of personal liberty but a framework where they risk infringing on the rights of others. "This often leads to robust debates about incitement, hate speech, blasphemy and their role in the political discourse, often in a manner more open to possible circumscription than would be acceptable in the United States," she says.

Even some who promote free expression worry about the United States taking a leading role in its promotion, because of the risk of it being seen elsewhere as an American value being imposed from without.

"The problem is freedom of expression has come to be seen as either an American or Anglo-Saxon construct, whereas we would all like to see it as a universal principle," says Kampfner, the British journalist. "There is a danger that if this value is seen as proselytized primarily by the United States, it will reinforce those who are suspicious of it."

But it may be that America's staunch adherence to free speech makes the United States uniquely well-suited to promote and defend the idea.

"The United States values a free press and should promote those values abroad," says Robert Mahoney, deputy director of the Committee to Protect Journalists.

"No Western country wants to appear to be lecturing other countries to uphold its values, but it's not an American construct," he says. "We have a duty to remind them of that, and we expect international bodies like the U.N. and countries like the United Kingdom and the European Union to do the same thing."

During his first trip abroad as secretary of State, John Kerry in February defended free speech — including the "right to be stupid" — as a virtue "worth fighting for."[26]

It's important that individuals and groups in foreign countries take the lead in explaining free-speech rights, "so it's not seen as a Western concept," says Reidy, the Index on Censorship editor.

"Certain human rights are not Western," he says, "they're universal. That's the whole point of human rights."

BACKGROUND

Refusal to *"Revoco"*

The struggle for free speech has been a long story about testing limits. Many of the most famous moments in the development of free speech in the Western world involved notable figures such as the French philosopher Voltaire, the Biblical translator William Tyndale and the Italian astronomer Galileo, who were variously exiled, executed or forced to recant things they had said or written.

"Governments in all places in all times have succumbed to the impulse to exert control over speech and conscience," writes Rodney A. Smolla, president of Furman University.[27]

The first great flowering of democracy and free speech occurred 500 years before the birth of Christ in the Greek city-state of Athens. The city pioneered the idea of government by consent, allowing the people the freedom to choose their own rules.

"Free speech was an inseparable part of the new Athenian order," Robert Hargreaves, who was a British broadcaster, writes in his 2002 book *The First Freedom*. "Never before had ordinary citizens been given the right to debate such vital matters as war and peace, public finance or crime and punishment."[28]

But although Athens embraced, off and on, the concept of government by consent, it did not yet accept the idea of individual free speech that might upset the prevailing order. Athens now may be remembered less for pioneering free speech than for trying and executing the great philosopher Socrates in 399 B.C., after he refused to recant his teachings.

Demanding that critics and heretics recant has been a persistent theme throughout history. After Martin Luther printed his *Ninety-Five Theses* in 1517, which criticized

CHRONOLOGY

1940s-1980s *New laws, international entities and court decisions expand free-speech rights.*

1946 French constitution upholds principle that "free communication of thought and of opinion is one of the most precious rights of man."

1948 United Nations adopts Universal Declaration of Human Rights, declaring "the right to freedom of opinion and expression" for all.

1952 U.S. Supreme Court extends First Amendment protections to movies.

1954 Congress effectively criminalizes the Communist Party.

1961 British jury allows Penguin to publish the novel *Lady Chatterly's Lover*, which had been on a list of obscene material.

1964 In landmark *New York Times v. Sullivan* decision, U.S. Supreme Court rules that public officials must prove "actual malice" on the part of journalists in order to sue for libel. . . . Free Speech Movement at University of California, Berkeley, insists that administrators allow campus protests.

1968 U.K. abolishes 400-year-old laws allowing for government censorship of theater performances.

1971 In the first instance of prior restraint on the press in U.S. history, a court blocks *The New York Times* from publishing the Pentagon Papers, but the Supreme Court OKs publication of the classified Vietnam War history.

1989 Iran's Islamic government issues a fatwa, or kill order, against *Satanic Verses* author Salman Rushdie forcing him into hiding for years. . . . Supreme Court upholds the right to burn the U.S. flag in protest.

2000s *In response to terrorist attacks, many Western countries limit civil liberties.*

2000 At the first meeting of the post-Cold War Community of Democracies, 106 countries pledge to uphold democratic principles, including freedom of expression

2005 George W. Bush administration ultimately fails in its year-long campaign to pressure *New York Times* not to publish a story about warrantless wiretaps

2006 More than 200 people die in violent protests across the Muslim world after the Danish newspaper *Jyllands-Posten* publishes cartoons satirizing the Prophet Muhammad. . . . United Kingdom bans language intended "to stir up religious hatred." . . . In response to July 2005 terrorist bombings of bus and subway system that killed more than 50 people, U.K. enacts Prevention of Terrorism Act, which curtails speech in the name of security. . . . Crusading Russian journalist Anna Politkovskaya, known for her coverage of the Chechen conflict, is assassinated.

2010s *In an age of new media, both rich and developing countries restrict speech that may offend.*

2010 WikiLeaks publishes thousands of sensitive documents related to U.S. diplomatic efforts in Iraq, Afghanistan and elsewhere. . . . Google announces it is pulling out of China due to government censorship of its service.

2012 U.S. Supreme Court finds the Stolen Valor Act unconstitutional; the 2006 law made it a crime to falsely claim to have won military decorations. . . . Members of the Russian punk band Pussy Riot are convicted of hooliganism for protesting President Vladimir Putin's policies in a Moscow church. . . . "Innocence of Muslims," an anti-Muslim video posted on YouTube, triggers riots in several Middle Eastern and North African countries. . . . Twitter blocks German access to posts by a banned neo-Nazi party, its first bow to "country-withheld content" regulations. . . . Inquiry on press abuses in Britain spurred by telephone-hacking scandal by media outlets calls for greater regulation. . . . Egyptian court sentences to death in absentia Florida pastor Terry Jones, who had offended Muslims through Quran burnings and promotion of an anti-Muslim film.

2013 Pfc. Bradley Manning pleads guilty to 10 charges of giving government secrets to WikiLeaks (Feb. 28). . . . Due to lack of support, Australia's ruling party withdraws a proposal to regulate the press (March 21). . . . Privately owned newspapers are distributed in Myanmar for the first time in 50 years (April 1). . . . Egyptian court drops charges against popular comedian Bassem Youssef, who had been accused of insulting the president (April 6).

clerical abuses, Cardinal Thomas Cajetan, the papal legate in Rome, asked him to say *revoco*, or "I recant," and all would be well. Luther refused.

Cajetan wanted to turn Luther over to Rome on charges of heresy, but Frederick III, the elector of Saxony, allowed him to stay. Luther's works became bestsellers. Not only was he a celebrity, but his writings helped spark the Protestant Reformation.

Eventually, Pope Leo X and the Holy Roman Emperor Charles V also asked Luther to recant his writings. He argued that he was defending works about the teachings of Christ and therefore was not free to retract them. He offered this famous defense: "Here I stand; God help me; I can do no other."[29] As a result, the pope excommunicated him, and the emperor condemned him as an outlaw.

Controlling the Press

Luther's writings were spread thanks to the advent of the printing press, a new technology that governments sought to control. The Star Chamber of the British Parliament in 1586 strictly limited the number of master printers, apprentices and printing presses that could operate in London. All books were required to be licensed by the archbishop of Canterbury or the bishop of London.

A few decades later, members of Parliament won the ability to speak and vote without royal restraint. This led to a freer press, as London printers began publishing journals that were largely accounts of Parliament but also contained news. By 1645, the printers were putting out an average of 14 separate weekly titles.[30]

A year earlier, the English poet John Milton had published his *Aereopagitica*, remembered as one of the most eloquent pleas for a free press ever penned. "Truth is strong next to the Almighty, she needs no policies, no stratagems nor licensing to make her victorious," Milton wrote in the treatise. "Give her but room, and do not bind her."

Although it grew out of ongoing debates about press licensing and limiting free speech, the *Aereopagitica* had little influence in its day. The press remained heavily regulated both in the United Kingdom and in its American colonies.

In 1734, a German-born printer in New York named John Peter Zenger published criticism of royalist Gov. William Cosby, calling him "a governor turned rogue" who was undermining the colony's laws. At Zenger's trial

the following year, attorney Andrew Hamilton argued that the judge and jury should not separately consider the questions of whether he had published the material and whether it was libelous, as was the practice at the time, but rather simply determine whether it could not be libel because it was true.

The jury's verdict of not guilty was considered an important precedent, but it would be 70 years before New York changed its libels laws so the question of truth could be entered into evidence.

William Blackstone, in his *Commentaries on the Laws of England* of 1769, laid the groundwork for the idea that there should be no licensing or prior restraint of the press, but that publishers could still face punishment after publication. This formed the basis for the thinking of the American Founders, who remained skeptical about a completely free press.

"License of the press is no proof of liberty," John Adams wrote in his *Novanglus Letters* of 1774. "When a people are corrupted, the press may be made an engine to complete their ruin . . . and the freedom of the press, instead of promoting the cause of liberty, will but hasten its destruction."

As U.S. president, Adams signed the Alien and Sedition Acts, which led to multiple arrests and convictions of printers and publicists (all Republicans, or political opponents of Adams). The law was overturned under Thomas Jefferson, who had been skeptical about the need for unbridled press but embraced it in his second inaugural, stating that the press needed no other legal restraint than the truth.

The principle that there was a right to disseminate facts in a democracy was crystallized in British philosopher John Stuart Mill's *On Liberty* of 1859. "News, independently gathered and impartially conveyed, was seen to be an indispensable commodity in a society where the people ruled themselves," Mill wrote.

Expanding Rights

The U.S. Supreme Court seldom examined the question of free speech during the 19th century, but justices began to expand its sense in the 20th century.

During World War I, more than 1,900 Americans were prosecuted under the Espionage Act of 1917 and the Sedition Act of 1918, which banned printing, writing and uttering of statements deemed disloyal or abusive of the U.S. government.

Free Speech Can Be Deadly in Russia

"Many journalists end up dead, assaulted or threatened."

Aleksei A. Navalny expects to go to jail. Last month, a Russian court announced it would schedule a trial against Navalny, who is accused of embezzling from a timber company, even though the case was dismissed last year for lack of evidence. Still, Navalny said, "Honestly, I am almost certain I am going to prison."[1]

Many of Navalny's supporters believe his real crimes were organizing protests in Moscow in 2011 and 2012, blogging and running a nonprofit group that operates websites that allow citizens to report incidents of government corruption.

Navalny, who announced on April 4 that he will run for president, is not the only activist to come under pressure from Russia's government. Since Vladimir Putin returned to the presidency last May, new restrictions have been imposed on Internet content, and fines of up to $32,000 have been imposed for participating in protests deemed illegal.

International nonprofit groups such as Amnesty International, Human Rights Watch and Transparency International have been ordered to register as foreign agents. All have refused, and their offices recently have been raided by government investigators.

Last month, Dmitry Gudkov, an opposition politician and one of only two members of the Russian parliament to support public protests such as those organized by Navalny, was accused of treason by some of his colleagues after he visited the United States in March. Gudkov's father was stripped of his seat in parliament last fall.

While cracking down on opposition voices, Putin's government has been able to rely on friendly state-run media coverage, including from Channel One, the nation's most widely watched television station. During his U.S. visit, Gudkov noted that Russian state-controlled media had accused him of treason and selling secrets.

While some countries try to crack down on independent media outlets through intimidation, Russia for the most part controls communications directly, with the state or its friends owning most of the major newspapers and broadcasters.

Arch Puddington, vice president for research at Freedom House, a Washington-based watchdog group, says what he calls the "Putin model" is widely practiced. "They buy television stations and turn them into mouthpieces of the government," he says.

It's a case of, "If you can't beat them, buy them," says Anthony Mills, deputy director of the International Press Institute in Austria.

Russia is not alone. In some Central Asian and Latin American countries, government-owned media are commonly used for propaganda and to negate foreign criticism.

In Turkey, most of the media are controlled by a few private companies, which leads more to collusion than intimidation, says former Rep. Tom Perriello, D-Va. "In Turkey, you have less of the situation of people being shaken down [or threatened] if they print this story," he says. "Instead, many of the TV companies are doing contracts with the government, so there's a financial interest in not wanting to irritate people in the . . . government."

In other countries, antagonism is the norm. According to Freedom House, Ecuadoran President Rafael Correa has

---

One case led to the famous formulation of Justice Oliver Wendell Holmes. "The most stringent protection of free speech would not protect a man in falsely shouting 'fire' in a crowded theater and creating a panic," Holmes wrote in his dissent in *Schenck v. U.S.* in 1919. "The question in every case is whether the words used are used in such circumstances and are of such a nature to create a clear and present danger that they will bring about the substantive evils that Congress has a right to prevent."

Although fewer dissenters were prosecuted during World War II there were still dozens. "The Roosevelt administration investigated suspects for their 'un-American' associations and employed a variety of legal devices to harass the dissenters and suppress the dissent," writes historian Richard W. Steele.[31]

During the 1940s and '50s, Congress did what it could to ban Communist Party activities in the United States, but after World War II, the sense that free speech was an inalienable right took deep hold in the

called the press his "greatest political enemy," which he says is "ignorant," "mediocre," "primitive," "bloodthirsty" and "deceitful."[2]

"Ecuador under its president of the last five years, Rafael Correa, has become one of the world's leading oppressors of free speech," Peter Hartcher, international editor for *The Sydney Morning Herald*, wrote last summer. "Correa has appropriated, closed and intimidated many media outlets critical of his government. He has sued journalists for crippling damages."[3]

Analysts say the Venezuelan government tries to own or control nearly all media, while vilifying and jailing independent journalists.

And in Russia, government harassment of independent voices is common. Only a few independent outlets operate, such as *Novaya Gazeta*, a newspaper co-owned by former Soviet President Mikhail Gorbachev, but they aren't widely read or heard except by law enforcement agencies that often arrest, beat and — according to watchdog groups — even kill journalists.[4]

The 2006 killing of Anna Politkovskaya, a *Novaya Gazeta* reporter noted for her coverage of the Chechen conflict, drew international attention, although no one has been convicted of her murder. "Russia is among the most dangerous countries in which to be a journalist," says Rajan Menon, a political scientist at City College of New York. "Many journalists end up dead, assaulted or threatened for looking into hot-button issues, especially corruption."

Russian activist Aleksei Navalny, a leading critic of President Vladimir Putin, addresses an anti-Putin rally in St. Petersburg on Feb. 12, 2012.

AFP/Getty Images/Olga Maltseva

In some countries, state-owned media criticize their own governments, says Robert Mahoney, deputy director of the Committee to Protect Journalists, citing the example of the BBC. But when nearly all media are owned by a few individuals or companies, it's not "good in the long term for a diverse and vibrant free press," he says.

Nor is it good when journalists fear they might be killed for digging into stories. In Russia, for instance, journalists are routinely killed with impunity. "There are 17 cases where journalists were killed in the last dozen years or so," Mahoney says, "and there have been no prosecutions."

— *Alan Greenblatt*

[1] Andrew E. Kramer, "With Trial Suddenly Looming, Russian Activist Expects the Worst," *The New York Times*, March 28, 2013, p. A4, www.nytimes.com/2013/03/28/world/europe/with-case-reopened-the-russian-activist-aleksei-navalny-expects-the-worst.html.

[2] "Freedom of the Press 2011: Ecuador," Freedom House, Sept. 1, 2011, www.freedomhouse.org/report/freedom-press/2011/ecuador.

[3] Peter Hartcher, "Hypocrisy Ends Hero's Freedom to Preach," *The Sydney Morning Herald*, Aug. 21, 2012, www.smh.com.au/opinion/politics/hypocrisy-ends-heros-freedom-to-preach-20120820-24ijx.html.

[4] Peter Preston, "Putin's win is a hollow victory for a Russian free press," *The Guardian*, March 10, 2012, www.guardian.co.uk/media/2012/mar/11/putin-win-russian-free-press.

country and the courts. It was even included in Article 19 of the Universal Declaration of Human Rights, adopted by the United Nations in 1948, which says: "Everyone has the right to freedom of opinion and expression; this right includes freedom to hold opinions without interference and to seek, receive and impart information and ideas through any media and regardless of frontiers."[32]

A series of lectures by American free-speech advocate Alexander Meiklejohn published in 1948 was hugely influential as a defense of the notion that free speech and democracy are intertwined. "The phrase 'Congress shall make no law . . . abridging the freedom of speech,' is unqualified," Meiklejohn wrote. "It admits of no exceptions. . . . That prohibition holds good in war and peace, in danger as in security."[33]

In the 1960s, the U.S. Supreme Court protected racist speech, as well as speech by advocates of integration. "A decision protecting speech by a Ku Klux Klan member cited a decision that protected an African-American

China Opens Up — But Just a Crack

Journalists' and dissenters' activities are still monitored.

It's been decades now since China opened up to the West. But it's still not completely open, especially with regard to freedom of speech and the press.

In recent months, angered by coverage it viewed as hostile, such as reports that the families of top government officials have enriched themselves while the officials have been in power, China has denied entry visas to reporters from media organizations such as *The New York Times*, Al-Jazeera English and Reuters.

Since October, it has blocked access within China to *The Times'* website, while Chinese hackers have broken into email accounts belonging to reporters from *The Times* and *The Wall Street Journal*, possibly to determine the sources of stories critical of government officials.

China has long maintained a "Great Firewall," blocking its citizens from accessing critical content from foreign sources. But the Chinese government is also at pains to block internal criticism from its own citizens and media, as well.

In any given year, China typically ranks in the world's top two or three countries in terms of how many journalists it imprisons.[1] "There's a certain level of very localized dissent allowed, but it can never be expressed directly at the regime," says Padraig Reidy, news editor for Index on Censorship, a free-speech advocacy group.

"You can say a local official is corrupt — maybe," Reidy says. "But you can't say the party is corrupt. That's the end of you."

Besides tracking journalists' activities, China's government also monitors activists' online postings. A recent study by computer scientist Dan Wallach of Rice University and several colleagues found that China could be employing more than 4,000 censors to monitor the 70,000 posts per minute uploaded to Weibo, the Chinese version of Twitter.[2]

The censors tend to track known activists and use automated programs to hunt for forbidden phrases. "Certain words you know are never going to get out of the gate," Wallach says. "Falun Gong" — a spiritual practice China has sought to ban — "those three characters you can't utter on any Chinese website anywhere in the country."

Weibo users are "incredibly clever" at coming up with misspellings and neologisms to sneak past the censors, Wallach says. For instance, a colloquial phrase for China, the Celestial Temple, is sometimes rewritten as "celestial bastard," using similar-looking characters.

But once such usage becomes widespread, the censors are quick to catch on and such terms also are quickly eradicated from websites. "China is definitely the market leader in technical tools for clamping down on free expression," says British journalist John Kampfner.

Aside from imprisonment and hacking attacks, China uses self-censorship to suppress criticism of the state, says Robert Mahoney, deputy director of the New York-based Committee to Protect Journalists. Reporters and others constantly worry about what sort of statements could trigger a crackdown.

"With self-censoring, journalists tend to be more conservative," Mahoney says. Such sensitivity to what censors will think extends even to Hollywood movies. Given the

---

antiwar state legislator, and the case of the klansman was, in turn, cited [in 1989] to protect a radical who burned the American flag as a political protest," writes Wake Forest law professor Michael Kent Curtis.[34]

In 1964, the Supreme Court limited libel suits brought by public officials, finding that the First Amendment required "actual malice" — that is, knowledge that information published was false.[35] Seven years later, a lower court blocked *The New York Times* from publish further portions of the Pentagon Papers, a government history of the Vietnam War — the first example in U.S. history of prior restraint.

The Supreme Court lifted the injunction. Justice Hugo Black wrote, "In revealing the workings of government that led to the Vietnam War, the newspapers nobly did precisely that which the Founders hoped and trusted they would do."[36]

After a long period of expansion, press freedoms and other civil liberties were challenged following the terrorist attacks of Sept. 11, 2001. Once again, free speech was

growing importance of the Chinese film market, the country's censors now review scripts and inspect sets of movies filmed in China to make sure that nothing offends their sensibilities.

"There were points where we were shooting with a crew of 500 people," said Rob Cohen, director of "The Mummy: Tomb of the Dragon Emperor," which kicked off a recent wave of co-productions between Chinese companies and American studios. "I'm not sure who was who or what, but knowing the way the system works, it's completely clear that had we deviated from the script, it would not have gone unnoticed."[3] The Academy Award-winning "Django Unchained" was initially cut to delete scenes of extreme violence, but censors blocked its scheduled April 12 release due to shots of full-frontal nudity.

In addition to carefully inspecting Western content coming into the country, China is seeking to export its model for rigid media control to other countries. "It's fascinating to look at Chinese investment in Africa," says Anthony Mills, deputy director of the Austria-based International Press Institute. "They've bought into a variety of media outlets in Africa."

While China can't impose censorship in Africa, its control of media outlets there helps ensure favorable coverage. Beijing is actively promoting its image abroad through news-content deals with state-owned media in countries including Zimbabwe, Nigeria, Cuba, Malaysia and Turkey, according to the South African Institute of International Affairs. "Countries that need Chinese trade, aid and recognition, and those with tense relations with the U.S., are more likely to be influenced by China's soft power," the institute concluded in a report last year.[4]

"China has this model in which the economic welfare and the perceived welfare of the state as a whole trump individual freedoms," Mills says.

Some Western observers, such as Reidy, believe China will eventually have to become more open, because capitalist investment demands a free flow of information.

But others wonder whether China's more authoritarian approach represents a challenge to the transatlantic model that has been fairly dominant around the globe since World War II, with freedom of expression seen as essential to democracy and economic growth.

Already, says former Rep. Tom Perriello, D-Va., residents of countries such as Turkey complain less about individual freedoms while the economy is growing.

"If you actually get to a point where China is associated with economic prosperity more than Western countries are, then people look differently at democracy and human rights," he says. "I wish they didn't, but that's part of the fear, that we can't assume there's this natural march toward more liberalism."

— Alan Greenblatt

---

[1]Madeline Earp, "Disdain for Foreign Press Undercuts China's Global Ambition," Committee to Protect Journalists, March 11, 2013, www.cpj.org/2013/02/attacks-on-the-press-china-tightens-control.php.

[2]"Computer Scientists Measure the Speed of Censorship on China's Twitter," *The Physics arXiv Blog*, March 6, 2013, www.technologyreview.com/view/512231/computer-scientists-measure-the-speed-of-censorship-on-chinas-twitter.

[3]Michael Cieply and Brooks Barnes, "To Get Movies Into China, Hollywood Gives Censors a Preview," *The New York Times*, Jan. 15, 2013, p. A1, www.nytimes.com/2013/01/15/business/media/in-hollywood-movies-for-china-bureaucrats-want-a-say.html.

[4]Yu-Shan Wu, "The Rise of China's State-Led Media Dynasty in Africa," South African Institute of International Affairs, June 2012, p. 11, www.saiia.org.za/images/stories/pubs/occasional_papers_above_100/saia_sop_%20117_wu_20120618.pdf.

---

seen as possibly undermining the government at a time when security concerns had become paramount. "Press freedoms are positively correlated with greater transnational terrorism," write University of Chicago law professor Posner and Harvard University law professor Adrian Vermeule. "Nations with a free press are more likely to be targets of such terrorism."[37]

For example, they cited a 2005 *New York Times* story on the so-called warrantless wiretapping program at the National Security Agency, which they argue alerted

terrorists that the United States was monitoring communications the terrorists believed were secure.[38] The Bush administration made similar arguments to The *Times*, which held the story until after the 2004 presidential election.

Worried that the administration would seek a federal court injunction to block publication, *The Times* first published the story on its website. "In the new digital world of publishing, there were no printing presses to stop," notes Samuel Walker, a University of Nebraska law professor.[39]

Ku Klux Klan members in Pulaski, Tenn., participate in a march honoring Nathan Bedford Forrest, a Confederate general who helped found the Klan, on July 11, 2009. The U.S. Supreme Court has ruled that even hate groups like the Klan have a constitutional right to express their racist views publicly.

CURRENT SITUATION

Government Secrets

With so much speech, commerce — and terrorist activity — taking place online, Congress is struggling to find an appropriate balance between security on the one hand and privacy and free-speech concerns on the other.

On April 18, the House passed the Cyber Intelligence Sharing and Protection Act, known by the acronym CISPA. The bill would give military and security agencies greater access to Americans' online activity by making it easier for private companies to share cyberthreat information with the government, allowing government and businesses to help each other out when they get hacked.

The nation's networks are already under attack from countries such as Iran and Russia, Texas GOP Rep. Michael McCaul, chair of the House Homeland Security Committee, told his colleagues during floor debate.[40]

"I think if anything, the recent events in Boston demonstrate that we have to come together to get this done," McCaul said, referring to the bombs that exploded near the finish line of the Boston Marathon three days earlier. "In the case of Boston, they were real bombs. In this case, they're digital bombs."[41]

But the bill's opponents said it represented a violation of privacy and free-speech rights, giving government agencies such as the FBI and CIA easy access to online accounts without warrants, chilling free expression. On April 16, the Obama administration threatened to veto the bill, if it were to reach the president's desk.[42]

The bill would allow Internet companies "to ship the whole kit and caboodle" of personal information to the government, including that which does not pertain directly to cyberthreats and "is none of the government's business," said California Rep. Nancy Pelosi, Democratic leader of the House.[43]

"I am disappointed. . . we did not address the concerns of the White House about personal information," Pelosi said. "It offers no policies and did not allow any amendments and no real solutions to uphold Americans' right to privacy."

The measure now goes to the U.S. Senate. A similar bill was unable to muster enough Senate votes last year to overcome a filibuster, and this year's outcome is uncertain.

Information Explosion

The explosion of information on the Internet and in online databases has made legal concerns about free speech more complicated, says Randall Bezanson, a law professor at the University of Iowa. For most of U.S. history, such concerns turned largely on the question of whether the government had the power to censor speech. Now, he says, regulating speech involves the government not just quashing the speech of individuals but in protecting documents and databases — its own, and others — from disclosure.

The Obama administration has learned that lesson well, he says, and is doing its best to keep state secrets secret. "Eric Holder, attorney general under President Barack Obama, has prosecuted more government officials for alleged leaks under the World War I-era Espionage Act than all his predecessors combined," Bloomberg News reported last fall.[44]

The administration was disturbed by the leak of thousands of diplomatic cables, which were published in 2010 by the whistleblower website Wiki-Leaks, founded by former Australian computer hacker Julian Assange.[45]

"The Julian Assange episode and those disclosures of pretty well unfiltered information, I think, scared people in government and raised a whole different specter of

Should journalists be regulated?

YES
Steven Barnett
Professor of Communications, University of Westminster, London, England

Written for *CQ Researcher*, April 2013

In an ideal world, a free press should not be constrained any more than free speech. Unfortunately, this is not an ideal world. Would-be terrorists seek to recruit supporters, grossly offensive material can reap huge financial rewards and some publications try to boost circulation and scoop competitors using immoral and even downright malicious methods.

Some methods, such as hacking into voicemails, are illegal in Britain. Others are not. Public outrage was sparked by atrocious behaviour that some British newspapers have sanctioned in the name of "journalism," such as splashing on the front page the private and intimate diaries of Kate McCann after the disappearance of her daughter Madeleine. Although Mrs. McCann begged the *News of the World* not to publish the diaries, the newspaper ignored her pleas. Such callous indifference to people's feelings had become institutionalized in some of Britain's best-selling newspapers.

What is required is not state control or statutory regulation. But the press must be held accountable for egregious abuses of its own privileged position within a democracy.

In the United Kingdom, Sir Brian Leveson, who chaired a judicial inquiry into press practices and ethics as a result of the phone-hacking scandal, recommended the moderate solution of voluntary self-regulation overseen by an autonomous body that would assess whether self-regulation was effective and independent. If so, news organizations choosing to belong would be entitled to financial incentives such as lower court costs and exemption from exemplary damages if sued. It is, I repeat, a voluntary incentive-based system, which is needed to protect ordinary people from amoral and sometimes vindictive practices that have no place in journalism.

Such proposals might feel uncomfortable in the land of the First Amendment, but it is exceptionally mild by European standards. In Finland, a Freedom of Expression Act mandates, among other things, that aggrieved parties have a right of reply or correction without undue delay. In Germany, newspapers are required to print corrections with the same prominence as the original report. Scandinavian countries have passed legislation on press ethics.

These countries are not rampant dictatorships. But they all, as will Britain, find a proper balance between unconstrained journalism and the rights of ordinary people not to have their misery peddled for corporate profit.

NO
Anthony Mills
Deputy Director, International Press Institute, Vienna, Austria

Written for *CQ Researcher*, April 2013

In any healthy democracy, the media play a watchdog role, holding elected officials accountable and serving the public interest by satisfying citizens' right to know what is being done in their name in the often not-so-transparent corridors of power. In the United States, for instance, the Watergate scandal was unearthed and covered, at not inconsiderable risk, by two young *Washington Post* reporters.

Not surprisingly, there are those in office for whom such media scrutiny is, to put it mildly, unwelcome. And, lo and behold, they become advocates for state regulation of the media. They may very well point to one or more examples of egregious, even criminal, journalist behavior as evidence of the need to exert greater control.

No one suggests that journalists are above the law. But when they engage in criminal behavior, they should be held accountable in criminal courts. The profession must not be overseen by the very elected officials whom it is supposed to hold to account. Surely, from the perspective of the politicians, that would be a conflict of interest.

The answer is self-regulation. That could be accomplished through independent regulatory bodies with the teeth to hold journalists ethically accountable or through ethical standards rigorously and systematically imposed by media outlets themselves as is the case in the United States, where the First Amendment right to freedom of the press is fiercely guarded. Professional peers must lead by example.

In the absence of self-regulation, or where it is not effectively implemented, the path is easily paved for statutory regulation, whether direct, or roundabout, in form. The aftermath of the *News of the World* phone-hacking scandal in the U.K., and the ensuing inquiry by Lord Justice Leveson, have amply demonstrated this. The U.K. press is set to be bound by statutory legislation for the first time in hundreds of years. That cannot be healthy for democracy, and other countries tend to follow the lead of their democratic "peers."

So it is incumbent upon everyone in the profession to resist any efforts to impose statutory regulation of the press by those upon whom the press is supposed to be keeping its watchful eye. But it falls upon the press to ensure that the standards it embraces are of the highest order of professionalism and integrity. Anything less offers cannon fodder for those targeting a free media.

what could be done and what the consequences are, and that has probably triggered a more aggressive approach in the Justice Department," Bezanson says.

On Feb. 28, Army Pfc. Bradley Manning, who leaked thousands of diplomatic, military and intelligence cables to WikiLeaks, pleaded guilty to 10 charges of illegally acquiring and transferring government secrets, agreeing to spend 20 years in prison. Manning pleaded not guilty, however, to 12 additional counts — including espionage — and faces a general court-martial in June.

Manning's case has made him a cause célèbre among some on the left who see him as being unduly persecuted. A similar dynamic is playing out in memory of American online activist and pioneer Aaron Swartz, who committed suicide in January while facing charges that could carry a 35-year prison sentence in a case involving his downloading of copyrighted academic journals.

In March, the entire editorial board of the *Journal of Library Administration* resigned over what one member described as "a crisis of conscience" over the 26-year-old Swartz's death.[46] The librarians were concerned not only about the Swartz case but the larger issue of access to journal articles, feeling that publishers were becoming entirely too restrictive in their terms of use.

In general, Bezanson says, courts are becoming less accepting of the idea that "information wants to be free," as the Internet-era slogan has it. The courts are not only more supportive of copyright holders but seemingly more skeptical about free speech in general, with the Supreme Court in recent cases having curbed some of the free-speech rights it had afforded to students and hate groups in previous decisions.

"The doctrine of the First Amendment is going to be more forgiving of regulated speech," Bezanson says.

Regulating the Press?

In other countries, concern is growing that freedom of speech and of the press have been badly abused in recent years. A phone-hacking scandal involving the *News of the World*, a British tabloid, shocked the United Kingdom in 2011 and has led to more than 30 arrests, as well as a high-profile inquiry chaired by Sir Brian Leveson, then Britain's senior appeals judge. Leveson's report, released in November, called for a new, independent body to replace the Press Complaints Commission, the news industry's self-regulating agency. The recommendations

triggered difficult negotiations among leaders of the United Kingdom's coalition government, which announced a compromise deal in March.

"While Lord Leveson was quite correct to call for a regulator with more muscle that can impose substantial fines for future misconduct, [Prime Minister] David Cameron pledged that he would resist the clamor for such measures to be backed by law," the *Yorkshire Post* editorialized. "Given that to do so would be to take the first step on the slippery slope toward censorship of the press, a weapon that has been employed by many a corrupt dictatorship around the globe, he was right to do so."[47]

The U.K. is not the only country considering new media regulations. In March, Australia's government proposed tighter regulation of media ownership and a new media overseer with statutory authority. "Australians want the press to be as accountable as they want politicians, sports people and business people," said Stephen Conroy, Australia's communications minister.[48]

Media executives argued that the proposals were draconian and amounted to the government's revenge for hostile coverage. "For the first time in Australian history outside wartime, there will be political oversight over the conduct of journalism in this country," said Greg Hywood, the CEO of Fairfax Media.[49]

In response to such criticisms, Australia's government quickly withdrew the proposals.

Reporters Under Attack

If journalists, commentators, artists and writers are feeling embattled in the English-speaking world, they face worse fates elsewhere. According to the Committee to Protect Journalists, 232 journalists around the world were imprisoned as of Dec. 1 — the highest total since the group began its survey work in 1990. And 70 journalists were killed while doing their jobs in 2012 — a 43 percent increase from the year before.[50]

According to the group, 49 journalists were imprisoned in Turkey alone in 2012, a record high, and more than were in jail in either Iran or China. Francis J. Ricciardone, the U.S. ambassador to Turkey, has been openly critical about the country's approach to free speech. "The responsibility of Turkey's friends and allies is to . . . to point out, with due respect, the importance of progress in the protection of freedom of expression for journalists and blog writers," State Department spokeswoman Victoria Nuland said at a news conference in February.[51]

In India freedom of expression is enshrined in the constitution, but with many provisos. And lately, India's judiciary has appeared to show little concern when the government has arrested people over their Facebook posts and remarks made at literary festivals. "Writers and artists of all kinds are being harassed, sued and arrested for what they say or write or create," writes Suketu Mehta, a journalism professor at New York University. "The government either stands by and does nothing to protect freedom of speech, or it actively abets its suppression."[52]

India — the world's most populous democracy — has slipped below Qatar and Afghanistan in Reporters Without Borders' press freedom index.[53]

In emerging economic powerhouses such as Turkey and India, along with Brazil, Mexico, South Africa and Indonesia, governments are "kind of floating" between two different models, says Kampfner, the *Freedom for Sale* author: the open-society approach favored by transatlantic democracies and a more authoritarian approach.

"I slightly fear it's going in the wrong direction in all of them," Kampfner says.

But there also have been signs recently that things may be improving in places for free-speech advocates. On April 1, for the first time in half a century, privately owned daily newspapers hit newsstands in Myanmar.[54]

In Syria, new newspapers have emerged to cover the civil war, countering bias from both government-controlled media and opposition-friendly satellite channels based in Qatar and Saudi Arabia.

"We need to get out of this Facebook phase, where all we do is whine and complain about the regime," said Absi Smesem, editor-in-chief of *Sham*, a new weekly newspaper.[55]

OUTLOOK

Shame, Not Laws?

It's always impossible to predict the future, but it's especially difficult when discussing free speech, which is now inextricably bound up with constantly changing technologies.

"I don't know what's next," says Reidy, the Index on Censorship news editor. "None of us five years ago

thought we would be spending our lives on Twitter." Still, Reidy says, the fact that so many people are conversing online makes them likely to equate blocking the Internet with more venerable forms of censorship, such as book burning.

"Within the next five years, you will have a lot of adults in the Western world who literally don't know what life is like without the Internet," he says. "That is bound to change attitudes and cultures."

Information technology is penetrating deeper into the developing world, says Kampfner, the British journalist and author. For instance, thanks to mobile technology African farmers can access more information they need about crop yields and prices. And with cell phones, everyone has better access to information on disasters.

However, "In terms of changing the political discourse, the jury is out," Kampfner says. "Every new technology, by its nature, is open to both use and abuse."

Activists wanting to use technology to spread information and governments trying to stop them play an ongoing "cat and mouse game," says Galperin, of the Electronic Frontier Foundation.

Given how easily commercial applications can track individuals' specific interests and movements online, it's not difficult to imagine that political speech will be tracked as well, Belarus-born writer and researcher Evgeny Morozov, a contributing editor at *The New Republic* and a columnist for *Slate*, contends in his 2011 book *The Net Delusion*. It's not the case, as some have argued, he says, that the need to keep the Internet open for commercial purposes will prevent regimes from stamping out other forms of online discourse.

"In the not so distant future, a banker perusing nothing but Reuters and *Financial Times*, and with other bankers as her online friends, would be left alone to do anything she wants, even browse Wikipedia pages about human-rights violations," he writes. "In contrast, a person of unknown occupation, who is occasionally reading *Financial Times* but is also connected to five well-known political activists through Facebook and who has written blog comments that included words like 'democracy' and 'freedom,' would only be allowed to visit government-run websites, or . . . to surf but be carefully monitored."[56]

In democratic nations, concerns about security and offending religious believers could lead to more restrictions — although not necessarily in terms of new laws, says Arch Puddington, vice president for research at Freedom House, but through shaming and "other informal methods" of disciplining unpopular ways of speaking.

"What you could have over the next 10 years in the U.S. and abroad is a distinction between rights and norms," says former Rep. Perriello, at the Center for American Progress Action Fund. "Having a legal right to say certain things does not actually mean one should say certain things."

Anthony Mills, the deputy director of the International Press Institute in Austria, suggests that the more things change, the more they will stay recognizably the same. "Unfortunately, in 10 years we'll still be having similar conversations about efforts by everyone from criminals to militants and government operatives to target the media and silence them," Mills says.

"But at the same time, . . . a variety of media platforms — of journalists and of media practitioners — will continue to defy that trend," he says. "I have no doubt that in the grand scheme of things, the truth will always come out. The dynamic of the flow of information is unstoppable."

Wallach, the Rice University computer scientist, is equally certain that despite all legal, political and technological ferment, the basic underlying tension between free expression and repressive tendencies will remain firmly in place.

"There will always be people with something to say and ways for them to say it," Wallach says. Likewise, "There will also always be people who want to stop them."

NOTES

1. Jonathan Turley, "Shut Up and Play Nice," *The Washington Post*, Oct. 14, 2012, p. B1, http://articles.washingtonpost.com/2012-10-12/opinions/35499274_1_free-speech-defeat-jihad-muslim-man.

2. For background, see Peter Katel, "Protecting Whistleblowers," *CQ Researcher*, March 31, 2006, pp. 265-288.

3. "Memorandum to the European Union on Media Freedom in Hungary," Human Rights Watch, Feb. 16, 2012, www.hrw.org/node/105200.

4. For background, see Kenneth Jost, "Unrest in the Arab World," *CQ Researcher*, Feb. 1, 2013, pp. 105-132; and Roland Flamini, "Turmoil in the Arab World," *CQ Global Researcher*, May 3, 2011, pp. 209-236.

5. Tom Gjelten, "Shutdowns Counter the Idea of a World-Wide Web," NPR, Dec. 1, 2012, www.npr.org/2012/12/01/166286596/shutdowns-raise-issue-of-who-controls-the-internet.

6. Jessica Chasmar, "French Jewish Group Sues Twitter Over Racist, Anti-Semitic Tweets," *The Washington Times*, March 24, 2013, www.washingtontimes.com/news/2013/mar/24/french-jewish-group-sues-twitter-over-racist-anti-.

7. Jean-Paul Marthoz, "Extremists Are Censoring the Story of Religion," Committee to Protect Journalists, Feb. 14, 2013, www.cpj.org/2013/02/attacks-on-the-press-journalism-and-religion.php. See also, Frank Greve, "Combat Journalism," *CQ Researcher*, April 12, 2013, pp. 329-352.

8. Chris York, "Pussy Riot Member Yekaterina Samutsevich Freed on Probation by Moscow Court," *The Huffington Post UK*, Oct. 10, 2012, www.huffingtonpost.co.uk/2012/10/10/pussy-riot-member-yekaterina-samutsevich-frees-probation-moscow-court_n_1953725.html.

9. Ethan Zuckerman, "The First Twitter Revolution?" *Foreign Policy*, Jan. 14, 2011, www.foreignpolicy.com/articles/2011/01/14/the_first_twitter_revolution.

10. Thomas Fuller, "E-mails of Reporters in Myanmar Are Hacked," *The New York Times*, Feb. 10, 2013, www.nytimes.com/2013/02/11/world/asia/journalists-e-mail-accounts-targeted-in-myanmar.html.

11. Yves Alexandre de Mountjoye, *et al.*, "Unique in the Crowd: The Privacy Bounds of Human Mobility," *Nature*, March 25, 2013, www.nature.com/srep/2013/130325/srep01376/full/srep01376.html.

12. Thomas Erdbrink, "Iran Blocks Way to Bypass Internet Filtering System," *The New York Times*, March 11, 2013, www.nytimes.com/2013/03/12/world/middleeast/iran-blocks-software-used-to-bypass-internet-filtering-system.html.

13. Andrew Higgins, "Danish Opponent of Islam Is Attacked, and Muslims Defend His Right to Speak," *The New York Times*, Feb. 28, 2013, p. A8, www.nytimes.com/2013/02/28/world/europe/lars-hedegaard-anti-islamic-provocateur-receives-support-from-danish-muslims.html.

14. Kenan Malik and Nada Shabout, "Should Religious or Cultural Sensibilities Ever Limit Free Expression?" Index on Censorship, March 25, 2013, www.indexoncensorship.org/2013/03/should-religious-or-cultural-sensibilities-ever-limit-free-expression/.

15. "Freedom of Thought 2012: A Global Report on Discrimination Against Humanists, Atheists and the Nonreligious," International Humanist and Ethical Union, Dec. 10, 2012, p. 11, http://iheu.org/files/IHEU%20Freedom%20of%20Thought%202012.pdf.

16. Asim Tanveer, "Pakistani Man Accuses Ambassador to U.S. of Blasphemy," Reuters, Feb. 21, 2013, http://news.yahoo.com/pakistan-accuses-ambassador-u-blasphemy-124213305.html.

17. Huma Yusuf, "The Censors' Salon," *Latitude*, March 14, 2013, http://latitude.blogs.nytimes.com/2013/03/14/in-lahore-pakistan-the-censors-salon/.

18. See "Speech to the United Nations General Assembly —"Practical progress towards realising those ideals in the world," Sept. 26, 2012, www.pm.gov.au/press-office/speech-united-nations-general-assembly-%E2%80%9Cpractical-progress-towards-realising-those-idea.

19. Turley, *op. cit.*

20. Aryeh Neier, "Freedom, Blasphemy and Violence," Project Syndicate, Sept. 16, 2012, www.project-syndicate.org/commentary/freedom--blasphemy--and-violence-by-aryeh-neier.

21. C. W. Nevius, "Free Speech Protects Offensive Ads on Muni," *The San Francisco Chronicle*, March 14, 2013, p. D1, www.sfgate.com/bayarea/nevius/article/Offensive-ads-on-Muni-protected-speech-4352829.php.

22. Clinton's remarks are available at www.state.gov/secretary/rm/2011/12/178511.htm.

23. Obama's remarks are available at www.whitehouse.gov/the-press-office/2012/09/25/remarks-president-un-general-assembly.

24. Anthea Butler, "Opposing View: Why 'Sam Bacile' Deserves Arrest," *USA Today*, Sept. 13, 2012, http://usatoday30.usatoday.com/news/opinion/story/2012-09-12/Sam-Bacile-Anthea-Butler/57769732/1.

25. Eric Posner, "The World Doesn't Love the First Amendment," *Slate*, Sept. 25, 2012, www.slate.com/articles/news_and_politics/jurisprudence/2012/09/the_vile_anti_muslim_video_and_the_first_amendment_does_the_u_s_overvalue_free_speech_.single.html.

26. Eyder Peralta, "John Kerry to German Students: Americans Have 'Right to Be Stupid,'" NPR, Feb. 26, 2013, www.npr.org/blogs/thetwo-way/2013/02/26/172980860/john-kerry-to-german-students-americans-have-right-to-be-stupid.

27. Rodney A. Smolla, *Free Speech in an Open Society* (1992), p. 4.

28. Robert Hargreaves, *The First Freedom* (2002), p. 5.

29. *Ibid.*, p. 51.

30. *Ibid.*, p. 95.

31. Richard W. Steele, *Free Speech in the Good War* (1999), p. 1.

32. See "The Universal Declaration of Human Rights," United Nations, www.un.org/en/documents/udhr/index.shtml#a19.

33. Alexander Meiklejohn, *Free Speech and Its Relation to Self-Government* (1948), p. 17.

34. Michael Kent Curtis, *Free Speech, 'The People's Darling Privilege': Struggles for Freedom of Expression in American History* (2000), p. 406.

35. David W. Rabban, *Free Speech in Its Forgotten Years* (1997), p. 372.

36. "Supreme Court, 6-3, Upholds Newspapers on Publication of Pentagon Report," *The New York Times*, July 1, 1971, www.nytimes.com/books/97/04/13/reviews/papers-final.html.

37. Eric A. Posner and Adrian Vermeule, *Terror in the Balance: Security, Liberty, and the Courts* (2007), p. 26.

38. James Risen and Eric Lichtblau, "Bush Lets U.S. Spy on Callers Without Courts," *The New York Times*, Dec. 16, 2005, www.nytimes.com/2005/12/16/politics/16program.html.

39. Samuel Walker, *Presidents and Civil Liberties From Wilson to Obama: A Story of Poor Custodians* (2012), p. 468.

40. For background, see Roland Flamini, "Improving Cybersecurity," *CQ Researcher*, Feb. 15, 2013, pp. 157-180.

41. Karen McVeigh and Dominic Rushe, "House Passes CISPA Cybersecurity Bill Despite Warnings From White House," *The Guardian*, April 18, 2013, www.guardian.co.uk/technology/2013/apr/18/house-representatives-cispa-cybersecurity-white-house-warning.

42. See the "Statement of Administration Policy" at www.whitehouse.gov/sites/default/files/omb/legislative/sap/113/saphr624r_20130416.pdf.

43. McVeigh and Rushe, *op. cit.*

44. Phil Mattingly and Hans Nichols, "Obama Pursuing Leakers Sends Warning to Whistle-Blowers," Bloomberg News, Oct. 17, 2012, www.bloomberg.com/news/2012-10-18/obama-pursuing-leakers-sends-warning-to-whistle-blowers.html.

45. For background, see Alex Kingsbury, "Government Secrecy," *CQ Researcher*, Feb. 11, 2011, pp. 121-144.

46. Russell Brandom, "Entire Library Journal Editorial Board Resigns," *The Verge*, March 26, 2013, www.theverge.com/2013/3/26/4149752/library-journal-resigns-for-open-access-citing-aaron-swartz.

47. "A Vital Test for Democracy," *Yorkshire Press*, March 19, 2013, www.yorkshirepost.co.uk/news/debate/yp-comment/a-vital-test-for-our-democracy-1-5505331.

48. Sabra Lane, "Stephen Conroy Defends Media Change Package," Australian Broadcasting Company, March 13, 2013, www.abc.net.au/am/content/2013/s3714163.htm.

49. Nick Bryant, "Storm Over Australia's Press Reform Proposals," BBC, March 19, 2013, www.bbc.co.uk/news/world-asia-21840076.

50. Rick Gladstone, "Report Sees Journalists Increasingly Under Attack," *The New York Times*, Feb. 15, 2013, p. A10, www.nytimes.com/2013/02/15/world/attacks-on-journalists-rose-in-2012-group-finds.html.

51. "U.S.: American Ambassador to Turkey Reiterating What Clinton Previously Said," *Today's Zaman*, Feb. 7, 2013, www.todayszaman.com/news-306435-us-american-ambassador-to-turkey-reiterating-what-clinton-previously-said.html.

52. Suketu Mehta, "India's Speech Impediments," *The New York Times*, Feb. 6, 2013, www.nytimes.com/2013/02/06/opinion/indias-limited-freedom-of-speech.html.

53. "Press Freedom Index 2013," Reporters Without Borders, fr.rsf.org/IMG/pdf/classement_2013_gb-bd.pdf.

54. Aye Aye Win, "Privately Owned Daily Newspapers Return to Myanmar," The Associated Press, April 1, 2013, www.huffingtonpost.com/huff-wires/20130401/as-myanmar-new-newspapers/.

55. Neil MacFarquhar, "Syrian Newspapers Emerge to Fill Out War Reporting," *The New York Times*, April 2, 2013, p. A4, www.nytimes.com/2013/04/02/world/middleeast/syrian-newspapers-emerge-to-fill-out-war-reporting.html.

56. Eugeny Morozov, *The Net Delusion* (2011), p. 97.

BIBLIOGRAPHY

Selected Sources

Books

Ghonim, Wael, *Revolution 2.0: The Power of the People Is Greater Than the People in Power*, Houghton Mifflin Harcourt, 2012.
A Google employee who became a leader in using social media to organize protests against the government in Egypt during the so-called Arab Spring of 2011 writes a memoir about those tumultuous times.

Hargreaves, Robert, *The First Freedom: A History of Free Speech*, Sutton Publishing, 2002.
The late British broadcaster surveys the long history of speech, from Socrates to modern times, highlighting the personalities and legal cases that eventually led to greater liberties.

Kampfner, John, *Freedom for Sale: Why the World Is Trading Democracy for Security*, Basic Books, 2010.

Visiting countries such as Russia, China, Italy and the United States, a British journalist examines how citizens in recent years have been willing to sacrifice personal freedoms in exchange for promises of prosperity and security.

Articles

Erdbrink, Thomas, "Iran Blocks Way to Bypass Internet Filtering System," *The New York Times*, March 11, 2013, www.nytimes.com/2013/03/12/world/middleeast/iran-blocks-software-used-to-bypass-internet-filtering-system.html.

Iran's Ministry of Information and Communications Technology has begun blocking the most popular software used by millions of Iranians to bypass the official Internet censoring system.

Malik, Kenan, and Nada Shabout, "Should Religious or Cultural Sensibilities Ever Limit Free Expression?" *Index on Censorship*, March 25, 2013, www.indexoncensorship.org/2013/03/should-religious-or-cultural-sensibilities-ever-limit-free-expression/.

An Indian-born British broadcaster (Malik) and an Iraqi art historian debate whether even the most offensive and blasphemous speech should be protected.

Mattingly, Phil, and Hans Nichols, "Obama Pursuing Leakers Sends Warning to Whistle-Blowers," Bloomberg News, Oct. 17, 2012, www.bloomberg.com/news/2012-10-18/obama-pursuing-leakers-sends-warning-to-whistle-blowers.html.

Attorney General Eric Holder has prosecuted more government officials for leaking documents than all his predecessors combined.

Posner, Eric, "The World Doesn't Love the First Amendment," *Slate*, Sept. 25, 2012, www.slate.com/articles/news_and_politics/jurisprudence/2012/09/the_vile_anti_muslim_video_and_the_first_amendment_does_the_u_s_overvalue_free_speech_.single.html.

In the wake of violent protests across the globe triggered by an anti-Muslim video that was produced in the United States, a University of Chicago law professor argues that freedom of expression must give way at times to other values.

Turley, Jonathan, "Shut Up and Play Nice," *The Washington Post*, Oct. 14, 2012, http://articles.washingtonpost.com/2012-10-12/opinions/35499274_1_free-speech-defeat-jihad-muslim-man.

A George Washington University law professor argues that freedom of speech is being eroded around the world as efforts to protect various groups against being offended become enshrined in law.

Reports and Studies

"Attacks on the Press: Journalism on the Front Lines in 2012," Committee to Protect Journalists, February 2013, www.cpj.org/2013/02/attacks-on-the-press-in-2012.php.

The latest edition of this annual report documents how more journalists are disappearing or being imprisoned in countries ranging from Mexico to Russia.

"Freedom of Thought 2012: A Global Report on Discrimination Against Humanists, Atheists and the Nonreligious," International Humanist and Ethical Union, Dec. 10, 2012, http://iheu.org/files/IHEU%20Freedom%20of%20Thought%202012.pdf.

The number of prosecutions for blasphemy is sharply on the rise, according to a global survey of laws regulating religious beliefs and expression.

Leveson, Lord Justice Brian, "An Inquiry Into the Culture, Practices and Ethics of the Press," *The Stationary Office*, Nov. 29, 2012, www.official-documents.gov.uk/document/hc1213/hc07/0780/0780.asp.

A judge appointed by the British prime minister to examine press abuses calls for greater regulation. "There is no organized profession, trade or industry in which the serious failings of the few are overlooked because of the good done by the many," Leveson writes.

Zhu, Tao, *et al.*, "The Velocity of Censorship: High-Fidelity Detection of Microblog Post Deletions," March 4, 2013, http://arxiv.org/abs/1303.0597.

A team of computer scientists examined the accounts of 3,500 users of Weibo, China's microblogging site, to see if it was being censored. The scientists found that thousands of Weibo employees were deleting forbidden phrases and characters.

For More Information

Access, P.O. Box 115, New York, NY 10113; 888-414-0100; www.accessnow.org. A digital-rights group, founded after protests against Iran's disputed 2009 presidential election, that fosters open communications.

Article 19, Free Word Centre, 60 Farringdon Road, London, United Kingdom, EC1R 3GA; +44 20 7324 2500; www .article19.org. A group named for a section of the Universal Declaration of Human Rights that designs laws and policies promoting freedom of expression.

Committee to Protect Journalists, 330 7th Ave., 11th Floor, New York, NY 10001; 212-465-1004; www.cpj.org. Documents attacks on journalists; publishes its findings and works to promote press freedom.

Freedom House, 1301 Connecticut Ave., N.W., 6th Floor, Washington, DC 20036; 202-296-5101; www.freedomhouse .org. An independent watchdog group founded in 1941 that advocates greater political and civil liberties.

Index on Censorship, Free Word Centre, 60 Farringdon Rd., London, United Kingdom, EC1R 3GA; +44 20 7324 2522; www.indexoncensorship.org. Founded in 1972 to publish stories of communist dissidents in Eastern Europe; promotes global free speech through journalistic reports and advocacy.

International Press Institute, Spielgasse 2, A-1010, Vienna, Austria; +43 1 412 90 11; www.freemedia.at. A global network of media executives and journalists founded in 1950, dedicated to promoting and safeguarding press freedoms.

Reporters Committee for Freedom of the Press, 1101 Wilson Blvd., Suite 1100, Arlington, VA 22209; 703-807-2100; www.rcfp.org. Provides free legal advice and other resources to journalists on First Amendment issues.

14

Islamic Sectarianism

Leda Hartman

Waving photos of dead relatives and friends, Pakistani Shiites in Quetta protest the rise in sectarian violence in the majority-Sunni country. Sunni extremists, who view Shiites as heretics, have carried out scores of bombings and shootings against minority Shiites in recent years.

O n July 18, in Damascus, the unthinkable happened: A bomb exploded at a meeting of the Syrian regime's innermost circle, killing four top officials in charge of putting down the country's 16-month-long rebellion.

But the nation's leader, President Bashar Assad, reportedly was not there. According to opposition forces and an American diplomat, Assad had retreated to the coastal town of Latakia, the stronghold of his own Alawite people.[1] In recent months as the insurgency has escalated, thousands of civilians have been killed by loyalist troops, and the fragile mosaic of Syrian society appears to have been shattered.

The rebels — mostly from the nation's majority Sunni Muslims — are rising up against nearly 100 years of rule by the minority Shiite Alawites, who have been aligned with Syria's Christians and Druze.*

"When countries are well-managed and citizens feel they have a say in political and economic developments, sectarian identities and tensions decrease and eventually disappear," wrote Rami Khouri, a columnist for the *Beirut Star*, Lebanon's English-language daily. "But when authoritarian gangs and oligarchic ruling families plunder their countries and treat their citizens like idiots without rights or feelings, sectarianism sprouts like the natural self-defense mechanism that it is."[2]

The dynamic that Khouri described is in full force in Syria and plays a role in other Muslim countries with sizable populations of both Sunnis and Shiites: Iraq, Lebanon, Bahrain, Pakistan and Yemen.

From *CQ Researcher*,
August 7, 2012.

---

*Shiites are often called Shia.

Sunnis Rule Most of Muslim World

The overwhelming majority of the world's 1.6 billion Muslims — 85 percent — are Sunnis. Shiites predominate in only three Middle Eastern countries — Iran, Iraq and Bahrain. Except for Iran, Sunnis have traditionally ruled over Shiites, even in places where Shiites held the majority. Currently, Syria is the only country in which Shiites rule over a Sunni majority. Experts fear that an upsurge in sectarian strife in Syria could trigger a proxy war that could spread throughout the region and eventually draw in Western nations.

Muslim Sectarian Hot Spots

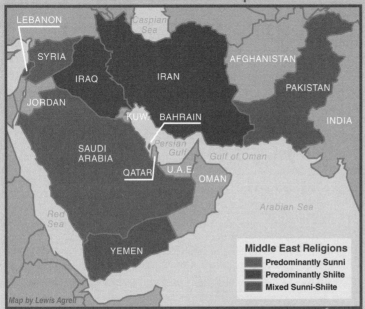

Map by Lewis Agrell

Middle East Religions
Predominantly Sunni
Predominantly Shiite
Mixed Sunni-Shiite

Predominantly Sunni Countries:

Pakistan — Eighty percent of the population is Sunni. The rest are Shiites and others.
Saudi Arabia — About 85 percent of the population is Sunni. Shiites predominate in the eastern oil-rich regions near Bahrain.
Syria — Shiite Alawites are the ruling elite, but 80 percent of the population is Sunni.

Predominantly Shiite Countries:

Bahrain — King Hamad and the ruling elite are Sunni, but 70 percent of the 1.2 million population is Shiite.
Iran — The only officially Shiite country; about 85 percent of the 70 million people are Shiite.
Iraq — Shiites make up 50 to 70 percent of the 31 million population.

Mixed Populations:

Lebanon — Has 18 recognized religious sects, including non-Muslims. Shiites make up 30 to 50 percent of the population.
Yemen — Population of 23 million is evenly split among Sunnis and Shiites.

Source: John R. Bradley, "The Ancient Loathing Between Sunnis and Shi'ites Is Threatening to Tear Apart the Muslim World," *Daily Mail*, March 2011, www.dailymail.co.uk/debate/article-1367435/ Middle-East-unrest-Sunni-Shiite-conflict-threatens-tear-Muslim-world-apart.html

"In many ways, sectarianism is the new politics of the Muslim world," observes Toby Jones, an associate professor of Middle East history at Rutgers University.

About 85 percent of the world's 1.6 billion Muslims — or 1.3 billion — are Sunnis, and the rest are Shiites. Four countries — Iran, Iraq, Bahrain and Azerbaijan — have Shiite majorities, but they are in power only in Iran and Iraq. Traditionally (except in Iran), Sunnis have ruled over Shiites, even when the Sunnis were in the minority. Syria is the only country in which a Shiite minority rules over Sunnis.

Sectarian conflict is not unique to Islam, of course. Experts cite bloody periods in Christian history such as the Reformation and the long conflict between Protestants and Catholics in Northern Ireland. In fact, Sunnis and Shiites have co-existed for centuries throughout the Muslim world.

But in the political vacuums that developed after the Iraq War and the Arab Spring, sectarian divisions have intensified, as previously disenfranchised groups from Islam's two branches have struggled for power.[3] "The problem is not in co-existing, but in who has the upper hand in terms of government control and oil money, things like that," explains Columbia University history professor Richard Bulliet.

Experts fear those struggles could spill over into neighboring countries, triggering a proxy war that could spread throughout the region and eventually draw in Western nations. The growing Sunni-Shiite conflict is damaging Islam's reputation as a religion of peace, according to nearly two-thirds of the Arabs surveyed in 2008 by Doha Debates, a Qatar-based free-speech forum. At least 77 percent of respondents blamed the United States for instigating sectarian tensions by invading Iraq and toppling the Sunni-led government of Saddam Hussein.[4]

Most mainstream Muslims want less division between the branches. "Moderate Muslims in Islam think that anybody who says there is only one God and Muhammad is his prophet is Muslim," says Gawdat Bahgat, a political science professor at National Defense University in Washington. "So moderate Muslims on both sides believe you should respect this and not question their beliefs."

In many places, however, Sunni-Shiite relations have deteriorated even further since the Doha poll. Sectarian violence — mainly Sunni attacks on Shiites — is on the upswing in Iraq, reflecting the political tug-of-war between the Shiite-controlled government and the Sunni opposition.[5] In Afghanistan, where sectarian attacks are rare, two Shiite shrines were bombed in December.[6] In March, the violence bled into Europe, when Belgium's biggest Shiite mosque was the target; the suspect was a member of the ultra-orthodox, hardline Sunni Salafist sect.[7] And since the Arab Spring began in 2011, many Shiite pro-democracy activists in Bahrain have been imprisoned and tortured by the minority Sunni monarchy.

In Syria, where the authoritarian Assad regime is Alawite — an offshoot of Shiism — most of its civilian victims have been Sunnis. In May, June and July, government forces and the Alawite militia, called the "shabiha," massacred hundreds of people in the Sunni villages of Houla, Qubair and Tremseh, and by mid-July the regime was bombing Syria's largest city, Aleppo.[8] The U.N.'s High Commissioner for Human Rights said both the shabiha and Syrian government could be prosecuted for crimes against humanity.[9]

While the sectarian strife in individual countries might be, as Bulliet says, a fight over who gains power or controls a country's natural resources, it's also part of a broader struggle over which group will dominate the Middle East. The struggles are, in a sense, proxy battles in the age-old religious and ethnic rivalry between the region's two centers of power: Iran, a Shiite Persian theocracy since its 1979 revolution, and Saudi Arabia, an Arab Sunni monarchy where the state religion is Wahhabism — an ultra-conservative form of Sunnism.

For instance, Iran supports the Shiite Alawite government in Syria, while Saudi Arabia supports the mostly Sunni opposition. Likewise, militant Islamic groups in the Middle East are divided along sectarian lines: Lebanon's Hezbollah and Iraq's Mahdi army are both Shiite, while Al Qaeda's terrorist network is made up of Sunnis from the hardline orthodox Wahhabi, Salafist and Deobandi sects.

Why is sectarianism on the upswing? For starters, says Bahgat, Muslims tend to identify themselves by their religion more than by their nationality. "In the United

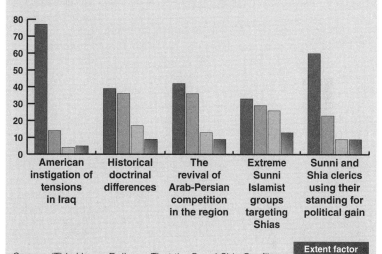

Muslims Say U.S. Worsened Sunni-Shiite Divide

More than three-quarters of Muslims surveyed in the Middle East blamed the 2003 U.S. invasion of Iraq for exacerbating Sunni-Shiite tensions in Iraq and the rest of the Middle East. Another factor was the age-old rivalry between Saudi Arabia, a Sunni Arab nation, and Iran, a country of Shiite Persians.

To what extent do you blame each of the factors for the Sunni-Shia conflict?

Source: "This House Believes That the Sunni-Shia Conflict Is Damaging Islam's Reputation As a Religion of Peace," Doha Debates, April 2008, clients.squareeye.net/uploads /doha/polling/shia_sunni.pdf; a total of 993 people from throughout the region responded to the survey.

Extent factor is to blame
■ A lot
□ A little
□ Not at all
■ Don't know

How to Tell a Sunni From a Shiite

Names and prayer styles often vary.

As with any religion, it's usually not considered polite to ask outright what branch of Islam someone belongs to. For most Muslims, it's a non-issue, because they live in countries that are predominantly Sunni.

But in countries such as Iraq and Lebanon, with mixed Sunni-Shiite populations, Muslims tend to look for subtle clues that indicate whether another Muslim is Sunni or Shiite.

A major indicator is geography. The overwhelming majority — about 85 percent — of the world's 1.6 billion Muslims are Sunni. But Shiites make up the majority in Iran, Azerbaijan, Bahrain and southern Iraq. There are also Shiite majorities in southern Lebanon, northern Yemen and the oil-producing region of eastern Saudi Arabia. And significant numbers live in Kuwait, Afghanistan, Pakistan and Syria.[1]

Names are another indicator. Ali and Hussein are popular among both Sunnis and Shiites, but have a special resonance for Shiites. Ali was the name of Muhammad's son-in-law, the man Shiites believe should have been his immediate successor. Hussein was the name of Ali's son, who was killed by the army of the caliph Yazid and is an important symbol of Shiite martyrdom.

Zulfikar — the name of Ali's sword — is a Shiite name. Zulfikar Ali Bhutto was prime minister of Pakistan from 1973-77. Although he was a secular, modernist Muslim, "Zulfikar" paired with the name "Ali" indicates a Shiite family background.

Other names are favored only by Sunnis. "There are certain names" — such as Abu Bakr, Omar, Osman or Yazid — "that a Shiite would never have," says Jonathan Brown, an assistant professor of Islamic Studies at Georgetown University's School of Foreign Service and a Muslim.

That's because those names refer to the three Muslim leaders who immediately succeeded Muhammad, bypassing Ali. In fact, the most powerful political state in Muslim history, the Sunni Ottoman Empire, derives from the name Osman.

In matters of worship, all Muslims believe in the five tenets of Islam: the declaration of faith, prayer, charity, fasting and pilgrimage to Mecca. All Muslims pray five times a day. But some Shiites allow some prayers to be combined, so they may pray only three times a day.[2]

"The style of praying also differs between the two branches. Shiites pray with their arms at their sides," says Brown, although a Sunni school of thought predominant throughout northern Africa prays that way, too. But if you are in Turkey, and people are praying with their arms by their sides, he says, they are probably Shiite. By contrast, most Sunnis pray by laying their right hand on top of the left, on their diaphragm, between the chest and the navel.

Also, Shiites pray by putting their foreheads on a little stone of compacted dirt or mud, which represents the earth of Karbala, the Iraqi city where Ali's son Hussein died. Unlike the Sunnis, Shiites commemorate Ashura, the day Hussein died, with ritual mourning processions that can include self-flagellation.

— *Leda Hartman*

[1]Vali Nasr, *The Shia Revival* (2006), pp. 12-13.

[2]"Sunni and Shi'a," BBC, Aug. 19, 2009, www.bbc.co.uk/religion/religions/islam/subdivisions/sunnishia_1.shtml.

States and most of the Western world, we define ourselves by our national identity," he explains. "We are Americans first. Christians and Jews, white and black, are second or third." In most Middle Eastern countries religious identity is more important. "They have not completely understood or accepted the concept of national identity," he added. "They are Shia or Sunni, Christian or Muslim. This is very clear in countries like Iraq and Lebanon."

The Middle East also lacks democratic institutions that could encourage people of different persuasions to live together peacefully. "The region is known for the mosaic structure of society," says Abdeslam Maghraoui, an associate professor of political science at Duke University. "The problem comes when you don't have procedures to say, 'Hey look, this is how we define our rights, this is how we can have a balance where you can fulfill your potential to be who you are without infringing on the rights of others.'"

Pluralism hasn't had a chance to develop in the Middle East because the region historically has been dominated by authoritarian powers that force people to jostle for position, says Jones, especially in oil-producing states where petroleum revenue is distributed as patronage. "The preference is not for reconciliation," he explains. "The preference is to protect access to a system of privilege."

But the most important factor, analysts say, may be the lack of trust. People from one sect don't trust that the other side would be fair if they were in power, and vice versa. In Iraq, for instance, the U.S. invasion deposed the Sunni Baath Party and opened the way for a Shiite-controlled government, leaving the Sunnis marginalized.

Such factors help explain why the situations in Egypt, Libya and Tunisia — where autocratic leaders were ousted during last year's Arab Spring — differ from what's happening in Syria and Bahrain. The North African countries are overwhelmingly Sunni, and sectarian divisions aren't much of an issue. But in Syria and Bahrain, where minority regimes rule over a majority of the opposite sect, the situation is more complex and much more volatile.

Meanwhile, unlike in Libya, Western powers are reluctant to step in with direct military action in Syria because they fear that a Syrian civil war could spill over into other countries where sectarian tensions simmer. However, on August 1, Reuters reported that President Obama had secretly authorized covert U.S. support for the rebels and that agencies such as the CIA are operating from a secret base in Turkey.[10]

Those fears appear to be well-founded. Sunnis from Iraq and Lebanon have gone to Syria to join the insurgents fighting the Alawite government.[11] There also have been fatal skirmishes in northern Lebanon between Sunnis who support the Syrian uprising and Alawites who back Assad.[12]

As the standoff in Syria continues, some fear that Islamic sectarianism in the Middle East could re-ignite Cold War-era animosities, as the United States and the other NATO powers call for Assad's ouster while Russia and China remain his ally.

Meanwhile, the human cost continues to rise unabated, and its after-effects may be felt for some time. Khalid Ali al-Sardi, a Sunni student at the University of Bahrain, told *New York Times* reporter Souad Mekhennet that he used to have Shiite friends who would come to his home to share a meal. Then, last year, he was badly beaten up by a group of Shiite protesters.

"Why did this happen to all of us here in Bahrain?" al-Sardi asks. "We thought Shiites and Sunnis had lived as brothers and sisters together. We all are losing. Why does no one see that?"[13]

As sectarian tensions escalate in the Middle East, here are some of the questions being debated by academics, Middle East experts and Muslims themselves:

Is the Sunni-Shiite split primarily about theology?

All Muslims believe in the five tenets of Islam: the declaration of faith, prayer, charity, fasting and making a pilgrimage to Mecca. But sectarian divisions emerged early in Islam, over who should succeed the Prophet Muhammad after his death.

A larger group of Muslims, who later became known as the Sunnis, chose one of Muhammad's companions, Abu Bakr. A smaller group, later known as the Shiites, supported Muhammad's son-in-law, Ali. The larger group won out, and throughout history, the Sunnis have maintained control of most of the Muslim world — even in places where Shiites comprise the majority — except in Iran and postwar Iraq.

Joshua Landis, director of the Center for Middle East Studies at the University of Oklahoma, sees religious differences as a major underpinning of today's sectarian conflict.

"It has a lot to do with theology," Landis maintains. "If you want to look at it ideologically, the easiest thing to do would be to compare it to a pre-Enlightened Europe. In a sense, the Middle East is in the midst of a pre-Enlightenment era. Theology and God still are the main sources of truth for most Middle Easterners. People take their religion seriously. It's driven by politics, but also by a world view where God is talking truth with a big 'T.'"

Although moderates from both branches accept one another without questioning each other's beliefs, in today's heated climate some Muslims, particularly Sunnis, disavow the others. "Many Sunnis believe Shia are Muslims," says Bahgat, at the National Defense University, but some extremist Sunnis believe the Shia "are not Muslims."

Theologically based violence is especially visible in Pakistan, where Shiite Iran and Sunni Saudi Arabia have vied for influence for decades and where most of the recent violence has been fomented by Sunnis targeting Shiites. Many Sunni extremists belong to the Deobandi sect, which inspired the Taliban, or have been educated in

Islam's Two Branches Have Many Offshoots

Eighty-five percent of the world's Muslims are Sunni, while the rest are Shiite. The split developed in the 7th century over who should succeed the Prophet Muhammad. Sunnis believed the best-qualified leader should succeed him, while Shiites believed Muhammad's blood descendants were his rightful successors. Since then, several small sects have broken off from mainstream Sunnism and Shiism. Some sects are more prevalent in certain countries.

Major Sunni Groups

Mainstream Sunnism includes four broad schools of thought, mainly divided along geographical lines. The Hanafi are prevalent in much of the Arab world and South Asia; the Hanbali in Saudi Arabia; the Maliki in North, Central and West Africa; and the Shafii, mainly in East Africa and Southeast Asia.

Salafists/Wahhabis — Practitioners of these ultra-conservative branches follow the practices of the early Muslims and distrust modernist interpretations of the Quran, Islam's holy book. Wahhabism — Saudi Arabia's state religion — began with an 18th-century Arabian scholar named Muhammad Ibn Abd al-Wahhab. Among other things, it provides the rationale for the global jihad against infidels espoused by today's terrorists and is known for its strict limits on women's rights. The terrorist group Al Qaeda is generally made up of Salafists and Wahhabis.

Deobandis — Based primarily in Pakistan and named after a city in northern India where it was founded, this ultra-conservative branch developed in the late 19th century in part as a response to British colonialism. The Deobandis believe Islamic societies have become too Westernized. Like Salafists, Deobandis restrict women's rights and regard Shiites as heretics. The extremist Taliban group, based in Pakistan and Afhganistan, is primarily Deobandi.

Major Shiite Sects

Twelvers — Centered in Iran, Shiism's largest mainstream sect recognizes 12 imams and believes the last imam — a messianic figure — will appear at the end of time to usher in peace and justice.

Ismailis — This geographically and ethnically diverse group of 15 million recognizes seven imams.

Zaidis — Mostly based in Yemen, this group recognizes only five imams. In belief and practice, the Zaidis are the Shiite group most similar to the Sunnis.

Alawites — This Shiite offshoot of 3 million followers is most prevalent in Syria. Their rituals incorporate elements of Christianity and other religions. Some mainstream Sunnis and Shiites don't consider them Muslims.

Alevis — Similar to the Alawites but based mostly in Turkey, the Alevis downplay formal rituals and stress gender equality.

Druze — Prevalent in Syria, Lebanon, Israel and Jordan, this group's secretive belief system includes elements of Christianity, Gnosticism and Zoroastrianism. Many mainstream Muslims view the Druze as non-Muslims.

Source: "The Sword and the Word," *The Economist*, May 2012, p. 67, www.economist.com/ node/21554513; "Deobandi Islam," GlobalSecurity.org, www.globalsecurity.org/military/intro/islam-deobandi.htm

"The Shia of Pakistan have not yet been officially declared a non-Muslim minority, but they have clearly lost their bid for power," wrote Vali Nasr, dean of The Johns Hopkins University's Paul H. Nitze School of Advanced International Studies (SAIS). "The extremist face of Sunnism has proven itself capable of reacting to the Shiite challenge, using violence but also theology and religious ideology to roll back Shiite gains."[15]

According to some experts, the power struggle is more important than theology in the sectarian conflict. In fact, the Sunni-Shiite schism after Muhammad's death was "purely political," wrote Islamic history scholars Bernard Lewis, professor emeritus of Near Eastern Studies at Princeton University, and Buntzie Ellis Churchill, the former president of the World Affairs Council of Philadelphia. It was "a dispute over the succession to the prophet Mohammed as the head of the Muslim state and community which he had founded."[16]

Geopolitics continues to be at the root of the conflict today, says Leena El-Ali, vice president of strategic development at Search for Common Ground, a Washington-based nongovernmental organization focusing on conflict resolution. "Very often we forget that what we describe in sectarian terms is actually a conflict about worldly political power, period," she says. "There are fault lines in certain countries whereby the political power is officially or de facto distributed along sectarian lines. So there you see people lining up behind different sorts of sectarian groupings because of the implications for political power."

El-Ali should know. She lived through the Lebanese civil war of 1975-90, when Christians, Sunnis and Shiites were all fighting each

madrassas (Islamic religious schools) built and financed by the hardline Saudi Wahhabis.[14]

other. "It sounded to the outside world that people were fighting over religion — 'mine is better than yours, you're a heretic' — and that was never, ever the issue," she says. "The issue was quite simply political power. And we run the risk now, when it comes to the Sunni-Shiite thing, to give the same wrong impression in some cases."

Sectarian divisions also have been exacerbated by economics, says Bahgat. "The minority in most countries are Shia who have been deprived of jobs and economic opportunities," he says. "So in many countries the Shia minority also happen to be the poor."

Are concerns about sectarian conflict overblown?

Although Muslim sectarian violence dominates today's headlines, some experts say it's important not to lose sight of the bigger picture, both numerically and historically.

"I think the norm in Islamic history is a relatively peaceful co-existence," says Charles Kurzman, professor of sociology at the University of North Carolina at Chapel Hill. "These communities have lived next to each other and even intermingled for centuries. They have intermarried in many communities, and we rarely see trouble rising to the level of communal violence."

Kurzman says nothing in the Sunni-Shiite split makes for inherent conflict, and for the overwhelming majority of Muslims, co-existence remains the norm. Even in the "handful of countries and cases" where violence does exist, he adds, the conflict has been triggered by external factors such as the U.S. invasion of Iraq or the Arab Spring movements in North Africa, which inspired similar movements in Bahrain and Syria.

Sheikh Mahmood Shaltoot, the grand imam of Al Azhar University in Cairo, Egypt, wrote in a 1959 *fatwa*, or Islamic legal opinion, that Shiism "is a school of thought that is religiously correct to follow in worship as are other Sunni schools of thought."[17]

Further, he continued, "Muslims must know this, and ought to refrain from unjust prejudice to any particular school of thought, since the religion of Allah and His Divine Law (Shari'ah) was never restricted to a particular school of thought."[18]

It's also important to compare Islamic sectarianism to religious conflicts in other times and places. Even the rivalry between the Sunni Ottoman Empire and Persia's Shiite Safavid dynasty during the 16th-18th centuries

Residents survey the damage caused by a truck bomb that killed 44 people in a market in Diwaniya, 95 miles south of Baghdad, on July 3, 2012. One of the latest in a series of sectarian attacks in Iraq, the bombing was near a Shiite mosque where pilgrims gather on their way to Karbala to celebrate the birthday of al-Mahdi, one of their most important imams. Sunni extremists were thought to have detonated the bomb.

"never reached the level of the bitter and bloody wars of religion that followed the Reformation in Europe," according to Lewis and Churchill.[19]

In his book *The Missing Martyrs*, Kurzman compares terrorist incidents around the world to other forms of violence and finds that terrorism represents only a tiny portion of the world's bloodshed. Thus, worries about Muslim sectarian tensions leading to violence and terrorism are exaggerated, he says.

"Both of these grand narratives are flawed," he says. "We would be better served to look at particular cases and also put these things in perspective. Not to ignore them — these are very real problems and have very real victims — but at the same time to recognize it's not nearly so bad as many of us feared it would be, and is not nearly the global tsunami that it may have appeared to be."

Others, however, note a sea change in the intensity and volatility of sectarian tension, especially when it's viewed in context with other issues.

"Is sectarianism — the fact that there's a Sunni-Shiite split — an inherently destabilizing fact in world politics? No, it's not," says Jonathan Brown, an assistant professor of Islamic studies at Georgetown University and a Muslim. "But, considering that sectarianism is fuel for a fire originally caused by political concerns, economic

CHRONOLOGY

Before 2011

1453-1924 *Sunni Ottoman Empire, headquartered in Istanbul, rules much of the Muslim world, stretching from Eastern Europe to the Arabian Peninsula and parts of North Africa.*

1501-1722 Safavids break away from Ottoman Empire and establish Shiite theocracy in Persia (modern Iran). They suppress Sunnism and other religions.

1783 Sunni Al Khalifa family expels Shiite Persians from Bahrain; establishes monarchy that rules over majority Arab Shiites.

1923 French take power in Syria and Lebanon and put Alawites — an unorthodox branch of Shiism — in charge of Syria and Maronite Christians in charge of Lebanon.

1932 Abdul-Aziz bin Saud establishes monarchy in Saudi Arabia, with ultra-orthodox Sunnism (Wahhabism) as the state religion. Minority Sunnis take power in Iraq.

1941 Lebanon declares its independence from France. . . . French mandate formally ends in 1943 but French power structure is retained.

1946 Syria becomes a sovereign state, but keeps French power structure.

1958 Iraq becomes a republic after military coup. Minority Sunnis take power.

1970s-1980s *The seeds of today's sectarian conflicts are planted in Syria, Pakistan, Iraq and Lebanon; Iranian Revolution creates a Shiite theocracy.*

1970 Alawite Hafez Assad seizes power in Syria. The Shiite Alawites rule majority Sunni population for more than 40 years, with support from Christian and Druze minorities.

1977 President Zulfikar Ali Bhutto, a secular Shiite, is ousted in a military coup in Pakistan.

1979 Shah of Iran abdicates; Ayatollah Ruhollah Khomeini establishes a Shiite theocracy. In Iraq, Sunni Baath leader Saddam Hussein seizes power. Gen. Zia ul-Haq, a fundamentalist Sunni, becomes president of Pakistan.

1981 Sunni monarchy in Bahrain puts down Shiite insurgency.

1982 Syria's Assad crushes uprising in Hama, a Sunni Muslim Brotherhood stronghold; thousands of civilians are killed. A militant Shiite group, Hezbollah, forms in Lebanon.

1980-1988 Iraq's Sunni leader Saddam Hussein invades Iran. Iraq's Shiites fight on the Iraqi side against Iran's Shiites. War ends in stalemate, with hundreds of thousands of deaths on each side.

1989 Ayatollah Khomeini dies.

1990s-2000s *Hardline Muslim extremist groups emerge; Sunni extremist group, Al Qaeda, attacks the United States, which then invades Afghanistan and Iraq.*

1990 North and South Yemen unite; Ali Abdullah Saleh becomes president of an autocratic regime.

1991 Saddam brutally suppresses Shiite uprising in southern Iraq, killing thousands. . . . United States establishes Fifth Fleet at a naval base in Bahrain.

1996 Sunni monarchy crushes second Shiite uprising in Bahrain.

2001 Al Qaeda hijacks four airliners and attacks targets in New York and Washington, killing 3,000 people. The United States retaliates by invading Al Qaeda safe-haven, Afghanistan. For the next 11 years U.S. battles Al Qaeda and the Sunni fundamentalist regime known as the Taliban.

2003 United States invades Iraq, claiming Saddam has weapons of mass destruction. Sunni Baath party is deposed and Shiite leader Nuri al-Maliki comes to power. Sunni Baathists and Al Qaeda launch anti-U.S. insurgency.

2006-2007 Sunni-Shiite violence in Iraq escalates.

2010 Bahrain arrests Shiite opposition leaders, claiming they are plotting to overthrow the Sunni monarchy.

Since Feb. 26, 2011

Feb. 17 Arab Spring movement, which began in December in Tunisia, migrates from Sunni-dominated North Africa to Bahrain, where it takes on a sectarian flavor. Majority Shiites demand equal rights from

Bahrain's Sunni monarchy, which cracks down hard on the protesters.

March 15 Sunni-led protests erupt against Syria's minority Alawite regime.

Nov. 23 Independent inquiry finds Iran was not involved in the Bahraini uprising, but that the government tortured and used excessive force against protesters.

Dec. 7 Sunnis bomb two Shiite mosques in Afghanistan.

Dec. 18 U.S. withdraws from Iraq.

Dec. 19 Shiite-controlled Iraqi government issues arrest warrant for Sunni vice president, Tariq al Hashemi, claiming he oversaw death squads. Hashemi denies the charges; flees Iraq.

April 20, 2012 Thousands of protesters, mostly Shiites, rally against Bahrain's Sunni monarchy. Riot police use tear gas and stun grenades.

May 13 Five people are killed in Tripoli, signaling an escalation of sectarian clashes in Lebannon.

May 21 A suicide bombing at a military rehearsal for Yemen's National Day parade kills nearly 100; extremist Sunnis claim responsibility.

May 26 Syrian military begin the first of three major assaults on Sunni villages, killing hundreds.

June 1 U.N. High Commissioner for Human Rights Navi Pillay says Syrian regime could face charges of crimes against humanity.

June 13 At least 70 Iraqis are killed in a wave of attacks targeting Shiite pilgrims. A militant Sunni group claims responsibility.

June 15 Russians ship defensive missile systems to Syria.

June 16 Car bombs target a Shiite pilgrimage in Baghdad, Iraq, killing 32.

June 18 Suicide bomber in Baquba, Iraq, targets a Shiite funeral, killing at least 15 and wounding 40. At least 130 Shiites are killed in sectarian attacks in June.

June 22 Some 25 members of Syria's Alawite militia are killed in Aleppo. Western intelligence officials warn that Sunni extremists have joined the rebel forces. Syria shoots down a Turkish fighter jet that inadvertently flew into Syrian air space.

June 24 Two high-level Syrian military officers join dozens of others who have defected to Turkey.

July 18 Rebel bombing in Damascus kills four top security officials, including the Defense minister.

July 24 Assad regime uses warplanes to bomb Aleppo, Syria's largest city, after rebel incursions there. . . . Death toll from sectarian attacks in Iraq reaches two-year monthly high of 325.

Aug. 1 Reuters says President Obama has secretly authorized covert U.S. support for the Syrian rebels.

concerns and strategic concerns — right now that is a very dangerous mixture of fire and fuel, which has been burning very fiercely for the last couple of years and will continue to do so."

That dynamic could not only cause increased armed conflict but also endanger the goals of the Arab Spring movement, he says. It could make "the anxieties of the regimes and the majority controlling groups supersede much nobler aspirations," he says, such as the protest movements "trying to better the lives of people and increase their ability to participate in government and demand accountability."

As an example, he cites the situation in Bahrain, where the ruling Sunni monarchy has defined the opposition as a Shiite uprising led by Iran. "The fact that

these people had legitimate grievances was forgotten," says Brown.

The sectarian label in Bahrain, among other places, has led to the torture and deaths of many people, adds Rutgers University's Jones. What's more, it has aggravated a religious divide that wasn't as bitter when the pro-democracy movement began. Jones says nonviolent activists could eventually turn to violence in desperation, or sectarian tension could become permanent or long-lasting in parts of the Middle East.

"What's more likely is that you'll have a generational, structural reality in which people identify along sectarian lines, and that will paralyze politics," Jones says. "That means the kinds of unrest we see in places like Syria, even in Iraq and in parts of the Gulf, will

Why Are the Sufis Under Attack?

Extremists see the tolerant mystics as heretics.

In early July, in northern Mali's fabled Timbuktu, members of the radical Islamist group Ansar Dine used picks and shovels to destroy the ancient mausoleums of several saints revered by the local Sufis.[1]

Technically, it wasn't a sectarian assault, since Ansar Dine is Sunni, as are Mali's Sufis, who practice a mystical form of Islam. But the two groups are as far apart as you can get in their approach to Islam.

Ansar Dine, along with its allies Al Qaeda and the Taliban, espouses an ultra-conservative, puritanical strain of Islam that is associated with the Wahhabi, Salafist and Deobandi sects of Sunnism. The movement began with the 18th-century Arabian scholar Muhammad Ibn Abd al-Wahhab.

"Wahhabi theology saw the world in white and black categories," wrote John Esposito, professor of religion and international affairs at Georgetown University, "Muslim and non-Muslim, belief and unbelief. They regarded all Muslims who did not agree with them as unbelievers to be subdued (that is, fought and killed) in the name of Islam." Thus, Wahhabism has provided the rationale for the global jihad against infidels espoused by today's terrorists.

Al-Wahhab formed an alliance with a tribal leader named Muhammad ibn Saud, who established the dynasty that still rules Saudi Arabia today. The Wahhabi interpretation of Islam is the country's official religion.[2]

Closely related to the Wahhabis are the Salafists, whose name comes from the Arabic phrase "those who have gone before," connoting a return to the purity of early Islam. The Salafist movement first developed in late 19th-century Egypt in reaction to the modernization and reform associated with foreign influence and has since spread to many parts of the Muslim world.[3]

At around the same time, the Deobandi movement emerged in northern India — partly in response to British colonialism — and spread to other South Asian countries, notably Pakistan and Afghanistan.[4]

At the other kinder, gentler end of the spectrum is Sufism. Grounded in traditional Muslim law and scholarship, it also incorporates a variety of mental and physical disciplines to achieve a direct and personal experience of God. Sufism's focus is on the esoteric, inner connection with the divine, perhaps most familiarly captured in the image of the dancing mystics known as the whirling dervishes, who are said to be "revolving in harmony with all things in nature."[5]

Sufis can be either Sunni or Shiite. They're inclusive in their outlook, even embracing local traditions and practices that may be somewhat outside the bounds of Islam.

The phrase that epitomizes Sufism is *sulk e kul*, or "peace with all," says Akbar Ahmed, an Islamic studies professor at American University and Pakistan's former ambassador to the United Kingdom. "Sufis believe we are all creatures of God, that there are many paths to God," Ahmed says. "You may be a Buddhist, a Christian, a Hindu. If you're striving to understand God, that's fine, and good luck to you."

Ahmed says it helps to view Muslims not in terms of Sunni and Shiite, but in terms of three groups: the literalists (the conservatives); the modernists (those who may speak English, wear Western dress and engage internationally while still maintaining their faith); and the mystics (the Sufis).

He illustrates these distinctions through the example of a traditional Sufi practice — chanting the name of God over and over. "Now, imagine there are 500 people chanting this, it's late at night, you've said your prayers, you're thinking of God," Ahmed says. "It's highly spiritual. But it almost smacks of something that's off the beaten path of orthodoxy. A literalist

more or less be a perennial problem, just waiting for the match to be ignited."

Is Sunni-Shiite reconciliation possible in the near future?

Jones, of Rutgers, doesn't see reconciliation on the near horizon, and he blames the Middle East's power structures.

Regional governments "have basically had to buy their way or co-opt their way or oppress their way into remaining in power," he says. And none of them has "the political will to stand above the fray and mediate.

"People want to talk to each other. They want to have relationships. But they don't have the space to create that," Jones observes.

. . . would say, 'What the hell is going on? This is not an Islamic ritual!' A modernist . . . would say, 'This is mumbo jumbo!' The Sufis would say in response, 'Well, we bless both of them. May their eyes be opened to the reality.'"

Such tolerance makes Sufis the target of extremists, especially the militant Salafists who comprise the majority of today's global terrorist groups. "Salafists and others who believe in a more orthodox brand of Islam harbor a particular animosity toward Sufism, whose mystical interpretation of the divine affords a more heterodox faith, steeped sometimes in local pre-Islamic traditions and a reverence for saints and wise men," wrote *Time* columnist Ishaan Tharoor.[6]

To Sunni extremists, Sufis — like Shiites — are infidels. And for the last generation, extremists in Pakistan have attacked Sufis almost as much as they have Shiites.

Sunni extremists — who recently declared northern Mali an independent nation called Azawad — have set their sights on the region's Sufis and in doing so have destroyed more than the ancient shrines.[7]

"The attack on Timbuktu's cultural heritage," says UNESCO's director general, Irina Bokova, "is an attack against this history and the values it carries — values of tolerance, exchange and living together, which lie at the heart of Islam. It is an attack against the physical evidence that peace and dialogue is possible."[8]

Still, Sufism continues to resonate with Muslims worldwide — both Sunnis and Shiites, literalists and modernists. Many see it as a potential bridge builder and a counterweight to extremism. In fact, in 2009, Tahroor reported, "the Algerian government announced it would promote the nation's Sufi heritage on radio and television in a bid to check the powerful influence of Salafism."[9]

When he's asked if the Muslim world can co-exist peacefully in the near future, Ahmed considers for a moment. Then he laughs gently. "Yes," he says, "if we listen to the mystics."

— *Leda Hartman*

STR/AFP/GettyImages

Islamist militants destroy an ancient Sufi shrine in Timbuktu, Mali, on July 1, 2012. Although the country's Sufis are Sunnis, extremist Sunni rebels in northern Mali consider the shrines idolatrous and have wrecked seven tombs — designated by UNESCO as world heritage sites.

[1] Rukmini Callimachi, "Islamists Continue Destroying Timbuktu Heritage," The Associated Press, July 2, 2012, http://hosted2.ap.org/APDEFAULT/cae69a7523db45408eeb2b3a98c0c9c5/Article_2012-07-02-AF-Mali-Timbuktu/id-995898803faf4d0da5de0b946e6fa2cb.

[2] John L. Esposito, *What Everyone Needs to Know about Islam* (2011), p. 54.

[3] Bernard Lewis and Buntzie Ellis Churchill, *Islam: the Religion and the People* (2009), pp. 158-159.

[4] Vali Nasr, *The Shia Revival* (2006), pp. 100-101.

[5] Esposito, *op. cit.*, p. 61. Also see "Sufism and Dervishes," www.whirlingdervishes.org.

[6] Ishaan Tharoor, "Timbuktu's Destruction: Why Islamists Are Wrecking Mali's Cultural Heritage," *Time*, July 2, 2012, http://world.time.com/2012/07/02/timbuktus-destruction-why-islamists-are-wrecking-malis-cultural-heritage/.

[7] For background, see John Felton, "Small Arms Trade," *CQ Global Researcher*, June 19, 2012, pp. 281-304.

[8] Ishaan Tharoor, "Can Sufism Defuse Terrorism and Radical Islam?" *Time*, July 22, 2009, www.time.com/time/world/article/0,8599,1912091,00.html.

[9] *Ibid.*

People also don't trust that they will be treated fairly by the other side if power switches hands because one side tends to have the power and wealth, and the other does not, he says.

"Iraq is your model for that," he says. The U.S. invasion led to the overthrow of Saddam Hussein's Sunni regime and resulted in establishment of a Shiite government, he says, which has become increasingly authoritarian. "We didn't have a change in the system. We had a change in sides for who controlled the system. That's exactly the dynamic that's feared across the region."

The University of Oklahoma's Landis is even more pessimistic. "In that core of the Middle East, we don't have a good example" of egalitarian co-existence. Even Lebanon, often touted as an egalitarian, multicultural society, has a dysfunctional government plagued by political paralysis and factional distrust, he says.

"People don't trust each other because they don't see where it works," says Landis. "The religious groups fight each other in a zero-sum game into complete submission, and it goes on for a decade or two, and hundreds or thousands of people are killed, and it makes misery." In comparison, a dictatorship might look preferable, he says.

El-Ali at Search for Common Ground agrees that issues of sectarianism get tangled up with concerns about access, privilege and power. Her goal is to untangle the web — to clarify exactly what needs to be fixed and in doing so, lower the temperature. "I am quite hopeful," she says.

Even in violence-wracked Syria, she says, "The issues are not Alawite versus Sunni. The issues are about living a life of dignity and freedom — free from fear — and where the law protects you and guarantees your rights."

To achieve that, all groups must work toward reform together, or the same inequality that existed before will just happen in reverse, she says. When she broaches this idea, she's often met with cynicism. But when she persists, she says, people begin to listen.

She's also encouraged by last year's Arab Spring. "For the first time in a very long time, the Arab seems to have shed his sense of victimhood," she says. "This has kind of shaken up things. The cynicism was always accompanied by a doomed response — 'The powers that be make all the decisions; you are kidding yourself' — and always blaming someone else and portraying oneself as a victim and powerless." But the members of the young generation that ushered in the awakening "don't want to be victims."

Other peacemakers turn to religion as a way to unite people, rather than divide them. "Even if you're devout, war can make you forget the positive, healing aspects of faith," says Qamar-ul Huda, a scholar of Islam and a senior program officer at the U.S. Institute for Peace, in Washington.

Huda works with religious leaders from different branches of Islam in several Muslim countries. He asks them how they developed their opinions of each other. Often, he finds that biases originate not from theology but from one's family, community, the political structure or a person's economic standing. Huda then stresses the common points in Islam that would resonate with any Muslim: the oneness of God; a sense of responsibility to the local and the global communities; the sacredness of each life; forgiveness and practicing reconciliation. And he then asks clerics — many of whom are afraid to call for reconciliation — what they're doing to alleviate the suffering around them.

"When you ask religious leaders, 'What are you doing?' either it's guilt, or they say, 'Yeah, right, we're not doing anything.' And they just jump up and say, 'Yeah, we need to do something. What can we do?'"

Huda has had some successes. In Pakistan, with its history of intense sectarian violence, people who wouldn't sit down with each other before now work together to head off conflict before it starts. He also has helped to develop a peace education curriculum for some of Pakistan's madrassas, which in some cases have been seen as incubators for terrorism.

"It's not a banana split every day," Huda says, "but there are wonderful things happening."

BACKGROUND

Roots of the Division

The division between Sunnis and Shiites stems from a dispute that erupted shortly after Muhammad's death in 632 over who would succeed him and lead the roughly 100,000 Muslims in the Arabian Peninsula.

The largest group — who would become known as Sunnis — favored Abu Bakr, one of Muhammad's close companions. A smaller group — who eventually would become the Shiites — favored Muhammad's cousin and son-in-law, Ali. The Sunnis wanted to choose the most-qualified person, while the Shiites wanted succession based on Muhammad's male descendants.[20]

Abu Bakr was selected as Islam's first caliph, or leader, probably because Ali, still in his early 30s, "lacked seniority within the Arabian tribal system," wrote researcher Febe Armanios.[21] Eventually, Ali became the Muslims' fourth leader after the second and third caliphs, Omar and Othman, were murdered. But tensions flared when the governor of Damascus took up arms against Ali for failing to prosecute Othman's killers. The two sides eventually agreed to a truce, but some of Ali's followers opposed it and murdered him while he was at prayer.[22]

The conflict continued into the next generation, when the governor's son, Yazid, became caliph, and Ali's son, Hussein, was asked to overthrow Yazid in 680. The two forces met near Karbala, in what is now Iraq. Hussein, who was vastly outnumbered, fought to the death and became a powerful symbol of martyrdom.

The Battle of Karbala remains a watershed event in Shiite history and is commemorated each year in a day of mourning called Ashura, when Shiites participate in public processions and perform symbolic acts of self-flagellation.[23]

Karbala not only led to the division of Islam into two branches but also shaped each branch's very different world views.

"Shiite rhetoric is couched in the rhetoric of a fight against injustice and tyranny, so at its root is the idea that the world is unjust and must be challenged," says Akbar Ahmed, an Islamic studies professor at American University in Washington, D.C., and Pakistan's former ambassador to the United Kingdom. Sunnism, on the other hand, "is the opposite. Sunni Islam is establishment Islam," he explains," and holds that "the world is what it is, and you must not disrupt it; you must not create chaos. So you see, straightaway you have a different attitude to how the world is seen."

The name Sunni refers to "one who follows the Sunnah," or the sayings, customs and judgments of Muhammad. The Sunnis are non-hierarchical, and their caliphs tended to be political rather than religious leaders. Shiite means simply "partisans of Ali." The Shiites venerate a series of imams, or spiritual leaders, who they believe are descendants of Muhammad, and their leaders can be both religious and political.[24]

Over time, divisions developed within each branch. The Sunni have four main schools of thought: the Hanafi, Maliki, Shafii and Hanbali, generally associated with different geographic areas.

The Shiites have three main groups, generally distinguished by how many imams each reveres. Twelvers — the largest Shiite group, comprising a majority in Iran, Iraq and Azerbaijan and substantial populations in Bahrain and Lebanon — venerate 12 imams. The Ismailis, a geographically and culturally diverse group, venerate seven; and the Zaydis, based mainly in Yemen, five.

There also are two distinct offshoots of mainstream Shiism: the Alawites and the Druze, whose beliefs incorporate elements of Christianity, Gnosticism and Zoroastrianism.[25] Some Sunnis and Shiites don't consider the Alawites to be Muslims, and even less so the Druze.[26]

Throughout Muslim history, empires and dynasties have defined themselves in religious and/or political terms. The most powerful was the Sunni Ottoman Empire, based in Turkey, which ruled a vast swath of the Mediterranean world from the 15th century to the end of World War I. At its height, it stretched from Eastern Europe to the Arabian Peninsula and parts of North Africa. The Shiite Safavid dynasty — centered in Persia (modern Iran) — ruled from the 16th-18th centuries.

The Safavids derived from a Sufi order that originated in Azerbaijan. When they took control of Persia in 1501, it was the first time that Persia had native rulers since the Arab Muslims conquered the country in 644. The Safavids established the Twelver branch of Shiism as the state religion and demanded that inhabitants either convert or leave.

Sunni-Shiite violence erupted twice during the Ottoman era. First, the Ottomans and the Safavids fought a long war for control of Iraq in the 17th century.[27] Then, in the 18th century the Wahhabis — ultra-orthodox Sunnis who had risen to power in the Arabian Peninsula — declared the Shiites heretics and mounted bloody attacks on them in the Iraqi cities of Najaf and Karbala.

"If you want to have a war with other Muslims," says Georgetown's Brown, "you'd better figure out a way to make them [heretics]; otherwise you can't have a holy war."

With that defeat the Sunnis have almost always ruled over the Shiites, except in Iran and for three centuries in North Africa and the Levant. "The really significant differences between the two arose from their different experience — the one of dominance, the other of subordination and all the social and psychological consequences of this difference," wrote Lewis.[28]

That dynamic has had a profound impact on sectarian relations throughout Islamic history.

Enter the Europeans

The presence of European powers in the Muslim world after World War I not only created animosity toward the West but also exacerbated sectarian divisions, largely because of how the Europeans granted power and privilege among the Arabs.

With the postwar fall of the Ottoman Empire — which the Arabs helped bring about — European powers established a "quasi-colonial network" in the Persian Gulf and the Levant, says Rutgers University's Jones. The exceptions were Turkey, which became an independent secular republic in 1923, and Saudi Arabia, which established itself as an independent kingdom in 1932.

The rest of the Arab lands were subjugated by Britain and France, which devastated Arab leaders who had been promised independence in exchange for helping to overthrow the Ottomans.[29] With the League of Nations' approval, Britain and France took control of what is now Iraq, Syria, Lebanon, Jordan, Israel and the Palestinian territories.[30]

The Europeans created a new power structure that favored minorities and disregarded the centuries-old Islamic social order, says Jones. "Over the course of the early to middle part of the 20th century, [the Europeans] used this as a colonial strategy — to empower the minority, bind them to the imperial power and make them dependent at the expense of the majority. It was divide and rule, absolutely," says Jones.

For example:

- In Iraq, the British put the minority Sunnis in power over the majority Shiites, a dynamic that persisted until the U.S.-backed coalition overthrew Saddam Hussein in 2003.
- In Syria, the French removed the ruling Sunni elites from power by brutally suppressing rebellion and replaced them with a coalition of minorities — including the Shiite Alawites, the religion of the current ruling family, the Assads.
- In Lebanon, the French distributed power along religious lines, largely favoring the Maronite Christians (Catholics based in the Middle East who trace their heritage back to a 4th-century monk).

The legacy of these arrangements is still at play in all three countries today, says Landis, of the University of Oklahoma. "We have seen bloody conflict in every one of these states, as the majority that was suppressed by the minority claws its way back to the top," he says.

Sectarian tensions eased somewhat in the 1950s and '60s, the heyday of the secular, anti-Western, pan-Arab nationalist movement. "A lot of Muslim activists who were trying to rally Muslims against Western colonialism and imperialism understood very clearly that you have to heal the Sunni-Shiite divide," observes Georgetown's Brown. "You can't resist the West if you are divided."

During the nationalist period, religious identity became weaker, and many Sunnis and Shiites intermarried, says the National Defense University's Bahgat. But nationalism declined after Israel defeated Egypt and its allies during the 1967 Six Day War. Traditional tribal attachments revived, political leaders turned back to their own countries' affairs and sectarian identities revived.

"Now with this failure of Arab nationalism," says Bahgat, "political Islam is on the rise."*

"In my opinion, there is nothing wrong with this," Bahgat continues. "People choose whatever they like. But with political Islam on the rise, people started thinking, 'I'm Shiite, Sunni or other sects.' This is how reconciliation is under attack now."

Modern Sectarianism

Three game-changing events shaped recent Muslim history before the Arab Spring occurred in 2011: the 1979 Iranian Revolution, the Iran-Iraq War (1980-88) and the U.S. invasion of Iraq in 2003.

"The Iranian Revolution was the genesis of modern sectarianism," says Rutgers' Jones. Spearheaded by the Shiite cleric Ayatollah Ruhollah Khomeini, the uprising ousted the iron-fisted, pro-Western Shah Mohammad Reza Pahlavi and created the modern world's first Islamic theocracy.[31]

"In one sweep," wrote historian J. E. Peterson, "the movement deposed an authoritarian monarch, reversed the process of secularization, trumpeted justice for the working classes and enforced the observance of a conservative view of Islam. It also initially espoused the spread of 'Islamic Revolution' to the rest of the region."[32]

At first, the rest of the Muslim world applauded the new Shiite state for standing up to the West. "Even if you are a Sunni and an Arab," says Georgetown's Brown, "it still resonates in some parts of your heart." But Khomeini's call for "relieving the oppressed people of the Earth" and his penchant for putting himself forward as the leader of the Muslim World threatened Sunni rulers, especially in Iraq and Saudi Arabia.[33]

In 1980, Saddam Hussein, whose secular Sunni regime ruled over a Shiite majority in Iraq, felt threatened by the new Shiite theocracy next door. He invaded Iran, with

---

*Political Islam is the movement to mix religion with politics, often involving a strict interpretation of Islamic law, known as Sharia.

financial help from Sunni monarchies in the Gulf States.[34] Hundreds of thousands died on both sides before the blood-bath ended in a stalemate in 1988. During the war, Iraqi Shiites had fought alongside their Sunni Iraqi compatriots against Iran's Shiites. But after the war, the Iraqi Shiites tried to overthrow Saddam but were viciously suppressed. Ironically, Iran was the only country that supported them.[35]

The Shiite majority eventually came to power in Iraq after the United States deposed Saddam in 2003, creating the world's only Arab country with a Shiite-dominated government and reviving Gulf State fears that their own restive Shiite populations might try to overthrow their Sunni rulers. The threat of sectarian civil war in Iraq seemed especially high in 2006 and 2007, as Sunnis bombed a Shiite shrine and a mobile phone video of Saddam's hanging showed him trading insults with his Shiite guards.[36]

Simmering Tensions

Sectarian conflict re-emerged during the late 20th century in other Muslim countries with mixed populations, especially where majority populations were oppressed by their minority rulers.

In Syria, Hafez Assad, an Alawite, became president after a military coup in 1970. In 1982 he brutally crushed a Muslim Brotherhood revolt in the predominantly Sunni stronghold of Hama, presaging today's civil war in Syria. Often described as one of the single deadliest acts by any modern Arab government against its own people, Assad (the father of today's president Bashar Assad) turned the full brunt of the military on Hama, killing from 10,000 to 40,000.[37]

In Bahrain, the disenfranchised Shiite majority twice tried unsuccessfully to overthrow the Sunni monarchy, in 1981 and 1996. And in 1975 civil war erupted in Lebanon — a multicultural mix of Christians, Sunnis, Shiites and Druze — and raged till 1990.

Muslims, who had become the majority in Lebanon, wanted more representation, but the French-installed Maronite Christians didn't want to relinquish power. Meanwhile, the militant Shiite group Hezbollah, allied with Iran, emerged in southern Lebanon in reaction to incursions by Israel and to the arrival of large numbers of Sunni Palestinian refugees from Israel.[38] At one point, all three groups were fighting each other. Today, an uneasy peace reigns in Lebanon.

Around the same time, sectarian conflict developed in northern Yemen. Historically, Sunnis and Shiites

A Sunni Muslim gunman fires during clashes that erupted in the Bab al-Tebbaneh neighborhood in Tripoli, Lebanon, on May 13, 2012, that killed three people, The fighting between members of Lebanon's Alawite minority, which supports Syrian President Bashar Assad, and members of Lebanon's Sunni majority, which supports the Syrian rebels, stoked fears that Syria's civil war could bleed into neighboring Lebanon.

there had lived in harmony, intermarrying and praying at each other's mosques. But that began to change in the 1980s, when ultra-orthodox Salafist Sunnis from Saudi Arabia settled along Yemen's northwestern border where the Zaidis, a Shiite sect, lived. At the time, the government was trying to reduce the influence of religion in Yemen. In response, some Zaidis formed a militant group called the Houthis, which opposed both the Salafists and the government. Occasionally, the tension turned violent.

"The leadership of the Zaidi community felt they were in danger of being eradicated," says Gregory Johnsen, a Yemen scholar at Princeton University. "So they fell back into a corner and lashed out."

Pakistan probably has experienced the worst deterioration of sectarian tranquility in the late 20th century. Like Yemen, Pakistan had a tradition of various religious communities living in harmony. But since the 1980s, thousands of people have been killed in sectarian violence, often perpetrated by ultra-conservative Sunnis against Shiites and Sufis.[39]

In the late 1970s, three events changed Pakistan's climate: a military coup in 1977 by Gen. Zia ul Haq; the 1979 Iranian Revolution and the Soviet invasion of Afghanistan in 1979.

Zia, a fundamentalist Sunni, deposed the secular, leftist Shiite president, Zulfikar Ali Bhutto, and used conservative Islam to legitimize his military regime. "He claimed that the state had been established in the name of Islam and that Islamization was the only way the state could attain its national identity," says Samina Ahmed, South Asia project director for the International Crisis Group, a nonprofit that advocates conflict resolution. Under Zia's regime, new laws encouraged discrimination against minority groups, including the Shiites, creating what Ahmed calls a "monster of extremism and intolerance."

Meanwhile, the revolution in neighboring Shiite Iran sparked a proxy war in Pakistan between Iran and Sunni Saudi Arabia. Both countries encouraged their own forms of sectarianism, says Naveed Ahmad, a Pakistani investigative journalist and academic. "The Saudi influence definitely filtered in, broadening all the rhetoric of Wahhabism, and claims that the Shia were infidels," he says. "The Iranian reaction was very open and very crude. They were talking the same way."

Another factor encouraged the violence. When the Soviets invaded Afghanistan, both Sunnis and Shiites sent fighters to vanquish their common enemy. But when they came home, they brought their weapons. "I was a very young student, going to school," Ahmad recalls, "and I knew that people . . . could get a good Kalashnikov anywhere in central or western Pakistan without much problem."

The violence began when the Sunnis attacked the Shiites, who set up their own militant groups in response. The conflict continued, and some would say worsened, under President Pervez Musharraf, who like Zia, took power in a military coup.

Now Musharraf has been replaced, and the militants are part of Pakistan's landscape, says Samina Ahmed. "If the state hadn't discriminated against the minority sects during the Zia years, would we have seen the violent conflict we see today between Sunni and Shiite?" she asks. "I don't think so."

CURRENT SITUATION

Syrian Powder Keg

Of all the countries in the Middle East, Syria has the most potential to set off a regional conflagration.

Syria's crisis pits the majority Sunnis against the ruling Shiite Alawites and their supporters, who have traditionally included Christians and Druze. The current leader, Bashar Assad — the younger son of Hafez Assad — had been trained as an ophthalmologist in London but returned to Syria to be groomed for succession after his older brother, Basil, died in a car accident in 1994. Bashar took power in 2000 after Hafez's death.

The current troubles began in March 2011 as an Arab Spring pro-democracy-style uprising against the 42-year-long Assad dynasty. Since then it has disintegrated into lethal sectarian conflict with a heavy civilian death toll. Pluralism and power-sharing seem impossible.

"So many Syrians — when you catch them in an off moment — will say, 'We're not prepared for democracy,'" says Landis, of the University of Oklahoma. "They'll say, 'Arabs are bloody-minded. They are little autocrats, and they need a strong leader. Otherwise they'll just kill themselves.'"

Indeed, more than 19,000 people have died since the uprising began, according to the Syrian Observatory for Human Rights; the United Nations said in May that 10,000 had died and 120,000 refugees had fled into Jordan, Iraq, Lebanon and Turkey.[40] Both sides have committed human-rights abuses.[41]

Even if the Assad regime falls, it's anyone's guess when and in what form stability will return to Syria, mainly because the opposition is not united. It consists of radical Islamists — who want to establish a theocratic Muslim caliphate across the Arab world — secularists, nonviolent protesters, armed rebels, expatriates and local residents.[42] Other minorities who are protected by the Alawites, including Christians and Druze, are afraid of being marginalized if a Sunni government takes power.[43] Even the Alawites are divided, with some condemning the regime's brutal crackdown.[44]

The conflict has spilled beyond Syria's borders. Starting in February, fatal skirmishes have erupted in northern Lebanon between Shiites and Sunnis. The rivalry between Iran and Saudi Arabia also plays a role: Iran counts Syria as its only Arab ally, while Saudi Arabia, Qatar and Turkey are helping fund the opposition's Free Syrian Army.[45] And recent intelligence confirms that members of Al Qaeda and other jihadists have joined the Sunni rebels.[46]

Meanwhile, CIA officers are in Turkey — Syria's weapons pipeline — trying to keep sophisticated weapons out of extremist hands.[47] Others worry who might gain access to the regime's chemical weapons if Assad falls.

Is sectarian reconciliation among Muslims likely anytime soon?

YES
Leena El-Ali
Vice President, Strategic Development Search for Common Ground

Written for *CQ Global Researcher*, August 2012

Until the Iraq War exploded onto our screens in 2003, I never heard talk of a Sunni-Shia divide, even during the 15-year civil war in my home country of Lebanon. The difference between Sunni and Shia was essentially a 7th-century disagreement about who should have succeeded Islam's prophet, Muhammad, as leader of the nascent Muslim community in Arabia.

Since the Iraq War, other factors have helped establish this consciousness of Sunni and Shia difference. One factor is the rise of Sunni extremist groups, such as Al Qaeda, which habitually pronounce on who is a real believer and who is not — a development that has directly harmed far more Muslims in numerous countries than it has Westerners.

Another factor was the 2005 assassination of former Lebanese Prime Minister Rafiq Hariri, a prominent and hugely influential Sunni leader, and the tense standoff that has developed between the Shia Hezbollah Party and the Sunni community over the investigation.

Finally, the Arab Spring has broadly pitted a ruling Sunni regime against a predominantly Shia population in Bahrain, and a ruling Shia regime (Alawite) against a majority Sunni population in Syria.

Grim as all this sounds, there is cause for optimism. First, the concept of a human being judging the quality or validity of another's belief is so antithetical to Islam that it would pretty much require the erasure of 13 centuries' worth of Muslim custom and tradition.

Secondly, all vying for political power — or for participation in it — is ultimately just that, even if it pits one sect against another along the way. This can happen even within the same religion. Witness Lebanon today, where after a 15-year Christian-Muslim civil war, we now have a Christian community that is split right down the middle, with half of it supporting the (Muslim) Sunni-led coalition and the other half the (Muslim) Shia-led one.

We can help bring about reconciliation sooner if we name the objectives of various groups rather than calling members of those groups names — even if religious ones. Calling one another names only delays the return to normal relations between the two sects of Islam, as practical considerations get mixed up with issues of identity. Moreover, it inflates the problem, given that nearly 90 percent of the world's Muslims are Sunni.

NO
Abbas Barzegar
Assistant Professor, Georgia State University; Affiliate, Middle East Institute

Written for *CQ Global Researcher*, August 2012

During the 20th century, sectarian affiliation was generally secondary to nationalist or pan-Islamic ideologies in the Middle East. Recently, however, the rapid rise of vitriolic sectarian rhetoric and violent outbursts have shocked most Middle East political analysts. Unfortunately, with escalating turmoil in the Muslim world, this is the most inopportune moment in modern history for Sunni-Shiite reconciliation.

Much of today's Islamic sectarian discord can be attributed to the consolidation of Shiite clerical rule in post-revolutionary Iran. Fearing Ayatollah Khomeini's plan to "export the revolution," most Arab states — especially the Gulf monarchies — instituted broad public-education campaigns to curb the revolution's appeal to the "Arab street."

The campaigns equated Sunni Islam with Arab national identities to the point that even pan-Islamist activism was trumped by sectarian parochialism. Anti-Shiite rhetoric took on the force of law. For example, even in Malaysia, typically cited as an example of Muslim pluralism, Shiism is illegal. In May 2012, Egyptian authorities shuttered a Shiite religious center in Cairo when fear of Shiite proselytism angered orthodox Sunni clerics.

But religious institutional rivalry pales in comparison to ideologies that sanction violence in the name of sectarian truth. Militant jihadists' treatises have revived medieval discourses of alleged humiliation and defeat, leading to terrible acts of violence in the name of self-defense. Similar allegations of Shiite sexual licentiousness, heresy and covert Iranian plots now abound in the Sunni opposition's rhetoric in Syria. Likewise, officials in Bahrain have skillfully framed the pro-democracy movement there as a cover for Iranian domination. Iran's geopolitical ambitions and well-financed Shiite evangelical campaign only add verisimilitude to such narratives.

Perhaps the acclaimed Lebanese director Nadine Labaki's latest film, "Where do we go now?" best demonstrates my pessimistic outlook on sectarian reconciliation. It is set in a fictitious Lebanese village inhabited by Christians and Muslims who get along well. Then, sectarian tension elsewhere leads to violence among the men, compelling the women to devise creative solutions to halt the hostility. The film illustrates how quickly dormant discourses of community identity can re-emerge to rearrange the social order.

I believe the sectarian tension in today's Middle East eschews anything but pragmatic cooperation between the Sunnis and Shiites.

A top Syrian official recently said that such weapons are only meant to be used against foreign "aggressors."[48]

The international community, meanwhile, seems paralyzed, with Russia and China continuing to stand behind the regime and the West and Gulf States calling for its ouster. Events on the ground seem to have simply outrun diplomacy. On Aug. 2, former U.N. Secretary-General Kofi Annan said he would resign as special Arab League envoy to Syria, complaining that international disunity is exacerbating the conflict.

"Eventually it's going to be okay, but it's going to be a hell of a struggle," says Landis. "And if you add in 10 years of civil war and instability — which all their neighboring countries faced when they went through the same effort to get rid of a minority and put the majority on top — it's miserable."

The single bright spot, ironically, seems to be within Syria itself, in the form of a multi-faith underground support and rescue network whose volunteers risk their lives to bring food, clothing and medical supplies to areas destroyed by the regime. "They [the regime] want to get rid of the idea that people can help each other," a participant told *The New York Times*. "They don't want there to be solidarity among the Syrian people."[49]

Regional Tensions

Sectarian fault lines have deepened elsewhere in the Middle East as well. In Iraq, for instance, suicide bombings against Shiites are on the rise, allegedly by Sunni militants linked to Al Qaeda. More than 325 people died just in July.[50]

Meanwhile, the government's unity is fragile. In December, the Shiite prime minister, Nuri al-Maliki, charged the Sunni vice president, Tariq al-Hashemi, with orchestrating anti-Shiite death squads. Hashemi denied the charges, calling them politically motivated, and fled to Turkey, which has refused to extradite him. Nevertheless, he is being tried in absentia in Baghdad. Maliki, meanwhile, is facing no-confidence calls in Parliament from critics who say he is concentrating too much power in his own hands.

A major Shiite-Sunni flashpoint in Iraq is the question of who will rebuild a shrine in Samarra — revered by both sects — which was destroyed in a 2006 bombing. In June a suicide car bombing targeted a Shiite religious office hoping to oversee the project, and a homemade bomb found in the offices of its Sunni counterpart was detonated by authorities.

"That the shrine is still a focus for Iraq's sectarian divisions illustrates how far Iraq is from salving its psychic wounds," wrote Tim Arango and Yasir Ghazi in *The New York Times*.[51]

Meanwhile, in tiny Bahrain, the restive Shiite majority says it has habitually been discriminated against by the country's minority Sunni monarchy. When a pro-democracy movement broke out in the early days of the Arab Spring, both Shiites and Sunnis were involved. But the monarchy lost no time in portraying the movement as an Iranian-backed Shiite uprising.

"The initial response was to claim that the Shiites . . . wanted to create an Islamic theocracy modeled on Iran's Islamic Republic," says Rutgers' Jones. "Of course, nothing could be further from the truth. But that kind of language justified a brutal crackdown [and] paralyzed American diplomacy and foreign policy in the region."

A November 2011 report by the Bahrain Independent Commission of Inquiry, an international panel commissioned by Bahrain's King Hamad bin Isa al Khalifa, found no evidence of Iranian involvement in the protests. But the report found that the government had used excessive force and torture against protesters. Moreover, on Aug. 1, the Cambridge, Mass.-based group Physicians for Human Rights claimed the Bahraini government has killed at least 30 civilians by "weaponizing" tear gas; the government denied the charges.[52] The United States has registered concern about those findings.[53] But, with a key U.S. naval base in Bahrain and a desire to maintain friendly access to the region's oil, the United States may be reluctant to upset the balance of power in the Gulf.[54]

"Imagining a political system that may not allow oil to flow as we want it to is too much of a risk," Jones maintains. "So the U.S. isn't going to let a little thing like human rights get in the way of that."

The commission's report created momentum to end the conflict, but that push now seems to have stalled, says Mariwan Hama-Saeed, a researcher at New York-based Human Rights Watch. He says the Bahraini government can't fairly negotiate with the opposition because many of its leaders are in jail — for demanding more political rights. "It's very tense," he says. "Nobody talks to anyone. Like friends from the other sect — even when they want to talk, they don't want to talk politics, or they're just silent. Everybody's scared."

Landis predicts the Shiites in Bahrain "will just have to suck their lemons." But others, such as Jones, worry about a turn towards radicalization, even terrorism. If that happens, Bahrain might agree to be annexed by its large, powerful, Sunni neighbor, Saudi Arabia.

That's exactly the plan a young Bahraini prince described to Columbia University's Bulliet a dozen years ago. "I said, 'You know, in the long run, your family is either going to have to share power, or turn the country over to Saudi Arabia, because you just can't stand up permanently to a substantial majority population,'" Bulliet says. "He said, 'Yes, that's what we're going to do. We're going to give up sovereignty and become part of Saudi Arabia.'"

Then, the prince began describing Shiites in the most racist terms possible, Bulliet adds. "And I thought, 'Wow, if that is the view [he has] grown up with — that the only way we can stand up to the vermin who inhabit our island is to give up sovereignty and become part of Saudi Arabia — then the Shiites can't win against them.'"

In poverty-stricken Yemen, there isn't much of a central government to rebel against — but factions on both sides of the sectarian divide are trying. In the south, the government is battling Al Qaeda. In the north, it's confronting the Houthi — militant Zaidis who oppose the government's alliance with the United States. The Houthi also are fighting the ultra-orthodox Sunni Salafists who have moved into their territory from Saudi Arabia.[55]

"It's a very complicated, murky picture," says Princeton's Yemen scholar Johnsen.

Such developments have weakened the traditional harmony that existed between the mainstream Sunnis and Shiites who make up the majority of Yemenis. Plus, the Persian-Arabian rivalry plays a role here as it does in other Middle Eastern hotspots.

"You have a kind of spectrum," says Laurent Bonnefoy, a political science researcher at the French Institute for the Near East in Jerusalem. "At one end of the spectrum you would have the Zaidi revivalists; at the extreme other end you would have the Salafists. They stigmatize each other as being led by Iran or Saudi Arabia." Still, Bonnefoy remains optimistic that the political process Yemen has adopted since the fall of its autocratic president, Ali Abdullah Saleh, in February will lead to stability.

Johnsen is less sanguine. "At this point, I'm not sure it's helpful to even talk about one Yemen anymore," he says. "There are several Yemens, and the country is slowly drifting apart."

In Pakistan, Sunni extremists continue to target Shiites, but "having spent decades turning a blind eye to . . . groups with a clear agenda based on hatred and intolerance, Pakistan's government appears helpless" to stop it, wrote blogger Mustafa Qadri in Britain's *Guardian*.[56]

Still, there are signs of hope, says the International Crisis Group's Ahmed. The two moderate parties that dominate the country's politics understand the need to reduce sectarian violence, she says. "If we see that process sustained," she adds, "then the political culture in Pakistan can go back to where it was — where the vast majority of moderate Pakistanis will not allow the extremists to hijack them."

OUTLOOK
Historical Process

Examples of harmony and reconciliation among Muslims of different branches abound.

Each year more than 2 million Muslims of every persuasion peacefully make the pilgrimage to Mecca, Muhammad's birthplace.[57] Muslim peacemaking clerics and conflict resolution experts work to build bridges between the branches. Muslims co-exist harmoniously in countries such as India, Azerbaijan and Oman.[58]

But the risk of continued violence in the heart of the Muslim world remains high. Looking ahead, much will depend on the course of the crises in Syria and Bahrain, the likelihood of maintaining stability in Iraq and Lebanon and the frequency of Sunni attacks on Shiites in Pakistan.

Jones of Rutgers University predicts that where disenfranchised groups — such as the Sunnis in Syria and the Shiites in Bahrain — have been met with violence by the ruling regime sectarian divisions will become permanent. "Part of what's so devastating and so dangerous about this is that the outcome is to make sectarianism more pronounced," he says. "This is toxic and it's structural, at this point." But it didn't have to be this way, he says. At the beginning of the Arab Spring people from different faiths and backgrounds united to push for equal rights.

El-Ali, at Search for Common Ground, hopes the Arab Spring will offer a different vision of the future. "The question is going to be, 'Is this young energy going to learn from the mistakes of previous generations that took to the streets in different parts of the region and tried to do things by force, and descended into mayhem and chaos?" she asks. That's why it's so important to offer a vision of the future in these countries, she adds, "to try to be builders and not destroyers."

Promoting education and economic development would help, says Bahgat of the National Defense University. He suggests that Islamic societies expose more people to different ways of life, without necessarily aping the Western model. This would help people of different persuasions accept each other, he says.

In the end, he says, Muslims may have little choice but to try to do just that. Western powers will come and go, but the people living in the Middle East will stay. "No sect will disappear," Bahgat says. "They will always live together — Sunni and Shia, Muslim and Jews. That is why they have to figure out how to have a peaceful relationship with each other."

With the heart of the Islamic world in flux, it's unclear what the future holds for the region. But most experts agree that for the foreseeable future the transition will be neither smooth nor nonviolent.

It took democratic nations centuries to get to the point where diverse populations live together in relative equality, points out Duke University's Maghraoui. "It was a struggle," he says, "bloody, convoluted. It went forward. It went backward. It was a process, a historical process. And in the Middle East, we have not seen this process. It has been dominated by authoritarian regimes, until the Arab Spring emerged."

NOTES

1. Damien McElroy, "Syria: Bashar al-Assad 'flees to Latakia,'" *The Telegraph*, July 19, 2012, www.telegraph.co.uk/news/worldnews/middleeast/syria/9412126/Syria-Bashar-al-Assad-flees-to-Latakia.html.

2. Rami Khouri, "Sectarianism starts at home," *The Globe and Mail*, July 26, 2011, www.nowlebanon.com/NewsArchiveDetails.aspx?ID=294678#ixzz21SuYGJtb.

3. For background on the Arab Spring, see Roland Flamini, "Turmoil in the Arab World," *CQ Global Researcher*, May 3, 2011, pp. 209-236.

4. "This House Believes the Sunni-Shia Conflict is Damaging Islam's Reputation as a Religion of Peace," The Doha Debates, April 29, 2008, http://thedohadebates.com/debates/item/?d=2&s=4&mode=opinions.

5. Kareem Raheem, "Iraq Attacks Kill at Least 53, Pilgrims Targeted," Reuters, June 13, 2012, www.reuters.com/article/2012/06/13/us-iraq-violence-idUSBRE85C05920120613.

6. "Shias Targeted in Afghan Shrine Blasts," *Al Jazeera*, Dec. 7, 2011, www.aljazeera.com/news/asia/2011/12/201112674650869183.html.

7. "The Sword and the Word," *The Economist*, May 12, 2012, www.economist.com/node/21554513.

8. "Houla: How a Massacre Unfolded," BBC, June 8, 2012, www.bbc.co.uk/news/world-middle-east-18233934.

9. Stephanie Nebehay, "Syrian Forces Face Prosecution for Houla — UN," Reuters, June 1, 2012, www.trust.org/alertnet/news/syrian-forces-face-prosecution-for-houla-un.

10. Khaled Yacoub Oweis, "Rifts Widen in Syrian Opposition," Reuters, May 21, 2012, www.reuters.com/article/2012/05/21/us-syria-opposition-idUSBRE84K1A220120521. Also see Mark Hosenball, "Obama Authorizes Secret U.S. Support for Syrian Rebels," Reuters, Aug. 1, 2012.

11. "Syria Boosts Fears of Sunni Shia War," UPI, April 19, 2012, www.upi.com/Top_News/Special/2012/04/19/Syria-boosts-fears-of-Sunni-Shiite-war/UPI-50411334854300/.

12. "North Lebanon Fighting Kills 1; Ninth in Five Days," Reuters, May 17, 2012, www.reuters.com/article/2012/05/17/us-lebanon-clashes-idUSBRE84G09N20120517.

13. Souad Mekhennet, "Bahrain's Shiite-Sunni Animosities Linger on Campus a Year After Clashes," *The New York Times*, March 28, 2012, www.nytimes.com/2012/03/29/world/middleeast/bahrains-shiite-sunni-animosities-linger-on-campus-a-year-after-clashes.html?pagewanted=all.

14. "Deobandi Islam," Global Security, www.global security.org/military/intro/islam-deobandi.htm.

15. Vali Nasr, *The Shia Revival* (2006), p. 168.

16. Bernard Lewis and Buntzie Ellis Churchill, *Islam: The Religion and the People* (2009), p. 61.

17. "Al-Azhar Verdict on the Shia," Al-Shia.org.

18. *Ibid.* For background, see Sarah Glazer, "Sharia Controversy," *CQ Global Researcher*, Jan. 3, 2012, pp. 1-28.

19. Lewis and Churchill, *op. cit.*, p. 65.

20. John L. Esposito, *What Everyone Needs to Know about Islam* (2011), p. 43. For background, see Kenneth Jost, "Understanding Islam," *CQ Researcher*, Nov. 3, 2006, pp. 913-936.

21. Febe Armanios, "Islam: Sunnis and Shiites," Congressional Research Service, Library of Congress, Feb. 23, 2004.

22. *Ibid.*

23. *Ibid.*

24. Lewis and Churchill, *op. cit.*, p. 62.

25. Armanios, *op. cit.* Also see Robert Mackey, "Syria's Ruling Alawite Sect," *The New York Times*, June 14, 2011, http://thelede.blogs.nytimes.com/2011/06/14/syrias-ruling-alawite-sect/.

26. "The Sword and the Word," *op. cit.*

27. "Safavid and Ottoman Eras," "History of the Middle East Database," www.nmhtthornton.com/mehistory database/safavid_and_ottoman_eras.php.

28. Lewis and Churchill, *op. cit.*

29. J. E. Peterson, "Introduction to the Middle East," *Political Handbook of the World* (2007), http://library.cqpress.com/phw/document.php?id=phw 2008-1000-43952-2033610&type=query&num=J .E.+Peterson&.

30. "Syria's Role in the Middle East," "PBS Newshour," Sept. 14, 2006, www.pbs.org/newshour/indepth_coverage/middle_east/syria/history.html.

31. For background, see D. Teter, "Iran Between East and West," *Editorial Research Reports*, Jan. 26, 1979, available at *CQ Researcher Plus Archive.*

32. Peterson, *op. cit.*

33. Mike Shuster, "The Partisans of Ali," NPR, Feb. 14, 2007.

34. Peterson, *op. cit.*

35. Shuster, *op. cit.*

36. Michael Scott Moore, "Was Saddam's Execution a Message to Shiites?" *Der Spiegel International*, Jan. 3, 2007, www.spiegel.de/international/the-world-from-berlin-was-saddam-s-execution-a-message-to-shiites-a-457559.html.

37. "1982: Syria's President Hafez al-Assad crushes rebellion in Hama," "From the Archive blog," *The Guardian*, www.guardian.co.uk/theguardian/from-the-archive-blog/2011/aug/01/hama-syria-massacre-1982-archive.

38. *Ibid.*

39. Alistair Lawson, "Pakistan's Evolving Sectarian Schism," BBC, Oct. 4, 2011.

40. "Syria troops hit back at rebels in Damascus and Aleppo," BBC, July 23, 2012, www.bbc.co.uk/news/world-middle-east-18943316. Also see Stephanie Nebehay and Tom Miles, "Tens of thousands flee Syria as fighting surges," Reuters, July 20, 2012.

41. Stephanie Nebehay and Mariam Karouny, "Both Sides in Syria Abuse Human Rights," Reuters, May 25, 2012, www.reuters.com/article/2012/05/24/us-syria-idUSBRE84N0ZJ20120524.

42. Khaled Yacoub Oweis, "Rifts Widen in Syrian Opposition," Reuters, May 21, 2012, www.reuters .com/article/2012/05/21/us-syria-opposition-idUSBRE 84K1A220120521.

43. Jack Healy, "Syrian Kurds Flee into Iraqi Refugee Limbo," *The New York Times*, March 8, 2012, www .nytimes.com/2012/03/09/world/middleeast/syrian-kurds-flee-into-iraqi-refugee-limbo.html?page wanted=all.

44. Neil MacFarquhar, "Syrian Alawites Divided by Assad's Response to Unrest," *The New York Times*, June 9, 2012, www.nytimes.com/2012/06/10/world/middleeast/syrian-alawites-divided-by-assads-response-to-unrest.html?pagewanted=all.

45. Eric Schmitt, "C.I.A. Said to Aid in Steering Arms to Syrian Opposition," *The New York Times*, June 21, 2012, www.nytimes.com/2012/06/21/world/middleeast/cia-said-to-aid-in-steering-arms-to-syrian-rebels.html?pagewanted=all. Also see Mark Landler and Neil MacFarquhar, "Heavier Weapons Push Syrian Crisis Toward Civil War," *The New York*

Times, June 12, 2012, www.nytimes.com/2012/ 06/13/world/middleeast/violence-in-syria-continues- as-protesters-killed.html?pagewanted=all.

46. Mark Hosenball, "As Militants Join Syria Revolt, Fears Grow over Arms Flow," Reuters, June 22, 2012, www.reuters.com/article/2012/06/22/us- syria-armsrace-idUSBRE85L0MS20120622.

47. Schmitt, *op. cit.*

48. "Syria threatens to use chemical weapons against foreign powers — video," *The Guardian*, July 24, 2012, www.guardian.co.uk/world/video/2012/ jul/24/syria-chemical-weapons-video?newsfeed=true.

49. "Syrians Defy Leaders to Aid Those in Need," *The New York Times*, May 14, 2012, www.nytimes .com/2012/05/15/world/middleeast/syria-aid- movement-defies-assad-government.html?page wanted=all.

50. "Iraq sees deadliest month in two years," BBC News, Aug. 1, 2012, www.bbc.co.uk/news/world-middle- east-19076257.

51. Tim Arango and Yasir Ghazi, "Violence Spreads in the Struggle for Baghdad Shrine," *The New York Times*, June 4, 2012, www.nytimes.com/2012/06/05/ world/middleeast/bombing-in-baghdad-linked-to- dispute-over-samarra-shrine.html.

52. "Report of the Bahrain Independent Commission of Inquiry," Bahrain Independent Commission of Inquiry, Nov. 23, 2011, www.bici.org.bh/ BICIreportEN.pdf. See also "Bahraini authorities 'weaponising' tear gas," BBC, Aug. 1, 2012, www.bbc .co.uk/news/world-middle-east-19078659.

53. "U.S. Statement at the Universal Periodic Review of Bahrain," U.S. Mission to the U.N. (Geneva), May 21, 2012, http://geneva.usmission.gov/2012/05/21/ bahrain/.

54. For background, see Jennifer Koons, "Future of the Gulf States," *CQ Global Researcher*, Nov. 1, 2011, pp. 525-548.

55. Chiara Onassis, "Yemen: The Sunni-Shia Divide, Sectarian Violence on the Rise," Bikyamasr.com, Feb. 27, 2012, http://bikyamasr.com/58961/yemen-the- sunni-shia-divide-sectarian-violence-on-the-rise/.

56. Mustafa Qadri, "Pakistan Is in Denial over Spreading Sectarian Violence," *Guardian*, April 19, 2012, www.guardian.co.uk/commentisfree/2012/ apr/19/pakistan-sectarian-violence.

57. Esposito, *op. cit.*, p. 22.

58. "The Sword and the Word," *op. cit.*

BIBLIOGRAPHY

Selected Sources

Books

Commins, David, *The Wahhabi Mission and Saudi Arabia*, Library of Modern Middle East Studies, 2009.
A professor of history at Dickinson College examines the rise of Wahhabism, a controversial hardline Sunni sect prevalent in Saudi Arabia, Afghanistan, Pakistan and other parts of the Muslim world. Commins also evaluates the challenge that radical militants in Saudi Arabia present to the Middle East.

Gonzalez, Nathan, *The Sunni-Shia Conflict: Understanding Sectarian Violence in the Middle East*, Nortia Press, 2009.
A lecturer in Middle East studies and international politics at California State University says Muslim sectarian rivalries are based on geopolitics rather than theology and contends that power vacuums allow regional leaders to use sectarianism for their own ends.

Haddad, Fanar, *Sectarianism in Iraq: Antagonistic Visions of Unity*, Hurst/Columbia University Press, 2011.
A Middle East scholar and analyst examines the relationship between Iraq's Shiites and Sunnis as it evolves from co-existence to conflict. He focuses on the Shiite uprising in 1991 and the fall of Saddam Hussein's Baath Party in 2003.

Hazleton, Lesley, *After the Prophet: The Epic Story of the Shia-Sunni Split in Islam*, Doubleday, 2009.
A veteran journalist describes the epic origins of the sectarian split that began while the Prophet Muhammad lay dying.

Johnsen, Gregory, *The Last Refuge: Yemen, al-Qaeda and America's War in Arabia*, W. W. Norton, 2012.
A Yemen scholar at Princeton University charts the rise, fall and resurrection of Al Qaeda in Yemen over the last 30 years. Johnsen brings readers inside the Sunni terrorist group's training camps and safe houses and examines successes and failures in fighting a new type of war in one of the most turbulent countries in the world.

Nasr, Sayyed Hossein, *The Heart of Islam: Enduring Values for Humanity*, Harper One, 2004.
A professor of Islamic Studies at The George Washington University and one of Islam's most respected intellectuals writes about the religion's core values.

Weiss, Max, *In the Shadow of Sectarianism: Law, Shi'ism, and the Making of Modern Lebanon*, Harvard University Press, 2010.
An assistant professor of history and Near East studies at Princeton University examines the complicated roots of Shiite sectarianism in Lebanon, going back to the French mandate after World War I.

Articles

Blanford, Nicholas, "In Lebanon, a Worrying Sectarian Spillover from Syria," *The Christian Science Monitor*, June 3, 2012, www.csmonitor.com/World/Middle-East/2012/0603/In-Lebanon-a-worrying-sectarian-spillover-from-Syria.
Analysts worry that sectarian violence in Syria could reignite civil war in Lebanon.

Diehl, Jackson, "Lines in the Sand: Assad Plays the Sectarian Card," *Foreign Affairs*, May/June 2012, www.worldaffairsjournal.org/article/lines-sand-assad-plays-sectarian-card.
A *Washington Post* foreign affairs specialist offers an explanation of how Syria has become the focal point of sectarian and regional conflict.

Feldman, Noah, "Choosing a Sect," *The New York Times Magazine*, March 4, 2007, www.cfr.org/religion-and-politics/choosing-sect/p12772.

A Harvard law professor at the Council on Foreign Relations explores the debate about whether the United States should side with one Islamic sect.

Reports and Studies

Blanchard, Christopher, "Islam: Sunnis and Shiites," *Congressional Research Service*, Jan. 28, 2009, www.fas.org/sgp/crs/misc/RS21745.pdf.
This study presents a history of the original split and a description of the differences and similarities between both branches, and the relationship to sectarian violence.

Jha, Saurav, "Saudi-Iranian Tensions Widening into Sunni-Shiite Cold War," *World Politics Review*, April 29, 2011.
The crisis in Bahrain has deepened the Saudi-Iranian Cold War, exacerbating regional tensions.

Kuwait Study Group: "Identity, Citizenship and Sectarianism in the GCC," Chatham House, February 2012, www.chathamhouse.org/sites/default/files/public/Research/Middle%20East/0212kuwaitsummary_identity.pdf.
This workshop summary examines the evolving identity of the Gulf States, particularly the authoritarian, male-dominated ruling regimes, juxtaposed with traditions of inclusiveness and multiculturalism.

Shuster, Mike, "The Partisans of Ali," NPR, www.npr.org/series/7346199/the-partisans-of-ali.
This five-part radio documentary traces the religious and historical differences between Sunnis and Shiites, and the impact of sectarian conflict.

For More Information

Center for Arab Unity Studies, P.O. Box 113-6001, Hamra, Beirut, Lebanon; +961 1 750084; www.caus.org. Researches Arab society and Arab unity without any partisan or government ties.

Center for Islamic Pluralism, 202-232-1750; www.islamic pluralism.org. A think tank that opposes the radicalization of Islam in America.

Center for Religious Freedom, 1319 18th St., N.W., Washington, DC 20036; 202-296-5101; www.freedom house.org/religion. Defends against religious persecution of all groups throughout the world.

Center for the Study of Islam and Democracy, 1050 Connecticut Ave., N.W., Suite 1000, Washington, DC 20036; 202-772-2022; www.islam-democracy.org. Merges Islamic and democratic political thought into modern Islamic discourse.

Conflicts Forum, Beirut, Lebanon; +961 3 803028; www.conflictsforum.org. Aims to shift Western opinion towards a deeper understanding of Islam and the Middle East.

Doha Debates, Qatar Foundation, P.O. Box 5825, Doha, Qatar; www.thedohadebates.com; Fax: +974 4454 1759. An independent public forum that conducts televised debates on controversial topics, with participants from all over the Arab world.

Institute for Social Policy and Understanding, 1225 I St., N.W., Suite 307, Washington, DC 20005; 202-481-8215; www.ispu.org. Provides analysis, insight and context on critical issues, especially those related to Muslims.

School of Sufi Teaching, London, England and centers worldwide; +44 20 8556-7713; www.schoolofsufiteaching .org. Offers instruction in teachings of Sufism.

Search for Common Ground, 1601 Connecticut Ave., Suite 200, Washington, DC 20009; 202-265-4300; www.sfcg .org. Nonprofit that advocates conflict resolution.

Voices From Abroad

RAMI KHOURI

Director, Issam Fares Institute for Public Policy Lebanon

The root causes

"When countries are well managed and citizens feel they have a say in political and economic developments, sectarian identities and tensions decrease and eventually disappear. But when authoritarian gangs and oligarchic ruling families plunder their countries and treat their citizens like idiots without rights or feelings, sectarianism sprouts like the natural self-defence mechanism that it is."

Globe and Mail (Canada), July 2011

India/*The National Herald*/Paresh Nath

SHEIKH YUSUF AL-QARADAWI

Islamic theologian, Egypt

Simply unacceptable

"Unfortunately, we have seen that in a big country, such as Iraq, another language, . . . the language of political sectarianism, is being used. This is a divisive sectarianism. The ummah, which was once united, is meant to be divided. . . . This is what Al-Maliki, those who are behind him, and his allies want to do. . . . This sectarianism is unacceptable."

Al Jazeera (Qatar), December 2011

MICHEL SULAYMAN

President, Lebanon

Liberating the youth

"It is critical in a diverse country such as Lebanon to draft laws that could liberate the youth from sectarianism, primarily the election law that is based on proportional representation and preserves the major characteristic of Lebanon's covenant of coexistence between the Lebanese."

The Daily Star (Lebanon), July 2011

SHEIKH KHALID BIN ALI AL KHALIFAH

Minister of Justice and Islamic Affairs, Bahrain

Things to consider

"There are societies that have turned political differences into issues of existence, and our priorities now are to implement consensus of the National Dialogue and make constitutional amendments in line with people's demands. . . . We can't stop preachers, because people will see it as targeting the whole congregation, and at the moment we are working with international organizations to train clergymen on the principles of giving speeches. There are some serious violations, and I agree with parliament that they have to be dealt with, but several factors have to be taken into consideration first."

Gulf Daily News (Bahrain), March 2012

ALHAJI MUHAMMAD SA'AD ABUBAKAR

Sultan of Sokoto state Nigeria

Stop blaming sects

"Most of the crises are not caused by the Boko Haram sect, so we have to ask ourselves, why is there violence in the northeast [of Nigeria]. Who are those behind them? The government must fish them out and tell us those responsible for the crises. This thing did not start today, stop blaming every violence on Boko Haram."

Daily Trust (Nigeria), July 2011

SHEIKH ANAS SUWAYD

Islamic cleric, Syria

Discrimination against Sunnis

"In Hims [Syria], there is sectarianism par excellence because the regime is discriminating against the Sunnis . . . in an unimaginable manner. Imagine that electricity is cut off for eight hours a day in all Sunni neighbourhoods in Hims, and the Sunni neighbourhoods are deprived of bread for days if people staged demonstrations, [but] bread would be passed secretly to them from other neighbourhoods."

Al Jazeera (Qatar), January 2012

WOLE SOYINKA

Author, Nigeria

Picking up the gauntlet

"The gauntlet of religious sectarianism has been thrown down. African leaders must pick it up, and lend succor to those who are plagued with this constriction of citizen choice."

The New Times (Rwanda), July 2012

WADAH KHANFAR

Former Director General Al Jazeera Network, Qatar

Preserving national character

"The Syrian popular consciousness has been able to protect the revolution from the virus of sectarianism and ethnicity by preserving its national character. . . . The Syrian street knows that the language of sectarianism will only serve the interests of the regime, and it will divert the revolution from the path of democracy."

The Guardian (England), February 2012

15

Climate Change

Jennifer Weeks

A villager rafts through flood waters in northeastern India on Sept. 25, 2012. Scientists say the negative effects of climate change, including flooding caused by sea-level rise, as well as heat waves and storms, will affect developing countries most severely because they are less prepared for disaster and have limited funds for disaster relief.

From *CQ Researcher*, June 14, 2013.

News reports last month marked a scientific milestone: Earth's atmosphere now contains more carbon dioxide (CO_2) than at any time in up to 3 million years.[1] And the average annual rate of increase for the past decade was more than twice as steep as during the 1960s.[2]

With carbon dioxide levels climbing at such a rapid pace, scientists said, it is clear that humans already have set dramatic climate change in motion. "Even if we all decided to stop emitting CO_2 immediately, it would take at least 20 years to start putting new [low-carbon or carbon-free] systems in place, and another 50 years for the climate to adjust," says Kevin Trenberth, a senior scientist at the National Center for Atmospheric Research in Boulder, Colo.

Carbon dioxide is a "greenhouse gas" (GHG) that traps heat in the atmosphere, warming Earth's surface. It is generated by natural sources such as wildfires and volcanic eruptions, and by human activities — primarily burning fossil fuels such as coal, oil and natural gas. Before the Industrial Revolution, Earth's atmosphere contained about 280 parts per million of CO_2. Now, numerous scientific studies warn, GHG concentrations have reached levels that will cause drastic warming with widespread consequences.[3]

"We cause global warming by increasing the greenhouse effect, and our greenhouse gas emissions just keep accelerating," climate scientist Dana Nuccitelli wrote in May. In a review of more than 4,000 peer-reviewed studies, Nuccitelli and others found that 97.1 percent endorsed the idea that human activities were contributing to climate change.[4]

Carbon Dioxide Concentrations on the Rise

The amount of carbon dioxide (CO_2) in the atmosphere reached 400 parts per million this spring, about a 25 percent increase since 1959. Scientists say CO_2 measurements, taken at an observatory in Mauna Loa, Hawaii, show that global carbon dioxide concentrations have climbed steadily in recent decades as a result of intensive fossil fuel combustion worldwide.

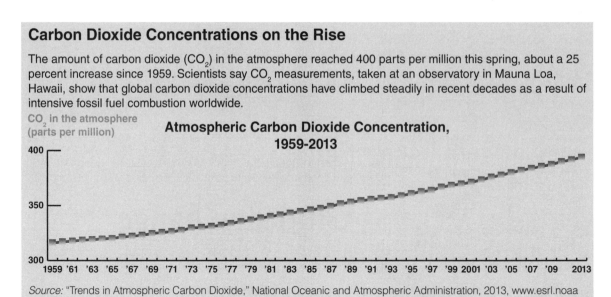

CO_2 in the atmosphere (parts per million)

Atmospheric Carbon Dioxide Concentration, 1959-2013

Source: "Trends in Atmospheric Carbon Dioxide," National Oceanic and Atmospheric Administration, 2013, www.esrl.noaa.gov/gmd/ccgg/trends

Other researchers say that while human activities may be warming the Earth, climate scientists are drawing conclusions that go beyond the evidence. "[T]here is no *prima facie* reason to think that global warming will make most extreme weather events more frequent or more severe. . . . Extreme events are by definition rare, and the rarer the event the more difficult it is to identify long-term changes from relatively short data records," said Judith Curry, chair of the School of Earth and Atmospheric Sciences at Georgia Tech, testifying to Congress in April.[5]

But many experts are deeply concerned. "The clock is ticking," said Jerry Melillo, a scientist at the Marine Biological Laboratory in Woods Hole, Mass., and chairman of a committee that published a national assessment earlier this year of the science and impacts of climate change.[6] According to the assessment, average U.S. temperatures have risen about 1.5° Fahrenheit since 1895, most of it in the past 20 years.

That change may not seem large, but small shifts can have big impacts. During the so-called Little Ice Age (1300s-1800s), when average temperatures fell by just under 1°C (1.8°F), widespread crop failures in Europe caused millions of deaths.[7] At the end of the last full-scale ice age about 10,000 years ago, average temperatures were only 5 to 9 degrees Fahrenheit cooler than modern levels, and much of North America and Europe was covered by glaciers.[8]

Recent warming already has caused significant changes. "Certain types of weather events have become more frequent and/or intense, including heat waves, heavy downpours, and, in some regions, floods and droughts," authors of the assessment report wrote. "Sea level is rising, oceans are becoming more acidic and glaciers and arctic sea ice are melting."[9]

During his 2008 presidential campaign, President Obama called for action to slow climate change, but prospects faded in 2010 after a Democratic controlled Congress failed to enact legislation and control of the House shifted to the GOP. Most congressional Republicans and some conservative Democrats oppose legislation to limit climate change.[10]

Campaigning for reelection in 2012, Obama supported developing all types of energy sources, including fossil fuels. In his second inaugural address in January he issued a strong call for action. Ignoring climate change, he said, "would betray our children and future generations."[11] In his State of the Union address in February he asked Congress to pass a "bipartisan, market-based solution to climate change." If not, Obama said, he would direct federal agencies to propose steps that could be taken through regulations.[12]

But the politics of climate change remain highly polarized. Some Republican politicians question the overwhelming scientific consensus that human actions are altering Earth's climate.[13] "All the things they're [the Obama administration] saying happened, they're all part of [former Vice President] Al Gore's science fiction movie, and they've all been discredited," said Oklahoma Sen. James Inhofe, former chairman of the Senate Environment and Public Works Committee.[14]

Others say the case is not proven, focusing on issues that researchers are still analyzing. "There is a great amount of uncertainty associated with climate science," wrote Rep. Lamar Smith of Texas, chairman of the House Science Committee.[15] And many legislators oppose measures that would raise fossil fuel prices. More than a dozen moderate and conservative Democrats joined Republicans in symbolic votes earlier this year against a carbon tax — which would raise the price of fossil fuels based on their carbon content — and for construction of the Keystone XL pipeline. The pipeline would facilitate development of Canadian "tar sand" oil and is opposed by many environmentalists who say it will enable greater use of fossil fuels.[16]

At the same time, polls show a growing share of Americans — including Republicans — believe climate change is occurring and support some kind of action. And some observers say Republican legislators' opposition is eroding.[17]

"There is a divide within the party," said Samuel Thernstrom, a scholar at the conservative American Enterprise Institute who served on the White House Council on Environmental Quality under President George W. Bush and has written that humans are

changing Earth's climate, with potentially severe effects. "The position that climate change is a hoax is untenable," he says.[18]

Other conservatives view climate change as a serious problem but question whether government actions — particularly through regulation — can slow it. "The real

Partisan Divide Is Wide on Climate Change

About 70 percent of Americans say there is solid evidence the Earth is warming, and about 40 percent say the planet is warming mainly because of human activity. The percentage of those with either view declined between 2006 and 2009-2010 but has risen since, including among Republicans. Nevertheless, the partisan divide over climate change remains wide: Fewer than 20 percent of Republicans believe human activity causes it. And although 42 percent of Republicans favor stricter environmental limits on power plants, significantly more Democrats and Independents want such restrictions.

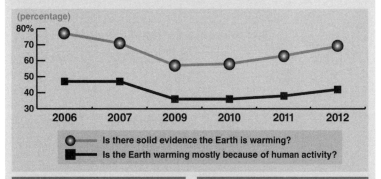

Percent Who Think the Earth Is Warming, by Party, 2013	
Yes	
Republicans	44%
Democrats	87%
Independents	68%
Yes, and mostly due to human activity	
Republicans	19%
Democrats	57%
Independents	43%

Percent Who Think Scientists Agree Human Activity Is Causing Climate Change, by Party, 2012	
Republicans	30%
Democrats	58%
Independents	45%
Percent Who Favor Setting Stricter Limits on Power Plants to Address Climate Change, by Party, 2013	
Republicans	42%
Democrats	72%
Independents	64%

Source: "Climate Change: Key Data Points From Pew Research," Pew Research Center, April 2013, www.pewresearch.org/2013/04/02/climate-change-key-data-points-from-pew-research

China, U.S. Emit the Most Carbon Dioxide

China emitted more carbon dioxide (CO_2) in 2011 than any other country. Its nearly 9 billion metric tons of carbon dioxide emissions were about 60 percent greater than the 5.5 billion metric tons emitted in the United States, which ranked second. Worldwide, CO_2 emissions from energy use totaled nearly 33 billion metric tons in 2011. Most carbon dioxide, a major source of heat-trapping greenhouse gases, comes from energy consumption. Emissions of other types of greenhouse gases — such as methane and nitrous oxide — are not included in these totals.

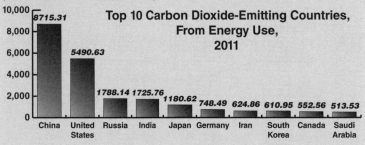

(millions of metric tons of carbon dioxide)

Top 10 Carbon Dioxide-Emitting Countries, From Energy Use, 2011

China	8715.31
United States	5490.63
Russia	1788.14
India	1725.76
Japan	1180.62
Germany	748.49
Iran	624.86
South Korea	610.95
Canada	552.56
Saudi Arabia	513.53

Source: "International Energy Statistics," Energy Information Administration, 2013, www.eia.gov/cfapps/ipdbproject/iedindex3.cfm?tid=90&pid=44&aid=8

obstacle to making meaningful emissions reductions is that it's unbelievably difficult to do," says Jonathan Adler, a professor of law and director of the Center for Business Law and Regulation at Case Western Reserve University. Adler describes himself as a conservative who believes that climate change is a serious problem, but is skeptical that government can mandate solutions. "We don't know how to do it at anything remotely approaching a cost that countries are willing to bear," he says. Instead, Adler favors policies that encourage energy innovation without prescribing specific technical solutions.

As Congress, the Obama administration and advocacy groups debate how to address climate change, here are some issues they are considering:

Are catastrophic climate change impacts inevitable?

Scientists say human activities have increased the amount of CO_2 in the atmosphere by more than 40 percent from pre-industrial levels. CO_2 remains in the atmosphere for years, so some climate change has already been set in motion. However, scientists and policymakers are debating how much climate change is inevitable.

During negotiations over the past decade, some officials — particularly from Europe — have called for limiting carbon emissions enough so global temperatures do not rise more than 2°C (3.6°F) above pre-industrial levels. That target recognizes that some climate change is unavoidable but strives to prevent more disastrous effects, such as large-scale melting of polar ice caps. The goal was noted at a 2009 climate conference in Copenhagen, although nations did not formally commit to reductions large enough to achieve it.[19]

Limiting warming to 2°C would require capping CO_2 concentrations at about 450 parts per million, a level the planet could hit by mid-century if emissions keep rising at current rates, scientists say. Warming could be limited to that level if governments make polluters pay for their carbon emissions, eliminate subsidies for fossil fuels and increase investments in energy efficiency and renewable energy, according to Maria van der Hoeven, executive director of the International Energy Agency, which works to help nations secure reliable, affordable and clean energy. "While ambitious, a clean energy transition is still possible," van der Hoeven said. "But action in all sectors is necessary to reach our climate targets."[20]

Other experts are more pessimistic. Sir Robert Watson, a British scientist and former chair of the Intergovernmental Panel on Climate Change (IPCC), an international organization established to advise governments on climate change science and impacts, argues that nations have 50-50 odds of limiting warming to 3°C (5.4°F), but should prepare for an increase of up to 5°C (9°F). At that level, scientists say the effects will be severe, especially for developing countries.

"When I was chairing the IPCC . . . we were hopeful that emissions would not go up at the tremendous rate they are rising now," Watson said in February.

While cost-effective and equitable solutions exist, he added, "political will and moral leadership is needed" to address climate change. And the substantial changes in policies, practices and technologies are "not currently under way."[21]

Climate scientist Trenberth of the National Center for Atmospheric Research (NCAR) also doubts that it will be possible to limit warming to 2°C. "But it matters enormously how rapidly we get to that number," he says. "The rate of change matters as much as the change itself. Getting to 2°C in 50 years is quite different than if it takes 200 years or longer."

Yet he believes it is still possible to limit the rate of warming to a pace that will allow societies to adapt. "We can slow things down enough to make a big difference and push the 2°C mark well into the 22nd century," Trenberth says.

To meet that target, nations would have to sharply cut fossil fuel use. "To stay at 2°C we can't emit more than 565 gigatons of carbon dioxide into the atmosphere by mid-century," he explains. "World CO_2 emissions in 2011 were 31.6 gigatons, which was a 3.2 percent increase from the year before. At current rates, we'll go through our limit in 16 years."*

Scientists say many of the effects of climate change will occur even if the planet warms by 2°C or less. "There's an impression that if we hold warming below two degrees we're safe, which is demonstrably false," says Christopher Field, a professor of global ecology at Stanford University and lead author of IPCC climate change assessment reports. "Climate change in the next 20 to 40 years will be the result of actions that are already baked into the system."

In the United States average temperatures are rising; frost-free seasons are lasting longer; precipitation is up in the Midwest, southern Plains and Northeast and down in parts of the Southeast, Southwest and Rocky Mountain states; and extreme weather events, such as heat waves and flooding, are becoming more frequent and intense.[22]

Some experts, such as James Hansen, who retired early this year as director of NASA's Goddard Institute for Space Studies, calls the 2-degree target "a prescription

Getty Images/Sean Gallup

A coal-fired power plant spews smoke over Mehrum, Germany, on March 4, 2013. Burning fossil fuels — such as coal, natural gas and oil — creates carbon dioxide (CO_2), a greenhouse gas that traps heat in the atmosphere, warming the Earth's surface. CO_2 is also generated by natural sources, such as volcanoes and wildfires.

for disaster." Hansen says nations should cut CO_2 emissions back sharply enough to reduce atmospheric concentrations to 350 parts per million — a level last seen in 1987 — to avoid effects such as melting most of the world's glaciers and ice caps.[23]

Other scientists share his perspective. "Two degrees is actually too much for ecosystems," Thomas E. Lovejoy, a professor of environmental science and policy at George Mason University, wrote in January. "A 2-degree world will be one without coral reefs (on which millions of human beings depend for their well-being)." At current warming levels, he noted, U.S. and Amazonian forests already have been heavily damaged. "The current mode of nibbling around the edges is pretty much pointless," he concluded.[24]

Is climate engineering a good idea?

As atmospheric concentrations of greenhouse gases climb and international negotiations fail to make progress, some say it is time to begin researching ways to alter Earth's climate system on a large scale to slow the rise of global temperatures, at least until nations make serious commitments to cut emissions.

---

*A gigaton is one billion tons.

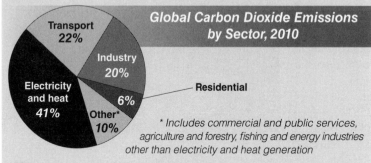

Electricity, Heat Generation Biggest CO_2 Sources

More than 40 percent of global carbon dioxide (CO_2) emissions in 2010 came from electricity and heat generation. The transportation and industrial sectors each accounted for about one-fifth of CO_2 emissions, the main component of human-generated greenhouse gases.

Global Carbon Dioxide Emissions by Sector, 2010

Transport 22%

Industry 20%

Electricity and heat 41%

Other* 10%

Residential 6%

*Includes commercial and public services, agriculture and forestry, fishing and energy industries other than electricity and heat generation

** Figures do not total 100 because of rounding.

Source: "CO_2 Emissions From Fuel Combustion," International Energy Agency, 2012, p. 9, www.iea.org/co2highlights/co2highlights.pdf

Various climate engineering schemes (also called geo-engineering) have been proposed, such as injecting particles into the atmosphere to reflect sunlight back into space or removing tons of carbon from the atmosphere and injecting it deep underground. But these concepts raise difficult technical, political and ethical questions, and some say they are unworkable or unnecessary.

The National Research Council concluded in 2010 that more research was needed on ways to reduce carbon emissions, such as improving energy efficiency, capturing and storing power plant emissions and developing more low-carbon energy sources. Geoengineering strategies "may also warrant attention, provided that they do not replace other research efforts," the authors wrote.[25]

Similarly, the Royal Society, Britain's national science academy, said in 2009 that "properly researched geoengineering methods . . . could eventually be useful to augment conventional mitigation [emission-reducing] activities, even in the absence of an imminent emergency."[26] Both academies emphasized that little was known about how well various geoengineering methods work or how easy they would be to deploy.

But some advocates are undeterred. Many cite the 1991 eruption of Mt. Pinatubo in the Philippines, which injected millions of tons of sulfur dioxide into the atmosphere.

There the gas formed sulfate particles, which reflected some of the sun's radiation back into space, lowering average global temperatures the following year by just under 1°C.

David Keith, a professor of physics and public policy at Harvard University, calls strategies to reduce incoming sunlight an imperfect but fast and cheap way to partly offset climate risk. "You can stop the warming or even do cooling if that's what you wanted to do," Keith said in January. "All the really hard problems [with geoengineering] are public policy problems."[27] For example, there are no broad international rules for governing geoengineering research or policies for assigning liability if an experiment harms natural resources or alters weather patterns.

Other scientists say geoengineering cannot be evaluated without better understanding of Earth's complex climate systems. For example, researchers at California's Scripps Institution of Oceanography have used shipboard generators to produce smoke (the same type used in skywriting) to see how it affects clouds on a small scale. They found that smoke particles brightened the clouds, making them more reflective, but that low clouds and multiple cloud layers made the process less effective.[28]

Clouds are still poorly understood, according to Scripps atmospheric chemistry professor Lynn Russell, lead author of the cloud brightening study. "Cloud droplets are measured in micrometers, but the heating and cooling that makes clouds appear occurs over areas of many kilometers. And droplets form in microseconds, but clouds form and dissipate in hours or days," she says. Computer models have trouble combining such large- and small-scale measurements, so they usually represent some variables well and approximate others, Russell notes.

Moreover, she says, scientists do not have good ways to measure some conditions that affect cloud formation, such as extremely high humidity or three-dimensional turbulence in the atmosphere. Nonetheless, Russell believes more small-scale experiments would be useful. "Before you think about investing money in long-term geoengineering studies, you need to know what's possible," she says.

Trenberth, of the National Center for Atmospheric Research, worries that adding particles to the atmosphere could harm Earth's weather and climate cycles. For example, an NCAR study of the impacts of the Mt. Pinatubo eruption found that besides temporarily lowering global temperatures, the event caused large declines in rainfall over land and extensive droughts worldwide.[29] "It was an extreme event," Trenberth says. "Geoengineering might cool off temperatures, but if it also shuts down parts of the weather and hydrological cycles, the cure could be worse than the disease."

In a recent article in the journal *Science*, Keith and UCLA law professor Edward Parson suggested governments start organizing modest field experiments in geoengineering to see how various techniques affect the atmosphere — on a scale small enough that it won't alter the climate — and start developing cooperative rules and limits.

"If research is blocked, then in some stark future situation where geoengineering is needed, only unrefined, untested and excessively risky approaches will be available," they contended.[30]

Should the United States adopt a carbon tax?

Although there is little prospect that Congress will adopt broad climate change legislation in the next several years, many liberal and conservative experts advocate taxing carbon — more specifically, the carbon content of fossil fuels. That would promote low-carbon and carbon-free fuels and technologies without having government agencies pick specific solutions, they argue.

"A carbon tax would encourage producers and consumers to shift toward energy sources that emit less carbon — such as toward gas-fired power plants and away from coal-fired plants — and generate greater demand for electric and flex-fuel cars and lesser demand for conventional gasoline-powered cars," wrote George P. Shultz, a former budget director, Treasury secretary and secretary of State during Republican presidential administrations, and Gary S. Becker, a Nobel laureate in economics and professor at the University of Chicago.[31]

A snorkeler views a coral reef near Mansuar Island, in eastern Indonesia's Papua region. The surrounding Raja Ampat archipelago, considered one of the most important biodiversity environments in the world, was nominated as a UNESCO World Heritage Site. A 2°C temperature rise would kill the world's remaining coral reefs, according to scientist Thomas Lovejoy of George Mason University.

AFP/Getty Images/Romeo Gacad

Nearly a dozen nations or regions have adopted some version of carbon taxes, including the Canadian province of British Columbia, Australia, Japan, South Africa, Switzerland, Norway, Sweden, Finland and Denmark.[32] In 2009-2010 Congress debated another way of pricing carbon: emissions trading through a so-called cap-and-trade system, which also has been adopted or is being considered by countries and regions in Europe, North America, Latin America and Asia.[33] The Waxman-Markey bill, which passed the House, would have created a U.S. emissions trading system, but it was never brought up in the Senate.*

Waxman-Markey illustrated the complexities of cap-and-trade systems, in which government agencies set a ceiling, or a cap, on total emissions of a pollutant, then issue emissions allowances to businesses that generate that pollutant. Companies must obtain allowances to cover all of their emissions or pay fines. Sources that reduce their emissions can sell their extra allowances, so they have a financial incentive to clean up their operations.

---

* The measure was named after its sponsors, Democratic Reps. Henry A. Waxman of California and Edward J. Markey of Massachusetts.

The Amazon rain forest — already being devastated by global warming — faces further damage from climate change. Scientists say a 2°C temperature rise would decrease water flow in the Amazon basin by 20-40 percent, causing widespread drought and other environmental problems.

Conservatives lobbied hard against Waxman-Markey, which they labeled "cap-and-tax" because government would keep the revenues from selling allowances. But many liberal activists also disliked the bill. They said it gave businesses permission to pollute. And most Americans had trouble understanding how the complex program would work or how it would benefit them.[34] Many observers say carbon taxes can be simpler and more understandable.

In addition, a carbon tax can be revenue-neutral, many supporters argue. Government could collect taxes on high-carbon fuels, either by taxing fuel producers (the simplest approach) or energy purchasers, then rebate the money to consumers when they file their annual income tax returns.

This approach "would make energy more expensive, but would greatly offset the regressive impact of increasing the cost of energy," says Adler of Case Western Reserve University. "It's also transparent. The more clearly we tax one thing and then send money directly back to people, the less ominous a carbon tax appears to be. Waxman-Markey was littered with special-interest giveaways, which magnified the suspicions that people have about this kind of legislation."

But many business interests strongly oppose a carbon tax, which they say would increase production costs, making their companies less competitive, especially if they compete with manufacturers in other countries where carbon isn't taxed. A study released earlier this year by the National Association of Manufacturers (NAM) contended that a carbon tax would reduce total U.S. manufacturing output by up to 15 percent in energy-intensive sectors. Higher production costs would put millions of jobs at risk and impel companies to reduce wages, which in turn would reduce workers' income. Eventually, workers would reduce their spending, which would dampen economic growth, the study said.[35]

"Manufacturers use one-third of all energy consumed in the U.S. and depend on reliable, low-cost energy sources to compete in a global marketplace," a coalition of manufacturing trade associations wrote to members of Congress in May, citing the NAM study.[36]

Industry representatives also say a carbon tax would hurt their ability to compete against fast-growing developing countries like China, which overtook the United States in 2006 as the world's largest GHG emitter. Earlier this year, however, China pledged to adopt its own carbon tax, although it has not yet offered details.[37]

Carbon tax advocates respond that emitting greenhouse gases imposes costs on society, in the form of climate change and all of its negative environmental effects. In their view, taxing carbon corrects an unfair advantage that fossil fuel producers reap when they are not required to pay the costs of carbon pollution.

"Oil and coal companies have been sending carbon pollution into the atmosphere since the Industrial Revolution. When these industries started, the risks were poorly understood. Today they know better," argued Sen. Sheldon Whitehouse, D-R.I., who has cosponsored legislation to impose a carbon tax. "On average, [economists'] estimates of the social cost of carbon are about $48 per ton of carbon dioxide — $48 per ton that these big businesses dodge and that we all pay for."

BACKGROUND

Measuring GHGs

Anthropogenic (human-driven) climate change is a relatively new scientific field, but it has deep roots. Scientists have understood for well over a century that Earth's climate has fluctuated between warm and cold phases

C H R O N O L O G Y

1890s-1950s *Scientists study weather and the role of heat-trapping greenhouse gases (GHGs).*

1896 Swedish chemist Svante Arrhenius develops first theory of human-caused climate change.

1945 U.S. military agencies start funding basic weather and climate research.

1950 The World Meteorological Organization is founded; it becomes a U.N. agency the next year.

1957 American geochemist Charles David Keeling begins measuring atmospheric carbon dioxide (CO_2) levels at Mauna Loa, Hawaii.

1980s *Environmentalists push for pollution limits in developed countries. Scientists warn that human activities are warming the planet.*

1988 Testifying before Congress, NASA scientist James Hansen warns that Earth's climate is warming with potentially disastrous impacts.

1987 Nations adopt the Montreal Protocol, setting international limits on gases that destroy Earth's ozone layer.

1988 U.N. creates Intergovernmental Panel on Climate Change (IPCC) to provide governments with expert views on climate change science.

1990s *Governments pledge to tackle climate change, but worry about costs.*

1990 First IPCC assessment report says global temperatures have risen and are likely to continue warming.

1992 At the Earth Summit in Rio de Janeiro, the United States and more than 150 other nations sign the Framework Convention on Climate Change (FCCC), pledging to cut all GHG emissions to 1990 levels by 2000.

1995 Second IPCC report finds scientific evidence of human-driven warming.

1997 FCCC member nations adopt the Kyoto Protocol, which requires developed countries to cut GHG emissions 5.2 percent, on average, by 2012. The Senate votes 95-0 not to adopt binding U.S. targets until developing nations also have to make cuts.

2000s-Present *Evidence mounts that human activities are warming the planet. Scientists find increasing evidence that climate change is altering weather patterns, ocean chemistry and other Earth systems.*

2001 Third IPCC report says major global warming is "very likely."

2005 The Kyoto Protocol enters into force after Russia ratifies it, leaving the United States and Australia as the only nonparticipating industrialized nations.

2006 Dutch Nobel laureate Paul Crutzen calls for active research into geoengineering.

2007 Fourth IPCC assessment finds with more than 90 percent certainty that human activities are warming the climate. . . . Australia ratifies Kyoto Protocol. . . . U.S. Supreme Court rules that the Environmental Protection Agency can regulate CO_2 as a pollutant.

2008 Newly elected President Barack Obama pledges quick action on climate change

2009-2010 Legislation creating a system of marketable permits to emit GHGs narrowly passes House (2009), fails to reach Senate floor. . . . Republicans win control of House in midterm elections.

2011 A conservative government announces that Canada will withdraw from the Kyoto Protocol because Canadian companies would have to buy too many carbon emission credits in order to meet the country's emission-control target.

2012 Kyoto Protocol member countries extend the agreement at the last minute and commit to developing a follow-on treaty requiring cuts from more countries by 2015.

2013 President Obama calls for action to slow climate change, pledging to use regulations if Congress will not pass legislation.

Global Warming Will Hit Poor the Hardest

"The heat must be turned down."

Will the planet warm by 2°C in coming decades, or 4 degrees — or even more? The question may seem trivial, but the difference could mean life or death for millions of people worldwide, especially in poor nations.

A 2012 report commissioned by the World Bank warned that while all countries will be affected by climate change, "the poor will suffer most, and the global community could become more fractured and unequal than today." That scenario is especially likely if the world warms by 4°C (7.2° F) above pre-industrial levels — the likely outcome if nations don't start cutting emissions sharply.[1]

"The projected 4°C warming simply must not be allowed to occur — the heat must be turned down," the report asserted.[2]

Scientists are still quantifying all of the potential impacts from a 4°C jump in temperature, but the report warns that risks from heat waves, altered rainfall patterns and drought will increase — even with a 2°C (3.6°F) temperature rise — and will be much more severe with 4°C of warming. For example:

- With a 2-degree rise in temperature, the average amount of water flowing yearly through the Danube, Mississippi and Amazon river basins would fall 20 to 40 percent, while flow in the Nile and Ganges river basins would rise by about 20 percent. With 4°C of warming, those changes would roughly double, increasing the likelihood and severity of droughts and flooding.

- If temperatures rise 1.5 to 2 degrees Celsius by 2050, the number of forest fires in the Amazon rain forest could double. With 4°C of warming, the number of fires would increase even more.[3]

Geophysical factors are part of why climate change will affect poor countries more than rich countries. Sea-level rise is likely to be 15 to 20 percent higher in the tropics than the average increase around the globe because of warming-related changes in ocean circulation patterns. And warming is expected to make tropical cyclones (hurricanes) more intense, while dry areas in many tropical and subtropical regions are likely to become drier as the climate warms.[4]

In addition, developing countries typically are less prepared for disasters and may not be able to provide adequate disaster relief to those whose lives will be uprooted by storms, floods or heat waves. According to the Intergovernmental Panel on Climate Change (IPCC), a scientific organization that advises national governments, more than 95 percent of deaths from natural disasters between 1970 and 2008 occurred in developing countries. However, economic losses were higher in wealthy countries, where more buildings and infrastructure were at risk.[5]

throughout history, and have studied factors that contribute to such changes.

For example, in 1864 Scottish physicist James Croll theorized that regular variations in Earth's orbit could trigger ice ages by changing how and where the sun's energy fell on the planet. Eighty years later Milutin Milankovic, a Serbian geophysicist, calculated these shifts more precisely and developed a theory of glacial periods, now known as Milankovic cycles.

Swedish chemist Svante Arrhenius was the first scientist to suggest that human activities could affect planetary climate cycles. In 1896 Arrhenius published the first explanation of how two greenhouse gases — CO_2 and water vapor — trapped heat in the atmosphere. He also recognized that humans were increasing CO_2 concentrations by burning fossil fuels, but assumed that it would take thousands of years for those activities to have a measurable impact.

In 1938 Guy Callendar, an English inventor, estimated that humans had added about 150 billion tons of CO_2 to the atmosphere since the 1880s. He collected temperature records from around the world and concluded that rising GHG concentrations were raising the planet's temperature. Like Arrhenius, he thought warming would benefit humans by extending growing seasons. "In any case, the return of the deadly glaciers should be delayed indefinitely," he wrote.[38]

The IPCC's definition of disaster risk is based on three factors:

- Weather and climate events, such as hurricanes or heat waves;
- Exposure — people living in areas where those events occur; and
- Vulnerability — whether victims have well-built homes or shelters, access to medical care, insurance and other resources to help them through the disasters.

"For the poor and vulnerable, a non-huge disaster can have huge consequences," says Christopher Field, a professor of global ecology at Stanford University and co-chair of the IPCC's working group on impacts, adaptation and vulnerability. For example, during urban heat waves the poor, elderly and infirm are much more likely to die than their more affluent neighbors.[6]

"Societies can moderate impacts of high heat by setting up cooling centers and increasing access to electricity for air conditioning, but if they're unprepared there can be very heavy loss of life," says Field.

Climate change threatens basic needs for the poor, such as access to clean drinking water and adequate food supplies. According to the World Bank report, 2°C to 2.5°C of warming would increase the rate of childhood stunting (failure to grow at normal rates because of undernourishment), especially in sub-Saharan Africa and South Asia, a problem likely to be more severe as warming increases. Higher temperatures also will expand the geographic ranges of many infectious diseases such as malaria, with higher risks for those without access to vaccinations and medical care.[7]

Climate change is a "clear and present danger . . . to our development plans and objectives and the health of economies large and small in all regions," United Nations Secretary-General Ban Ki-moon said in April. "The poor and vulnerable are the ones most hit and targeted, but no nation will be immune."[8]

— *Jennifer Weeks*

[1]"Turn Down the Heat: Why a 4ºC Warmer World Must Be Avoided," Potsdam Institute for Climate Impact Research and Climate Analytics, (prepared for the World Bank), November 2012, p. xviii, http://climate change.worldbank.org/sites/default/files/Turn_Down_the_heat_Why_a_4_degree_centrigrade_warmer_world_must_be_avoided.pdf.

[2]*Ibid.*

[3]*Ibid.*, p. xvi.

[4]*Ibid.*, p. xiii.

[5]"Managing the Risks of Extreme Events and Disasters to Advance Climate Change Adaptation," Intergovernmental Panel on Climate Change, 2012, p. 7, http://ipcc-wg2.gov/SREX/images/uploads/SREX-SPMbrochure_FINAL.pdf.

[6]For example, see Micah Maidenburg, "The 1995 Heat Wave Reflected Chicago's 'Geography of Vulnerabilty,' " *ChicagoNow.com*, July 20, 2011, www.chicagonow.com/chicago-muckrakers/2011/07/the-1995-heat-wave-reflected-chicagos-geography-of-vulnerability/.

[7]"Turn Down the Heat," *op. cit.*, p. xvii.

[8]"Climate change is a 'clear and present danger,' says UN Chief," United Nations, April 19, 2013, www.unmultimedia.org/radio/eng lish/2013/04/climate-change-is-a-clear-and-present-danger-to-human kind-says-un-chief/.

But after further study, scientists began to worry about where all of the excess CO_2 would go. In 1957 Roger Revelle and Hans Suess of California's Scripps Institution of Oceanography published a study showing that most human-generated CO_2 emissions up to that time had been absorbed by the world's oceans. But the oceans were nearing their capacity for absorbing CO_2, so the gas was accumulating in the atmosphere, they contended, with unknown results.

"[H]uman beings are now carrying out a large-scale geophysical experiment," Revelle and Suess warned. "Within a few centuries we are returning to the atmosphere and oceans the concentrated organic carbon [that was] stored in sedimentary rocks over hundreds of millions of years."[39]

Climate science expanded rapidly in the 1950s and 1960s. International research groups in the United States, England, Mexico and elsewhere began designing general models to simulate the many complex processes that created Earth's climate, such as ocean currents and wind patterns. Scientists used these models to test theories about how the system might change in response to natural or manmade events.

French, Danish, Swiss, Russian and U.S. scientists drilled into ice sheets in Greenland and Antarctica and analyzed air bubbles from thousands of years earlier to

AFP/Getty Images/Nicholas Kamm

President Obama has called for cutting emissions of heat-trapping gases from power plants and other sources and pledged to use regulations if Congress fails to act. Environmental advocates say the president could take other steps as well, including rejecting the proposed Keystone XL crude oil pipeline from Alberta, Canada, and tightening restrictions on hydraulic fracturing, or fracking.

determine how the atmosphere's composition had changed over time. A growing body of research showed that many processes shaped global climate patterns, and that human actions could disrupt the system.

Calls for Action

In the late 1960s public concerns about pollution and over-development in industrialized countries triggered a global environmental movement. Governments began setting standards for air and water quality, waste management and land conservation.

Congress established the Environmental Protection Agency (EPA) in 1970 and a wave of major environmental laws followed, including the Clean Air and Clean Water acts, the Endangered Species Act and the National Environmental Policy Act, which required federal agencies to consider the environmental impacts of major government projects. A 1972 international conference on the environment in Stockholm set lofty goals for international cooperation and led to creation of the United Nations Environment Programme.

Global climate change had not yet become a policy issue, but scientists were drawing more connections between

atmospheric GHG concentrations, rising temperatures and alarming potential consequences, such as a melting and breaking apart of Antarctic ice sheets. By the early 1980s, many prominent scientists were warning that heavy fossil fuel use was warming the planet, with possible widespread effects.[40]

By the late 1980s, environmental groups were calling for reductions in fossil fuel use. But critics argued that scientific evidence for climate change was uncertain and that reducing emissions would seriously harm economic growth by forcing businesses and households to use more expensive low-carbon energy sources.

Western Europe, with its strong Green parties, pressed for an international agreement to limit GHGs. In 1992 nations signed the Framework Convention on Climate Change (FCCC) at the Earth Summit in Rio de Janeiro, Brazil. The treaty called for voluntarily reducing GHGs to 1990 levels, but did not set binding national limits or timetables.

Climate Wars

As it became clear that nonbinding pledges would not slow rising GHG concentrations, the focus shifted to numerical limits. In 1997 nations adopted the Kyoto Protocol, which required developed countries to reduce their GHG emissions, on average, by 5.2 percent below 1990 levels by 2012. It also created programs to slow emission growth in developing countries, including international trading of emission allowances and credits for wealthy countries that paid for emission reduction projects in developing countries.[41]

The framework recognized that developed countries were responsible for virtually all warming above pre-industrial levels that had already occurred, but fast-growing developing nations such as China, India and Brazil also were becoming major emitters. But the U.S. Senate made clear that it would not ratify the pact unless developing countries also were required to make binding reduction pledges. Accordingly, President Bill Clinton, who had signed the Kyoto Protocol in 1997, never submitted it to the Senate for ratification, although both he and Vice President Al Gore supported action to address climate change.

The prospect of national legislation to cut GHG emissions energized fossil-fuel interests, which were funding work by some conservative think tanks and media outlets to discredit scientific evidence of a human role in climate change. As long as the scientific evidence was uncertain, these advocates argued, it did not make sense to limit GHG emissions. Over time, the Republican Party came to strongly oppose government efforts to address climate change.[42]

Shortly after he was sworn into office, Republican President George W. Bush (2001-2009) renounced Clinton's decision to sign the Kyoto agreement and said cutting GHG emissions would harm the U.S. economy. Bush's presidency was also marked by what many observers came to refer to as "climate wars" — harsh debates over the accuracy of climate science. "There is still a window of opportunity to challenge the science," Republican political consultant Frank Luntz wrote in a 2002 strategy memo. To prevent voters from supporting action to slow climate change, he argued, politicians should "continue to make the lack of certainty a primary issue in the debate."[43]

Despite these arguments, some national leaders — including Republicans — pressed for the United States to take action. In 2003, 2005 and 2007, Sens. John McCain, R-Ariz., and Joseph Lieberman, D-Conn., introduced bills to create a cap-and-trade system for reducing U.S. carbon emissions. And some major corporations began endorsing carbon controls. "We know enough to act on climate change," the U.S. Climate Action Partnership (an alliance of major corporations including Alcoa, DuPont and General Electric) said in January 2007.[44]

Also in 2007 the IPCC and former Vice President Gore — who had argued strongly for action on climate change in the Academy Award-winning documentary *An Inconvenient Truth* — were awarded the Nobel Peace Prize, a sign of strong international concern about climate change.[45]

Obama's Record

Many observers expected progress on climate change after Obama was elected in 2008. As a candidate, he had pledged to support clean-energy options and work for passage of a national cap-and-trade system to limit GHG emissions.

Initially, however, Obama's attention was consumed by the worldwide recession that had begun in 2007. Obama's major legislative successes in 2009 were economic rescue measures, including a $787 billion economic stimulus package and a bailout plan for U.S.

automakers. In such economic circumstances, proposing policies that would raise the price of fossil fuels was much more challenging than it would have been in a strong economy.

In June 2009 the House passed the Waxman-Markey cap-and-trade bill by a narrow 219-212 margin.[46] Many environmental advocates hailed it as a first step, but others complained it set what they saw as weak emissions limits and allowed polluters to "offset" some of their emissions by paying for cleanup projects elsewhere.[47]

Without strong support from the public or liberal environmentalists, and with conservatives labeling it an "energy tax," Senate Democratic leaders opted not to bring the bill up for consideration.[48] Then in the 2010 midterm elections Republicans won control of the House, making it effectively impossible to enact climate change legislation. Conservative legislators, particularly those affiliated with or seeking support from the conservative anti-tax Tea Party movement, challenged numerous laws and regulations as government intrusions into private decisions — including previously uncontroversial policies such as efficiency standards for light bulbs.[49]

Obama's main climate-related success was negotiating tighter fuel efficiency and greenhouse gas pollution standards for new cars and trucks. These changes, announced in 2011, were projected to cut U.S. oil use by 12 billion barrels and avoid 6 billion metric tons of CO_2 emissions — equivalent to all of U.S. emissions in 2010.[50]

During the 2012 presidential race, Obama and his GOP opponent, former Massachusetts Gov. Mitt Romney, largely avoided the topic of climate change. (Romney had supported state GHG limits as governor, then reversed his position shortly before leaving office.) Instead, they both emphasized producing energy from as many sources as possible, including coal, oil and natural gas. Obama also advocated more government support for solar, wind and other renewable energy sources, while Romney called for leaving energy choices up to the market.[51]

Just before the election, New York City Mayor Michael Bloomberg, an independent who had been courted by both campaigns, endorsed Obama, partly because he believed Obama was more likely to act to slow climate change. Bloomberg made his announcement just after Superstorm Sandy, an immense hurricane, flooded parts of Manhattan and devastated coastal New Jersey.

Geoengineering Proposals Would Alter Earth's Climate

Scientists say the controversial techniques demand more study.

Shooting small particles into Earth's upper atmosphere to reflect incoming sunlight back into space. Dumping large quantities of iron into the oceans to stimulate the growth of pollution-eating plankton. Those are just two of the futuristic methods engineers have considered as ways to keep the planet from overheating.

So-called geoengineering techniques involve large-scale efforts to alter Earth's climate system in order to reduce the impact of climate change. They fall into two broad categories: Managing the amount of energy from the sun that falls on Earth's surface, and scrubbing millions of tons of heat-trapping carbon dioxide (CO_2) from the atmosphere.

Strategies designed to control the amount of heat from the sun striking the Earth include:

- Injecting small reflective particles, such as sulfates, into the upper atmosphere to reflect some sunlight back to space.
- Spraying salt water into the lower atmosphere, which makes clouds brighter and more reflective (water vapor in the atmosphere condenses around salt particles, increasing the number of droplets in clouds).
- Installing reflective objects in space between the Earth and sun; and
- Increasing the percentage of Earth's surface covered with light-colored, reflective surfaces, through such techniques as painting millions of roofs white.

Engineers believe shooting reflective particles into the atmosphere would be the most cost-effective and feasible approach, but some scientists worry that it could change rain and snowfall patterns, damage the Earth's ozone layer or increase air pollution.[1]

Strategies for removing carbon dioxide from the atmosphere include planting more forests, which consume and store carbon as trees grow; "fertilizing" the oceans by dumping large quantities of iron to stimulate the growth of plankton, which absorbs CO_2 as it multiplies; and capturing CO_2 by passing air through "scrubbers" that remove carbon dioxide. The CO_2 would then be injected into deep underground reservoirs.

No international treaty or agency governs geoengineering, and many critics say efforts to manipulate weather and climate on such massive scales could threaten human health, forests or fisheries.

One widely publicized geoengineering experiment was conducted by Russ George, an American businessman who has tried several ocean-fertilization experiments, seeking to demonstrate that by locking CO_2 up in the deep ocean a company can generate marketable "carbon credits." But studies have not yet shown that ocean fertilization actually removes significant amounts of carbon from the atmosphere, so he doesn't have any buyers yet.

Spain and Ecuador barred George from their ports after he sought to carry out ocean fertilization experiments near the Galápagos and Canary islands, which officials contended would pollute the seas and threaten biodiversity.[2] Controversy over his proposals spurred the United Nations to adopt a moratorium on ocean fertilization experiments. Nonetheless, George dumped 100 metric tons of iron sulphate off Canada's west coast last fall, generating a large plankton bloom. He said international treaties barring ocean dumping and actions that might threaten biodiversity were "mythology" and did not apply to his activities.[3]

"Our climate is changing. And while the increase in extreme weather we have experienced in New York City and around the world may or may not be the result of it, the risk that it might be — given this week's devastation — should compel all elected leaders to take immediate action," Bloomberg said.[52]

CURRENT SITUATION

Bypassing Congress

With Congress sharply divided along party lines, observers see little prospect for legislation to address climate change during Obama's second term. But environmental

The Canadian government belatedly launched an investigation into George's experiment, which was partly funded by a native Haida community on the coast in hopes that a plankton bloom would help restore traditional salmon runs.[4] But the president of the Haida Nation, Guujaw, denounced the village's action. "Our people, along with the rest of humanity, depend on the oceans and cannot leave the fate of the oceans to the whim of the few," he said.[5]

In its last major climate change assessment report, the Intergovernmental Panel on Climate Change (IPCC) called geoengineering techniques such as ocean fertilization "speculative" and noted that many of the potential environmental side effects had yet to be studied, no detailed cost estimates existed and there was no legal or political framework for implementing such projects.[6] The IPCC held an expert workshop on geoengineering in 2011, and its next assessment, scheduled to be published in late 2014, will consider the science, potential impacts and uncertainties of geoengineering in more detail.

Meanwhile, many nations are concerned about how geoengineering strategies could affect climate cycles and natural resources. A 2012 report for the U.N. Convention on Biological Diversity (an international treaty signed by 193 countries that aims to protect Earth's natural resources) concluded that few proposed geoengineering strategies had been well researched and no good systems had been designed for regulating them. In short, the report concluded, much more study was needed.[7]

Large-scale application of geoengineering techniques "is near-certain to involve unintended side effects and increase sociopolitical tensions," the report observed. "While technological innovation has helped to transform societies and improve the quality of life in many ways, it has not always done so in a sustainable manner."[8]

— *Jennifer Weeks*

AFP/Getty images/Arlan Naeg

The 1991 eruption of Mt. Pinatubo in the Philippines caused global temperatures to drop temporarily by nearly 1°C by sending millions of tons of sulfur dioxide into the atmosphere. The gas formed sulfate particles, which reflected some of the sun's radiation back into space.

[2]Kalee Thompson, "Carbon Discredit," *Popular Science*, July 1, 2008, www.popsci.com/environment/article/2008-07/carbon-discredit?single-page-view=true.

[3]Martin Lukacs, "World's Biggest Geoengineering Experiment 'Violates' UN Rules," *The Guardian*, Oct. 15, 2012, www.guardian.co.uk/environment/2012/oct/15/pacific-iron-fertilisation-geoengineering.

[4]"B.C. Village's Ocean Fertilization Experiment Probed," CBC News, March 28, 2013, www.cbc.ca/news/canada/british-columbia/story/2013/03/27/bc-iron-restoration-fifth-estate.html.

[5]"West Coast Ocean Fertilization Project Defended," CBC News, Oct. 22, 2012, www.cbc.ca/news/canada/british-columbia/story/2012/10/19/bc-ocean-fertilization-haida.html.

[6]"Climate Change 2007: Mitigation of Climate Change," Intergovernmental Panel on Climate Change, section 11.2.2, 2007, www.ipcc.ch/publications_and_data/ar4/wg3/en/ch11s11-2-2.html.

[7]"Impacts of Climate-Related Geoengineering on Biological Diversity," Convention on Biodiversity, April 5, 2013, pp. 3, 9, www.cbd.int/doc/meetings/sbstta/sbstta-16/information/sbstta-16-inf-28-en.pdf.

[8]*Ibid.*, p. 8.

[1]"IPCC Expert Meeting on Geoengineering," Intergovernmental Panel on Climate Change, June 20-22, 2011, pp. 19-20, www.ipcc.ch/pdf/supporting-material/EM_GeoE_Meeting_Report_final.pdf.

advocates say he can make significant progress through executive actions and regulations.

"By far the most important step the president can take is using his authority under the Clean Air Act to finalize carbon pollution limits for new power plants [i.e., plants not yet constructed] and develop limits for existing power plants," says David Goldston, government affairs director for the Natural Resources Defense Council (NRDC), a national environmental advocacy group. "That could reduce CO_2 output from power plants by 25 percent."

The EPA proposed a carbon pollution standard for new power plants in 2012 after the Supreme Court ruled

USGS Climate Change in Mountain Ecosystems Program

The glaciers at Glacier National Park in Montana (above) are melting, along with many of the world's other glaciers and Arctic ice. Some officials have called for limiting temperature increases to 2° C, but some climate experts say even that could cause most of the world's glaciers and ice caps to melt.

But in April the EPA put the new rule on hold indefinitely after energy companies said it would effectively kill any new coal-fired power plants. Agency officials said the rule would be rewritten to provide more flexibility.[56] And during her confirmation hearings this spring to be administrator of EPA, Gina McCarthy said the agency was not developing GHG regulations for existing power plants.[57]

Environmentalists also suggest other steps Obama could take to limit GHG emissions, including:

- Rejecting the proposed Keystone XL pipeline, which would carry crude oil from tar sand deposits in Alberta, Canada, to refineries on the U.S. Gulf Coast. "Tar sand oil is far more polluting than traditional fossil fuels," says Goldston.
- Further tightening energy efficiency standards for appliances, electronics and other equipment.
- Maintaining robust funding for renewable energy research and development; and
- Regulating the environmental impacts of hydraulic fracturing, or "fracking," for natural gas, including limits on methane emissions.[58] Methane, the main component of natural gas, is a greenhouse gas, and critics contend that methane leaks from fracking operations contribute significantly to climate change, although energy companies say the problem can be managed.[59]

Any new regulations could face legal challenges, especially if industry says they would cost too much to implement. But Goldston believes courts will uphold reasonable climate protection rules. "Everyone knows there will be challenges, but there's no reason that well-written standards shouldn't survive in court," he says.

Republican opposition to greenhouse gas regulations figured prominently in debate over Obama's choice of McCarthy as EPA administrator. McCarthy currently heads the agency's Air and Radiation program (a position for which the Senate confirmed her by voice vote in 2009) and has also worked for Republican governors in Massachusetts and Connecticut. Her nomination was praised by business leaders: Gloria Bergquist, vice president of the Alliance of Automobile Manufacturers, called her a "pragmatic policymaker" who "accepts real-world economics."[60]

But Republicans on the Senate Environment and Public Works Committee asked McCarthy more than

in 2007 that the agency had authority to regulate carbon dioxide as a pollutant under the Clean Air Act.[53] The proposed standard would limit carbon emissions from fossil-fuel-burning power plants to 1,000 pounds of CO_2 per megawatt-hour of electricity generated.[54]

According to the agency, new natural gas plants should be able to meet the standard without additional controls. But coal-fired plants emit carbon dioxide at about twice that rate, so new coal plants would need extra pollution controls. Because the price of natural gas has dropped sharply in recent years, the EPA and Department of Energy (DOE) expect that new power plants likely will burn gas, so they don't expect the coal plant rule to affect energy prices or reliability.[55]

AT ISSUE

Should the United States adopt a carbon tax?

YES William G. Gale
Co-Director,
Urban-Brookings Tax Policy Center

From "The Tax Favored by Most Economists," Brookings Institution, March 12, 2013, www.brookings.edu/research/opinions/2013/03/12-taxing-carbon-gale

Looking for a public policy that would improve the . . . economy, lower our dependence on foreign oil, reduce pollution, slow global warming, allow cuts in government spending and decrease the long-term deficit? Then a carbon tax is what you want. . . .

Energy consumption [involves] substantial societal costs — including air and water pollution, road congestion and climate change. Since many of these costs are not directly borne by those who use fossil fuels, they are ignored when energy production and consumption choices are made, resulting in too much consumption and production of fossil fuels. Economists have long recommended a tax on fossil-fuel energy sources as an efficient way to address this problem. . . .

Most analyses find that a carbon tax could significantly reduce emissions. Tufts University economist Gilbert Metcalf estimated that a $15 per ton tax on CO_2 emissions that rises over time would reduce greenhouse gas emissions by 14 percent. . . .

A carbon tax . . . has been implemented in several other countries, including the Scandinavian nations, the Netherlands, Germany, the United Kingdom and Australia. . . . Estimates suggest that a well-designed tax in the United States could raise . . . up to 1 percent of GDP, [which] could . . . address the country's . . . medium- and long-term budget deficits.

A carbon tax could [also reduce U.S.] dependence on foreign sources of energy and [create] better market incentives for energy conservation, the use of renewable energy sources and the production of energy-efficient goods. . . .

Two problems are sometimes raised in response to a federal carbon tax proposal. The first is its impact on low-income households, who use most of their income for consumption. However, this . . . could be offset [through] refundable income tax credits or payroll tax credits.

The second concern is whether the U.S. should act unilaterally. Without cooperation from the rest of the world, critics fear that a U.S. carbon tax would reduce economic activity here and make little difference to overall carbon emissions or levels. This view . . . discounts the experience of other countries that unilaterally created carbon taxes; there is no evidence that they paid a significant price, or any price at all, in terms of economic activity levels.

No one is claiming the carbon tax is a perfect outcome. But relative to the alternatives, it has an enormous amount to offer.

NO Kenneth P. Green
Senior Director, Energy and Natural Resources
Studies, Fraser Institute, Calgary, Canada

From "Why a Carbon Tax is Still a Bad Idea," American Enterprise Institute, Aug. 28, 2012

Taxes on carbon are not simply taxes on consumption, they're a tax on production as well, since energy is a primary input to production. Taxing both production and consumption seems like a poor way to stimulate your economy, reduce your costs of production or make your exports more competitive.

Carbon taxes are regressive. Poorer people spend a higher portion of their household budget on energy than do the better off. [Unless] you were to posit redistributing the tax to the poor, higher energy costs [will] slap the lower-end of the income spectrum hard.

Taxing carbon gets you virtually no climate or health benefit unless it exists within some binding, international carbon control regime, which is unlikely. China and India will dominate global carbon emissions for the next century, while emissions in the developed world are already level or in decline. And, global negotiations over carbon controls have become a farce in which developing countries fish for wealth and intellectual property transfers, while developed countries make promises they have little intention of keeping.

Carbon taxes would put a share (potentially a large share) of the U.S. tax system under the influence of bureaucrat-scientists at the U.N. You can guarantee that there would be steady pressure to tax carbon at ever-higher rates (and transfer some of that booty to developing countries!). Do we really want "the science" of climate change as developed by the U.N. setting our tax rates?

We already have a vast array of regulations aimed at reducing carbon emissions, [so] new carbon taxes would represent double-taxation. You're already paying carbon taxes in the additional costs of new vehicles with higher fuel emission standards, more expensive appliances that aim to conserve energy, renewable energy standards that raise your cost of electricity, etc.

For the record, I'm a "lukewarmer" [on global warming] and I've written (since 1998) that some resilience-building actions would be wise in the face of climate risk, but a carbon tax? In the real world, like other eco-taxes, carbon taxes would quickly morph into just another form of taxation that feeds the ever-hungry maw of big government.

---

*Green was a policy analyst at the American Enterprise Institute when he wrote this commentary.

1,100 questions for the record during her confirmation process — seven times as many as McCarthy's predecessor, Lisa Jackson, faced. The Republican Policy Committee contended that McCarthy had "played a central role in authoring environmental regulations that could effectively ban the use of coal as an energy source," alluding to the carbon standards for new power plants. The committee also charged that EPA was working to undercut approval of the Keystone XL pipeline by criticizing the State Department's environmental review of the project.[61]

All eight committee Republicans voted against McCarthy's nomination, which was supported by all 10 Democrats. The nomination could face a Republican filibuster on the Senate floor. A *Boston Globe* editorial said the GOP was trying to "bully the EPA into lowering pollution standards." If McCarthy is eventually confirmed, *The Globe* observed, she will face looming challenges — in particular, rising GHG emissions.[62]

Public Concern

Recent polls show that while climate change remains a divisive issue, the public is much less polarized than Congress, with a majority of respondents believing global warming is occurring. And while Democrats are more likely than Republicans to believe in global warming, some polls show that Republicans increasingly agree. For instance:

• A March Gallup poll found that 66 percent of Americans believe global warming has already begun or will begin soon or within their lifetimes. And the share of those who believe human activity causes climate change has jumped from 50 percent in 2010 to 57 percent today.[63]

• An April Pew Research Center poll found that 69 percent of Americans believe there is solid evidence Earth is warming (including 44 percent of Republicans), and 42 percent believe it is caused mostly by human activity. Both beliefs have been increasing since about 2010.[64]

• A University of Michigan study conducted last fall found that the percentage of Republicans who believe in global warming rose from 33 percent in 2010 to 51 percent in 2012.[65]

• Similarly, a George Mason University survey in January found that 52 percent of Republicans and

Republican-leaning independents believe climate change is occurring.[66]

However, Stephen Ansolabehere, a professor of government at Harvard University who has conducted numerous surveys of public views about energy and climate change, says "the public is of two minds about climate change. People generally accept that it's happening, but they don't see it as an urgent issue." The Gallup survey, for instance, found that 64 percent of respondents did not see climate change as a threat to them or their lifestyles, while the Pew poll found that only 33 percent of respondents called global warming a "very serious" problem.

Since climate change is not considered an impending crisis, surveys indicate Americans are only willing to make minor sacrifices to deal with it. Ansolabehere has found that respondents, on average, would spend only $10 per month to shift to low-carbon energy sources. "That's an important first step, but it's only a modest one," he says.

Polls also suggest that many Americans do not support broad national, taxpayer-supported solutions. In a March survey commissioned by Stanford University, respondents were asked who should pay for projects to protect coastal communities from flooding, such as building sea walls and manmade dunes. More than 80 percent said such projects should be funded by raising local property taxes for those who live near shorelines.[67]

More extreme weather events could convince Americans that climate change is an imminent threat. "Big galvanizing examples can change public opinion across generations in a lasting way," says Ansolabehere. "The cleanest examples are the accident at Three Mile Island, which completely reset the nuclear power industry in the United States, and Chernobyl, which did the same in Europe. But Hurricane Sandy plus droughts in Texas and the Midwest are starting to make people realize they need to be concerned about weather."

Indeed, wrote Trenberth, at the National Center for Atmospheric Research, and Princeton's Michael Oppenheimer, "There is conclusive evidence that climate change worsened the damage caused by Superstorm Sandy. Sea levels in New York City harbors have risen by more than a foot since the beginning of the 20th century. Had the storm surge not been riding on higher seas, there would have been less flooding and less damage.

Warmer air also allows storms such as Sandy to hold more moisture and dump more rainfall, exacerbating flooding."[68]

OUTLOOK

Adapting and Leading

As the impacts of climate change become increasingly clear, scientists say the United States must spend more money and resources to help the nation adapt to extreme weather and other climate-related events.

"Water will be one of the biggest pressure points on society," says NCAR's Trenberth. "The intensity and frequency of rain and storms will increase, with longer dry spells. Even if we get the same average amount of precipitation yearly, the way it's distributed over time will become harder to manage, and shortages will be more likely."[69]

Rising sea levels are also highly likely. "Storm surges, high tides and flood events all are amplified by rising seas. A few inches of sea level rise can make a big difference in the amount of damage," says Stanford's Field.

Other effects could be devastating for many regions. "Droughts are becoming longer or more severe in some parts of world, but shortening in others," says Field. Hurricane frequency "probably won't change, but more storms will grow to the most damaging levels. Tornadoes are a very active area of research, and we may see some new results over the next decade."

As the science of climate change improves, prospects for leadership from the United States or other major greenhouse gas emitters remain murky. Environmental advocates hope for strong action from the Obama administration, especially on power plant emissions. "President Obama took very important actions in his first term, especially raising mileage standards for passenger cars," says the NRDC's Goldston. "That policy will save money, reduce fuel consumption, and cut a large chunk of carbon pollution. Power plant standards are the next logical step."

Others see promoting innovative low-carbon energy sources and technologies as a better long-term strategy. "We need ways to drive down the cost of decarbonization, and regulatory mandates aren't likely to do that," says Adler of Case Western Reserve University. "Encouraging more innovation is the way to get large developing countries onto a low-carbon development path. Going after energy subsidies, especially for high-carbon fuels, would also help. So would reducing regulatory barriers that impede nontraditional energy sources like offshore wind energy, tidal power, solar generation on federal lands and next-generation nuclear reactors."

Meanwhile, environmentalists and policymakers are closely watching China, the world's largest GHG source. "If China puts a price on carbon, that could really change the international dynamic," says Arvind Subramanian, a senior fellow at the Center for Global Development, a research center in Washington, D.C. "And if China becomes a leader in green technologies, that would have an even bigger impact. It could make developed countries fear that they were losing leadership and rouse the United States into stronger action."

Field would like to see more emphasis on potential profits from building low-carbon economies. "There are rich and exciting prospects for developing new technologies that will help us solve the climate problem," Field says. "I'd like to shift away from viewing climate policies as scary economic choices and frame them as exciting business opportunities. One person's risk is another person's opportunity to capture markets."

NOTES

1. Justin Gillis, "Carbon Dioxide Level Passes Long-Feared Milestone," *The New York Times*, May 10, 2013, www.nytimes.com/2013/05/11/science/earth/carbon-dioxide-level-passes-long-feared-milestone.html?hp.

2. John Vidal, "Large Rise in CO_2 Emissions Sounds Climate Change Alarm," *The Guardian*, March 8, 2013, www.guardian.co.uk/environment/2013/mar/08/hawaii-climate-change-second-greatest-annual-rise-emissions.

3. For recent overviews see "Climate Change Science Overview," U.S. Environmental Protection Agency, April 22, 2013, www.epa.gov/climatechange/science/overview.html; and "Climate Change: Evidence, Impacts, and Choices," National Research Council, 2012, http://nas-sites.org/americasclimatechoices/files/2012/06/19014_cvtx_R1.pdf.

4. John Cook, *et al.*, "Quantifying the Consensus on Anthropogenic Global Warming in the Scientific Literature," *Environmental Research Letters*, vol. 8, 2013, http://iopscience.iop.org/1748-9326/8/2 /024024.

5. Testimony before the Subcommittee on Environment, House Committee on Science, Space and Technology, April 25, 2013, p. 8, http://science .house.gov/sites/republicans.science.house.gov/files/ documents/HHRG-113-SY18-WState-JCurry-201 30425.pdf.

6. Melillo's comments are from the American Association for the Advancement of Science annual conference, Feb. 18, 2013. The draft report is online at "Draft Climate Assessment Report," National Climate Assessment and Development Advisory Committee, January 2013, http://ncadac.globalchange.gov, and is scheduled to be finalized later in 2013.

7. "Research Highlight: The Little Ice Age Was Global, Scripps Researchers Say," *Explorations Now*, June 7, 2012, http://explorations.ucsd.edu/research-high lights/2012/research-highlight-the-little-ice-age-was-global-scripps-researchers-say/; Edna Sun, "Little Ice Age," *Scientific American Frontiers*, Feb. 15, 2005, www.pbs.org/saf/1505/features/lia.htm.

8. "The Current and Future Consequences of Global Change," National Aeronautics and Space Administration, http://climate.nasa.gov/effects.

9. "Draft Climate Change Assessment Report," *op. cit.*, p. 3, http://ncadac.globalchange.gov/download/ NCAJan11-2013-publicreviewdraft-chap1-execs um.pdf.

10. For background see Marcia Clemmitt, "Energy and Climate," *CQ Researcher*, July 24, 2009, pp. 621-644.

11. "Inaugural Address by President Barack Obama," Jan. 21, 2013, www.whitehouse.gov/the-press-office/2013/01/21/inaugural-address-president-barack-obama.

12. "Remarks by the President in the State of the Union Address," Feb. 12, 2013, www.whitehouse.gov/the-press-office/2013/02/12/remarks-president-state-union-address.

13. John Cook, *et al., op. cit.* See also "Consensus: 97% of Climate Scientists Agree," National Aeronautics and Space Administration, http://climate.nasa.gov/ scientific-consensus.

14. Roger Aronoff, "The Greatest Hoax? Global Warming, Says Sen. James Inhofe," *AIM Report*, May 30, 2012, www.aim.org/aim-report/the-great est-hoax-global-warming-says-sen-james-inhofe/.

15. Lamar Smith, "Overheated Rhetoric on Climate Change Doesn't Make for Good Policies," *The Washington Post*, May 19, 2013, http://articles .washingtonpost.com/2013-05-19/opinions/39 376700_1_emissions-carbon-dioxide-climate-change.

16. Andrew Restuccia and Darren Goode, "Obama's Achilles' Heel on Climate: Senate Democrats," *Politico*, March 25, 2013, www.politico.com/ story/2013/03/obamas-achilles-heel-on-climate-senate-democrats-89295.html.

17. See "Continuing Partisan Divide in Views of Global Warming," Pew Research Center, April 2, 2013, p. 4, www.people-press.org/files/legacy-pdf/4-2 -13%20Keystone%20Pipeline%20and%20 Global%20Warming%20Release.pdf; and Lydia Saad, "Americans' Concerns About Global Warming on the Rise," *Gallup Politics*, April 8, 2013, www.gall up.com/poll/161645/americans-concerns-global-warming-rise.aspx. For details, see "Gallup Poll Social Series: Environment," March 7-10, 2013, question 25, www.usclimatenetwork.org/resource-database/poll-global-warming-fears-rising.

18. Coral Davenport, "The Coming GOP Civil War Over Climate Change," *National Journal*, May 9, 2013, www.nationaljournal.com/magazine/the-com ing-gop-civil-war-over-climate-change-20130509. For a sample of Thernstrom's position see "Resetting Earth's Thermostat," American Enterprise Institute, June 2008, www.aei.org/files/2008/06/27/200806 27_OTIThernstrom.pdf, p. 2.

19. William R. Moomaw, "Can the International Treaty System Address Climate Change?" Fletcher Forum of World Affairs, vol. 37, no. 1, winter 2013, p. 109, www.fletcherforum.org/wp-content/uploads/2013/02/ Moomaw_37-1.pdf. For more background on limiting warming to 2°C see Samuel Randalls, "History of the 2°C Climate Target," *WIREs Climate Change*, vol. 1, July/August 2010, http://wires.wiley.com/WileyCDA/ WiresArticle/wisId-WCC62.html.

20. "Limiting the Long-Term Increase of Global Temperature to 2° Celsius is Still Possible," International Energy Agency, Aug. 17, 2012, www.iea.org/newsroomandevents/news/2012/august/name,30638,en.html.

21. Alex Kirby, "Ex-IPCC Head: Prepare for 5°C Warmer World," *Climate Central*, Feb. 17, 2013, www.climatecentral.org/news/ex-ipcc-head-prepare-for-5c-warmer-world-15610.

22. "Draft Climate Assessment Report," *op. cit.*, pp. 25-26.

23. Mark Fischetti, "2-Degree Global Warming Limit is Called a 'Prescription for Disaster,'" *Scientific American.com*, Dec. 6, 2011, http://blogs.scientificamerican.com/observations/2011/12/06/two-degree-global-warming-limit-is-called-a-prescription-for-disaster/. For more on the 350 target, see http://350.org/en.

24. Thomas E. Lovejoy, "The Climate Change Endgame," *The New York Times*, Jan. 21, 2013, www.nytimes.com/2013/01/22/opinion/global/the-climate-change-endgame.html.

25. "Advancing the Science of Climate Change," National Research Council, 2010, p. 174, www.nap.edu/catalog.php?record_id=12782.

26. *Geoengineering the Climate: Science, Governance and Uncertainty* (2009), p. 56, http://royalsociety.org/uploadedFiles/Royal_Society_Content/policy/publications/2009/8693.pdf.

27. "David Keith on Climate Change and Geo-Engineering as a Solution," *Harvard PolicyCast*, Jan. 23, 2013, https://soundcloud.com/harvard/david-keith-on-climate-change.

28. Lynn M. Russell, "Offsetting Climate Change by Engineering Air Pollution to Brighten Clouds," *The Bridge*, Winter 2012, www.nae.edu/File.aspx?id=67680.

29. Kevin E. Trenberth and Aiguo Dai, "Effects of Mount Pinatubo Volcanic Eruption on the Hydrological Cycle as an Analog of Geoengineering," *Geophysical Research Letters*, vol. 34, Aug. 1, 2007, www.cgd.ucar.edu/cas/adai/papers/TrenberthDai_GRL07.pdf.

30. Edward A. Parson and David W. Keith, "End the Deadlock on Governance of Geoengineering Research," *Science*, vol. 339, March 15, 2013, www.keith.seas.harvard.edu/preprints/163.Parson.Keith.DeadlockOnGonvernance.p.pdf.

31. George P. Shultz and Gary S. Becker, "Why We Support a Revenue-Neutral Carbon Tax," *The Wall Street Journal*, April 7, 2013, http://online.wsj.com/article/SB10001424127887323611604578396401965799658.html.

32. "Mapping Carbon Pricing Initiatives: Development and Prospects," The World Bank, May 2013, http://www-wds.worldbank.org/external/default/WDSContentServer/WDSP/IB/2013/05/23/000350881_20130523172114/Rendered/PDF/779550WP0Mappi0til050290130morning0.pdf, pp. 57-58.

33. *Ibid.*, p. 43.

34. Theda Skocpol, "Naming the Problem: What It Will Take to Counter Extremism and Engage Americans in the Fight Against Global Warming," Harvard University, January 2013, http://www-wds.worldbank.org/external/default/WDSContentServer/WDSP/IB/2013/05/23/000350881_20130523172114/Rendered/PDF/779550WP0Mappi0til050290130morning0.pdf, pp. 45-55.

35. "Economic Outcomes of a U.S. Carbon Tax: Executive Summary," National Association of Manufacturers, March 2013, www.nam.org/~/media/ECF11DF347094E0DA8AF7BD9A696ABDB.ashx, p. 1.

36. National Association of Manufacturers, www.nam.org/~/media/9C72C0E7823B4E558DF3D49B65114615.ashx.

37. "China to Introduce Carbon Tax: Official," Xinhua, Feb. 19, 2013, http://news.xinhuanet.com/english/china/2013-02/19/c_132178898.htm; Adele C. Morris, *et al.*, "China's Carbon Tax Highlights the Need for a New Track of Carbon Talks," East Asia Forum, March 19, 2013, www.eastasiaforum.org/2013/03/19/chinas-carbon-tax-highlights-the-need-for-a-new-track-of-climate-talks/.

38. G. S. Callendar, "The Artificial Production of Carbon Dioxide and its Influence on Temperature," in Bill McKibben, ed., *The Global Warming Reader* (2011), p. 37.

39. Roger Revells and Hans E. Suess, "Carbon Dioxide Exchange between Atmosphere and Ocean and the Question of an Increase of Atmospheric CO_2 During the Past Decades," in McKibben, *ibid.*, pp. 41-42.

40. For a chronology of climate change research see "The Discovery of Global Warming: Timeline," American Institute of Physics, www.aip.org/history/climate/timeline.htm.

41. For background, see Jennifer Weeks, "Carbon Trading," *CQ Global Researcher*, Nov. 1, 2008, pp. 295-320.

42. Carolyn Lochhead, "How GOP Became Party of Denial on Global Warming," *The San Francisco Chronicle*, April 28, 2013, www.sfchronicle.com/politics/article/How-GOP-became-party-of-denial-on-warming-4469641.php; and Riley E. Dunlap and Aaron M. McRight, "Organized Climate Change Denial," *The Oxford Handbook of Climate Change and Society* (2011).

43. Oliver Burkeman, "Memo Exposes Bush's New Green Strategy," *The Guardian*, March 3, 2003, www.guardian.co.uk/environment/2003/mar/04/usnews.climatechange.

44. "A Call for Action," U.S. Climate Action Partnership, Jan. 22, 2007, p. 2, www.us-cap.org/ClimateReport.pdf.

45. "Nobel Peace Prize Citation," *The Guardian*, Oct. 12, 2007, www.guardian.co.uk/environment/2007/oct/12/gorecitation.

46. A cap-and-trade system sets a ceiling on emissions and requires large GHG sources to buy marketable allowances to cover their emissions.

47. For a survey of views see "The Waxman-Markey Bill: A Good Start or a Non-Starter?" *Yale Environment 360*, June 18, 2009, http://e360.yale.edu/feature/the_waxman-markey_bill_a_good_start_or_a_non-starter/2163/.

48. Bryan Walsh, "Why the Climate Bill Died," *Time*, July 26, 2010, http://science.time.com/2010/07/26/why-the-climate-bill-died/.

49. Mark Clayton, "House Republicans fail to save 30-cent light bulbs from extinction," *The Christian Science Monitor*, July 12, 2011, www.csmonitor.com/USA/Politics/2011/0712/House-Republicans-fail-to-save-30-cent-light-bulbs-from-extinction. For background, see Peter Katel, "Tea Party Movement," *CQ Researcher*, March 19, 2010, pp. 241-264, updated May 23, 2011.

50. The White House, July 29, 2011, www.whitehouse.gov/blog/2011/07/29/president-obama-announces-new-fuel-economy-standards.

51. John M. Broder, "Both Romney and Obama Avoid Talk of Climate Change," *The New York Times*, Oct. 25, 2012, www.nytimes.com/2012/10/26/us/politics/climate-change-nearly-absent-in-the-campaign.html?pagewanted=all.

52. Michael R. Bloomberg, "A Vote for a President to Lead on Climate Change," Bloomberg News, Nov. 1, 2012, www.bloomberg.com/news/2012-11-01/a-vote-for-a-president-to-lead-on-climate-change.html.

53. *Massachusetts v. Environmental Protection Agency*, 549 U.S. 497, 2007, www.supremecourt.gov/opinions/06pdf/05-1120.pdf. In 2009 EPA issued a formal determination that carbon pollution threatened American's health and welfare by contributing to climate change, laying the ground for issuing regulations to limit carbon emissions.

54. "Proposed Carbon Pollution Standards for New Power Plants," U.S. Environmental Protection Agency, March 27, 2012, http://epa.gov/carbonpollutionstandard/pdfs/20120327factsheet.pdf, p. 2.

55. *Ibid.*, p. 3.

56. John M. Broder, "E.P.A. Will Delay Rule Limiting Carbon Emissions at New Power Plants," *The New York Times*, April 12, 2013, www.nytimes.com/2013/04/13/science/earth/epa-to-delay-emissions-rule-at-new-power-plants.html.

57. Erica Martinson and Jennifer Epstein, "Where's President Obama's Climate Agenda?" *Politico*, May 25, 2013, www.politico.com/story/2013/05/obama-climate-change-agenda-91877.html.

58. For background see Daniel McGlynn, "Fracking Controversy," *CQ Researcher*, Dec. 16, 2011, pp. 1049-1072.

59. Kevin Begos, "EPA Methane Report Could Reshape Fracking Debate," *The Boston Globe*, April 29, 2013, www.bostonglobe.com/business/2013/04/28/

epa-methane-report-further-divides-fracking-camps/Ft7DVUvAHE6zctsgbcGuZN/story.html.

60. Daniel J. Weiss, *et al.*, "EPA Nominee Gina McCarthy Has Strong History of Bipartisan leadership," *Climate Progress*, April 10, 2013, http://thinkprogress.org/climate/2013/04/10/1846181/epa-nominee-gina-mccarthy-has-strong-history-of-bipartisan-leadership/.

61. "Questions for EPA Nominee Gina McCarthy," Republican Policy Committee, April 11, 2013, www.rpc.senate.gov/policy-papers/questions-for-epa-nominee-gina-mccarthy.

62. "Under Fire, EPA Nominee Can't Give Ground on Climate Change," *The Boston Globe*, May 17, 2013, www.bostonglobe.com/editorials/2013/05/16/epa-nominee-can-give-ground-climate-change/4fTQci7wlXK1mJw0qYH6kO/story.html.

63. See Lydia Saad, "Americans' Concerns About Global Warming on the Rise," *Gallup Politics*, April 8, 2013, www.gallup.com/poll/161645/americans-concerns-global-warming-rise.aspx. For details, see "Gallup Poll Social Series: Environment," March 7-10, 2013, question 25, www.usclimatenetwork.org/resource-database/poll-global-warming-fears-rising.

64. See "Continuing Partisan Divide in Views of Global Warming," Pew Research Center, April 2, 2013, p. 4, www.people-press.org/files/legacy-pdf/4-2-13%20Keystone%20Pipeline%20and%20Global%20Warming%20Release.pdf.

65. Christopher Borick and Barry G. Rabe, "The Fall 2012 National Surveys on Energy and the Environment: Findings Report for Belief-Related Questions," The Center for Local, State, and Urban Policy, Gerald R. Ford School of Public Policy, University of Michigan, March 2013, http://closup.umich.edu/files/nsee-climate-belief-fall-2012.pdf.

66. "A National Survey of Republicans and Republican-leaning Independents on Energy and Climate Change," George Mason University Center for Climate Change Communication, April 2, 2013, http://climatechangecommunication.org/sites/default/files/reports/Republicans%27_Views_on_Climate_Change_2013.pdf.

67. "2013 Stanford Poll on Climate Adaptation," Stanford Woods Institute for the Environment, March 2013, pp. 10-12, http://woods.stanford.edu/research/public-opinion-research/2013-Stanford-Poll-Climate-Adaptation.

68. Michael Oppenheimer and Kevin Trenberth, "Will we hear Earth's alarm bells?" *The Washington Post*, June 9, 2013, p. A19. Oppenheimer is a professor of geosciences and international affairs at Princeton University. Trenberth is a distinguished senior scientist at the National Center for Atmospheric Research.

69. For background, see Peter Katel, "Water Crisis in the West," *CQ Researcher*, Dec. 9, 2011, pp. 1025-1048.

BIBLIOGRAPHY

Selected Sources

Books

Guzman, Andrew T., *Overheated: The Human Cost of Climate Change*, **Oxford University Press, 2013.**
A University of California, Berkeley, law professor explores the consequences of climate change, including deaths from flooding, water shortages, strains on global food supplies and growing competition for resources.

Hamilton, Clive, *Earthmasters: The Dawn of the Age of Climate Engineering*, **Yale University Press, 2013.**
An ethics professor at Australia's Charles Sturt University describes geoengineering proposals and considers how these concepts could alter humans' relationship with Earth.

Mann, Michael E., *The Hockey Stick and the Climate Wars: Dispatches from the Front Lines*, **Columbia University Press, 2012.**
A prominent climate scientist at Penn State University describes well-funded efforts to discredit climate science.

Mattoo, Aaditya, and Arvind Subramanian, *Greenprint: A New Approach to Cooperation on Climate Change*, **Center for Global Development, 2013.**
A World Bank research manager (Mattoo) and a global development scholar propose new strategies for achieving global cooperation on climate change.

McKibben, Bill, ed., *The Global Warming Reader*, Penguin, 2011.

A prominent journalist and climate activist provides a collection of articles and documents about climate change, from its 19th-century discovery to the present day.

Articles

Ansolabehere, Stephen, and David M. Konisky, "The American Public's Energy Choice," *Daedalus*, vol. 141, no. 2, Spring 2012.

Political scientists at Harvard and Georgetown universities, respectively, contend that American attitudes about energy are largely unrelated to views about climate change, so the most politically efficient way to reduce greenhouse gas emissions may be to regulate the burning of fossil fuels.

Drajem, Mark, "Obama Will Use Nixon-Era Law to Fight Climate Change," Bloomberg News, March 15, 2013, www.bloomberg.com/news/2013-03-15/obama-will-use-nixon-era-law-to-fight-climate-change.html.

The Obama administration is reportedly preparing to direct federal agencies to consider global warming impacts when they review major projects under the National Environmental Policy Act, which industry leaders say could delay infrastructure projects.

Gillis, Justin, "Carbon Dioxide Level Passes Long-Feared Milestone," *The New York Times*, May 10, 2013, www.nytimes.com/2013/05/11/science/earth/carbon-dioxide-level-passes-long-feared-milestone.html?hp.

In the spring of 2013 atmospheric concentrations of carbon dioxide reached 400 parts per million, the highest level in perhaps 3 million years.

Moomaw, William R., "Can the International Treaty System Address Climate Change?" Fletcher Forum of World Affairs, vol. 37, no. 1, Winter 2013, www.fletcherforum.org/wp-content/uploads/2013/02/Moomaw_37-1.pdf.

A professor of international environmental policy and contributor to past global climate assessments argues that a new approach is needed for international progress, led by the United States and China.

Parson, Edward A., and David W. Keith, "End the Deadlock on Governance of Geoengineering Research," *Science*, vol. 339, March 15, 2013, pp. 1278-1279, www.sciencemag.org/content/339/6125/1278.

A professor of law at UCLA (Parson) and a professor of applied physics at Harvard (Keith) call for creating rules and procedures to allow geoengineering research to proceed.

Reports and Studies

"Draft Climate Assessment Report," National Climate Assessment and Development Advisory Committee, January 2013, http://ncadac.globalchange.gov/.

A draft of a report mandated under the Global Change Research Act of 1990, finds that climate change already affects the United States in several ways, causing — among other things — more frequent extreme weather events and damage to ocean life.

"The Global Climate Change Regime," Council on Foreign Relations, updated March 22, 2013, www.cfr.org/climate-change/global-climate-change-regime/p21831.

A broad overview of the international framework for addressing climate change finds that the system is underdeveloped and offers options to strengthen it, according to a prominent think tank.

Hansen, J., M. Sato, and R. Ruedy, "Global Temperature Update Through 2012," NASA Goddard Institute for Space Studies, Jan. 15, 2013, www.nasa.gov/pdf/719139main_2012_GISTEMP_summary.pdf.

NASA scientists report that global surface temperature in 2012 was 1° Fahrenheit warmer than the 1951-1980 average, continuing a long-term warming trend since the mid-1970s.

For More Information

Center for Global Development, 1800 Massachusetts Ave., N.W., 3rd floor, Washington, DC 20036; 202-416-4000; www.cgdev.org. An independent think tank that works to reduce global poverty and inequality through research and outreach to policymakers.

National Association of Manufacturers, 733 10th St., N.W., Suite 700, Washington, DC 20001; 800-814-8468; www.nam.org. An industrial trade association representing small and large American manufacturers.

National Center for Atmospheric Research, P.O. Box 3000, Boulder, CO 80307; 303-497-1000; www.ncar.ucar.edu. A federally funded research and development center devoted to service, research and education in the atmospheric sciences, including weather, climate and atmospheric pollution.

Natural Resources Defense Council, 40 West 20th St., New York, NY 10011; 212-727-2700; www.nrdc.org.

A national environmental advocacy group that lobbies and conducts public education on issues including ways to combat global climate change.

Scripps Institution of Oceanography, University of California at San Diego, 9500 Gilman Dr., La Jolla, CA 92023; 858-534-3624; www.sio.ucsd.edu. Center for ocean and Earth science research, including atmosphere and climate.

U.S. Global Change Research Program, 1717 Pennsylvania Ave., N.W., Suite 250, Washington, DC 20006; 202-223-6262; www.globalchange.gov. A congressionally mandated program that coordinates and integrates climate change research across 13 government agencies and publishes scientific assessments of potential impacts in the United States from global warming.

16

Global Hunger

Tom Price

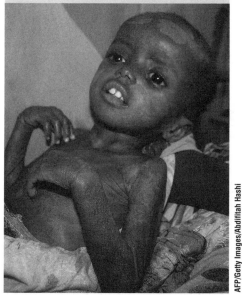

A severely malnourished girl convalesces at a hospital in Mogadishu, Somalia, on July 15, 2014. Food is scarce in the country, where civil war has been raging for years. Affluent countries sent some 5 million metric tons of food to the world's hungry in 2012, mostly for emergency relief. The United States donated the most — 44 percent of the total.

From *CQ Researcher*,
August 8, 2014.

As radical Islamists overran the Iraqi city of Mosul in mid-June, taxi driver Abdel Hady, his wife and their six children began walking north toward the relatively peaceful autonomous region of Kurdistan, sleeping in the homes of generous strangers along the way.

When the Hadys arrived at the Garmava refugee camp three days later, workers were pitching tents and digging latrines to prepare for some of the 300,000 or more Iraqis who had fled combat zones the previous week alone, joining 250,000 Syrians already in Kurdish territory.

More than 2.5 million Syrians have fled that country's bloody civil war to neighboring Kurdistan, Turkey, Jordan and Lebanon, and the Iraqi conflict is expected to produce 1.5 million more refugees, straining local resources and draining the budgets of United Nations (U.N.) relief agencies and humanitarian organizations.[1] Feeding the Syrian refugees alone costs $38 million to $40 million a week, dramatically demonstrating how warfare contributes to global hunger.[2]

But such conflicts represent only a fraction of the food shortages that today leave 842 million people around the world undernourished. That figure is down from just over 1 billion in 1992, due to new agricultural technology that has enabled global food supplies to outstrip population growth. The number of hungry people worldwide dropped by 26 million — 3 percent — in 2013 alone,

Hunger Concentrated in Sub-Saharan Africa, Southeast Asia

Seven African countries, Timor Leste in Southeast Asia and Haiti in the Caribbean have the world's highest concentrations of hunger, or daily undernourishment.* Twenty-one other countries — including 14 African nations, Iraq, North Korea and Guatemala — have "high" rates of undernourishment, with 25 percent to 35 percent of their population classified as hungry.

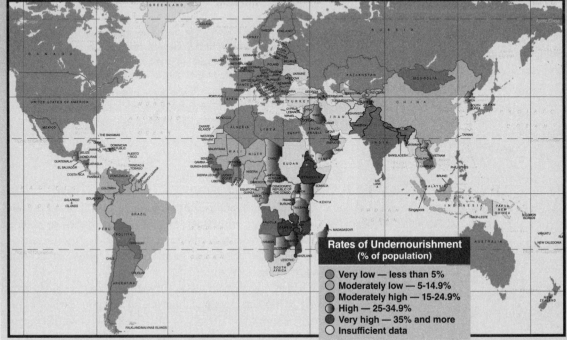

Rates of Undernourishment
(% of population)

- Very low — less than 5%
- Moderately low — 5-14.9%
- Moderately high — 15-24.9%
- High — 25-34.9%
- Very high — 35% and more
- Insufficient data

* Undernourishment is defined as not having enough calories (energy) to meet minimum physiological needs for an active life. It is a less visible form of hunger than starvation, which the World Food Programme calls acute hunger.

Source: "Hunger Map 2013," World Food Programme, United Nations, http://tinyurl.com/plddrmr

according to the U.N. Food and Agriculture Organization (FAO).[3] The FAO defines hunger, or undernourishment, as "not having enough food for an active and healthy life" or not being able to meet "dietary energy requirements."[4]

Still, 12 percent of the Earth's population does not get enough to eat. Most of the hungry are in the developing world, and 70 percent are small farmers or agricultural laborers who can't grow sufficient food to feed their families or sell to others. [5] The problem is severest in sub-Saharan Africa, where one in four goes hungry, but that is down from one in three in the early '90s.[6]

Experts worry that over the long term, expanding middle classes in rapidly developing countries such as

China and India will raise demand for more expensive foods that overtax the environment, further boosting food prices. And climate change and modern industrial agricultural practices threaten future agricultural production and the environment in a variety of ways, scientists say.

Currently, hunger kills nearly 3.1 million children under 5 each year — 45 percent of all deaths in that age range. One-sixth of the children in developing countries — 100 million — are underweight. [7] Hunger also helps to truncate adults' lives. Life expectancy in Africa is 58, for instance, compared with 67 in Southeast Asia, 68 in the Eastern Mediterranean and 79 in the United States.[8]

Paradoxically, the Earth produces more food than its inhabitants need, but the food is unevenly distributed. In the United States and other affluent countries, more people are overweight or obese than hungry — the result of eating too much high-calorie food and getting insufficient exercise. Obesity also is growing in rapidly developing countries such as China, where childhood obesity rose from 1.5 percent of the child population in 1989 to 6.9 percent of boys and 2.8 percent of girls last year.[9]

"One billion people in the world don't have enough food, while one billion people eat too much," said World Wildlife Fund Senior Vice President Jason Clay.[10]

Experts say hunger has a number of causes, including war, poverty, population growth, poor farming practices, government corruption, ineffective food distribution, inclement weather, climate change and waste. "Short-term hunger usually is due to natural disaster or war," says Christopher Barrett, director of the School of Applied Economics and Management at Cornell University, who researches hunger and poverty. "Chronic hunger is related to chronic poverty."

Due to inadequate technology and resources, for instance, Africa's agricultural productivity is less than half the world average and is rising at half the rate of the continent's population growth.[11]

Some anti-hunger activists say affluent nations also add to the world hunger problem. Government subsidies to growers in wealthy nations can depress world commodity prices, they say, reducing the earnings of small-scale farmers in developing nations. Promoting plant-based biofuel also drives up world food prices, making it more expensive for the poor. Consuming meat- and dairy-rich diets increases the cost of food by diverting food and land to feeding and raising animals. In addition, critics say certain aspects of the donor countries' aid policies exacerbate hunger, such as a U.S. provision requiring food aid to be shipped on U.S.-flagged vessels, which are often more expensive than other ships.

United States and U.N. Are Largest Food Donors

The United States delivered nearly 2.2 million metric tons of food aid in 2012, more than twice the combined amount of the next three largest donors — Japan, Brazil and Canada. The United Nations and European Commission, the largest international government organizations, together provided more than 700,000 metric tons.

Largest Food Donors, Countries, 2012		Largest Food Donors, International Organizations, 2012	
Country	Total Food Aid (in metric tons)	Type of Organization	Total Food Aid (in metric tons)
United States	2,195,285	United Nations	565,796
Japan	406,585	European Commission	137,002
Brazil	334,294	Others	86,192
Canada	293,293	International Government	60,075
China	243,381	Nongovernmental	40,443
Germany	168,486	Private	28,003
Australia	72,817		
Russia	61,606		
United Kingdom	59,876		
Sweden	47,343		

Source: "Table 6, Food Aid Deliveries in 2012 by Donor and Category (Mt — Cereals In Grain Equivalent)," Food Aid Flows 2012 Report Annex Tables, World Food Programme, United Nations, p. 16, http://tinyurl.com/llklkap

About a third of the world's food is wasted, the FAO estimates.[12] "In the undeveloped world, the waste happens before the food gets to people," said North Dakota farmer Roger Johnson, president of the National Farmers Union. "The food rots" because of lack of roads and proper storage facilities. In the developed world, he said, waste is due to "the staggering amount of food that's thrown out after it gets to our plates."

Food production and distribution are hampered in many countries by prolonged conflict and political instability, such as in Nepal, incomplete land reform, as in Tajikistan, and population growth and extreme poverty in countries like Uganda, according to the FAO.[13] Erratic rainfall and more frequent droughts have exacerbated hunger in the Sahel, the arid region just south of the Sahara Desert where 20 million people have inconsistent access to food and 5 million children face acute malnutrition, according to the U.S. Agency for International Development (USAID).[14]

Countries that are winning the war against hunger have governments that are consistently committed to "long-term rural development and poverty reducing plans," says the FAO. For instance, in Bangladesh, Ghana and Nicaragua, hunger has been cut in half in the last two decades through economic growth and freer trade, the agency said. Ghana and Nicaragua also have enjoyed political stability and high world prices for their exports.[15]

Speaking to a gathering of African diplomats in 2010, Johnnie Carson, then U.S. assistant secretary of State for African affairs, said that "our ability to achieve our shared long-term goals of democracy, stability and prosperity on the continent depends entirely on the integrity and effectiveness of African leadership."[16]

Most food aid responds to emergencies, rather than chronic hunger. Affluent countries sent just over 5 million metric tons of food to the hungry in 2012, 70 percent of which was for emergency relief. The biggest donor, the United States, contributed 2.2 million tons — 44 percent of the total, and more than four times as much as the next-biggest donor, Japan, which gave 407,000 tons.[17]

The United States will spend about $3.5 billion on international food aid and agricultural development programs this year. The Food for Peace program receives almost $1.5 billion of that, used primarily to buy U.S. farmers' commodities, which are shipped abroad as emergency relief. Another $600 million provides cash for such emergency relief activities as giving food vouchers to individuals and purchasing food near where it is consumed.

The Obama administration's Feed the Future initiative — which supports development programs led by farmers and local, regional and national governments in the developing world — gets about $1.1 billion. The rest supports child and school feeding activities, increased agricultural productivity and expanded trade in agricultural products.

Almost all of the U.S. emergency relief is distributed by the U.N.'s World Food Programme; non-emergency relief is supplied by nongovernmental organizations. A small amount is distributed directly by the United States, such as when the military responds to natural disasters.[18]

Back at the Garmava refugee camp, a Mosul police officer named Taha and his wife Shahla (who declined to give their last names to a reporter) faced a key danger posed by inadequate nutrition: Shahla was about to give birth.[19] "The people who are especially vulnerable to hunger are those in the first 1,000 days — from the beginning of pregnancy to age 2," says Richard Leach, president and CEO of the World Food Program USA, an independent nonprofit that supports the U.N.'s World Food Programme through fundraising and advocacy in the United States. If mothers and children don't receive adequate nutrition then, he says, the children "won't develop intellectually or physically to the degree that they could have."

Maternal undernourishment followed by inadequate childhood nutrition causes stunting — abnormally short growth. Stunting affected 160 million children in the developing world — 28 percent — in 2011, down from 45 percent in 1990.[20]

Children's health is affected by the quality of the food they eat as well as the quantity. Not consuming enough Vitamin A impairs growth, increases vulnerability to infection and is the leading cause of childhood blindness. Iron deficiency impedes children's intellectual development and women's chances of successful pregnancy.[21]

As government officials, relief workers, advocates and scholars debate the best ways to attack hunger, here are some of the questions they are addressing:

Are developed countries' aid policies making hunger worse?

Anti-hunger activists cheered when Congress in 2012 adopted a modest reform to U.S. international food-aid programs by lowering a requirement that 75 percent of food be shipped on U.S.-flagged vessels. By this spring, the cheers had morphed into complaints, as the House moved to repeal the reform.

That legislation — which cleared the House April 1 and awaits Senate consideration — illustrates activists' contention that developed countries' aid policies and lifestyles make hunger worse or lessen the effectiveness of food-aid programs.[22]

The critics especially cite U.S. aid policies that rely heavily on purchasing food from American farmers rather than using cash to acquire food near where it will be consumed. Most of the purchased food is given to the hungry, usually through the World Food Programme. But in some cases, commodities may be "monetized" — or sold on the market and the proceeds used for developmental activities. Because of the cost of purchasing commodities in the United States and shipping them overseas, critics say it would be more efficient in both cases to buy food near where it's consumed and to allocate cash to pay for development programs.

Even the 2012 shipping change had fallen far short of activists' desires. It still required that half of U.S. food aid be transported on the more-expensive U.S.-flagged ships, costing $75 million more per year than if the shipping were open to global competition, according to Cornell's Barrett and Erin C. Lentz, assistant professor of international relations at Bucknell University.[23]

Authors of the House legislation repealing the change — Reps. Duncan Hunter, R-Calif., and Elijah Cummings, D-Md. — said requiring the food to be transported on U.S. ships supports a Merchant Marine that is "essential to sustaining our military."[24] But the Defense and Transportation departments told the House Foreign Affairs Committee that the preference is unnecessary.[25]

The requirement "forces a huge premium price on ocean shipping and generates windfall profits for a handful of shipping lines, most [of them] foreign owned" despite being U.S.-flagged, says Barrett, who has studied the matter in depth. Even without the shipping markup, locally bought food is often faster and cheaper to deliver, he says.

"For the same [aid] budget," says agricultural economics professor Michael Carter, "we can save millions more people." Carter, of the University of California-Davis, directs a research consortium funded by USAID.

But several nonprofits and companies that grow, process and ship the food defend existing commodities programs. In a letter to Congress during last year's debate on reauthorization of a major farm bill, several of them wrote: "Growing, manufacturing, bagging, shipping and transporting nutritious U.S. food creates jobs and economic activity here at home, provides support for our U.S. Merchant Marine, essential to our national defense sealift capability, and sustains a robust domestic constituency for these programs not easily replicated in alternative foreign aid programs."[26]

Rep. Jeff Duncan, R-S.C., asked: "How is wiring cash to someone in a developing country a good idea instead of giving them wholesome, nutritious commodities grown by hard-working Americans?"[27]

As for the criticisms of monetization programs, a 2012 study commissioned by the Alliance for Global Food Security — a coalition of 14 relief and development organizations, some of which engage in monetization — found that properly managed monetization transactions can avoid pitfalls while providing benefits that cash-only support cannot.

Informa Economics — a Memphis-headquartered firm that conducts agriculture-related research — analyzed five monetization programs and found that they were designed not to compete with local production or disrupt commercial trade. Although the sales were made at fair-market value, the study concluded, the programs were able to offer the recipient countries other benefits, such as flexible payment terms. As a result, some recipients were able to make the purchases despite volatile exchange rates and avoid higher shipping costs associated with low-volume sales, the researchers said.[28]

The key is using "the right tool at the appropriate place," says Leach, of the World Food Program USA. "There are countries like Sudan that do not have access to food" and need to have it shipped in. "In Syria, it's much better to buy food regionally," because it's difficult to move commodities through a combat zone.

Shipping U.S. commodities also can make sense when responding to a nearby disaster in the Americas, Barrett says. And when the need is for foods fortified with vitamins and minerals, "you can start to enjoy the efficiency of modern American food processing."

Aside from advanced nations' aid policies, their agricultural subsidies, biofuel mandates and eating habits also can aggravate hunger, critics say.

Farm subsidy programs "tend to reduce worldwide commodity prices, hurting farmers in the developing world," said Daniel Sumner, an agricultural economics professor at the University of California-Davis and director of the University of California Agricultural Issues Center.[29]

Supporters of farm subsidies say they help stabilize U.S. agriculture production. Critics should "feel lucky we don't have runs on grocery stores," said Rep. Tim Walz, D.-Minn.[30]

And donating U.S.-grown commodities — or selling them at below-market prices — can also depress local crop prices, says Robert Rector, a senior research fellow at the Heritage Foundation, a conservative think tank in Washington. "You have to be careful not to undermine domestic production," Rector says. "Cheap and free food takes away from the [local] market, particularly if you're doing it consistently."

Critics say subsidies and mandates promoting biofuels such as corn-based ethanol — designed to reduce greenhouse gas emissions and lower American and European dependence on foreign oil — raise food prices and divert food to fuel production. Action Against Hunger, an international relief and development organization, said the amount of U.S. corn being converted into biofuels could feed 570 million people a year.[31]

Converting food to fuel "poses risks to ecosystems and biodiversity," said the U.N. Intergovernmental Panel on Climate Change, which previously supported biofuel production.[32]

Oxfam, an international relief and advocacy organization, has called for Europe and the United States to end their biofuel mandates and subsidies, which are projected to total between $9.2 billion and $11.5 billion in Europe in 2015, says Damon Vis-Dunbar, project and communications manager for the International Institute for Sustainable Development, a Canadian-based research organization with offices in the United States, Europe and China. The United States, which offered $6.6 billion in subsidies in 2010, cut them to around $1 billion in 2012.[33]

To meet Europe's biofuel demand, companies are planting land in developing countries that would be better used feeding the poor who live nearby, Oxfam said.[34]

Biofuels corporate executive Paul Beckwith argued that the ethanol mandate has stimulated important investment that has put the United States ahead of the world in getting "new advanced renewable energy into commercialization." Beckwith is CEO of Butamax Advanced Biofuels, a joint venture of BP and DuPont that develops biofuel manufacturing technology.[35]

The affluent world's appetite also taxes the environment and threatens the developing world's access to sufficient food, critics say. For instance, raising animals for consumption is far less efficient than using land to grow food plants — and that much-coveted steak is the least efficient of all.

Every 100 calories of grain fed to an animal produces only about 40 new calories of milk, 22 calories of eggs, 12 of chicken, 10 of pork or three of beef, according to Jonathan Foley, who is leaving his position as director of the University of Minnesota's Institute on the Environment on Aug. 15 to become executive director of the California Academy of Sciences.[36] By another reckoning, it takes about a pound of feed to produce a pound of farmed fish, but seven to make a pound of beef.[37]

Despite the relative efficiency of farmed fish, affluent diners' desire for wild-caught seafood — along with pollution and global warming — is depleting wild fish populations, which in turn threatens the livelihoods of poor fishermen who compete with sophisticated fleets from developed countries.

The International Programme on the State of the Ocean at Oxford University has declared the planet "at high risk of entering a phase of extinction of marine species unprecedented in human history."[38] For instance, overfishing — both legal and illegal — threatens the scalloped hammerhead shark, used in shark fin soup, a delicacy in many Asian countries.[39]

Is climate change making hunger worse?

Oxfam has called climate change "the single biggest threat to fighting hunger."[40]

Scientists have issued dire warnings about the threat global warming poses to humanity's ability to feed itself in the future, and they cite damage that's already occurring. The World Food Programme says climate change could wipe out two-thirds of Africa's arable land by 2025, boost food prices by 50 to 90 percent by 2030 and raise the risk of hunger by 10 to 20 percent by 2050.[41]

But when it comes to climate change, agriculture is both a victim and a villain. Farming is a major source of greenhouse gases — including methane, carbon dioxide and nitrous oxide — which scientists say are warming the planet. Agriculture emits more greenhouse gases than all forms of transportation combined. Fuel-burning farm machinery emits carbon dioxide. Cattle release large amounts of methane, fertilizer emits nitrous oxide and soil releases carbon dioxide (CO_2) when cultivated.[42]

Some say a warming planet and more atmospheric CO_2 will reduce hunger by improving agricultural productivity. "Plants love warmth and sunshine," says Dennis Avery, a senior fellow at the conservative Heartland and Hudson institutes and director of Hudson's Center for Global Food Issues. "Both animals and vegetation have a much greater tolerance for temperature changes than the [widely used scientific] models would have us believe."

Describing CO_2 as "like fertilizer for plants," which breathe it in like animals breathe oxygen, Avery says doubling atmospheric CO_2 concentrations would increase crop yields by about 35 percent.

Similarly, Andrei Illarionov, a senior fellow at the libertarian Cato Institute, points out that in warmer places "there is usually more precipitation than in drier areas, the cost of heating and volume of food required to sustain human life [are] lower, while vegetation and [ice-free] navigation periods are longer, and crops' yields are higher."[43]

Arguing that the Earth simply is in the warm period of a routine climate cycle, Avery says the greater threat to food production will occur during the next Ice Age.

Other climate-change skeptics contend that proposed responses to global warming, such as switching to biofuels production, can threaten food supplies.

Scientists agree that CO_2 by itself could increase plant yields, but most say the damage to food done by greenhouse gases will outweigh the benefits. For instance, two recent studies found that higher CO_2 levels diminish plants' nutritional value and resistance to pests.[44]

More broadly, scientists warn that rising temperatures, more drought, and more violent weather will lead to diminished agricultural yields, particularly in warmer regions where many of the poor live.

This past May was the hottest on record, according to the National Oceanic and Atmospheric Administration (NOAA).[45] The first decade of this century was the hottest in recorded history, and temperatures are even higher so far this decade, according to the University Corporation for Atmospheric Research, a consortium based in Boulder, Colo., that manages the National Center for Atmospheric Research.[46]

Already, according to the American Association for the Advancement of Science (AAAS), heat waves and extreme storms are becoming worse and more frequent. The Greenland and Antarctic ice sheets are melting more rapidly. The oceans are absorbing growing amounts of carbon dioxide, which makes them more acidic and degrades coral reefs where millions of marine species live.[47]

Meanwhile deserts are expanding. The growing Sahara Desert has been destroying crops and leaving

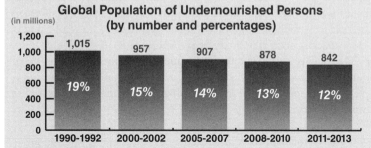

Global Hunger on the Decline

The number of undernourished people worldwide fell from more than 1 billion in 1992, one-fifth of the global population, to 842 million in 2013, or 12 percent.

Global Population of Undernourished Persons (by number and percentages)

(in millions)

1990-1992	2000-2002	2005-2007	2008-2010	2011-2013
1,015	957	907	878	842
19%	15%	14%	13%	12%

Source: "Hunger Portal," U.N. Food and Agriculture Organization, undated, http://tinyurl.com/yz2bcrh

farmers in West Africa without food.[48] To escape rising temperatures, plants and animals are migrating toward the poles, up mountainsides and deeper into the sea. Droughts this year devastated crops in Brazil's southeast and in California, which grows nearly half of America's fruits, vegetables and nuts.[49] Global wheat and corn productivity is declining.[50]

"We're facing the specter of reduced yields in some of the key crops that feed humanity," said Rajendra Pachauri, chairman of the U.N.'s climate change panel. The panel's report warned that altered ocean chemistry could cause fish extinctions, and changes in climate could threaten apple orchards in Washington, cherry orchards in California and coffee crops in Central and South America, often tended by subsistence farmers who depend on their coffee crops for survival.[51]

Are genetically modified crops needed to end hunger?

A group of farmers and activists this spring protested at the office of Philippine Agriculture Secretary Proceso Alcala, calling on him to block tests of so-called "golden rice," a genetically modified grain designed to combat vitamin A deficiency in the developing world. Last year, about 400 protesters tore down fences surrounding a golden rice test field and ripped the plants from the ground.

"There are not enough studies to ensure the safety of golden rice to humans," Chito Medina, national coordinator of the Filipino activist group known by its acronym

MASIPAG, said in explaining the protests. "To plant the genetically engineered rice, or the golden rice, is a real threat to the environment," he said.[52]

The Philippine protesters represent just one of numerous campaigns worldwide opposing genetically modified organisms (GMOs). Scientists make genetically modified (GM) plants and animals by adding genes that introduce specific traits — such as pest resistance — to the organism. Opponents fear GMO plants could harm humans, animals or the environment. They paint GMOs as part of a plot by Western agribusiness to control farming in the developing world.

So far, their actions have produced mixed results: GMOs are common in the United States, rare in Europe and subject to heated debate in the developing world.

Golden rice was created in 1999 by Ingo Potrykus of the Swiss Federal Institute of Technology and Peter Beyer of the University of Freiburg in Germany. They inserted genes from a daffodil and a bacterium into rice to enable it to generate beta-carotene, which the human body converts into vitamin A. Later, beta-carotene production was boosted by replacing the daffodil gene with one from corn.

The Philippines-based nonprofit International Rice Research Institute, which is developing the rice, said field trials there met beta-carotene goals but produced a lower yield than varieties currently in use. The institute is continuing research focused on yield.[53]

Proponents say GM foods are safe and essential to ease hunger and meet the demands of a growing world population, particularly as developing countries' become more affluent and demand more and higher-quality food. GM crops, they say, increase yields, survive with less fertilizer and pesticides and can be more nutritious. Scientists are working on drought-tolerant corn, sweet potatoes with high beta-carotene content, bacteria-resistant bananas, cassava varieties that resist viruses and contain added beta-carotene and other nutrients, and corn that requires less fertilizer.

GM plants grow on more than half of U.S. farmland, represent nearly all of America's soybeans and 70 percent of its corn and are common in Canada.[54] However, European countries effectively ban GMOs, with some exceptions. Some GMO animal feed can be imported, for example, and Spain, Portugal, the Czech Republic, Romania and Slovakia grow some genetically modified crops.[55]

More than half the acreage planted in GM crops last year was in developing countries, 87 percent of that in Brazil, Argentina, India, China and South Africa. Only three other African countries — Sudan, Egypt and Burkina Faso — grow GM crops, partly due to fear among farmers in other African countries that GM crops can't be sold in Europe.[56]

Some countries refuse to accept GMOs as food aid, says Steve Taravella, the World Food Programme's senior spokesman in the United States. And some donor nations prohibit their aid money from being used to purchase GM food, Taravella adds.

Richard Roberts — a Nobel laureate for genetic research and chief scientific officer for a company that makes genetic-research supplies — called opposition to GM crops a "crime against humanity," because the foods are needed to feed the hungry.[57]

Michael Purugganan, a professor of genomics and biology and dean for science at New York University, lamented the "misinformation" circulated by GM opponents. "The genes they inserted to make the vitamin [in golden rice] are not some weird manufactured material but are also found in squash, carrots and melons," he said.[58]

The AAAS has noted that the World Health Organization, the American Medical Association, the U.S. National Academy of Sciences, the British Royal Society and "every other respected organization that has examined the evidence" has concluded that eating GM plants is no riskier than eating plants bred with traditional farming technology.[59]

Opponents, however, contend that there are better ways to feed the hungry. "Most GMOs are not used to solve hunger" but to increase the profitability of industrial farming, says Greenpeace USA researcher Mark Floegel. "We have [other] technologies that subsistence farmers could use to make their lives better."

Paul Johnston and Dave Santillo, scientists in Greenpeace International's Science Unit, argued that history proves the need for caution in using GMOs. Citing the ill effects of "one-time 'wonder chemicals,' such as PCBs and many pesticides," they contended that "new problems continue to emerge from chemicals put into widespread use without the drawbacks having been fully investigated." Thus, they said, "If you are in doubt about the consequences of what you intend to do, then don't do it."[60]

Others take a more nuanced approach. GMO technology can be used "for good or bad," says Walter Willett, chair of Harvard University's Department of Nutrition. GMOs used in the United States probably don't pose health threats, he says, but they also probably don't produce a significantly higher yield. Noting the need to increase global food production, he adds, "I wouldn't take them off the table."

Oxfam is "agnostic about GMOs," says Gawain Kripke, Oxfam America's policy director. Most GM products brought to market so far primarily benefit industrial farming, he notes, but he finds attempts to enrich plants' nutrients "pretty interesting."

Similarly, World Food Program USA's Leach says, "We will accept food from a country if that country would use that food to feed its own population, and we will take that food into any country that will accept it."

Farmers in Burkina Faso in West Africa have found that GM cotton "cuts pesticide and labor costs," the University of California's Carter says. That shows that "small-scale farmers can potentially make good use of at least some of these technologies," he adds.

However, in the United States insects have developed resistance to GM cotton, which initially allowed farmers to use less pesticide. So pesticide use is rising, according to Charles Benbrook, research professor at Washington State University's Center for Sustaining Agriculture and Natural Resources. Similarly, corn engineered to tolerate Monsanto's Roundup herbicide requires increasing amounts of the product to kill weeds that have developed resistance, he said.[61]

BACKGROUND

Early Famines

History records serious famine in every part of the world. Egyptian stone carvers chronicled lengthy droughts and famines in the third millennium B.C. They also portrayed the first recorded hunger-relief efforts — by the Egyptian upper class.

In *Famine: A Short History*, Irish economist Cormac Ó Gráda identifies multiple causes of hunger, including too much or too little rain, extreme temperatures, conflict, overpopulation, poverty, ideology and autocratic governments. Often the causes converged, as when conflict

coincided with poor harvests, or drought struck an impoverished community. Famine most frequently hit the poor and seldom occurred in democracies.

The Old Testament book of Nehemiah, likely written in the fifth century B.C., describes overpopulation compelling the poor to sell their children because there was not enough food. The Punic Wars triggered famine in Rome in the first century B.C. Heavy rains and low temperatures brought famine to Europe in the early 14th century A.D. Authoritarian communist government policies turned poor harvests into mass starvation in the Soviet Union and China in the 20th century and continue to do so in North Korea.[62]

Ó Gráda, an economics professor at University College Dublin, chronicles famines throughout history, including in Turkey (499-501), Bengal (1176), Japan (1229-32), Mexico (1454), Africa (often) and, of course, in Ireland, during the potato famine in the 1840s and '50s, one of the best known.[63]

Potato blight struck Ireland's potatoes — the primary sustenance of half the population — in 1845. The fungus-like micro-organism, carried to Ireland from Mexico, devastated the crop and led to the deaths of more than 750,000 Irish over the next decade. Two million people fled to England, Canada or the United States.[64] During the latter part of the century, 50 million people died in famines in India, China, Korea, Brazil, Russia, Ethiopia and Sudan.[65]

Ireland's Great Hunger marked the beginning of the end of peacetime famine in Europe, except for Russia. The last natural famine in Western Europe was in Finland in 1867-68.[66]

Previously, societies had responded to hunger with personal and religious philanthropy. Some governments imposed price controls, distributed food and subsidized migration to places without food shortages. In the 19th and 20th centuries nongovernment relief organizations emerged, as did major advances in agricultural technology.[67]

In the United States, the 1862 Morrill Act funded state colleges and universities focused on agriculture and mechanical arts. The U.S. government also established the Cooperative State Research, Education and Extension Service to disseminate agricultural research findings.[68] In 1883, the Department of Agriculture began research on boosting agricultural production.[69] And, in 1905, German chemist Fritz Haber enabled a gigantic leap in agricultural yield by extracting nitrogen from air, which permitted the manufacture of nitrogen-based synthetic fertilizer.[70]

Advances in transportation, storage, medicine and the understanding of nutrition as well as the spread of democracy also helped end peacetime famine in developed countries. In the developing world, hunger was lessened and dealt with more quickly because of the growth of relief organizations, creation of inexpensive nutrient-dense foods that could be stored and transported easily and the expansion of communication technology that enabled news of food emergencies to spread rapidly.

Residents of affluent countries were eating more, including more expensive food. Per capita annual meat consumption in Germany, for instance, rose from less than 44 pounds before 1820 to almost 115 pounds by the early 20th century. In 1800 a typical European consumed 2,000 calories a day, which rose to 3,000 calories by the early 20th century.

In the mid-20th century, nearly 60 percent of the world's population lived in countries with an average daily diet of less than 2,200 calories. By the mid-'80s, only 10 percent did.[71]

Manmade Famine

Some of the most notorious 20th-century famines were substantially caused by humans.

In 1932-33, for instance, an estimated 6 million to 8 million people died — many of starvation — during Russian dictator Josef Stalin's violent push to collectivize agriculture and turn the Soviet Union into an industrial power. Beginning in 1929, small peasant farms were forced into collectives of up to 247,000 acres. Many peasants resisted, and the government cracked down brutally. As farm production fell by 40 percent, the state seized and exported grain to raise funds for industrial equipment, leaving peasants without enough to eat.[72]

Mao Tse-tung pressed the same disastrous policies on Communist China 25 years later. Between 1958 and 1962, 36 million starved to death.[73]

In the late 1960s, between 500,000 and 2 million people — many of them children — died of starvation during civil war in Nigeria. Warfare disrupted food supplies, and the Nigerian government blocked relief shipments into the breakaway region of Biafra.[74]

In the early 1980s, several factors converged to create severe famine in Ethiopia. The country was struggling to

recover from drought-caused famine in the 1970s when another drought hit. Poor farming techniques worsened the effects, leading to deforestation, soil erosion and expanding deserts. Civil war — between Ethiopia's Marxist dictatorship and rebels in the north — compounded the suffering.

The government tried to keep news of the starvation from the world. But after the BBC televised images of the devastation, relief supplies flowed into the country. The government then blocked shipments to rebel-controlled areas, and diverted food from starving Ethiopians to the army. An estimated 1 million people died in 1984-85.[75]

Relief Efforts

The United States led relief efforts in Ethiopia, just as it had around the world since early in the century, especially after World War II.[76] The United Nations, created after that war, also facilitated international relief programs.

The U.N. established the FAO in 1945 and the International Children's Emergency Fund (UNICEF) in 1946. It added the World Food Programme in 1961, the U.N. Development Programme in 1966 and the U.N. Population Fund in 1969.[77] The World Bank got into the act in 1973, when bank President Robert McNamara set a goal of reducing malnutrition and poverty in the developing world by making loans for agricultural and rural development.[78]

In 1954, the United States institutionalized its relief efforts by creating the Food for Peace program, under which Congress authorized the purchase of surplus commodities from American farmers for resale at low prices overseas. The process was designed to help both U.S. farmers and the hungry abroad. It also provided the basis for a later debate about whether shipping commodities across the ocean was the best way to aid the hungry. Over the years, the program's emphasis shifted from sales, which essentially ceased during the 1990s, to donations.

The postwar era also fostered scientific and technological advances that led to an unprecedented increase in agricultural productivity. In 1944, American biologist Norman Borlaug went to Mexico to work in a Rockefeller Foundation-funded program that launched what became the "Green Revolution" of high-yield farming.[79] In 1953, American biochemist James Watson and British biophysicist Francis Crick described the double-helix structure of DNA, which paved the way for mapping the genetic code and creating genetically modified organisms.[80]

CHRONOLOGY

1845-1984 *As technology and anti-hunger organizations fight famine, wars and other human actions become leading causes of hunger.*

1845 Potato blight causes Irish famine that kills 750,000 and sends millions of refugees to England, Canada and United States.

1862 U.S. government begins to support agricultural research and education.

1868 End of Finnish famine marks last in heart of Europe.

1905 German chemist Fritz Haber "fixes" nitrogen from air, enabling manufacture of modern fertilizer.

1929 Soviet Union begins forcing farmers into collectives while pushing industrial development, leading to collapse of agricultural production and 6 to 8 million deaths, many from starvation.

1944 American biologist Norman Borlaug begins research that leads to "Green Revolution" of high-yield farming.

1945 U.N. establishes Food and Agriculture Organization (FAO).

1953 American biochemist James Watson and British biophysicist Francis Crick describe the structure of DNA, enabling eventual creation of genetically modified organisms.

1954 Congress authorizes purchase of surplus commodities for resale at low prices overseas to feed the hungry.

1958 Communist China copies Soviet Union's collectivism/industrialization efforts; 36 million starve.

1961 U.N. creates World Food Programme to distribute food to the hungry.

1967 Secessionist war in Nigeria's Biafra state leads to 500,000 to 2 million starvation deaths.

1973 Scientists create first genetically engineered organism; World Bank begins to address hunger.

1984 Drought, poor farming practices and civil war cause famine that kills 1 million Ethiopians.

1994-2014 *New agricultural technologies incite controversy; anti-hunger organizations focus on sustainability.*

1994 Food and Drug Administration approves sale of genetically modified (GM) food.

2000 Genes from genetically engineered StarLink corn, approved only for animal feed, are found in taco shells after farmers sell the corn for human consumption.

2002 GM crops in United States produce 4 billion pounds more food and fiber with less pesticide per acre than conventional plants, raise farm income by $1.5 billion.

2006 To help protect wildlife habitat, World Wildlife Fund works with food companies to promote efficient farming practices.

2007 Overuse of Green Revolution techniques in India have made Punjab state's agriculture "unsustainable and nonprofitable," according to local officials. World Food Programme, with support from the Bill & Melinda Gates and Howard Buffett foundations, begins teaching better agricultural practices to poor farmers and buying their crops for use in relief deliveries.

2009 Obama administration launches Feed the Future program that seeks leadership from developing countries and taps private-sector expertise of nonprofit and profit-making organizations to promote agricultural development.

2011 Study finds high-tech sensors can increase crop yields while reducing fuel consumption and fertilizer and pesticide overuse.

2012 Farmers raise more fish than beef for the first time.

2013 FAO counts 842 million hungry people worldwide — 26 million fewer than in 2012.

2014 Climate-change threat to food production underscored by University Corporation for Atmospheric Research report that this decade is on track to being hottest ever recorded.

Videographer Farmers Promote Best Practices

Locally produced videos have credibility.

The scene — played out thousands of times across rural India — led one journalist to liken poor farmers to the late Indian filmmaker Satyajit Ray.[1] After a crash course in filmmaking, farmers set up tripods and use small, battery-powered, digital cameras to record interviews with fellow farmers about their best agricultural practices. They then edit their work to eight- to 10-minute presentations.

Finally, with a tiny, battery-powered projector and perhaps a sheet stretched between trees, they show the videos to other indigenous farmers at bus stops, temples, schools, street corners or local government offices — anywhere they find farmers with time on their hands and an interest in learning how to grow more food at less cost in environmentally friendly ways. Sometimes government workers attend the meetings and distribute materials needed to implement the suggested practices.[2]

The program is organized and supported by Digital Green, the brainchild of Indian-American Rikin Gandhi, who got the idea about a decade ago while researching technology for emerging markets at Microsoft Research India.

Traditional government agricultural extension programs, provided via broadcast or print media, don't reach many small-scale farmers, many of whom are illiterate. So Gandhi decided to combine the high technology of making videos with low-tech means of distributing them to farflung rural communities. The equipment is small enough to fit into a backpack for transport by bicycle or on foot.[3]

Gandhi figured farmers would be more likely to listen to their peers. So, while the information comes from experts, farmers tell about their own experiences using the new technologies. Having locals produce the videos adds to the films' credibility, Gandhi said, and enables the films to be shot in the local languages.

"Farmers listen to farmers," says Jason Clay, senior vice president at the World Wildlife Fund, "They listen to their neighbors and to people who speak their language." Worldwide, farmers speak about 6,000 different languages, he says.

When the videos are shot by farmers, Gandhi said, other farmers "instantly connect with it."[4] "The first questions farmers often ask when they see these videos are, 'What is the name of the farmer in the video?' and 'Which village is he or she from?' " he said.[5]

Farmers adopt the new techniques about 45 percent of the time, compared to a 33 percent rate for traditional agricultural extension programs in India, according to Digital Green. Microsoft Research India also found that the program spent $3.70 to get a single farmer to adopt a new practice, while traditional approaches cost $38.[6]

One farmer who adopted a new technique after attending a Digital Green presentation was Chaitan Gadaba, from Putpandi in eastern India, who learned how to grow okra with minimal irrigation. He had been cultivating rice on a portion of his land, and leaving the rest fallow for lack of water. After watching the video, he began planting all of his property.[7]

Similarly, farmers in Karnataka in western India learned to use the azolla fern as cattle fodder to increase milk yields. Originally shot in the Kannada language, the video was later produced in Hindi for farmers in Madhya Pradesh, some 600 miles away, where the practice became popular as well, Gandhi said.[8]

Both advances later faced criticisms that they may do more harm than good.

Borlaug, who won the 1970 Nobel Peace Prize, focused on using conventional breeding processes to develop disease-resistant and high-yield wheat varieties.[81] The advances were accompanied by development of chemical fertilizers and pesticides, improved irrigation techniques and increased use of mechanized equipment. Agricultural productivity soared.

Mexico became self-sufficient in wheat during the 1950s, with yields increasing sixfold between 1950 and 1970.[82] In India, wheat yields tripled between the mid-'60s and mid-'90s.[83]

Overall, the Green Revolution has saved up to 1 billion people from starvation, according to former U.S. Agriculture Secretary Dan Glickman and former U.N. World Food Programme Executive Director Catherine Bertini.[84]

Launched in 2006, Digital Green had reached 20 villages by 2008. By 2009 it had spun off as an independent nonprofit.[9] Since then, the organization has produced more than 2,800 videos in over 20 languages and shown them to more than 330,000 farmers in 3,000 villages. It operates in eight Indian states and in Ethiopia, Ghana, Mozambique and Tanzania.[10] Gandhi wants to reach 10,000 villages by next year.[11] The videos are available at www.digital green.org.

A case study by the OneWorld Foundation India called Digital Green "a viable solution to the major problems afflicting government agricultural extension programs," which require a "huge number of staff" and "usually restrict their interactions to the richer, more enterprising farmers within a village."[12]

Gawain Kripke, policy director at Oxfam America, the U.S. affiliate of the international relief and advocacy organization, says Digital Green adopts a key concept in agricultural development: Education should be embraced, directed and delivered by farmers themselves.

"You don't just arrive with new seeds and say try this," Kripke explains. "You invite them to ask questions and request support for what they're trying to do. You can't come to grow maize if they want to grow mangos."

— *Tom Price*

Farmers in the central Indian state of Madhya Pradesh, one of the country's most undeveloped regions, shoot a video on chemical treatment of paddy seeds being grown in a nursery, to be shown to other farmers interested in environmentally friendly, lower-cost farming methods.

[1]Rajiv Rao, "Aspiring astronaut helps farmers," *Business Standard* (India), Aug. 9, 2011, http://tinyurl.com/l5cqevt.

[2]*Ibid.*; "Case Study: Digital Green," Governance Knowledge Centre, Department of Administrative Reforms and Public Grievances, Ministry of Personnel, Public Grievances and Pensions, Government of India, June 2011, http://tinyurl.com/qayfl8p.

[3]David Bornstein, "Where YouTube Meets the Farm," *The New York Times*, April 3, 2013, http://tinyurl.com/ozbjohp.

[4]M. J. Prabu, "Video clippings educate on methods practised elseware," *The Hindu*, Feb. 17, 2011, http://tinyurl.com/qchfubr.

[5]"Tech-based Farming Advice Should Stay People-Centred," *SciDev.Net* (London), Nov. 20, 2013, http://tinyurl.com/obp2u4a.

[6]Bornstein, *op. cit.*

[7]"Latest technology helps ryots get good yield," *The Hindu*, Aug. 4, 2011, http://is.gd/Tmi1Yq.

[8]Geeta Padmanabhan, "When farmers turn filmmakers," *The Hindu*, Sept. 18, 2013, http://tinyurl.com/o9uh6so.

[9]Rao, *op. cit.*; Priyanka Golikeri, "MIT alumnus chucks space dreams for terra firma," *DNA India*, March 24, 2011, http://tinyurl.com/lmmp8hn; "Ashoka Innovators For The Public: Rikin Gandhi," Ashoka, http://tinyurl.com/kxhlwlr.

[10]"An Innovative Platform for Rural Development," *Digital Green*, http://tinyurl.com/pzqv99k.

[11]Padmanabhan, *op. cit.*

[12]"Case Study: Digital Green," *op. cit.*

Genetic Engineering

It took 41 years for Watson and Crick's DNA breakthrough to bring genetically engineered food to market. Scientists created the first genetically engineered organism, a bacterium, in 1973. Calgene — a California-based company that is now a subsidiary of Monsanto — patented the genetically modified FlavrSavr tomato in 1989, but it didn't get Food and Drug Administration approval for sale until 1994. Two years later, Monsanto introduced Roundup Ready soybeans, which could survive when the fields were sprayed with the company's Roundup weed killer.

By 2002, U.S. farmers were producing 4 billion pounds more food and fiber per acre with GM crops than with conventional plants, reducing pesticide use by 46 million pounds and raising farm income by $1.5 billion, according to the National Center for Food and Agricultural Policy, a Washington-based research and education institution.[85]

Freezing Food's Footprint to Save Wildlife

"The biggest threat to biodiversity is agricultural sprawl."

A few years ago, the World Wildlife Fund (WWF) took a look around the globe and determined that one of the biggest threats to wildlife is habitat loss, and the biggest threat to wildlife habitat is the human appetite.

Tigers no longer live in areas of Malaysia and Sumatra that have been converted to oil palm plantations, for instance. And oil palm cultivation has driven the Sumatran rhino from parts of Malaysia, Sumatra and Borneo.[1]

Overall, the fund says, habitat loss is a major hazard for 85 percent of species on the International Union for Conservation of Nature's list of threatened and endangered species. During the 1990s, more than 230 million acres of forests — 2.4 percent of the world's total — were cut down, almost 70 percent for conversion to agriculture.[2] Between 1960 and 2000, the globe's cultivated land grew by 13 percent.[3] And conservationists worry that demand for farmland will soar in the future.

Earth's population — currently 7 billion — is expected to grow to 9 billion or more by the middle of this century, notes Jason Clay, the organization's senior vice president for market transformation. And as economic growth creates larger middle classes in places like China and India, those populations will consume greater amounts of food, especially more animal protein. Thus, by mid-century individuals may require twice as much food as they do now — counting what they consume and the food consumed by the animals they eat, Clay says.

Without greatly improved productivity and more environmentally friendly farming techniques, "the biggest threat to biodiversity becomes agricultural sprawl," Clay says. "Wildlife need homes, too."

So the WWF set out to "freeze the footprint of food," as Clay puts it, by promoting more efficient agricultural practices: producing more crops on existing cropland, thus halting the conversion of natural habitat to farmland.

The fund's goal is to improve the efficiency of all food producers — from the largest conglomerate to the smallest subsistence farmer — so they use less land, water, fertilizer and pesticides. The organization decided to focus first on companies that produce or trade in 15 commodities whose cultivation poses the biggest threat to wildlife habitat, including soy, sugar, palm oil, beef and farmed salmon.

"We needed to find the business case for change," Clay says, a case he says can be found in the value of intangible assets such as a company's reputation. "Killing that last population of orangutans can affect your corporate value," he says. "So companies see this as a huge risk."

WWF negotiators also argued that producing more food on the same land — or in the same water — was good for the bottom line.

Currently, with support from the Mars food corporation, the WWF also is working with the Beijing Genomic Institute to map the genomes of Africa's most important food crops, such as yams, plantains and cassava. The findings will be released in the public domain, so plant breeders can use the information to improve African crops.

"The goal is to produce better materials" so farmers can "double, triple or quadruple productivity" in areas where hunger is most common, Clay says.

The information can be used to improve plants either through genetic engineering or traditional breeding.

Farmers also got an unintentional boost from the 1973 Arab oil embargo. As the embargo pushed up the cost of oil-based fertilizer, pesticides and fuel, governments turned to plant-based ethanol as an alternative fuel. In 1975, Brazil required that ethanol from sugarcane be blended with gasoline. The United States exempted ethanol from gasoline taxes in 1978.[86]

In 2007, the United States required that an increasing amount of ethanol be blended with gasoline — from 9 billion gallons in 2008 to 36 billion by 2022. Last year, the Environmental Protection Agency, which implements the law, required fuel producers to use 14 billion gallons of corn-based ethanol and 2.75 billion from nonfood sources, such as wood or inedible parts of the corn plant.

The United States, Brazil and later European countries were aiming to reduce dependence on foreign oil and cut carbon pollution caused by burning fossil fuels. By 2011, ethanol production was consuming 40 percent of

Breeders can identify plants with favorable genetic traits, then use traditional techniques to reproduce them.

The fund also has worked on food-related issues with such industry giants as Wal-Mart, Coca-Cola, General Mills and Kellogg. Now it is focusing on trade associations in order to have a broader, faster impact, Clay says. "Working with companies one by one is not fast enough," he says.

Among other things, the WWF has encouraged industries to have their practices evaluated by independent certification organizations. For example, 15 salmon-farming companies, which represent 70 percent of global production, have committed to having all of their practices meet third-party standards for minimizing environmental damage by 2020, Clay says.

Members of the Consumer Goods Forum — a 400-member international trade association of manufacturers, retailers and service providers whose business lines range from food to beer to laundry supplies — have agreed to stop contributing to deforestation in their production and acquisition of beef, soy, paper and palm-oil products, he says. The fund also is helping palm-oil processors enable their small-scale suppliers to implement environment-friendly practices, he says.

WWF's market transformation program has become "a bit of a model for others, including Oxfam," says Oxfam America Policy Director Gawain Kripke. "We launched a campaign a couple years ago — called Behind the Brands — that's modeled on what WWF has done, but with a slightly different focus."

Oxfam rates how companies treat land, water, climate, women, farmers and workers and then asks its supporters to contact the companies demanding improvement. "We're actually having constructive engagement with these companies," Kripke says. "They've done stuff we think is really positive in the last couple of years."

Coca-Cola, for instance, raised its score for how fairly it treats land issues from 1, the lowest, in 2013 to 7, the highest,

Forest habitats for endangered Sumatran tigers have been lost to conversion to massive oil palm plantations in Malaysia and Indonesia, leading environmentalists to call "agricultural sprawl" the biggest threat to the planet's biodiversity.

this year by requiring its sugar suppliers to respect the property rights of small-scale farmers, who often have their land seized by larger organizations, Oxfam reported.[4]

— *Tom Price*

[1]"Palm oil & biodiversity loss," World Wildlife Fund, http://tinyurl.com/oce8a9t.

[2]"Impact of habitat loss on species," World Wildlife Fund, http://tinyurl.com/pgv3ota. For background, see Reed Karaim, "Vanishing Biodiversity," *CQ Researcher*, Nov. 6, 2012, pp. 497-520.

[3]Hugh Turral, "Climate change, water and food security," U.N. Food and Agriculture Organization, 2011, p. 31, http://tinyurl.com/nlh3q5b.

[4]"Race to the top: One year of looking Behind the Brands," Oxfam International, Feb. 26, 2014, http://tinyurl.com/acxglfh. For background, see Jina Moore, "Resolving Land Disputes," *CQ Researcher*, Sept. 11, 2011, pp. 421-446.

the U.S. corn crop, which rose to 44 percent last year, according to Sen. Dianne Feinstein, D-Calif. Critics began bemoaning the unintended consequences of ethanol use: higher food prices and disappointing environmental benefits.[87]

Unintended Consequences

Genetic engineering and the Green Revolution produced other unintended consequences.

Many people's fears of GM crops were heightened in 2000 when genes from genetically modified StarLink corn — approved only for use in animal feed — were found in taco shells. Some farmers admitted selling the corn for human consumption.[88] The same year, Roundup-resistant weeds were found in Delaware. Three years later, bollworms resistant to GM cotton were discovered in the South.[89]

The modern agriculture spawned by the Green Revolution — including large, industrialized farms that replant the same crops in the same places year after year — has overused chemicals, drained aquifers, depleted soil, threatened wildlife and biodiversity, spewed greenhouse gases and created its own pesticide-resistant crops.

Even small-scale farmers in India have discovered the Green Revolution's downside. Beginning in the 1960s, high-yield seeds, fertilizer, pesticides and irrigation multiplied productivity in Punjab and made the state the breadbasket of a nation that had transformed itself from a land of starvation to a food exporter. Over the decades, however, Punjab's farmers depleted the soil, created pesticide-resistant insects and weeds and polluted the water sources with chemicals. In 2007, the Punjab State Council for Science and Technology reported that "the most stunning example of the Green Revolution in India . . . has become unsustainable and non-profitable."[90]

Pat Mooney, executive director of the ETC Group, an Ottawa-based organization that studies how technologies affect the poor, says the Green Revolution "deserves credit for having produced a lot more wheat and rice and maize. Some people might otherwise not have been fed." But, he adds, "it became a one-size-fits-all model. In the long term it caused a lot of damage and ended up focusing on yields beyond nutrition."

A review of academic literature conducted by Barrett of Cornell and others found that the Green Revolution led to some poor people consuming a calorie-rich but nutrition-poor diet. "From the 1970s to the mid-1990s, the price of staple foods [such as rice and wheat] decreased relative to the price of micronutrient rich foods [such as vegetables] in much of Asia," they wrote. As a result, the poor were eating more grain and fewer vegetables, they said.[91]

Barrett also notes other Green Revolution shortcomings. "In initially making water available essentially for free to farmers, it pretty much guarantees they will overuse water," he says. He also notes the overuse of chemicals.

But, he adds, "The Green Revolution had an amazing effect. It increased per capita calorie availability. It drove down food prices. There's no better way to fight hunger than to bring down the price of the food, and the Green Revolution achieved that more than anything before or since."

The Green Revolution was much less successful in Africa, where countries lacked good roads or railways to transport food to market or to distribute high-yield seeds, fertilizers and pesticides. African governments also did not offer farmers the support provided by Asian governments, such as credit, training and subsidies.[92] And since independence, many African countries have suffered from government corruption, authoritarianism, anti-free market ideologies and strife, U.S. Assistant Secretary of State for African Affairs Carson lamented in 2010.

"Mismanagement, embezzlement of state revenues and centralized approaches to economic management precipitated economic decline and the deterioration of infrastructure and government services," Carson said. However, since the 1990s, he said, a growing number of African countries have "liberalized their economies, embraced market reforms and adopted pro-business policies."[93]

CURRENT SITUATION

Sustainable Food

The Senate Environment and Public Works Committee is considering a proposal to repeal the mandate that results in nearly half of America's corn crop being burned as motor fuel. Supporters of the legislation say the mandate diverts food to fuel and drives up food prices.

Cosponsored by liberal California Democrat Feinstein, and conservative Oklahoma Republican Sen. Tom Coburn, the measure would eliminate the requirement that an increasing amount of corn-based ethanol be blended into the nation's gasoline. However, it would continue a mandate for burning so-called advanced biofuels, which are made from inedible vegetation.

Feinstein said she still supports shifting to low-carbon fuels, but opposes the corn mandate because it raises the cost of food and damages the environment. Coburn called for letting "market forces, rather than political and parochial forces, determine how to diversify fuel supplies."[94]

The bill fits into a larger movement that emphasizes sustainable food production that uses environmentally friendly agriculture and boosts the resiliency of small-scale farmers in the developing world when they face drought and other challenges, says Leach of World Food Program USA. The efforts include providing drought- and pest-resistant seeds, teaching more effective farming techniques and combining relief with development projects.

The most effective attacks on hunger and its effects, Cornell's Barrett says, are providing health care for children and women of childbearing age, educating

Should hunger programs ban genetically modified food?

YES
Éric Darier, Ph.D.
Food for Life Campaigner,
Greenpeace International

Written for *CQ Researcher*, August 2014

The biotech industry has been exploiting food crises to promote genetically modified (GM) crops, claiming they can solve world hunger. People experiencing hunger should have decent solutions, not be used to promote controversial technologies. Even in emergency situations, desperate people should have the right to choose what they eat.

Greenpeace opposes the deliberate release of GM organisms into the environment. They can multiply and cross-breed and pose a threat of irreversible damage to biodiversity and ecosystems. Furthermore, we don't know if GM crops are safe to eat, especially over the long term. Therefore, with regard to GM foods, it is urgent that we apply the "precautionary principle," which could be summarized as "in case of doubt, leave it out."

Genetic modification makes crops prone to unexpected effects. Evaluating food safety requires looking for such effects, which is extremely difficult, if not impossible, as reflected in the ongoing controversy surrounding the assessment of the safety of GM crops.

U.S. food aid containing GM grains has been used to provide famine relief. Greenpeace is most concerned about the potential uncontrolled environmental spread of GM organisms into the affected countries. Notably, the United States has not joined 167 other countries in ratifying the U.N. Cartagena Protocol on Biosafety, a treaty regulating the movement of GM organisms among nations.

Millions of people around the world suffer from food shortages, high food prices and hunger, due to several factors: industrial farming, bad harvests, inadequate access to food due to poverty and inequality, rising oil prices, changing consumption patterns, commodities speculation and the rush to produce unsustainable biofuels.

Instead, ecological farming enables and encourages communities to produce enough food to feed themselves while fostering sustainable farming and healthy food.

There are many ecological alternatives to GM crops. The U.N. agriculture assessment known as IAASTD recommended policies that would lead to scaling up ecological agriculture. More recently, the report of the U.N. special rapporteur on the right to food urged governments to "move away from business as usual" and to tackle the systemic failure of the current food system.

Let people choose which ecological agriculture solutions best allow them to feed themselves while protecting nature. GM crops are part of the problem, not the solution.

NO
Dennis T. Avery
Environmental Economist and Senior Fellow,
Heartland Institute; Co-Author, Unstoppable: Global
Warming Every 1,500 Years

Written for *CQ Researcher*, August 2014

GM crops produce more food during good years and have the potential to resist drought and disease more effectively than traditional crops. They are ideal for famines and emergencies.

Pessimists say we can't yet trust GM foods, but they've turned up no valid dangers. In fact, the European Commission in 2010 said GM is slightly safer than conventional crops because of the targeted research conducted on them.

Aside from hunger emergencies, GM is also critically important to meeting the enormous food challenge of the next 40 years. The world must roughly double its food output, quickly, in order to feed a larger, more affluent population. (After 2050, world population will begin a slow, steady decline as increasingly literate women live in cities where it is expensive to raise a child.)

Ideally, we will be able to double food output without plowing under wildlife habitat equal to the land area of South America — just to produce low-yield crops. The world's prime farmland is already under cultivation, so farmers must redouble per-acre yields on existing fields. More nitrogen fertilizer and herbicides can be used in Africa, but most of the world's farmland is already using today's high-tech inputs. That leaves a major food-supply gap that only higher-yield new technology — such as biotechnology — can fill.

The last time the world faced such a problem, during the Little Ice Age (1300-1850 AD), it was also solved with technology. Governments ordered farmers to rotate crops and livestock on the same land to maintain soil nitrogen. Better sailing ships brought Europe crops such as corn and potatoes from the New World and cold-tolerant turnips from China as a feed crop. Drought-tolerant New World corn was planted across China. Food production surged, averting famine — except in France, where people claimed potatoes were poisonous. Famine then brought on the French Revolution.

A California biotech researcher believes he has found a one-gene solution to a massive Third World food problem. The soil in about half of the world's tropical cropland is naturally saturated with toxic aluminum. Traditional crop plants struggle to survive in the toxic soils, but the researcher has devised a way to genetically modify plants to thrive on the same soils. However, the scientist is being discouraged due to public GM mistrust in wealthy, aid-donor countries.

children and investing in boosting poor farmers' agricultural productivity.

The Obama administration, U.N. agencies and private relief organizations are adopting policies based on the theory that increasing small farmers' productivity while protecting the environment can lift them out of poverty while reducing hunger and boosting the local economy.

"Half of hungry people globally are small-scale farmers," Leach says. "We can take them out of hunger by creating economic opportunity."

For six years the U.N. World Food Programme has been teaching developing-world farmers better techniques, helping to organize them into associations to store and distribute food more efficiently and providing access to credit. The agency then purchases their crops to provide food relief for the hungry.

The goal is to "get them producing the quantity and quality they need to feed themselves, then to sell to the World Food Programme and then to graduate to selling to the marketplace," Leach explains.

Feed the Future

The Obama administration's efforts to push a similar approach in U.S. hunger programs have had a "transformative impact on the whole international community," Leach says.

Similarly, Oxfam's Kripke describes Obama as "a real leader across the world in pushing agriculture development as a priority." Unfortunately, he adds, "many other donors haven't really been following very effectively."

Called Feed the Future, the U.S. approach assumes that anti-hunger and antipoverty programs are most effective when embraced and led by developing world farmers and their local, regional and national governments. It also seeks to tap expertise of both nonprofit and profit-making private organizations.

The administration, for instance, has asked the Agriculture Department and college agriculture schools to research technologies to enable small farmers to increase productivity. In addition, the New Alliance for Food Security and Nutrition, launched in 2012 by the Group of Eight leading industrial nations,* now includes 10 African countries and more than 160 companies

that have pledged to invest more than $15 billion in African agriculture.

Carter, the UC-Davis researcher, credits the administration for targeting assistance to the specific needs of various farmer groups, such as by conducting research into the most effective and affordable farming techniques for a small geographic area. "It's one thing to move to the frontier of what's technologically possible," he says, "and it's another to put resources into situations where farmers can exploit what's available."

Barrett cites increased funding for agriculture research as key to the program. Overall, according to Barrett, the $1.1-billion Feed the Future program is "a step in the right direction, but is severely underfunded."

"We should be spending more for preventative action than for curative treatment," he says, suggesting that "$10 billion is in the neighborhood of what's needed."

Cornell's Barrett is also optimistic about a trend in which relief agencies acquire food from local and regional sources rather than shipping commodities from donor countries. In the United States, the 2014 farm bill took modest steps in that direction by increasing the amount of aid that can be provided in cash instead of commodities or that can be used to purchase food near where it's consumed.

Corporations also are pitching in. Wal-Mart, for instance, helps farmers in Mexico and Central America follow more sustainable practices and improve their post-harvest food handling, where much waste occurs. The Keurig Green Mountain coffee company helps coffee growers in Mexico, Central America and Africa diversify their crops to combat seasonal hunger.[95]

Corporate involvement is doubly important, according to Clay of the World Wildlife Fund, because "when companies like Wal-Mart or McDonald's make commitments to sustainability, their supply chains follow suit."

Reversing Damage

Private organizations also are moving to overcome environmental damage caused by modern agriculture, which affects the Earth's future ability to feed itself.

Some advocates are looking to the sea as a source of food, because water covers 70 percent of the globe but provides less than 2 percent of the planet's food. They face significant obstacles, however. Many ocean areas have been overfished, and fish farms pose significant pollution challenges.[96]

Farmers raised more fish than beef for the first time in 2012, harvesting more than 70 million tons of

---

* The eight were France, Germany, Italy, Japan, the United Kingdom, Canada, Russia and the United States. Russia was expelled after its seized Crimea this year.

seafood — 14 times what they produced in 1980. But, just as agriculture has destroyed wildlife habitat, depleted soil and polluted fresh water supplies on land, aquaculture has destroyed mangroves to create shrimp farms and released fertilizers, pesticides, antibiotics and fish waste into oceans.[97]

To avoid aquaculture's downsides, some farmers are raising fish in tanks on land; others are adopting environmentally friendly practices at sea.

In landlocked western Virginia, for instance, Blue Ridge Aquaculture has devised a land-based fish farming method that produces 12,000 pounds of antibiotic- and hormone-free tilapia each day. Company president Bill Martin describes his indoor fish farming process as having "as close to zero impact on the oceans as we can get."

Others are working to minimize the impact of their ocean-based fish farms. Off the coast of Panama, for instance, Open Blue raises hundreds of thousands of cobia in cages 60 feet below the Caribbean. Ocean currents flush the pens to provide the fish with clean water and to dilute waste. The farm does not use antibiotics, and researchers have not found waste outside the farm.

To the north, off Canada's British Columbia coast, University of Victoria researchers are raising sablefish (also called black cod) while keeping the Pacific Ocean clean. Down-current from the fish pens, baskets of shellfish eat the fish excretions. Sugar kelp grow next to the baskets and consume almost all of the remaining nitrates and phosphorus. Eighty feet below, sea cucumbers ingest the waste that falls to the sea floor.[98]

Farmers who grow crops and livestock on land are deploying "precision-agriculture" technology to increase yields while decreasing environmental damage. Global Positioning System devices attached to farm equipment detect precise locations where water, fertilizer or pesticides are needed. Other machines drag sensors over and through soil to measure treatment needs.

Precise measurements enabled New Zealand farmer Hugh Wigley to cut his lime use by 40 percent, for instance. Wigley, who also supplies precision equipment to other farmers, says one client discovered he didn't need to spread any lime on land where he had been using about two tons per acre.[99]

A 2011 Agriculture Department study found that precision agriculture has enabled farmers to reduce the damage caused by runoff of fertilizers and pesticides, reduced fuel consumption and increased crop yields.[100]

OUTLOOK

Solvable Problem

While food production has been growing more quickly than consumption, experts worry that expanding middle classes in countries such as China and India will boost demand for more expensive foods that put a greater strain on the environment than cheaper foods. That could drive already-rising food prices higher, making it harder for the poorest of the poor to purchase enough to eat.

Fulfilling demand for meat — especially beef — will divert food to animal feed and put added pressure on the environment. In addition, climate change could disrupt the growth of crops and livestock. But technological advances promise to enable farmers to increase yields while protecting the environment. And many experts are optimistic that hunger not caused by conflict or natural disaster can be eliminated.

"Hunger is a solvable problem," Leach of World Food Program USA says. "We are smarter now in terms of understanding the causes of hunger and in having creative strategies to address hunger. And there's greater understanding by the private sector about how to enhance their businesses and at the same time have positive social impact."

Big remaining challenges include addressing climate change and creating "better mechanisms to prevent conflict," Leach adds.

Cornell's Barrett also expects the private sector to contribute to reducing hunger. Rising food prices are drawing more private investment into production, he says. And reducing agriculture's threat to the environment goes hand in hand with reducing farmers' costs, he says.

"As you develop products that are greener and lower-cost, farmers adopt them pretty quickly," Barrett explains. "They're doing a better job of dosing inorganic fertilizers precisely so we reduce inorganic runoff to waterways. People are figuring out better ways to control pests with natural predators and natural secretions from plants. And we're doing a much better job developing efficient machinery."

Unfortunately, these improvements are not occurring fast enough to meet expected future demand, he adds. Kripke, of Oxfam, agrees. As to whether poor farmers will benefit from increasing food demand, Kripke says, "It's possible. It's not inevitable."

Clay, of the World Wildlife Fund, worries that rising food prices — which may be good for farmers — will "leave people with less money in a real bad way." But he's hopeful today's young adults will tackle hunger because "they care a lot about [how their food is] produced and knowing that it's produced sustainably."

Mooney, of the ETC Group, contends that affluent eaters must change their habits, and relief organizations must teach the poor how to grow their own food and eat more healthily. "We've got to adapt our consumer habits to our planet and to our health needs, which means we need to reduce our meat and dairy consumption," he says.

Developed nations waste food because "you go to the grocery once a week and buy all sorts of stuff, and it spoils in the back of the refrigerator," Mooney says. Shoppers should visit the store more frequently and buy less on each trip, he says.

Large-scale farms will continue to produce a substantial amount of the world's food, Mooney says. But "that doesn't mean it has to be highly chemical farming." Small-scale farmers probably will adapt to climate change more easily than large agricultural corporations, if researchers focus on small-scale agriculture's needs, he says.

Avery of the Heartland and Hudson institutes predicts that large-scale, high-tech agriculture will not be replaced. "We need more food and more high-value food, and we have to think about tripling the yield of crops and livestock on the good land that we currently farm, because there's no more good land," he says.

Without continued technological advances — including with GMOs and chemicals —"we will have more famine, and there will be loss of wildlife habitat on a massive scale" as more land is allocated to farming, Avery says.

NOTES

1. Abigail Hauslohner, "U.N. agency raises disaster designation in Iraq as refugees flood into Kurdistan," *The Washington Post*, June 18, 2014, http://tinyurl.com/k7deo5v; Mac McClelland, "How to Build a Perfect Refugee Camp," *The New York Times*, Feb. 13, 2014, pp. MM-24, http://tinyurl.com/ljnvc3v.

2. Olivia Ward, "Canadian aid timely for starving children," *The Toronto Star*, May 30, 2014, p. A10, http://tinyurl.com/nrmc86w.

3. "The State of Food Insecurity in the World: The multiple dimensions of food security," Food and Agriculture Organization of the United Nations, 2013, http://tinyurl.com/njzqzjp.

4. *Ibid.*

5. "The State of Food Insecurity in the World 2013," Food and Agriculture Organization of the United Nations (executive summary), 2013, http://tinyurl.com/nq8n pru; "Wake up before it is too late: Make agriculture truly sustainable now for food security in a changing climate," U.N. Conference on Trade and Development, September 2013, http://tinyurl.com/kly4c3r.

6. "The State of Food Insecurity in the World 2013," *op. cit.*

7. "Hunger Statistics," World Food Programme, http://tinyurl.com/lhjx45.

8. "World Health Statistics 2014 Part III: Global Health Indicators," World Health Organization, http://tinyurl.com/q5fgmmx.

9. Chris Otter, "Feast and Famine: The Global Food Crisis," *Origins: Current Events in Historical Perspective*, Ohio State University, Vol. 3, Issue 6, March 2010, http://tinyurl.com/l988h56. Also see "Table: Age-standardised regional and national estimates of the prevalence of overweight and obesity combined and obesity alone for girls, boys, men, and women for 2013, for 188 countries and 21 GBD regions" in "Global, regional, and national prevalence of overweight and obesity in children and adults during 1980-2013," *The Lancet*, May 29, 2014, http://tinyurl.com/k8slkbu.

10. Jason Clay, "Freezing the Footprint of Food," World Wildlife Fund, Oct. 23, 2012, http://tinyurl.com/kohxm3k.

11. Andrew C. Revkin, "It's Time for Africa's Green Revolution, Focused on Corn," *The New York Times* (blog), April 10, 2014, http://tinyurl.com/kdn4kqx.

12. Brian Jones, "Wasting food can eat away the future," *Canberra Times*, April 5, 2014, p. B9, http://tinyurl.com/oyezt6e.

13. "The State of Food Insecurity in the World 2013," *op. cit.*; Mark Koba, "A hungry world: lots of food, in too few places," CNBC, July 22, 2013, http://tinyurl.com/n8trpyp.

14. Chris Thomas, "Improving nutrition, building resilience for families, societies," USAID, May 22, 2014, http://tinyurl.com/kfqwn9d.

15. "The State of Food Insecurity in the World 2013," *op. cit.*

16. Johnnie Carson, "Africa: Remarks at the African Diplomatic Corp's Celebration of Africa Day," U.S. State Department Documents and Publications, May 25, 2010, http://tinyurl.com/39o78ar.

17. "Food Aid Flows 2012 Report," World Food Programme, United Nations, December 2013, http://tinyurl.com/jwcl2tn.

18. Statistics from interview with Alan Jury, senior adviser to World Food Program USA.

19. Hauslohner, *op. cit.*

20. Miguel I. Gómez, *et al.*, "Post-green revolution food systems and the triple burden of malnutrition," Food Policy, October 2013, Vol. 42, pp. 129-138, http://tinyurl.com/ozugl6n.

21. *Ibid.*

22. "H.R. 4005 — Coast Guard and Maritime Transportation Act of 2014," Library of Congress, http://tinyurl.com/ozso9el.

23. Christopher B. Barrett and Erin C. Lentz, "Highway Robbery on the High Seas," *The Hill*, May 29, 2014, http://tinyurl.com/l9t7gp7.

24. Elijah E. Cummings and Duncan D. Hunter, "Food aid supports sea-lift abilities," *The Washington Post*, May 17, 2013, p. A16, http://tinyurl.com/ls4c9jd.

25. "Senator Coons introduces bill to reform and modernize America's food aid program," Office of Sen. Christopher Coons, June 3, 2014, http://tinyurl.com/lab8wf9.

26. Letter to Sens. Debbie Stabenow and Thad Cochran, wheatworld.org, March 21, 2013, http://tinyurl.com/nwav3dq.

27. Steve Baragona, "Congress Debates Limiting US Farmers' Role in Food Aid," Voice of America News, June 18, 2013, http://tinyurl.com/oswob8b.

28. "The Value of Food Aid Monetization: Benefits, Risks and Best Practices," *Informa Economics*, November 2012.

29. Daniel A. Sumner, "Picking on the Poor, How US Agricultural Policy Hurts the Developing World," AmericanBoondoggle.com, http://tinyurl.com/ko62jfk.

30. Tim Krohn, "Farm bill up against misperceptions, lawmakers say," *The* [Mankato, Minnesota] *Free Press*, Feb. 19, 2014, http://tinyurl.com/m5p9nyl.

30. *Ibid.*

31. James Phelan, "U.S. Food Aid: To Ship Food or Send Cash — the Obama Administration Weighs In," Action Against Hunger, April 9, 2013, http://tinyurl.com/mw3wpxo.

32. Dennis T. Avery, "Column: Biofuels have fallen out of fashion," *Orange County Register*, May 8, 2014, http://tinyurl.com/q5c2kgp.

33. "Direct federal financial Interventions and Subsidies in Energy in fiscal Year 2010," U.S. Energy Information Administration, Aug. 1, 2011, http://tinyurl.com/nvm97sz; Robert Pear, "After Three Decades, Tax Credit for Ethanol Expires," *The New York Times*, Jan. 1, 2012, http://tinyurl.com/a3ve67x.

34. Timothy Spence, "Europe Worsening Hunger Worldwide," Inter Press Service, May 31, 2011, http://tinyurl.com/plzmtup. For background see Jina Moore, "Resolving Land Disputes," *CQ Researcher*, Sept. 6, 2011, pp. 421-446.

35. "National Journal Holds a Policy Summit on Biofuels Mandate," *Political Transcript Wire*, Oct. 9 2013, http://tinyurl.com/nctkqo4.

36. Jonathan Foley, "A Five-Step Plan to Feed the World," *National Geographic*, undated. http://tinyurl.com/l3b2jaw.

37. Joel K. Bourne, Jr., "How to Farm a Better Fish," *National Geographic*, June 2014, http://tinyurl.com/l5hbosw. For background, see Daniel McGlynn, "Whale Hunting," *CQ Researcher*, June 29, 2012, pp. 573-596.

38. Richard Black, "World's oceans in 'shocking' decline," BBC News, June 20, 2011, http://tinyurl.com/oqtyo9p. Also see Reid Wilson, "Fisheries at Risk as Oceans Acidify," *The Washington Post*, July 31, 2014, p. A3, http://tinyurl.com/pqwtvk7.

39. "The IUCN Red List of Threatened Species: *Sphyrna lewini*," International Union for Conservation of Nature, http://tinyurl.com/qexdyos.

40. "4 steps food companies can take to help stop climate change," Oxfam, May, 20, 2014, http://tinyurl.com/ow3ffrm.

41. "7 Facts About Climate Change And Hunger," World Food Programme, United Nations, Dec. 4, 2011, http://tinyurl.com/7zw9c4u.

42. Foley, *op. cit.*

43. Andrei Illarionov, "A Few Notes on Climate Change," The Cato Institute, Dec. 11, 2009, http://tinyurl.com/ourmqpg.

44. Eli Kintisch, "High CO2 Makes Crops Less Nutritious," *National Geographic*, May 7, 2014, http://tinyurl.com/p3ud8fc.

45. Terrell Johnson and Jon Erdman, "World's Hottest May Is Now May 2014: NOAA," The Weather Channel, June 23, 2014, http://tinyurl.com/kcnjgpn.

46. "How Much Has the Global Temperature Risen in the Last 100 Years?" The University Corporation for Atmospheric Research, http://tinyurl.com/a8gygt3.

47. Fiona Harvey, "Rate of ocean acidification due to carbon emissions is at highest for 300m years," *The Guardian*, Oct. 2, 2013, http://tinyurl.com/o55anz3.

48. Coral Davenport, "Climate Change Deemed Growing Security Threat by Military Researchers," *The New York Times*, May 13, 2014, http://tinyurl.com/q9jnvak.

49. Winnie Byanyima, "World 'woefully unprepared' for climate impacts on food," Oxfam International, March 25, 2014, http://tinyurl.com/oxwbatz.

50. Justin Gillis, "Panel's Warning on Climate Risk: Worst Is Yet to Come," *The New York Times*, March 31, 2014, http://tinyurl.com/mstxs6b.

51. Alex Renton, "How climate change will wipe out coffee crops — and farmers," *The* (London) *Observer*, March 29, 2014, http://tinyurl.com/pdgl6wb. Also see The Associated Press, "Cost of change," *The Denver Post*, April 1, 2014, p. A-14.

52. Rio N. Araja, "Golden rice entry blocked," *Manila Standard Today*, May 1, 2014, http://tinyurl.com/pvblyoh; Amy Harmon, "Golden Rice: Lifesaver?"

The New York Times, Aug. 24, 2013, p. SR1, http://tinyurl.com/nvannmk.

53. "What is the status of the Golden Rice project coordinated by IRRI?" International Rice Research Institute, March 2014, http://tinyurl.com/la6moer.

54. Richard Roberts, "GMOs are a key tool to addressing global hunger," *The Boston Globe*, May 23, 2014, http://tinyurl.com/q5gespx. See also Reed Karaim, "Farm Subsidies," *CQ Global Researcher*, May 1, 2012, pp. 205-228.

55. Marjorie Olster, "Key points in the genetically modified food debate," The Associated Press, Aug. 2, 2013, http://tinyurl.com/mkuwj2b; "Beyond Promises: Top 10 Facts about Biotech/GM Crops in 2013," International Service for the Acquisition of Agri-biotech Applications, http://tinyurl.com/mjopzge. For background, see Jason McLure, "Genetically Modified Food," *CQ Researcher*, Aug. 31, 2012, pp. 717-740.

56. Sharon Schmickle, "Hungry African nation at center of a food debate," *The Washington Post*, Oct. 8, 2013, p. A10, http://tinyurl.com/k2wmkfl; "Beyond Promises: Top 10 Facts about Biotech/GM Crops in 2013," *op. cit.*

57. Roberts, *op. cit.*

58. Harmon, *op. cit.*

59. Ginger Pinholster, "AAAS Board of Directors: Legally Mandating GM Food Labels Could 'Mislead and Falsely Alarm Consumers,'" American Association for the Advancement of Science, Oct. 25, 2012, http://tinyurl.com/no6eyt9.

60. Paul Johnston and David Santillo, "Precaution is simply common sense," Greenpeace International, May 24, 2012, http://tinyurl.com/pgj29pa.

61. Carey Gillam, "Pesticide use ramping up as GMO crop technology backfires: study," Reuters, Oct 1, 2012, http://tinyurl.com/9etfaj5.

62. Cormac Ó Gráda, *Famine: A Short History* (2009), http://tinyurl.com/6slof8r. Also see Joohee Cho, "North Korean Prison Camp Atrocities Detailed in UN Report," ABC News, Feb. 17, 2014, http://tinyurl.com/o23wb4w.

63. Ó Gráda, *op. cit.*

64. "The Irish Potato Famine," *Digital History*, University of Houston, http://tinyurl.com/jwwnh96.

65. Otter, *op. cit.*

66. Ó Gráda, *op. cit.*

67. Robert Denning, "Review: Famine: A Short History," *Origins: Current Events in Historical Perspective*, Ohio State University, October 2009, http://tinyurl.com/pv26cvv.

68. For background, see Tom Price, "Science in America," *CQ Researcher*, Jan. 11, 2008, pp. 25-48.

69. See Jennifer Weeks, "Farm Policy," *CQ Researcher*, Aug. 10, 2012, pp. 693-716.

70. "Fritz Haber," Chemical Heritage Foundation, undated, http://tinyurl.com/m6b7w4w.

71. Otter, *op. cit.*

72. "Ukraine: The famine of 1932-33," *Encyclopaedia Britannica*, http://tinyurl.com/k4eumoo; David P. Lilly, "The Russian Famine of 1932-1933," The Center for Volga German Studies, Concordia University, http://tinyurl.com/k6mafp8.

73. Yang Jisheng, "China's Great Shame," *The New York Times*, Nov. 13, 2012, http://tinyurl.com/n7m3drb; Anne Applebaum, "When China Starved," *The Washington Post*, Aug. 12, 2008, http://tinyurl.com/l63626u.

74. "The Biafran War," Inventory of Conflict and Environment, American University, http://tinyurl.com/n5c235o.

75. Tony Hall with Tom Price, *Changing the Face of Hunger* (2006); "Ethiopian Famine 25th Anniversary — Questions and Answers," ONE, Oct. 23, 2009, http://tinyurl.com/m6akc5v.

76. Denning, *op. cit.*

77. See Tom Price, "Assessing the United Nations," *CQ Global Researcher*, March 20, 2012, pp. 129-152.

78. See Mary H. Cooper, "World Hunger," *CQ Researcher*, Oct. 25, 1991, pp. 801-824. Also see Marcia Clemmitt, "Global Food Crisis," *CQ Researcher*, June 27, 2008, pp. 553-576.

79. Tina Rosenberg, "A Green Revolution, This Time for Africa," *The New York Times*, April 9, 2014, http://tinyurl.com/kc6v4zf.

80. For background, see Jason McLure, "Genetically Modified Food," *CQ Researcher*, Aug. 31, 2012, pp. 717-740.

81. "Our History," International Maize and Wheat Improvement Center, http://tinyurl.com/q79dynr.

82. *Ibid.*

83. Rosenberg, *op. cit.*

84. Dan Glickman and Catherine Bertini, "Saving A Billion People from Starvation," *The Huffington Post*, Sept. 18, 2009, http://tinyurl.com/nkdjx8n.

85. McLure, *op. cit.*

86. For background, see Sarah Glazer, "Rising Food Prices" *CQ Global Researcher*, Oct. 18, 2011, pp. 499-524.

87. Charles Kenny, "Congress Wakes Up to the Bad News About Biofuels," *BloombergBusinessweek*, Jan. 6, 2014, http://tinyurl.com/pfmg6e8; "Feinstein, Coburn Introduce Bipartisan Bill to Eliminate Corn Ethanol," Office of Sen. Dianne Feinstein, Dec. 12, 2013, http://tinyurl.com/pal8nyz.

88. Andrew Pollack, "Altered Corn Surfaced Earlier," *The New York Times*, Sept. 4, 2001, http://tinyurl.com/qg5nu24.

89. McLure, *op. cit.*

90. Kenneth Weiss, "In India, agriculture's Green Revolution dries up," *Los Angeles Times*, July 22, 2012, http://tinyurl.com/luofrj2.

91. Miguel I. Gómez, *et al.*, *op. cit.*

92. Revkin, *op. cit.*

93. Carson, *op. cit.*

94. Office of Sen. Dianne Feinstein, *op. cit.*

95. Andrew C. Revkin, "A Coffee Seller Seeks to Cut Hunger Among Coffee Growers," *The New York Times*, Oct. 9, 2012, http://tinyurl.com/m8o4enb; "Food Security," Keurig Green Mountain, http://tinyurl.com/k5ln3r7.

96. Alan Ward, "Weighing Earth's Water from Space," National Aeronautics and Space Administration, Dec. 23, 2003, http://tinyurl.com/qxjjoqa.

97. Bourne, *op. cit.*

98. *Ibid.*

99. Tim Cronshaw, "Soil mapping technology a big step forward," *The* (Christchurch, New Zealand) *Press*, July 4, 2014, p. 15.

100. David Schimmelpfennig and Robert Ebel, "On the Doorstep of the Information Age: Recent Adoption of Precision Agriculture," U.S. Dept. of Agriculture Economic Research Service, August 2011, http://tinyurl.com/m8qan98.

BIBLIOGRAPHY

Selected Sources

Books

Buffett, Howard G., *40 Chances: Finding Hope in a Hungry World*, Simon & Schuster, 2013.
A philanthropist and son of billionaire investor Warren Buffett analyzes how the well-fed world should fight hunger and poverty.

Falcon, Walter, and Rosamond Naylor, eds., *Frontiers in Food Policy: Perspectives in Sub-Saharan Africa*, Stanford Center on Food Security and the Environment, 2014.
Experts at an agricultural development symposium address various aspects of hunger and rural poverty in the hungriest region on Earth.

Gratton, Lynda, *The Key: How Corporations Succeed by Solving the World's Toughest Problems*, McGraw-Hill, 2014.
A professor of management practice at London Business School argues that global problems such as hunger cannot be solved without help from major corporations and their executives.

Ó Gráda, Cormac, *Famine: A Short History*, Princeton University Press, 2009.
An economics professor at University College, Dublin, traces the history of hunger from ancient Egypt onward.

Thurow, Roger, *The Last Hunger Season: A Year in an African Farm Community on the Brink of Change*, Public Affairs, 2012.
A senior fellow for global agriculture and food policy at the Chicago Council on Global Affairs tells the stories of four small-scale farmers in western Kenya and concludes that relief and development organizations are headed in the right direction.

Articles

Barrett, Christopher B., and Erin C. Lentz, "Highway Robbery on the High Seas," *The Hill*, May 29, 2014, http://tinyurl.com/l9t7gp7.
The director of Cornell University's School of Applied Economics and Management (Barrett) and an assistant professor of international relations at Bucknell University lament that hungry people go unfed because Congress requires at least half of U.S. food aid to be shipped in U.S.-flagged vessels. The American vessels tend to be more expensive, so less food can be purchased when they are used.

Bourne, Joel K., Jr., "How to Farm a Better Fish," *National Geographic*, undated, http://tinyurl.com/l5hbosw.
A former senior editor for *National Geographic* explores environmentally friendly approaches to fish farming.

Otter, Chris, "Feast and Famine: The Global Food Crisis," *Origins: Current Events in Historical Perspective*, March 2010, http://tinyurl.com/l988h56.
An assistant professor of history at Ohio State University provides a historical perspective on the modern paradox of global hunger and widespread obesity.

Rosenberg, Tina, "When Food Isn't the Answer to Hunger," The New York Times, April 24, 2013, http://tinyurl.com/n7b7ndm.
Monetary aid can better solve hunger than food aid under certain circumstances.

Reports and Studies

"Case Study: Digital Green," Governance Knowledge Centre, Department of Administrative Reforms and Public Grievances, Ministry of Personnel, Public Grievances and Pensions, Government of India, June 2011, http://tinyurl.com/qayfl8p.
A case study prepared for the Indian government evaluates Digital Green, a nonprofit that uses information technology to educate poor farmers about agricultural practices.

"The State of Food Insecurity in the World 2013," U.N. Food and Agriculture Organization, Sept. 1, 2013, http://tinyurl.com/mbt7g5g.

An annual U.N. report says the world is approaching the U.N.'s 2015 hunger-reduction target, but achieving it would require "considerable and immediate additional efforts."

"Wake up before it is too late: Make agriculture truly sustainable now for food security in a changing climate," U.N. Conference on Trade and Development, September 2013, http://tinyurl.com/kly4c3r.
A U.N. agency report says farmers should grow a larger variety of crops and reduce fertilizer use, while food-aid organizations should support small-scale farmers and consumption of locally grown food.

"What is the status of the Golden Rice project coordinated by IRRI?" International Rice Research Institute, March 2014, http://tinyurl.com/la6moer.

A nonprofit explains the challenges of developing "golden rice," a genetically modified grain designed to combat blindness and other ailments due to Vitamin-A deficiency.

Schimmelpfennig, David, and Robert Ebel, "On the Doorstep of the Information Age: Recent Adoption of Precision Agriculture," Economic Research Service, U.S. Department of Agriculture, August 2011, http://tinyurl.com/m8qan98.
Government economists evaluate farmers' use of technology such as optical sensors and GPS systems to more accurately fertilize, protect and water their crops.

For More Information

Center for Global Food Issues, P.O. Box 202, Churchville, VA, 24421; 540-337-6354; www.cgfi.org. Project of the conservative Hudson Institute think tank that promotes free trade in agricultural products and contends that agricultural productivity is key to environmental conservation.

ETC Group, 180 Metcalfe St., Suite 206, Ottawa, ON K2P 1P5, Canada; 613-241-2267; www.etcgroup.org. Research and advocacy group that studies how new technologies, especially in agriculture, affect the poor.

Food and Agriculture Organization, Viale delle Terme di Caracalla, 00153 Rome, Italy; 39-06-57051; www.fao.org/home/en. U.N.'s chief agency for food and agriculture issues; compiles statistics and publishes reports on hunger.

Oxfam International, Second Floor, 228-240 Banbury Road, Oxford OX2 7BY, United Kingdom; 44-1865-339-100; www.oxfam.org. U.S. affiliate: **Oxfam America**, 226

Causeway St., Fifth Floor, Boston, MA 02114-2206; 800-776-9326; www.oxfamamerica.org. Global relief, development and advocacy organization.

World Food Programme, Via Cesare Giulio Viola 68,?Parco dei Medici, 00148 Rome, Italy; 39-06-65131; www.wfp.org. U.N. agency that is the world's largest anti-hunger organization, distributing 58 percent of the world's food aid in 2012.

World Food Program USA, 1725 I St., N.W., Suite 510, Washington, DC 20006; 202-627-3737; www.wfpusa.org. An independent nonprofit organization that supports the U.N.'s World Food Programme.

World Wildlife Fund, 1250 24th St., N.W., Washington, DC 20037; 202-293-4800; www.worldwildlife.org. Wildlife conservation organization that sees agricultural expansion as a threat to wildlife habitat.